A Sanskrit Grammar Text
basic principles, rules and formats
with reference tables and vocabulary

ॐ

परमात्मने नमः

अथ

revised edition 2011

ISBN 978-0-473-15391-5

Contents

Introduction to Sanskrit

The *Sanskrit* language was spoken before it was written and in India it may be seen in a number of different scripts. The most common is called *Devanagari* and this is the one used here. As in English, this has some variations in the fonts used but these differences are quickly overcome. The script is syllabic i.e. each symbol represents a syllable rather than a letter. In the alphabet, the vowel *a* is added to consonants e.g. *ka, pa, ja.* The consonants cannot be pronounced without a vowel. Here is the Sanskrit alphabet

ॐ

अ इ ऋ ऌ उ

ए ओ ऐ औ

क च ट त प

ख छ ठ थ फ

ग ज ड द ब

घ झ ढ ध भ

ङ ञ ण न म

य र ल व

श ष स

ह

This is the traditional way of presenting the alphabet - starting with *oṁ,* from which all sounds are derived, then the vowels in order of manifestation. Beneath the primary vowels are the consonants in mouth position families vertically, They are uttered with the mouth position of that vowel and each consonant is followed by the short vowel *a.*

Because there are more letters in the Sanskrit alphabet than in English, it is necessary to create extra English letters by the addition of dots and dashes. Using these it is possible to write Sanskrit in English letters. This process is called transliteration. The de-code is shown on the next page with a pronunciation guide.

Measure is important in pronunciation so the correct measures need to be practiced precisely. The vowels अ *a* इ *i* ऋ *ṛ* ऌ *ḷ* उ *u,* are sounded very short (*hraswa*) and also have a long measure (*dīrgha* p.3) which is twice as long. Anything longer is termed *pluta.*

notes for the alphabet table on the left.

- The left column is called *kaṇṭha* meaning throat. The mouth and throat are open and unrestrained.
- The next is *tālu* meaning palatal with the back of the tongue raised toward the palate.
- The middle column is called *mūrdha* meaning high in which the tip of the tongue reaches toward but does not touch the roof of the mouth.
- The next is *danta* meaning teeth. The tongue is just behind the teeth.
- The last is *oṣṭhau* meaning two lips in which the sound is controlled by the lips.

Sir William Jones, speaking to the Asiatic Society in Calcutta (now Kolkata) on February 2, 1786, said: The Sanskrit language, whatever be its antiquity, is of a wonderful structure; more perfect than the Greek, more copious than the Latin, and more exquisitely refined than either, yet bearing to both of them a stronger affinity, both in the roots of verbs and in the forms of grammar, than could possibly have been produced by accident; so strong, indeed, that no philologer could examine them all three, without believing them to have sprung from some common source, which, perhaps, no longer exists.

Pronunciation

अ a as u in but

आ ā a in master

इ i i in fix

ई ī ee in feel

उ u u in suit

ऊ ū oo in pool

ऋ ṛ or ॠ ri in river

ॠ or ॠ ṝ ree in reed

ऌ ḷ lry in jewelry

ए e a in evade

ऐ ai y in my

ओ o o in oh

औ au ou in loud

क् k k in kite

ख् kh kh in blockhead

ग् g g in good

घ् gh gh in loghouse

ङ् ṅ ng in sing

च् c ch in check

छ् or च्छ ch chh in catch him

ज् j j in jam

झ or झ jh dgeh in hedgehog

ञ् ñ n in lunch

ट् ṭ t in true

ठ् ṭh th in anthill

ड् ḍ d in drum

ढ् ḍh dh in red-haired

ण् ṇ 2nd n in none

त् t t in water

थ् th th in fat-head

द् d d in dice

ध् or ध् dh dh in adhere

न् n n in not

प् p p in put

फ् ph ph in uphill

ब् b b in bear

भ् bh bh in abhor

म् m m in mother

य् y y in you

र् r r in red

ल् or ल l l in love

व् v w in water

श् ś sh in sure

ष् ṣ sh in show

स् s s in sit

ह् h h in hard

ं ṁ m in hum

: ḥ h in oh

avagrahaḥ ऽ or (') i.e. an apostrophe in transliteration - a mark of hiatus - i.e. this symbol is shorthand for the letter "*a*" that is not otherwise shown nor is pronounced due to the rules of grammar.

The *hraswa* (short) and *dīrgha* (long) forms of vowels are shown as -
a अ *ā* आ *i* इ *ī* ई *u* उ *ū* ऊ *ṛ* ऋ or ॠ *ṝ* ॠ or ॠ *ḷ* ऌ
The vowels
ए *e* ओ *o* ऐ *ai* औ *au* are each made up of two vowels *(a + i, a+u, a+e, a+o* respectively) and so they naturally have two measures. There is provision for an undefined protracted measure (*pluta*) which is seldom met with in grammar but is practised to attain purity in sounding. The technique is to sound the vowel as a continuous tone with correct mouth position while listening carefully to the sound. This will enable the tone to refine.

Numerals

१ २ ३ ४ ५ ६ ७ ८ ९ ०

1 2 3 4 5 6 7 8 9 0

Other symbols and sounds

The *visarga* - a small measure of expelled air is represented by a colon : or in transliteration a *ḥ* . e.g. रामः *rāmaḥ*

Anunāsika is a form of vowel nasalization, often represented by an *anusvara*. (A sound uttered simultaneously with mouth and nose is assigned the attribute *anunāsika.*)

Anusvara

In Sanskrit, a nasalized sound is represented as an *anusvara*, a dot above the letter.

Nasalization of a preceding vowel (represented by *ṁ* or *ṃ)* is a nasal sound related to the mouth position of the following consonant (either within a word or across a word boundary).

e.g. *aṁkita* would be pronounced *aṅkita, kaṁpita* would be pronounced *kampita.*

An *m* is realized as *m* before vowels or at a natural sound break e.g. at the end of a sentence.

In the Monier-Williams Dictionary the transliterated form is the letter *ṃ*or in many other documents *ṁ* except when followed by *ś, ṣ, s, or ḥ* , when it is represented by *ṉ*.

Candrabindu ँ(meaning "moon-dot") having the form of a dot inside the lower half of a circle. It usually means that the previous vowel is nasalized.

In Vedic Sanskrit it is used instead of *anusvara* to represent the sound called *anunāsika* when the next word starts with a vowel. It usually occurs where in earlier times a word ended in -*ans*. (Vedic Sanskrit is prior to about 500BC. After this time the language became more regular and became known as Classic Sanskrit. Most Sanskrit texts, like this one, refer to Classic Sanskrit.)

In Classical Sanskrit it only seems to occur over a *lla* conjunct consonant, to show that it is pronounced as a nasalized double *l*, which occurs where *-nl-* have become assimilated in sandhi (the rules for joining letters).

Reading or writing vowels other than short *a*.
If vowels other than *a* are added to a consonant they are shown like this-

long *a* — *ā* vertical stroke to the right ा *kā* का *dhā* धा *yā* या *gā* गा *śā* शा

short *i* — *i* joined vertical stroke to the left ि *ni* नि *bhi* भि *yi* यि *gi* गि *śi* शि

long *i* — *ī* joined vertical stroke to the right ी *cī* ची *tī* ती *vī* वी *gī* गी *śī* शी

short *u* — ु symbol below *ku* कु *ru* रु *śu* शु *gu* गु

long *u* — *ū* ू symbol below *rū* रू *hū* हू *śū* शू

short *ṛ* — ृ symbol below *kṛ* कृ *dhṛ* धृ *hṛ* हृ *gṛ* गृ *śṛ* शृ

long *ṝ* — ॄ symbol below *kṝ* कॄ *tṝ* तॄ *hṝ* हॄ

short *ḷ* — ऌ symbol below *kḷ* कॢ *mḷ* मॢ

long *ḹ* — ॣ (a theoretical construct) ॡ *kḹ* कॣ

e (a+i) — े symbol above *ke* के *te* ते *ye* ये *ge* गे *śe* शे

ai (a+a+i) — ै symbol above *tai* तै *kai* कै *sai* सै *gai* गै *śai* शै

o (a+u*)* — ो stroke to the right + symbol above *ko* को *co* चो *bho* भो *go* गो *śo* शो

au (a+a+u) — ौ stroke to the right + symbol above *tau* तौ *nau* नौ *vau* वौ *gau* गौ

The omission of an initial *a* is shown by inserting an *avagraha (*ऽ*)*. e.g. तेऽपि *te'pi*
A consonant without vowel attached is shown with a *halanta* mark (like a diagonal comma). e.g. ल् र् भ् झ्

The Alphabet (with transliteration)

ॐ

अ a　इ i　ऋ ṛ　ऌ ḷ　उ u

ए e　ओ o　ऐ ai　औ au

क ka　च ca　ट ṭa　त ta　प pa

ख kha　छ cha　ठ ṭha　थ tha　फ pha

ग ga　ज ja　ड ḍa　द da　ब ba

घ gha　झ jha　ढ ḍha　ध dha　भ bha

ङ ṅa　ञ ña　ण ṇa　न na　म ma

य ya　र ra　ल la　व va

श śa　ष ṣa　स sa

ह ḥ

Sounds

	ए		ओ	
	ऐ		औ	
क	च	ट	त	प
ख	छ	ठ	थ	फ
ग	ज	ड	द	ब
घ	झ	ढ	ध	भ
ङ	ञ	ण	न	म
ह	य	र	ल	व
	श	ष	स	

The consonants marked thus are unaspirated (*alpaprāṇāḥ*) (pl). Those marked like this are aspirated. Aspirated (*mahāprāṇāḥ*)(pl) means that the sound is followed by a release of air, heard as a breathiness in the sound of chalk or ghost, *kh* in blockhead, *ch* in catch him, *gh* in loghouse, *jh* in hedgehog, ṭh in anthill, *ḍh* in redhead, *th* in fathead, *dh* in adhere, ph in uphill. the full details are on the next page

अ	इ	ऋ	ऌ	उ
	ए		ओ	
	ऐ		औ	
क	च	ट	त	प
ख	छ	ठ	थ	फ
ग	ज	ड	द	ब
घ	झ	ढ	ध	भ
ङ	ञ	ण	न	म
ह	य	र	ल	व
	श	ष	स	

The consonants marked thus are said to be "voiced", and these sounds "unvoiced". Although sounds may be described as either **voiceless** (**unvoiced**) or **voiced**, there can in fact be degrees of voicing (see below).

A voiced sound is one in which the vocal cords vibrate, and a voiceless sound is one in which they do not. Voicing is the difference between pairs of sounds such as [s] and [z] in English. If one places the fingers on the voice box (ie the location of the Adam's apple in the upper throat), one can feel a vibration when one pronounces *zzzz*, but not when one pronounces *ssss*. Vowels are usually voiced. Consonants may be voiced or unvoiced.

A **voiced** sound is produced when air expelled from the lungs causes the vocal folds to vibrate. This produces a fundamental tone accompanied by several non-harmonic overtones.

Voiced sounds are said to be *saṁvāraḥ* (contracted, closing of the throat), *nādaḥ* (sounding, supported by sound),and *ghoṣaḥ* (soft, sonant).

Unvoiced sounds are said to be *vivāraḥ* (open, expansion), *śvāsaḥ* (sighing, supported by breath), *aghoṣaḥ* (hard, soundless, non-sonant).

The vocal vibration is varied to produce intonation and tone. Tone and intonation are not conveyed well by voiceless sounds, with their lax vocal folds, but the changes in airflow are still audible.

ङ ञ ण न म

These letters are the nasals. Each is pronounced nasally (*anunāsika*) using the mouth position of its parent vowel directly above in the alphabet diagram.

श ष स ह

These letters are the sibilants or *ūṣmanaḥ*

ह य र ल व

These letters are called the *antaḥsthāḥ* (pl) or semi-vowels. *Antaḥsthaḥ* means standing between. They stand between the vowels and consonants.

क	च	ट	त	प
ख	छ	ठ	थ	फ
ग	ज	ड	द	ब
घ	झ	ढ	ध	भ
ङ	ञ	ण	न	म

The 25 consonants are called *sparśa* (meaning contact) because they require contact to be pronounced correctly.
The vowels are called *svarāḥ* (pl).

Families of Sounds - Inner and Outer Effort

The methods of articulation (sounding) have been traditionally specified in rules that are grouped by the different kinds of inner or outer effort.
The sounds of the alphabet are grouped in families according to mouth position and method of articulation —सवर्ण. (*savarṇa* - having the same family).

Inner effort

आभ्यन्तर (*ābhyantara* -interior, inner part,)

प्रयत्न (*pra* - towards, *yatna* effort, activity of will, work, endeavour)

Vowels can be sounded continuously because the airflow is not stopped or restricted much so the स्वर method of articulation प्रयत्न is said to be विवृत्त (open) .

The व्यञ्जन or consonants are sometimes called stops because the sound (airflow) is stopped to define the sound. Different sounds are made by stopping at different places - throat, palate, roof of the mouth, teeth, lips. The letters are grouped by families according to these positions and these are called *ābhyantara prayatna* meaning internal effort of the mouth/throat in producing articulate utterance.

....

The following terms define other aspects of this प्रयत्न or articulation.

....

स्पृष्ट means touched, formed by complete contact of the organs of utterance and applies to the व्यञ्जन or consonants क् – म् which are said to be स्पर्श -touching.

....

ईषत्स्पृष्ट -means formed by slight contact and applies to the अन्तःस्थ य् र् ल् व्

....

ईषद्विवृत्ति -means slightly open and applies to the ऊष्मन् - ह् श् ष् स्

....

Outer effort

The *bāhya prayatnas* or outer methods of articulation are best considered in 3 groups.

....

1. The **voiced** sounds have the characteristics : संवार closed, नादresonant, घोष voiced and are those of the consonant grouping - *haś* (व्यञ्जन प्रत्याहार हश्) .

The Voiced sounds are those which create sound through tension of the vocal cords - (something which can be tested by lightly placing a finger on the throat while making sounds).

2. The **unvoiced** sounds have the characteristics : विवार open, श्वास, with breath, अघोष unvoiced and are those of the खर् consonant grouping (व्यञ्जन प्रत्याहार खर्)

3. **Aspirated** महाप्राण (large breath), or unaspirated अल्पप्राण (small breath)

The aspirated letters are the 2nd and 4th lines of the consonants i.e.

ख छ ठ थ फ घ झ ढ ध भ + ह् श् ष् स्

The unaspirated letters are the 1st, 3rd and 5th lines of the consonants i.e.

क च ट त प ग ज ड द ब ङ ञ ण न म +य् र् ल् व्

....

3. The 3 accents of the vowels or (singular) - स्वर

उदात्त high pitch, अनुदात्त low pitch, स्वरित combination of pitch

light and heavy emphasis लघु = light गुरु = heavy

a light *svara* is *laghu (*ह्रस्व स्वर लघु) i.e. is sounded lightly. A *guru* sound is sounded with more weight.

There are 4 rules to indicate the *guru* vowels.

- a short *svara* followed by a *saṁyoga* is sounded *guru* (*saṁyoga* = 2 consonants together) i.e. The vowel before the *saṁyoga* is sounded as *guru.*
- a double measure *svara is sounded guru*
- a short *svara* followed by a *visarga* is sounded *guru*
- a short *svara* followed by a single *vyañjana* at the end of a sentence or line is sounded *guru.*

Conjunct Consonants (*saṁyoga*)

Where 2 consonants are in direct contact a general rule is –

- If the first to be joined ends with a vertical stroke then it is placed first with the loss of the vertical. *n* + *ta* = न्त
- If the first does not end with a vertical stroke then the following consonant is joined underneath with loss of its vertical stroke *d* + *va* = द्व
- There are other variations and exceptions.

There are many possibilities and sometimes it may be necessary to consult or look up a table. There are many type fonts for reproducing Sanskrit so if something unusual arises then sometimes it is necessary to do some detective work. Different combinations may be assessed for sensibility or different renditions of a text consulted to discover the truth. This list is far from exhaustive as it only covers consonants with the vowel *a.* Note that the listings are in English alphabetical order and that n and s are listed under ṅ,ñ,ṇ,n and ś,ṣ,s

ब्ब *bba* ब्भ *bbha* ब्द *bda* ब्ध *bdha* भ्र *bhra* ब्ज *bja* ब्न *bna* ब्र *bra* भ्य *bhya*
च्च *cca* च्छ *ccha* च्छ्र *cchra* च्छ्व *cchva* च्म *cma* च्ञ *cña* छ्य *chya* च्य *cya*
छ्र *chra* द्ब *dba* द्भ *dbha* द्भ्य *dbhya* द्द *dda* द्ध *ddha* द्ध्न *ddhna* द्द्र *ddra*
द्द्व *ddva* ध्व *dhva* द्ध्य *ddhya* द्ग *dga* ड्ग *ḍga* द्ग्र *dgra* द्ग्य *dgya* ध्म *dhma*
ढ्म *ḍhma* ध्न *dhna* ध्र *dhra* ध्य *dhya* ढ्य *ḍhya* द्म *dma* द्न *dna* द्र *dra*
द्र्य *drya* द्व *dva* द्व्य *dvya* द्य *dya* ड्य *ḍya*
ग्भ *gbha* ग्द *gda* ग्ध *gdha* घ्म *ghma* घ्न *ghna* घ्र *ghra* घ्य *ghya* ग्ल *gla* ग्म *gma*
ग्न *gna* ग्र *gra* ग्र्य *grya* ग्व *gva* ग्य *gya*
ह्ल *hla* ह्म *hma* ह्न *hna* ह्ण *hṇa* ह्र *hra* ह्व *hva* ह्य *hya*
ज्ज *jja* ज्झ *jjha* ज्ज्व *jjva* ज्म *jma* ज्ञ *jña* ज्ञ्य *jñya* ज्र *jra* ज्य *jya* ज्व *jva*
ख्र *khra* क्क *kka* क्ख *kkha* क्ल *kla* क्म *kma* क्न *kna* क्र *kra* क्श *kśa* क्ष *kṣa* क्ष्म
kṣma क्ष्य *kṣya* क्ष्व *kṣva* क्त *kta* क्थ *ktha* क्त्र *ktra* क्त्व *ktva* क्त्य *ktya*
क्व *kva* ख्य *khya*
ल्क *lka* ल्ल *lla* ल्व *lva* ल्य *lya*
म्ब *mba* म्भ *mbha* म्ल *mla* म्न *mna* म्प *mpa* म्र *mra* म्य *mya*
ङ्ग *ṅga* ङ्घ *ṅgha* ङ्क *ṅka* ङ्क्ष *ṅkṣa* ङ्म *ṅma*
ञ्च *ñca* ञ्छ *ñcha* ञ्ज *ñja*
ण्त्य *ṇtya* ण्थ *ṇtha* ण्ड *ṇḍa* ण्ढ *ṇḍha* ण्ण *ṇṇa* ण्म *ṇma* ण्य *ṇya* ण्व *ṇva*
न्द *nda* न्द्ध्य *nddhya* न्द्द्र *nddra* न्ध *ndha* न्ध्र *ndhra* न्म *nma* न्न *nna* न्र *nra*
न्स *nsa* न्त *nta* न्थ *ntha* न्त्र *ntra* न्त्य *ntya* न्व *nva* न्य *nya*
फ्य *phya* प्ल *pla* प्म *pma* प्न *pna* प्र *pra* प्स *psa* प्त *pta* प्त्य *ptya* प्य *pya*
र्ध *rdha* र्ज *rja* र्क *rka*

श्च *śca* श्ल *śla* श्न *śna* श्र *śra* श्र्य *śrya* श्व *śva* श्व्य *śvya* श्य *śya*

ष्क *ṣka* ष्क्र *ṣkra* ष्म *ṣma* ष्ण *ṣṇa* ष्ण्य *ṣṇya* ष्प्र *ṣpra* ष्प *ṣpa* ष्त *ṣta* ष्ठ *ṣṭha*

ष्ठ्य *ṣṭhya* ष्ट्र *ṣṭra* ष्ट्र्य *ṣṭrya* ष्ट्व *ṣṭva* ष्ट्य *ṣṭya* ष्व *ṣva* ष्य *ṣya*

स्थ *stha* स्क *ska* स्ख *skha* स्म *sma* स्म्य *smya* स्न *sna* स्प *spa* स्फ *spha*

स्र *sra* स्त *sta* स्त्र *stra* स्त्व *stva* स्त्य *stya* स्य *sya* स्व *sva*

थ्य *thya* त्थ *ttha* त्क *tka* त्म *tma* त्म्य *tmya* त्न *tna* त्प *tpa* त्र *tra* त्र्य *trya* त्स *tsa*

त्स्न *tsna* त्स्य *tsya* त्त *tta* त्त्र *ttra* त्व *tva* त्त्व *ttva* त्त्य *ttya* त्य *tya*

ठ्र *ṭhra* ट्क *ṭka* ट्य *ṭya*

व्र *vra* व्य *vya*

य्व *yva* य्य *yya*

Punctuation

The ***virāma*** symbol | is used to indicate the end of a sentence segment or the first line of a *sūtra*. It could be thought of as a comma

pūrna virāma || is used at the end of a sentence or *śloka* (stanza) like a full stop.

Parts of a Sentence

Sanskrit is a very orderly language which has many similarities to English and many English words are easily seen to be derived from it. It has verbs, nouns, pronouns, adjectives, adverbs, prefixes and suffixes, prepositions etc, and these are organised in sentences but governed by different rules.

It is convenient to consider words as originating from roots or *dhātu*s. Words are formed by adding letters to these according to rules. By further adding suffixes or prefixes the root can provide many related meanings. The principal (Monier-Williams) dictionary is organised alphabetically by *dhātu*s.

A word is identified by its stem and its function is identified by looking at the suffix (*pratyaya*). The sentence has a subject and an object which relate to the verb in the normal way. The subject is usually at the start of a sentence which develops like an English sentence, though the verb is usually at the end. Adjectives come before nouns, and adverbs are used in a normal manner. Participles usually function like adjectives and there is a sprinkling of words which do not change their form (*nipāta*) such as *ca* – which means 'and'.

The alphabet and its order must be learned because the alphabet contains many orderly relationships which have practical uses. It is also easier to learn in sound "families" which are organised together. The rules of grammar were laid out by Pāṇini long ago but are not easy to understand in their original form. This text is arranged for ease of reference. Tables will be introduced in the text for practical reference.

नामरूपैव
नाम name रूप shape, form एव only
everything exists in name and shape only

नामन् (nominal), क्रिया (verb), उपसर्ग (verbal prefix), निपात (particle)

These are the 4 kinds of words which according to पतञ्जलि were born together

Word Classification

नामन् *nāman* – the nominals or naming words. There are 4 types described in more detail below. They include nouns, adjectives, pronouns and adverbs.

क्रिया *kriyā* is the sanskrit word for verbs and they are formed from roots called *dhātu.*

For instance the *dhātu* for *kriyā* is *kṛ* 300/3 - to do, make, perform, accomplish, cause, effect, prepare, undertake. Strictly speaking, to be correct, the meaning should be listed as do, make etc., because "to" do is the infinitive form of the verb but the meanings are easily understood as they are listed.

विशेषण *viśeṣaṇa* - an adjective

क्रिया विशेषण *kriyāviśeṣaṇa* - a word which expands the remainder in a *kriyā* (verb) bringing out a previously unmanifest quality in the verb (Adverb). (Indeclinable)

kṛdanta –(*pāṇini s* name for) participles

उपसर्ग *upasarga* - a particle joined to a verb and indicating the direction of the action. Practically it may be thought of as a pre-fix

निपात *nipāta* – an indeclinable particle . ..all adverbs plus particles and interjections 549/2 irregular form, exception e.g. *ca* and

Nominals

- the 4 categories of नामन् or nominal are:

नामन् संज्ञा सर्वनामन् विशेषण

नामन् **name in general, including proper names**

e.g. Jim, (a proper name) and nouns such as tree, house, dog

संज्ञा सम् + ज्ञा सम् all together as one ज्ञा to know

to know all together as one. A संज्ञा is a नामन् which contains all knowledge of the thing named; being the true name it is the first type of नामन् . *Pāṇini* uses them as classifications e.g. *vṛddhi, guṇa, anunāsika*

सर्वनामन् सर्व + नामन् सर्व all, everyone

नामन् name – सर्वनामन् **the name of all** (we know these as pronouns)

examples अहम् and its variations – I, me, mine, thou, thee, thine, etc. also which, who

विशेषण – The adjective brings out a quality of a नामन e.g. The beautiful girl speaks. The yellow ball bounced high. - lit. " **the act of expanding the remainder**"

विशेषण वि + शेष + ण

वि to expand शेष remainder ण the act of . In English this is an adjective.

The act of expanding the remainder, - bringing out an unmanifested quality and making it manifest; The unmanifest Absolute is the remainder.

The nouns are derived from the same *dhātu* (roots) as other Sanskrit words so they are found in the dictionary after the *dhātu* discussion and indicated by m, n or f. Adjectives are indicated by mfn. which implies they can change gender to match the noun they are associated with.

- Nominals may be masculine (m), feminine (f) or neuter (n) (neither masculine or feminine).
- Different gender nouns have different endings. e.g. *rāma**ḥ*** (m), *sīt**ā*** (f) , *mitr**am*** (n)
- There are also different endings for different functions. e.g. *mitr**am*** - a friend, mitreṇa - with a friend
- These different functions are called *vibhakti* (which describes the modification and systematic regulation for the declension of nouns and the conjugation of verbs).
- These forms are then declined in tables.
- The tables also indicate whether the word describes a singular, dual or more-than-two situation (number).
- the tables use traditional forms which are regular and typical. The first form given is *rāmaḥ* . *Rāmaḥ* was the hero of an epic story well known in India hence the first word is first case (the subject), singular, and masculine.
- The dictionary entry sometimes uses a different (citation) form as its first entry for a word and if necessary adds another form to indicate which declension should be used. e.g. *ātman (ā)* , this indicates that the declension starts at *ātmā,* i.e. this is the 1st case, singular, nominative. Bucknell clarifies this in Part II, A (c).

Nouns *(nāman)*

This table shows in English the ways a noun may be used in a sentence. On the left side are the case numbers and their names. On the right is the traditional Sanskrit understanding of the meaning which is discussed later. Sanskrit grammar expresses number in singular (***ekavacana),*** dual ***(dvivacana)*** and plural ***(bahuvacana).***

	***ekavacana* speaking of one**	***dvivacana* speaking of two**	***bahuvacana* speaking of many**	***kāraka* characteristic**
***prathamā* (1st) subject vocative**	*Rāmaḥ* as agent O *Ràma*	two *Rāmas* O two *Rāmas*	many *Rā* O many *Rāmas*	*kartṛ* *sambodhana*
***dvitīyā (2nd)* object**	*Rāma* as object	two *Rāmas*	many *Rāmas*	*karma*
***tṛtīyā* (3rd) instrumental**	by/with *Rāmaḥ*	by/with two *Rāmas*	by/with many*Rāmas*	*karaṇa*
***caturthā* (4th) for the sake of**	for the sake of *Rāmaḥ*	for the sake of two *Rāmas*	for the sake of many *Rāmas*	*saṁpradāna*
***pañcamī* (5th)**	from *Rāmaḥ*	from two *Rāmas*	from many *Rāmas*	*apādāna*
***ṣaṣṭī* (6th)**	for the use of *Rāmaḥ*	for the use of two *Rāmas*	for the use of many *Rāmas*	*sambandha*
***saptamī* (7th)**	in or on *Rāmaḥ*	in or on two *Rāmas*	in or on many *Rāmas*	*adhikaraṇa*

Here is the Sanskrit declension of राम: *(Rāmaḥ)* - a typical masculine declension*

prathamā (1st)	राम:	रामौ	रामा:
vocative	हे राम	हे रामौ	हे रामा:
dvitīyā(2nd)	रामम्	रामौ	रामान्
tṛtīyā (3rd)	रामेण	रामाभ्याम्	रामै:
caturthī (4th)	रामाय	रामाभ्याम्	रामेभ्य:
pañcamī (5th)	रामात्	रामाभ्याम्	रामेभ्य:
ṣaṣṭī (6th)	रामस्य	रामयो:	रामाणाम्
saptamī (7th)	रामे	रामयो:	रामेषु

***Declension** means describing the forms of case, number and gender in a regular format.
The most common formats are those of *rāma* – masculine (m), *sītā* – feminine (f), *and mitram* neuter(n) . These are given with other common forms in standard format. Sometimes the vocative is shown with the 1st case but from here on it will be after 7th.

Number - speaking of one *ekavacana,* two *dvivacana*, or many *bahuvacana*

Gender

The Sanskrit word for gender is *liṅga* and there are three of them .
puṁliṅga – masculine, *strīliṅga* – feminine, and *napuṁsakaliṅga* neuter.
Gender applies to nouns, adjectives, and pronouns so the noun gender is found from the dictionary and the appropriate gender specific *vibhakti* ending is applied. Adjectives match the gender of the noun and pronoun gender is applied as required.

vibhakti

The 7 concepts of *vibhakti* define the part which a *nāman* plays in an action. These concapts are given as brief expressions which alter the perspective from which one approaches the use of language

- प्रथमा (1st) nominative case (subject). कर्तृ – is the "agent".
  स्वतन्त्रः कर्तृ He who has the system (for the action), within himself is the कर्तृ – or agent of the action.

- द्वितीया (2nd) accusative case कर्मन् (object) कर्तुरीप्सिततमं That which is most beloved of the agent is कर्म *karma* (the object)

- तृतीया (3rd) instrumental case करण (by, with, tool associated)
  साधकतमं करणम् That which is most propitious (for the completion of work) is करण *karaṇa*

- चतुर्ती (4th) dative case संप्रदान (for, to) कर्मणायमभिप्रैति सः संप्रदानम् With whom the mind intends to associate the action as a sacrifice, offering or gift that very person is संप्रदानम्

- पञ्चमी (5th) ablative case अपादान (from, through)
  ध्रुवमपायेऽपादानम् The eternal unmoving from which all movement comes is अपादानम् (the Self within, all action comes from the Self अप moving away from.)

- षष्ठी (6th) genitive case सम्बन्ध (bound together) That which is associated with one of the actors is सम्बन्ध .

- सप्तमी (7th) locative अधिकरण (place of action, in, under, below, above, behind)
  आधारोऽधिकरणम् The substratum, the substance of the Absolute is अधिकरण
  Occasionally सम्बोधन , the vocative case, is considered in conjunction with विभक्ति (e.g. Oh Rāma !) That name which awakens attention in the person addressed is सम्बोधन. The six विभक्ति excepting सम्बन्ध are referred to as being कारके i.e. directly related to the action expressed by the क्रिया (verb).

> # सत्यम् ज्ञानम् अनन्तम् ब्रह्म
> Truth knowledge infinite Brahman (is)

Practical use of vibhakti -the ways in which the 7 cases (*vibhakti)* may be interpreted

prathamā (1st)

- is used to state the existence of something and its name.
- It identifies the "agent" of the action.
- is used with roots *bhū, as,* and *kṛ* when something becomes, is, or is made into something

dvitīyā (2nd)

- states the *karma* or object of the sentence
- may state the destination of a verb of motion
- may express "fallen into", "gone to" as a state – happiness or other words ending in ness, ship, hood. i.e. he went to angriness – (was angry)

tṛtīyā (3rd)

- carries the sense of "by means of" - the instrument that brings about the action.
- is used in the sense "with", "together with" –especially with *saha*
  words such as *rahit* (without) and *vinā* (devoid of) attract *tṛtīyā*
- is used with words like "filled", "enough"
- sometimes has the sense of cause or reason for
  with "*kim*" etc. has the sense of "what use.... or purpose"
- a *tṛtīyā* ending is often used to form an adverb. e.g. with happiness - happily

caturthī (4th)

- is used for the person or purpose to which the action is dedicated
- in the act of giving and often of bowing, the recipient is stated in the dative.
- the word *artha* has the dative sense at the end of a compound
- can be used in the sense of leads to

pañcamī (5th)

- is used mainly in the sense of "away from"
- when there is fear from something or protection from something
- with directional words like *dūre, bahi, pūrvam, anya*
- to state the source of something
- as a way of saying "because of" or "due to"
- is used with certain verbs as "stops" (from)

ṣaṣṭī (6th)

- primary use is the genitive case
- can be used to do the work of almost any vibhakti
- since there is not a verb meaning to have in Sanskrit *ṣaṣṭī* is used
- is used with words for (for the sake of, a little of and full or filled with), sometimes is used to take the place of another *vibhakti* with words like "dear," and "known" his, her, and their are not usually supplied but should be included in a translation

saptamī (7th)

- locative case. indicates where something occurs.
- indicates the time when something occurs
- there may be the sense of "among"
- is used for the person or thing to which an emotion is directed
- with words like "capable" or "skilful in" , that in which there is skill or ability is expressed.
- some words such as "placed" and "gone to" have the locative sense at the end of a compound
- may have the sense of "concerning" or "in the matter of"

Declension – masculine

rāma m

1	*rāmaḥ*	*rāmau*	*rāmāḥ*
2	*rāmam*	*rāmau*	*rāmān*
3	*rāmeṇa*	*rāmābhyām*	*rāmaiḥ*
4	*rāmāya*	*rāmābhyām*	*rāmebhyaḥ*
5	*rāmāt*	*rāmābhyām*	*rāmebhyaḥ*
6	*rāmasya*	*rāmayoḥ*	*rāmāṇām*
7	*rāme*	*rāmayoḥ*	*rāmeṣu*
voc	*rāma*	*rāmau*	*rāmāḥ*

hari m. brown n. of *Viṣṇu-Kṛṣṇa*

1	*hariḥ*	*harī*	*harayaḥ*
2	*harim*	*harī*	*harīn*
3	*hariṇā*	*haribhyām*	*haribhiḥ*
4	*haraye*	*haribhyām*	*haribhyaḥ*
5	*hareḥ*	*haribhyām*	*haribhyaḥ*
6	*hareḥ*	*haryoḥ*	*harīṇām*
7	*harau*	*haryoḥ*	*hariṣu*
voc	*hare*	*harī*	*harayaḥ*

guru m. teacher

1	*guruḥ*	*gurū*	*guravaḥ*
2	*gurum*	*gurū*	*gurūn*
3	*guruṇā*	*gurubhyām*	*gurubhiḥ*
4	*gurave*	*gurubhyām*	*gurubhyaḥ*
5	*guroḥ*	*gurubhyām*	*gurubhyaḥ*
6	*guroḥ*	*gurvoḥ*	*gurūṇām*
7	*gurau*	*gurvoḥ*	*guruṣu*
voc	*guro*	*gurū*	*guravaḥ*

dhātṛ m. creator

1	*dhātā*	*dhātārau*	*dhātāraḥ*
2	*dhātāram*	*dhātārau*	*dhātṝn*
3	*dhātrā*	*dhātṛbhyām*	*dhātṛbhiḥ*
4	*dhātre*	*dhātṛbhyām*	*dhātṛbhyaḥ*
5	*dhātuḥ*	*dhātṛbhyām*	*dhātṛbhyaḥ*
6	*dhātuḥ*	*dhātroḥ*	*dhātṝṇām*
7	*dhātari*	*dhātroḥ*	*dhātṛṣu*
voc	*dhātaḥ*	*dhātārau*	*dhātāraḥ*

pitç m. father

1	*pitā*	*pitarau*	*pitaraḥ*
2	*pitaram*	*pitarau*	*pitṝn*
3	*pitrā*	*pitṛbhyām*	*pitṛbhiḥ*
4	*pitre*	*pitṛbhyām*	*pitṛbhyaḥ*
5	*pituḥ*	*pitṛbhyām*	*pitṛbhyaḥ*
6	*pituḥ*	*pitroḥ*	*pitṝṇām*
7	*pitari*	*pitroḥ*	*pitṛṣu*
voc	*pitaḥ*	*pitarau*	*pitaraḥ*

suhṛd m. friend, kind-hearted

1	*suhṛt*	*suhṛdau*	*suhṛdaḥ*
2	*suhṛdam*	*suhṛdau*	*suhṛdaḥ*
3	*suhṛdā*	*suhṛdbhyām*	*suhṛdbhiḥ*
4	*suhṛde*	*suhṛdbhyām*	*suhṛdbhyaḥ*
5	*suhṛdaḥ*	*suhṛdbhyām*	*suhṛdbhyaḥ*
6	*suhṛdaḥ*	*suhṛdoḥ*	*suhṛdām*
7	*suhṛdi*	*suhṛdoḥ*	*suhṛtsu*
v	*suhṛt*	*suhṛdau*	*suhṛdaḥ*

ātman m. self

1	*ātmā*	*ātmānau*	*ātmānaḥ*
2	*ātmānam*	*ātmānau*	*ātmanaḥ*
3	*ātmanā*	*ātmabhyām*	*ātmabhiḥ*
4	*ātmane*	*ātmabhyām*	*ātmabhyaḥ*
5	*ātmanaḥ*	*ātmabhyām*	*ātmabhyaḥ*
6	*ātmanaḥ*	*ātmanoḥ*	*ātmanām*
7	*ātmani*	*ātmanoḥ*	*ātmasu*
v	*ātman*	*ātmānau*	*ātmānaḥ*

rājan m. king

1	*rājā*	*rājānau*	*rājānaḥ*
2	*rājānam*	*rājānau*	*rājāaḥ*
3	*rājñā*	*rājabhyām*	*rājabhiḥ*
4	*rājñe*	*rājabhyām*	*rājabhyaḥ*
5	*rājñaḥ*	*rājabhyām*	*rājabhyaḥ*
6	*rājñaḥ*	*rājñoḥ*	*rājñām*
7	*rājñi*	*rājñoḥ*	*rājasu*
voc	*rājan*	*rājānau*	*rājānaḥ*

jñānin m. wise man, knower

1	*jñānī*	*jñāninau*	*jñāninaḥ*
2	*jñāninam*	*jñāninau*	*jñāninaḥ*
3	*jñāninā*	*jñānibhyām*	*jñānibhiḥ*
4	*jñānine*	*jñānibhyām*	*jñānibhyaḥ*
5	*jñāninaḥ*	*jñānibhyām*	*jñānibhyaḥ*
6	*jñāninaḥ*	*jñāninoḥ*	*jñāninām*
7	*jñānini*	*jñāninoḥ*	*jñāniṣu*
v	*jñānin*	*jñāninau*	*jñāninaḥ*

sumanas m. good-minded, well-disposed

1	*sumanāḥ*	*sumanasau*	*sumanasaḥ*
2	*sumanasam*	*sumanasau*	*sumanasaḥ*
3	*sumanasā*	*sumanobhyām*	*sumanobhiḥ*
4	*sumanase*	*sumanobhyām*	*sumanobhyaḥ*
5	*sumanasa*	*sumanobhyām*	*sumanobhyaḥ*
6	*sumanasaḥ*	*sumanasoḥ*	*sumanasām*
7	*sumanasi*	*sumanasoḥ*	*sumanaḥsu*
v	*sumanaḥ*	*sumanasau*	*sumanasaḥ*

dhīmat m. wise, intelligent

1	*dhīmān*	*dhīmantau*	*dhīmantaḥ*
2	*dhīmantam*	*dhīmantau*	*dhīmataḥ*
3	*dhīmatā*	*dhīmadbhyām*	*dhīmadbhiḥ*
4	*dhīmate*	*dhīmadbhyām*	*dhīmadbhyaḥ*
5	*dhīmataḥ*	*dhīmadbhyām*	*dhīmadbhyaḥ*
6	*dhīmataḥ*	*dhīmatoḥ*	*dhīmatām*
7	*dhīmati*	*dhīmatoḥ*	*dhīmatsu*
v	*dhīman*	*dhīmantau*	*dhīmantaḥ*

Feminine Nouns

sītā f.

1	*sītā*	*sīte*	*sītāḥ*
2	*sītām*	*sīte*	*sītāḥ*
3	*sītayā*	*sītābhyām*	*sītābhiḥ*
4	*sītāyai*	*sītābhyām*	*sītābhyaḥ*
5	*sītāyāḥ*	*sītābhyām*	*sītābhyaḥ*
6	*sītāyāḥ*	*sītayoḥ*	*sītānām*
7	*sītāyām*	*sītayoḥ*	*sītāsu*
v	*sīte*	*sīte*	*sītāḥ*

svasṛ f. sister

1	*svasā*	*svasārau*	*svasāraḥ*
2	*svasāram*	*svasārau*	*svasṝḥ*
3	*svasrā*	*svasṛbhyām*	*svasṛbhiḥ*
4	*svasre*	*svasṛbhyām*	*svasṛbhyaḥ*
5	*svasuḥ*	*svasṛbhyām*	*svasṛbhyaḥ*
6	*svasuḥ*	*svasroḥ*	*svasṝṇām*
7	*svasari*	*svasroḥ*	*svasṛṣu*
v	*svasaḥ*	*svasārau*	*svasāraḥ*

mati f. devotion, prayer

1	*matiḥ*	*matī*	*matayaḥ*
2	*matim*	*matī*	*matīḥ*
3	*matyā*	*matibhyām*	*matibhiḥ*
4	*matyai, mataye*	*matibhyām*	*matibhyaḥ*
5	*matyāḥ mateḥ*	*matibhyām*	*matibhyaḥ*
6	*matyāḥ mateḥ*	*matyoḥ*	*matīnām*
7	*matyām matau*	*matyoḥ*	*matiṣu*
v	*mate*	*matī*	*matayaḥ*

mahat m. great

1	*mahān*	*mahāntau*	*mahāntaḥ*
2	*mahāntam*	*mahāntau*	*mahataḥ*
3	*mahatā*	*mahadbhyām*	*mahadbhiḥ*
4	*mahate*	*mahadbhyām*	*mahadbhyaḥ*
5	*mahataḥ*	*mahadbhyām*	*mahadbhyaḥ*
6	*mahataḥ*	*mahatoḥ*	*mahatām*
7	*mahati*	*mahatoḥ*	*mahatsu*
v	*mahān*	*mahāntau*	*mahāntaḥ*

Feminine Nouns

nadī f. river

1	*nadī*	*nadyau*	*nadyaḥ*
2	*nadīm*	*nadyau*	*nadīḥ*
3	*nadyā*	*nadībhyām*	*nadībhiḥ*
4	*nadyai*	*nadībhyām*	*nadībhyaḥ*
5	*nadyāḥ*	*nadībhyām*	*nadībhyaḥ*
6	*nadyāḥ*	*nadyoḥ*	*nadīnām*
7	*nadyām*	*nadyoḥ*	*nadīṣu*
v	*nadi*	*nadyau*	*nadyaḥ*

mātṛ f. mother

1	*mātā*	*mātarau*	*mātaraḥ*
2	*mātaram*	*mātarau*	*mātṝḥ*
3	*mātrā*	*mātṛbhyām*	*mātṛbhiḥ*
4	*mātre*	*mātṛbhyām*	*mātṛbhyaḥ*
5	*mātuḥ*	*mātṛbhyām*	*mātṛbhyaḥ*
6	*mātuḥ*	*mātroḥ*	*mātṝṇām*
7	*mātari*	*mātroḥ*	*mātṛṣu*
v	*mātaḥ*	*mātarau*	*mātaraḥ*

vāk f. speech

1	*vāk*	*vākau*	*vākaḥ*
2	*vākam*	*vākau*	*vākaḥ*
3	*vākā*	*vāgbhyām*	*vāgbhiḥ*
4	*vāke*	*vāgbhyām*	*vāgbhyaḥ*
5	*vākaḥ*	*vāgbhyām*	*vāgbhyaḥ*
6	*vākaḥ*	*vākoḥ*	*vākām*
7	*vāki*	*vākoḥ*	*vṣkṣu*
v	*vāk*	*vākau*	*vṣkaḥ*

dhenu f. cow

1	*dhenuḥ*	*dhenū*	*dhenavaḥ*
2	*dhenum*	*dhenū*	*dhenūḥ*
3	*dhenvā*	*dhenubhyām*	*dhenubhiḥ*
4	*dhenvai, dhenave*	*dhenubhyām*	*dhenubhyaḥ*
5	*dhenvāḥ, dhenoḥ*	*dhenubhyām*	*dhenubhyaḥ*
6	*dhenvāḥ, dhenoḥ*	*dhenvoḥ*	*dhenūnām*
7	*dhenvāḥ dhenoḥ*	*dhenvoḥ*	*dhenuṣu*
v	*dheno*	*dhenū*	*dhenavaḥ*

Neuter Nouns

phalam n. fruit

1	*phalam*	*phale*	*phalāni*
2	*phalam*	*phale*	*phalāni*
3	*phalena*	*phalābhyām*	*phalaiḥ*
4	*phalāya*	*phalābhyām*	*phalebhyaḥ*
5	*phalāt*	*phalābhyām*	*phalebhyaḥ*
6	*phalasya*	*phalayoḥ*	*phalānām*
7	*phale*	*phalayoḥ*	*phaleṣu*
v	*phala*	*phale*	*phalāni*

karman n. act, action

1	*karma*	*karmaṇī*	*karmāṇi*
2	*karma*	*karmaṇī*	*karmāṇi*
3	*karmaṇā*	*karmabhyām*	*karmabhiḥ*
4	*karmaṇe*	*karmabhyām*	*karmabhyaḥ*
5	*karmaṇaḥ*	*karmabhyām*	*karmabhyaḥ*
6	*karmaṇaḥ*	*karmanoḥ*	*karmaṇām*
7	*karmaṇi*	*karmanoḥ*	*karmasu*
v	*karma*	*karmaṇī*	*karmāṇi*

nāman n. name

1	*nāma*	*nām(a)nī*	*nāmāni*
2	*nāma*	*nām(a)nī*	*nāmāni*
3	*nāmnā*	*nāmabhyām*	*nāmabhiḥ*
4	*nāmne*	*nāmabhyām*	*nāmabhyaḥ*
5	*nāmnaḥ*	*nāmabhyām*	*nāmabhyaḥ*
6	*nāmnaḥ*	*nāmnoḥ*	*nāmnām*
7	*nām(a)ni*	*nāmnoḥ*	*nāmasu*
v	*nāma(n)*	*nām(a)nī*	*nāmāni*

manas n. mind

1	*manaḥ*	*manasī*	*manāṁsi*
2	*manaḥ*	*manasī*	*manāṁsi*
3	*manasā*	*manobhyām*	*manobhiḥ*
4	*manase*	*manobhyām*	*manobhyaḥ*
5	*manasaḥ*	*manobhyām*	*manobhyaḥ*
6	*manasaḥ*	*manasoḥ*	*manasām*
7	*manasi*	*manasoḥ*	*manaḥsu*
v	*manaḥ*	*manasī*	*manāṁsi*

madhu n spring, sweet

1	*madhu*	*madhunī*	*madhūni*
2	*madhu*	*madhunī*	*madhūni*
3	*madhunā*	*madhubhyām*	*madhubhiḥ*
4	*madhune*	*madhubhyām*	*madhubhyaḥ*
5	*madhunaḥ*	*madhubhyām*	*madhubhyaḥ*
6	*madhunaḥ*	*madhunoḥ*	*madhūnām*
7	*madhuni*	*madhunoḥ*	*madhuṣu*
v	*madhu*	*madhunī*	*madhūni*

dhanus n. bow

1	*dhanuḥ*	*dhanuṣī*	*dhanuṁsi*
2	*dhanuḥ*	*dhanuṣī*	*dhanuṁsi*
3	*dhanuṣā*	*dhanurbhyām*	*dhanurbhiḥ*
4	*dhanuṣe*	*dhanurbhyām*	*dhanurbhyaḥ*
5	*dhanuṣaḥ*	*dhanurbhyām*	*dhanurbhyaḥ*
6	*dhanuṣaḥ*	*dhanuṣoḥ*	*dhanuṣām*
7	*dhanuṣi*	*dhanuṣoḥ*	*dhanuḥṣu*
v	*dhanuḥ*	*dhanuṣī*	*dhanuṁsi*

dhīmat n. wise, intelligent

1	*dhīmat*	*dhīmatī*	*dhīmanti*
2	*dhīmat*	*dhīmatī*	*dhīmanti*
3	*dhīmatā*	*dhīmadbhyām*	*dhīmadbhiḥ*
4	*dhīmate*	*dhīmadbhyām*	*dhīmadbhyaḥ*
5	*dhīmataḥ*	*dhīmadbhyām*	*dhīmadbhyaḥ*
6	*dhīmataḥ*	*dhīmatoḥ*	*dhīmatām*
7	*dhīmati*	*dhīmatoḥ*	*dhīmatsu*
v	*dhīmat*	*dhīmatī*	*dhīmanti*

mahat n. great

1	*mahat*	*mahatī*	*mahānti*
2	*mahat*	*mahatī*	*mahānti*
3	*mahatā*	*mahadbhyām*	*mahadbhiḥ*
4	*mahate*	*mahadbhyām*	*mahadbhyaḥ*
5	*mahataḥ*	*mahadbhyām*	*mahadbhyaḥ*
6	*mahataḥ*	*mahatoḥ*	*mahatām*
7	*mahati*	*mahatoḥ*	*mahatsu*
v	*mahat*	*mahatī*	*mahānti*

Adjectives

विशेषण – An adjective brings out the qualities of a नामन् e.g. The beautiful girl sits. The yellow ball bounced over the fence- lit. " **the act of expanding the remainder**"

Adjectives are placed before the noun they describe and will have the same number, gender and case. In the Monier-Williams Dictionary (MWD) the adjectival meaning of a word is given first and because they can have any gender they are identified by the letters mfn. at the start of the entry. Similarly in Sanskrit script the word may be followed by a ° symbol to the right and above to indicate the possibility of being declined in any gender. The same word acting as a noun may be found later in the entry with its specific gender. This meaning will likely have some difference from the adjectival meaning and the meanings for each gender may be considerably different. Therefore care is needed to ascertain the correct meaning.

Most adjectives decline like nouns as they have the basic endings. However there are many words indicated as mfn. in the dictionary that are actually participles that can be used as adjectives. As shown in the participle section, most of these can be declined to match the noun that they are describing but some have unusual endings like *an*, *ant* or *at* that require variations to the declension. Here are examples – alternatives are shown together

bhavant – being

	singular	dual	plural
	m. n.	m. n.	m. n.
1st case	*bhavan bhavat*	*bhavantau bhavantī*	*bhavantaḥ bhavanti*
2nd	*bhavantam bhavat*	*bhavantau bhavantī*	*bhavataḥ bhavanti*
3rd	*bhavatā*	*bhavadbhyām*	*bhavadbhiḥ*
4th	*bhavate*	*bhavadbhyām*	*bhavadbhyaḥ*
5th	*bhavataḥ*	*bhavadbhyām*	*bhavadbhyaḥ*
6th	*bhavataḥ*	*bhavatoḥ*	*bhavatām*
7th	*bhavati*	*bhavatoḥ*	*bhavatsu*
voc.	*bhavan bhavat*	*bhavantau bhavantī*	*bhavantaḥ bhavanti*

adant – eating

1	*adant adant*	*adantau adantī*	*adantaḥ adanti*
2.	*adantam adant*	*adantau adantī*	*adantaḥ adanti*
3.	*adantā*	*adandbhyām*	*adandbhiḥ*
4.	*adante*	*adandbhyām*	*adandbhyaḥ*
5.	*adantaḥ*	*adandbhyām*	*adandbhyaḥ*
6.	*adantaḥ*	*adantoḥ*	*adantām*
7.	*adanti*	*adantoḥ*	*adantsu*
voc.	*adant adant*	*adantau adantī*	*adantaḥ adanti*

-mant and *–vant*

pacumant possessing cattle

	m.	n.	m.	n.	m.	n.
1	*pacumant*	*pacumant*	*pacumantau*	*pacumantī*	*pacumantas*	*pacumanti*
2	*pacumantam*	*pacumant*	*pacumantau*	*pacumantī*	*pacumatas*	*pacumanti*
3	*pacumantā*		*pacumandbhyām*		*pacumandbhiḥ*	
4	*pacumante*		*pacumandbhyām*		*pacumandbhyaḥ*	
5	*pacumantaḥ*		*pacumandbhyām*		*pacumandbhyaḥ*	
6	*pacumantaḥ*		*pacumantoḥ*		*pacumantām*	
7	*pacumanti*		*pacumantoḥ*		*pacumantsu*	
voc	*pacumant*	*pacumat*	*pacumantau*	*pacumantī*	*pacumantas*	*pacumanti*

bhagavat fortunate, blessed (having good fortune)

	m.	n.	m.	n,	m.	n.
1	*bhagavān*	*bhagavat*	*bhagavantau*	*bhagavatī*	*bhagavantaḥ*	*bhagavanti*
2	*bhagavantam*	*bhagavat*	*bhagavantau*	*bhagavatī*	*bhagavataḥ*	*bhagavanti*
3	*bhagavatā*		*bhagavadbhyām*		*bhagavadbhiḥ*	
4	*bhagavate*		*bhagavadbhyām*		*bhagavadbhyaḥ*	
5	*bhagavataḥ*		*bhagavadbhyām*		*bhagavadbhyaḥ*	
6	*bhagavataḥ*		*bhagavatoḥ*		*bhagavatām*	
7	*bhagavati*		*bhagavatoḥ*		*bhagavatsu*	
voc.	*bhagavat*		*bhagavantau*	*bhagavatī*	*bhagavantaḥ*	*bhagavanti*

Comparatives and Superlatives

The comparative is usually formed by adding *tara* to the masculine stem of the adjective.
e.g. *puṇya* pure *puṇyatara* purer
The superlative is formed by adding *tama* to the masculine stem of the adjective
e.g. *puṇya* pure *puṇyatama* purest

Some adjectives have *īyas* added for the comparative and *iṣṭha* for the superlative.
e.g. *laghu* light *laghīyas* lighter *laghiṣṭha* lightest
or simply *yas* and *ṣṭha*

सर्वेभावन्तुसुखिनः सर्वे सन्तु निरामयाः ।
सर्वे भद्राणि पश्यन्तु मा कश्चित् दुःखभाग्भवेत् ॥

All be happy, all be without disease;
All have well-being; none be in misery of any kind

Prefixes- including -upasarga(s)

upasarga 210/2 m. a *nipāta* or particle joined to a verb or noun denoting action...
These are used like prefixes and are said to 'change the direction' of the action.

a gives a negative or contrary sense (changes to *an* before a vowel), absence of a quality or attribute, e.g. *an-eka* not one, *an-anta* endless, *a-sat* not good, *a-paśyat* not seeing

ā to, until, as far as, right up to, near, near to, towards, strong affirmation, With roots like *gam, yā, i* (to go), 1. *dā* to give, it reverses the action; e.g. *ā-gacchati* he comes, *ā-datte* he takes

abhi to, towards, into, over, upon, moving towards, approaching

adhi 20/2 expresses above, over and above, besides

anu after, along, alongside, lengthwise, near to, subordinate to, with

apa away, off, back, down

api 55/1 expresses placing near or over, uniting to, annexing, reaching to, proximity, as a separable adv. and, also, besides, surely, very, even, even now, also, moreover

ati 12/2 beyond, over, excessively, too, exceedingly, very, passing, going, excessive, intense, beyond, surpassing

ava 96/1 off, away, down

dus evil, ill, bad, difficult, hard, slight, inferior, opp. to *su*

ku- a prefix indicating badness, smallness, deficiency,

ni prefix to verbs or nouns, down, back, into, within, (with nouns has a sense of negation or privation e.g. down-hearted).

nis 543/2 ind. out, forth, away. also used as a prefix to verbs and nouns in which case it takes the meanings- out of, away from, without, destitute of, free from, also may be used as a strengthening particle – entirely, (very liable to be changed to *niḥ, nir, niś, niṣ,* or *nī)*

para(m) more correctly part of a compound – far, distant, remote, beyond, highest, supreme, chief,

parā away, off, aside, along, on

pari 591/2 round, around, about, round about, fully, abundantly richly, against, opposite, in the direction of

pra before, forward, in front, on, forth (forwards direction)

prati towards, near to, against, in opposition to, down, upon, back again, towards (after a word in 2nd case)

sa 1111/2 with, together or along with, accompanied by, added to, having, possessing, containing, having the same,

saha 1193/2 2. together with, with, along with, (with 5th) jointly, in common, in company,

sam with, together with, along with, altogether, (opp. to *vi*)

su 5. 1219/3 ind. good, much, greatly, very, right, virtuous, beautiful, easy, (opp. to *dus)*

sva part of many compounds and declinable – own, one's own, my own, our own etc.

ud expresses superiority in place, rank, station, power; up, upwards, upon, on, over, above. May also express separation and disjunction: out, out of, from, off, away, away from, apart, (also seen as *ut, ul, uj, uc,*

upa towards, near to, by side of, with, together with, under, down, (opp. to *apa*)

vi in two parts, asunder, apart, outwards, in all directions. expresses division, distinction, distribution, arrangement, order, opposition, deliberation (opp. to sam)

Pronouns (*sarvanāman* – name for all)

The personal pronouns for "I" and "you" (1st person and 2nd person) are without gender. Others have one of the three genders. Each pronoun has a base word. In compound words the base of a pronoun is given rather than a declined word. This has the practical effect of shortening the compound and the meaning is usually clear from the context.

Options are given in brackets. (Some are enclitic i.e. may not be used at the start of a sentence. and may not be followed by articles such as *ca* (and) or *vā* (or)). As always be aware that final *s* > *ḥ*

Personal Pronouns

Base (in composition) *mad* and *asmad*. Base (in composition) *tvad* and *yuṣmad*

1st p	**I**	**we two**	**we**		2nd p	**you**	**you two**	**you (pl).**
1	*aham*	*āvām*	*vayam*		*1*	*tvam*	*yuvām*	*yūyam*
2	*mām (mā)*	*āvām (nau)*	*asmān (nas)*		2	*tvām (tvā)*	*yuvām (vām)*	*yuṣmān (vas)*
3	*mayā*	*āvābhyām*	*asmābhis*		*3*	*tvayā*	*yuvābhyām*	*yuṣmābhis*
4	*mahyam(me)*	*āvābhyām (nau)*	*asmabhyam (nas)*		*4*	*tubhyam(te)*	*yuvābhyām (vām)*	*yuṣmabhyam (vas)*
5	*mat*	*āvābhyām*	*asmat*		*5*	*tvat*	*yuvābhyām*	*yuṣmat*
6	*mama (me)*	*āvayos (nau)*	*asmākam (nas)*		*6*	*tava (te)*	*yuvayos (vām)*	*yuṣmākam (vas)*
7	*mayi*	*āvayos*	*asmāsu*		*7*	*tvayi*	*yuvayos*	*yuṣmāsu*

Demonstrative pronouns Base (in composition) *tad*

(Demonstrative pronouns distinguish something as being further from or nearer to the speaker. e.g. 'that' is further away than 'this'. That [*tad*] is used for people or things that are further away. Other distinctions are given with each table.)

he **that**

masc.	*saḥ*	*tau*	*te*		neut.	*tat*	*te*	*tāni*
	tam	*tau*	*tān*			*tat*	*te*	*tāni*
	tena	*tābhyām*	*taiḥ*			*tena*	*tābhyām*	*taiḥ*
	tasmai	*tābhyām*	*tebhyaḥ*			*tasmai*	*tābhyām*	*tebhyaḥ*
	tasmāt	*tābhyām*	*tebhyam*			*tasmāt*	*tābhyām*	*tebhyam*
	tasya	*tayoḥ*	*teṣām*			*tasya*	*tayoḥ*	*teṣām*
	tasmin	*tayoḥ*	*teṣu*			*tasmin*	*tayoḥ*	*teṣu*

she

fem.	*sā*	*te*	*tāḥ*
	tām	*te*	*tāḥ*
	tayā	*tābhyām*	*tābhiḥ*
	tasyai	*tābhyām*	*tābhyaḥ*
	tasyāḥ	*tābhyām*	*tābhyaḥ*
	tāsyāḥ	*tayoḥ*	*tāsām*
	tasyām	*tayoḥ*	*tāsu*

Possessive adjectives are formed by adding *iyaḥ* to the bases of the personal pronouns –

madiyaḥ, yā, yam -mine

tvadiyaḥ, yā, yam -your

tadiyaḥ, yā, yam -his, her, its

asmadiyaḥ, yā, yam - our

yuṣmadiyaḥ, yā, yam - your

tadiyaḥ, yā, yam -their

Enclitic Pronouns

	masculine			*neuter*			*feminine*		
	singular			dual			plural		
2nd	*enam*	*enau,*	*enān*	*enat*	*ene*	*enāni*	*enām*	*ene*	*enāḥ*
3rd	*enena*			*enena*			*eneyā*		
6th/7th		*enayoḥ*			*enayoḥ*			*enayoḥ*	

Demonstrative pronouns continued (this and that)

stem ***etad*, this, (very near)**

masc.	*eṣaḥ*	*etau*	*ete*		neut.	*etat*	*ete*	*etāni*
	etam	*etau*	*etān*			*etat*	*ete*	*etāni*
	etena	*etābhyām*	*etaiḥ*			*etena*	*etābhyām*	*etaiḥ*
	etasmai	*etābhyām*	*etebhyaḥ*			*etasmai*	*etābhyām*	*etebhyaḥ*
	etasmāt	*etābhyām*	*etebhyaḥ*			*etasmāt*	*etābhyām*	*etebhyaḥ*
	etasya	*etayoḥ*	*eteṣām*			*etasya*	*etayoḥ*	*eteṣām*
	etasmin	*etayoḥ*	*eteṣu*			*etasmin*	*etayoḥ*	*eteṣu*

fem.	*eṣa*	*ete*	*etāḥ*
	etām	*ete*	*etāḥ*
	etayā	*etābhyām*	*etābhiḥ*
	etasyai	*etābhyām*	*etābhyaḥ*
	etasyāḥ	*etābhyām*	*etābhyaḥ*
	etasyāḥ	*etayoḥ*	*etāṣām*
	etasyām	*etayoḥ*	*eteṣu*

stem ***idam*, this (indefinitely)**

masc.	*ayam*	*imau*	*ime*		neut	*idam*	*ime*	*imāni*
	imam	*imau*	*imān*			*idam*	*ime*	*imāni*
	anena	*ābhyām*	*ebhiḥ*			*anena*	*ābhyām*	*ebhiḥ*
	asmai	*ābhyām*	*ebhyaḥ*			*asmai*	*ābhyām*	*ebhyaḥ*
	asmāt	*ābhyām*	*ebhyaḥ*			*asmāt*	*ābhyām*	*ebhyaḥ*
	asya	*anayoḥ*	*eṣām*			*asya*	*anayoḥ*	*eṣām*
	asmin	*anayoḥ*	*eṣu*			*asmin*	*anayoḥ*	*eṣu*

stem ***idam*, this (indefinitely)**

fem.	*iyam*	*ime*	*imāḥ*
	imām	*ime*	*imāḥ*
	anayā	*ābhyām*	*ābhiḥ*
	asyai	*ābhyām*	*ābhyaḥ*
	asyāḥ	*ābhyām*	*ābhyaḥ*
	asyāḥ	*anayoḥ*	*āsām*
	asyām	*anayoḥ*	*āsu*

***adas*, that (mediate i.e in between, neither near nor far)**

masc.	*asau*	*amū*	*amī*		**neut.**	*adaḥ*	*amū*	*amūni*
	amum	*amū*	*amūn*			*adaḥ*	*amū*	*amūni*
	amunā	*amūbhyām*	*amībhiḥ*			*amunā*	*amūbhyām*	*amībhiḥ*
	amuṣmai	*amūbhyām*	*amībhyaḥ*			*amuṣmai*	*amūbhyām*	*amībhyaḥ*
	amuṣmāt	*amūbhyām*	*amībhyaḥ*			*amuṣmāt*	*amūbhyām*	*amībhyaḥ*
	amuṣya	*amuyoḥ*	*amīṣām*			*amuṣya*	*amuyoḥ*	*amīṣām*
	amuṣmin	*amuyoḥ*	*amīṣu*			*amuṣmin*	*amuyoḥ*	*amīṣu*

***adas*, that** (mediate)

fem.	*asau*	*amū*	*amūḥ*	
	amūm	*amū*	*amūḥ*	
	amuyā	*amūbhyām*	*amūbhiḥ*	
	amuṣyai	*amūbhyām*	*amūbhyaḥ*	
	amuṣyāḥ	*amūbhyām*	*amūbhyaḥ*	
	amuṣyāḥ	*amuyoḥ*	*amūṣām*	
	amuṣyām	*amuyoḥ*	*amūṣu*	

the relative pronoun *yad* who, or which, (relates to another part of the sentence)

masc.	*yaḥ*	*yau*	*ye*		neut.	*yat*	*ye*	*yāni*
	yam	*yau*	*yān*			*yat*	*ye*	*yāni*
	yena	*yābhyām*	*yaiḥ*			*yena*	*yābhyām*	*yaiḥ*
	yasmai	*yābhyām*	*yebhyaḥ*			*yasmai*	*yābhyām*	*yebhyaḥ*
	yasmāt	*yābhyām*	*yebhyaḥ*			*yasmāt*	*yābhyām*	*yebhyaḥ*
	yasya	*yayoḥ*	*yeṣām*			*yasya*	*yayoḥ*	*yeṣām*
	yasmin	*yayoḥ*	*yeṣu*			*yasmin*	*yayoḥ*	*yeṣu*

the relative pronoun *yad* (fem.)

fem.	*yāḥ*	*ye*	*yāḥ*
	yām	*ye*	*yāḥ*
	yayā	*yābhyām*	*yābhiḥ*
	yasyai	*yābhyām*	*yābhyaḥ*
	yasyāḥ	*yābhyām*	*yābhyaḥ*
	yasyāḥ	*yayoḥ*	*yāsām*
	yasyām	*yayoḥ*	*yāsu*

ātman, self, is declined like Brahman, '*ātmānam ātmanā paśya*' "see thyself by thyself" but is used in the singular even when referring to 2 or 3 persons.
svaḥ, svā, svam is a reflexive adjective(see next page). *svam putram* "his own son".

Interrogative pronouns based on *kim*, who or which

masc.	*kaḥ*	*kau*	*ke*		neut.	*kim*	*ke*	*kāni*
	kam	*kau*	*kān*			*kim*	*ke*	*kāni*
	kena	*kābhyām*	*kaiḥ*			*kena*	*kābhyām*	*kaiḥ*
	kasmai	*kābhyām*	*kebhyaḥ*			*kasmai*	*kābhyām*	*kebhyaḥ*
	kasmāt	*kābhyām*	*kebhyaḥ*			*kasmāt*	*kābhyām*	*kebhyaḥ*
	kasya	*kayoḥ*	*keṣām*			*kasya*	*kayoḥ*	*keṣām*
	kasmin	*kayoḥ*	*keṣu*			*kasmin*	*kayoḥ*	*keṣu*

base *kim* who or which

fem.	*kā*	*ke*	*kāḥ*
	kām	*ke*	*kāḥ*
	kayā	*kābhyām*	*kābhiḥ*
	kasyai	*kābhyām*	*kābhyaḥ*
	kasyāḥ	*kābhyām*	*kābhyaḥ*
	kasyāḥ	*kayoḥ*	*kāṣām*
	kasyām	*kayoḥ*	*kāsu*

***Sarva* all**

m	*sarvaḥ*	*sarvau*	*sarve*	n	*sarvam*	*sarve*	*sarvāṇi*
	sarvam	*sarvau*	*sarvān*		*sarvam*	*sarve*	*sarvāṇi*
	sarveṇa	*sarvābhyām*	*sarvaiḥ*		*sarveṇa*	*sarvābhyām*	*sarvaiḥ*
	sarvasmai	*sarvābhyām*	*sarvebhyaḥ*		*sarvasmai*	*sarvābhyām*	*sarvebhyaḥ*
	sarvasmāt	*sarvābhyām*	*sarvebhyaḥ*		*sarvasmāt*	*sarvābhyām*	*sarvebhyaḥ*
	sarvasya	*sarvayoḥ*	*sarveṣām*		*sarvasya*	*sarvayoḥ*	*sarveṣām*
	sarvasmin	*sarvayoḥ*	*sarveṣu*		*sarvasmin*	*sarvayoḥ*	*sarveṣu*
v	*sarva*	*sarvau*	*sarve*		*sarva*	*sarve*	*sarvāṇi*

fem.	*sarvā*	*sarve*	*sarvāḥ*
	sarvām	*sarve*	*sarvāḥ*
	sarvayā	*sarvābhyām*	*sarvābhiḥ*
	sarvasyai	*sarvābhyām*	*sarvābhyaḥ*
	sarvasyāḥ	*sarvābhyām*	*sarvābhyaḥ*
	sarvasyāḥ	*sarvayoḥ*	*sarvāsām*
	sarvasyām	*sarvayoḥ*	*sarvāsu*
voc.	*sarve*	*sarve*	*sarvāḥ*

Reflexive Pronouns -

In English, the reflexive pronouns are myself, yourself, himself, herself, itself, oneself, ourselves, yourselves, and themselves. In the statements "**I** see **him**" and "**She** sees **you**", the objects are not the same persons as the subjects, and regular pronouns are used. However, when the person being seen is the same as the person who is seeing, the reflexive pronoun is used: "**I** see **myself**" or "**She** sees **herself**". (Wikipedia)

svayam (self) is indeclinable and may express any person or number. – myself, himself, etc.
e.g.*svayam vṛtavān* - I chose it myself, you chose it yourself or he chose it himself.
svayam vṛtavatī - she chose it herself
svayam vṛtavantaḥ – we, you, they chose it by our, your, themselves
usually used in 1st case but also 3rd, 6th and may mean spontaneously

Indefinites from Pronouns (see Indefinite Statements following Adverbs),

Indefinites may be formed by adding *cit, cana,* or *api* to the pronoun base *kim.* e.g.

kaḥ + cit (kaścit) ind. any, *yaḥ kaścit* whosoever,
or *kaḥ + cana (kaścana)* ind. some, somebody,
or *kaḥ + api (ko'pi)* = a certain man, some man, something (m),
e.g. *kaścit mām vadati* - he says something to me,

kā + cit (kācit) or *kā+ cana (kācana) or kā +api (kāpi)* = a certain woman, any, some woman, something (f), e.g. *kācana mām śṛṇoti* - someone (f.) hears me,

kim + cit (kiñcit) or *kim + cana (kiñcana)* or *kim +api (kimapi)* = a certain thing, some thing, e.g
vane kimapi carati - in the forest something walks

kṛdanta -(having a *kṛt* ending - includes) participles

English –

- participles are formed from verbs and function as adjectives or verbs
- they may relate to the past, present or future
- present participles are usually formed by adding –ing e.g. swimming, fishing
- past participles are usually formed by adding –ed e.g. fished, swam, was swimming
- participles may act as adjectives e.g. the <u>satisfied</u> customer, the <u>spoken</u> word
- verbal forms - e.g. the customer <u>was satisfied</u>, the word <u>was spoken</u>

Sanskrit-

present active	present middle	present passive
future active	future middle	future passive (gerundive)
past active		past passive
perfect active	perfect middle	

gerund (conjunctive, absolute)
infinitive

- participles are formed from verb roots but do not take verb endings. Those that decline take primary nominal endings according to gender and number
- most participles are declined (not the gerund)

past passive participle (ppp) (*bhūte kṛdanta*)This is formed by taking the root or a weak form of it and adding ***-ta, -ita, -āta,*** or ***-na***
na ciraṁ supto 'smi I have not slept long
rāmo rājagṛhaṁ gataḥ Rāma has gone to the palace

(Reminder: There is a system of vowel grade or strengthening by adding one or two measures of *a*. The vowel plus *a* is referred to as being *guṇa* or with *ā* is called *vṛddhi*. This involves *sandhi* changes so if unsure refer to a table.)

- ppp's are adjectives, and so must agree with a nominal in number and gender.. Since they end in *a* they are declined like *-a (puṁliṅga), -am (napuṁsakaliṅga.), -ā (strīliṅga).*
- ppp's often function as a verb, appearing in and agreeing with the first case
- ppp's may be used in a past passive sense, agreeing with the direct object which would be in the first case- *aśvo bālena labdaḥ* – the horse was obtained by the boy
- intransitive verbs (not taking a direct object e.g. arrive, snore) – ppp' s sometimes have an active sense, agreeing with the agent e.g. *Rāmo vanaṁ gataḥ.* Rāma went to the forest. or *sītā vanaṁ gatā.* Sītā went to the forest.
- a ppp may act as an adjective alone or as part of a compound e.g. *iṣṭaṁ phalam* desired reward or *iṣṭa-phalam* desired reward (*karmadhārya*) Note it is used in its base form (without gender). Gender is established by the final member.
- a ppp may have a present relevance referring to a past yet uncompleted action, e.g. *tyaktām kanyām paśyāmi* "I see the abandoned girl" or an action completed in the past but addressed in the present e.g. *kim naś chinnam* "What of ours is cut". meaning - "What's it to me?"

dhātu	1st pers/singular	past passive participle	
iṣ	*icchati*	*iṣṭa*	desired, liked, wished,
kṛ	*karoti, kurute*	*kṛta*	done, made

gam	*gacchati*	*gata*	gone, departed, dead,
gup	*gopāyati*	*gupta*	protected, guarded, concealed, secret,
cint	*cintayati(te)*	*cintita*	thought, considered, imagined,
cur	*corayati (te)*	*corita*	stolen
ji	*jayati*	*jita*	conquered, acquired, subdued,
tan	*tanoti, tanute*	*tata*	stretched, extended, expanded,
tud	*tudati (te)*	*tunna*	pushed, struck, goaded, hit
tyaj	*tyajati*	*tyakta*	abandoned, left
dṛś(paś)	*paśyati*	*dṛṣṭa*	seen, perceived, noticed,
nī	*nayati-te*	*nīta*	led, guided, brought, obtained,
paṭh	*paṭhati*	*paṭhita*	read, recited, studied,
pā	*pibati*	*pīta*	drunk, sucked, sipped, quaffed,
prach	*pṛcchati*	*pṛṣṭa*	asked, inquired, questioned,
budh	*bodhati-te*	*buddha*	known, awakened, expanded, understood,
bhāṣ	*bhāṣate*	*bhāṣita*	spoken, uttered,
bhū	*bhavati*	*bhūta*	been, become, fit, proper,
man	*manyate*	*mata*	thought, believed, imagined,
ram	*ramate*	*rata*	enjoyed, pleased, amused,
labh	*labhate*	*labdha*	obtained, taken, seized, caught,
vad	*vadati*	*udita*	spoken, spoken to, addressed,
			risen, ascended
vas	*vasati*	*uṣita*	lived, retired or resorted to, time (spent),
śubh	*śobhate*	*śobhita*	shined, adorned or embellished,
sev	*sevate*	*sevita*	served, visited, followed, frequented,
sthā	*tiṣṭhati*	*sthita*	established, situated, abiding in,
smi	*smayate*	*smita*	smiled, blossomed, expanded,
smṛ	*smarati*	*smṛta*	remembered, recollected, thought of,
has	*hasati*	*hasita*	laughed, mocked, ridiculed, excelled,
hā	*jahāti*	*hīna*	abandoned, left behind, excluded,
hu	*juhoti*	*huta*	offered, sacrificed, sacrified to,

other less common forms are-

dhātu /class				
dah	(1)	burn	*dagdha*	burnt
duh	(2)	milk	*dugdha*	milked
nah	(4)	bind	*naddha*	bound
lih	(2)	lick	*līḍha*	licked, tasted,
ruh	(1)	climb, mount	*rūḍha*	climbed, mounted
sah	(1)	endure	*soḍha*	endured, conquered, overcome,
vah	(1)	carry	*voḍha*	carried, led home married,
yuj	(7)	join	*yukta*	joined
dviṣ(	2)	hate	*dviṣṭa*	hated, disliked,
nind	blame		*nindita*	blamed
cumb	kiss		*cumbita*	kissed, touched softly,
śaṅk	doubt		*śaṅkita* doubted	
vac	say		*ukta*	said, spoken,
cal	move		*calita*	moved, gone, walked,
jīv	live		*jīvita*	lived, enlivened,
likh	write		*likhita*	written, drawn,
pat	fall		*patita*	fallen, descended,
khād	eat		*khādita*	eaten, devoured,
kup	be angry		*kupita*	angry, provoked, offended,

bādh	oppress	*bādhita*	oppressed, anulled
chid	cut	*chinna*	cut
bhid	split	*bhinna*	separated, split
pad	move	*panna*	fallen down, gone,
pṝ	fill	*pūrṇa*	filled
tṝ	cross	*tīrṇa*	crossed

A past passive participle may be the basis of an adjective or a noun (often a neuter noun).

dhātu	**adjective**	**noun**
kṛ do	*kṛta* done	*kṛta* *(n)* action
gai sing	*gīta* sung	*gītā* *(f)* song
budh awake	*buddha* awakened	*Buddha (m)* sage
sam + dhā together + put	*saṁhita* collected	*saṁhitā* collectedness, unity
sam + kṛ together+make	*saṁskṛta* perfected	*saṁskṛta (n)* sanskrit language

note: many roots add an *i* before *ta* e.g. *kup → kupita, cal → calita*
some roots lose the nasal before *ta* e.g. *gam → gata, man → mata*
some gain a vowel measure plus ***n*** e.g. *kam → kānta śam→ śānta*
There are also other variations mostly to do with internal sandhi or irregularity.
example *mayā pustakaṁ* ***paṭhitam*** A book **was read** by me.

The past active participle (*ktavatu*) is used as a past tense in the active construction (*kartari prayoga*) and agrees with the subject in number and gender. It is formed by adding *vat/vant* to the past passive participle and operates as a simple past tense. It is used in the first case following the pattern of *dhīmat* and the feminine ends in *–vatī* and declines like *nadī.* See examples below.
e.g. *jita → jitavat* conquered
and is declined like *dhīmat*

Masculine	*jitavān*	*jitavantau*	*jitavantaḥ*
	jitavantam	*jitavantau*	*jitavataḥ*
Neuter	*jitavat*	*jitavatī*	*jitavanti*
Feminine	*jitavatī*		etc.

Arjuna vanaṁ gatavān *Arjuna* went to the forest
sītā vanaṁ gatavatī *Sītā* went to the forest

ktvānta – the gerund (*-tvā*) or *lyabanta* (*-ya*)

- The *ktvānta* indicates prior action e.g. having gone, having spoken. In English they are known as gerunds. Note that they are also frequently translated like a past passive participle e.g. spoken, gone, received, deleted
- This applies whether the main verb is past, present or future.
- A series of gerunds may be used but should be in sequential order and followed by a main verb.
- Reference is usually to the subject.
- That which goes with the Gerund e.g. the 2nd case is usually placed immediately before it.
- The gerund is not declined. (Because its form is unchanging it is sometimes called the absolutive.)
- It is formed by adding *tvā* after the *dhātu* as below.
- If there is a prefix then *ya* is added instead of *tvā*.
- The gerund is frequently used to mark successive dependent clauses with prior or same time action. A subsequent independent clause often delivers the conclusions of the previous actions.

examples ... *yaj jñātvā mokṣyase ' śubhāt*
.. which having known thou shalt be released from evil BG 9/1
...*te puṇyam āsādya* (*ā* + √*sad* attaining, having attained) *surendralokam*
they attaining the pure world of the chief of the gods

prefix/root	*1st /singular*	*ktvānta/ gerund*	*meaning*
ā + gam	*āgacchati*	*āgamya* *āgatya*	having come *tya* alternative (special rule)
gam	*gacchati*	*gatvā*	having gone
cint	*cintayati –te*	*cintayitvā*	having thought (typical of Class 10)
ji	*jayati*	*jitvā*	having conquered
dṛś (paś)	*paśyati*	*dṛṣṭvā*	having seen
paṭh	*paṭhati*	*paṭhitvā*	having read
prach	*pṛcchati*	*pṛṣṭvā*	having asked
bhāṣ	*bhāṣate*	*bhāṣitvā*	having said
bhū	*bhavati*	*bhūtvā*	having been
man	*manyate*	*matvā*	having thought, thinking, considering,
labh	*labhate*	*labhdvā*	having obtained, having received,
vad	*vadati*	*uditvā*	having said, having spoken,
vas	*vasati*	*uṣitvā*	having lived (n.b.extra *i* for some roots) after dwelling, staying, residing,
sev	*sevate*	*sevitvā*	having served

sthā	*tiṣṭhati*	*sthitvā*	having stood, being situated, remaining,
smṛ	*smarati*	*smṛtvā*	having remembered, remembering

vartamāne kṛdanta – the present participle

- *Rāma*, going to the forest, sees a deer. "Going" is a present participle. The most common form is *-an* as in *gacchan* going, *svapnan* sleeping,

- The present participle (e.g. going) forms a dependent clause subordinate to the main verb and, when recognized, should be translated as a subordinate or relative clause (as above). If the translation is simply as an adjective, the meaning of the sentence may be misunderstood.

Consider the sentence *vanaṁ gacchatā rāmeṇa mūnirdṛśyate* (*Rama*, going to the forest, sees the sage). The principal clause is *Rama* sees the sage. *rāmeṇa mūnirdṛśyate.* However *gacchatā is* in the third/singular/masculine form because it is a present participle of the root *gam* and has to agree with the noun it modifies - *rāmeṇa.*
Vanam is 2nd/single/neuter and is therefore the focus of the action of the root *gam* as expressed in the participle form *gacchatā.*

- The present participle expresses an action still in progress at the time of the action of the independent or main verb. i.e. the actions are more or less simultaneous. e.g. (While) going to the forest, he saw the sage.
  A common construction is "*yadā* (when)(present participle e.g. flying) ... *tadā* (then)...." .
  The present participle may effectively substitute for relative clauses.

- Like the gerund, it is always subordinate to another finite verb or its equivalent i.e. it can never substitute for the principal verb of a sentence or an independent clause.
  e.g. the phrases *rāmo vanaṁ gatvā*, Rama, having gone to the forest... or *rāmo vanaṁ gacchan* Rama, going to the forest... are incomplete on their own and require an independent clause to complete them. e.g. .....found Sita, or ....saw a friend

- The present participle acts as an adjective and a verb. It is nominal in that it is adjectival and so should be in grammatical agreement in case, number and gender with the nominal it modifies. It is verbal in that it can take a direct object (if formed from a transitive verb).

- The present participle is unusual in that it reflects the 'voice' (*ātmane* or *parasmai pada*) of the root. Active roots take the present active participle and middle roots take the present middle participle. Passive roots have a present passive participle. The present active and the present middle participles are used the same way but are formed differently.

<u>Active</u> (*parasmaipada*) present participle formation and declension

The stem of the present active participle is formed by taking the 3rd person plural form of the present indicative and dropping the final *i*. e.g.

bhū	*bhavanti*	*bhavant*	being
ad	*adanti*	*adant*	eating
hu	*juhvati*	*juhvat*	offering
div	*dīvyanti*	*dīvyant*	playing
su	*sunvanti*	*sunvant*	pressing
tud	*tudanti*	*tudant*	pushing
tan	*tanvanti*	*tanvant*	stretching

Sandhi rules state that a word may not end with 2 consonants so in practice
bhavant becomes *bhavan*
adant becomes *adan* and so on

- note: *juhvat* not *juhvant* – typical of class 3 verbs
- like an adjective the present participle stem is declined in gender, number and case.
- The present participle occurs in active (*parasmaipada*) middle (*ātmanepada*) and passive forms. The present active and the present middle participles are used the same way but are formed differently.

Paradigms - there are 3 paradigms - 1 per gender

The masculine follows the *–at* (or *-ant*) declension pattern. e.g. see *dhīmat* in the vibhakti section but note the exception that 1st/single/masculine regularly ends in *–an* (not *–ān* as in *dhīmān*).

Masculine *bhavant* being

1st	*bhavan*	*bhavantau*	*bhavantaḥ*
2nd	*bhavantam*	*bhavantau*	*bhavataḥ*
3rd	*bhavatā*	*bhavadbhyām*	*bhavadbhiḥ*
4th	*`bhavate*	*bhavadbhyām*	*bhavadbhayaḥ*
5th	*bhavataḥ*	*bhavadbhyām*	*bhavadbhayaḥ*
6th	*bhavataḥ*	*bhavatoḥ*	*bhavatām*
7th	*bhavati*	*bhavatoḥ*	*bhavatsu*
voc.	*bhavan*	*bhavantau*	*bhavantaḥ*

examples
antakāle ca mām eva smaran muktvā kalevaram
antakāle at the time of death *ca* and *mām eva* me indeed
smaran (pres. act. part. √*smṛ* remembering, thinking on or of) *muktvā* (gerund √*muc* having relinquished, having been liberated from), *kalevaram* (2/s/m the body)

And at the hour of death, remembering me, having relinquished the body.....BG 8/5

yogaṁ yuñjan madāśrayaḥ
yogaṁ (yoga 2/s/m) *yuñjan* (pres.part. 1/s/m √*yuj* practising, performing) *madāśrayaḥ* (me dependent 1/s/m)
practising yoga dependent on me BG 7/1

yatatām api siddhānām
yatatām (of the striving, pres. act. part. √*yat* 6/pl) *api* (even, though,) *siddhānām* (of the perfected 6/pl/m)
even of the striving and perfected BG 7/3

Feminine The feminine forms of the participle are formed by suffixation of *ī* to either the strong or weak stem (depending on the verb class [*gaṇa*]) and are declined as :

1	*gacchantī*	*gacchantyau*	*gacchantyaḥ*
2	*gacchantīm*	*gacchantyau*	*gacchantīḥ*
3	*gacchantyā*	*gacchantībhyām*	*gacchantībhiḥ*
4	*gacchantyai*	*gacchantībhyām*	*gacchantībhyaḥ*
5	*gacchantyāḥ*	*gacchantībhyām*	*gacchantībhyaḥ*
6	*gacchantyāḥ*	*gacchantyoḥ*	*gacchantīnām*
7	*gacchantyām*	*gacchantyoḥ*	*gacchantīṣu*
sam.	*gacchanti*	*gacchantyau*	*gacchantyaḥ*

The *ī* is added :

a. to the strong stem in Classes 1,4 and 10
 e.g. root *vad* m. stem *vadant* f.stem *vadantī*

b. to the strong or weak stem in Class 6 and for roots of Class 2 ending in *ā*
 e.g. root *tud* m.stem *tudant* f. stem *tudantī / tudatī*
 root *yā* m.stem *yānt* f. stem *yāntī /yātī*

c. to the weak stem for the other Classes (3, 5, 7, 8, and 9).
 e.g. root *kṛ* m. stem *kurvant* f.stem *kurvatī*
 root *chid* m. stem *chindant* f.stem *chindatī*

- **Neuter** The neuter is usually formed from the weak stem *-at*. It is declined as neuter stems in *-vant* or- *mant* except 1st, 2nd and voc. dual have an *n* before the *t*.

1st	*bhavat*	*bhavantī*	*bhavanti*
2nd	*bhavat*	*bhavantī*	*bhavanti*
voc.	*bhavat*	*bhavantī*	*bhavanti*

or

gacchat	*gacchantī*	*gacchanti*
gaccht	*gacchantī*	*gacchanti*
gacchatā	*gacchadbhyām*	*gacchadbhiḥ*
gacchate	*gacchadbhyām*	*gacchadbhyaḥ*
gacchataḥ	*gacchadbhyām*	*gacchadbhyaḥ*
gacchataḥ	*gacchatoḥ*	*gacchatām*
gacchati	*gacchatoḥ*	*gacchatsu*
gacchat	*gacchantī*	*gacchanti*

Middle (*ātmanepada*) present participles

- The stem form of the middle voice or *ātmanepada* is generated by:

a. adding *-māna* to present stems of verb classes 1,4,6 and 10 e.g. √ *bhāṣ* → *bhāṣamāṇa,* √*man* → *manyamāna*

b. adding *āna* to present stems of verb classes 2. 3, 5, 7, 8, 9
e.g. √ *dvṣ* →*dvṣāṇa,* √ *kṛ* → *kurvāṇa*

- The present middle participle is declined the same as masculine (-*a*) neuter (-*a*) and feminine (-*ā*) . The 1st case *ātmanepada* single endings are m. *aḥ*, n *am*, f. *ā*. and they decline in a straightforward manner as per these paradigms. The *ātmanepada* present participle is used in the same way as the *parasmaipada* present participle.

- some common forms of this participle are identical with some common verb forms so care needs to be taken to resolve ambiguity. Reference to context is always important.

- The present participle stem for *as* is *sant* (m), *sat* (n), and *sati* (f)

example *abhi syāma mahato manyamānān* (2/pl)
may we surpass those thinking themselves great

The present passive participle (*karmaṇi* or *bhave* form) is formed from the passive stem, with the ending *māna* for all classes. The termination *te* of the first person singular present passive is replaced by *māna* e.g. from root *gam* passive *gamyate* present passive part. *gamyamāna.* being gone to

dā	*dīyate*	*dīyamāna*	being given
kṛ	*kriyate*	*kriyamāna*	being done

Special applications of the present participle

- The present participle is frequently used to express continuous action with *asti* is, *bhavati* becomes, *āste* sits , *tiṣṭhati* stands, *vartate* goes on,
- √ *as (*participles mfn. *sant, sat, satī)* being - may be used (with *api*) to indicate a situation contrary to normal expectation. The use of *api* implies concession.
e.g. *rājaputraḥ sannapi sa na dhīraḥ .*

Even though he is a prince, he is not wise. (He may be a prince, but he is not a wise man.)

This construction may be used with *api* and the present participle of any root to convey the sense of "even though".

"*aparādhe kṛte 'pi ca na me kopaḥ",* and even in the case of an offense committed, there is no anger on my part.

The same construction may be used with other participles.

There is a special construction used when the subject of the relative clause is different from the subject of the other clause. e.g. The weather being satisfactory, the plane took off.
This is referred to as Absolute Construction and there are 2 kinds of these.

- subject and participle are in the 7th (locative) case (known as *sati saptamī*) . This location could be of realm, condition or circumstance. In the sentence "*stīrṇe barhiṣi samidhāne agnau'* "when the *barhis* (a sacrificial gift) is strewn and the fire kindled" both the participle

stīrṇi (strewn) in the first clause and the subject *agnau* (fire), in the second are in the 7th case. In these instances the 7th case is referring to time and could be translated as 'while' or 'when'.
"*have tvā sūra udite have madhyaṁdine divaḥ*" I call to thee at the arisen sun (when the sun has risen), I call at midtime of the day.
"*na hanyate hanyamāne śarīre*" he is not slain when the body is slain, B.G. 2/20
na not *hanyate* is slain *hanyamāne* in being slain (7/s/m pres.mid. part. √han) *śarīre* (7/s/m) in the body

- subject and participle are in the 6th case (known as *sataḥ ṣaṣṭhī*).
  In the 6th case the use is disparaging e.g. *rājño bhāṣamāṇasya bālo' hasat.*
  The boy laughed while the king was speaking.

Future active (*-yat, -yant,*) and middle (*-māna*) participles *(bhaviṣyatkāle kṛdanta)*
The future participles describe an action that has not happened but may in the future. They are declinable. The future active and middle participles are formed from the simple future stem in the same way as the present participles are formed from a *gaṇa* stem. e.g. (feminine ending in brackets)

dhātu	**class**	**1/s/future**	**fut. act. part.**	**fut. mid. part.**	**english**
gam	1P	*gamiṣyati*	*gamiṣyat (yantī)*		will be going
sev	1A	*seviṣyate*		*seviṣyamāṇa (ā)*	will be serving
sthā	1P	*sthāsyati*	*sthāsyat (yantī)*		will be standing
dā	3PA	*dāsyati (e)*	*dāsyat (yantī)*	*dāsyamāna (ā)*	will be giving
bhū	1P	*bhaviṣyati*	*bhāviṣyat (yantī)*		will be becoming/creating/causing
yudh	4A	*yotsyate*		*yotsyamāna (ā)*	fight

aham vadiṣyantaṁ naraṁ paśyāmi I see the man who will be speaking

Future passive participle (gerundive) *kṛtya* suffixes *-ya, -anīya, or -tavya*

- expresses obligation or necessity – what should or ought to be done
- in a sentence where the gerundive acts as a verb, the sentence is put in passive construction *(karmaṇi prayoga)*. In this construction the object is in the 1st case, and the agent (*kartṛ)* of action is in the 3rd or sometimes 6th case. e.g.
  example *tenāpi śabdaḥ kartavyaḥ* lit. a noise is to be made by him also
  or in English 'he too (also) will surely make a noise'
- An active English sentence must be recast in the passive before using the gerundive as a verb. e.g. The king must lead the horse. becomes The horse is to be led by the king.
- The gerundive is usually in the nominative case.
- The gerundive agrees in person, number and case with the object of action.
- If there is no object of action, the gerundive is declined in the 1/s/n. e.g.
  "I must go." becomes *mayā gantavyam* "It is to be gone by me." – see 2nd dot point

- The gerundive may be used as an imperative – *gantavyam* Go. (It is to be gone.) There are 3 alternative suffixes though these are not all applicable in some cases. The alternatives - *-ya, -anīya, or -tavya* have the same meaning.

	anīya	***tavya***	***ya***	
āp	*āpanīya*	*āptavya*	*āpya*	to be obtained
iṣ	*eṣaṇīya*	*eṣitavya*	*eṣya*	to be chosen
kṛ	*karaṇīya*	*kartavya*	*kārya*	to be done
gam	*gamanīya*	*gantavya*	*gamya*	to be gone
gup	*gopanīya*	*goptavya*	*gopya*	to be protected
cint	*cintanīya*	*cintavitavya*	*cintya*	to be thought
cur	*coranīya*	*coravitavya*	*corya*	to be stolen
jan		*janitavya*	*janya*	to be born
ji		*jetavyajitya,*	*jeya*	to be conquered
tan		*tanitavya*	*tanya*	to be stretched
tud			*todya*	to be pushed
tṝ	*tāraṇīya*	*taritavya*	*tāvya*	to be crossed
tyaj	*tyajanīya*	*tyaktavya*	*tyājya*	to be abandoned
dā	*dānīya*	*dātavya*	*deya*	to be given
div		*devitavya*		to be played
dṛś	*darṣanīya*	*draṣṭavya*	*dṛśya*	to be seen
dhā	*dhānīya*	*dhātavya*	*dheya*	to be placed
nī	*nayanāya*	*netavya*	*neya*	to be lead
paṭh	*pañhanāya*	*paṭhitavya*	*pāṭhya*	to be read
pā	*pānīya*	*pātavya*	*peya*	to be drunk
prach		*praṣṭavya*	*pṛcchya*	to be asked
budh	*bodhanāya*	*bodhitavya*	*bodhya*	to be known
bhāṣ	*bhàùanāya*	*bhāṣitavya*	*bhāṣya*	to be spoken

bhū	*bhavanīya*	*bhavitavya*	*bhāvya*	should be
man	*mānanīya*	*mantavya*	*mānya*	to be thought
muc	*mocanīya*	*moktavya*	*mocya*	to be released
yuj	*yojanīya*	*yoktavya*	*yojya*	to be united
ram	*ramanīya*	*rantavya*	*ramya*	to be enjoyed
labh	*labhanīya*	*labdhavya*	*labhya*	to be obtained
vad	*vādanīya*	*vaditavya*	*vadya*	to be spoken
vas	*vāsanīya*	*vastavya*	*vāsya*	to be lived
śubh	*śobhanīya*			to be shined
śru	*śravaṇīya*	*śrotavya*	*śravya*	to be heard
su	*sotavya*			to be pressed
sev	*sevanāya*	*sevitavya*	*sevya*	to be served
sthā		*sthātavya*	*stheya*	to be established
smi	*smayanīya*	*smetavya*	*smāya*	to be smiling
smṛ	*smaraṇīya*	*smartavya*	*smarya*	to be remembered
has	*hasanīya*	*hasitavya*	*hāsya*	to be laughing
hā		*hātavya*	*heya*	to be abandoned
hu		*hotavya*	*havya*	to be offered

hantavyo*'smi na te rājan* you must not (i.e. do not) kill me O king

tatastenāpi śabdaḥ ***kartavyaḥ***
then he too will surely make a noise

yajñadānatapaḥkarma na ***tyājyaṁ*** *kāryam eva tat ..*
Acts of sacrifice, giving and austerity are not **to be abandoned** but rather performed.. BG18/5

etāny api tu karmāṇi saṅgaṁ tyaktvā phalāni ca ***kartavyānīti*** *me pārtha niścitam matam uttamam.*
These actions are **to be performed**, however abandoning attachment to the fruits. This is my definite and highest belief BG 18/6

dātavyamiti "(it is) **to be given**" BG 17/20

The gerundive is used idiomatically to indicate probability. The form *bhavitavyam* is frequently use in the sense of very likely, probably, undoubtedly.
tayā saṁnihitayā bhavitavyam
she must be (is likely) near

used as a weak imperative
āgantavyam Come!

Gerundives, like other adjectives may sometimes become nouns.

√*kṛ*	→	*kāryam*	duty, what is to be done
√*pā*	→	*peyam*	beverage, what is to be drunk

The Perfect Participle –*vāṁs*

This is a form more commonly seen in Vedic Sanskrit that serves as a past active participle (i.e. can be translated identically).

masculine formation -*vāṁs* is added to the weak form of the perfect stem.
√*kå* → *cakṛvāṁs*

If the stem is monosyllabic the suffix is spaced from the stem by the insertion of vowel *i*.

√*sthā* → *tasthivāṁs*	stood
√*tap* → *tepivāṁs*	heated

Masculine Paradigm for *vidvāṁs* - a wise or learned man

vidvān	*vidvāṁsau*	*vidvāṁsaḥ*
vidvāṁsam	*vidvāṁsau*	*viduṣaḥ*
viduṣā	*vidvadbhyām*	*vidvadbhiḥ*
viduṣe	*vidvadbhyām*	*vidvadbhyaḥ*
viduṣaḥ	*vidvadbhyām*	*vidvadbhyaḥ*
viduṣaḥ	*viduṣoḥ*	*viduṣām*
viduṣi	*viduṣoḥ*	*vidvatsu*
vidvan	*vidvāṁsau*	*vidvāṁsaḥ*
napun		
vidvat	*viduṣī*	*vidvāṁsi*
strī		

viduṣī declension as *devī (*standard f. *ī* paradigm)

Adverbs

Kriyāviśeṣaṇa - a word which expands the remainder in a kriyā bringing out a previously unmanifest quality in the verb (Adverb)

Adverb – A word that describes a verb, an adjective or another adverb. e.g. The band played *loudly* and *inaccurately*. – describing the word played. An adverb normally describes how, when, where or in what degree the action of a verb takes place.
Think *carefully*. Come *tomorrow*.
Comparatives and superlatives are created from adverbs – *fast, faster, fastest.*

Adverbs in sanskrit may be indeclinable or have special terminations.
Most pronouns have some adverbial forms. Also adjectives may be used in an adverbial sense.

Adverbs of manner tell how e..g. swiftly, boldly etc. Adjectives do not have a termination reserved for adverbial use - instead the 2nd/sing/napun may be used . e.g.
śīghram calati - he moves a swift (moving) - he moves swiftly. Also the instrumental case is frequently used - *viṣādena* with dejection, - dejectedly;
vacanaiḥ - by words -verbally.

Ordinary case terminations are frequently used in an adverbial sense e.g.

2nd *ciram*	a long time
3rd *cireṇa*	in a long time
4th *cirāya*	for a long time
5th *carat*	long ago
6th *cirasya*	a long time
7th *cire*	long

adverbial terminations can have the sense of - ablative (from), temporal (time), causal (cause), modal (how), effective (the effect), or locative (location).

taḥ	with an ablative meaning (from)
tataḥ	thence
yataḥ	whence
itaḥ	hence
ataḥ	hence
kutaḥ	Whence?
amutaḥ thence	
mattaḥ	from me
ammataḥ	from us
bhavattaḥ	from your Honour
parvataḥ	before (in a general local or temporal sense)
sarvataḥ	always
agrataḥ	before, like agre
abhitaḥ	around, near
ubhayataḥ	on both sides
paritaḥ	all round
gramataḥ	from the village
ajñānataḥ	from ignorance

-tra,	locative
tatra,	there
yatra	where
kutra	*Where?*

-atra here
amutra there, in the next world
ekatra at one place together
satrā with
satraṁ with (see saha)

-ha locative
kuha Where?
iha here
saha with

-dā temporal
tadā then, and *tadānim*
yadā when, whenever
kadā when?
anyadā at another time, sometimes, once
sarvadā always, at all times
ekadā at one time
sadā always
idā later
idānīm now

-rhi temporal and causal
etarhi at this time
karhi at what time?
yarhi wherefore
tarhi therefore, at that time

-tāt, local
praktāt in front
purastāt before
adharastāt below
parastāt afterwards, further away, towards, beyond, from afar off, hereafter, later,
adhastāt below
upariṣtāt above

-ā, and *āhi* local
dakṣināhi in the South
dakṣinā in the South
uttarāhi in the North
uttarā in the North
antarā or *raṁ* or *reṇa* between
purā in the East, in front, formerly
paścā behind, (or *paścāt*)

-tar local
prātar early, in the morning
sanutar in concealment

-thā modal
tathā thus
yathā as
sarvathā in every way
ubhayathā in both ways
anyathā in another way
anyatarathā in one of two ways

itarathā in the other way
vṛttā vainly ?
tham *katham* how?
ittham thus
tha in *atha* thus

-*sāt* effective
rājasāt (*rājño'dhīnam* dependent on the king)
bhasmasāt reduced to ashes
agnisāt reduced to fire

-*dhā* *mudhā* ind. in vain, uselessly, wrongly, falsely
instrumental case of obsolete noun ending in consonant
-*ṣā* *mṛṣā* ind. in vain, uselessly, wrongly, falsely, untruth personified ,
instrumental case of obsolete noun ending in consonant

other
upasargas are indeclinable and have an adverbial nature
antar within, between, amongst, in the interior

-*caḥ* adverbs of quantity

ekacas one by one
akṣaracas syllable by syllable
sarvacas wholly
stambacas by bunches

-*vat* signifying - after the manner of, like
pūrvavat as of old
manuṣvat as Manu did
aṅgirasvat like Aṅgiras

Interrogative	Relative	Correlative	Other
kaḥ? who?	*yaḥ* who	*saḥ* he, that	*ayam* this *asau* that
kva? where?	*yatra* where	*tatra* there	*atra, iha* here
kutra? (to) where?			
kutaḥ from where?	*yataḥ* from where	*tataḥ* from there	*itaḥ* from here, in this direction
kutaḥ? for what reason?	*yataḥ* because	*tataḥ* therefore	
ataḥ hence, for this reason			
kadā? when?	*yadāc* when	*tadā* then	
idānīm, adhunā now			
katham? how?	*yathā* as	*tathā, evam* so, thus	*ittham, evam* in this way
kidṛśa? of what kind	*yadṛśa* of that kind, such (a)	*ādṛśa* of this kind, such (a)	
kiyant? how much	*yāvant* as much as	*tāvant* so much	*iyant* this much
kiyacciram for how long?	*yāvat* as long as, while	*tāvat* for so long	*iyacciram* for this long
kiyantaṁ kālam for how long?		*iyantaṁ kālam* for this long	
	yadi if	*tat* (etc.) then	
	cet if	*tat* then	
	yady api even if	*tathā* even so	
	kāmam granted that	*punar* nevertheless	

Expression of the Indefinite (Examples) (also see Indefinites under Pronouns)

anya (or *eka*)... *anya* the one.... the other
anyatama mfn one of several, someone,
akiñcana mfn without anything, utterly destitute, disinterested, (*am*) n. that which is worth nothing,
anyatas ind. from anywhere, from another direction, otherwise, elsewhere, to another place,
kaccit(d) is it that? has it? has this? used in questions expecting the answer 'yes',
ibc. marks the uselessness, badness or defectiveness of anything e.g. *-akṣara* n. a bad letter, bad writing,
with *na* in no way or manner,
kadā 248/1 when? *na kadā cana* not at any time so-ever, never,
kadā cid once on a time, one day, *kadā cid api na* never,
kadācana at any time, at any time whatsoever
kadācana at any time
kadācit sometime,
kadāpi ever (after *na*) never
kaḥ who?
kāle kāle ind. from time to time, sometimes,
kaṁcana someone, something, (2nd)
karhicit 260/1 at any time
kaścana 240/3 any, anyone at all, in any way
kaścit 240/3 anyone, someone,
kasmin in what?
katama mfn who or which of many, often a strengthened substitute for *ka,* the superlative affix imparting emphasis, occasionally 'who or which of two', when 'followed by *ca* and preceded by *yatama* an indefinite expression is formed', e.g. *yatamad eva katamac ca vidyāt,* "he may know anything whatsoever".
katham or *kathā* ind. how? in what way? *katham etat* how's that, *kathaṁ nu* how indeed,
katham api somehow,
kathaṁ cana in any wise whatsoever (emphasizing a preceding negation),
katham api somehow,
katham-cana ind. in some way
katipaya mfn indef. several, some, a few,
kecit some
kenacit by someone or something,
kim what? *kimapi* anything
kiṁcit (*kim cit)* anything, something,
kiñcanna jāyate (na kiñcit jāyate) nothing whatsoever is born, (*Māṇḍūkya Up.K. III.48)*
kim punas tu but what besides, how much more
kena by whom or what? *kenāpi* by any,
kimartham why?
kiṁ ca moreover
kimiti wherefore? why? *kimiva* wherefore? *kiṁ tu* but, however
kiṁ vā perchance?
kutra where?
kutrāpi somewhere, *kva cid* anywhere, in any case, ever, (with *na*) never,
na kaścijjāyate jīvaḥ (na jīvaḥ kaḥ cit jāyate) no individual being whichsoever is born
nakis 1. no one, 2. nothing, 3. never, *na kutaścid* ind. from nowhere, *na kiṁcid* nothing,
sapta in comp. for *saptan*, seven, also may express an indefinite plurality, e.g. 71, 72
vāram vāram ind. sometimes
yad anyat kiṁ cana whatever else

Kriyā - Verbs 320/3 doing, performing, activity, (in gram.) action (as the general idea expressed by any verb), verb.

Kriyā is the sanskrit word for verbs and they are formed from roots (√) called *dhātu.* For instance the *dhātu* for *kriyā* is *kṛ* 300/3 - to do, make, perform, accomplish, cause, effect, prepare, undertake. Because "to" do is the infinitive form of the verb the meaning should be listed as do, make etc., but the meanings are easily understood as they are listed.

The grammarians divided the verbs into 10 classes according to the way they are conjugated (changing the form of a verb for grammatical purposes). However in reality most verbs fit into a few of these classes. The class for each verb is identified in the dictionary entry as 1-10.

There are also special endings for causative (causing), desiderative (desiring), intensive (intensifying), and denominative (derived from nominatives, e.g. behaving like... , treating someone like..., wishing for or doing whatever is expressed by the noun.) These will be dealt with in due course.

Verbs can be identified in 4 ways – tense/mood, voice, person and number.

Tense The tenses and modes are grouped together in ten *lakāra* (891/3 see 1. *la* – the letter or sound *la.* Each name for a tense begins with l.) The present tense is called *laṭ.*

the tenses are:

present	*laṭ*	he leads
perfect	*liṭ*	an action that occurred in the remote past or was not witnessed by the speaker
periphrastic future	*luṭ*	not of today
simple future	*lṛṭ*	he will
subjunctive	*leṭ*	if he were leading
imperative	*loṭ*	let him lead, lead!
imperfect	*laṅ*	common past tense, 'not of today', he led
optative or potential	*liṅ*	he should lead
aorist	*luñ*	events in the very recent past or with present relevance
conditional	*lṛṅ*	"future in the past" he would have

Person ***(puruṣa)*** Verbs are conjugated in 3 'Persons' – he she or it, you, and I. These are listed in the reverse order from English. Verb stems typically develop from the *dhātu* by adding the vowel *a* . For instance- The *dhātu vas* has an *a* added (after *vas*) becoming the stem *vasa* and following suffixes for each 'person'. – *ti* – he, she or it, *si*- you, and *ami* for I, (present tense). e.g. *vasati* he, she, or it lives or dwells.

dhātu vas to live	*prathamā* (meaning 1st)	*vasati*	he, she, or it lives
	madhyamā (middle)	*vasasi*	you live
	uttamā (best or last)	*vasāmi*	I live (*vasa* + *ami* =*vasāmi*)

These statements are in the present tense (time), indicative mood (indicating – used for an ordinary objective sentence. , active (an ordinary statement such as "he lives") and singular.

In a text book this could be listed as pres/indic/act/1st/s and it is sometimes listed as the citation case in academic texts. Some typical uses:

√*pṛach* ask	*pṛcchati*	he asks or she asks
√*smṛ* remember	*smarasi*	you remember
√*gam* go	*gacchāmi*	I go or I am going

The *dhātu* may look significantly different from the citation case but is always related and there is consistency within classes and declension. e.g. *gacchati, pṛcchati, smarati*

Number The verb and subject must agree in number so Sanskrit has endings for single, dual and plural. Dual *(dvivacana)* verbs apply to 2 of anything. e.g. English – we both go, Sanskrit – *gacchavaþ* - i.e. we (2) go.

So now we need a total of 9 present tense endings to include dual and plural as seen below.

The present indicative active (*laṭ*) – (indicative means – a statement)

nayati he, she, it leads	*nayataḥ* they (2) lead	*nayanti* they plural lead
nayasi you (sing.) lead	*nayathaḥ* you (2) lead	*nayatha* you (pl) lead
nayāmi I lead	*nayāvaḥ* we (2) lead	*nayāmaḥ* we (pl) lead

Voice (*upagraha*) There are 3 voices – active, middle and passive.

Active (*kartari prayoga)* The active voice is the one we most commonly use and is called ***parasmaipada*** (589/1 "word for another" the transitive or active verb and its terminations). This is used when the fruit of an action goes to another person (*para*) e.g. He bought a hen (for Bob).

The verb *as* "is" is often understood or assumed*if the predicate (the part of the sentence which relates to the subject) is a noun *i.e. It is meant but not written.

Middle If the fruit of an action comes back to the agent (*ātman*) then the ***ātmanepada*** or middle endings are used. e.g. He has a hen. The verb implies an action belonging or reverting to self. However over time the difference has become blurred between active and passive so that the use of one or the other is sometimes apparently determined by metre. *ātmanepada* verbs may have originally expressed states e.g. *edhate* he grows, *modate* he rejoices, *śete* he lies down. Some verbs are conjugated in both active and middle voices and some in one only. The present tense system has a special passive inflection. Outside this the middle forms are sometimes used in a passive sense.

Verbs which may be used in both the active and middle forms take the appropriate form e.g. *pacati*, he cooks, *pacate* he cooks for himself , *yajati* he sacrifices, *yajate* he sacrifices for himself.

Passive (*karmaṇi prayoga)* {*karmaṇi* 259/3 mfn. connected with or being in the action}, {*prayoga* 688/2 2. (in gram.) an applicable or usual form} In a passive construction the verb relates directly to the *karman* or object. e.g. The book is read by the boy. In *sanskrit* the object (book) would be in the nominative or 1st case and the agent of the action (the boy) would be in the instrumental or 3rd case (or sometimes 6th case). The verb would have a passive termination.

Active compared with passive-

active form *bodhati* he knows,

passive form *budhyate* he is known.

bhāve prayoga This is an abstract construction related to the passive construction that is not used in English. In this the verb is passive but the direct object is missing, or abstract. e.g. *mayā gamyate* – It is gone by me (I go).

Passive verb terminations are formed by the process –

- root + *ya* + *ātmanepada* endings.
- every class forms the passive in this way
- the passive may take present, imperfect and imperative endings

example – active *bālaḥ pustakaṁ paṭhati* the boy reads the book

passive -*pustakaṁ bālena paṭhyate* the book is read by the boy

In the passive sentence *pustakam* is in the nominative case.

In the Monier-Williams Dictionary after a *dhātu* will be a large A, P, or U indicating whether the verb conjugates as *ātmanepada* , *parasmaipada* or both (*ubhayapada*).

Verbal prefixes are common and are said to 'change the direction' of the meaning.

Here is the conjugation and construction for the passive form of - √*paṭh* to be read, or recited or taught or mentioned,

paṭhyate	*paṭhyete*	*paṭhyante*
paṭh+ya+te	*paṭh+ya+ite*	*paṭh+ya-a+ante*
paṭhyase	*paṭhyethe*	*paṭyadhve*
paṭh+ya+se	*paṭh+ya+ithe*	*paṭh+ya+dhve*
paṭhye	*paṭhyāvahe*	*paṭhyāmahe*
paṭh+ya+i	*paṭh+ya+ā+vahe*	*paṭh+ya+ā+mahe*

Present middle or *parasmaipada* of √*nī* to lead

nayate	*nayete*	*nayante*
nayase	*nayethe*	*nayadhve*
naye	*nayāvahe*	*nayāmahe*

Present passive

nīyate	*nīyete*	*nīyante*
nīyase	*nīyethe*	*nīyadhve*
nīye	*nīyāvahe*	*nīyāmahe*

Imperfect (past) active tense (*laṅ*)

The imperfect is a simple past narrative tense e.g. he ran, they ate, we talked.

It is not used where progression or duration need to be expressed (e.g. he was working, or he used to make) because these may be expressed through the present tense or a present tense participle possibly with particle *sma* added. e.g. *praviśanti sma* they entered. Quite frequently a past passive or active participle is used instead of a verb.

anayat	*anayatām*	*anayan*
anayaþ	*anayatam*	*anayata*
anayam	*anayāva*	*anayāma*

Imperfect (past) middle

anayata	*anayetām*	*anayanta*
anayathāḥ	*anayethām*	*anayadhvam*
anaye	*anayāvahi*	*anayāmahi*

Imperfect (past) passive

anīyata	*anīyetām*	*anīyanta*
anãyathāḥ	*anīyethām*	*anīyadhvam*
anīye	*anīyāvahi*	*anīyāma*

The Perfect Tense (*liṭ*)

The perfect is traditionally used for remote past action not witnessed by the speaker

e.g. *bhagavān uvāca* the Lord said

It may express a fact which is the result of a past event or it may state or summarize past facts. It is usually in the *prathamā puruṣa* form but other forms exist. It may be formed in either of two ways through re-duplication of the root or through a combination of an auxiliary or 'helping' verb and a specially formed noun. Only the first option will be discussed.

Re-duplication refers to repetition of a part of the root. e.g. from √*budh* is made the reduplicated stem *bu-budh* . Using *nayati* (to lead) the forms are:

Active

nināya	*ninyatuḥ*	*ninyuḥ*
ninetha	*ninyathuḥ*	*ninya*
ninãya	*ninyiva*	*ninyima*

Middle

ninye	*ninyāte*	*ninyire*
ninyiṣe	*ninyāthe*	*ninyidhve*
ninye	*ninyivahe*	*ninyimahe*

Passive

ninye	*ninyāte*	*ninyire*
ninyiṣe	*ninyāthe*	*ninyidhve*
ninye	*ninyivahe*	*ninyimahe*

Note: The singular active stems are "strong" i.e. have an extra measure of "*a*"

Here is the first person single in the present (active and middle) and the perfect from some common roots.

root	present	perfect	English
ad	*atti*	*āda*	he ate
as	*asti*	*āsa*	he was
āp	*āpnoti*	*āpa*	he obtained
āste	*āste*	*āsa*	he sat
iṣ	*icchati*	*iyeṣa*	he desired
kṛ	*karoti/kurute*	*cakāra/cakre*	he did
gam	*gacchati*	*jagāma*	he went
jan	*jāyate*	*jajñe*	he was born
jñā	*jānāti/jānīte*	*jajñau/jajñe*	he knew
tan	*tanoti/tanute*	*tatāna/tene*	he stretched
tud	*tudati/te*	*tutoda*	he pushed
tṝ	*tarata*	*tatāra*	he crossed
tyaj	*tyajati*	*tatyāja*	he abandoned
dā	*dadāti/date*	*dadau*	he gave
div	*dīvyati*	*dideva*	he played
dṛṣ/paś	*paśyati*	*dadarśa*	he saw
dhā	*dadhāti/dhatte*	*dadhau/dadhe*	he placed
nī	*nayati/te*	*ninīya*	he led
paṣh	*paṣhati*	*papau*	he read
pad	*padyate*	*pede*	he went
pā	*pibati*	*papau*	he drank
prach	*pṛcchati*	*papracha*	he asked
budh	*bodhati/te*	*bubodha/bubudhe*	he knew
bhāṣ	*bhāṣate*	*babhāṣe*	he spoke
bhū	*bhavati*	*babhūva*	he was
man	*manyate*	*mene*	he thought
muc	*muñcati/te*	*mumoca/mumuce*	he released
yuj	*yunakti/yu-kte*	*yuyoja/yuyuje*	he united
ram	*ramate*	*reme*	he enjoyed
labh	*labhate/ti*	*lebhe*	he obtained
vac	*vakti*	*uvāca*	he spoke
vad	*vadati*	*uvāda*	he spoke
vas	*vasati*	*uvāsa*	he lived
vraj	*vrajati*	*vavrāja*	he walked
śubh	*śobhate*	*śuśubhe*	he shone
śru	*śṛṇoti*	*śuśrāva*	he heard
su	*sunoti/sunute*	*suṣāva*	he pressed
sev	*sevate*	*siṣeve*	he served
sthā	*tiṣṭhati*	*tasthau*	he stood
smi	*smayate*	*siṣmiye*	he smiled
smṛ	*smarati*	*sasmāra*	he remembered
han	*hanti*	*jaghāna*	he killed
has	*hasati*	*jahāsa*	he laughed
hā	*jahāti*	*jahau*	he abandoned
hu	*juhoti*	*juhāva*	he offered

Note: for a verb root ending in *ā* the Perfect ending is *a.*
Perfect forms may be made from causative and other derivative forms by a method not shown.

The Aorist Tense (*luṅ*)

This is another past tense that refers only to actions of today. It is rare to find it in Classical Sanskrit.

Examples of the paradigms are given later in this chapter.

The Simple Future Tense (*lṛṭ*) – Sometimes the present indicative will indicate the immediate future e.g. *gacchāmi* – I will go, but usually the simple future is used.

- *devas ced varṣiṣyati dhanyam vapsyamaḥ* , if it rain we shall sow rice,
- *dasyati* he will give.
- it is formed by adding *sya* or *iṣya* to the strengthened root.
- most roots are strengthened by adding *guṇa* changes to the vowel.
- the standard active and middle endings are then added
- note that *s* becomes *ṣ* when immediately preceded by any vowel except *a* or *ā*

3rd person examples

gam	*gamiṣyati*	he will go
gup	*gopsyati*	he will protect
cint	*cintayiṣyati –te*	he will think
ji	*jeṣyati*	he will conquer
nī	*neṣyati -te*	he will lead
paṭh	*paṭhiṣyati*	he will read
paś	*drakṣyati*	he will see
prach	*prakṣyati*	he will ask
budh	*bodhiṣyati –te*	he will know
bhū	*bhaviṣyati*	he will be
man	*maṁṣyate*	he will think
labh	*lapsyate*	he will obtain
vad	*vadiṣyati*	he will speak
vas	*vatsyati*	he will live
śubh	*śobhiṣyati*	he will shine
sthā	*sthāsyati*	he will stand
smṛ	*smariṣyati*	he will remember

The Imperative (*loṭ*) The imperative is used as a command, demand, instruction or injunction. i.e. when one person is asking or telling another to do something. It uses the present stem. The 2nd case is used as expected e.g. *tuda* strike !, but the 1st and 3rd are used often in place of the Optative e.g. *icchāmi bhavān bhuṅktàm* I wish your honour may eat.
Often translated as 'let' or 'may' in English. e.g. 'let it be done', 'may he follow',

gacchāma 1/pl/impv/act "we must go" or "let us go".

imperative active

prathama	*gacchatu*	*gacchatām*	*gacchantu*
madhyama	*gaccha*	*gacchatam*	*gacchata*
uttama	*gacchāni*	*gacchāva*	*gacchāma*

Imperative middle

prathama	*labhatām*	*labhetām*	*labhantām*
madhyama	*labhasva*	*labhethām*	*labhadhvam*
uttama	*labhai*	*labhāvahai*	*labhāmahai*

- the imperative verb is negated by *mā* rather than *nā*

The Optative(*liṅ*) The optative is used for what should or ought to be done. It is also used for what might or could be the case now, in the future or even in the past. It expresses uncertainty which has an unreality about it. e.g. it might rain, it could rain, it should rain. The optative (sometimes called the potential), may express hope, expectation, advice, a soft command or a contingency. Sometimes *kadācit* (perhaps) may be added to emphasize uncertainty. The context is always important when studying the relevant meaning. The optative may also express a remote possibility e.g. if he were to do, if he were doing. Examples of the paradigms are given later in this chapter.

The Infinitive (*tumannanta*) In English the infinitive is preceded by "to" e.g. to go, to ski, to laugh. In Sanskrit it is considered as an indeclinable participle. The ending *-tum* is used as below *guṇa* of root + *tum* or *itum* e.g.

root	present	infinitive	english
ad	*atti*	*attum*	to eat
āp	*āpnoti*	*āptum*	to obtain

ās	*āste*	*āsitum*	to sit
iù	*icchati*	*eùñum*	to desire
kṛ	*karoti, kurute*	*kartum*	to do
gam	*gacchati*	*gantum*	to go
jīv	*jīvati*	*jīvitum*	to live

The Causative **- (*ṇijanta*)** This modification of the verb form indicates the cause of an action.

saḥ kaṭaṁ karoti	he makes a mat
saḥ kaṭaṁ kārayati	he causes (someone) to make a mat
	or, he has a mat made

A causative is constructed by strengthening the root (*guṇa* or *vṛddhi*) until it is *guru* (heavy) and adding the suffix *–aya.*

examples	*kṛ*	*kārayati*	causes to make or do
	bh	*ūbhāvayati*	causes to be
	gam	*gamayati*	causes to go (example with light first syllable)
	tvar	*tvarayati*	causes to hurry (light first syllable)

Note that the promoter of the action would be in first case and the one who performs it in the 3rd case. *saḥ devadattena kaṭaṁ kārayati* - he causes the making of a mat through the instrumentality of *Devadatta.*

Most verbs ending in *ā* and some others also add *-p* bfore suffix *–aya* hence we get

sthāpayati establishes

ropayati raises

other examples

√*nī*	lead	*nāyayati*	causes to lead
√*plu*	swim	*plāvayati*	he makes swim
√*smi*	laugh	*smāyayati*	he makes laugh
√*vid*	know	*vedayati*	he makes know
√*budh*	know	*bhodayati*	he makes know
√*kḷp*	be able	*kalpayati*	he renders fit
√*pat*	fall	*pātayati*	he fells
√*dṛś*	see	*darśayati*	causes to see, shows

The suffix *–aya* is constructed from *-ay* with the thematic vowel.

Causative verbs are conjugated like Class 10, *cur*

svara	*a, ā*	*i, ī*	*u, ū*	*ṛ*	*ṝ*	strengthened becomes

guõa	*a, ā*	*e*	*o*	*ar*	*al*	strengthened becomes
vṛddhi	*ā*	*ai*	*au*	*ār*	*āl*	

Reduplication See Class 3 below

***The Desiderative*- (sannanta)** The desiderative indicates the sentiment 'wanting to ....'./ It is formed by adding the suffix *sa* or *ṣa* (if appropriate) and prefixing a reduplicative syllable consisting of the first consonant of the root (sometimes modified) and a vowel (usually *i* but *u* if the root has a *u* in it).

root	present	desiderative	English
ad	*atti*	*jighatsati*	wishes to eat
āp	*āpnoti*	*īpsati*	wishes to obtain
ās	*āste*	*āsisiṣati*	wishes to sit
bhāṣ	*bhāṣate*	*bibhāṣiṣati*	wishes to speak
bhū	*bhavati*	*bubhūṣati*	wishes to be
budh	*bodhati/te*	*bubhutsati*	wishes to know
dā	*dadāti, date*	*ditsati*	wishes to give
dhā	*dadhāti,dhatte*	*dhitsati*	wishes to place
dhṛ	*dharati/te*	*didhīrṣati*	wishes to hold
dṛś/ paś	*paśyati*	*didṛkṣati*	wish to see
gam	*gacchati*	*jigamiṣati*	wishes to go
gai	*gāyati*	*jigāsati*	wishes to sing
gup	*gopāyati*	*jugupsati*	wishes to protect
han	*hanta*	*jighāṁsati*	wishes to kill
has	*hasati*	*jihasiṣati*	wishes to laugh
hā	*jahāti*	*jihāsati*	wishes to abandon
hu	*juhoti*	*juhūṣati*	wishes to offer
i	*eti*	*iyiṣati*	wishes to go
iṣ	*icchati*	*eṣiṣiṣati*	wishes to choose
jan	*jāyate*	*jijaniṣate*	wishes to be born
ji	*jayati*	*jijigīṣati*	wishes to conquer
jīv	*jīvati*	*jijīviṣati*	wishes to live
jñā	*jānāti, jānīte*	*jijñāsati*	wishes to know
kṛ	*karoti/kurute*	*cikīrṣati*	wishes to do or make
labh	*labhate*	*lipsate*	wishes to find/obtain

man	*manyate*	*mīmāṁsate*	wishes to think
muc	*muñcati/te*	*mumukṣati*	wishes to release
nī	*nayati/te*	*ninīṣati*	wishes to lead
pā	*pibati*	*pipāsati*	wishes to drink
pad	*padyate*	*pitsati*	wishes to go
paṭh	*paṭhati*	*pipaṭhiṣati*	wishes to read
prach	*pṛcchati*	*pipṛchiṣati*	wishes to ask
jīv	*jivati*	*jijīviṣati*	wishes to live
śak	*śaknoti*	*śikṣati*	wishes to be able
sev	*sevate*	*siseviṣati*	wishes to serve
smi	*smayate*	*sismayiṣati*	wishes to smile
sṛj	*sṛjati*	*sisṛkṣati*	wishes to create
śru	*śṛnoti*	*śuśrūṣati*	wishes to hear
sthā	*tiṣṭhati*	*tiṣṭhāsati*	wishes to stand
tan	*tanoti, tanute*	*titāmsati*	wishes to stretch
tud	*tudati tudate*	*tututsati*	wishes to push
tṝ	*tarati*	*titirṣati*	wishes to cross
tuṣ	*tuṣyati*	*tutukṣati*	wishes to satisfy
vac	*vakti*	*vivakṣati*	wishes to speak
vad	*vadati*	*vivadiṣati*	wishes to speak
vas	*vasati*	*vivatsati*	wishes to live
viś	*viśati*	*vivikṣati*	wishes to enter

There is also an adjectival form arrived at by changing the final *a* of the stem to *u*.

root	desiderative stem	adjective	English
jñā	*jijñāsa*	*jijñāsu*	wishing to know
jñā	*jijñāsa*	*jijñāsā** (nominal)	the desire to know
kṛ	*cikīrṣa*	*cikīrṣu*	wishing to do or make
yudh	*yuyutsa*	*yuyutsu*	eager to fight

***The Denominative Verb Form* (*nāmadhātu*)** (noun-root). These are verbs that are derived from nouns and adjectives. The English equivalent could be "Sailing a boat" , or "The sky darkens". A common indicator of the *nāmadhātu* is the suffix *ya* added to a nominal stem followed by a personal ending. e.g. *namas* obeisance *namas-ya-ti* he makes obeisance or homage

gopā cow-herd	*gopā-ya-ti*	acts like a herdsman

Denominatives are conjugated like the 10th class with either active or middle endings.

If the verb is intransitive then the *a* preceding the *ya* is lengthened
e.g. from adjective *śithila* loose comes *śithila -ya-ti* makes loose, loosens
or *śithilā-ya-te* becomes loose (most *nāmadhātu* are *ātmanepada*).

There are many exceptions but the basic rules above are generally consistent.. The meanings of nouns or adjectives converted to verbs are varied but typical ones are-

be like or act like e.g.	*rājāyate*	acts like a king
use, make or perform	*pṛtanāyati*	fights (from fight)
desire	*aśvāyati*	desires a horse or horses (from horse)
regard as or treat as	*svāmīyati*	regard as a lord or master (from *svàmãn*)

deva	*devayati*	is pious
kathā	*kathayati*	tells the story
namas	*namasyati*	pays homage
putra	*putrīyati*	desires a son
tapas	*tapasyati*	practises austerities

***The Intensive Verb Form* (*yaḍanta*)** The intensive, (sometimes called a frequentative), - – is used to give a sense of repetition or intensification.
It is formed through strong re-duplication forms of the *abhyāsa* syllable .(*abhyāsa* 76/3 m. the act of adding anything, what is prefixed, the first syllable of a re-duplicated radical, re-duplication, repetition). They are of 2 types.
One (*parasmaipada* only) adds the personal endings immediately to the reduplicated stem and is conjugated like a verb of the 3rd class. e.g.

$\sqrt{}$*bhū (*be*)* → *bobhoti.*

The other (*ātmanepada* only) adds *ya* in the same way as the passive to the reduplicated stem.

$\sqrt{}$*bhū* → *bobhūyate*

It can only be made from of one syllable, that don't begin with a vowel and are not of the tenth *gaṇa.* e.g.

other examples	√*vid* know	*vevetti* or *vevidīti*	
	impf.	*avevet*	
	impv		*vevedītu* or *vevettu*
	cekriyate		he does repeatedly
	dedīyate		he gives generously

The Conditional Mood (lṛṅ) This is a way of expressing 'would have, .. had been ' through a modification of the future tense to refer it to the past. i.e. it is a past form of the future. It deals with hypotheses or situations contrary to fact and is called *atipattau lṛṇ*. *Atipattau* refers to a lapsed action, one not coming to pass. An *a* is prefixed to the future tense word which is then followed by imperfect endings. e.g.

gamiṣyati	he will go	becomes	*agamiṣyat*	he would have gone
bhaviṣyati	he will become		*abhaviṣyat*	he would have become or, it would have been
tyakṣyati	it will leave		*atyakṣayat*	it would have left

The Benedictive or Precative (*āśir liṅ* –the optative of blessing)

A rare form used for uttering blessings or prayers or expressing a wish or contingency. It is formed by adding the optative suffix *–yā* plus the original aorist sign *–s* to the root.

e.g. from √*bhū*	*bhūyāt*	*bhūyāstām*	*bhūyāsus*
	bhūyās	*bhūyāstām*	*bhūyāsta*
	bhūyāsam	*bhūyāstām*	*bhūyāsma*

The injunctive mood A mood in Sanskrit characterized by secondary endings but no augment, and usually looks like an augmentless aorist or imperfect. It typically stood in a main clause and had a subjunctive or imperative meaning; for example, it could indicate intention, e.g. *indrasya nú vīryā̀ṇi prá* ***vocam*** "Indra's heroic deeds **will/shall I** now **declaim**" (Beekes 1995. It was obligatory for use in prohibitions, where it follows *mā́*. In later Classical Sanskrit, only the use after *mā* remained (there were no accents in Classical Sanskrit). (Wikipedia)

Classification of Verbs There are 10 classes divided according to how their roots are modified before certain terminations are added. This classification refers to how verbs form their present tense and derivatives and has no relevance to aorist for instance. Some roots appear in more than one class because they can form their present stem in more than one way. For practical purposes these 10 can be dealt with in 2 groups.

- bases in which an *a* is inserted between the stem and the ending –classes 1, 4, 6 and 10.

In this First Conjugation the stems are formed by adding *a, ya,* or *aya* depending on which o the 4 thematic classes a root belongs to. Thus *bhū* changes to *bhav +a = bhava* to which is added the personal ending.

Note: Whenever the thematic vowel *-a-* is followed by an ending beginning with m + vowel as in *-mi, maḫ, and -ma* the *-a-* is lengthened to *ā.*

- all other bases (athematic)
  - bases which insert *nu, u, or nā* between the root and the terminations
  - bases without intermediate elements before terminations

Each class is named after one root from its class – usually the first of its kind in *Pāṇini*'s version of the *Dhātu Paṭha*. For instance the first class is called *bhvādi gaṇa (bhū ādi gaṇa). (ādi* 136/3 beginning with). About half of all roots belong to this class. In the dictionary *bhū* is classified 1P – meaning class 1, *parasmaipada.* An *ātmanepada* verb would be indicated by "Ā".

Stems in this class are formed by the process - *guṇa* of root plus *a* = stem

.

Reminder : There is a process by which roots are strengthened. In most cases the root is strengthened by adding 'a' (the thematic vowel) and this is the *guṇa* form. Addition of another *'a'* creates the *vṛddhi* form. "Strengthened" simply means one or 2 vowels have been added so the meaning changes and the new word is looked up in the dictionary in the usual way.

Here are some examples: in the middle row *a* has been added, in the 3rd row an additional *a* has been added.

root	***guṇa* (stronger)**	***vṛddhi* (strongest)**
vid	*veda*	*vaidya*
div	*deva*	*daivika*
yuj	*yoga*	*yaugika*
dhṛ	*dharma*	*dhārmika*

<u>There are 10 classes</u> (*gaṇa*) **<u>of verbs – this is a summary of how they are structured</u>**

# ***gaṇa***	**stem**	**present**	**English**
1. bhū (p)	*guṇa* of root + *a*	*bhava + ti*	he is
2. ad (p)	*guṇa* of root (strong)	*at + ti*	he eats
	root (weak)	*at + taḥ*	those two eat
3. hu (p)	*abhyāsa* ✱ + *guṇa* of root (strong)	*juho + ti*	he offers
	abhyāsa + root (weak)	*juhu +taḥ*	those two offer
4. div (p)	root + *ya*	*dīvya + ti*	he plays
5. su (u)	*root + no* (strong)	*suno+ ti*	he presses
	root + nu (weak)	*sunu+taḥ*	those two press
6. tud (u)	*root + a*	*tuda + ti*	he pushes
7. rudh (u)	*na* after vowel of root (strong)	*ruṇaddhi*	he blocks
		ruṇadh + ti	
	n after vowel of root (weak)	*runndhaḥ*	those two block
		rundh + taḥ	those two block
8. tan (u)	*root + o* (strong)	*tano + ti*	he stretches
	root + u (weak)	*tanu + taḥ*	those two stretch
9. krī	*root + na* (strong)	*krīṇā + ti*	he buys
	root + nī (weak)	*krīṇī + taḥ*	those two buy
10. cur (u)	*guṇa* of root + *aya*	*corayati*	he steals

abhyāsa ✱ doubling – see reduplication under Class 3 p.60

Class 2,3,5,7,8 and 9 differences for the present indicative, imperfect and imperative

The present indicative, imperfect and imperative endings are almost the same for all classes in *parasmaipada*, (the 2nd /singular is *hi* in classes 2,3,7and 9). but the *ātmanepada* endings are different. It is practical to consult tables for these rather than try and remember them.

Class 1 stems

root	guṇa form	stem		1st person	
smṛ	*smar* *	*smara*	remember	*smarati*	he remembers
vad	*vad*	*vada*	speak	*vadati*	he speaks
śubh	*śobh**	*śobha*	shine	*śobhate*	he shines

- *This is a general rule also true of other classes that add *guṇa* to the root vowel.
- If the *guṇa* of the root is *e* or *o* then the *e* appears as *ay* (from *a + i)* and the *o* appears as *av* (from *a + u)*. The a is then added e.g.

ji	*je*	*jaya*	conquer	*jayati*	he conquers
bhū	*bho*	*bhava*	be	*bhavati*	he is
nī	*ne*	*naya*	lead	*nayati*	he leads

- some stems are formed from the *vṛddhi* of the root, and there are other forms e.g.

gam		*gaccha*	go	*gacchati*	he goes
sthā		*tiṣṭhā*	stand	*tiṣṭhati*	he stands
pā		*piba*	drink	*pibati*	he drinks

Class 2 *ad gaṇa* – The second class is called the root class because its present stem is the root. The root takes *guṇa* in strong forms. The stem of class 2 is formed by-

root (for weak forms)

of root (for strong forms). The most common form of this verb is *as* .

*ad (*eat)

atti	*attaḥ*	*adanti*
ad+ti	*ad +tas*	*ad+anti*
atsi	*atthah*	*attha*
ad+si	*ad +ths*	*ad+tha*
admi	*advaḥ*	*admaḥ*
ad+mi	*ad+vas*	*ad+ mas*

Class 3 *hu gaṇa* (offer) The present stem is formed by *abhyāsa,* which means "doubling" The root is repeated and this is referred to as re-duplication. The first syllable is considered to be the *abhyāsa* syllable followed by the root which is in strong *guṇa* form. The formation of Class 3 stems is –
abhyāsa + root (weak forms)
abhyāsa + *guṇa* of root (strong forms)

Re-duplication rules

- the vowel and first consonant of the root are repeated
- The first syllable usually appears in a weaker form e.g. root *dā* becomes *dadā*
- an aspirated syllable becomes unaspirated. *dhā* (put) becomes *dadhā*
- the vowel *ṛ* is changed to *i* e.g. *bhṛ (* carry) becomes - *bibhṛ*
- only the first consonant of a conjunct is repeated *tyaj - tatyāja,*
- if the root begins with an s followed by a stop (*sparśa*) *sthā* → *tiṣṭha*
- a *kaṇṭha* consonant turns into a *tālu* *kṛ* → *cakara*
- an *h* turns into *j* *hā* → *jaha*

example *hu* offer

juhoti	*juhutaḥ*	*juhvati*
juhosi	*juhuthaḥ*	*juhutha*
juhomi	*juhuvaḥ*	*juhumaḥ*

Class 4 (*div gaṇa*) -is formed by root + ya
man + *ya* = *manya* think *manyate* he thinks

Class 5 *su gaṇa* – this is formed exactly like Class 8 except *nu* and *no* are added instead of *u* and *o*. i.e.
root + *nu* for weak forms (dual and plural)
root + *no* for strong forms (singular)
example – root *śru* (Note: *śru* becomes *śr* before adding *nu* or no)

śṛṇoti	*śṛṇutaḥ*	*śṛṇvanti*
śṛṇo+ti	*śṛṇu+tas*	*śṛṇu+anti*
śṛṇosi	*śṛṇuthaḥ*	*śṛṇutha*
śṛṇu+si	*śṛṇu+ṭhas*	*śṛṇu+tha*

śṛṇomi	*śṛṇuvaḥ*	*śṛṇumaḥ*
śṛṇo +mi	*śṛṇu+vas*	*śṛṇu+mas*

āpnoti is another Class 5 verb

Class 6_(*tud gaṇa*) – is formed by root + a

tud + a = tuda push, strike, hit, goad *tudati* he pushes etc.

Class 7_*rudh gaṇa* – the present stem in strong forms is formed by adding *na* between the vowel and final consonant of the root. In weak forms *n* is added. Example *yuj* (unite)

yuj +an yunaj (strong)

yuj +n yuñj (weak)

yunakti	*yuṅktaḥ*	*yuñjanti*
yunaksi	*yuṅkthaḥ*	*yuṅktha*
yunajmi	*yuñjvaḥ*	*yuñjmaḥ*

Class 8_(*tan gaṇa*) root + *u* for weak forms (dual and plural)

root + *o* for strong forms (singular)

tan + o = tano (strong form) *tanoti* he stretches

tan + u = tanu (weak form) *tanvanti* they stretch

Class 8 conjugation example

<u>*tanoti*</u>	*tanutaḥ*	*tanvanti*
tan+o+ti	*tan+u+tas*	*tan+u+anti*
<u>*tanosi*</u>	*tanuthaḥ*	*tanutha*
tan+o+si	*tan+u+tha*	*tan+u+tha*
<u>*tanomi*</u>	*tanuvaḥ*	*tanumaḥ*
tan+o+mi	*tan+u+vas*	*tan+u+mas*

- strong forms are underlined
- endings are the same
- in the 2/s *si* turns into *śi* because of vowel *o*
- the ending *anti* turns *u* in to *v* e.g. *tanvanti*

- in the dual or plural the u may be optionally deleted before v or m e.g. *tanumaḥ* or *tanmaḥ, tanuvaḥ* or *tanvaḥ*

- dictionary entry - √*tan* cl. 8 U The U indicates that this verb is *ubhayapada* which means it is regularly used with *parasmaipada* and *ātmanepada* endings.
- There are only 8 roots in this class.
- *kṛ* is an irregular class 8 verb conjugated as

karoti	*kurutaḥ*	*kurvanti*
karosi	*kuruthaḥ*	*kurutha*
karomi	*kurvaḥ*	*kurmaḥ*

- when *kṛ* is prefixed by *sam* or *pari* the *kṛ* becomes *skṛ* e.g. *saṁskṛta*

Class 9 *krī gaṇa (krī* buy) The 9th class forms its stem by adding *nā* in strong forms and *nī* in weak forms.

Few of the roots in class 9 are used except the important root *jñā* (know).

jānati	*jānitaḥ*	*jānanti*
jānāsi	*jānīthaḥ*	*jānītha*
jānāmi	*jānīvāḥ*	*jānīmaḥ*

note that before *anti* the *nī* loses the *ī*

Class 10 (*cur gaṇa*) – is formed by *guṇa* of root + *aya*

cur + *aya* = *coraya* *steal* *corayati* he steals

cint + *aya* = *cintaya* think *cintayati* he thinks

(*cint* does not take *guṇa* because there are 2 consonants following the vowel.)

Verb ConjugationTables

The following pages contain examples of the verb conjugations.
These examples are arranged by Class *(gaṇa)* from 1 to 10.
The examples have been chosen for their usefulness as commonly used words and preferably with spiritual/philosophical significance. Sometimes this has resulted in 'theoretical' words being shown. i.e. the word may not exist in practical use but is shown in order to illustrate the method of construction. Also note that these examples do contain some irregularities. An outstanding website is the 'Sanskrit Grammarian' of Gerard Huet. If the verb root and class are entered the full conjugation is shown complete with participles and alternatives.

In the tables 'active' = *parasmaipada*
'middle' = *ātmanepada*
The participles and indeclinables for the verb are also included here.
Some verbs have additional 'causative', 'desiderative' or 'intensive' conjugations and these have also been shown together with their own sets of participles and indeclinables. This is to help track down unusual variations of words.

Some additional verbs are included e.g. √*paś* 'to see' because it unusually changes to √*dṛṣ* for some tenses. This is listed at the end of the section.

Sometime alternative words are available. These are indicated by the (/ or |) symbols connecting them.
Examples are in the following order-

class 1 *smṛ* remember, recollect, call to mind, think of

class 1 *bhū* –to be, become, come into being, exist, stay, abide, happen,

class 2 *as* to be , live, exist, be present, take place, happen, abide, dwell, stay, belong to

class 2 *vid* to know, understand, perceive, learn, become acquainted with, be conscious of, have a correct notion of,

class 3 *dā* give, bestow, grant, yield, impart, present, offer to, hand over, give back, pay (a fine),

class 4 *budh* (also conjugates as class 1) to wake, wake up, be awake, to observe, heed, attend to,

class 5 *śru* to hear, listen, attend to anything, study, learn, be attentive, be obedient,

class 6 *vid* find, discover, obtain,acquire (see also *vid* class 2 – know, understand)

class 7 *yuj* to yoke, join, unite, harness, prepare, arrange, employ, concentrate upon, be absorbed in meditation,

class 8 *kṛ* - to do, make, act, perform, cause, work at, build

class 9 *jñā* - know, understand, have knowledge, perceive, experience, recognise, know as,

class 10 *cint* to think, reflect, consider, reflect upon, care for, find out,

paś/dṛṣ to see, behold, look at, regard, consider, see with the mind, learn, understand, see by intuition, (√*paś* is used for the present, imperfect, optative and imperative tenses)

Here are examples of how the classes are conjugated

Conjugations class 1 *smṛ* remember, recollect, call to mind, think of

			active				middle				passive	
		singular	dual	plural		singular	dual	plural		singular	dual	plural
present	1st 2nd 3rd	*smarati* *smarasi* *smarāmi*	*smarataḥ* *smarathaḥ* *smarāvaḥ*	*smaranti* *smaratha* *smarāma*		*smarate* *smarase* *smare*	*smarete* *smarethe* *smarāvahe*	*smarante* *smaradhve* *smarāmahe*		*smaryate* *smaryase* *smarye*	*smaryete* *smaryethe* *smaryāvahe*	*smaryante* *smaryadhve* *smaryāmahe*
imperfect		*asmarat* *asmaraḥ* *asmaram*	*asmaratām* *asmaratam* *asmarāva*	*asmaran* *asmarata* *asmārama*		*asmarata* *asmarathāḥ* *asmare*	*asmaretām* *asmarethām* *asmarāvahi*	*asmaranta* *asmaradhvam* *asmarāmahi*		*asmaryata* *asmaryathāḥ* *asmarye*	*asmaryetām* *asmaryethām* *asmaryāvahi*	*asmaryanta* *asmaryadhvam* *asmaryāmahi*
simple fut.		*smariṣyati* *smariṣyasi* *smariṣyāmi*	*smariṣyataḥ* *smariṣyathaḥ* *smariṣyāvaḥ*	*smariṣyanti* *smariṣyatha* *smariṣyāmaḥ*		*smariṣyate* *smariṣyase* *smariṣye*	*smariṣyete* *smariṣyethe* *smariṣyāvahe*	*smariṣyante* *smariṣyadhve* *smariṣyāmahe*				
imperative		*smaratu* *smara* *smarāṇi*	*smaratām* *smaratam* *smarāva*	*smarantu* *smarata* *smarāma*		*smaratām* *smarasva* *smarai*	*smaretām* *smarethām* *smarāvahai*	*smarantām* *smaradhvam* *smarāmahai*		*smaryatām* *smaryasva* *smaryai*	*smaryetām* *smaryethām* *smaryāvahai*	*smaryantām* *smaryadhvam* *smaryāmahai*
perfect		*sasmāra* *sasmaritha* *sasmāra or sasmara*	*sasmaratuḥ* *sasmarathuḥ* *sasmariva*	*sasmaruḥ* *sasmara* *sasmarima*		*sasmare* *sasmariṣe* *sasmare*	*sasmarāte* *sasmarāthe* *sasmarivahe*	*sasmarire* *sasmaridhve* *sasmarimahe*				

Conjugation *bhū* – Class 1 to be, become come into being, exist, stay, abide, happen,

		active			middle			passive		
		singular	dual	plural	singular	dual	plural	singular	dual	plural
present	1st 2nd 3rd	*bhavati* *bhavasi* *bhavāmi*	*bhavataḥ* *bhavathaḥ* *bhavāvaḥ*	*bhavanti* *bhavatha* *bhavāmaḥ*	*bhavate* *bhavase* *bhave*	*bhavete* *bhavethe* *bhavāvahe*	*bhavante* *bhavadhve* *bhavāmahe*	*bhūyate* *bhūyase* *bhūye*	*bhūyete* *bhūyethe* *bhūyāvahe*	*bhūyante* *bhūyadhve* *bhūyāmahe*
optative		*bhavet* *bhaveḥ* *bhaveyam*	*bhavetām* *bhavetam* *bhaveva*	*bhaveyuḥ* *bhaveta* *bhavema*	*bhaveta* *bhavethāḥ* *bhaveya*	*bhaveyātām* *bhaveyāthām* *bhavevahi*	*bhaveran* *bhavedhvam* *bhavemahi*	*bhūyeta* *bhūyethāḥ* *bhūyeya*	*bhūyeyātām* *bhūyeyāthām* *bhūyevahi*	*bhūyeran* *bhūyedhvam* *bhūyemahi*
imperative		*bhavatu* *bhava* *bhavāni*	*bhavatām* *bhavatam* *bhavāva*	*bhavantu* *bhavata* *bhavāma*	*bhavatām* *bhavasva* *bhavai*	*bhavetām* *bhavethām* *bhavāvahai*	*bhavantām* *bhavadhvam* *bhavāmahai*	*bhūyatām* *bhūyasva* *bhūyai*	*bhūyetām* *bhūyethām* *bhūyāvahai*	*bhūyantām* *bhūyadhvam* *bhūyāmahai*
imperfect		*abhavat* *abhavaḥ* *abhavam*	*abhavatām* *abhavatam* *abhavāva*	*abhavan* *abhavata* *abhavāma*	*abhavata* *abhavathāḥ* *abhave*	*abhavetām* *abhavethām* *abhavāvahi*	*abhavanta* *abhavadhvam* *abhavāmahi*	*abhūyata* *abhūyathāḥ* *abhūye*	*abhūyetām* *abhūyethām* *abhūyāvahi*	*abhūyanta* *abhūyadhvam* *abhūyāmahi*
perfect		*babhūva* *babhūvitha* or *babhūtha* *babhūva**	*babhūvatuḥ* *babhūvathuḥ* *babhūviva*	*babhūvuḥ* *babhūva* *babhūvima*						

* the reduplicative *ba* is irregular instead of *bu*

		active			middle			passive		
		singular	dual	plural	singular	dual	plural	singular	dual	plural
aorist	1st 2nd 3rd	*abhūt* *abhūḥ* *abhūvam*	*abhūtām* *abhūtam* *abhūva*	*abhūvan* *abhūta* *abhūma*	 *abhāvi*					
periphrastic fut. indic.		*bhavitā* *bhavatāsi* *bhavitāsmi*	*bhavitārau* *bhavitāsthaḥ* *bhavitāsvaḥ*	*bhavitāraḥ* *bhavitāstha* *bhavitāsmaḥ*						
simple fut. indicative		*bhaviṣyati* *bhaviṣyasi* *bhaviṣyāmi*	*bhaviṣyataḥ* *bhaviṣyathaḥ* *bahaviṣyāvaḥ*	*bhaviṣyanti* *bhaviṣyatha* *bhaviṣyāmaḥ*	*bhaviṣyate* *bhaviṣyase* *bhaviṣye*	*bhaviṣyete* *bhaviṣyethe* *bhaviṣyāvahe*	*bhaviṣyante* *bhaviṣyadhve* *bhaviṣyāmahe*			
conditional indicative		*abhaviṣyat* *abhaviṣyaḥ* *abhaviṣyam*	*abhaviṣyatām* *abhaviṣyatam* *bhaviṣyāva*	*abhaviṣyan* *abhaviṣyata* *abhaviṣyāma*	*abhaviṣyata* *abhaviṣyathāḥ* *abhaviṣye*	*abhaviṣyetām* *abhaviṣyethām* *abhaviṣyāvahi*	*abhaviṣyanta* *abhaviṣyadhvam* *abhaviṣyāmahi*			

past passive participle	*bhūta* m.n. *bhūtā* f.
past active participle	*bhūtavat* m.n. *bhūtavatī* f.
present active participle	*bhāvat* m.n. *bhāvantī* f.
present middle participle	*bhāvamāna* m.n. *bhāvamānā* f.
present passive participle	*bhūyamāna* m.n. *bhūyamānā* f.
future active participle	*bhāviṣyat* m.n. bhāviṣyantī f.
future middle participle	*bhāviṣyamāna* m.n. *bhāviṣyamāṇā* f.
future passive participle	*bhoya or bhāvitavya* or *bhavanīya* m.n. *bhoyā* f. or *bhāvitavyā* or *bhavanīyā*
perfect active participle	*babhūvaḥ* m.n. *babhūṣī* f.
perfect middle participle	*babhūvāna* m.n. *babhūvānā* f.
Indeclinables:	*bhāvitum* infinitive, *bhūtvā* –gerund/absolutive, -*bhūya* –gerund/absolutive

Conjugation *bhū* Class 1 (Causative)

		active			middle			passive		
		singular	dual	plural	singular	dual	plural	singular	dual	plural
present causative	1st 2nd 3rd	*bhāvayati* *bhāvayasi* *bhāvayāmi*	*bhāvayataḥ* *bhāvayathaḥ* *bhāvayāvaḥ*	*bhāvayanti* *bhāvayatha* *bhāvayāmaḥ*	*bhāvayate* *bhāvayase* *bhāvaye*	*bhāvayete* *bhāvayethe* *bhāvayāvahe*	*bhāvayante* *bhāvayadhve* *bhāvayāmahe*	*bhāvyate* *bhāvyase* *bhāvye*	*bhāvyete* *bhāvyethe* *bhāvyāvahe*	*bhāvyante* *bhāvyadhve* *bhāvyāmahe*
causative optative		*bhāvayet* *bhāvayeḥ* *bhāvayeyam*	*bhāvayetām* *bhāvayetam* *bhāvayeva*	*bhāvayeyuḥ* *bhāvayeta* *bhāvayema*	*bhāvayeta* *bhāvayethāḥ* *bhāvayeya*	*bhāvayeyātām* *bhāvayeyāthām* *bhāvayevahi*	*bhāvayeran* *bhāvayedhvam* *bhāvayemahi*	*bhāvyeta* *bhāvyethāḥ* *bhāvyeya*	*bhāvyeyātām* *bhāvyeyāthām* *bhāvyevahi*	*bhāvyeran* *bhāvyedhvam* *bhāvyemahi*
causative imperative		*bhāvayatu* *bhāvaya* *bhāvayāni*	*bhāvayatām* *bhāvayatam* *bhāvayāva*	*bhāvayantu* *bhāvayata* *bhāvayāma*	*bhāvayatām* *bhāvayasva* *bhāvayai*	*bhāvayetām* *bhāvayethām* *bhāvayāvahai*	*bhāvayantām* *bhāvayadhvam* *bhāvayāmahai*	*bhāvyatām* *bhāvyasva* *bhāvyai*	*bhāvyetām* *bhāvyethām* *bhāvyāvahai*	*bhāvyantām* *bhāvyadhvam* *bhāvyāmahai*
imperfect (causative)		*abhāvayat* *abhāvayaḥ* *abhāvayam*	*abhāvayatām* *abhāvayatam* *abhāvayāva*	*abhāvayan* *abhāvayata* *abhāvayāma*	*abhāvayata* *abhāvayathāḥ* *abhāvaye*	*abhāvayetām* *abhāvayethām* *abhāvayāvahi*	*abhāvayanta* *abhāvayadhvam* *abhāvayāmahi*	*abhāvyata* *abhāvyathāḥ* *abhāvye*	*abhāvyetām* *abhāvyethām* *abhāvyetām*	*abhāvyanta* *abhāvyadhvam* *abhāvyāmahi*
causative future		*bhāvayiṣyati* *bhāvayiṣyasi* *bhāvayiṣyāmi*	*bhāvayiṣyataḥ* *bhāvayiṣyathaḥ* *bhāvayiṣyāvaḥ*	*bhāvayiṣyanti* *bhāvayiṣyatha* *bhāvayiṣyāmaḥ*	*bhāvayiṣyate* *bhāvayiṣyase* *bhāvayiṣye*	*bhāvayiṣyete* *bhāvayiṣyethe* *bhāvayiṣyāvahe*	*bhāvayiṣyante* *bhāvayiṣyadhve* *bhāvayiṣyāmahe*			
causative periphrastic future		*bhāvayitā* *bhāvayitāsi* *bhāvayitāsmi*	*bhāvayitārau* *bhāvayitāsthaḥ* *bhāvayitāsvaḥ*	*bhāvayitāraḥ* *bhāvayitāstha* *bhāvayitāsmaḥ*						

Causative participles *bhū*

past passive participle — *bhāvita* m.n. *bhāvitā* f.
past active participle — *bhāvitavat* m.n. *bhāvitavatī* f.
present active participle — *bhāvayat* m.n. *bhāvayantī* f.
present middle participle — *bhāvayamāna* m.n. *bhāvayamānā* f.
present passive participle — *bhāvyamāna* m.n. *bhāvyamānā* f.
future active participle — *bhāvayiṣyat* m.n. bhāvayiṣyantī f.
future middle participle — *bhāvayiṣyamāna* m.n. *bhāvayiṣyamāṇā* f.
future passive participle — *bhāvya* or *bhāvavitavya* or *bhāvanīya* m.n. *bhāvyā* or *bhāvavitavyā* or *bhāvanīyā* f.
Indeclinables: *bhāvitum* - infinitive, *bhāvayitvā* –gerund/absolutive, *bhāvavyyām* –gerund/absolutive

Conjugation Class 1 **(Intensive)** ***bhū***

		active				middle		
		singular	**dual**	**plural**		**singular**	**dual**	**plural**
present intensive	1st	*bobhoti/bobhavīti*	*bobhotaḥ/bobhavtaḥ*	*bobhavati*		*bobhūyate*	*bobhūyete*	*bobhūyante*
	2nd	*bobhoṣi/bobhavīṣi*	*bobhothaḥ/bobhavthaḥ*	*bobhotha/bobhavtha*		*bobhūyase*	*bobhūyethe*	*bobhūyadhve*
	3rd	*bobhomi, bobhavīmi*	*bobhovaḥ/bobhavvaḥ*	*bobhomaḥ/bobhavmaḥ*		*bobhūye*	*bobhūyāvahe*	*bobhūyāmahe*
optative intensive		*bobhoyāt/bobhavyāt*	*bobhoyātām/bobhavyātām*	*bobhoyuḥ/bobhavyuḥ*		*bobhūyeta*	*bobhūyeyātām*	*bobhūyeran*
		bobhavyāḥ	*bobhoyatām/bobhavyātam*	*bobhoyāta/bobhavyāta*		*bobhūyethāḥ*	*bobhūyeyāthām*	*bobhūyedhvam*
		bobhoyām/bobhovyām	*bobhoyāva/bobhavyātām*	*bobhoyāma/bobhavyāma*		*bobhūyeya*	*bobhūyevahi*	*bobhūyemahi*
imperative intensive		*bobhotu, bobhavītu*	*bobhotām/bobhavtām*	*bobhavatu*		*bobhūyatām*	*bobhūyetām*	*bobhūyeran*
		bobhohi/bobhavdhi	*bobhotam/bobhavtam*	*bobhota/bobhavta*		*bobhūyasva*	*bobhūyethām*	*bobhūyedhvam*
		bobhavāni	*bobhavāva*	*bobhavāma*		*bobhūyai*	*bobhūyāvahai*	*bobhūyāmahai*
imperfect intensive		*abobhot*	*abobhotām/abobhavtām*	*abobhavuḥ*		*abobhūyata*	*abobhūyetām*	*abobhūyanta*
		abobhoḥ/ abobhaviḥ/ abobhavīt	*abobhotam/abobhavtam*	*abobhota/abobhavta*		*abobhūyathāḥ*	*abobhūyethām*	*abobhūyadhvam*
		abobhavam	*abobhova/abobhavva*	*abobhoma/abobhavma*		*abobhūye*	*abobhūyāvahi*	*abobhūyāmahi*

Intensive Participles
present active participle *bobhavat* m.n. *bobhavatī* f.
present middle participle *bobhūyamāna* m.n. *bobhūyamānā* f.

Conjugation *as* class 2 to be , live, exist, be present, take place, happen, abide, dwell, stay, belong to

			active				middle				passive	
		singular	dual	plural		singular	dual	plural		singular	dual	plural
present	1st	*asti*	*staḥ*	*santi*		*ste*	*sāte*	*sate*				
	2nd	*asi*	*sthaḥ*	*stha*		*se*	*sāthe*	*dhve*				
	3rd	*asmi*	*svaḥ*	*smaḥ*		*he*	*svahe*	*smahe*				
		syāt	*syātām*	*syuḥ*								
optative		*syāḥ*	*syātam*	*syāta*								
		syām	*syāva*	*syāma*								
imperative		*astu*	*stām*	*santu*								
		edhi	*stam*	*sta*								
		asāni	*asāva*	*asāma*								
imperfect		*āsīt*	*āstām*	*āsan*								
		āsīḥ	*āstam*	*āsta*								
		āsam	*āsva*	*āsma*								
perfect		*āsa*	*āsatuḥ*	*āsuḥ*								
		āsitha	*āsathuḥ*	*āsa*								
		āsa	*āsiva*	*āsima*								
periphrastic future		*astā*	*astārau*	*astāraḥ*								
		astāsi	*astāsthaḥ*	*astāstha*								
		astāsmi	*astāsvaḥ*	*astāsmaḥ*								

present active participle m.n. *sat* f. *satī*
future passive participle m.n. *asya* f. *asyā*
future passive participle m.n. *asanīya* f. *asanīyā*
perfect active participle m. n. *āsivaḥ* f. *āsuṣī*

Conjugation *vid* Class 2 to know, understand, perceive, learn, become acquainted with, be conscious of, have a correct notion of

		active			middle			passive		
		singular	dual	plural	singular	dual	plural	singular	dual	plural
present indicative	1st 2nd 3rd	*vetti* *vetsi* *vedmi*	*vittaḥ* *vitthaḥ* *vidvaḥ*	*vidanti* *vittha* *vidmaḥ*	*vitte* *vitse* *vide*	*vidāte* *vidāthe* *vidvahe*	*vidate* *viddhve* *vidmahe*	*vidyate* *vidyase* *vidye*	*vidyete* *vidyethe* *vidyāvahe*	*vidyante* *vidyadhve* *vidyāmahe*
present optative		*vidyāt* *vidyāḥ* *vidyām*	*vidyātām* *vidyātam* *vidyāva*	*vidyuḥ* *vidyāta* *vidyāma*	*vidīta* *vidīthāḥ* *vidīya*	*vidīyātām* *vidīyāthām* *vidīvahi*	*vidīran* *vidīdhvam* *vidīmahi*	*vidyeta* *vidyethāḥ* *vidyeya*	*vidyeyātām* *vidyeyāthām* *vidyevahi*	*vidyeran* *vidyedhvam* *vidyemahi*
present imperative		*vettu* *viddhi* *vedāni*	*vittām* *vittam* *vedāva*	*vidantu* *vitta* *vedāma*	*vittām* *vitsva* *vedai*	*vidātām* *vidāthām* *vedāvahai*	*vidatām* *viddhvam* *vedāmahai*	*vidyatām* *vidyasva* *vidyai*	*vidyetām* *vidyethām* *vidyāvahai*	*vidyantām* *vidyadhvam* *vidyāmahai*
imperfect indicative		*avet* *avet* *avedam*	*avittām* *avittam* *avidva*	*avidan* *avitta* *avidma*	*avitta* *avitthāḥ* *avidi*	*avidātām* *avidāthām* *avidvahi*	*avidata* *aviddhvam* *avidmahi*	*avidyata* *avidyathāḥ* *avidye*	*avidyetām* *avidyethām* *avidyāvahi*	*avidyanta* *avidyadhvam* *avidyāmahi*
perfect indicative		*veda* *vettha* *veda*	*vittuḥ* *vitthuḥ* *vidva*	*viduḥ* *vida* *vidma*						
future		*vediṣyati* */ vetsyati* *vediṣyasi* */vetsyasi* *vediṣyāmi* */ vetsyāmi*	*vediṣyataḥ* */ vetsyataḥ* *vediṣyathaḥ* */ vetsyathaḥ* *vediṣyāvaḥ* */ vetsyāvaḥ*	*vediṣyanti* */vetsyanti* *vediṣyatha /vetsyatha* *vediṣyāmaḥ* */vetsyāmaḥ*	*vediṣyate* */vetsyate* *vediṣyase* */vetsyase* *vediṣye* */vetsye*	*vediṣyete* */vetsyete* *vediṣyethe* */vetsyethe* *vediṣyāvahe* */vetsyāvahe*	*vediṣyante* */vetsyante* *vediṣyadhve* */vetsyadhve* *vediṣyāmahe* */vetsyāmahe*			
aorist indicative		*avedīt* *avedīḥ* *avediṣam*	*avediṣṭām* *avediṣṭam* *avediṣva*	*avediṣuḥ* *avediṣṭa* *avediṣma*	*avediṣṭa* *avediṣṭāḥ* *avediṣi*	*avediṣātām* *avediṣāṭhām* *avediṣvahi*	*avediṣata* *avedhidhvam* *avediṣmahi*			
periphrastic fut. indic.		*veditā/vettā* *veditāsi/vettāsi* *veditāsmi/vettāsmi*	*veditārau* */vettārau* *veditāsthaḥ* */vettāsthaḥ* *veditāsvaḥ* */vettāsvaḥ*	*veditāraḥ/vettāraḥ* *veditāstha/vettāstha* *veditāsmaḥ/vettāsmaḥ*						

passive participle *vidita* m.n. *viditā* f. past active participle *viditavat* m.n. *viditavatī* f.

present active participle *vidat* m.n. *vidatī* f. present middle participle *vidāna* m.n. *vidānā* f.
present passive participle *vidyamāna* m.n. *vidyamānā* f. future active participle *vetsyat* m.n. *vetsyantī* f.
future middle participle *vediṣyamāna* m.n. *vediṣyamāṇā* f. future passive participle *vettavya* or *veditavya* or *vedya* m.n. *vetyā* or *veditavyā* or *vedyā* or *vettavyā* f.
perfect active participle *vidvaḥ* or *vidivaḥ* m.n. *viduṣī* f.
Indeclinables: *veditum or vettum* infinitive, gerund/absolutive *viditvā* or , *-vidya*

Causative Conjugation class 2 *vid*

		active			middle			passive		
		singular	dual	plural	singular	dual	plural	singular	dual	plural
present indicative	1st 2nd 3rd	*vedayati* *vedayasi* *vedayāmi*	*vedayataḥ* *vedayathaḥ* *vedayāvaḥ*	*vedayanti* *vedayatha* *vedayāmaḥ*	*vedayate* *vedayase* *vedaye*	*vedayete* *vedayethe* *vedayāvahe*	*vedayante* *vedayadhve* *vedayāmahe*	*vedyate* *vedyase* *vedye*	*vedyete* *vedyethe* *vedyāvahe*	*vedyante* *vedyadhve* *vedyāmahe*
present optative		*vedayet* *vedayeḥ* *vedayeyam*	*vedayetām* *vedayetam* *vedayeva*	*vedayeyuḥ* *vedayeta* *vedayema*	*vedayeta* *vedayethāḥ* *vedayeya*	*vedayeyātām* *vedayeyāthām* *vedayevahi*	*vedayeran* *vedayedhvam* *vedayemahi*	*vedyeta* *vedyethāḥ* *vedyeya*	*vedyeyātām* *vedyeyāthām* *vedyevahi*	*vedyeran* *vedyedhvam* *vedyemahi*
present imperative		*vedayatu* *vedaya* *vedayāni*	*vedayatām* *vedayatam* *vedayāva*	*vedayantu* *vedayata* *vedayāma*	*vedayatām* *vedayasva* *vedayai*	*vedayetām* *vedayethām* *vedayāvahai*	*vedayantām* *vedayadhvam* *vedayantām*	*vedyatām* *vedyasva* *vedyai*	*vedyetām* *vedyethām* *vedyāvahai*	*vedyantām* *vedyadhvam* *vedyāmahai*
imperfect indicative		*avedayat* *avedayaḥ* *avedayam*	*avedayetām* *avedayatam* *avedayāva*	*avedayan* *avedayata* *avedayāma*	*avedayata* *avedayathāḥ* *avedaye*	*avedayetām* *avedayethām* *avedayāvahi*	*avedayanta* *avedayadhvam* *avedayāmahi*	*avedyata* *avedyathāḥ* *avedye*	*avedyetām* *avedyethām* *avedyāvahi*	*avedyanta* *avedyadhvam* *avedyāmahi*
futureindicative		*vedayiṣyati* *vedayiṣyasi* *vedayiṣyāmi*	*vedayiṣyataḥ* *vedayiṣyathaḥ* *vedayiṣyāvaḥ*	*vedayiṣyanti* *vedayiṣyatha* *vedayiṣyāmaḥ*	*vedayiṣyate* *vedayiṣyase* *vedayiṣye*	*vedayiṣyete* *vedayiṣyethe* *vedayiṣyāvahe*	*vedayiṣyante* *vedayiṣyadhve* *vedayiṣyāmahe*			
peri. future		*vedayitā* *vedayitāsi* *vedayitāsmi*	*vedayitārau* *vedayitāsthaḥ* *vedayitāsvaḥ*	*vedayitāraḥ* *vedayitāstha* *vedayitāsmaḥ*						

past passive participle *vedita* m.n. *veditā* f. past active participle *veditavat* m.n. *veditavatī* f.
present active participle *vedayat* m.n. *vedayantī* f. present middle participle *vedayamāna* m.n. *vedayamānā* f.
present passive participle *vedayamāna* m.n. *vedayamānā* f. future active participle *vedayiṣyat* m.n. *vedayiṣyantī* f.
future middle participle *vedayiṣyamāna* m.n. *vedayiṣyamāṇā* f. future passive participle *vedya* or *vedanīya* or *vedayitavya* m.n. *vedyā* or *vedanīyā* or *vedayitavyā* f.
Indeclinables: *vedāyitum* infinitive, *veditvā* –gerund/absolutive, *-vedya* –gerund/absolutive, *vedayyām* peri. perf.

Intensive Conjugation class 2

			active				middle				passive	
		singular	dual	plural		singular	dual	plural		singular	dual	plural
present	1st	*vevetti/vevidīti*	*vevittaḥ*	*vevidati*		*vevidyate*	*vevidyete*	*vevidyante*				
	2nd	*vevetsi/vevidīṣi*	*vevithaḥ*	*vevittha*		*vevidyase*	*vevidyethe*	*vevidyadhve*				
	3rd	*vevedmi/vevidīmi*	*vevidvaḥ*	*vevidmaḥ*		*vevidye*	*vevidyāvahe*	*vevidyāmahe*				
imperfect		*avevet*	*avevittām*	*aveveduḥ*		*avevidyata*	*avevidyetām*	*avevidyanta*				
		avevet/avevidīḥ/avevidīt	*avevittam*	*avevitta*		*avevidyathāḥ*	*avevidyethām*	*avevidyadhvam*				
		avevedam	*avevidva*	*avevidma*		*avevidye*	*avevidyāvahi*	*avevidyāmahi*				
optative		*vevidyāt*	*vevidyātām*	*vevidyuḥ*		*vevidyeta*	*vevidyeyātām*	*vevidyeran*				
		vevidyāḥ	*vevidyātam*	*vevidyāta*		*vevidyethāḥ*	*vevidyeyāthām*	*vevidyedhvam*				
		vevidyām	*vevidyāva*	*vevidyāma*		*vevidyeya*	*vevidyevahi*	*vevidyāmahi*				
imperative		*vevedītu/vevettu*	*vevittām*	*vevidatu*		*vevidyatām*	*vevidyetām*	*vevidyantām*				
		veviddhi	*vevittam*	*vevitta*		*vevidyasva*	*vevidyethām*	*vevidyadhvam*				
		vevedāni	*vevedāva*	*vevedāma*		*vevidyai*	*vevidyāvahai*	*vevidyāmahai*				

present active participle *vevidat* m.n. *vevidatī* f.

present middle participle *vevidyamāna* m.n. *vevidyamānā*

Desiderative Conjugation class 2

			active				middle				passive	
		singular	dual	plural		singular	dual	plural		singular	dual	plural
present	1st 2nd 3rd	*vividiṣati/vivitsati* *vividiṣasi/ vivitsasi* *vividiṣāmi/vivitsāmi*	*vividiṣataḥ/vivitsataḥ* *vividiṣathaḥ/vivitsathaḥ* *vividiṣāvaḥ/vivitsāvaḥ*	*vividiṣanti/vivitsanti* *vividiṣatha/vivitsatha* *vividiṣāmaḥ/vivitsāmaḥ*								
imperfect		*avividiṣat/avivitsat* *avividiṣaḥ/avivitsaḥ* *avividiṣam/avivitsam*	*avividiṣatām/avivitsatām* *avividiṣatam/avivitsatam* *avividiṣāva/avivitsāva*	*avividiṣan/avivitsan* *avividiṣata/avivitsata* *avividiṣāma/avivitsāma*								
optative		*vividiṣet/vivitset* *vividiṣeḥ/vivitseḥ* *vividiṣeyam/vivitseyam*	*vividiṣetām/vivitsetām* *vividiṣetam/vivitsetam* *vividiṣeva/vivitseva*	*vividiṣeyuḥ/vivitseyuḥ* *vividiṣeta/vivitseta* *vividiṣema/vivitsema*								
imperative		*vividiṣatu/vivitsatu* *vividiṣa/vivitsa* *vividiṣāni/vivitsāni*	*vividiṣatām/vivitsatām* *vividiṣatam/vivitsatam* *vividiṣāva/vivitsāva*	*vividiṣantu/vivitsantu* *vividiṣata/vivitsata* *vividiṣāma/vivitsāma*								
perfect		*vividiṣa/vivitsa* *vividiṣitha/vivitsitha* *vividiṣa/vivitsa*	*vividiṣatuḥ/vivitsatuḥ* *vividiṣathuḥ/vivitsathuḥ* *vividiṣiva/vivitsiva*	*vividiṣuḥ/vivitsuḥ* *vividiṣa/vivitsa* *vividiṣima/vivitsima*								

past passive participle *vividiṣita* or *vivitsita* m.n. *vividiṣitā* or *vivitsitā* f.

past active participle *vividiṣitavat* or *vivitsitavat* m.n. *vividiṣitavatī* or *vivitsitavatī* f.

present active participle *vividiṣat* or *vivitsat* m.n. *vividiṣantī* or *vivitṣantī* f.

perfect active participle *vividiṣvaḥ* or *vivitsvaḥ* m.n. *vivividuṣuṣī* or *vivitsuṣī*

Indeclinables: gerund/absolutive, *-vividiṣitvā or vivitsivā, --vividiṣiya or –vivitsiya*

Infinitive *vividiṣitum, vivitsitum,*

Conjugation *dā* class 3 give, bestow, grant, yield, impart, present, offer to, hand over, give back, pay (a fine), give up, sell, speak, place, put

		active			middle			passive		
		singular	dual	plural	singular	dual	plural	singular	dual	plural
present indicative	1st 2nd 3rd	*dadāti* *dadāsi* *dadāmi*	*dattaḥ* *datthaḥ* *dadvaḥ*	*dadati* *dattha* *dadmaḥ*	*datte* *datse* *dade*	*dadāte* *dadāthe* *dadvahe*	*dadate* *daddhve* *dadmahe*	*dīyate* *dīyase* *dīye*	*dīyete* *dīyethe* *dīyāvahe*	*dīyante* *dīyadhve* *dīyāmahe*
present optative		*dadyāt* *dadyāḥ* *dadyām*	*dadyātām* *dadyātam* *dadyāva*	*dadyuḥ* *dadyāta* *dadyāma*	*dadīta* *dadīthāḥ* *dadīya*	*dadīyātām* *dadīyāthām* *dadīvahi*	*dadīran* *dadīdhvam* *dadīmahi*	*dīyeta* *dīyethāḥ* *dīyeya*	*dīyeyātām* *dīyeyāthām* *diyevahi*	*dīyeran* *dīyedhvam* *dīyemahi*
present imperative		*dadātu* *dehi* *dadāni*	*dattām* *dattam* *dadāva*	*dadatu* *datta* *dadāma*	*dattām* *datsva* *dadai*	*dadātām* *dadāthām* *dadāvahai*	*dadatām* *dadhvam* *dadāmahai*	*dīyatām* *dīyasva* *dīyai*	*dīyetām* *dīyethām* *dīyāvahai*	*dīyantām* *dīyadhvam* *dīyāmahai*
imperfect indicative		*adadāt* *adadāḥ* *adadām*	*adattām* *adattam* *adadva*	*adaduḥ* *adatta* *adadma*	*adatta* *adatthāḥ* *adadi*	*adadātām* *adadāthām* *adadvahi*	*adadata* *adaddhvam* *adadmahi*	*adīyata* *adīyathāḥ* *adīye*	*adīyetām* *adīyethām* *adīyāvahi*	*adīyanta* *adīyadhvam* *adīyāmahi*
future		*dāsyati* *dāsyasi* *dāsyāmi*	*dāsyataḥ* *dāsyathaḥ* *dāsyāvaḥ*	*dāsyanti* *dāsyatha* *dāsyāmaḥ*	*dāsyate* *dāsyase* *dāsye*	*dāsyete* *dāsyethe* *dāsyāvahe*	*dāsyante* *dāsyadhve* *dāsyāmahe*			
periphrastic future		*dātā* *dātāsi* *dātāsmi*	*dātārau* *dātāsthaḥ* *dātāsvaḥ*	*dātāraḥ* *dātāstha* *dātāsmaḥ*						
perfect		*dadau* *daditha/* *dadātha* *dadau*	*dadatuḥ* *dadathuḥ* *dadiva*	*daduḥ* *dada* *dadima*	*dade* *dadiṣe* *dade*	*dadāte* *dadāthe* *dadivahe*	*dadire* *dadidhve* *dadimahe*			
aorist		*adāsīt/adāt* *adāsīḥ/adāḥ* *adāsam/adām*	*adāstām/adātām* *adāstam/ adātam* *adāsva/ adāva*	*aduḥ/adāsuḥ* *adāsta adāta* *adāsma/* *adāma*	*adiṣṭa/adāyi* *adiṣṭhāḥ* *adiṣi*	*adiṣātām* *adiṣāthām* *adiṣvahi*	*adiṣata* *adiṣṭhvam* *adiṣmahi*			

past passive participle *datta* m.n. *dattā* f. past active participle *dattavat* m.n. *dattavatī* f.
present active participle *dadat* m.n. *dadatī* f. present middle participle *dadāna* m.n. *dadānā* f.
present passive participle *dīyamāna* m.n. *dīyamānā* f. future active participle *dāsyat* m.n. *dāsyantī* f.
future middle participle *dāsyamāna* m.n. *dāsyamāṇā* f. future passive participle *dātavya* or *deya* or *dānīya* m.n. *dātavyā* or *deyā* or *dānīyā* f.
perfect active participle *dadivaḥ* m.n. *daduṣī* f. perfect middle participle *dadāna* m.n. *dadānā* f.
Indeclinables: *dātum* infinitive, gerund/absolutive *dattvā* or *dāyam* or *-dāya*

Causative Conjugation ***dā*** **class 3**

		active			middle			passive		
		singular	dual	plural	singular	dual	plural	singular	dual	plural
present	1st 2nd 3rd	*dāpayati* *dāpayasi* *dāpayāmi*	*dāpayataḥ* *dāpayathaḥ* *dāpayāvaḥ*	*dāpayanti* *dāpayatha* *dāpayāmaḥ*	*dāpayate* *dāpayase* *dāpaye*	*dāpayete* *dāpayethe* *dāpayāvahe*	*dāpayante* *dāpayadhve* *dāpayāmahe*	*dāpyate* *dāpyase* *dāpye*	*dāpyete* *dāpyethe* *dāpyāvahe*	*dāpyante* *dāpyadhve* *dāpyāmahe*
optative		*dāpayet* *dāpayeḥ* *dāpayeyam*	*dāpayetām* *dāpayetam* *dāpayeva*	*dāpayeyuḥ* *dāpayeta* *dāpayema*	*dāpayeta* *dāpayethāḥ* *dāpayeya*	*dāpayeyātām* *dāpayeyāthām* *dāpayevahi*	*dāpayeran* *dāpayedhvam* *dāpayemahi*	*dāpyeta* *dāpyethāḥ* *dāpyeya*	*dāpyeyātām* *dāpyeyāthām* *dāpyevahi*	*dāpyeran* *dāpyedhvam* *dāpyemahi*
imperative		*dāpayatu* *dāpaya* *dāpayāni*	*dāpayatām* *dāpayatam* *dāpayāva*	*dāpayantu* *dāpayata* *dāpayāma*	*dāpayatām* *dāpayasva* *dāpayai*	*dāpayetām* *dāpayethām* *dāpayāvahai*	*dāpayantām* *dāpayadhvam* *dāpayāmahai*	*dāpyatām* *dāpyasva* *dāpyai*	*dāpyetām* *dāpyethām* *dāpyāvahai*	*dāpyantām* *dāpyadhvam* *dāpyāmahai*
imperfect		*adāpayat* *adāpayaḥ* *adāpayam*	*adāpayatām* *adāpayatam* *adāpayāva*	*adāpayan* *adāpayata* *adāpayāma*	*adāpayata* *adāpayathāḥ* *adāpaye*	*adāpayetām* *adāpayethām* *adāpayāvahi*	*adāpayanta* *adāpayadhvam* *adāpayemahi*	*adāpyata* *adāpyathāḥ* *adāpye*	*adāpyetām* *adāpyethām* *adāpyāvahi*	*adāpyante* *adāpyadhve* *adāpyāmahe*
future		*dāpayiṣyati* *dāpayiṣyasi* *dāpayiṣyāmi*	*dāpayiṣyataḥ* *dāpayiṣyathaḥ* *dāpayiṣyāvaḥ*	*dāpayiṣyanti* *dāpayiṣyatha* *dāpayiṣyāma*	*dāpayiṣyate* *dāpayiṣyase* *dāpayiṣye*	*dāpayiṣyete* *dāpayiṣyethe* *dāpayiṣyāvahe*	*dāpayiṣyante* *dāpayiṣyadhve* *dāpayiṣyāmahe*			
periphrastic future		*dāpayitā* *dāpayitāsi* *dāpayitāmi*	*dāpayitārau* *dāpayitāsthaḥ* *dāpayitāsvaḥ*	*dāpayitāraḥ* *dāpayitāstha* *dāpayitāsmaḥ*						
conditional		*adāsyat* *adāsyaḥ* *adāsyam*	*adāsyatām* *adāsyatam* *adāsyāva*	*adāsyan* *adāsyata* *adāsyāma*	*adāsyata* *adāsyathāḥ* *adāsye*	*adāsyetām* *adāsyethām* *adāsyāvahi*	*adāsyanta* *adāsyadhvam* *adāsyāmahi*			

past passive participle	*dāpita* m.n. *dāpitā* f.	past active participle	*dāpitavat* m.n. *dāpittavatī* f.
present active participle	*dāpayat* m.n. *dāpayantī* f.	present middle participle	*dāpayamāna* m.n. *dāpayamānā* f.
present passive participle	*dāpyamāna* m.n. *dāpyamānā* f.	future active participle	*dāpayiṣyat* m.n. *dṣpayiṣyantī* f.
future middle participle	*dāpayiṣyamāna* m.n. *dāpayiṣyamāṇā* f.		
future passive participle	*dāpya* or *dāpayitavya* or *dāpanīyā* m.n. *dāpyā* or *dāpanīyā* or *dāpayitavyā* f.		
perfect active participle	*dadivaḥ* m.n. *daduṣī* f.		
perfect middle participle	*dadāna* m.n. *dadānā* f.		
Indeclinables:	*dāpayitum* infinitive,	gerund/absolute *dāpayitvā* *-dāpayya* periphrastic perfect *dāpayyām*	

Desiderative Conjugation ***dā*** **class 3**

			active			middle			passive	
		singular	dual	plural	singular	dual	plural	singular	dual	plural
present	1st	*ditsati*	*ditsataḥ*	*ditsanti*						
	2nd	*ditsasi*	*ditsathaḥ*	*ditsatha*						
	3rd	*ditsāmi*	*ditsāvaḥ*	*ditsāmaḥ*						
imperfect		*aditsat*	*aditsatām*	*aditsan*						
		aditsaḥ	*aditsatam*	*aditsata*						
		aditsam	*aditsāva*	*aditsāma*						
optative		*ditset*	*ditsetām*	*ditseyuḥ*						
		ditseḥ	*ditsetam*	*ditseta*						
		ditseyam	*ditseva*	*ditsema*						
imperative		*ditsatu*	*ditsatām*	*ditsantu*						
		ditsa	*ditsatam*	*ditsata*						
		ditsāni	*ditsāva*	*ditsāma*						
perfect		*diditsa*	*diditsatuḥ*	*diditsuḥ*						
		diditsitha	*diditsathuḥ*	*diditsa*						
		diditsa	*diditsiva*	*diditsima*						

past passive participle	*ditsita* m.n. *ditsitā* f.	past active participle	*ditsitavat* m.n. *ditsitavatī* f.
present active participle	*ditsat* m.n. *ditsantī* f.		
perfect active participle	*diditsvaḥ* m.n. *diditsuṣī* f.	Indeclinables: gerund/absolutive *ditsitvā,* *-ditsiya*	

Conjugation *budh* class 4 (also conjugates as class 1) to wake, wake up, be awake, to observe, heed, attend to, perceive,

			active			**middle**			**passive**	
		singular	**dual**	**plural**	**singular**	**dual**	**plural**	**singular**	**dual**	**plural**
present	1st 2nd 3rd	*budhyati* *budhyasi* *budhyāmi*	*budhyataḥ* *budhyathaḥ* *budhyāvaḥ*	*budhyanti* *budhyatha* *budhyāmaḥ*	*budhyate* *budhyase* *budhye*	*budhyete* *budhyethe* *budhyāvahe*	*budhyante* *budhyadhve* *budhyāmahe*	*budhyate* *budhyase* *budhye*	*budhyete* *budhyethe* *budhyāvahe*	*budhyante* *budhyadhve* *budhyāmahe*
optative		*budhyet* *budhyeḥ* *budhyeyam*	*budhyetām* *budhyetam* *budhyeva*	*budhyeyuḥ* *budhyeta* *budhyema*	*budhyeta* *budhyethāḥ* *budhyeya*	*budhyeyātām* *budhyeyāthām* *budhyevahi*	*budhyeran* *budhyedhvam* *budhyemahi*	*budhyeta* *budhyethāḥ* *budhyeya*	*budhyeyātām* *budhyeyāthām* *budhyevahi*	*budhyeran* *budhyedhvam* *budhyemahi*
imperative		*budhyatu* *budhya* *budhyāni*	*budhyatām* *budhyatam* *budhyāva*	*budhyantu* *budhyata* *budhyāma*	*budhyatām* *budhyasva* *budhyai*	*budhyetām* *budhyethām* *budhyāvahai*	*budhyantām* *budhyadhvam* *budhyāmahai*	*budhyatām* *budhyasva* *budhyai*	*budhyetām* *budhyethām* *budhyāvahai*	*budhyantām* *budhyadhvam* *budhyāmahai*
imperfect		*abudhyat* *abudhyaḥ* *abudhyam*	*abudhyatām* *abudhyatam* *abudhyāva*	*abudhyan* *abudhyata* *abudhyāma*	*abudhyata* *abudhyathāḥ* *abudhye*	*abudhyetām* *abudhyethām* *abudhyāvahi*	*abudhyanta* *abudhyadhvam* *abudhyāmahi*	*abudhyata* *abudhyathāḥ* *abudhye*	*abudhyetām* *abudhyethām* *abudhyāvahi*	*abudhyanta* *abudhyadhvam* *abudhyāmahi*
future		*bhotsyati* *bhotsyasi* *bhotsyāmi*	*bhotsyataḥ* *bhotsyathaḥ* *bhotsyāvaḥ*	*bhotsyanti* *bhotsyatha* *bhotsyāmaḥ*	*bhotsyate* *bhotsyase* *bhotsye*	*bhotsyete* *bhotsyethe* *bhotsyāvahe*	*bhotsyante* *bhotsyadhve* *bhotsyāmahe*			
periphrastic future		*boddhā* *boddhāsi* *boddhāsmi*	*boddhārau* *boddhāsthaḥ* *boddhāsvaḥ*	*boddhāraḥ* *boddhāstha* *boddhāsmaḥ*						
perfect		*bubodha* *bubodhitha* *bubodha*	*bubudhatuḥ* *bubudhathuḥ* *bubudhiva*	*bubudhuḥ* *bubudha* *bubudhima*	*bubudhe* *bubudhiṣe* *bubudhe*	*bubudhāte* *bubudhāthe* *bubudhivahe*	*bubudhire* *bubudhidhve* *bubudhimahe*			
aorist		*abhausīt/* *abodhīt* *abhautsīḥ/* *abodhīḥ* *abhautsam/* *abodhiṣam*	*abauddhām/* *abodhiṣṭām* *abauddham/* *abodhiṣṭam* *abhautsva/* *abodhiṣva*	*abhautsuḥ/* *abodhiṣuḥ* *abauddha/* *abodhiṣṭa* *abhautsma/* *abodhiṣma*	*abodhiṣṭa/* *abuddha* *abodhiṣṭāḥ/* *abuddhāḥ* *abhutsi/* *abodhiṣi*	*abhutsātām/* *abodhiṣātām* *abhutsāthām/* *abodhiṣāthām* *abhutsvahi/* *abodhiṣvahi*	*abhutsata/* *abodhiṣata* *abodhidhvam/* *abuddhvam* *abhutsmahi/* *abodhiṣmahi*	**benedictive** *budhyāt* *budhyāḥ* *budhyāsam*	**benedictive** *budhyāstām* *budhyāstam* *budhyāsva*	**benedictive** *budhyāsuḥ* *budhyāsta* *budhyāsma*

past passive participle *buddha* m.n.*buddhā* f. past active participle *buddhavat* m.n. *buddhavatī* f.
present active participle *buddhyat* m.n. *buddhyantī* f. present middle participle *buddhyamāna* m.n. *buddhyamānā* f.
present passive participle *buddhyamāna* m.n. *buddhyamānā* f. future active participle *bhotsyat* m.n. *bhotsyantī* f.
future middle participle *bhotsyamāna* m.n. *bhotsyamāṇā* f. future passive participle *bodhya, boddhavya, bodhanīya* m.n. *bodhyā, boddhavyā, bodhanīyā* f.
perfect active participle *bubudhvaḥ* m.n. *bubudhuṣī* f. perfect middle participle *bubudhāna* m.n. *bubudhānā*
Indeclinables: *boddhum* infinitive, *buddhvā*,–gerund/absolutive, *-budhya* –gerund/absolutive

Conjugation *budh* class 4 to perceive, (causative)

		active			middle			passive	
	singular	dual	plural	singular	dual	plural	singular	dual	plural
present 1st 2nd 3rd	*bodhayati* *bodhayasi* *bodhayāmi*	*bodhayataḥ* *bodhayathaḥ* *bodhayāvaḥ*	*bodhayanti* *bodhayatha* *bodhayāmaḥ*	*bodhayate* *bodhayase* *bodhaye*	*bodhayete* *bodhayethe* *bodhayāvahe*	*bodhayante* *bodhayadhve* *bodhayāmahe*	*bodhyate* *bodhyase* *bodhye*	*bodhyete* *bodhyethe* *bodhyāvahe*	*bodhyante* *bodhyadhve* *bodhyāmahe*
optative	*bodhayet* *bodhayeḥ* *bodhayeyam*	*bodhayetām* *bodhayetam* *bodhayetām*	*bodhayeyuḥ* *bodhayeta* *bodhayema*	*bodhayeta* *bodhayethāḥ* *bodhayeya*	*bodhayeyātām* *bodhayeyāthām* *bodhayevahi*	*bodhayeran* *bodhayedhvam* *bodhayemahi*	*bodhyeta* *bodhyethāḥ* *bodhyeya*	*bodhyeyātām* *bodhyeyāthām* *bodhyevahi*	*bodhyeran* *bodhyedhvam* *bodhyemahi*
imperativ e	*bodhayatu* *bodhaya* *bodhayāni*	*bodhayatām* *bodhayatam* *bodhayāva*	*bodhayantu* *bodhayata* *bodhayāma*	*bodhayatām* *bodhayasva* *bodhayai*	*bodhayetām* *bodhayethām* *bodhayāvahai*	*bodhayantām* *bodhayadhvam* *bodhayāmahai*	*bodhyatām* *bodhyasva* *bodhyai*	*bodhyetām* *bodhyethām* *bodhyāvahai*	*bodhyantām* *bodhyadhvam* *bodhyāmahai*
imperfect	*abodhayat* *abodhayaḥ* *abodhayam*	*abodhayatām* *abodhayatam* *abodhayāva*	*abodhayan* *abodhayata* *abodhayāma*	*abodhayata* *abodhayathāḥ* *abodhaye*	*abodhayetām* *abodhayethām* *abodhayāvahi*	*abodhayanta* *abodhayadhvam* *abodhayāmahi*	*abodhyata* *abodhyathāḥ* *abodhye*	*abodhyetām* *abodhyethām* *abodhyāvahi*	*abodhyanta* *abodhyadhvam* *abodhyāmahi*
future	*bodhayiṣyati* *bodhayiṣyasi* *bodhayiṣyāmi*	*bodhayiṣyataḥ* *bodhayiṣyathaḥ* *bodhayiṣyāvaḥ*	*bodhayiṣyanti* *bodhayiṣyatha* *bodhayiṣyāmaḥ*	*bodhayiṣyate* *bodhayiṣyase* *bodhayiṣye*	*bodhayiṣyete* *bodhayiṣyethe* *bodhayiṣyāvahe*	*bodhayiṣyante* *bodhayiṣyadhve* *bodhayiṣyāmahe*			
periphrastic future	*bodhayitā* *bodhayitāsi* *bodhayitāsmi*	*bodhayitārau* *bodhayitāsthaḥ* *bodhayitāsvaḥ*	*bodhayitāraḥ* *bodhayitāstha* *bodhayitāsmaḥ*						

: passive participle *bodhita* m.n.*bodhitā* f. past active participle *bodhitavat* m.n. *bodhitavatī* f.

present active participle *bodhayat* m.n. *bodhayantī* f. present middle participle *bodhayamāna* m.n. *bodhayamānā* f.

Class 4 causative participle examples present passive participle -*bodhyamāna* m.n. *bodhayamānā* f.
future active participle *bodhayiṣyat* m.n. *bodhayiṣyantī* f.
future middle participle *bodhayiṣyamāna* m.n. *bodhayiṣyamāṇā* f.
future passive participle *bodhya, bodhanīya bodhayitavya* m.n. *bodhyā, bodhanīyā, bodhayitavyā* f.
Indeclinables: *bodhayitum* infinitive, -*bodhya* –gerund/absolutive , periphrastic perfect *bodhayyām*

Intensive Conjugation example Class 4 √*budh* to perceive

		active			middle			passive	
	singular	dual	plural	singular	dual	plural	singular	dual	plural
present 1st 2nd 3rd	*bobhoddhi/* *bobhudhīti* *bobhotsi/* *bobhudhīṣi* *bobhodhmi/* *bobhudhīmi*	*bobhuddhaḥ* *bobhuddhaḥ* *bobhudhvaḥ*	*bobhudhati* *bobhuddha* *bobhudhmaḥ*						
optative	*bobhudhyāt* *bobhudhyāḥ* *bobhudhyām*	*bobhudhyātām* *bobhudhyātam* *bobhudhyāva*	*bobhudhyuḥ* *bobhudhyāta* *bobhudhyāma*						
imperative	*bobhodhītu/* *bobhoddhu* *bobhuddhi* *bobhodhāni*	*bobhuddhām* *bobhuddham* *bobhodhāva*	*bobhudhatu* *bobhuddha* *bobhodhāma*						
imperfect	*abobhot* *abobhot/* *abobhudhīḥ/* *abobhudhīt* *abobhodham*	*abobhuddhām* *abobhuddham* *abobhudva*	*abobhodhuḥ* *abobhuddha* *abobhudhma*						

present active participle: *bobhudhat* m.n. *bobhudhatī* f.

Desiderative Conjugation Class 4 √*budh* to perceive

		active			middle			passive	
	singular	dual	plural	singular	dual	plural	singular	dual	plural
present 1st 2nd 3rd	*bubhutsati* *bubhutsasi* *bubhutsāmi*	*bubhutsataḥ* *bubhutsathaḥ* *bubhutsāvaḥ*	*bubhutsanti* *bubhutsatha* *bubhutsāmaḥ*	*bubhutsate* *bubhutsase* *bubhutse*	*bubhutsete* *bubhutsethe* *bubhutsāvahe*	*bubhutsante* *bubhutsadhve* *bubhutsāmahe*			
optative	*bubhutset* *bubhutseḥ* *bubhutseyam*	*bubhutsetām* *bubhutsetam* *bubhutseva*	*bubhutseyuḥ* *bubhutseta* *bubhutsema*	*bubhutseta* *bubhutsethāḥ* *bubhutseya*	*bubhutseyātām* *bubhutseyāthām* *bubhutsevahi*	*bubhutseran* *bubhutsedhvam* *bubhutsemahi*			
imperfect	*abubhutsat* *abubhutsaḥ* *abubhutsam*	*abubhutsatām* *abubhutsatam* *abubhutsāva*	*abubhutsan* *abubhutsata* *abubhutsāma*	*abubhutsata* *abubhutsathāḥ* *abubhutse*	*abubhutsetām* *abubhutsethām* *abubhutsāvahi*	*abubhutsanta* *abubhutsadhvam* *abubhutsāmahi*			
imperative	*bubhutsatu* *bubhutsa* *bubhutsāni*	*bubhutsatām* *bubhutsatam* *bubhutsāva*	*bubhutsantu* *bubhutsata* *bubhutsāma*	*bubhutsatām* *bubhutsasva* *bubhutsai*	*bubhutsetām* *bubhutsethām* *bubhutsāvahai*	*bubhutsantām* *bubhutsadhvam* *bubhutsāmahai*			
perfect	*bububhutsa* *bububhutsitha* *bububhutsa*	*bububhutsatuḥ* *bububhutsathuḥ* *bububhutsiva*	*bububhutsuḥ* *bububhutsa* *bububhutsima*	*bububhutse* *bububhutsiṣe* *bububhutse*	*bububhutsāte* *bububhutsāthe* *bububhutsivahe*	*bububhutsire* *bububhutsidhve* *bububhutsimahe*			

Desiderative past passive participle *bubhutsita* m.n. *bubhutsitā* f. past active participle *bubhutsitavat* m.n. *bubhutsitavatī* f.
present active participle *bubhutsat* m.n. *bubhutsantī* f. present middle participle *bubhutsamāna* m.n. *bubhutsamānā* f.
future passive participle *bubhutsanīya, bubhutsya, bubhutsitavya,* m.n. *bubhutsanīyā, bubhutsyā, bubhutsitavyā,* f.
perfect active participle *bububhutsvaḥ* m.n. *bububhutsuṣī* f. perfect middle participle *bububhutsāna* m.n. *bububhutsānā* f.
:clinables: *bubhutsitum* infinitive, *bubhutsitvā,* - *bububhutsiyā* –gerund/absolutive

Primary Conjugation Class 5 √*śru* to hear, listen, attend to anything, study, learn, be attentive, be obedient,

		active			middle			passive	
	singular	dual	plural	singular	dual	plural	singular	dual	plural
present 1st 2nd 3rd	*śṛṇoti* *śṛṇoṣi* *śṛṇomi*	*śṛṇutaḥ* *śṛṇuthaḥ* *śṛṇvaḥ/* *śṛṇuvaḥ*	*śṛṇvanti* *śṛṇutha* *śṛṇmaḥ/* *śṛṇumaḥ*	*śṛṇute* *śṛṇuṣe* *śṛṇve*	*śṛṇvāte* *śṛṇvāthe* *śṛṇvahe/* *śṛṇuvahe*	*śṛṇvate* *śṛṇudhve* *śṛṇmahe/* *śṛṇumahe*	*śrūyate* *śrūyase* *śrūye*	*śrūyete* *śrūyethe* *śrūyāvahe*	*śrūyante* *śrūyadhve* *śrūyāmahe*
optative	*śṛṇuyāt* *śṛṇuyāḥ* *śṛṇuyām*	*śṛṇuyātām* *śṛṇuyātam* *śṛṇuyāva*	*śṛṇuyuḥ* *śṛṇuyāta* *śṛṇuyāma*	*śṛṇvīta* *śṛṇvīthāḥ* *śṛṇvīya*	*śṛṇvīyātām* *śṛṇvīyāthām* *śṛṇvīvahi*	*śṛṇvīran* *śṛṇvīdhvam* *śṛṇvīmahi*	*śrūyeta* *śrūyethāḥ* *śrūyeya*	*śrūyeyātām* *śrūyeyāthām* *śrūyevahi*	*śrūyeran* *śrūyedhvam* *śrūyemahi*
imperfect	*aśṛṇot* *aśṛṇoḥ* *aśṛṇavam*	*aśṛṇutām* *aśṛṇutam* *aśṛṇva/* *aśṛṇuva*	*aśṛṇvan* *aśṛṇuta* *aśṛṇma/* *aśṛṇuma*	*aśṛṇuta* *aśṛṇuthāḥ* *aśṛṇvi*	*aśṛṇvātām* *aśṛṇvāthām* *aśṛṇvahi/* *aśṛṇuvahi*	*aśṛṇvata* *aśṛṇudhvam* *aśṛṇmahi/* *aśṛṇumahi*	*aśrūyata* *aśrūyathāḥ* *aśrūye*	*aśrūyetām* *aśrūyethām* *aśrūyāvahi*	*aśrūyanta* *aśrūyadhvam* *aśrūyāmahi*
imperative	*śṛṇotu* *śṛudhu/śṛṇu* *śṛṇavāni*	*śṛṇutām* *śṛṇutam* *śṛṇavāva*	*śṛṇvantu* *śṛṇuta* *śṛṇavāma*	*śṛṇutām* *śṛṇuṣva* *śṛṇavai*	*śṛṇvātām* *śṛṇvāthām* *śṛṇvāvahai*	*śṛṇvatām* *śṛṇudhvam* *śṛṇavāmahai*	*śrūyatām* *śrūyasva* *śrūyai*	*śrūyetām* *śrūyethām* *śrūyāvahai*	*śrūyantām* *śrūyadhvam* *śrūyāmahai*
perfect	*śuśrāva* *śuśrotha* *śuśrāva/* *śuśrava*	*śuśruvatuḥ* *śuśruvathuḥ* *śuśruva*	*śuśruvuḥ* *śuśruva* *śuśruma*	*śuśruve* *śuśruṣe* *śuśruve*	*śuśruvāte* *śuśruvāthe* *śuśruvahe*	*śuśruvire* *śuśrudhve* *śuśrumahe*			
future	*śroṣyati* *śroṣyasi* *śroṣyāmi*	*śroṣyataḥ* *śroṣyathaḥ* *śroṣyāvaḥ*	*śroṣyanti* *śroṣyatha* *śroṣyāmaḥ*	*śroṣyate* *śroṣyase* *śroṣye*	*śroṣyete* *śroṣyethe* *śroṣyāvahe*	*śroṣyante* *śroṣyadhve* *śroṣyāmahe*			

periphrastic future	*śrotā* *śrotāsi* *śrotāsmi*	*śrotārau* *śrotāsthaḥ* *śrotāsvaḥ*	*śrotāraḥ* *śrotāstha* *śrotāsmaḥ*						

1st aorist	*aśrauṣīt /* *aśravat/* *aśuśruvat*	*aśrauṣṭām/* *aśravatām/* *aśuśruvatām*	*aśrauṣuḥ/* *aśravan/* *aśuśruvan*	*aśroṣṭa/* *aśrāvi/* *aśuśruvata*	*aśroṣātām/* *aśuśruvetām*	*aśroṣata/* *aśuśruvanta*			
2nd	*aśrauṣiḥ/* *aśravaḥ/* *aśuśruvaḥ*	*aśrauṣtam/* *aśravatam/* *aśuśruvatam*	*aśrauṣṭa/* *aśravata/* *aśuśruvata*	*aśroṣṭhāḥ/* *aśuśruvathāḥ*	*aśroṣāthām/* *aśuśruvethām*	*aśroḍhvam/* *aśuśruvadhvam*			
3rd	*aśrauṣam/* *aśravat/* *aśuśruvam*	*aśrauṣva/* *aśravāva/* *aśuśruvāva*	*aśrauṣma/* *aśravāma/* *aśuśruvāma*	*aśroṣi/* *aśuśruve*	*aśroṣvahi/* *aśuśruvāvahi*	*aśroṣmahi/* *aśuśruvāmahi*			

past passive participle *śruta* m.n. *śrutā* f. past active participle *śrutavat* m.n. *śrutavatī* f.
present active participle *śṛṇvat* m.n. *śṛṇvatī* f. present middle participle *śṛṇvāna* m.n. *śṛṇvāṇā* f.
present passive participle *śrūyamāna* m.n. *śrūyamānā* f. future active participle *śroṣyat* m.n. *śroṣyantī* f.
future middle participle *śroṣyamāna* m.n. *śroṣyamāṇā* f. future passive participle *śrotavya, śroya, śravanīya* m.n. *śrotavyā, śroyā śravanīyā* f.
perfect active participle *śuśruvaḥ* m.n. *śuśrūṣī* f. perfect middle participle *śuśrvāṇa* m.n. *śuśrvāṇā*
Indeclinables: *śrotum* infinitive, *śrutvā,*–gerund/absolutive, *śrāvam, - śrutya* –gerund/absolutive

Causative Conjugation Class 5 √*śru*

		active			middle			passive	
	singular	dual	plural	singular	dual	plural	singular	dual	plural
present 1st 2nd 3rd	*śrāvayati* *śrāvayasi* *śrāvayāmi*	*śrāvayataḥ* *śrāvayathaḥ* *śrāvayāvaḥ*	*śrāvayanti* *śrāvayatha* *śrāvayāmaḥ*	*śrāvayate* *śrāvayase* *śrāvaye*	*śrāvayete* *śrāvayethe* *śrāvayāvahe*	*śrāvayante* *śrāvayadhve* *śrāvayāmahe*	*śrāvyate* *śrāvyase* *śrāvye*	*śrāvyete* *śrāvyethe* *śrāvyāvahe*	*śrāvyante* *śrāvyadhve* *śrāvyāmahe*
optative	*śrāvayet* *śrāvayeḥ* *śrāvayeyam*	*śrāvayetām* *śrāvayetam* *śrāvayeva*	*śrāvayeyuḥ* *śrāvayeta* *śrāvayema*	*śrāvayeta* *śrāvayethāḥ* *śrāvayeya*	*śrāvayeyātām* *śrāvayeyāthām* *śrāvayevahi*	*śrāvayeran* *śrāvayedhvam* *śrāvayemahi*	*śrāvyeta* *śrāvyethāḥ* *śrāvyeya*	*śrāvyeyātām* *śrāvyeyāthām* *śrāvyevahi*	*śrāvyeran* *śrāvyedhvam* *śrāvyemahi*
imperfect	*aśrāvayat* *aśrāvayaḥ* *aśrāvayam*	*aśrāvayatām* *aśrāvayatam* *aśrāvayāva*	*aśrāvayan* *aśrāvayata* *aśrāvayāma*	*aśrāvayata* *aśrāvayathāḥ* *aśrāvaye*	*aśrāvayetām* *aśrāvayethām* *aśrāvayāvahi*	*aśrāvayanta* *aśrāvayadhvam* *aśrāvayāmahi*	*aśrāvyata* *aśrāvyathāḥ* *aśrāvye*	*aśrāvyetām* *aśrāvyethām* *aśrāvyāvahi*	*aśrāvyanta* *aśrāvyadhvam* *aśrāvyāmahi*
imperative	*śrāvayatu* *śrāvaya* *śrāvayāṇi*	*śrāvayatām* *śrāvayatam* *śrāvayāva*	*śrāvayantu* *śrāvayata* *śrāvayāma*	*śrāvayatām* *śrāvayasva* *śrāvayai*	*śrāvayetām* *śrāvayethām* *śrāvayāvahai*	*śrāvayantām* *śrāvayadhvam* *śrāvayāmahai*	*śrāvyatām* *śrāvyasva* *śrāvyai*	*śrāvyetām* *śrāvyethām* *śrāvyāvahai*	*śrāvyantām* *śrāvyadhvam* *śrāvyāmahai*
future	*śrāvayiṣyati* *śrāvayiṣyasi* *śrāvayiṣyāmi*	*śrāvayiṣyataḥ* *śrāvayiṣyathaḥ* *śrāvayiṣyāvaḥ*	*śrāvayiṣyanti* *śrāvayiṣyatha* *śrāvayiṣyāmaḥ*	*śrāvayiṣyate* *śrāvayiṣyase* *śrāvayiṣye*	*śrāvayiṣyete* *śrāvayiṣyethe* *śrāvayiṣyāvahe*	*śrāvayiṣyante* *śrāvayiṣyadhve* *śrāvayiṣyāmahe*			
periphrastic future	*śrāvayitā* *śrāvayitāsi* *śrāvayitāsmi*	*śrāvayitārau* *śrāvayitāsthaḥ* *śrāvayitāsvaḥ*	*śrāvayitāraḥ* *śrāvayitāstha* *śrāvayitāsmaḥ*						

Causative participles for *śru* (Class 5)

past passive participle	*śrāvita* m.n. *śrāvitā* f.	past active participle	*śrāvitavat* m.n. *śrāvitavatī* f.
present active participle	*śrāvvayat* m.n. *śrāvayantī* f.	present middle participle	*śrāvayamāna* m.n. *śrāvayamāṇā* f.
present passive participle	*śrāvyamāna* m.n. *śrāvyamāṇā* f.	future active participle	*śrāvayiṣyat* m.n. *śrāvayiṣyantī* f.

future middle participle *śrāvayiṣyamāna* m.n. *śrāvayiṣyamāṇā* f.
future passive participle *śrāvya, śrāvaṇīya, śrāvayitavya* m.n. *śrāvyā, śrāvaṇīyā, śrāvayitavyā* f.
Indeclinables: *śrāvayitum* infinitive, - *śrāvya, śrāvitvā,*–gerund/absolutive,
P 'phrastic Perfect *śrāvayyām*

Desiderative Conjugation for √*śru* (Class 5) to hear

	active			middle			passive		
	singular	dual	plural	singular	dual	plural	singular	dual	plural
present 1st 2nd 3rd	*śuśrūṣati* *śuśrūṣasi* *śuśrūṣāmi*	*śuśrūṣataḥ* *śuśrūṣathaḥ* *śuśrūṣāvaḥ*	*śuśrūṣanti* *śuśrūṣatha* *śuśrūṣāmaḥ*	*śuśrūṣate* *śuśrūṣase* *śuśrūṣe*	*śuśrūṣete* *śuśrūṣethe* *śuśrūṣāvahe*	*śuśrūṣante* *śuśrūṣāadhve* *śuśrūṣāmahe*			
optative	*śuśrūṣet* *śuśrūṣeḥ* *śuśrūṣeyam*	*śuśrūṣetām* *śuśrūṣetam* *śuśrūṣeva*	*śuśrūṣeyuḥ* *śuśrūṣeta* *śuśrūṣema*	*śuśrūṣeta* *śuśrūṣethāḥ* *śuśrūṣeya*	*śuśrūṣeyātām* *śuśrūṣeyāthām* *śuśrūṣevahi*	*śuśrūṣeran* *śuśrūṣedhvam* *śuśrūṣemahi*			
imperfect	*aśuśrūṣat* *aśuśrūṣaḥ* *aśuśrūṣam*	*aśuśrūṣatām* *aśuśrūṣatam* *aśuśrūṣāva*	*aśuśrūṣan* *aśuśrūṣata* *aśuśrūṣāma*	*aśuśrūṣata* *aśuśrūṣathāḥ* *aśuśrūṣe*	*aśuśrūṣetām* *aśuśrūṣethām* *aśuśrūṣāvahi*	*aśuśrūṣanta* *aśuśrūṣadhvam* *aśuśrūṣāmahi*			
imperative	*śuśrūṣatu* *śuśrūṣa* *śuśrūṣāṇi*	*śuśrūṣatām* *śuśrūṣatam* *śuśrūṣāva*	*śuśrūṣantu* *śuśrūṣata* *śuśrūṣāma*	*śuśrūṣatām* *śuśrūṣasva* *śuśrūṣai*	*śuśrūṣetām* *śuśrūṣethām* *śuśrūṣāvahai*	*śuśrūṣantām* *śuśrūṣadhvam* *śuśrūṣāmahai*			
perfect	*śuśuśrūṣa* *śuśuśrūṣitha* *śuśuśrūṣa*	*śuśuśrūṣatuḥ* *śuśuśrūṣathuḥ* *śuśuśrūṣiva*	*śuśuśrūṣuḥ* *śuśuśrūṣa* *śuśuśrūṣima*	*śuśuśrūṣe* *śuśuśrūṣiṣe* *śuśuśrūṣe*	*śuśuśrūṣāte* *śuśuśrūṣāthe* *śuśuśrūṣivahe*	*śuśuśrūṣire* *śuśuśrūṣidhve* *śuśuśrūṣimahe*			

Desiderative participles for *śru* (Class 5)

past passive participle *śuśrūṣita* m.n. *śuśrūṣitā* f.

past active participle *śuśrūṣitavat* m.n. *śuśrūṣitavatī* f.

present active participle *śuśrūṣat* m.n. *śuśrūṣantī* f.

present middle participle *śuśrūṣamāna* m.n. *śuśrūṣamānā* f.

present passive participle *śrāvyamāna* m.n. *śrāvyamānā* f.

future passive participle *śuśrūṣaṇīya, śuśrūṣya śuśrūṣitavya,* m.n. *śuśrūṣaṇīyā, śuśrūṣyā śuśrūṣitavyā* f.

perfect active participle *śuśuśrūṣvaḥ* m.n. *śuśuśrūṣuṣī* f.

perfect middle participle *śuśuśrūṣāṇa* m.n. *śuśuśrūṣāṇā* f.

Indeclinables: *śuśrūṣitum* infinitive, *śuśrūṣitvā,* absolutive, *śuśrūṣiya* absolutive

Conjugation class 6 *vid* find, discover, obtain,acquire (see also *vid* class 2 – know, understand)

		singular	dual	plural		singular	dual	plural		singular	dual	plural
present	1st 2nd 3rd	*vindati* *vindasi* *vindāmi*	*vindataḥ* *vindathaḥ* *vindāvaḥ*	*vindanti* *vindatha* *vindāmaḥ*		*vindate* *vindase* *vinde*	*vindete* *vindethe* *vindāvahe*	*vindante* *vindadhve* *vindāmahe*		*vidyate* *vidyase* *vidye*	*vidyete* *vidyethe* *vidyāvahe*	*vidyante* *vidyadhve* *vidyāmahe*
imperfect		*avindat* *avindaḥ* *avindam*	*avindatām* *avindatam* *avindāva*	*avindan* *avindata* *avindāma*		*avindata* *avindathāḥ* *avinde*	*avindetām* *avindethām* *avindāvahi*	*avindanta* *avindadhvam* *avindāmahi*		*avidyata* *avidyathāḥ* *avidye*	*avidyetām* *avidyethām* *avidyāvahi*	*avidyanta* *avidyadhvam* *avidyāmahi*
optative		*vindet* *vindeḥ* *vindeyam*	*vindetām* *vindetam* *vindeva*	*vindeyuḥ* *vindeta* *vindema*		*vindeta* *vindethāḥ* *vindeya*	*vindeytām* *vindeyāthām* *vindevahi*	*vinderan* *vindedhvam* *vindemahi*		*vidyeta* *vidyethāḥ* *vidyeya*	*vidyeyātām* *vidyeyāthām* *vidyevahi*	*vidyeran* *vidyedhvam* *vidyemahi*
imperative		*vindatu* *vinda* *vindāni*	*vindatām* *vindatam* *vindāva*	*vindantu* *vindata* *vindāma*		*vindatām* *vindasva* *vindai*	*vindetām* *vindethām* *vindāvahai*	*vindantām* *vindadhvam* *vindāmahai*		*vidyatām* *vidyasva* *vidyai*	*vidyetām* *vidyethām* *vidyāvahai*	*vidyantām* *vidyadhvam* *vidyāmahai*
future		*vetsyati* *vetsyasi* *vetsyāmi*	*vetsyataḥ* *vetsyathaḥ* *vetsyāvaḥ*	*vetsyanti* *vetsyatha* *vetsyāmaḥ*		*vetsyate* *vetsyase* *vetsye*	*vetsyete* *vetsyethe* *vetsyāvahe*	*vetsyante* *vetsyadhve* *vetsyāmahe*				
periphrastic future		*vettā* *vettāsi* *vettāsmi*	*vettārau* *vettāsthaḥ* *vettāsvaḥ*	*vettāraḥ* *vettāstha* *vettāsmaḥ*								
perfect		*viveda* *viveditha* *viveda*	*vividatuḥ* *vividathuḥ* *vividiva*	*vividuḥ* *vivida* *vividima*		*vivide* *vividiṣe* *vivide*	*vividāte* *vividāthe* *vividivahe*	*vividire* *vivididhve* *vividimahe*				
aorist		*avidat* *avidaḥ* *avidam*	*avidatām* *avidatam* *avidāva*	*avidan* *avidata* *avidāma*		*avidata* *avidathāḥ* *avide*	*avidetām* *avidethām* *avidāvahi*	*avidanta* *avidadhvam* *avidāmahi*				

past passive participle *vinna* , *vitta* m.n. *vinnā vittā* f. past active participle *vittavat vinnavat* m.n. *vtitavatī vinnavatī* f.
present active participle *vindat* m.n. *vindantī* f. present middle participle *vindamāna* m.n. *vindamānā* f.
present passive participle *vidyamāna* m.n. *vidyamānā* f. future active participle *vetsyat* m.n. *vetsyantī* f.
future middle participle *vetsyamāna* m.n. *vetsyamāṇā* f. future passive participle *vedya* or *vedanīya* or *vettavya* m.n. *vedyā* or *vedanīyā* or *vettavyā* f.
ect active participle *vividvaḥ* m.n. *vividuṣī* f. perfect middle participle *vividāna* m.n. *vividānā*
clinables: *vettum* infinitive, *vintvā vittvā, -vidya* –gerund/absolutive,

Primary Conjugation Class 7 √*yuj* to yoke, join, unite, harness, prepare, arrange, employ, concentrate upon, be absorbed in meditation,

	active			middle			passive		
	singular	dual	plural	singular	dual	plural	singular	dual	plural
present 1st 2nd 3rd	*yunakti* *yunakṣi* *yunajmi*	*yuṅktaḥ* *yuṅkthaḥ* *yuñjvaḥ*	*yuñjanti* *yuṅktha* *yuñjmaḥ*	*yuṅkte* *yuṅkṣe* *yuñje*	*yuñjāte* *yuñjāthe* *yuñjvahe*	*yuñjate* *yuṅgdhve* *juñmahe*	*yujyate* *yujyase* *yujye*	*yujyete* *yujyethe* *yujyāvahe*	*yujyante* *yujyadhve* *yujyāmahe*
optative	*yuñjyāt* *yuñjyāḥ* *yuñjyām*	*yuñjyātām* *yuñjyātam* *yuñjyāva*	*yuñjyuḥ* *yuñjyāta* *yuñjyāma*	*yuñjīta* *yuñjīthāḥ* *yuñjīya*	*yuñjīyātām* *yuñjīyāthām* *yuñjīmahi*	*yuñjīran* *yuñjīdhvam* *yuñjīmahi*	*yujyeta* *yujyethāḥ* *yujyeya*	*yujyeyātām* *yujyeyāthām* *yujyevahi*	*yujyeran* *yujyedhvam* *yujyemahi*
imperfect	*ayunak* *ayunak* *ayunajam*	*ayuṅktām* *ayuṅktam* *ayuñjva*	*ayuñjan* *ayuṅkta* *ayuñjma*	*ayuṅkta* *ayuṅkthāḥ* *ayuñji*	*ayuñjātām* *ayuñjāthām* *ayuñjvahi*	*ayuñjata* *ayuṅgdhvam* *ayuñjmahi*	*ayujyata* *ayujyathāḥ* *ayujye*	*ayujyetām* *ayujyethām* *ayujyāvahi*	*ayujyanta* *ayujyadhvam* *ayujyāmahi*
imperative	*yunaktu* *yuṅgdhi* *yunajāni*	*yuṅktām* *yuṅktam* *yuajāva*	*yuñjantu* *yuṅkta* *yunajāma*	*yuṅktām* *yuṅkṣva* *yunajai*	*yuñjātām* *yuñjāthām* *yunajāvahai*	*yuñjatām* *yuṅgdhvam* *yunajāmahai*	*yujyatām* *yujyasva* *yujyai*	*yujyetām* *yujyethām* *yujyāvahai*	*yujyantām* *yujyadhvam* *yujyāmahai*
future	*yokṣyati* *yokṣyasi* *yokṣyāmi*	*yokṣyataḥ* *yokṣyathaḥ* *yokṣyāvaḥ*	*yokṣyanti* *yokṣyatha* *yokṣyāmaḥ*	*yokṣyate* *yokṣyase* *yokṣye*	*yokṣyete* *yokṣyethe* *yokṣyāvahe*	*yokṣyante* *yokṣyadhve* *yokṣyāmahe*			
periphrastic future	*yoktā* *yoktāsi* *yoktāsmi*	*yoktārau* *yoktāsthaḥ* *yoktāsvaḥ*	*yoktāraḥ* *yoktāstha* *yoktāsmaḥ*						
perfect	*yuyoja* *yuyojitha* *yuyoja*	*yuyujatuḥ* *yuyujathuḥ* *yuyujiva*	*yuyujuḥ* *yuyuja* *yuyujima*	*yuyuje* *yuyujiṣe* *yuyuje*	*yuyujāte* *yuyujāthe* *yuyujivahe*	*yuyujire* *yuyujidhve* *yuyujimahe*			
aorist 1st 2nd 3rd	*ayaukṣīt/* *ayokṣīt/* *ayujat* *ayaukṣīḥ/* *ayokṣīḥ/* *ayujaḥ* *ayaukṣam/* *ayokṣam/* *ayujam*	*ayauktām/* *ayoktām/* *ayujatām* *ayauktam/* *ayoktam/* *ayujatam* *ayaukṣva/* *ayokṣva* *ayujāva*	*ayaukṣuḥ/* *ayokṣuḥ/* *ayujan* *ayaukta/* *ayokta/* *ayujata* *ayaukṣma/* *ayokṣma/* *ayujāma*	*ayujata/* *ayukta* *ayujathāḥ/* *ayukthāḥ* *ayuje/* *ayukṣi*	*ayujetām/* *ayukṣātām* *ayujethām/* *ayukṣāthām* *ayujāvahi/* *ayukṣvahi*	*ayujanta/* *ayukṣata* *ayujadhvam/* *ayugdhvam* *ayujāmahi/* *ayukṣmahi*			

Primary participles for √*yuj* (Class 7)

past passive participle *yukta* m.n. *yuktā* f. past active participle *yuktavat* m.n. *yuktavatī* f.
present active participle *yuñjat* m.n. *yuñjatī* f. present middle participle *yuñjāna* m.n. *yuñj ānā* f.
present passive participle *yujyamāna* m.n. *yujyamānā* f. future active participle *yokṣyat* m.n. *yok ṣyantī* f.
future middle participle *yokṣyamāna* m.n. *yokṣyamāṇā* f. future passive participle *yojya,yoktavya,* yojanīya m.n. *yoktavyā,yojyā* *yojanīyā* f.
perfect active participle *yuyujvaḥ* m.n. *yuyujūṣī* f. perfect middle participle *yuyujāna* m.n. *yuyujānā* f.
Indeclinables: *yoktum* infinitive, *yuktvā,–* - *yujya* –gerund/absolutive

Causative conjugation for √*yuj*

		active			middle			passive	
	singular	dual	plural	singular	dual	plural	singular	dual	plural
present 1st 2nd 3rd	*yojayati* *yojayasi* *yojayāmi*	*yojayataḥ* *yojayathaḥ* *yojayāvaḥ*	*yojayanti* *yojayatha* *yojayāmaḥ*	*yojayate* *yojayase* *yojaye*	*yojayete* *yojayethe* *yojayāvahe*	*yojayante* *yojayadhve* *yojayāmahe*	*yojyate* *yojyase* *yojye*	*yojyete* *yojyethe* *yojyāvahe*	*yojyante* *yojyadhve* *yojyāmahe*
optative	*yojayet* *yojayeḥ* *yojayeyam*	*yojayetām* *yojayetam* *yojayeva*	*yojayeyuḥ* *yojayeta* *yojayema*	*yojayeta* *yojayethāḥ* *yojayeya*	*yojayeyātām* *yojayeyāthām* *yojayevahi*	*yojayeran* *yojayedhvam* *yojayemahi*	*yojyeta* *yojyethāḥ* *yojyeya*	*yojyeyātām* *yojyeyāthām* *yojyevahi*	*yojyeran* *yojyedhvam* *yojyemahi*
imperfect	*ayojayat* *ayojayaḥ* *ayojayam*	*ayojayatām* *ayojayatam* *ayojayāva*	*ayojayan* *ayojayata* *ayojayāma*	*ayojayata* *ayojayathāḥ* *ayojaye*	*ayojayetām* *ayojayethām* *ayojayāvahi*	*ayojayanta* *ayojayadhvam* *ayojayāmahi*	*ayojyata* *ayojyathāḥ* *ayojye*	*ayojyetām* *ayojyethām* *ayojyāvahi*	*ayojyanta* *ayojyadhvam* *ayojyāmahi*
imperative	*yojayatu* *yojaya* *yojayāni*	*yojayatām* *yojayatam* *yojayāva*	*yojayantu* *yojayata* *yojayāma*	*yojayatām* *yojayasva* *yojayai*	*yojayetām* *yojayethām* *yojayāvahai*	*yojayantām* *yojayadhvam* *yojayāmahai*	*yojyatām* *yojyasva* *yojyai*	*yojyetām* *yojyethām* *yojyāvahai*	*yojyantām* *yojyadhvam* *yojyāmahai*
future	*yojayiṣyati* *yojayiṣyasi* *yojayiṣyāmi*	*yojayiṣyataḥ* *yojayiṣyathaḥ* *yojayiṣyāvaḥ*	*yojayiṣyanti* *yojayiṣyatha* *yojayiṣyāmaḥ*	*yojayiṣyate* *yojayiṣyase* *yojayiṣye*	*yojayiṣyete* *yojayiṣyethe* *yojayiṣyāvahe*	*yojayiṣyante* *yojayiṣyadhve* *yojayiṣyāmahe*			
periphrastic future	*yojayitā* *yojayitāsi* *yojayitāsmi*	*yojayitārau* *yojayitāsthaḥ* *yojayitāsvaḥ*	*yojayitāraḥ* *yojayitāstha* *yojayitāsmaḥ*						

Causative participles for √*yuj* (Class 7)

: passive participle *yojita* m.n. *yojitā* f. past active participle *yojitavat* m.n. *yojitavatī* f.
;ent active participle *yojayat* m.n. *yojayantī* f. present middle participle *yojayamāna* m.n. *yojayamānā* f.

present active participle *yojayat* m.n. *yojayantī* f. present middle participle *yojayamāna* m.n. *yojayamānā* f.
present passive participle *yojyamāna* m.n. *yojyamānā* f. future active participle *yojayiṣyat* m.n. *yojayi ṣyantī* f.
future middle participle *yojayiṣyamāna* m.n. *yojayiṣyamāṇā* f.
future passive participle *yojya,yojayitavya, yojanīya* m.n. *yojayitavyā,yojyā yojanīyā* f.
perfect active participle *yuyujvaḥ* m.n. *yuyujūṣī* f. perfect middle participle *yuyujāna* m.n. *yuyujānā*
Indeclinables: *yojayitum* infinitive, *yojitvā, -yojya yojayyām* –gerund/absolutive

Desiderative conjugation for √*yuj*

		active			middle			passive	
	singular	dual	plural	singular	dual	plural	singular	dual	plural
present 1st 2nd 3rd	*yuyukṣati* *yuyukṣasi* *yuyukṣāmi*	*yuyukṣataḥ* *yuyukṣathaḥ* *yuyukṣāvaḥ*	*yuyukṣanti* *yuyukṣatha* *yuyukṣāmaḥ*						
optative	*yuyukṣet* *yuyukṣeḥ* *yuyukṣeyam*	*yuyukṣetām* *yuyukṣetam* *yuyukṣeva*	*yuyukṣeyuḥ* *yuyukṣeta* *yuyukṣema*						
imperfect	*a yuyukṣat* *a yuyukṣaḥ* *a yuyukṣam*	*a yuyukṣatām* *a yuyukṣatam* *a yuyukṣāva*	*ayuyukṣan* *ayuyukṣata* *ayuyukṣāma*						
imperative	*yuyukṣatu* *yuyukṣa* *yuyukṣāṇi*	*yuyukṣatām* *yuyukṣatam* *yuyukṣāva*	*yuyukṣantu* *yuyukṣata* *yuyukṣāma*						
perfect	*yuyuyukṣa* *yuyuyukṣitha* *yuyuyukṣa*	*yuyuyukṣatuḥ* *yuyuyukṣathuḥ* *yuyuyukṣiva*	*yuyuyukṣuḥ* *yuyuyukṣa* *yuyuyukṣima*						

Desiderative participles for √*yuj* (Class 7)
past passive participle *yuyukṣita* m.n. *yuyukṣitā* f. past active participle *yuyukṣitavat* m.n. *yuyukṣitavatī* f.
present active participle *yuyukṣat* m.n. *yuyukṣantī* f.
future passive participle *yuyukṣanīya yuyukṣya yuyukṣitavya* m.n. *yuyukṣanīyā yuyukṣyā, yuyukṣitavyā* f.
perfect active participle *yuyuyukṣvaḥ* m.n. *yuyuyukṣuṣī* f.
Indeclinables: *yuyukṣitum* infinitive, *yuyukṣitvā,* - *yuyukṣiya* –gerund/absolutive

Conjugation *kṛ* -class 8 to do, make, act, perform, cause, work at, build

		active			middle			passive		
		singular	dual	plural	singular	dual	plural	singula	dual	plural
present	1st 2nd 3r	*karoti* *karoṣi* *karomi*	*kurutaḥ* *kuruthaḥ* *kurvaḥ*	*kurvanti* *kurutha* *kurmaḥ*	*kurute* *kuruṣe* *kurve*	*kurvāte* *kurvāthe* *kurvahe*	*kurvate* *kurudhve* *kurmahe*	*kriyate* *kriyase* *kriye*	*kriyete* *kriyethe* *kriyāvahe*	*kriyante* *kriyadhve* *kriyāmahe*
optative		*kuryāt* *kuryāḥ* *kuryām*	*kuryātām* *kuryātam* *kuryāva*	*kuryuḥ* *kuryāta* *kuryāma*	*kurvīta* *kurvīthāḥ* *kurvīya*	*kurvīyātām* *kurvīyāthām* *kurvīvahi*	*kurvīran* *kurvīdhvam* *kurvīmahi*	*kriyeta* *kriyethāḥ* *kriyeya*	*kriyeyātām* *kriyeyāthām* *kriyevahi*	*kriyeran* *kriyedhvam* *kriyemahi*
imperative		*karotu* *kuru* *karavāni*	*kurutām* *kurutam* *karavāva*	*kurvantu* *kuruta* *karavāma*	*kurutām* *kuruṣva* *karavai*	*kurvātām* *kurvāthām* *karavāvahai*	*kurvatām* *kurudhvam* *karavāmahai*	*kriyatām* *kriyasva* *kriyai*	*kriyetām* *kriyethām* *kriyāvahai*	*kriyantām* *kriyadhvam* *kriyāmahai*
imperfect		*akarot* *akaroḥ* *akaravam*	*akurutām* *akurutam* *akurva*	*akurvan* *akuruta* *akurma*	*akuruta* *akuruthāḥ* *akurvi*	*akurvātām* *akurvāthām* *akurvahi*	*akurvata* *akurudhvam* *akurmahi*	*akriyata* *akriyathāḥ* *akriye*	*akriyetām* *akriyethām* *akriyāvahi*	*akriyanta* *akriyadhvam* *akriyāmahi*
perfect		*cakāra* *cakartha* *cakara / āra*	*cakratuḥ* *cakrathuḥ* *cakṛva*	*cakruḥ* *cakra* *cakṛma*	*cakre* *cakṛṣe* *cakre*	*cakrāte* *cakrāthe* *cakṛvahe*	*cakrire* *cakṛdhve* *cakṛmahe*			

		active			middle		
		singular	dual	plural	singular	dual	plural
aorist	1st 2nd 3rd	*akārṣit* *akārṣīḥ* *akārṣam*	*akārṣṭām* *akārṣṭam* *akārṣva*	*akārṣuḥ* *akārṣṭa* *akārṣma*	*akṛta* *akṛthāḥ* *akri/ akṛṣi*	*akrātām/ akṛṣātām* *akrāthām/akṛṣāthām* *akṛṣvahi/akṛvahi*	*akrata/akṛṣata* *akṛdhvam/akṛḍhvam* *akṛṣmahi/akṛmahi*
periphrastic future.		*kartā* *kartāsi* *kartāsmi*	*kartārau* *kartāsthaḥ* *kartāsvaḥ*	*kartāraḥ* *kartāstha* *kartāsmaḥ*			
simple fut.		*kariṣyati* *kariṣyasi* *kariṣyāmi*	*kariṣyataḥ* *kariṣyathaḥ* *kariṣyāvaḥ*	*kariṣyanti* *kariṣyatha* *kariṣyāmaḥ*	*kariṣyate* *kariṣyase* *kariṣye*	*kariṣyete* *kariṣyethe* *kariṣyāvahe*	*kariṣyante* *kariṣyadhve* *kariṣyāmahe*

conditional		*akariṣyat* *akariṣyaḥ* *akariṣyam*	*akariṣyatām* *akariṣyatam* *akariṣyāva*	*akariṣyan* *akariṣyata* *akariṣyāma*		*akariṣyata* *akariṣyathāḥ* *akariṣye*	*akariṣyetām* *akariṣyethām* *akariṣyāvahi*	*akariṣyanta* *akariṣyadhvam* *akariṣyāmahi*	
injunctive		*kārṣīt* *kārṣīḥ* *kārṣam*	*kārṣṭām* *kārṣṭam* *kārṣva*	*kārṣuḥ* *kārṣṭa* *kārṣma*		*kṛta* *kṛthāḥ* *kri/kṛṣi*	*krātām/kṛṣātām* *krāthām/kṛṣāthām* *kṛṣvahi/kṛvahi*	*krata/kṛṣata* *kṛdhvam/kṛḍhvam* *kṛṣmahi/kṛmahi*	

Primary Participles √*kṛ* (Class 8)

past passive participle	m. *kṛta*	f. *kṛtā*
past active participle	m.n. *kṛtavat*	f. *kṛtavatī*
present active participle	m.n. *kurvat*	f. *kurvatī*
present middle participle	m.n. *kurvāṇa*	f. *kurvāṇā*
present passive participle	m.n. *kriyamāṇa*	f. *kriyamāṇā*
future active participle	m.n. *kariṣyat*	f. *kariṣyantī*
future middle participle	m.n. *kariṣyamāṇa*	f. *kariṣyamāṇā*
future passive participle	m.n. *kartavya, kārya, karaṇiya*	f. *kartavyā, kāryā, karaṇīyā*
perfect active participle	m.n. *cakṛvaḥ*	f. *cakruṣī*
perfect middle participle	m.n. *cakrāṇa*	f. *cakrāṇā*
infinitive	*kartum*	
gerund/ absolutive	*kṛtvā, kāram, -kṛtya*	

Conjugation *kṛ* Class 8 (Causative)

		active			middle			passive		
		singular	dual	plural	singular	dual	plural	singular	dual	plural
present indicative	1st	*kārayati*	*kārayataḥ*	*kārayanti*	*kārayate*	*kārayete*	*kārayante*	*kāryate*	*kāryete*	*kāryante*
	2nd	*kārayasi*	*kārayathaḥ*	*kārayatha*	*kārayase*	*kārayethe*	*kārayadhve*	*kāryase*	*kāryethe*	*kāryadhve*
	3rd	*kārayāmi*	*kārayāvaḥ*	*kārayāmaḥ*	*kāraye*	*kārayāvahe*	*kārayāmahe*	*kārye*	*kāryāvahe*	*kāryāmahe*
present optative		*kārayet*	*kārayetām*	*kārayeyuḥ*	*kārayeta*	*kārayeyātām*	*kārayeran*	*kāryeta*	*kāryeyātām*	*kāryeran*
		kārayeḥ	*kārayetam*	*kārayeta*	*kārayethāḥ*	*kārayeyāthām*	*kārayedhvam*	*kāryethāḥ*	*kāryeyāthām*	*kāryedhvam*
		kārayeyam	*kārayeva*	*kārayema*	*kārayeya*	*kārayevahi*	*kārayemahi*	*kāryeya*	*kāryevahi*	*kāryemahi*
present imperative		*kārayatu*	*kārayatām*	*kārayantu*	*kārayatām*	*kārayetām*	*kārayantām*	*kāryatām*	*kāryetām*	*kāryantām*
		kāraya	*kārayatam*	*kārayata*	*kārayasva*	*kārayethām*	*kārayadhvam*	*kāryasva*	*kāryethām*	*kāryadhvam*
		kārayāṇi	*kārayatām*	*kārayāma*	*kārayai*	*kārayāvahai*	*kārayāmahai*	*kāryai*	*kāryāvahai*	*kāryāmahai*
imperfect indicative		*akārayat*	*akārayatām*	*akārayan*	*akārayata*	*akārayetām*	*akārayanta*	*akāryata*	*akāryetām*	*akāryanta*
		akārayaḥ	*akārayatam*	*akārayata*	*akārayathāḥ*	*akārayethām*	*akārayadhvam*	*akāryathā*	*akāryethām*	*akāryadhvam*
		akārayam	*akārayāva*	*akārayāma*	*akāraye*	*akārayāvahi*	*akārayāmahi*	*akārye*	*akāryāvahi*	*akāryāmahi*
future indicative		*kārayiṣyati*	*kārayiṣyataḥ*	*kārayiṣyanti*	*kārayiṣyate*	*kārayiṣyete*	*kārayiṣyante*			
		kārayiṣyasi	*kārayiṣyathaḥ*	*kārayiṣyatha*	*kārayiṣyase*	*kārayiṣyethe*	*kārayiṣyadhve*			
		kārayiṣyāmi	*kārayiṣyāvaḥ*	*kārayiṣyāmaḥ*	*kārayiṣye*	*kārayiṣyāvahe*	*kārayiṣyāmahe*			
future periphrastic		*kārayitā*	*kārayitārau*	*kārayitāraḥ*						
		kārayitāsi	*kārayitāsthaḥ*	*kārayitāstha*						
		kārayitāsmi	*kārayitāsvaḥ*	*kārayitāsmaḥ*						

past passive participle m.n. *kārita* f. *kāritā*
past active participle m.n. *kāritavat* f.*kāritavatī*
present active participle m.n. *kārayat* f.*kārayantī*
present middle participle m.n. *kārayamāṇa* f.*kārayamāṇā*
present passive participle m.n. *kāryamāṇa* f.*kāryamāṇā*
future active participle m.n. *kārayiṣyat* f.*kārayiṣyantī*
future middle participle m.n. *kārayiṣyamāṇa* f.*kārayiṣyamāṇā*
future passive participle m.n. *kārya, kāraṇīya, kārayitavya* f.*kāryā, kāraṇīyā, kārayitavyā*
infinitive *kārayitum* gerund/absolutive *kāritvā, -kārya* periphrastic perfect *kārayyām*

Conjugation *kṛ* Class 8 (Desiderative)

		active				middle				passive		
		singular	dual	plural		singular	dual	plural		singular	dual	plural
present desiderative	1st	*cikīrṣati*	*cikīrṣataḥ*	*cikīrṣanti*		*cikīrṣate*	*cikīrṣete*	*cikīrṣante*				
	2nd	*cikīrṣasi*	*cikīrṣathaḥ*	*cikīrṣatha*		*cikīrṣase*	*cikīrṣethe*	*cikīrṣadhve*				
	3rd	*cikīrṣāmi*	*cikīrṣāvaḥ*	*cikīrṣāmaḥ*		*cikīrṣe*	*cikīrṣāvahe*	*cikīrṣāmahe*				
optative desiderative		*cikīrṣet*	*cikīrṣetām*	*cikīrṣeyuḥ*		*cikīrṣeta*	*cikīrṣeyātām*	*cikīrṣeran*				
		cikīrṣeḥ	*cikīrṣetam*	*cikīrṣeta*		*cikīrṣethāḥ*	*cikīrṣeyāthām*	*cikīrṣedhvam*				
		cikīrṣeyam	*cikīrṣeva*	*cikīrṣema*		*cikīrṣeya*	*cikīrṣevahi*	*cikīrṣemahi*				
imperative desiderative		*cikīrṣatu*	*cikīrṣatām*	*cikīrṣantu*		*cikīrṣatām*	*cikīrṣetām*	*cikīrṣantām*				
		cikīrṣa	*cikīrṣatam*	*cikīrṣata*		*cikīrṣasva*	*cikīrṣethām*	*cikīrṣadhvam*				
		cikīrṣāṇi	*cikīrṣāva*	*cikīrṣāma*		*cikīrṣai*	*cikīrṣāvahai*	*cikīrṣāmahai*				
imperfect desiderative		*acikīrṣat*	*acikīrṣatām*	*acikīrṣan*		*acikīrṣata*	*acikīrṣetām*	*acikīrṣanta*				
		acikīrṣaḥ	*acikīrṣatam*	*acikīrṣata*		*acikīrṣathāḥ*	*acikīrṣethām*	*acikīrṣadhvam*				
		acikīrṣam	*acikīrṣāva*	*acikīrṣāma*		*acikīrṣe*	*acikīrṣāvahi*	*acikīrṣāmahi*				
perfect desiderative		*cicikīrṣa*	*cicikīrṣatuḥ*	*cicikīrṣuḥ*		*cicikīrṣe*	*cicikīrṣāte*	*cicikīrṣire*				
		cicikīrṣitha	*cicikīrṣathuḥ*	*cicikīrṣa*		*cicikīrṣiṣe*	*cicikīrṣāthe*	*cicikīrṣidhve*				
		cicikīrṣa	*cicikīrṣiva*	*cicikīrṣima*		*cicikīrṣe*	*cicikīrṣivahe*	*cicikīrṣimahe*				

past passive participle m.n. *cikīrṣita* f. *cikīrṣitā*
past active participle m.n. *cikīrṣitavat* f. *cikīrṣitavatī*
present active participle m.n. *cikīrṣat* f. *cikīrṣantī*
present middle participle m.n. *cikīrṣamāṇa* f. *cikīrṣmāṇā*
perfect active participle m.n. *cikīrṣvaḥ* f. *cikīrṣuṣī*
infinitive *cikīrṣitum* gerund/absolutive *cikīrṣitvā* - *cikīrṣiya*

Conjugation ***jñā*** class 9 - know, understand, have knowledge, perceive, experience, recognise, know as,

		active			middle			passive		
		singular	dual	plural	singular	dual	plural	singular	dual	plural
present indicative	1st 2nd 3rd	*jānāti* *jānāsi* *jānāmi*	*jānītaḥ* *jānīthaù* *jānīvaù*	*jānanti* *jānītha* *jānīmaḥ*	*jānīte* *jānīñe* *jāne*	*jānāte* *jānāthe* *jānīvahe*	*jānate* *jānīdhve* *jānīmahe*	*jñāyate* *jñāyase* *jñāye*	*jñāyete* *jñāyethe* *jñāyāvahe*	*jñāyante* *jñāyadhve* *jñāyāmahe*
present optative		*jānīyāt* *jānīyḥ* *jānīyām*	*jānīyātām* *jānīyātam* *jānīyāva*	*jānīyuḥ* *jānīyāta* *jānīyāma*	*jānīta* *jānīthāḥ* *jānīya*	*jānīyātām* *jānīyāthām* *jānīvahi*	*jānīran* *jānīdhvam* *jānīmahi*	*jñāyeta* *jñāyethaḥ* *jñāyeya*	*jñāyeyātām* *jñāyeyāthām* *jñāyevahi*	*jñāyeran* *jñāyedhvam* *jñāyemahi*
present imperative		*jānātu* *jānīhi* *jānāni*	*jānītām* *jānītam* *jānāva*	*jānantu* *jānīta* *jānāma*	*jānītām* *jānīñva* *jānai*	*jānātām* *jānāthām* *jānāvahai*	*jānatām* *jānīdhvam* *jānāmahai*	*jñāyatām* *jñāyasva* *jñāyai*	*jñāyetām* *jñāyethām* *jñāyāvahai*	*jñāyantām* *jñāyadhvam* *jñāyāmahai*
imperfect indicative		*ajānāt* *ajānāḥ* *ajānām*	*ajānītām* *ajānītam* *ajānīva*	*ajānan* *ajānīta* *ajānīma*	*ajānīta* *ajānīthāḥ* *ajāni*	*ajānātām* *ajānāthām* *ajānīvahi*	*ajānata* *ajānīdhvam* *ajānīmahi*	*ajñāyata* *ajñāyathaḥ* *ajñāye*	*ajñāyetām* *ajñāyethām* *ajñāyāvahi*	*ajñāyanta* *ajñāyadhvam* *ajñāyāmahi*
future		*jñāsyati* *jñāsyasi* *jñāsyāmi*	*jñāsyataḥ* *jñāsyathaḥ* *jñāsyāvaḥ*	*jñāsyanti* *jñāsyatha* *jñāsyāmaḥ*	*jñāsyate* *jñāsyase* *jñāsye*	*jñāsyete* *jñāsyethe* *jñāsyāvahe*	*jñāsyante* *jñāsyadhve* *jñāsyāmahe*			
periphrastic future		*jñātā* *jñātāsi* *jñātāsmi*	*jñātārau* *jñātāsthaḥ* *jñātāsvaḥ*	*jñātāraḥ* *jñātāstha* *jñātāsmaḥ*						
perfect		*jajñau* *jajñitha/jajñātha* *jajñau*	*jajñatuḥ* *jajñathuḥ* *jajñiva*	*jajñuḥ* *jajña* *jajñima*	*jajñe* *jajñiñe* *jajñe*	*jajñāte* *jajñāthe* *jajñivahe*	*jajñire* *jajñidhve* *jajñimahe*			
aorist		*ajñāsīt/ajñāt* *ajñāsiḥ/ajñāḥ* *ajñāsiṣam/ajñām*	*ajñāsiṣṭām/ ajñātām* *ajñāsiṣṭam/ ajñātam* *ajñāsiṣva/ajñāva*	*ajñāsiṣuḥ/ ajñuḥ* *ajñāsiṣṭa/ ajñāta* *ajñāsiṣma/ ajñāma*	*ajñeṣṭa/ajñāyi* *ajñeṣṭhāḥ* *ajñeṣi*	*ajñeṣātām* *ajñeṣāthām* *ajñeṣvahi*	*ajñeṣata* *ajñedhvam* *ajñeṣmahi*			

past passive participle *jñāta* m.n. *jñātā* f. past active participle *jñātavat* m.n. *jñātavatī* f. present active participle *jānat* m.n. *jānatī* f.
present middle participle *jānāna* m.n. *jānānā* f. present passive participle *jñāyamāna* m.n. *jñāyamānā* f. future active participle *jñāsyat* m.n. *jñāsyantī* f.
future middle participle *jñāsyamāna* m.n. *jñāsyamāṇā* f. future passive participle *jñātavya* or *jñeya* or *jñānīya* m.n. *jñeyā* or *jñātavyā* or *jñānīyā* f.
...fect active participle *jajñivaḥ* m.n. *jajñuñī* f. perfect middle participle *jajñāna* m.n. *jajñānā* f.
...clinables: *jñātum* infinitive, gerund/absolutive *jñātvā* or , *-jñāya*

Causative Conjugation ***jñā*** **class 9 (Note** there are unshown variations. Partic. Where the first *ā* becomes *a*)

		active			middle			passive		
		singular	dual	plural	singular	dual	plural	singular	dual	plural
present	1st 2nd 3rd	*jñāpayati* *jñāpayasi* *jñāpayāmi*	*jñāpayataḥ* *jñāpayathaḥ* *jñāpayāvaḥ*	*jñāpayanti* *jñāpayatha* *jñāpayāmaḥ*	*jñāpayate* *jñāpayase* *jñāpaye*	*jñāpayete* *jñāpayethe* *jñāpayāvahe*	*jñāpayante* *jñāpayadhve* *jñāpayāmahe*	*jñāpyate* *jñāpyase* *jñāpye*	*jñāpyete* *jñāpyethe* *jñāpyāvahe*	*jñāpyante* *jñāpyadhve* *jñāpyāmahe*
imperfect		*ajñāpayat* *ajñāpayaḥ* *ajñāpayam*	*ajñāpayatām* *ajñāpayatam* *ajñāpayāma*	*ajñāpayan* *ajñāpayata* *ajñāpayāma*	*ajñāpayata* *ajñāpayathāḥ* *ajñāpaye*	*ajñāpayetām* *ajñāpayethām* *ajñāpayāvahi*	*ajñāpayanta* *ajñāpayadhvam* *ajñāpayāmahi*	*ajñāpyata* *ajñāpyathāḥ* *ajñāpye*	*ajñāpyetām* *ajñāpyethām* *ajñāpyāvahi*	*ajñāpyanta* *ajñāpyadhvam* *ajñāpyāmahi*
optative		*jñāpayet* *jñāpayeḥ* *jñāpayeyam*	*jñāpayetām* *jñāpayetam* *jñāpayeva*	*jñāpayeyuḥ* *jñāpayeta* *jñāpayema*	*jñāpayeta* *jñāpayethāḥ* *jñāpayeya*	*jñāpayeyātām* *jñāpayeyāthām* *jñāpayevahi*	*jñāpayeran* *jñāpayedhvam* *jñāpayemahi*	*jñāpyeta* *jñāpyethāḥ* *jñāpyeya*	*jñāpyeyātām* *jñāpyeyāthām* *jñāpyevahi*	*jñāpyeran* *jñāpyedhvam* *jñāpyemahi*
imperative		*jñāpayatu* *jñāpaya* *jñāpayāni*	*jñāpayatām* *jñāpayatam* *jñāpayāva*	*jñāpayantu* *jñāpayata* *jñāpayāma*	*jñāpayatām* *jñāpayasva* *jñāpayai*	*jñāpayetām* *jñāpayethām* *jñāpayāvahai*	*jñāpayantām* *jñāpayadhvam* *jñāpayāmahai*	*jñāpyatām* *jñāpyasva* *jñāpyai*	*jñāpyetām* *jñāpyethām* *jñāpyāvahai*	*jñāpyantām* *jñāpyadhvam* *jñāpyāmahai*
future		*jñāpayiṣyati* *jñāpayiṣyasi* *jñāpayiṣyāmi*	*jñāpayiṣyataḥ* *jñāpayiṣyathaḥ* *jñāpayiṣyāvaḥ*	*jñāpayiṣyanti* *jñāpayiṣyatha* *jñāpayiṣyāmaḥ*	*jñāpayiṣyate* *jñāpayiṣyase* *jñāpayiṣye*	*jñāpayiṣyete* *jñāpayiṣyethe* *jñāpayiṣyāvahe*	*jñāpayiṣyante* *jñāpayiṣyadhve* *jñāpayiṣyāmahe*			
periphrastic future		*jñāpayitā* *jñāpayitāsi* *jñāpayitāsmi*	*jñāpayitārau* *jñāpayitāsthaḥ* *jñāpayitāsvaḥ*	*jñāpayitāraḥ* *jñāpayitāstha* *jñāpayitāsmaḥ*						

Causative Aorist not shown.

past passive participle *jñāpita* m.n. *jñāpitā* f.
past active participle *jñāpitavat* m.n. *jñāpitavatī* f.
present active participle *jñāpayat* m.n. *jñāpayantī* f.
present middle participle *jñāpayamāna* m.n. *jñāpayamānā* f.
present passive participle *jñāpyamāna* m.n. *jñāpyamānā* f.
future active participle *japayiṣyat* m.n. *jñapayiṣyantī* f.
future middle participle *jñāpayiṣyamāna* m.n. *jñāpayiṣyamāṇā* f.
future passive participle *jñāpatavya* or *jñāpya* or *jñāpanīya* m.n. *jñāpyā* or *jñāpatavyā* or *jñāpanīyā* f.

periphrastic perfect *jñāpayyām*

Indeclinables: *jñāpayitum* infinitive, *jñāpitvā*, - *jñāpya*, *jñāpayyām* gerund/absolutive

Desiderative Conjugation ***jñā***

		active				middle				passive	
		singular	dual	plural		singular	dual	plural		singular	dual	plural
present	1st	*jijñāsate*	*jijñāsete*	*jijñāsante*								
	2nd	*jijñāsase*	*jijñāsethe*	*jijñāsadhve*								
	3rd	*jijñāse*	*jijñāsāvahe*	*jijñāsāmahe*								
imperfect		*ajijñāsata*	*ajijñāsetām*	*ajijñāsanta*								
		ajijñāsathāḥ	*ajijñāsethām*	*ajijñāsadhvam*								
		ajijñāse	*ajijñāsāvahi*	*ajijñāsāmahi*								
optative		*jijñāseta*	*jijñāseyātām*	*jijñāseran*								
		jijñāsethāḥ	*jijñāseyāthām*	*jijñāsedhvam*								
		jijñāseya	*jijñāsevahi*	*jijñāsemahi*								
imperative		*jijñāsatām*	*jijñāsetām*	*jijñāsantām*								
		jijñāsasva	*jijñāsethām*	*jijñāsadhvam*								
		jijñāsai	*jijñāsāvahai*	*jijñāsāmahai*								
perfect		*jijijñāse*	*jijijñāsāte*	*jijijñāsire*								
		jijijñāsiṣe	*jijijñāsāthe*	*jijijñāsidhve*								
		jijijñāse	*jijijñāsivahe*	*jijijñāsimahe*								

past passive participle *jijñāsita* m.n. *jijñāsitā* f. past active participle *jijñāsitavat* m.n. *jijñāsitavatī* f.
present middle participle *jijñāsamāna* m.n. *jijñāsamānā* f.
future passive participle *jijñāsanīya, jijñāsya, jijñāsitavya* m.n. *jijñāsanīyā, jijñāsyā, jijñāsitavyā* f.
Indeclinables: infinitive *jijijñāsitum* gerund/absolutive *jijñāsitvā* or , *-jijñāsiya*

Conjugation √*cint* (class 10) to think, reflect, consider, reflect upon, care for, find out,

		active			middle			passive		
		singular	**dual**	**plural**	**singular**	**dual**	**plural**	**singular**	**dual**	**plural**
present	1st 2nd 3rd	*cintayati* *cintayasi* *cintayāmi*	*cintayataḥ* *cintayathaḥ* *cintayāvaḥ*	*cintayanti* *cintayatha* *cintayāmaḥ*	*cintayate* *cintayase* *cintaye*	*cintayete* *cintayethe* *cintayāvahe*	*cintayante* *cintayadhve* *cintayāmahe*	*cintyate* *cintyase* *cintye*	*cintyete* *cintyethe* *cintyāvahe*	*cintyante* *cintyadhve* *cintyāmahe*
optative		*cintayet* *cintayeḥ* *cintayeyam*	*cintayetām* *cintayetam* *cintayeva*	*cintayeyuḥ* *cintayeta* *cintayema*	*cintayeta* *cintayethāḥ* *cintayeya*	*cintayeyātām* *cintayeyāthām* *cintayevahi*	*cintayeran* *cintayedhvam* *cintayemahi*	*cintyeta* *cintyethāḥ* *cintyeya*	*cintyeyātām* *cintyeyāthām* *cintyevahi*	*cintyeran* *cintyedhvam* *cintyemahi*
imperative		*cintayatu* *cintaya* *cintayāni*	*cintayatām* *cintayatam* *cintayāva*	*cintayantu* *cintayata* *cintayāma*	*cintayatām* *cintayasva* *cintayai*	*cintayetām* *cintayethām* *cintayāvahai*	*cintayantām* *cintayadhvam* *cintayāmahai*	*cintyatām* *cintyasva* *cintyai*	*cintyetām* *cintyethām* *cintyāvahai*	*cintyantām* *cintyadhvam* *cintyāmahai*
imperfect		*acintayat* *acintayaḥ* *acintayam*	*acintayatām* *acintayatam* *acintayāva*	*acintayan* *acintayata* *acintayāma*	*acintayata* *acintayathāḥ* *acintaye*	*acintayetām* *acintayethām* *acintayāvahi*	*acintayanta* *acintayadhvam* *acintayāmahi*	*acintyata* *acintyathāḥ* *acintye*	*acintyetām* *acintyethām* *acintyāvahi*	*acintyanta* *acintyadhvam* *acintyāmahi*

past passive participle *cintita* m.n. *cintitā* f. past active participle *cintitavat* m.n. *cintitavatī* f.

present active participle *cintayat* m.n. *cintayantī* f. present middle participle *cintayāna* m.n. *cintayānā* f.

future passive participle *cintayitavya* or *cintya* or *cintanīya* m.n. *cintyā* or *cintayitavyā* or *cintanīyā* f.

Indeclinables:, gerund/absolutive *cintitvā* or , -*cintya*

Periphrastic perfect *cintayām*

Conjugation *dṛṣ class 1* see, behold, look at, regard, consider, see with the mind, learn, understand, see by intuition, (√*paś* is used for the present, imperfect, optative and imperative tenses). Conditional not shown.

			active				middle		
		singular	dual	plural		singular	dual	plural	
present indicative	1st 2nd 3rd	*paśyati* *paśyasi* *paśyāmi*	*paśyataḥ* *paśyathaḥ* *paśyāvaḥ*	*paśyanti* *paśyatha* *paśyāmaḥ*		*paśyate* *paśyase* *paśye*	*paśyete* *paśyethe* *paśyāvahe*	*paśyante* *paśyadhve* *paśyāmahe*	present active participle *paśyat* m.n. *paśyantī* f. present middle participle *paśyamāna* m.n. *paśyamānā* f.
imperfect		*apaśyat* *apaśyaḥ* *apaśyam*	*apaśyatām* *apaśyatam* *apaśyāva*	*apaśyān* *apaśyata* *apaśyāma*		*apaśyata* *apaśyathāḥ* *apaśye*	*apaśyetām* *apaśyethām* *apaśyāvahi*	*apaśyanta* *apaśyadhvam* *apaśyāmahi*	
optative		*paśyet* *paśyeḥ* *paśyeyam*	*paśyetām* *paśyetam* *paśyeva*	*paśyeyuḥ* *paśyeta* *paśyema*		*paśy eta* *paśyethāḥ* *paśyeya*	*paśyeyātām* *paśyeyāthām* *paśyevahi*	*paśyeran* *paśyedhvam* *paśyemahi*	
imperative		*paśyatu* *paśya* *paśyāṇi*	*paśyatām* *paśyatam* *paśyāva*	*paśyantu* *paśyata* *paśyāma*		*paśyatām* *paśyasva* *paśyai*	*paśyetām* *paśyethām* *paśyāvahai*	*paśyantām* *paśyadhvam* *paśyāmahai*	
future		*drakṣyati* *drakṣyasi* *drakṣyāmi*	*drakṣyataḥ* *drakṣyathaḥ* *drakṣyāvaḥ*	*drakṣyanti* *drakṣyatha* *drakṣyāmaḥ*		*drakṣyate* *drakṣyase* *drakṣye*	*drakṣyete* *drakṣyethe* *drakṣyāvahe*	*drakṣyante* *drakṣyadhve* *drakṣyāmahe*	
periphrastic future		*draṣṭā* *draṣṭāsi* *draṣṭāsmi*	*draṣṭārau* *draṣṭāstaḥ* *draṣṭāsvaḥ*	*draṣṭāraḥ* *draṣṭāstha* *draṣṭāsmaḥ*					
perfect		*dadaśa* *dadarśitha/dadraṣṭha* *dadarśa*	*dadṛśatuḥ* *dadṛśathuḥ* *dadṛśiva*	*dadṛśuḥ* *dadṛsa* *dadṛṣima*		*dadṛśe* *dadṛśiṣe* *dadṛśe*	*dadṛśāte* *dadṛśāthe* *dadṛśivahe*	*dadṛśire* *dadṛśidhve* *dadṛṣimahe*	

			active				middle	
Aorist	1st 2nd 3rd	*adrākṣīt* *adrākṣīḥ* *adrākṣam*	*adrākṣṭām* *adrākṣṭam* *adrākṣva*	*adrākṣuḥ* *adrākṣṭa* *adrākṣma*				

Pāṇini

"Sanskrit is the conscious language, and all others are distorted, losing their consciousness in course of time." *śrī śāntānanda sarasvatī*

The great grammarian Pāṇini regularised the language by writing the laws of grammar in about 4000 *sūtra* s. The document was so important that it marks the transition between earlier Sanskrit (now known as Vedic) and all subsequent (Classic) Sanskrit. There had been earlier grammarians and there are later grammarians but *Panini*'s document is so comprehensive logical and masterful that it set the standard. However it is difficult to understand because of complexity and extreme brevity. An abbreviated and re-ordered set of rules called the *Laghu-siddhānta-kaumudī* (A Short Elucidation of the Laws of Grammar) was subsequently written by *Varadarāja. Laghu* means short or light. This is an exposition used as the basis for this summary. It states the important *sūtra* s with a commentary indicating how they are applied. It has been said with authority that all natural laws are held within the Sanskrit Grammar and that to understand the profundity of these it is necessary to follow Panini and that the *Laghu-siddhānta-kaumudī* is a recommended way to do this. Here is a brief outline of the first chapter and the beginning of the second. The study of Panini's work is a significant and worthy study on its own but not easy because the brevity can lead to ambiguity. It is best tackled with a good teacher. The Sanskrit *sūtra* s have generally been omitted for clarity and the *sūtra* numbering is that used in the translation by James R Ballantyne.

The document opens with the *Maheśvarāṇi Sutrāṇi*, said to have been revealed to Panini This contains 14 letter groupings which contain all the letters of the alphabet. In addition it contains 42 *pratyāhāras** which are used as abbreviations to explain the grammar. The contents of the *pratyāhāras* are given at the end of this chapter.

महेश्वराणि सुत्राणि

अइउण् ।१। ऋऌक् ।२। एओङ् ।३। ऐऔच् ।४।
हयवरट् ।५। लण् ।६। ञमङणनम् ।७। झभञ् ।८।
घढधष् ।९। जबगडदश् ।१०। खफछठथचटतव् ।११।
कपय् ।१२। शषसर् ।१३। हल् ।१४।।

pratyāhāra* (in grammar) the comprehension of a series of letters or roots etc., into one syllable by combining for brevity the first member with the *anubandha of the last member, a group of letters so combined e.g. *ac* (which contains all the vowels) or *hal* (which contains all the consonants). **anubandha* –an indicatory letter attached to roots etc., marking some peculiarity in their inflection.

Pāṇini Chapter 1 Names

This chapter defines grammatical terms and relates sounds to mouth positions and inner and outer effort or activity.

The *sūtra* numbers indicated by bold numbers are those of *Varadarāja* not Panini . The *Maheśvarāṇi Sutrāṇi* provides names for groups of consecutive sounds used in the subsequent *sūtra* s. Each *sūtra* takes identity from its first and last letters alone. Thus the first *sūtra* (***aiuṇ***) is known as ***aṇ*** These names are called *pratyāhāra* (meaning) –'the comprehension of a series of letters or roots etc., into one syllable by combining for brevity the first member with the .. .last member.'

For brevity there are special kinds of *sūtras* for stating the rules of grammar, to explain for understanding and to indicate statements that govern following groups of *sūtra*s. Additionally some *vibhakti* endings are used to indicate the name of the replacement sound (1st), that after which there is replacement (5th), that which is replaced (6th), and that before which there is replacement (7th).

1-8 In an *upadeśa* (an "original utterance" like any of the *Maheśvarāṇi* words above), of Panini a final consonant (*hal*) is called ***'it'*** (indicatory). This means it is their as an indicator only and is not considered a substantial part of the word so in *an* above the effective letters are *a, i, u*.

Hal is a *pratyāhāra* that includes all the consonants so if Panini wants to say something about all the consonants he just refers to *hal.*

A short *a* has been added to consonants so that they may be articulated but the bare consonants are intended. e.g. from *sūtra hayaravat* only *h,y,r,v* is intended. So the *a* letters are '*it'* as is also the *a* in *laṇ.*

Another example is the *pratyāhāra* ***ak*** which represents the letters *a,i u, ṛ, ḷ,* starting with *a* and with the indicatory ending *k.* Thus the *k* sound is not included and so is effectively "not seen" . This latent effect of being "not seen" is given the name *lopa. ac* is the name o the *pratyāhāra* for all the vowels, *hal* is the name for all the consonants and *al* includes all letters.

A word which is not seen in a *sūtra* but which is necessary to make sense of it must be obtained from a previous *sūtra* . Panini assumes that previous aphorisms are remembered and applied appropriately.

9 -15 The duration of any vowel sound (*ac*) is called *hrasva* (short), *dīrgha* (long) or *pluta* (extended). Each of these has 3 measures of pitch known as the distinctions of *udātta* (high pitch), *anudātta* (low pitch) and *svarita* (a combination of high and low pitch). Each of these nine forms may be expressed as a nasal or non-nasal thus giving 18 variations of the sound. Sound produced by the mouth and nose together is called *anunāsika. A,i,u* and *ṛ* each have 18 ways of being pronounced e.g. ***a*** x 3(duration) x 3 (pitch) x2 (nasal) =18 but *ḷ* has 12 because it has no *dīrgha* (long) measure. The *ec* sounds (*e, o, ai* and *au*) also have 12 because there is no short (*hraswa*) measure. Sounds that use the same mouth position and method of are known as being *savarṇa* (same family). There is also a *savarṇa* relationship between *ṛ* and *ḷ*.

The mouth positions for the sounds are.

कण्ठ *kaṇṭha* (throat) *a,k,kh,g,gh,ṅ,h* अ column (+*visarga*)

तालु *tālu* (palate) *i,c,ch,j,jh,ī,y,ś* इ column

मूर्ध *mūrdhā* (roof of the mouth) *ṛ,ṭ,ṭh,ḍ,ḍh,ṇ,r,ṣ* ऋ column

दन्ता: *dantāḥ* (teeth) *t,th,d,dh,n,l,s* ऌ column

ओष्ठौ *oṣṭhau* (lips) *u,p,ph,b,bh,m*, and उ column

उपध्मानीय *upadhmānīya* (to do with blowing or breathing)

नासिक *nāsikā* (nose) *ṅ,ñ,ṇ,n,m*

कण्ठतालु *kaṇṭhatālu* throat/palate *e,ai*

कण्ठोष्ठ *kaṇṭhoṣṭha* throat/lips *o, au*

दन्तोष्ठम् *dantoṣṭham* teeth/lips *v*

अ	इ	ऋ	ऌ	उ
क	च	ट	त	प
ख	छ	ठ	थ	फ
ग	ज	ड	द	ब
घ	झ	ढ	ध	भ
ङ	ञ	ण	न	म
ह	य	र	ल	व
	श	ष	म	

जिह्वामूलीय *jihvāmūlīya* - this is an infrequently seen symbol sometimes used instead of *visarga* before *ka* or *kha*. It looks like a saucer over an inverted saucer. The same symbol used instead of visarga before *pa* or *pha* is called *upadhmānīya*.

16 There are two kinds of articulation activity (*prayatnaḥ*)–
inner (*ābhyantara*),(5 types), and outer (*bāhya*), (11 types).

Inner types of activity or effort – contact, slight contact etc., describes the tongue position relative to the upper part of the mouth.

contact स्पृष्ट (*spṛṣṭa*) for contact sounds –the स्पर्षा: (*sparṣāḥ*). *halanta* क् to म्

slight contact ईषत्स्पृष्ट (*īṣatspṛṣṭa*)the semi-vowels अन्त:स्था:(*antaḥsthāḥ*)*y v r l*

slightly open ईषद्विवृत्त (*īṣadvivṛta*) the sibilants ऊष्मान: (*ūṣmaṇ*) ह्, श्, ष्, म्,

open विवृत्त (*vivåta*) for vowels स्वरा: (*svarāḥ*)

closed -in reality the short (*hraswa*) *'a'* is closed i.e. vocal cords contracted but in the context of grammar only it is said to be open.

Outer types of activity or effort

open विवार: (*vivāraḥ*) — closed संवार: (*saṁvāraḥ*)

with breath श्वास: (*śvāsaḥ*) — resonant नाद: (*nādaḥ*)

voiced घोष: (*ghoṣaḥ*) — unvoiced अघोष: (*aghoṣaḥ*)

unaspirated अल्पप्राण (*alpaprāṇaḥ*) — aspirated महाप्राण: (*mahāprāṇaḥ*)

high (*udātta*) accent — not high (*anudātta*) accent

high/low (*svarita*) accent

खर् *khar* sounds are open, with breath, unvoiced

हश् *haś* sounds are closed, resonant, voiced

The first, third and fifth sounds in each alphabet consonant column and
यन् *yan* sounds *y, v, r, l,* are unaspirated.

The second and fourth sounds in each alphabet consonant column
and the शल् *śal* sounds *ś, ṣ, s* and *h* are aspirated

अ इ ऋ ऌ उ ए ओ ऐ औ *khar* (unvoiced) **क च ट त प** **ख छ ठ थ फ** ग ज ड द ब घ झ ढ ध भ ङ ञ ण न म ह य र ल व **श ष स**	अ इ ऋ ऌ उ ए ओ ऐ औ क च ट त प ख छ ठ थ फ *haś* (voiced) **ग ज ड द ब** **घ झ ढ ध भ** **ङ ञ ण न म** **ह य र ल व** श ष स	अ इ ऋ ऌ उ ए ओ ऐ औ *yan* *(antaḥsthāḥ)* क च ट त प ख छ ठ थ फ ग ज ड द ब घ झ ढ ध भ ङ ञ ण न म ह **य र ल व** श ष स	अ इ ऋ ऌ उ ए ओ ऐ औ क च ट त प ख छ ठ थ फ *śal (uṣmāṇaḥ)* ग ज ड द ब घ झ ढ ध भ ङ ञ ण न म **ह** य र ल व **श ष स**	**अ इ ऋ ऌ उ** **ए ओ** **ऐ औ** **क च ट त प** ख छ ठ थ फ (unaspirated) **ग ज ड द ब** घ झ ढ ध भ **ङ ञ ण न म** ह **य र ल व** श ष स	अ इ ऋ ऌ उ ए ओ ऐ औ (aspirated) क च ट त प **ख छ ठ थ फ** ग ज ड द ब **घ झ ढ ध भ** ङ ञ ण न म **ह** य र ल व **श ष स**

the shaded areas represent letters in the indicated groups

The sounds in the list beginning with *k* and ending with *m* are called *sparśāḥ.*
The *yan* sounds (semi-vowels) are called *antaḥstāḥ*. (in-between)
The *śal* sounds (sibilants) are called *ūṣmāṇāḥ.*
The *ac* sounds (vowels) are called *svarāḥ.*
The character (short *u* over long *u*) before *k,kh,* like a half *visarga* is called *jihvāmūlīya* and before *p* or *ph* like a half *visarga* is called *upadhmānīya*. A dot following a vowel is called *anusvara*, two dots following (colon) are called *visarga*.

17 अण् *aṇ* sounds- (there are 2 possible lists of *an* sounds. This is the only time the longer grouping is used) *a, i, u, ṛ, ḷ, e, o, ai, au, ha, ya, va, ra, la*) and those followed by an *it hraswa u (ku, cu, ṭu, tu, pu*) stand for sounds *savarṇa* with them*
i.e *ku* stands for *k, kh, g, gh, ṅ,* *cu* stands for *c, ch, j, jh, ñ* and similarly for others.
a , i, and *u,* are each the name for 18 forms
Note: These forms and the following numbers of forms include all appropriate measures i.e. [sound length], accents and nasals.

ṛ and *ḷ* each have thirty forms एच् *ec* letters have twelve forms
y, v, l, have two forms (nasal and non-nasal)
therefore *y, v, l,* are each the names of two forms
*provided it is not being prescribed for another use such as a substitute, affix or augment

18 संहिता (*saṁhitā)* is the name of sounds drawn very close together.

19 हल (*hal)* sounds with nothing in between are called *saṁyoga*

20 That which has a सुप् *sup* or a तिङ् *tiṅ* ending is called a पद *pada* (fully developed word)

sup represents the 21 case endings for nominals
tiṅ represents the 18 endings for verbs

Pāṇini **Chapter 2 The harmonious joining of final and initial vowels**

Note: The next 3 chapters deal with the sandhi (harmonious joining of final and initial letters) of firstly vowels, then consonants, and then the joining of final *visarga*s with other letters.

21 *iko yaṇaci* With the help of the following *sūtra*s this comes to mean-
In place of an *ik* before an *ac* there is a *yaṇ.* (the most similar *yaṇ* is substituted)
an example is given *sudhī* the wise + *upāsya* to be worshipped > *sudhyupāsya*
y (a *yaṇ*) has replaced *ī* (an *ik* letter). The result is harmonious, natural and sounds like the original. The following table shows which *ik* (first column) would be replaced by what .

अस्ति+एव =अस्त्येव

तु+अपि =त्वपि

मातृ+आसीत् =मात्रासीत्

इ	>	य्
उ	>	व्
ऋ	>	र्
ऌ	>	ल्

22 When a term is in the seventh case there is a grammatical change to the preceding letter.
This refers to the previous *sūtra* where *ac* is in the 7th case as *aci*. Thus it adds meaning to the previous *sūtra* by indicating that the change happens to the letter prior to the *ac* that starts the second word.

23 In (that) place nearest (sound). Let the most similar (sound) be the substitute.
Another explanatory *sūtra* for number 21 indicating that the most similar of the *yaṇ* sounds should be substituted for the *ik* sound. As per the table above.

24 A *yar* letter (all consonants except *h*) may optionally (according to tradition) be doubled after an *ac* but not before a subsequent *ac*. Thus by duplication of the letter *dh* arises *sudhdhyupāsya*. Conditional phrase providing an option and explanation for #21.

25 Instead of the letters (*pratyāhāra*) called *jhal* there shall be *jaś* (*pratyāhāra*) if *jhaś* (*pratyāhāra*) follow i.e. instead of *jha, bha, gha, ḍha, dha, ja, ba, ga, ḍa, da, kha, pha, cha, ṭha, tha, ca, ṭa, ta, ka, pa, śa, ṣa, sa, ha*
there is *ja, ba, ga, ḍa, da,*
if followed by *jha, bha, gha, ḍha, dha, ja, ba, ga, ḍa, da*
The *sūtra* comment carries on – **This is clear. Thus in placeof *dh* in the example there is *d*** so the example would now read *suddhy-upāsya*

26 Let there be *lopa* of a final of a word which ends with a *saṁyoga*
If a word ends with 2 consonants then the last is dropped.

27 Let a substitute take the place of only the final letter of that indicated in the 6th case e.g. *suddhy* becomes *suddh* but

28 For a final yan this is prohibited
so because *y* is a *yan* the *y* remains in *suddhy* and the final result is *suddhy-upāsya*

29 In place of *e, o, ai au* there are *ay, av, āy* and *āv*
Instead of an *ec* letter let there be *ay, av, āy* and *āv* if an *ac* follows.
e > *ay,* *o* > *av,* *ai* > *āy,* *au* > *āv*

30 If a rule concerns equal numbers of originals and substitutes then let their mutual order be that of their numbering. Thus as *e* > *ay, o* > *av, ai* > *āy, au* > *āv* so in the examples;
hare +e = haraye, viṣno +e = viṣnave, nai +aka = nāyaka, pau + aka = pāvaka

31 *av* and *āv* shall be substituted for corresponding *o* and *au* before an affix beginning with *y*.
Thus *go + yam = gavyam,* belonging to a cow, ***nau + yam = nāvyam*** accessible by boat

32 (except) in the sense of distance if *go* is followed by *yūti* (though this is not an affix) the the *o* of *go* becomes *av* ***go + yūti = gavyūti*** (about 4 miles)

33 Short *a, and eṅ (e* and *o)* are called *guṇa....*
Let short *a, e* and *o* be called *guṇa*

34 A vowel followed by the letter t, and a vowel following the letter t of that time measure.
A vowel followed by the letter *t* and a vowel following the letter *t* are to be pronounced with that same time measure name alone. (Limits the effect of 17 above.)

35 When *ac* comes after *a* or *ā* let *guṇa* be the single substitute for both. Examples-

> **The mouth positions for *a* and *i* combining produce *e***
> ***upa + indra = upendra (a +i = e)*** born after Indra (Kṛṣṇa)
> **The mouth positions for *a* and *u* combining produce *o***
> ***gaṅga + udakam = gaṅgodakam (a +u = o)*** the water of the Ganges

Note: From previous *sūtra* s: nearest substitute applies
any time measure of *i, u,* results in *e* or *o* respectively
Note: Following *sūtra* s restrict the operation of this *sūtra* to *a* followed by *ic*, (*i, u, ṛ, ḷ, e, o, ai, au*).
There are many more *sūtra* s along these lines. Lack of space prevents these being explained more adequately but it can be seen that it is a complex subject and requires discussion to fully understand.

Pratyāhāras

Here are the *pratyāhāras* from the *Maheśvarāṇi Sutrāṇi.*

1	*ak*	*a i u ṛ ḷ*
2	*ac*	*a i u ṛ ḷ e o ai au* all vowels
3	*aṭ*	*a i u ṛ ḷ e o ai au ha ya wa ra*
4	*aṇ*	*a i u*
5	*an*	*a i u ṛ ḷ e o ai au ha ya wa ra la*
6	*am*	*a i u ṛ ḷ e o ai au ha ya wa ra la ña ma ṅa ṇa na*
7	*al*	all the letters
8	*aś*	*a i u ṛ ḷ e o ai au ha ya va ra la ña ma ṅa ṇa na jha bha gha ḍha dha ja ba ga ḍa da*
9	*ik*	*i u ṛ ḷ*
10	*ic*	*i u ṛ ḷ e o ai au*
11	*iṇ*	*i u*
12	*uk*	*u ṛ ḷ*
13	*eṅ*	*e o*
14	*ec*	*e o ai au*
15	*aic*	*ai au*
16	*khay*	*kha pha cha ḍha tha ca ḍa ta ka pa*
17	*khar*	*kha pha cha ṭha tha ca ṭa ka pa śa ṣa sa* –unvoiced consonants having the qualities *vivāra* (open*) śvāsa* (with breath*) agoṣa* (unvoiced)
18	*ṅam*	*ṅa ṇa na*
19	*cay*	*ca ṭa ta ka pa*
20	*car*	*ca ṭa ta ka pa śa ṣa sa*
21	*chav*	*cha ṭha tha ca ṭa ta*
22	*jaś*	*ja ba ga ḍa da*
23	*jhay*	*jha bha gha ḍha dha ja ba ga ḍa da kha pha cha ṭha tha ca ṭa ta ka pa*
24	*jhar*	*jha bha gha ḍha dha jaba ga ḍa da kha pha cha ṭha tha ca ṭa ta ka pa śa ṣa sa*
25	*jhal*	*jha bha gha ḍha dha ja ba ga ḍa da kha pha cha ṭha tha ca ṭa ta ka pa śa ṣa sa ha*
26	*jhaś*	*jha bha gha ḍha dha ja ba ga ḍa da*
27	*jhaṣ*	*jha bha gha ḍha dha*
28	*baś*	*ba ga ḍa da*
29	*bhaṣ*	*bha gha ḍha dha*
30	*may*	*ma ṅa ṇa na jha bha gha ḍha dha ja ba ga ḍa da kha pha cha ṭha tha ca ṭa ta ka pa*
31	*yañ*	*ya va ra la ña ma ṅa ṇa na jha bha*
32	*yaṇ*	*ya va ra la (*the *antaḥstha)*
33	*yam*	*ya va ra la ña ma ṅa ṇa na*
34	*yay*	*ya va ra la ña ma ṅa ṇa na jha bha gha ḍha dha ja ba ga ḍa da kha pha cha ṭha tha ca ṭa ta ka pa* (all consonants except the sibilants)
35	*yar*	*ya va ra la ña ma ṅa ṇa na jha bha gha ḍha dha ja ba ga ḍa da kha pha cha ṭha tha ca ṭa ta ka pa śa ṣa sa* (all consonants except *ha*)
36	*ral*	*ra la ña ma ṅa ṇa na jha bha gha ḍha dha ja ba ga ḍa da kha pha cha ṭha tha ca ṭa ta ka pa śa ṣa sa*

		(all consonants except *ya* and *va*)
37	*val*	*va ra la ña ma ṅa ṇa na jha bha gha ḍha dha ja ba ga ḍa da kha pha cha ṭha tha ca ṭa ta ka pa śa ṣa sa* (all consonants except *ya*)
38	*vaś*	*va ra la ña ma ṅa ṇa na jha bha gha ḍha dha ja ba ga ḍa da*
39	*śar*	*śa ṣa sa*
40	*śal*	*śa ṣa sa ha* (the *ūṣmanāḥ* sounds)
41	*hal*	*ha ya va ra la ña ma ṅa ṇa na jha bha gha ḍha dha ja ba ga ḍa da kha pha cha ṭha tha ca ṭa ta ka pa śa ṣa sa ha*
42	*haś*	*ha ya va ra la ña ma ṅa ṇa na jha bha gha ḍha dha ja ba ga ḍa da* (The voiced consonants. They are *saṁvāra* (closed), *nāda* (resonant) and *ghoṣa* (voiced).

Abbreviated External (between words) Sandhi Rules

Most sanskrit sandhi may be addressed by using the shortened rules on the next 2 pages and the tables on the following page. Otherwise a more complete set of rules follows.

A final letter and an initial letter are joined except as specified. e.g. There are no sandhi changes if the first word ends in a vowel and the next begins with a consonant. i.e. the gap between the words remains.

Ac (Vowel) Sandhi

1. Final *i, u, ṛ,* before any initial vowel is replaced by its nearest *yan (y, v, r).* e.g.
   namati + api = namatyapi

2. Final *e, o, ai, au,* before any initial vowel is replaced by *ay, av, aay, aav* respectively.
   e.g. *hare + iti = harayiti*

3. When any length of *a* is followed by any length of an *ik (i, u ṛ, ḷ,),* the sandhi is *e,o,ar,al.*

Final *a /ā* +	initial *i/ī combine to become*	*= e*	*parama + īśvara = parameśvara*
a /ā +	*u/ū combine to become*	*= o*	*sītā + utiṣṭhati = sītotiṣṭhati*
a /ā +	*ṛ/ṝ combine to become*	*= ar*	*mahā + ṛṣi = maharṣi*
a / ā +	*ḷ combine to become*	*= al*	*tava + ḷkāra = tavalkāra*

thus both sounds combine to become one sound

4. When final *a/ā* is followed by *e* or *ai* then both are replaced by *ai*
   atra + eva =atraiva *kṛṣṇa +aiśvarya = kṛṣṇaiṣvarya*
   when final *a/ā* is followed by *o* or *au* then both are replaced by *au*
   gaṅgā + ojas = gaṅgaujas *putra + aumya = putraumya*

5. When any *ak (a,i,u,ṛ,ḷ),* letter of any length is followed by the same *ak* letter regardless of length the *saṁdhi* is the *dīrgha* form.
   a or *ā* + *a* or *ā* = *ā* *atra + ākāśaḥ = atrākāśaḥ*

6. When *e* or *o* at the end of a word is followed by a short *a*, the *a* disappears. This is indicated by an *avagraha* symbol. e.g. *puṣpe + asti = puṣpe'sti* पुष्पे⊠ ऽस्ति

7. When *ay* or *āy* are followed by an *ac* the final *y* disappears but there is no further joining up. (ay and āy come from application of rule 2).
   rathay + icchati = ratha icchati

8. *ī,ū,* and *e* as dual endings are not subject to sandhi.

9. Sandhi is not applied to the final vowel of an interjection (usually a vocative)
   e.g. *he arjuna* (O Arjuna)

Hal (Consonant) Sandhi

1. Final त्
2. ् followed by क् ख् त् थ् प् फ् ष् स् joins directly e.g.

तत् + करोति = तत्करोति   but

when त is followed by च् or छ् it is replaced by च्, तत् + च = तच्च

or when followed by श् it is replaced by च and श् is replaced by छ्

तत् + शृनोति = तच्छृनोति

Final त् followed by a स्वर् or most हश् letters is replaced by द. e.g.

तत् + इति = तदिति

If त् is followed by a ज् or झ् , it is replaced by ज् , तत् + जगत् =तज्जगत्

If त् is followed by a न् or म् it is replaced by न् ,

तत् + न =तन्न, तत् + मम = तद्मम → तन्मम

When त् is followed by a ह् it is replaced by द and the ह् is replaced by ध्

तत् + हस्त: = तद्धस्त:

3. Final न् followed by most व्यञ्जन or a स्वर remains unchanged
4. If न is preceded by a short स्वर and followed by any स्वर it is doubled

अभवन् + इति =अभवन्निति , तस्मिन् + एव = तस्मिन्नेव

5. Final म् followed by a व्यञ्जन is replaced by an अनुस्वार, रामम् + वा = रामं वा

Visarga sandhi   Apply the following rules in the listed sequence

1. A *visarga* remains a *visarga* before all *khar* letters except for these cases below.
A *visarga* before *t* or *th* is replaced by halanta *s* e.g. *rāmaḥ + tat = rāmastat*
A visarga before *ṭ* or *ṭh* is replaced by halanta *ṣ* e.g. *rāmaḥ + ṭīkā = rāmaṣṭīkā*
A visarga before *c* or *ch* is replaced by halanta *ś* e.g. *rāmaḥ + ca = rāmaśca*

2. If the *visarga* has a short *a* before and after then apply 2a.
If it has short *a* before and is followed by a *haś* then apply 2b.
2a *aḥ + a* is replaced by *o'* e.g. *rāmaḥ + asti = rāmo'sti*
2b *aḥ + haś* is replaced by *o + haś* e.g. *rāmaḥ + bhavati = rāmo bhavati*

3. A *visarga* preceded by an *ic* (any *svara* except *a* or *ā*) and followed by an *ac* or a *haś* is replaced by *r* e.g. *hariḥ + eva = harireva, guruḥ + mama = gururmama*
4. Applies to situations not covered by 1,2,3. A *visarga* is elided, but there is no subsequent sandhi if the elision produces 2 adjacent *svarāḥ*.
4a *aḥ* before any *ac* except short *a* becomes *a* e.g. *naraḥ + eva = nara eva*
4b *āḥ* before any *ac* or *haś* becomes *ā. e.g. narāḥ + bhavanti = narā bhavanti*
5. *saḥ* and *eṣaḥ* lose the *visarga* if followed by a *hal* (any consonant).
e.g. *saḥ + bhavati* becomes *sa bhavati*,

nb. do not apply *ac* sandhi after applying *visarga* sandhi

अ इ ऋ ऌ उ ए ओ ऐ औ *khar* (unvoiced) क च ट त प ख छ ठ थ फ ग ज ड द ब घ झ ढ ध भ ङ ञ ण न म ह य र ल व श ष स	अ इ ऋ ऌ उ ए ओ ऐ औ क च ट त प ख छ ठ थ फ *haś* (voiced) ग ज ड द ब घ झ ढ ध भ ङ ञ ण न म ह य र ल व श ष स	
अ इ ऋ ऌ उ *ac* all vowels ए ओ ऐ औ क च ट त प ख छ ठ थ फ ग ज ड द ब घ झ ढ ध भ ङ ञ ण न म ह य र ल व श ष स	अ इ ऋ ऌ उ *ak* the simple vowels ए ओ ऐ औ *ec* क च ट त प ख छ ठ थ फ ग ज ड द ब घ झ ढ ध भ ङ ञ ण न म ह य र ल व श ष स	अ इ ऋ ऌ उ *ik* ए ओ *eṅ* ऐ औ क च ट त प ख छ ठ थ फ ग ज ड द ब घ झ ढ ध भ ङ ञ ण न म ह य र ल व *yaṇ* श ष स

Sandhi - definition MW 144/3 *(saṁdhi)* mfn. -containing a conjunction or transition from one to the other. junction, connection, combination, euphonic junction of final and initial letters in grammar (every sentence being regarded as a euphonic chain, a break in which occurs at the end of a sentence and is denoted by a *virāma* or *avasāna,* 'stop'. This euphonic combination causes modifications of the final and initial letters of the separate words of a sentence and in the final letters of roots and stems when combined with endings).

Without familiarity with the basic rules of *sandhi* it is impossible to understand a *Sanskrit* sentence. The *sandhi* rules are grouped as external (between words), or internal (within words), and sub-grouped to vowels, consonants and *visarga sandhi* .

External Sandhi Rules When is *sandhi* applied? All words are joined together except if:

- the word ends in a *svara* and is followed by a consonant.
- the word ends in an *anusvara*
- the word ends in a *visarga*
- the word ends a sentence

Vowel (*ac*) Sandhi

The general rule is 2 vowels should not come into direct contact. This is usually managed by replacing the 2 vowels by one in a harmonious way. This can be done by:

- the combination of the 2 vowels into one
- change of the prior vowel to a consonant which then forms a single syllable with the remaining vowel
- loss of one of the vowels

Vowel Sandhi Rules

The study of *Pāṇini's* work regarding sandhi is beyond the scope of this work so only the briefest indications are given of a few *sūtra* s. The rules should be applied in sequence.

1. The *sūtra* from *Pāṇini 'iko yaṇāci'* translates as

'In place of an *ik* letter (*i,u,ṛ,ḷ,*) before an *ac* (any vowel) there is a corresponding *yan* (*y,r,l,w*) letter.'

Final *i,* or *ī* + initial vowel = *y* +(any) vowel	*namati + api = namatyapi*
Final *u,* or *ū* + initial vowel = *v* + (any) vowel	*guru + atha = gurvatha*
Final *ṛ* + initialvowel = *r* + (any) vowel	*pitṛ + eka = pitreka*

2. *Pāṇini – eco'yavāyāvaḥ*

An *ec* (*e,o,ai,au,*) letter before an *ac* (any vowel) is replaced by *ay, av, āy, āv* respectively.

hare + iti = harayiti

viṣṇo + idam = viṣṇavidam

tasmai + eva = tasmāyeva

rāmau + asti = rāmāvasti

Note that the prior sound is replaced while the following *ac* remains unchanged.

Exception –if *e* or *o* are followed by a short *a* then the *e* or *o* remains but the *a* disappears and to indicate this has happened an *avagraha* (') is inserted in its place.

e + a = e + avagraha *puṣpe +asti = puṣpe'sti*

viṣṇo + arhati = viṣṇo'rhati

Supplementary rule – When *ay* or *āy* are followed by an *ac* then the *y* disappears and the words are not joined.

e + vowel = a + vowel	*grāme+ iti* →	*grāmay iti*	→	*grāma iti*
ai + vowel = āy + vowel	*tasmai + atra* →	*tasmāy atra*	→	*tasmā atra*

3. *Pāṇini - ādguṇaḥ* With the help of previous utterances this has been translated as - 'When any form of *a* is followed by an *ac* there is *guṇa* in place of both.' The meaning of *guṇa* is explained elsewhere but is concerned here with the measure of vowel *a*. Consequently the practical meaning becomes-

When any length of *a* is followed by any length of an *ik (i, u ṛ, ḷ,)*, the sandhi is *e,o,ar,al,* respectively.

a + ī = e *parama + īśvara = parameśvara*

a + u = o *sītā + utiṣṭhati = sītotiṣṭhati*

a + ṛ = ar *maha + ṛṣi = maharṣi*

a + ḷ = al *tava + ḷakāra = tavalakāra*

Note: Both sounds combine to form one new sound.

There are other modifying or limiting *sūtra* s from *Pāṇini* that prevent untoward effects from previous *sūtrāṇi* or add precision. e.g.

Pāṇini – uraṇraparaḥ 'When an *aṇ* letter takes the place of *ṛ* there is a following *r*.

(ii) a long final *ā* produces *ar* or *al* as above not *ār* or *āl.*

Pāṇini – vṛddhireci 'When any form of *a* is followed by (or before) an *ec* there is *vṛddhi* in place of both.'(*Vṛddhi* is to do with the strongest measure of the vowel *a* so the meaning becomes –

4.When any length of final *a* is followed by an *ec* (*e,ai,o,au,*) letter, the sandhi is *ai* when *e* or *ai* follow and *au* when *o* or *au* follow.

a + e = ai *atra + eva = atraiva* (right here)

a + o = au *gaṅga + ojas = gaṅgaujas*

a + ai = ai *kṛṣṇa + aiśvarya = kṛṣṇaiśvarya*

a + au =au *putra + aumya = putraumya*

Both sounds combine to form one sound.

5. **When an *ak* (*a,i,u,ṛ,ḷ,*) letter of any length is followed by the same *ak* letter of any length then the sandhi form is the *dirgha* form**

a + a = ā, *a + ā = ā* , *ā + a = ā* , *ā + ā = ā*

atra + ākāśaḥ = atrākāśaḥ

śrī + īśaḥ = śrīśaḥ

tu + uttiṣṭhati = tūttiṣṭhati

kartṛ + ṛṇām = kartṛṇām

kanyā + api = kanyāpi

6. **When a final *eṅ* (*e,o*) is followed by *hraswa a* the *a* disappears. This is indicated by substituting an *avagraha.*** ऽ

puṣpe + asti = puṣpe'sti पुष्पेऽस्ति

viṣṇo + arhati = viṣṇo'rhati विष्णोऽर्हति

Notes:

- The vowels *–i, ī, u,ū,* and *e* are not subject to sandhi when they serve as dual endings. e.g. *bāle āgacchataḥ* the 2 girls come, needs no *sandhi.*
- The final vowel of a particle or an interjection (usually a vocative) needs no sandhi e.g. *aho aśva* (O horse!)
- There are no sandhi changes if the first word ends in a vowel (excluding *ḥ* and *ṁ)* and the second word begins with a consonant. i.e. the gap between words remains.
- The *i* or *ī* of pronoun *amī* is not subject to sandhi.

Vowel Sandhi can be determined from the following chart.
Note: 'o' is not shown as a final because it is so rare

Final Vowels →		*a, ā*	*i, ī*	*u, ū*	*ṛ*	*e*	*ai*	*au*
Initial Vowels ↓	*a*	*ā*	*ya*	*va*	*ra*	*e '*	*ā a*	*āva*
	ā	*ā*	*y ā*	*v ā*	*r ā*	*a ā*	*ā āà*	*ā v ā*
	i	*e*	*ā*	*vi*	*ri*	*a i*	*ā i*	*ā vi*
	ī	*e*	*ī*	*vī*	*rī*	*a ī*	*ā ī*	*ā vī*
	u	*o*	*yu*	*ū*	*ru*	*a u*	*ā u*	*ā vu*
	ū	*o*	*yu*	*ū*	*rū*	*a ū*	*ā ū*	*ā vū*
	ṛ	*ar*	*yṛ*	*vṛ*	*ṝ*	*a ṛ*	*ā ṛ*	*ā vṛ*
	e	*ai*	*ye*	*ve*	*re*	*a e*	*ā e*	*ā ve*
	ai	*ai*	*yai*	*vai*	*rai*	*a ai*	*ā ai*	*ā vai*
	o	*au*	*yo*	*vo*	*ro*	*a o*	*ā o*	*ā vo*
	au	*au*	*yau*	*vau*	*rau*	*a au*	*ā au*	*ā vau*

Notes:

- Enter the chart with the last letter of the first word and the first letter of the second word. The answer is substituted for both. e.g. –e + a- = ai
- Under *e* , and *ai* above are 2 letters separated by a space. This indicates that the words remain separate and indicates the last letter of the first word and the first letter of the second word.
- The apostrophe (') represents the missing letter a. This is termed *avagraha* meaning separation. Missing means it is neither seen nor pronounced.

examples *i + ū = yū,* *ṛ+ i = ri,* *i + u = yu,* *au + o = ā vo*

Consonant *(hal)* Sandhi Table

Permitted final letters across the top. Initial letters of the next word down the right side.

k	*ṭ*	*t*	*p*	*ì*	*n*	*m*	*ḥ/r* except *āḥ/ḥ*	*āḥ*	*aḥ*	Initial letters ↓
k	*ṭ*	*t*	*p*	*ṅ*	*n*	*ṁ*	*ḥ*	*āḥ*	*aḥ*	*k/kh*
g	*ḍ*	*d*	*b*	*ṅ*	*n*	*ṁ*	*r*	*ā*	*o*	*g/gh*
k	*ṭ*	*c*	*p*	*ṅ*	*ṁ ś*	*ṁ*	*ś*	*āś*	*aś*	*c/ch*
g	*ḍ*	*ḍ*	*b*	*ṅ*	*ṇ*	*ṁ*	*r*	*ā*	*o*	*j/jh*
k	*ṭ*	*ṭ*	*p*	*ṅ*	*ṁṣ*	*ṁ*	*ṣ*	*āṣ*	*aṣ*	*ṭ /ṭh*
g	*ḍ*	*ò*	*b*	*ṅ*	*ṇ*	*ṁ*	*r*	*ā*	*o*	*ḍ/ḍh*
k	*ṭ*	*t*	*p*	*ṅ*	*ṁs*	*ṁ*	*s*	*ās*	*as*	*t/th*
g	*ḍ*	*d*	*b*	*ṅ*	*n*	*ṁ*	*r*	*ā*	*o*	*d/dh*
k	*ṭ*	*t*	*p*	*ṅ*	*n*	*ṁ*	*ḥ*	*āḥ*	*aḥ*	*p/ph*
g	*ḍ*	*d*	*b*	*ṅ*	*n*	*ṁ*	*r*	*ā*	*o*	*b/bh*
ṅ	*ṇ*	*n*	*m*	*ṅ*	*n*	*ṁ*	*r*	*ā*	*o*	*nasals n/m*
g	*ḍ*	*d*	*b*	*ṅ*	*n*	*ṁ*	*r*	*ā*	*o*	*y/v*
g	*ḍ*	*d*	*b*	*ṅ*	*n*	*ṁ*	*zero 1*	*ā*	*o*	*r*
g	*ḍ*	*l*	*b*	*ṅ*	*ll 2*	*ṁ*	*r*	*ā*	*o*	*l*
k	*ṭ*	*c ch*	*p*	*ṅ*	*ñ ś/ch*	*ṁ*	*ḥ*	*āḥ*	*aḥ*	*ś*
k	*ṭ*	*t*	*p*	*ṅ*	*n*	*ṁ*	*ḥ*	*āḥ*	*aḥ*	*ṣ/s*
gg h	*ḍḍ h*	*dd h*	*bb h*	*ṅ*	*n*	*ṁ*	*r*	*ā*	*o*	*h*
g	*ḍ*	*d*	*b*	*ṅ/ṅ3*	*n/nn 3*	*m*	*r*	*ā*	*a 4*	*vowels*
k	*ṭ*	*t*	*p*	*ṅ*	*n*	*ṁ*	*ḥ*	*āḥ*	*aḥ*	*zero*

1 – *ḥ or r* disappears and if *a/i/u* precedes, these lengthen to *ā/ī/ū*

2 e.g. *tān* + *lokān* = *tāl lokān*

3 Doubling occurs if the preceding vowel is short.

4 Except *aḥ* + *a* =*o*

Note : Zero refers to the lowest grade of vowel strength.

Hal (Consonant) Sandhi

- Only a vowel or a single consonant may end a word. If there is more than one then all except the first are dropped. There are only 8 allowable absolute final consonants i.e. that have no sound following in a sentence or as a single word. *k, ṭ, t, p, ṅ, n, m,* and *visarga*
- *Hal* sandhi is not applied until the word termination has been reduced to one permissible letter.
- Final *s* becomes a *visarga*. See *visarga sandhi*
- ***k, t, ṭ,* and *p*** Note that these are the first in each family of consonants except the palatal. Other consonants are replaced by the first in that family.

    anuṣṭubh → anuṣṭup, *suhṛd → suhṛt*

    Palatals cannot appear in absolute final position.

    c → k *vāc → vāk*

    j → ṭ or k *bhiṣaj → bhiṣak ,* *virāj → virāṭ*

    A final consonant before a vowel beginning the following word or before a voiced consonant (*haś*) must be voiced. Consequently ***k, t, ṭ,* and *p*** may need to be replaced by their voiced equivalents-

    -k → -g, *-ṭ → -ḍ,* *-t → -d,* *-p → -b*

Sandhi changes by final letter

1. Final त् followed by क् ख् त् थ् प् फ् ष् स् joins directly e.g.

    तत् + करोति = तत्करोति

    but when त is followed by च् or छ् it is replaced by च्, तत् + च = तच्च

    or when followed by श् it is replaced by च and श् is replaced by छ्

    तत् + शृनोति = तच्छृनोति

Final त् followed by a स्वर or most हश् letters is replaced by द. e.g.तत् + इति = तदिति

If त् is followed by a ज् or झ् , it is replaced by ज् , तत् + जगत् =तज्जगत्

If त् is followed by a nasal it optionally changes to the nasal of its own family.

तत् + न =तन्न, तत् + मम → तद्मम → तन्मम

When त् is followed by a ह् it is replaced by द and the ह् is replaced by ध्

e.g. तत् + हस्त: = तद्धस्त:

-*t* before *l-* is changed to -*l* as in *tal labhate*

2. Final न् followed by most व्यञ्जन or a स्वर remains unchanged.

3. If न् is preceded by a short स्वर and followed by any स्वर it is doubled.

अभवन् + इति =अभवन्निति , तस्मिन् + एव = तस्मिन्नेव

-*n* before *c-/ch- or t-/th- or ṭ-/ṭh-*

the *n* is dropped, the prior vowel is nasalised and *ś, ṣ, or s* respectively is interposed.

e.g. *kumārān ca → kumārāṁśca*

-*n* following *-c or -j* within a word is changed to *ñ.* thus, *yācñā,* or *yajñā*

-*n* of √*han* is lost before endings beginning with *t-/th-* e.g. *hatha* 2/pl/pres, *hata* ppp.

-*n* before *j-* → *ñ*

-*n* before *l-* → nasalised *-l* usually written as an *l* with *candrabindu* above

-*n* before *ś-* → *ñ* and the *ś* nearly always → *ch-* e.g. *tān śatrūn →tāñchatrūn*

-*n followed by -n, -m, -y, -v, with prior r, ṛ, ṝ, or ṣ* changes to *ṇ.* Intervening sounds may prevent this taking place i.e. a palatal (except *c*), cerebral, or dental. When there are two -*n*- s juxtaposed both become cerebral. e.g. *karṇa, akṣiṇi, nāriṇām, ṛṣiṇa, rūpeṇa, rāmāyaṇa, niṣaṇṇa*

-*n* following -*ṣ* becomes *ṇ* as in *tṛṣṇa* or *uṣṇa*

4.Final म् followed by a व्यञ्जन is replaced by an अनुस्वार e.g.

रामम् + वा = रामं वा

Other occurrences, options and exceptions

-*k* to -*ṅ* may occur e.g. *vāṅ me* for *vāk me*

-*p* before a voiced palatal *j-* is assimilated to → *-b* - *ap+ ja abja* born in water

This is more common in compounds than between words.

k, t, ṭ, p before *h-* is changed to *-g, - ḍ, -d, -b* respectively and the *h-* is changed to *gh-, ḍh-, dh-, bh-* respectively. *e.g. vāk hi → vāgghi, śarat hi → śaraddhi*

-gh (representing *h), -dh, -bh* followed by *t- or th-* become *-gdh-, -ddh-, -bdh-* as in *dagdha, digdha, buddha, buddhi, boddhum, banddhum, labdha, labdhvā*

ch- is doubled following a short vowel e.g. *eṣa cchāgaḥ* Note an aspirated consonant is doubled by adding the preceding un-aspirated equivalent.

Visarga sandhi

- ***s*** The most common of the consonant finals, *s* becomes *visarga* in absolute final position. It could be thought of as unstable.

1. A *visarga* remains a *visarga* before all *khar* letters except for the special cases below.
A *visarga* before *t* or *th* is replaced by halanta *s* e.g. *rāmaḥ + tat = rāmastat*
A *visarga* before *ṭ* or *ṭh* is replaced by halanta *ṣ* e.g. *rāmaḥ + ṭīkā = rāmaṣṭīkā*
A *visarga* before *c* or *ch* is replaced by halanta *ś* e.g. *rāmaḥ + ca = rāmaśca*

2. If rule 1 does not apply then rule 2a applies if the *visarga* has a short *a* before and after.
2a *aḥ + a* is replaced by *o'*
e.g. *rāmaḥ + asti = rāmo'sti*
2b *aḥ + haś* is replaced by *o + haś* e.g. *rāmaḥ + bhavati = rāmo bhavati*

3. A *visarga* preceded by an *ic* (any *svara* except *a* or *ā*) and followed by an *ac* or a *haś* is replaced by *r* e.g. *hariḥ + eva = harireva*
guruḥ + mama = gururmama
If two *r s* would result then the first one is dropped and the prior vowel if short is lengthened eg *nṛpatī ramate*

4. Applies to situations not covered by 1,2,3. A *visarga* is elided, but there is no subsequent sandhi if the elision produces 2 adjacent *svarāḥ.*
4a *aḥ* before any *ac* except short *a* becomes *a* e.g. *naraḥ + eva = nara eva*
4b *āḥ* before any *ac* or *haś*becomes *ā*
e.g. *narāḥ + bhavanti = narā bhavanti*

5. *saḥ* and *eṣaḥ* lose the *visarga* if followed by a *hal* (any consonant) or an *ic.*
When they occur before *a* then rule 2a above applies.
nb. do not apply *ac* sandhi after applying *visarga* sandhi

bhoḥ an exclamatory particle loses its *visarga* before vowels and voiced consonants.

e.g. *bho indra*

r Original final *r* becomes *visarga* and sometimes behaves like final *s.*

punar → *punaḥ*

Internal sandhi (within a word)

Because the Sanskrit words we use are already formed it is not necessary to go deeply into the rules for construction of words. Some essential rules are given but the main principle is that the rules enable practical pronunciation of words which would otherwise require difficult or impractical changes of mouth position. The changes smooth out these changes to accommodate the flow of speech. For instance the past passive participle of root *budh* – (awake) could be *budhta* but is in fact *buddha* (awakened) because it assimilates the voicing and aspiration of the final sound of the root.

frequent occurrences -	*i* or *ī* change to *iy*	*dhī+i = dhiyi* 7/s in thought
	u or *ū* change to *uv*	*bhū+i =bhuvi 7/s* on earth
	ṝ changes to *ir*	*gṝ + ati = girati* he swallows

ṝ before a final consonant changes to *īr*
ṝ after *oṣṭau* letters changes to *ūr*
ṛ after a single consonant but before *y* changes to *ri*
e ai o au before suffixes beginning with vowels or y change to *ay āy av āv* respectively

Final verbal and nominal stems do not change before terminations beginning with vowels.
e.g. *prāñc-aḥ* eastern, *vacāni* let me speak
Nominals or verbal stems ending in consonants lose that consonant if they are followed by a termination consisting of a single consonant. (Remember you cannot finish a word with 2 consonants). The remaining consonant is treated according to external sandhi. Thus *prāñc* + *s* becomes *prāṅ* by the following process.

- the *s* is dropped
- the *tālu* letters change to *kaṇṭha* because a palatal may not end a word =*prāṅk*
- the *k* is dropped because 2 consonants may not end a word = *prāṅ* eastern

Aspirated letters followed by any letters except vowels, semi-vowels or nasals lose their aspiration e.g. *rundh* + *dhve* = *runddhve.* But if a voiced final aspirate is followed by *t* or *th* of a suffix the combination becomes voiced and the aspiration is transferred to the initial of the ending.
e.g. *budh* + *ta* → *buddha, rundh* + *tas* →*runddhas, labh* + *ta* → *labdha,*
Also *h* coming initially from *gh* is treated similarly – from *duh* →*dugdha*
However the final consonant of a root or stem e.g. √*vac* or the noun *vāc,* may not be changed for a number of reasons. e.g. *uvāc-a.* said (perfect tense)
or *vāc* may → *vāk or vāg* depending on the next sound, e.g. *vāg-bhyam, vāk-ṣu*

The following table describes conditions causing *s* to change to *ṣ*

Preceding letters *i, ī, u,ū, ṛ,ṝ, e, ai, o, au, k, r,*	regardless of intervening letters *ṁ* or *ḥ*	cause a following *s* to change to ṣ	unless it is a final letter or followed by *r*

e.g. *deveṣu, agniṣu, dikṣu, adikṣam, havīṁṣi, haviḥṣu*

If the following sound is *t, th,* or *n* this also becomes *mūrdha* .

thus *tisthati* becomes *tiṣṭhati*

Note that there are exceptions to the rule.

A similar rule relates to *n* changing to *ṇ*

Preceding letters *r, ṛ, ṝ, ṣ*	regardless of intervening *k, kh, g, gh, ṇ, p, ph, b, bh, m, v, y, h, ṁ*, or any vowels	cause a subsequent *n* to change to *ṇ*	if followed by any vowels or *n, m, y, v*.

e.g. *sad* (sit) + prefix *ni* = *nisanna* (seated)

from the first table this becomes *niṣanna*

from the second it becomes *niṣaṇṇa*

These rules do not apply between the components of compound words but do apply with prefixes, verbal prefixes and suffixes.e.g. *guru* + *su* = *guruṣu*. There are exceptions to these rules.

-*c*- within a word is doubled to *cch* e.g. *gacchati*

If -*h*- is followed by *s*

or roots beginning with *d*- are followed by *t, th, dh*, then

k, t, ñ, p before *h*- is changed to -*g*, - *ḍ*, -*d*, -*b* respectively and the *h*- is changed to *gh-, ḍh-, dh-, bh-* respectively. *e.g.leh* + *si* = *lekṣi, dah* + *syati* = *dhakṣyati* he will burn. These examples may appear to be wrong and confusing but are the result of the application of all the appropriate rules.

-*m*- before suffixes beginning with *v*- changes to *n* *e.g. ja-+gam+vān* → *jaganvān*

-*n*- is not changed by following *y* or *v* e.g. *hanyamane* being killed, *tanvan* stretching

-as final of a root becomes *anusvāra* before *s*

-sometimes becomes *t* as a final of roots or nominal stems

-*s*- between consonants (partic. dentals) -s- may be lost e.g. *utthita* for *utsthita*

after *k* -*s*- may be lost, e.g. *abhaksta* → *abhakta*

after -*dh* -*s*- is lost (In this example the -*dh* then combines with following *t-/th-* into *-ddh)* *abudhsta* becomes *abuddha*

as a final root or nominal stem letter becomes *t* before the *s* of many verbal suffixes e.g. *vas* becomes *vat-syati* will dwell,

A consonant following *r* or *l* is often doubled e.g. *alppa* for *alpa*, *arttha* for *artha*. Sometimes a consonant that theoretically should be doubled is written as single. e.g. *pattra*, or *patra*

समास - Compound words

Sanskrit is full of compound words which have the generic name *samāsa*. They may be composed of 2 to 10 or even more words.

As a general rule, all words except the last drop their *pratyaya* (endings). They appear in that form which is their base or stem, and when they have more than one, their *pada* base . (That used for 3rd to 7th cases and 2nd pl. when a noun has 2 bases.)

....

> The principal part is called the *pradhāna* -680/3 (in gram.) the principal member of a compound, as opposed to *upasarjana* 210/2 (in gram.) subordinate or secondary

There are a number of different types. Sometimes a compound may be of 2 types depending on how it is used in a sentence. The Sanskrit name for each type of compound is a traditional example of that type.

***bahuvrīhi (much-riced) compound* – neither member is principal.**
The name 'much-riced' is a description of an individual as wealthy (i.e. one who has much rice), so it is a good example of a compound which is always adjectival to a noun or pronoun, either expressed or implicit. *Bahuvrīhi* compounds frequently take suffixes. The last member is a noun and the first usually an adjective. It may often be translated by placing the word 'having' in front. It's structure can most simply be explained by examples. A typical form is -"He whose B (last member) is A (first member)".

e.g. दिर्घनासिकः one whose nose is long

or

"One by whom something is somethinged"

त्यक्ताहङ्कार one by whom *ahaṃkāra* has been abandoned

i.e. "This of which the B (last member) is A (first member)".

redneck – he whose neck is red
bluebeard – he whose beard is blue
hardhat – he whose hat is hard

mahāratha – he whose chariot is mighty
dhṛtarāṣṭra – proper name – he by whom the kingdom is held
mahābāho – vocative – o thou whose arms are mighty
anantarūpa – that of which the form is unending
avyaktādīni – such that their beginnings are unmanifest

translation process

- look up the 2 parts in the dictionary to establish independent meanings
- translate as a *karmadhāraya tatpuruṣa* eg steady wisdom
- translate as a *bahuvrīhi samāsa* eg he of steady wisdom

The last word of a *bahuvrīhi* compound takes the gender of the word to which it is related.

When a past participle comes first ambiguity can occur and should be resolved by context or other references.

dvandva (copulative) compound – **both members are principal**
dvaṁdva 503/2 pair, couple, male and female, a pair of opposites, a copulative compound or any compound in which the members if uncompounded would be in the same case and connected by the conjunction "and"

there are 2 kinds *itaretara* and *samāhāra*

itaretara (164/3 one with another, mutual, respective) The members are viewed separately. The termination could be dual or plural depending on the number of words forming the compound and it takes the gender of the final member.

rāmasīte – *rāma* and *sītā*	1/du/f
hastyaśvau an elephant and a horse	1/du/m
śuklakṛṣṇau black and white	1/du/m

अश्वगजबालनराः नृत्यन्ति horses, elephants, children and men are dancing 1/pl/m

samāhāra- (1163/3 summing up, sum, totality, collection, conjunction or connecting of words or sentences (as by the particle ca), a compound, (esp. applied to a *dvandva* whose last member is in the neuter gender or to a *dvigu*, when it expresses an aggregate.) The members are viewed as a whole and the ending is usually singular. e.g.

sukha-duḥkam – happiness and suffering	1/s/n
hastyaśvam – horses and elephants (in an army)	1/s/n
gavāśvam – a cow and a horse	1/s/n

....

tatpuruṣa compound – **2nd member is principal** a compound of words which would normally have different case endings in which the last member is qualified by the first. It has a nominal function. e.g. *tatpuruṣa* his servant (the servant of the Absolute).
In *tatpuruṣa* the word *tat* is the base for the personal pronoun hence alternative personal pronouns may be deduced from it.
The last word may be a noun, participle or adjective (if capable of governing a noun).

A *tatpuruṣa* compound is one in which the final element, whether adjective or substantive, is merely further defined by what precedes it. To analyze it in English we often use a preposition, for instance
home-made - made in the home
hand-made - made by the hand
In Sanskrit the *vibhakti* relationships are used.
Here they are arranged by *vibhakti* (case).

1. blackbird, girlfriend,
2. sword-fight, hand-written

3. man-eating, door-stop,
4. dining-room
5. book-learning
6. status-symbol
7. side-door.

e.g. doghouse – a house for a dog, is a *tatpuruṣa* in the 4th case (4th case expresses to or for)

mountain peak – the peak of a mountain (6th case)
jīvaloka – living, world, the world of the living
rājendra – *rāja*, king, *indra*, chief, chief of kings
tatpuruṣa – his servant

the compound is also named after the case of the first member

द्वितीया ॥ अचलगतः gone to the mountain

तृतीया ॥ देवदत्तः given by God

चतुर्ती ॥ ध्यानशाला room for meditation

पञ्चमी ॥ स्वर्गपतितः fallen from heaven

षष्ठी ॥ रामदूतः messenger of Rāma

सप्तमी ॥ जलस्थः standing in the water

vyadhikaraṇa tatpuruṣa a compound that refers to different objects. The first member would be in a different case than the second if dissolved. There are 6 types corresponding to *vibhakti* 2 to 7 e.g. *tatpuruṣa* – his servant

……………………………..

karmadhāraya tatpuruṣa compound – both members refer to the same object and therefore would be in the same case if the compound were dissolved. e.g. *nīlotpalam* (*nīla* + *utpalam*) blue lotus. If the first member is a number it is called a ***dvigu.*** **)** The last word ending is often changed to masculine e.g. *rajan* king to *rajaḥ* but there are many other rules for these endings (refer Muller para 520), e.g. *mahāt* always becomes *mahā* e.g. *mahārājaḥ* great king.

There are 3 combinations
adjective + noun e.g. highway, or *mahādhana* – great wealth
noun+ noun e.g. gentleman-thief, or *rājarṣi* – king-sage
adjective+adjective – pale-red, or *uttarapūrva* – north-east

dvigu a ***karmadhāraya*** **compound that starts with a number e.g.**
dvigu - two cows
triloka – the 3 worlds
triguṇa – the 3 *guṇāḥ*

upapada (subordinate word). The second member is an adjusted verbal root . e.g. *jalamuc* water-dropping i.e. a cloud, *somapā* soma-drinking . Bases ending in a short vowel usually take a final *t.* e.g. *viśvajit* all-conquering from *ji* to conquer. *brahma-vit* – the knower of Brahman, *kumbha-kāra* a pot-maker or potter, *jala-da* a cloud, one who gives water. Although the last member is formed from a verb it is declined as a noun.

…………………………………..

upamāna *karmadhāraya* states a comparison e.g.
candramukham – a moonlike face

……………………………...........

nañ in which *na* is reduced to *a* or *an*
avidyā – ignorance

………………………………

prādi the first member is an *upasarga* . The compound is used as a nominal.
anusvāra – after sound

……………………………..

gati – (347/3 a term for prepositions and some other adverbial prefixes when immediately connected with the tenses of a verb or verbal derivatives) The first member is the prefix and the compound is used as a nominal.
antaryāmin – inner ruler

………………

aluk – *samāsa* case endings are retained e.g. *ātmanepadam* a word for one-self

………………..

amreḍita (iterative) Repetition of a word expresses repetition.
e.g. *dive-dive* day by day

avyayībhāva* compound- 1st member is principal.** (111/3 "unchangeable state", an indeclinable compound). This compound begins with an indeclinable (avyaya)*** and consequently the whole word is indeclinable and is used as an adverb.
yathānāma – my name
yathā –(according to) + *dharmam* – according to justice or law,
avyaybhāva – unchangeable state - indeclinable

यथाकालम् – according to time – i.e. at the proper time

prati – a variety of meanings e.g. towards as in पर्त्यग्नि facing the fire

every as in प्रतिदिनम् every day

upa – up to - उपतीरम् up to or near the shore

anu – following after अनुरथम् after the chariot

antar – within अन्तर्गिरि within a mountain

special case – *saha* often changes to *sa* सस्मितम् with a smile

kevala This is the name used for a compound which does not fit into any other category.

other remarks

A ***karmadhāraya*** *tatpuruṣa* compound may become a ***bahuvrīhi*** compound depending on how it is used. e.g. *nīlotpalam* (*nīla + utpalam*) "blue lotus" is a *tatpuruṣa* compound but in the phrase *nilotpalam saraḥ"* a blue lotus lake" it becomes an adjective and is therefore a *bahuvrīhi* compound.

There is no limit to the size of a Sanskrit compound. Many long compounds are made up of smaller compounds strung together. Hence analysis usually begins by identifying and translating the smaller units in a compound. This leads to seeing how the compound is built up.

A number of forms are used at the end of compounds that would never be used as words by themselves. In particular, many verbal roots are used, predominantly with an active participial sense. Roots in *ā* and certain others are simplified so as to end in *a*, and are inflected like *kānta* – thus *kāla-jña*, from *jñā.* It is also common for the root to be extended by *a* or for a *t* to be added. Monier-Williams in his dictionary uses the abbreviation ifc. specifically for final compound endings. ifc= in final compounds.

arthaḥ – (purpose) is used adverbially at the end of compounds, usually in the accusative case *artham* – for the sake of, *kim-artham* – for the sake of what, for what purpose, why

If pronouns are used as prior members of a compound, they are put in base forms, which are used regardless of the case, gender, or number of the pronoun.
mad- I *asmad*-we *tvad*- you *yuṣmad*-you *tad*- he, she, it, they

a comparative compound lotusfoot – a foot like a lotus

More examples of compounds

अश्वमुखः horse faced
उग्रःमुख grim-faced
त्रिःशीर्ष three-headed
कृश्नाःवर्ण black-coloured

dhṛtarāṣṭra – proper name – he by whom the kingdom is held
mahārathās 'those whose chariots are great' –great warriors 1/pl/m BV
kāmātmanas 272/3 whose very essence is desire, whose selves are desirous, given to lust, sensual

kāmarūpam desire-form, having the form of desire, which has the form of desire
lābhasamtuṣṭaḥ one who has found contentment
mahāratha – he whose chariot is mighty
phalahetavas those who are motivated by the fruit of action
prasannacetasas of him whose mind is tranquil
tadbuddhayas they whose minds are absorbed in
vigataspṛhas - gone away desire, whose desire has gone away
vītarāgabhayakrodhas- whose passion, fear and anger have departed

Dvandva a pair or couple
jayājayau victory and defeat (1/2/dual/ m *dvandva* comp.)
lābhālabhau gain and loss, (dual *dvandva* compound)

Tat-puruṣa
buddhibheda fragmentation of the mind
indriyārthan sense-objects, objects of the senses
janmakarmaphalapradām birth, action, fruit, offering offering rebirth as the fruit of action 2/s/f
karma-bandha bondage of karma
veda-vāda-ratās delighting in the doctrines of the *Veda* 1/pl/m
yajñabhāvitas sacrifice produced, brought into being by sacrifice, *yajña* + ppp √*bhū*

Syntax – grammar and traditional practices

Word Order

The basic structure in a sentence is- subject (with adjuncts), object (with adjuncts), verb but much of the literature is poetic and poets change the order as poets will.

- a vocative usually comes first
- adverbs are frequently near the beginning
- a word in the sixth case precedes its nominative
- adjectives precede their nouns
- a relative clause precedes a principal clause
- if the subject is a pronoun it may not be expressed (i.e. is assumed) unless required for emphasis
- 'is' is frequently omitted e.g. a sentence might read 'the wind (is) strong'. Where there is no verb the verb 'to be' should be assumed.

Number

Sanskrit grammar is arranged in singular, dual and plural.
ekavacana – speaking of one, *dvivacana* –speaking of two and *bahuvacana* – speaking of many
The last word in a compound expresses number for the compound
e.g. *jayājayau* victory and defeat (1/2/dual/ m *dvandva* comp.)
hastyaśvau an elephant and a horse
hastyaśvāḥ - horses and elephants
but a singular word may express a collective sense
hastyaśvam – horses and elephants (in an army)
strījana womenfolk, women
dual is often used for things occurring in pairs e.g. *oṣṭhau* lips
some nouns are used only in the plural e.g. *prāṇāḥ* life

Person

Verbs are conjugated in 3 'Persons' – he she or it, you, and I. These are listed in the reverse order from English.

Prathama means first and is expressed as he, she or it but one should remember it as representing the *puruṣa*, the first in the universe, visible or otherwise. *Puruṣa* is the light that illumines everything so that it can be he, she or it.

Madhyama (you) is the superlative of *madhya* meaning middle, middlemost, central, hence it represents the Supreme Self standing in front and not different from your own Self.

Uttama means first or best and as such it represents your own Self expressed as I or we.

Time

bhūtakāla past tense comes from *bhūta* a past participle from the root *bhū* become and 2.*kāla* 278/1 meaning time. Similarly in
vartamānakāla present tense, *vartamāna* is a present participle (see vocab). and in *bhaviṣyatkāla* future tense, the term *bhaviṣyat* is a future participle 'about to become'.

Rules of Concord

- adjectives agree with their nominal in case, gender and number
- verbs agree with the subject (normal construction) in case and number
- pronouns may agree in case, gender and number as appropriate
- When the particle *vā* (or) joins two nominatives the verb agrees with the nearest nominative.
- A dual or plural adjective that agrees with m. and f. substantives is put in masculine but when neuters are included it is put in the neuter.
- A singular collective noun is followed by a singular verb.

Articles

There is no true definite or indefinite article like 'a' or 'the' in Sanskrit.
Eka (one) sometimes serves like 'a' or *ekadā* as once.
Sa (that) may be seen as 'the' depending on its use.

Rules for application of *anusvara*-

(a) *Halanta m* at the end of a word
1. Is unchanged *(m)* when a vowel or nothing follows (end of sentence)
2. becomes *anusvara* (*ṁ*) compulsorily when followed by *ś, ṣ,* or *s*
3. becomes *parasavarna* nasal (a nasal of the same mouth position as the following letter) if followed by any consonant except a sibilant or *ḥ*

(b) The rules above also apply to a compound

(c) Within a word
1. *halanta n* or *m* followed by any consonant (not nasals or semi-vowels) must be changed to *anusvara.*
2. when *anusvara* is followed by any consonant except a sibilant then the *anusvara* must be sounded as the *parasavarna* e.g. *śāṁ* + *ta* = *śānta*

strengthening – the process of guṇa or vṛddhi

- Root strengthening to form verbs or nominatives is a factor which affects sandhi processes of word derivation. In most cases the root is strengthened by adding '*a*' and this is the *guṇa* form. Addition of another '*a'* creates the *vṛddhi* form. (Exception: short '*a*' is not changed in *guṇa.*) "Strengthened" simply means one or 2 vowels have been added. Consequently the meaning changes and the new word is looked up in the dictionary in the usual way.

- Here are some examples: in the middle row *a* has been added, in the 3rd row another *a* has been added.

  - root *guṇa vṛddhi*

    vid veda vaidya

    div deva daivika

    yuj yoga yaugika

    dhṛ dharma dhārmika

Locative and Genitive Absolute

An absolute phrase is one containing a participle the subject of which is different from the main verb subject. e.g. 'Having driven home, we had dinner.' When translated the construction is often changed to an adverbial clause. e.g. 'We had dinner after the drive home.' A special construction (called *sati saptami* or Locative Absolute *)* may be used in Sanskrit. The subject is put in the seventh (locative) case and the participle agrees with it in case, gender and number. This is mostly used where the meaning is 'while, when, since or although' .

e.g. *sainikeṣu iṣūn kṣipatsu senāpatiraśvamāruḍhaḥ*
sainikeṣu the soldiers (7/pl/m) *iṣūn* arrows (2/pl/m) *kṣipatsu* throwing or shooting (present participle 7/pl/m) *senāpatiraśvamāruḍhaḥ* the general mounted his horse,

the subject (soldiers) and the participle (shooting) are in the seventh case indicating the translation - 'While the soldiers were shooting arrows the general mounted his horse.'

The genitive absolute (*sataḥ ṣaṣṭhī)* is a clause implying contempt or a slighting.

e.g. *pasyato mūrkhasya* 'while a fool was looking on',
pasyataḥ past participle in the 6th case *mūrkhasya* 6/s/m

assumption of the verb 'to be'

The verb *as* "to be" may often be assumed if there is no obvious verb and the predicate (the part of the sentence which relates to the subject) is a noun. e.g. "My sister (is) a nurse."

names of countries from names of people

- The plural of the name of a people designates countries and regions e.g. *Madrāḥ* – the land of the *Madra*

nouns from verbs

kṛt vṛtti - These are nouns formed by adding primary suffixes to verb roots thus forming *kṛdanta* (i.e. having a *kṛd* ending). As we may remember this includes participles.
e.g. *yoga* is formed from √*yuj* + suffix *a*

derivative nouns

Secondary suffixes added to nouns form derivative nouns and adjectives called *taddhitānta* i.e. *taddhita* ending
taddhita is an example of this *tad+ dhita* means 'good for that or him'

relationships

There are different ways in which relationships may be treated but one of the most common for descendants is –

Many patronymics (son or descendant of) are formed by *vṛddhi* in the initial syllable of the stem + suffix *a* added to the stem . e.g. the son of *Subhadrā* is *Saubhadraḥ*. In this case the *u* in *Subhadrā* is strengthened by the addition of *a* to become *au* in *Saubhadraḥ* . *Vāsudeva (Kṛṣṇa),* is the son of *Vasudeva.*

Similarly a descendant of *Divodāsa* might be called *Daivodāsa.* If the stem ends in *u* then *guṇa* of this vowel also applies. e.g. *Puru* becomes *Pauravaḥ.*
The feminine equivalent would end in *ī.* Thus the daughter of *Drupada* is *Draupadī.*

The same mechanism is also used for other relationships e.g.
śaivaḥ a follower of *śiva*
śaibhyaḥ king of the *śibi*
Vāsavaḥ (Indra) chief of the *Vasus*

abstract nouns

Many abstract nouns are formed by either

a. adding *ya* to a neuter stem e.g. *sat + ya = satyam* truth
b. or with a feminine *tā* ending e,g, *devatā* = divinity

However the dictionary should be used for guidance as there are alternative uses for many suffixes and common usage may have evolved a different meaning. Over a hundred uses have been listed for some suffixes.

Consonant endings

A word may end in a consonant but not with two consecutive consonants. Final consonants are dropped off from the end until there is only one remaining.
e.g. *agacchant* would become *agacchan.*

Affixes and suffixes

As *Pāṇini* has over 1800 rules regarding *pratyaya* it is necessary to abbreviate to some basic classifications and examples.

.

Definitions

Pratyaya - Almost every Sanskrit word is made up of a base plus additions and the additions are often suffixes. The Sanskrit word for suffix is *pratyaya* in the sense of subsequent word or sound. It appears that in earlier times the term was used more freely to mean prefixes, suffixes, augments and more. Thus a *vibhakti pratyaya* is a case ending. It is derived from *prati* -√*i* to go towards or against and thus means 'that which follows'.

(An affix is a morpheme that is attached to a stem to form a word. Affixes may be derivational, like English *-ness* and *pre-*, or inflectional, like English plural *-s* and past tense *-ed*. They are bound morphemes by definition; prefixes and suffixes may be separable affixes. Wikipedia)

Suffixes are of 6 main types *–kṛt, taddhita, sup, tiṅ, strī and sanādi* .
An affix usually comes after a stem and these may be treated as suffixes.

kṛt is the name for a primary suffix and also a name for a noun formed in this way. *Kṛt* is formed from the *dhātu* √*kṛ* and is itself an example of this type. Note that the suffix '*t*' is added directly to the root and this is why it is said to be primary.
Kṛt mostly denote agency or an action related to the *dhātu* but there are exceptions. There are also the so-called zero (a modern term) suffixes or affixes which are totally elided when added to a root but may leave an indication of their influence through a modification of the stem. Conjugational endings are also added to the *dhātu* but are classified as *tiṅ*.
Primary suffixes such as *–a,* and *-ana,* usually influence the root vowel to strengthen to the mid level (*guṇa*) but if *ā* is present this may change to the strong (*vṛddhi*) level .

sanādi derivative verbal

strī feminine affixes

sup 1227/2 a *pratyāhāra* used as a term for all or any one of the 21 nominal case-terminations. Each set of 3 affixes of *sup* and *tin* has a descriptive *vibhakti* as also some *taddhita* affixes.

taddhita 434/2 m. an affix forming (derivative) nouns from other nouns. *taddhita* is an example of this and means 'good for that or him' .

tiṅ 446/1 a collective name for the personal (verbal) terminations, ending with *tiṅ*, an inflected verbal base

zero *0* the zero suffix is a concept invented to describe the situation where a word consists of the verbal root alone except for a possible *upasarga.* They are mostly nouns expressing the action of the root and are listed here under z. They also occur at the end of compounds to identify the agent of the action. In this case they may take any gender.

Most grammarians list suffixes as primary or secondary. A primary suffix forms a substantive from a root (primary or derivative e.g. it may have a pre-fix) and usually indicates agency or action related to the *dhātu,* however there are forms which may express any other *kāraka* e.g. instrumental, dative etc.

A secondary suffix could be seen as anything added after a primary suffix. They are sometimes added to the roots of pronouns, case forms, phrases and (rarely) indeclinables. Adding a suffix may cause changes to the stem. Some of the more common changes are –

Before a suffix beginning with a vowel or with *y* (which is treated as if it were *i*), final *a*- and *i*- vowels are regularly lost altogether; final u becomes *av. Vṛddhi* strengthening of an initial syllable of the stem frequently occurs as with primary suffixes.

Most secondary suffixes create adjectives of great variety often indicating relationship or connection. e.g. secondary suffix *–a.*

ayasa of metal, *mānasa* relating to the mind, *saumanasa* (from *sumanas*) friendliness, *aṅgirasa* of the *aṅgiras* family, *hāstina* elephantine, *brāhmana* priest from *brahman*.

The fully detailed rules are too numerous for this work but if needed are available for instance in Whitney's Sanskrit Grammar.

Listed below are examples of suffixes in English alphabetical order. The notes explain some stem changes that occur when suffixes or affixes are added. It must be stressed that there are many alternative meanings so the dictionary, context and reflection are important for effective translation.
Somtimes a bare stem is used, particularly at the end of a compound e.g. *duh* milking, *yudh* fight, fighter, *dviṣ* hater, enemy

Notes: 1. G= *guṇa* 1st strengthening of a vowel and V=*vṛddhi* 2nd strengthening of a vowel, P= primary stem and S=secondary stem. (Shown in some examples for illustrative purpose).

Modern theory suggests that *guṇa* is standard and there is a weakening and a strengthening (rather than weak + two stages of strengthening).

suffix	**root**	**stem**	**meaning/ notes**
-a	√*yuj* yoke	*yug-a*	yoke
	√*dih* stroke	*deh-a*	body
	√*muh* be confused	*moh-a*	delusion
	vi-√*kram* step out, attack	*vi-kram-a*	courage
	ni-√*vas* dwell	*ni-vās-a*	dwelling
	sam-√*tuṣ* be satisfied	*saṁ-toṣ-a*	satisfaction
	vi-śiṣ leave apart	*vi-śeṣ-a*	difference
	√*īś* rule	*iś-a*	ruler, lord
	√*kṛ* do/make	*kara/kāra* (ifc.)	doer, maker, agent
		bhāskaraḥ	light-maker, sun
		kumbhakāra	pot-maker, potter
	√*mih* emit fluid/urinate	*megha*	cloud

The use of primary suffix *–a* causes a final *ca* family consonant to change to the *ka* family e.g. √*sarj* send forth *sarga* creation, creation of the world,
vi√*sarj* send forth *visarga* emission, sending forth,

-a 2ndary. Primary stem changes to *Vṛddhi* in the 1st syllable
often means 'coming from' *putra* a son, child→*pautra* a grandson

ay (=√i)		*āyas-a* pertaining to metal, metallic	
√bhī	fear	*bhayam*	sickness, disease,
√bhid	split	*bheda*	separation, distinction
√bhū	be	*bhava/bhāva*	being, state
√bhuj	enjoy	*bhoga*	enjoyment
buddha		*bauddh-a*	connected with the Buddha follower of B, buddhist
√ji	conquer	*jaya*	conquest, victory
√kup	be angry	*kopa*	anger
√krudh	be angry	*krodha*	anger
√lubh	be greedy	*lobha*	greed
sam + ā + √gam	come together	*samāgamaù*	meeting
√sṛj	emit	*sarga*	creation
√śuc	grieve	*śoka* grief	
sumanas	a friend	*saumanas-a*	friendliness (abstract)
√tyaj	leave	*tyāga*	abandonment, renunciation
ud + √i	go up	*udaya*	rising up, success
vi + √śiṣ	distinguish	*viśeṣa*	distinction
vi + √suj	release	*visarga*	release
√vid	know	*veda*	knowledge
√yuj	join	*yoga*	mental concentration

2ndary **Vṛddhi 1st syll. + Guṇa of final –u**

manu	man	*mānava*	pertaining to man, human
kuru	*Kuru*	*kaurava*	descendant of *Kuru*

Vaiśvāmitra son of *Viśvamitra*

-ā usually feminine adjectives or action nouns

√bhāṣ	speak	*bhāṣā*	speech, language
√cint	think	*cintā*	thought, anxiety
√hiṁs	injure	*hiṁs-ā*	injury
√krīḍ	play	*krīḍā*	sport, play
√kṣudh	be hungry	*kṣudh-ā*	hunger
√man	think	*mīmāṁsā*	inquiry
√nam	bow	*namaḥ*	homage, a bow
		kāntā	beloved

-aḥ 2ndary *stem changes to Vṛddhi 1st syll. where appropriate.*
Forms mostly action nouns.

√man	think	*manaḥ*	mind, thought
√vac	speak	*vacaḥ*	speech
√tap	burn	*tapaḥ*	perform austerity

-aka often used to show smallness, sometimes used to indicate the material from which something is made,
janaka, generating, begetting, father *khanaka* digger, excavator, *aśvaka* little horse, colt, pony,

-an mostly masc agent nouns

√ah		*ah-an*	*n. day*
√rāj	rule	*rāj-an*	rul-er, king

√*takṣ* hew, make from wood *takṣ-an* hew-er, carpenter
prati-√div play against *prati-div-an* dice opponent

-ana *may* indicate a noun of action in the following way
jñāna = *jñā* –know + suffix *ana* = the act of knowing, knowledge.
It forms these nouns from many roots
Some of these nouns may indicate the object of an action, some the locus and some the agent.
nirvāṇa = *nir-vā* blow out + *suffix –ana* = the act or process of blowing out or going out
vyākaraṇa – grammatical analysis or grammar
vy-ā- √*kṛ* - undo, separate, sever, analyze + *ana* the act of

√*ās*	sit	*ās-ana*	sitting, seat
√*bhuj*	enjoy	*bhoj-ana*	enjoying;food, what is enjoyed
√*dā*	give	*dāna*	giving, gift
√*dṛś*	see	*darś-ana*	sight seeing, showing,(causing to see)
√*gam*	*go*	*gamana*	going
√*han*	kill	*hanana*	killing
√*kṛp*	lament	*kṛpana*	lamenting, miserable
√*rakṣ*	protect	*rakṣaṇa*	protection
√*nī*	lead	*nay-ana*	leading, eye as leader
√*pā*	drink	*pānam*	drinking, drink
śru	hear	*śravanam*	hearing
√*sthā*	stand	*sthāna(m)*	standing, place
√*vac*	speak	*vacanam*	speech
√*vāh*	carrying	*vāhana*	conveying, vehicle

-āna participles of middle and passive value – present, perfect or aorist
-ani √*dyut* shine dyotani splendour, brightness
-ānī 2ndary forms the fem. of the names of deities *Indrānī* wife of *Indra*
-ant or –at makes present and future participles active
√*ad* *adant or adat* eating
-anīya gerundive

-as

√*vac*	speak	*vac-as*	speech
√*tij*	be sharp	*tej-as*	sharpness, tip (of flame), splendour
√*tap*	be warm	*tap-as*	heat, internal warmth, austerity
√*man*	think	*man-as*	mind
√*prī*	please	*prayas*	pleasure
√*cakṣ*	look upon	*cakṣ-as*	eye
√*nam*	bow	*nam-as*	bowing, obeisance
√*sṛ*	flow	*sar-as*	lake

-at see *–ant* above
- *āyana* 2ndary Primary stem changes to *Vṛddhi* in the 1st syllable
descended from... e.g. *Kati* S. *Kāty-āyana* a descendant of *Kati*
-āyī wife of *agnāyī* wife of *agni*
-bha 2ndary forms the names of animals *gardabha* ass, *vṛṣabha* bull
-dās causing, bringing about 1/pl/m
-dhi √*budh* be awake *buddhi* intellect, mental faculty
-enya *virenya* manly, *kīrtenya* famous
-eya Primary stem changes to *Vṛddhi* in the 1st syllable
descended from.... *Draupadī* *Draupad-eya* a son of *Draupadī*
Kuntī *Kaunt-eya* a son of *Kuntī*

Saramā Sāram-eya descendant of *Saramā*

-i *akṣ* penetrate, pervade *akṣi* eye
√*kṛṣ* plow *kṛṣ-i* plowing
√*ruc* please *ruc-i* pleasure, brightness
√śuc flame *śuc-i* flaming, bright

-i 2ndary Primary stem changes to *Vṛddhi* in the 1st syllable
descended from... e.g. *Marut* *Mārut-i* descended from the *Maruts*
Satyaka *Sātyak-i* son of *Satyaka*
Somadatta *Saumadatta-i* son of *Somadatta*

ī 2ndary mostly feminine adjectives from other masculine and neuter terminations
√*nad* roar *nadī* flowing water, a river

-ika Primary stem changes to *Vṛddhi* in the 1st syllable
pertaining to... *veda* *vaid-ika* pertaining to the *Veda*s
dharma *dhārm-ika* relating to *dharma*
nyāya (logic system) *naiyāy-ika* connected with this system or 1st/s/m a follower of this system

-ika, -ka,- uka 2ndary can mean pertaining to as in *sāttvika* or *tāmasika* though *ka* is often used as a diminutive and is also added to many nouns and adjectives to form others with the same meaning. *putrika* little daughter

-in the suffix *–in* denotes an agent but also has regard (through common usage in the past) to in what way the agency is expressed e.g. as a matter of habit, an agent who performs the action over and over again, one who has been agent for the action in the past, one who has taken a vow to perform the action, or as simple agent.
2ndary possessive adjectives- *aṣvin* possessing horses, *bhagin* fortunate

-in possessing *pakṣa* a wing *pakṣ-in* possessing wings winged, 1/s/m a bird
hasta hand *hast-in* possessing hands 1/s/m an elephant (referring to the trunk as a hand)
bala strength *balin* strong (possessing strength)
dhanin possessing wealth

-īna 2ndary no change in meaning, added to weak stem of adjectives in *añc*
pratyañc backward, westward *pratīc-īna* backward, western

-is neuter action nouns
√*arc* shine *arc-is* flame, light
√*hu* offer *hav-is* oblation
√*jyut* shine *jyot-is* light
√*ṛc* gleam *arc-is* flame

-iṣṭha intensive adjectives, superlative
-iyas intensive adjectives

-iya secondary suffix, similar to *ya*, which see

-īya 2ndary possessive adjectives

parvatīya mountains (having mountains), *tadīya* his

mad- *mad-īya* belonging to me

asmad-asmad-īya belonging to us

tvad- *tvad-īya* belonging to you

yuṣmad *yuṣmad-īya* belonging to you (pl)

tad- *tad-īya* belonging to him, her, it

-īyāṁs comparative

-ka 2ndary forms adjectives and diminutives

often added to *bahuvrīhi* compounds without changing the meaning

rājan a king *rāja-ka* a little or petty king, a princeling

aśva a horse *aśva-ka* a nag

putra a son *putra-ka* little son, sometimes a form of endearment

pertaining to, *asmāka* ours, *yuṣmāka* yours, bhāvatka your worship's, *antika* near

widely used to make nouns and adjectives having the same meaning as the original- *astaka* home, *dūraka* distant, *nagnaka* naked, *nāsikā* nostril

added to a possessive adjectival compound *sapatnīka* with his spouse

-kata *utkata* exceeding the usual measure, *nikata* nearness, proximity

-la 2ndary adjectives and diminutives *kapila* brown (monkey-coloured), *bahula* abundant,

vṛṣala little man or man of low caste

-ma forms some superlatives, *avama* lowest, *madhyama* middlemost, *añcama* fifth

-maya being made of, consisting of, abounding in

kāṣṭha wood *kāṣṭha-maya* made of wood

tejas splendour, majesty *tejo-maya* abounding in splendour or majesty

-ma √*bhā* shine *bhāma* light, brightness, *bhīma* terrible

dhīma m. smoke

2ndary also has a superlative value and forms ordinals

-man √*kṛ* do *kar-man* n. action

√*jan* be born *jan-man* birth

√*viś* enter, settle down *veś-man* dwelling (an entering, settling down, settlement, *brahman* prayer

-mant replaces *vant* after stems ending in *i,ī, u, ū, ṛ, o, iṣ, uṣ* and sometimes after stops,

see *vant, avimant* possessing sheep, *yavamant* rich in barley, *jyotiṣmant* full of brightness, *virukmant* shining, *asimant* with knives, *agnimant* having fire, *mātṛmant* having a mother,

-māna present and future participles, with middle or passive value

-mat and *–vat* 2ndary. indicate having, possessed of

buddhimat – possessed of intelligence, wise

dhanavat – possessed of wealth, wealthy

jñānavat – possessed of knowledge *jñānavān* 1/s/m

jñānavantaḥ 1/pl/m *jñānavantam* 2/s/m

rūpayat – having the form

rasāvat – having the essence

smṛtimat – possessed of memory, wise
bhaga fortune *bhaga-vat* having good fortune, blessed
dayā compassion *dayā-vat* having compassion, compassionate
saṁtāpa sorrow *saṁtāpa-vat* having sorrow, sorrowful
śrutimat having ears, having hearing
aṁśu ray, beam *aṁśu-vat* rich in rays, radiant, m. the sun
jyotis light *jyotiṣ-mat* possessing light, luminous
agnimat maintaining the sacred fire

-maya 2ndary. consisting of *manomaya* consisting of mind

-mi √*bhū* become, exist *bhūmi* earth, *raśmi* m. ray, *-mī* f.
lakṣmī f. prosperity

-min or *–vin* indicates possession
go a cow *go-min* possessing cows
sva one's own property *svā-min* an owner or master
tapas austerities *tapas-vin* practising austerities, an ascetic
yaśas glory *yaśas-vin* possessing glory, glorious
tejas splendour, majesty *tejas-vin* splendid, majestic

-na forms perfect passive participles like *-ta* from many roots some as *–ina* or
–
una
mlāna, līna, pūrna, bhinna, some optionally take *–ta e.g. vinna or vita*
also adjectives and substantives *kṛṣṇa* black, *varṇa* colour,
parṇa wing, *tṛṣṇa* f. thirst

-nas *arṇas* a wave

-ni √*hā* to leap away *hāni* abandonment, *agni* fire, *śreṇi* f. line

-nu √*vac* speak *vagnu* sound, *dhenu* f. cow, *bhānu* m. light, *sūnu m.* sun

-ra many adjectives, some nouns, sometimes with a preceding vowel
√*śak* be able *śak-ra* mighty (able),
√*vaj* be strong *ug-ra* mighty, (terrible)
√*śuc* be bright, glow *śuk-ra* bright,
rudra – name of a god, *abhra* n. cloud
2ndary also forms comparatives from prepositions and adjectives
kṣipra quick, *avara* lower, *dhūmra* grey from *dhūma* smoke

-ri *bhūri* abundant

-ru sometimes with a preceding vowel
bhīru timid, *aṣru* n. a tear (as in crying)

-sa with or without preceding union vowel *gṛtsa* clever

-ṣa adjectival *etaṣa* variegated, *bāliṣa* childish

-śas according to (adverbial suffix)

-sna *tīkṣṇa* sharp

-snu adjective derivatives, plus from causative stems
jiṣṇu victorious

-stha fixed, abiding in

-ta,-na form passive participles from transitive verbs i.e. they qualify something as having endured the action expressed by (a transitive) verb
e.g. *datta* – given, *ukta* –spoken, *kṣīṇa* -destroyed
when made from an intransitive verb the participle has only an indefinite past sense (i.e. not passive) e.g. *gata* gone, *bhūta* been, *patita* fallen.
-na often used to mean -the act of

Generally this suffix is added to the bare root with appropriate sandhi changes but in some cases particularly where joining would be awkward the suffix becomes *ita* to ease the joining.
e.g. all those ending in two consonants – *ubj ubjita, valg valgita,*
some roots ending in one consonant – *cak cakita, ac acita also acna, pat patita, cup cupita*

√*vṛ*	cover	*var-na*	colour (lit. covering)
√*yaj*	worship	*yajña*	worship
√*svap*	sleep	*svapna*	sleep
√*tṛṣ*	be thirsty	*tṛṣ-nā*	thirst
√yac	request	*yācñā*	request

also in a more general sense *sita* cold, *asita* black, *hasta* m. hand

-tā - ness, feminine abstract nouns indicating the quality of 'being so and so'
e.g. *devatā* divinity, *vīratā* manliness, *puruṣatā* human nature, *bandhutā* relationship, *vasutā* wealth, *puruṣatā* human nature
for neuter see *tva,*

-tama- 2ndary indicates superlative, takes gender *vibhakti* e.g.
priyatamā kanyā the dearest daughter

-tana 2ndary added to adverbs of time to make adjectives

purā	formerly	*purā-tana*	belonging to a former time, ancient
śvas	tomorrow	*śvas-tana*	belonging to the morrow
sanā	of old, always	*sanā-tana*	eternal, *nūtana* present

-tara- indicates comparative, take gender vibhakti e.g.
priyataram mitram a dearer friend

-tas √*ri or rī* release *retas* seed

-tavat this ending is added to roots or stems forming words with a past sense that act like a past tense active verb. These words take gender and number.
Masculine words decline like *dhīmat* e.g.
1/s/m = *dhīmān* etc. (note *m* for *v* as appropriate),
Feminine words add an *ī* and decline like *nadī*
examples - *rāmaḥ gatavān* Rāma went
sītā gatavatī Sītā went
tau khāditavantau they both ate
nāryau khāditavatyau the two ladies ate

-tavya gerundive

-taya a few adjectives meaning 'of so many kinds or divisions'

-tha 2ndary √*nī* to lead *nītha* leader, leading, *artha* aim, object, *tirths* ford, *gāthā* f. song
forms ordinals from a few numerals *cathurtha* fourth

-ti mostly feminine action nouns

√*dṛṣ*	see	*dṛṣ-ṭi*	sight, vision
√*gam*	go	*ga-ti*	path, way, going
√*jan*	be born	*jā-ti*	birth, genus, caste f.
√*man*	think	*ma-ti*	thought
√*muc*	free	*mukti*	muk-ti liberation, freedom
pra + √*āp*	*attain*	*prāpti*	attainment, acquisition
√*pri*	be glad	*pri-ti*	pleasure

	pra-√kṛ presuppose	*pra-kṛ-ti* nature, matter (what is presupposed, hence original condition of things)
	√puṣ thrive, be nourished	*puṣṭi* well nourished
	√śam be quiet,	*śān-ti* quiet, peace
	√vac speak	*ukt-ti* speaking
	√bhū be, become	*bhūti* well-being f.
-tiḥ		
	ut+√pad be born, arise, originate	*utpat-tiḥ* birth, arising,origin
	vi+√pad experience misfortune	*vipat-tiḥ* misfortune
	sam + √pad experience good fortune	*saṁpat-tiḥ* good fortune
-tnu	adjective derivatives, plus from causative stems	*jiṣṇu* victorious

-tṛ denotes *kartṛ* i.e. *tṛ* indicates the root as agent

√kṛ	do, make	*kar-tṛ*	doer, maker, grammatical subject
√dā	give	*dā-tṛ*	giver

also relationships *mātṛ* mother, *pitṛ* father

-tra –trā indicates the root as the instrument of the action means of doing,

√nay	to go, to lead, protect,	*nāya*	guidance, direction,
√vas	wear	*vas-tra*	garment
√pā	drink	*pā-tra*	cup (means of drinking)
√pat	fly	*pat-tra*	wing (means of flying)
√śas	cut	*śas-tra*	knife, sword(means of cutting)
√nī	lead, guide	*ne-tra*	eye (means of leading or guiding)
√mā	measure	*mā-trā*	measure
√daṁś	bite	*daṁś-trā*	large tooth, tusk, (means of biting)
√man	think	*mantra*	prayer, reflection

-tu forms the stem of infinitives (*tum*) *tantu* – thread, also substantives

√dhā	generate	*dhātu*	constituent part

hetu cause, *vāstu* dwelling, *gantum* to go

-tva conveys meaning like the English suffix –ness e.g. happiness (feminine *tā*) added to a nominal forms an abstract noun

sat (existence) becomes *sattva* (purity, consciousness)
nitya (eternal) becomes *nityatva* (eternity)
amṛta (immortal) becomes *amṛtatva* (immortality)

forms nouns from prepositions and adverbs *nitya* constant, *amātya* companion

-tva or tā indicates abstract qualities, -having the nature of

amṛta	immortal	*amṛta-tva*	immortality
go	a cow	*go-tva*	cowness, the quality

or condition of being a cow, *patitva* husbandry, *bhrātṛtva* brotherhood

-tvā a past participle indicating a completed action, *gatvā* having gone,
-tvāt or *tvād* = *tva* (having the nature of) + (5th/s from) = by reason of, because,
-tvana neuter abstracts as with *-tva*
-tya a class of adjectives from particles e.g. *nitya* own, *amātya* companion

-tya	2ndary	*nitya* constant, eternal *aputra* not having a son *aputra-tā* a condition of being son-less
-u		adjectives, agent- nouns and often makes adjectives with the value of present participles √*sādh* come or lead straight to one's goal — *sādh-u* good, (lit. leading straight to the goal) √*vas* shine — *vas-u* excellent, (shining, splendid) √*svad* be savoury — *svād-u* savoury, tasting good *tanu* thin, *bāhu* arm, *hanu* f. jaw, *jānu* n. knee
-ū		*f. tanū* body, *camū* army
-uka		derivatives with the meaning and construction of a present participle *bhāvuka* being, becoming
-una		*taruṇa* young, *mithuna* pair, *śakuna* bird
-us		√*cakṣ* look upon — *cakṣ-us* eye √*dhan* set in motion — *dhan-us* bow (that which sets the arrow in motion √*tap* be hot — *tap-us* heat, hot
-va		*keṣava* hairy, *rājīva* striped, *dhruva* fixed, *sarva* all, *aśva* horse
-vāṁs		participles of the re-duplicated perfect in *vas* form their strong stem with *vāṁs* 1/s/m *cakṛvān* 1/du/m *cakṛvāṁsau* 1/pl/m *cakṛvāṁsaḥ,* the middle with *vat,* the weakest with *uṣ* *cakṛvas* having done (from √*kṛ*),
-van		agent words, adjectives and nouns to a short final vowel a *t* is added before the suffix √*yaj* worship — *yajvan* offering √*san* gain, acquire — *satvan* warrior, *grāvan* m. stone *parvan* n. joint
	2ndary	indicates possession *maghavan* bountiful, *atharvan* fire priest
-vana		*nivana* downwards *pravaṇa* slope, declivity, depth
-vant		possessive adjectives e.g. *putravant* of whom there is a son i.e. having a son, *patnīvant* with spouse, *sakhivant* having friends, *saptarṣivant* accompanied by the seven sages also often means like, resembling, e.g. *māvant* like me, *indrasvant* like *Indra, nṛvant* manly, *paravant* dependent, *vivasvant* shining
-vantas		1/pl/m having, rich in, tending toward
-vara		√*kṛ* make, do, — *karvara* a deed
-varī		√*yaj* worship — *yajvarī* worshipping, a worshipper
-vat		often indicates like or similar to. e.g. *putravat* – like a boy, like a child, derivatives from prepositions/ particles of direction *arvāvat* proximity, *udvat* height, elevation, also see *–mat,* also indicates possession *prajāvat* having offspring, *nabhasvat* cloudy
-vi		derivatives *jāgṛvi* awake
-vin	2ndary.	adjectives indicating possession as for *–in* *tapasvin* heated, *tejasvin* brilliant forms adjectives indicating possession *yaśasvin* glorious
- ya		is used in the formation of a gerund whenever there is an *upasarga* or as an adjective in the sense of 'relating to', masculine patronymics and neuter abstracts (with *vṛddhi* in first syll.), *traiguṇya* – pertaining to the 3 *guṇā*

or forms neuter abstract nouns e.g. *sat* (existence) becomes *satyam* truth

-*ya* gerundive *kārya* to be done,

secondary –*ya* suffixes are usually adjectives and have great variety in application
aṣvya equine, *durya* of the door, *narya* manly, *divya* heavenly,
kavya wise, *satya* true, grāmya of the village, *somya* relating to *soma,*
hṛdya of the heart, *vidyutya* of the lightning, *karmaṇya* active,
apsavya of the waters, *budhnya* fundamental, *ādya* edible,

-*ya* 2ndary. Primary stem changes to *Vṛddhi* in the 1st syllable , pertaining, relating to

deva	god	*daiv-ya*	relating to the gods, divine
grīvā	the neck	*graiv-ya*	pertaining to the neck

-*ya* 2ndary. . Primary stem changes to *vṛddhi* in the 1st syllable; descended from...

aditi	infinity as a goddess	*ādit-ya*	son of *Aditi*
neuter abstracts			
adhipati	overlord	*ādhipat-ya*	overlordship
paṇḍita	a scholar	*pāṇḍit-ya*	learning, erudition
subhaga	a happy person	*saubhāg-ya*	happiness

car walk, *ācar* follow a path, practice, *ācara* custom, rules of conduct, *ācārya* one who knows the *ācāra,*

-*ya* no stem changes

brahman	a priest	*brahman-ya*	pious
aśva	a horse	*aśva-ya*	relating to horses, equine
pitṛ	father	*pitr-ya*	relating to one's father, paternal

-*yu* √*yaj* to worship *yajyu* pious
manyu m. anger, *mṛtyu* death

zero a verbal root used as a noun expressing the action of the verb.

ā + √*pad*	undergo misfortune	*āpad*	f. calamity, misfortune
√*dṛś*	see	*dṛś*	f. sight
pari + √*sad*	sit around	*pariṣad (-t)*	f. assembly
sam + √*sad*	sit together	*saṁsad (-t)*	f. assembly
upa+ni+ √*sad*	sit down near	*upaniṣad (-t)*	f. *upaniṣad*
√*yudh*	fight	*yudh*	f. fight, battle

used at the end of a compound to identify the agent of the action and able to take appropriate gender

√*jñā*	know	*sarvajñaḥ*	knower of everything
√*ji*	conquer	*indrajit*	conquerer of Indra
√*dā*	give	*varadaḥ*	boon giver, *Brahmā*

Sanskrit Vocabulary

This dictionary is in English alphabetical order.
The words are in *prātipadika* or stem form like the Monier-Williams Dictionary e.g. without any endings added. Some have endings including "*s*" which is the precursor for a visarga, or "*ḥ*" an actual visarga. The vocabulary contains all the words or word components from the Bhagavad Gita except for a few of the less important names of warriors etc. Many compounds are included but for compounds such as *suṣuptābhimānī* it will be necessary to look up the components *suṣupta* and *abhimānī.*

a 1a/1 1. the first letter of the alphabet, 2. a vocative particle, e.g. *a ananta* O Viṣṇu 3. a prefix having a negative or contrary sense, *a-sat* not good, (before a vowel *an*),

ā as a prefix to verbs, to, unto, at; it may reverse the action of the verb e.g. go becomes come, 126/1 a particle of assent, as an adverb after words expressing a number or degree –fully, really, indeed

abaddha 59/3 unbound, unrestrained, at liberty, not yet visible,

abāhya 60/1 mfn not exterior, internal, without an exterior,

abbā f. a mother,

abbindu m. a drop of water, a tear,

abda m. 'water-giving', a year, a cloud, the grass,

abdhi m. ocean

ābdika mfn annual, yearly, - *ābdika* ..-ennial, lasting .. years

ābhā P. *ābhāti,* to shine or blaze towards, to irradiate, outshine, illumine f. light, appearance,

abhāgya 61/1 unfortunate, wretched, unfortunately

abhakta one who is not a devotee

ābharaṇa 1/2/s/n ornament or decoration

ābhāṣa m. speech, talking, a saying, proverb, introduction, preface,

ābhāsa 145/2 splendour, light, appearance, reflection, semblance, looking like, understood, as a reflection of *Brahman* , including personal aspects. reflection (of the Self)

abhāva 60/3 non-existence, destruction, absence, proof from non-existence, annihilation, death, privation,

abhavat became

abhāvayat mfn non-perceiving, non-concentrating, un-meditative, unwise, unconscious,

abhaya mfn absence of fear, fearless, f. *(ā)* fearlessness

abhi prefix, to, towards, into, over, upon, moving towards, approaching as a prefix to nouns not derived from verbs expresses superiority, intensity as an adverb or prep. (with 2nd.) to, towards, in the direction of, against, into, for, for the sake of, on account of, before, in front of

abhi- √*bhū* 66/3 overcome, overpower

abhibhūya (gerund)overpowering, subduing 67/1*(am*) /n. superiority

abhi-bhava 66/3 mfn. overpowering, powerful

abhicāra m. employment of spells for a malevolent purpose, exorcising, incantation, magic,

abhicāraka m. a magician,

abhidhā f. name, appellation, the literal power or sense of a word, a word, sound,

abhidhāsyati he shall set forth, shall explain, 1/s/fut/act *abhi* √*dhā*

abhidhīyate 63/2 it is called or explained 1/s/pres/indic/pass *abhi* √*dhā*

abhihitā 74/1mfn. named, called, spoken

abhijānāti recognizes, perceives, knows, is or becomes aware of comes to know or realize

1/s/pres/indic/act *abhi√jñā*
abhijāta 62/2 born, produced, well-born,
abhijāyate is born, is produced, is reborn, is born again *abhi√jan* 1/s/pres/indic/pass
abhijña mfn conversant with, knowing, skilful, clever, understanding, remembrance, recollection,
abhijñā 62/2 mfn knowing, skilful, clever, understanding,
abhijñānam n. remembrance, recollection, knowledge, ascertainment, a sign or token of remembrance, any sign or token serving as a proof, recognition
abhijñānāti recognizes, knows, perceives, is or becomes aware of
abhikrama 61/2 m. stepping near, effort, approaching, assault, attack, ascending, undertaking, attempt
abhilāṣa m. desire, wish, covetousness, affection,
abhimāna 67/1 pride, egoistic feeling, self-conceit, arrogance, arrogating to one-self, obsession, self-respect,
abhimānī " the claimant of the experience" HH " unless there is an *abhimānī*, pleasure and pain, even if registered by the witness, will have no effect."
abhimānin 67/2 thinking of oneself, imagining oneself to be, laying claim to,
abhimukha mfn face towards
abhi√nand 63/3 rejoices, delights,
abhinaya m. (indication of a passion or purpose by look, gesture, etc.), acting, dramatic action (expressive of sentiment), stream forth,
abhinetṛ m. actor, one who brings near,f. *tā*
abhiniveśa 64/2 m. attachment, application, intentness, study, affection, devotion, determination, tenacity,
abhipravṛtta 66/1 mfn. being performed, advancing, proceeding,
abhiprāya m. aim, purpose, intention, wish, opinion,
ābhīra m. cowherd, (sometimes incorrectly *abhira*), name of a people,
abhirakṣantu 3/pl/impv protect!
abhirakṣita (*abhi √rakṣ*) guarded, protected
abhirata 68/1 pleased or contented with, attentive to, performing
abhiṣeka m. anointing, coronation,
abhiṣicyatām let (him) be anointed, impv.
abhisaṁ √dhā 72/3 to take aim at, to aim at, have in view 2. f. speech, declaration,
abhisaṁdhāya having in view, having in mind
abhisara m. a companion,
abhisāra m. attack, assault, meeting, rendezvous (of lovers),
abhisaraṇa n. meeting, rendezvous,
abhiṣekaḥ anointing, coronation, sprinkling,
abhiṣikta mfn anointed
abhitaḥ ind. near to towards, near, all around, around, on both sides, before and after (all with 2nd),
abhi √vad address or salute with reference, declare with reference to, express by, say, speak, to present oneself to (4th case.)
abhivadet may talk to, 1/s/opt/act see above
abhiyoga 68/1 m application, energetic effort, exertion, perseverance in, constant practice, attack, assault,
abhiyukta 68/1 applied, intent on, the steadfast, united to yoga
ābhoga m. satiety, enjoyment, fulness, completion, expanse, (G) immediate experience, engrossed attachment of the mind to one thing,
abhra 79/3 n. water-bearer, cloud, thunder-cloud, rainy weather, sky
abhyadhika 75/3 pre-eminent, extraordinary
abhyahanyanta 1/pl/impf/pass *√han* they sounded
abhyantara 75/3 being inside of, interior
abhyāsa 76/3 2. repeated, mental repetition, "practice, knowledge into action by repetition" HH 2. *abhy* + √2. *as asya* ind. 76/3 to concentrate one's attention on, practice, study,

abhyasūyā f. indignation, anger, envy, jealousy
abhyasūya (*ti*) 77/1 to show indignation, be indignant at, speaks evil of, sneers at,
abhyasūyaka having envy, the envious, or indignant
abhyudaya 78/2 m. sunrise or rise of luminaries, beginning, commencing, increase, prosperity, good result
abhyudita 78/2 mfn. 1. risen, arisen, rising (said of the sun or moon), 'one over whom, while sleeping, the sun has risen', engaged in combat, 2. expressed (in words)
abhyutthāna 78/1 n. rising from a seat through politeness, gaining a high position, rising, setting out, rise, origin, birth, gaining efficacy, power, *abhy-ut-thā*
abja mfn born in water, a conch, the moon, (*am*) n. a lotus,
ābrahma 145/1 ind. up to or including brahma, *ābrahma* 145/1 ind. up to or including brahma,
stamba 1257/3 a clump or tuft of grass, *paryanta* 607/1 bounded by *ābrahmastambaparyanta* from *Brahmā* to a tuft of grass
abravīt he said, spoke, 1/s/impf/act √*brū*
abuddhimat mfn unintelligent,
ācakṣva (V) (V) kindly inform, kindly calculate, please describe, please tell,
acala mfn. not moving, immovable m. a mountain,
acalā f. the earth
acāpalam freedom from restlessness, steadiness 1/s/n
acara mfn not moving, (substantive) a plant (as distinguished from an animal)
ācara 484/3 to be practised or performed, 1/s/pres/part. √*car*
ācāra 131/3 2/s good conduct, good behaviour, acting lawfully
ācarata undertaking, moving towards
acarat walked
ācarati he does, he behaves, he practices 1/s/pres/indic/act *ā*√*car*
ācārya m. 'knowing or teaching the *ācāra* or rules', a spiritual guide or teacher, master
ācāryopāsanam n. sitting with a teacher, attendance on a teacher
accha 9/1 mfn not shaded, not dark, clear, transparent,
acchedya mfn not to be pierced or cut, not able to be cut, indivisible,
acetas *9/1* mfn. imprudent, unconscious, insensible, the non-discriminating
acintayat he or she thought
acintya 9/1mfn. unthinkable, unimaginable
acira mfn not of long duration, brief, instantaneous, recent, ind. not long, not for long, not long ago, soon, speedily,
acirāt mfn brief, soon
acireṇa ind. soon
acit 8/3 without understanding, irreligious, bad
acyuta 9/2 imperishable, unshaken, not fallen, permanent, unchanging one, name of *Viṣṇu*, *Kṛṣṇa*
adadāt gave
adagdha mfn unburnt
adahat he, she or it burned
adāhayat set alight 1/s/past/imperf/act
adāhyas not to be burned *a*√*dah*
adakṣiṇam 17/3 not dexterous, not handy, not right, left, inexperienced, simple-minded, not offering a present to the priest
adambha mfn. free from deceit, m. straightforwardness
adambhitva 18/1 n. sincerity, unpretentiousness
ādāna 136/3 7/s taking, receiving
ādara 138/1m. respect, regard, notice, care, trouble,
ādāya 136/3 1. mfn. taking, seizing, 2. ind. having taken, with, along with
ādarśa 18/1 *adarśa* for *ādarśa* m. a mirror Apte 79/3 1.showing, displaying, 2. a mirror.
ādarśamadhyasthe 470/3 *darśa* looking at,

viewing. root *dṛś* 491/1 to see, -*madhya* in the middle, standing between, belonging to neither or both parties 7/s (ref. A and C) existing in a mirror,

adarśana 18/1 not seeing, a latent condition, beyond the range of vision

adas, adaḥ pron. 1/s/n this, that

ādau in the beginning 7/s of *ādi*

ādatte 136/2 give to one self, take, accept, receive from, seize, take back,

adbhuta 19/1 wonderful, marvellous

ādbika mfn annual, additional, subsequent, later, surpassing, superior,

ādeśa 137/3 m. advice, instruction, account, information, declaration, injunction, precept, rule, command, order, foretelling, soothsaying, 'instruction through analogy',

adeśakāle in the wrong place and time

adha 19/3 ind. used mainly as an inceptive particle, now, then, therefore, moreover, and

adhaḥśākha (whose) branches are below,

adhama 19/3 lowest, vilest, worst, (often ifc. e.g. *narādhama* the lowest of men,

adhara mfn lower, inferior, West,
m. the lower lip, the lip,
n. the lower part, a reply, the vulva

ādhāra 139/1 support, prop, stay, the power of sustaining or the support given, substratum, reservoir, pond, (in phil. and gram.) comprehension, location, the sense of the locative case, ifc. belonging or relating to, the subject in a sentence,

adharma injustice, wrong, against the law,cheating, sin, unrighteousness, f. (*ā*) unrighteousness,

adharedhyus ind. the day before yesterday,

adharottara mfn lower and higher, worse and better, topsy-turvy, nearer and further, upside-down,

adhas 20/1 ind. below, down, in the lower region, beneath, under,

adhastāt ind. below, the lower region, the nadir,

ādhatsva keep! place!
2/s/impv/mid *ā√dhā*

adhāvat ran

ādhāya having placed or put, placed, put gerund *ā√dhā* 138/2

adhi 1. m. anxiety

adhi 2. *(upasarga* – indeclinable prefix to nouns and verbs) 20/2, expresses above, over, besides,
a separable adverb or preposition,
(with 5th) – over, from above, from, from the presence of, after, for, instead of,
(with 7th) – over, on, at, in comparison with,
(with 2nd) over upon concerning,
also 'different'
as a figure of speech

ādhi m. a receptacle, place, situation, a pledge, deposit, hire, rent, an attribute, title, epithet, 2. anxiety, pain, mental anguish,

ādhibhautika 138/3 belonging or related to created beings, elementary, derived or produced from the primitive elements, material

adhibhūta Supreme Being, aggregate of physical elements, the spiritual or fine substratum of material or gross objects, the all-penetrating influence of the Supreme Spirit,
'the transitoriness of the elements-' nature, (*am*) ind. on material objects, 'with regard to natural things',

adhidaiva 21/1 Supreme God, the divine agent operating in material objects 'beyond Indra and other gods' , (*am*) ind. on the subject of the deity or the divine agent,

ādhidaivika 138/3 relating to or proceeding from gods or from spirits, proceeding from divine or supernatural agencies

adhigacchati 20/3 *adhi* +√ *gam* to go up to, approach , obtain, he/she/it obtains, finds, discovers, attains, goes

adhika 20/2 mfn. additional, subsequent, later, superior, going beyond,

adhikāra m. authority, government, administration, rule, jurisdiction, prerogative, right, privilege, ownership, property, a subject, topic, (in gram.) a governing rule, (the influence of which over any number of succeeding rules is called *anu-vṛtti*),

adhīkāra m. superintendence over, interest, business, affair, authorization, capability, authority, duty, right,

adhikaraṇa 20/3 n. the act of placing at the head, supremacy, (in phil.) a substratum; a subject (e.g. *ātman* is the *adhikaraṇa* of knowledge), (in gram.) location, the sense of the locative case, relationship of words in sentence (which agree together).

adhikatara greater, surpassing, (comparative)

adhikṣepa m. abuse, insult, dismissal,

adhīna mfn resting on or in, situated, depending on, subject to, subservient to,

ādhipatya 138/3 n. supremacy, sovereignty power

adhiṣṭāna 22/2 standing by being at hand, a position, site, residence, abode, seat, the locus, the body

adhiṣṭāya controlling, governing, standing over, gerund *adhi* √*sthā*

adhiyajña m. chief sacrifice, lord of sacrifice, 'he who is to be propitiated by sacrifice' mfn relating to a sacrifice, (*am*) ind. on the subject of sacrifice,

ādhmāta mfn puffed up, blown up, inflated, sounding, burnt,

adho'dhaḥ below (with 2nd),

adhruva 23/3 mfn. not fixed, uncertain, doubtful, impermanent

adhunā 22/3 ind. at this time, now , immediately

ādhunika mfn present, current, modern,

adhvan m. way, road, f. *adhvā*

āḍhya mfn abounding in, wealthy, rich,

adhyakṣa 23/1 mfn. perceptible, observable, exercising supervision. m. an eye-witness, inspector, superintendent

adhyāropa 23/1 m. (in Vedanta phil.) wrong attribution, erroneous transferring of a statement from one thing to another

ādhyāsa Grimes p. 13, super-imposition; illusion; false-attribution... e.g. a rope seen as a snake and with all the qualities of snake. super-imposing ignorance and the empirical world upon the Absolute- hence not being aware of the Absolute

adhyātma 23/2 n. the Supreme Spirit, own, belonging to self, ind. concerning self or individual personality, 'in the context of the soul, with regard to the indwelling Self', (Gam.), pertaining to the self,

adhyātmacetas 23/2 m. one who meditates on the Supreme Spirit

adhyātmajñāna 23/2 knowledge of the Supreme Spirit or of the Self

adhyātmavidyā f. knowledge of the Supreme Spirit or of *ātman*

adhyātmayoga 'the yoga of the unity of the Self' HH 'to clarify the world and to put everything in perspective from multiplicity to singularity' HH

ādhyātmika 139/3 relating to Self or to the soul, relating to the Supreme Spirit, spiritual, holy,

adhyāya m. study, reading, a lesson, lecture, chapter, study, proper time for reading or a lesson, ifc. a reader,

adhyāyaka m. one who has studied the Vedas, a teacher,

ādhyayana study, recitation, 'the knowledge that arises from studying the scriptures' (Gam.),

adhyeṣyate will study, will recite 1/s/fut/mid *adhi* √*i*

-ādi m. the first (of a series)

ādi 136/3 beginning with, etc, and so on e.g. *ādi śaṅkara* the original or first *śaṅkara, pl. ādīni*

ādideva primal god, existing from the

beginning

aditi mfn not tied, free, boundless, unbroken, entire, unimpaired, happy, f. having nothing to give, destitute, a goddess ('infinity' or 'the Eternal and Infinte Expanse', mother of the *āditya* s and of the gods), boundlessness, immensity, inexhaustible abundance, unimpaired, condition, perfection, creative power, a cow, milk, the earth, m. devourer, death,

āditya (s) m. months of the year, 7 divine powers, 12 as representing the sun in the months of the year, name of the sun god, belonging to or coming from the *āditya,* son of Aditi, mfn belonging to or coming from,

ādityavāra 137/1 Sunday *āditya* the name for seven deities of the heavenly sphere, the chief of whom is *Varuna* to whom the name *āditya* is particularly applicable, the name of a god in general, particularly *Sūrya* the sun.

adri m. a mountain, a stone, a rock, a stone for pounding soma, a slingstone, a thunderbolt, a mountainous cloud, a tree, the sun,

adroha m. freedom from malice or hatred

adṛś mfn blind,

adṛṣṭa 18/3 unseen, unforeseen, not experienced, unperceived, beyond the reach of observation or consciousness, fate, destiny,

adṛṣyat 18/3 mfn invisible

advaita 19/3 mfn destitute of duality, sole, unique, non-duality, identity of spirit and matter, the ultimate truth, the philosophy by that name,

advaitavāda monism, the doctrine of *advaita*

advaya 19/2 mfn not 2, without a second, only, unique, as One, the ultimate Truth, One without a second, n. non-duality, unity,

adveṣṭṛ non-hater, not an enemy, a friend

adya 19/1 today, nowadays, now, to this day

ādya 1. 137/1 being at the beginning, first primitive, primal, ifc.

āgacchā come!

agacchat went

āgacchat came

āgacchati comes, arrives

agada mfn not having disease, well, healthy, whole, wholesome, m. medicine,

agādha – 4/3 deep, unfathomable, a hole,

āgama 'a coming', approaching, m. a grammatical augment, (N) an authoritative statement, (G) scripture, what has come down from tradition, revealed scripture, recognized scriptures in particular fields, traditionally 28 in number but hundreds are spoken of,

āgamana n. a coming

āgamiṣyati will come

āgamya having come

āgantu m. arrival, a stranger, guest, mfn anything adding or adhering, incidental, accidental,

āgas n. sin, (orig. a slip),

agāra 4/3 n. a house, apartment,

āgata 129/2 mfn come, arrived, come to or into, entered, reached

āgatya having come

agāyat sang

agha name of a demon, 6/3 mfn. bad, dangerous, sinful, impure, sin, impurity, pain, suffering

aghāta no injury, no damage,

āghāta 130/3 m. striking, a blow, killing, misfortune, pain,

aghāya 7/1 Nom. P. *aghāyati* to intend to injure

agni 5/1 m. fire, sacrificial fire, the god of fire, the element fire , has the property *rūpa* – form, shape, beauty, a symbol of consciousness

agra mfn top, tip, first, chief, best, the nearest end, the beginning, n. foremost point, tip, front, top, summit, surface, point, the nearest end, the climax or best part, goal, aim, multitude, a weight, a measure of food given as alms, remainder, sharpness (fig.),

agrahāyaṇa m. commencement of the year (about November 12th), name of a month,

agraṇīḥ m. leader,

agratas ind. in front, before, in the beginning, (with 6th) in presence of

agre (7th agra) in front, before, in presence of (with 6th), beginning, in the beginning, in the first place, first, tip, end, in the presence of,

agrya mfn foremost, best,

√*ah* 1. to say, speak, express
2.cl 5 P. to pervade or occupy

āḥ a particle expressing joy or indignation

aha particle, certainly, of course, namely, for *ahan* in compounds,

āha he said 1/s/perf/act, √*ah* say, speak

ahaituka 125/3 mfn. causeless, unexpected, having no motive, disinterested

aham 124/2 pron. 1/s I

ahaṃkāra 124/2 conception of one's individuality, ego, pride,

ahaṃkāriṇī conceited, proud, thinking of "me" and "mine"

ahaṁkṛta 124/2 egotistic, conscious of one's individuality

ahan or *ahaḥ* a day,

ahar 124/3 a day

āhāra 162/3 mfn ifc. bringing near, procuring, going to fetch, being about to fetch, m. food, taking food, eating, employing, use, taking,

ahasat laughed

āhava 163/1m. challenge, war, battle, sacrificing, sacrifice,

ahi m. 125/1 a snake

ahipati m. lord of the snakes (*Vāsuki*),

ahita 125/2 mfn. unfit, improper, noxious, hostile, m. an enemy

ahimsā 125/2 f. harmlessness of thought speech and action, non-violence

āhnika mfn daily, a day's work etc,

aho 126/1 ind. 'Oh my!', Oh!, alas

aho aho ind. expression of surprise or alarm, like "Oh my"

āhṛtya 163/1 ind. p. having fetched or brought, having offered, to be fetched or offered,

ā√*hu* to sacrifice, offer oblation, sprinkle *ājuhoti, ājuhote*

ā√*hū* Cl 1 *–hvayati* to call to, summon, invite,

āhus they say, they assert, 1/pl/perf √*ah*

āhuta mfn offered as an oblation, sacrificed, laid in the fire as a corpse, offering made to men, hospitality, nourishment of all created beings,

āhuti 162/3 f. offering oblations with fire to the deities, oblation, offering,

āhūyatām let (him) be called (impv)

aikya n. oneness, unity, harmony, sameness, identity, identity of the soul or of the universe with the deity, an aggregate, sum,

airāvata 'produced from the ocean' the name of Indra's elephant 234/2

aiśvara 234/3 mfn. relating to a mighty lord or king, powerful, majestic (*am*) n. supremacy, might

aiśvarya glory, glory of wealth, 234/3 the state of being a mighty lord, sovereignty, supremacy, dominion, superhuman power (eight listed), power, lordliness

aitihāsika m. teller of legends, mfn traditional,

aja 9/3 1. m. a drove, a driver, mover, instigator, leader, a ram, 2. not born, existing from all eternity, eternal,

ajānanta not knowing, ignorant of

ajasra 10/1 not to be obstructed, perpetual, said of fire (not dying out),

ajasram ind. perpetually, for ever

ajayat conquered

ājāyate (*ā*√*jan*) is born, begets,

ajina 10/2 the hairy skin of a(black) antelope or of a tiger

ājīva 133/1 livelihood, subsisting through, living by, *ājīvam* ind. for life, throughout life *ajña* 10/3 mfn. not knowing, ignorant, inexperienced, unconscious, unwise

ājñā a command, order,

ajñāna 10/3 n. non-cognizance, ignorance, spiritual ignorance, mfn ignorant, unwise, (- *āt*) ind. ignorantly

ajñānajam born of ignorance

ajñāta mfn unknown, unexpected, unaware, (*am*) ind. without the knowledge of,

ājuhoti, ājuhote see *ā√hu*

ājya 133/2 n. melted or clarified butter

akāma 2/1 mfn. desireless

akāṇḍa mfn accidental, causeless, unexpected, without a trunk, ind. (*e*) causelessly, unexpectedly

ākāṅkṣ 126/3 to desire, longing for, to expect , *ākāṅkśet* 1/s/pres/opt/act. he should desire

ākāṅkṣa mfn (in gram.) requiring a word or words to complete the sense, (*ā*) f. desire, wish, (also as for mfn),

akāra 1/1 the letter or sound *a*

ākara m. one who scatters, i.e. distributes abundantly, accumulation, abundance, 2. a mine, a rich source of anything, *-ja* produced in a mine, a mineral,

ākāra m. make, shape, appearance, form, category, expression of the face (furnishing a clue to the disposition of the mind),

akāraṇa 2/ mfn. causeless, n. absence of a cause, ind. causelessly

akārin 2/1 mfn. inactive, not performing, an evil-doer, neglecting duty,

akarot 1/s/past imperf./act. made or did, built

ākarṇya 126/2 ind. to give ear to, listen to. part. hearing, having heard,

ākarṣa m. attraction, playing with dice, a die, an organ of sense, fascination

akartṛ 1/3 not an agent, (of the Absolute), not active

akārya not to be done, improper,

ākaṣa m. a touchstone,

ākāśa 126/3 the ether, sky, or atmosphere, the element space, the first great element (having the property Sound). 'not visible',

akasmāt ind. suddenly, unexpectedly, accidentally, without apparent cause,

ākasmika 126/3 causeless, unforeseen, unexpected, sudden, accidental

akathayat told

akāya 2/1 mfn. bodiless, incorporeal

ākha m. a spade, a pitfall,

akhādat ate

akhaṇḍa 4/1 not fragmentary, whole, complete, "the unlimited is pervading everywhere and there is no end to it, and this is what does exist in reality. This is the substratum. It always remains the same and always remains one. It has no division. Therefore it is called *akhaṇḍa.*" HH

akhila 4/2 without a gap, complete, completely, whole, entire, (*ena)* ind. completely

ākhyā f. name, at end of compounds – 'having ... as name'

ākhyāhi tell! speak! 2/s/impv. *ā√khyā*

ākhyāna n. report, tale, story,

ākhyāta ppp. told, explained, has been spoken of

akiñcana 2/2 without anything, utterly destitute.

akīrtatikara m. causing ill-fame,

akīrti 2/2 f. ill-fame, disgrace

akledyas not to be wetted *a√klid*

akrama mfn not happening successively, happening at once, m. want of order, confusion,

ākrama m. m. approaching, attaining, obtaining, overcoming,

akriya 3/1 inactive, abstaining from religious rites, impious

akrodha absence of anger, '*krodha* is anger or rage. Anger or rage is instrumental to violence. Therefore not to be agitated, not to fall into rage is to avoid violence. ...to be enraged and to be violent is against the law.'

akrośat cried out

ākrośati he scolds, cries out in anger

akśta 2/2 unprepared, an act never before committed, spontaneous

ākṛti f. make, shape,

ākṛtī 127/3 f. form, shape,

akśtrima 2/3 1/s/m inartificial, unmade, not created,

akṛtsna 2/3 mfn incomplete

akṣa m. an axle or wheel, pivot, axis, die *3.* 3/2 an organ of sense, sensual perception, son of *Rāvaṇa,* knowledge, religious knowledge, a lawsuit, a person born blind,

akṣama mfn unfit, unable to endure, impatient, incompetent, envious,

akṣan n. eye,

akṣara 3/2 mfn. imperishable, unalterable, m. a sword, n. (*am*) a syllable, a sound, a word

akṣaya 3/2 exempt from decay, imperishable

ākṣepa 128/3blame, allusion, reviling, abuse, harsh speech, objection, drawing together, convulsion, applying, laying, throwing away, giving up, removing,

akṣi n. the eye, the number two, (*ī*) n. du. the sun and moon,

akñipat threw

akñobhya 4/1mfn unagitated, unmoved, imperturbable,

akñubdha 331/3 m. unperturbed

ākula 127/2 mfn. confounded, confused, agitated, distressed,

akurvan 1/pl/past imperf/act. they (many) made or did (dual – *akurutām*)

akurvata they did √*kṛ* 1/imperf/mid

akuśala 2/2/ inauspicious, evil (*am*) n. evil, an evil word

alabhata found,

alaka m. a curl or lock of hair,

alakṣya 94/1 invisible, unobserved, not indicated

alakta m. red lac, a resin from insects,

alam 94/2 ind. enough, sufficient enough of (with 4th), 56/1 no need of, needless

ālamba 153/2 m. that on which one rests, support, prop, depending on,

ālambanam n. depending upon or resting on, supporting, sustaining, a yogic exercise, silent repetition of a prayer, the 5 qualities distinguishable by the senses, form, sound, smell, taste and touch

alaṅkāra 94/2 the act of decorating, (in rhetoric) embellishment of sense or sound

ālāpa m. talk, conversation,

alasa 94/3 inactive, idle, lazy, dull,

ālasya 153/3 n. idleness, sloth, want of energy

ālaya a house, dwelling

ali m. a black bee, scorpion, crow, a cuckoo, liquor,

alīka 95/1 , not pleasing, disagreeable

ālocya mfn to be considered or reflected on, ind. having considered or reflected on,

āloka m. looking, seeing, beholding, sight, aspect, vision, light, lustre, splendour, praise, flattery,

ālokya 154/2 mfn beholding, ind. having seen,

aloluptva 95/2 free from desire

alpa mfn small, tiny, mean,

alpamedha 95/3 of little understanding, ignorant, silly

ām ind. yes

amala mfn 81/1 spotless, stainless, clean, shining, pure

amānitva 81/2 modesty, humility, absence of pride or arrogance

amanyata he thought 1/s/impf/mid √*man*

amara mfn immortal, m. an immortal, a god,

amarṣa 81/1 impatience, anger, passion

amātya m. a King's minister

āmaya 146/2 sickness, disease,

amāyā f. without guile, sincerity,

amba/ambā a mother, good woman, as title of respect, a name for several

goddesses,
ambara 83/2 n. sky, atmosphere, ether, circumference, compass, neighbourhood, apparel, garment,
ambhas n. water, the celestial waters, power, fruitfulness, a world, n.pl. a collective name for gods, men, Manes and Asuras,
ambhodhi 84/1 the ocean,
ambu n. water,
ambuvega m. water currents, esp.swift currents,
amedhya 83/1 mfn impure, foul, n. faeces,
amī pronoun 1/pl those,
amilat (+3rd) met
āmiṣa n. flesh, food, meat, prey,
amita mfn immeasurable, boundless, infinite, unmeasured, *(am)* ind. immensely
amitābha of unmeasured splendour, m.pl.
amla 841/1 mfn sour, acid, m. n. sour curds,
āmoda mfn gladdening, m. fragrance,
amogha mfn unfailing, unerring, m. the not erring or not failing,
āmra n. the mango fruit,
amṛta 82/2 mfn. immortal, imperishable, beautiful, beloved, m. (as) an immortal, a god, f. (*ā*) a goddess, a plant, liquor, n. (*am*) world of immortality, immortality, the nectar conferring immortality, ambrosia, nectar-like food, infinity
amṛtatva (or °tatā) 82/2 n. immortality
amṛtatvāya 4/s/n for immortality
aṁśa 1a/1 m. a share, portion, the portion of a sacrifice that goes to the gods,
aṁsa m. shoulder,
aṁsin m. sharer, heir,
aṁśu m. a shoot of the soma plant, a shooting ray of light, a ray,
aṁśuka n. cloth, garment,
aṁśuman grandson of King Sagara
aṁśumat mfn radiant, shining,
amuc -*k* f. not setting at liberty,
amuḍha 82/1 not perplexed, m. the intelligent man,
amuka mfn such and such a person or thing, a thing or person referred to without name, so an so,
amukta mfn not loosed, not let go, not liberated from birth and death,
amuktavat as if not free,
amukti f. non-liberation,
amūra mfn not ignorant, wise, intelligent, sharp-sighted,
amutra 82/1 in the other world, in the life to come,
an- occasionally (before a vowel) substituting for *a* as a negative,
ana a pronoun stem related to *idam* (this)
ana m. breath, respiration,
anabhisaṁdhāya without interest in, not aiming at, without regard for,
anabhisneha mfn. 26/1 without affection, cold, non- desirous
anabhiṣvaṅgas absence of clinging, non-attachment, without self-identification such as 'I am this, or I am that'
anabhyudita not expressed, not uttered, (Gam.)
anādara 28/1 indifferent, calm, m. disrespect,contemptuous neglect,
anādi mfn, not having a beginning, eternal, existing from eternity, ind. perpetually, incessantly,
anāditva n. beginninglessness
anādimat 28/1 mfn. having no beginning,
anaḍvah m. a bull, a breeding bull,
anagha 24/2 mfn. sinless, faultless (*Kṛṣṇa)*
anahamvādin 27/2 mfn free from self-conceit, not given to asserting his ego,
anala 26/2 m. fire, god of fire, wind, digestive power,
anamat bowed
anāmaya 28/2 mfn. free from disease, healthy, salubrious, not pernicious n. health
ānana n. mouth, face, entrance, door,
ānanda 139/3 pure happiness, bliss,
ānandavigraha embodied bliss, embodiment of bliss,
ānandamaya 140/1 consisting of bliss or

happiness
ānandamayakoṣa the 'bliss sheath',
ānandena blissfully, very happily
ananta 25/1 mfn limitless, boundless, eternal, infinite, endless
anantamahāmbhodhi *ananta* 25/1 boundless, limitless, *mahā* 794/2,3 great, *ambhodhi* 84/1 receptacle of waters, the ocean, the great limitless ocean
anantara mfn having no interior, having no interstice or interval or pause, uninterrupted, unbroken, continuous, immediately adjoining, contiguous, next of kin, compact, close, (*as*) m. a neighbouring rival, a rival neighbour, (*am*) n. contiguousness, Brahma or the supreme soul (as being of one entire essence), *(am)* ind. straight away, after (time),
ananya 25/2 not another, not different, identical, self, identical, without a second, undeviating,
ananyayogena with single-minded concentration, with undivided concentration,
anapekṣa 25/3 mfn. indifferent, impartial, careless
anārabhya mfn. improper or impractical, to be commenced or undertaken,
anārambha 28/2 m. absence of beginning, non-commencement, not attempting or undertaking, having no commencement,
anartha 26/2 nonsense, having no meaning, non-value, worthless, evil, bad, (L) non-advantage, disadvantage,
anārya 28/3 mfn not honourable or respectable, inferior, (not Aryan)
anāsakti yoga 'the yoga of detachment, which comes through understanding the unity of object and subject of observation. This makes everything and every action blissful and then all else does not exist. ' HH76
'Objects of the material world need no change and the actions of the subtle world of mind need no change. The change takes place in the *bhāva*, the emotional level. Once understanding is achieved, once knowledge is gained fully, then alone change will follow'.
'Only if one could change one's centre of understanding that all observed things and the observer are the same, then one could have achieved all changes; for the view of the world, of the beauty and the action will all change diametrically'.
anaśanam n. abstinence from food, fasting
anaśnan fasting
anāśayat destroyed
anāśrita 29/1 mfn. not supported, detached, independent, not depending on
anasūya 27/2 not spiteful, not envious, absence of ill-will or envy, not sneering or scoffing
anasūyanta not sneering, not spiteful, not speaking ill of, pres. part.
anātha mfn having no master or protector, widowed, fatherless, helpless, poor, (*am*) n. want of a protector, helplessness,
anavacchinna 26/3 not intersected, not interrupted, unbounded,
anavalokayan not looking toward, not looking, 1/s/m pres/caus/act part. *an ava √lok*
anavāpta unattained, not attained, not reached, mfn *an ava √āp*
anavadhāna 26/3 inattention, inadvertence, inattentive, careless
ānaya bring! m. leading to, leading to a teacher, √*nī*
ānayat brought
ānayati brings,
anayat led
anāśayat (he/she) destroyed
anayoḥ of these two 6/du/m
aṇḍa n. an egg, a testicle, the scrotum,
aṇḍaja mfn. egg-born, as m. a bird, a fish, a snake,
aṇḍaka m. the scrotum, (*am*) n. an egg,
aṇḍakāra mfn egg-shaped, oval, elliptical,

m. an ellipsis,
√*andh* cl 10 *andhayati* make blind
andha 44/3 mfn blind, blinding, dark, (*am*)n. darkness, dark water, water
andhakāra m.n. darkness,
anejat 42/2 mfn. not moving, immovable √*ej*
aneka mfn many, several,
anekadhā in many ways, in various ways,
anekarūpa mfn. multiform, of various kinds or sorts
anekaśas 42/2 mfn not one, many, much, *an* not + *eka* ind. one, in great numbers
aneke, anekāni many
anena pron. 3/s/m or n by this, from this, with this
aṅga n. a limb, member, body, person, form ind. a particle implying attention, assent or desire, and sometimes impatience, sometimes rendered by well, indeed, true, please, rather, quick,
aṅgāra m. coal, charcoal,
aṅgī√1.*kṛ* to take the side of, agree to, assent, promise, confess,
aṅgiras a sage
aṅgadam 7/3 an armlet,
aṅguli f. a finger, a toe, the thumb, the big toe, the finger-like tip of an elephant's trunk,
aṅgulīyam a ring
aṅguṣṭha 8/2 m. the thumb, the great toe, a thumb's breadth,
aṅgana 8/1 2/s/f the act of walking, any woman or female, a woman with well-rounded limbs, the female elephant of the north
aṅgin embodied, principal, chief,
aṅgiras a sage
aṅguli m. (*ī*) f. finger, toe
aṅgulīyam a ring
aniccha 29/2 mfn. undesirous, unwilling
anicchā f. absence of wish or desire, indifference
anīhita- *31/1*disagreeable displeasing unwished,
anīkam army, fighting force, appearance, face, edge, 2/s/m or n
anila 30/1 m. air or wind, the god of wind, one of the demi-god *Vasus*
anirdeśya 30/1 undefinable, inexplicable, incomparable, indescribable,
anirvacanīya mfn unutterable, indescribable,' neither identical with nor different from', 'neither real nor unreal', relating to the ontological existence of the world, not determinable as either real or unreal,
anirvācya 30/1 unutterable, indescribable
aniṣṭa undesired, disagreeable, unapproved, unlawful,
anīśvara mfn without a superior, unchecked, paramount, powerless, unable, godless, atheistic, *tā* f. or *tva* n. absence of a supreme ruler,
anitya 29/2 impermanent, transient, occasional, incidental, irregular, unusual, unstable, uncertain, destructible, (*am*) ind. occasionally,
aniyama 29/3 absence of rule or fixed order, uncertainty, doubt
aṇīyaṁsa more minute, smaller, subtler, m comparative,
a-niyata 29/3 mfn. not regulated uncontrolled, uncertain, unrestricted
añjali 11/1 m. a reverent gesture,
aṅka m. 1. the lap body-fold, the lap, 2. the hip bend that carried babies may be rested on, 3. hook, 4. a mark or sign like a pot-hook,
aṅkura 7/2 a sprout, a shoot, a blade
aṅkuśa a goad, esp. an elephant goad,
anna 45/1 mfn. eaten, n. food, food in a mystical sense, water
annamayakoṣa 45/1 m. the food sheath, the gross material body,
anirviṇṇa 30/1 mfn. not downcast
ano ind. no, not,
anṛta 42/2 n. mfn not true, false and with all the qualities of snake. super-imposing ignorance and the empirical world upon the Absolute- hence not being aware of the

Absolute (refers to the story of a rope being seen as a snake),

anta 42/3m. end, limit, termination, border, inner part, inside, internal, certainty, *ante* in the end,

antagatam end-gone, come to an end

antaḥ 42/3 ind. inner part, inside

antaḥkaraṇa 43/1 the internal organ, the seat of feeling and thought, the mind, the thinking faculty comprising *buddhi, citta, manas*, and *ahaṅkāra*

antaḥsukhas he who has happiness within

antakāla 42/3 time of death, death

antaḥpuram n. inner apartment, inner stronghold, citadel,

antar ind. 43/2 within, between, amongst, inside, interior, within

antara 43/3 mfn being in the interior, interior, near, related, different from, n. the interior, a hole, opening, the interior part of a thing, the contents, soul, heart, supreme soul, interval, intermediate space or time, period, term, distance (between two things), the difference, representation

antarā 44/1in the middle, inside, amidst, among, between, within,
except, without, assoc with case 2.

antareṇa between, without, regarding, except, with reference to (with 2nd), on account of,

antareṣu in between

antarjyotis mfn he who has light within,

antarpuram the women's quarters,

antataḥ ind. finally

antavat 43/1 mfn. having an end or term, limited, perishable, containing a word which has the meaning of anta, ind. like the end, like the final of a word

ante ind. finally, in the end,

antevāsin 43/1 mfn dwelling near the boundaries, dwelling close by, m. a pupil who dwells near or in the house of his teacher, a disciple,

antika 44/2 mfn.near, proximate, n. vicinity, proximity, near, (*am*) ind. until, near to, into the presence of, etc.
2. reaching to, reaching to the end of, lasting till, until

antima mfn last, final, ultimate, ifc. immediately following, very near,

aṇu 11/3 mfn fine, minute, atomic, an atom of matter or of time, subtle ind. minutely

anu 31/1 prefix after, along, alongside, lengthwise, near to, subordinate to, with,
(when prefixed to nouns, especially in adverbial compounds) according to, severally, each by each, orderly, methodically, one after another, repeatedly,
as a separable adverb – after, afterwards, thereupon, again, further, then, next
mfn = *aṇu*
m. a non-Aryan man,
of a non-Aryan tribe,

anubaddha mfn bound to, obliged to, connected with, related to, belonging to, followed by,

anubandha 36/2 m. binding, connection, consequence, inevitable result, consequence accruing,
sequence, an indicatory letter or syllable attached to roots etc., (marking some peculiarity in their inflection).

anubandhin 36/3 connected with, attached, resulting, permanent, having in its train or as a consequence

anubhava m. perception, apprehension, fruition, understanding, impression on the mind not derived from memory, experience, knowledge from personal observation or experiment, result, consequence, cognition, consciousness, custom, usage, (*am*) ind. at every birth,
(N) perception by intuition,
-siddha mfn established by experience or perception,

anubhāva m. experience, becoming an atom, firm opinion, indication of a feeling (by a gesture), belief, dignity, ascertainment, authority, good resolution,

anubhavati feels, experiences

anu√bhū 36/3 to enclose, embrace, to be after, attain, equal, to be useful, to help, to notice, perceive, understand, to experience, attempt,
mfn perceiving, understanding,

anubhūta mfn experienced, perceived understood, apprehended, resulted, followed as a consequence; that has experienced, tasted, tried or enjoyed,

anubhūti 36/3 f. perception, knowledge from any source but memory, (in phil.) knowledge gained by perception by the senses, inference, comparison and verbal authority. G40 direct apprehensions, experience which reveals new knowledge, experience

anucara mfn following, attending,
m. companion, follower, servant,

anu √cint 32/2 to meditate, consider, recall to mind,

anucintayan meditating, thinking of pres/act/caus/part 1/s/m

anudarśanam 33/2 keeping in view or in mind, consideration, n.

anudhāvati runs after, pursues

anudvegakara 33/3 not causing apprehension not overawing

anudvigna 33/3 mfn. free from apprehension or anxiety, easy in mind

anugacchati 1/s/pres/ind/act follows,

anugraha 32/1 favour, kindness, showing favour, conferring benefits

anuja mfn born after, later, younger,
m. younger brother

anujñā f. assent, permission

anu √kamp 31/1 to sympathise with, be compassionate

anukampā f. compassion, with compassion, causeless mercy, (V)

anukūla mfn favourable, following the bank or slope, according to the current, agreeable, conformable, friendly, kind, well-disposed, a good husband

anulepana n. 38/1 anointing the body, unguent so used

anumāna n. the act of inferring, inference, reflection, consideration, guess, conjecture, one of the means of obtaining true knowledge, the forming of a conception,

anumantā f. permitter, consenter

anumati f. approbation, favour (of gods to the pious), grace (personified), M. approval, consent, permission,

anunaya m. conciliation, salutation, courtesy, civility, showing respect or adoration to a guest or deity, humble entreaty or supplication, reverential deportment, regulation of conduct, discipline, tuition, mfn conciliatory, kind, *(am)* ind. fitly, becomingly,

anupakārin 34/2 mfn. not assisting, disobliging, ungrateful, not making a return for benefits received,

anupaśya mfn.keeping in view, perceiving, seeing, following with looks,

anupaśyāmi I foresee, I anticipate, consider, notice, look at, keep in view, 3/spres/indic/act *anu √paś*

anupaśyati he/she realizes, looks at, notices, discovers, reflects upon, takes as, look upon as, sees, keeps in view, follow with looks,

anu√prach to ask, to inquire after,

anuprapanna 35/3 following after, conformed to, conforming to

anupurva mfn regular, orderly, in successive order from the beginning,

anupūrveṇa ind. regularly,

anurāga m. attachment, affection, love, passion, red colour,

anurajyate is fond of (with 6th)

anu√rañj to be attached or devoted

anurañjyate becomes attracted

anurodha m. obliging or fulfilling the wishes of anyone, means for winning the affection of, compliance, considerance, respect, reference or bearing of a rule, conformity,
ifc. with regard to, according to,

anurūpā 37/3 following the form,
corresponding, like, fit,
anusajjate he or she is attached or clings onto, /s/pres/indic/mid *anu √sañj*
anusaṁtati f. continuation,
anusarati follows – an instruction
anu √śās 39/2 to rule, govern, teach, direct,
anuśāsita mfn defined by rule, directed
anusātam ind. according to delight,
anuśīlana n. constant practice or study (of a science etc.), repeated and devoted service, exercise,
anuśiṣṭa mfn. 39/3 taught, revealed, done according to law, instructed
anuśiṣṭi f. instruction, teaching, ordering
anuśiṣyāt it/he/she should be taught, 1/s/opt/act
anusmara remember! think of 2/s impv/act *anu √smṛ*
anusmaran meditating on, thinking about pres/act/part
anusmarati remembers
anusmaret he should meditate on or call to mind 1/s/opt/act
anusṛta mfn followed, conformed to,
anusṛtya ind. following, imitating, searching out
anu √śuc 39/3 to mourn over, regret, bewail
anuśuśruma we have heard, we have heard repeatedly, 3/pl/perf/act *anu√śru*
anuṣṭhita 40/1 mfn. done, practised,
anutāpa m. repentance, heat, remorse,
anutiṣṭhanti practises, follows, carries out
anuttama 33/1 mfn. unsurpassed, incomparably the best or chief, excellent, excessive
anuvartana 39/1 n. obliging, serving or gratifying another, compliance, obedience, following, result, concurring, continuance, continues
anuvartate he, she, it follows 1/s/pres/indic/mid *anu √vṛt*
anviccati searches after,
anuvidhīyate it is guided, ordered, regulated,
1/s/pres/pass *anu vi √ dhā*
anvaicchat searched after
anvaicchatām (they two) searched
anvaśocas you have mourned
anu a śocas 2/s/impf/act *anu √śuc*
anvaya 46/1 m. following, succession, connection, association, logical connection of cause and effect, syntax, natural order of words, proposition and conclusion, race, family, positive knowledge as opposed to *vyatireka* – (knowledge gleaned through negation and process of elimination).
anviccha seek!, wish for, desire 2/impv/act *anu √iṣ*
anvita 47/2 gone along with, accompanied by, reached by the mind, understood, joined, endowed with
anvicchati searches after,
anya mfn other, another,
*anya (*or *eka)... anya*
the one.... the other,
another person, one of a number,
anyac ca and another thing, moreover,
anyad n. different, other, another
anyatama mfn any one of many, either, any
anyatara mfn either, one of two,
anyathā 45/3 ind. otherwise, in a different manner, otherwise
ānyati brings
anyatra ind. aside from, otherwise, elsewhere, apart from
anyāyena by unjust or foul means, illegally,
anye 1/pl/m others, other
anye-dyus ind. on the next day,
anyonya 46/1 one another, mutual
anyonyādhyāsa 'When two things of different nature come together, they influence each other. The interchange of their qualities is known as *anyonyādhyāsa,* that is inter-superimposition.'
apa prefix away, off, back, down
āpa 142/2 n. water, the waters, mfn obtaining, ifc. to be obtained,
āpada 1/s/m hardship
āpadā f. misfortune, calamity, ind. through mistake or error, unintentionally, distress,

āpāda m. remuneration, reward, arriving at,
apādāna, am, n. taking away, removal, ablation, a thing from which another thing is removed, 'The eternal unmoving from which all movement comes'
apaharati carries away
apahṛta 53/3 mfn. taken away, stolen
apahṛtya having taken away or carried off
apaśyat (he or she) saw
apaharati carries away
apahṛt° taken away, carried off
apaiśuna 56/3 n. absence of slander,, absence of vilification
apalāyana n. not retreating or fleeing
apamāna 50/2 m. dishonour, disrespect, disgraced,
apāṇa 54/2 m. that of the 5 vital airs which goes downwards and out at the anus, G48 'carrying downwards breath', inspired breath, outbreath, inhalation, digestive energy. The life breath which removes all waste from the human system. excreting
āpaṇa m. market, shop, commerce, trade,
āpāna mfn one who has reached, n. a tavern, the act of drinking, a drinking party, banquet, 142/2
āpanika m. shopkeeper, merchant,
āpanna 143/1 mfn entered, got in, gained, obtained, acquired, afflicted, unfortunate,
apanudyāt it should remove, it should take away/dispel 1/s/opt/act
apāpa 54/2 mfn. sinless, virtuous, pure
-viddha not afflicted with evil
apara 50/2 mfn. 1. having nothing beyond or after, having no rival or superior,
2. other, another, posterior, later, latter, following, inferior, lower, distant, opposite *aparā* the west, lower, inferior, inferior (used in the Upanishads to describe knowledge relating to the phenomenal world), (*am*) n. the future, ind. in future, for the future, again, moreover, in the west of (5th), (*eëa* with 2nd) ind. behind, west, to the west of,
aparādha m. crime, sin, offence,
aparādhin one guilty of offence, mfn offending, criminal, guilty,
aparam see *apara*
apara brahman " a synonym for *saguṇa brahman*" HH
aparādhin one guilty of offence
aparājita mfn unconquered, invincible
aparaspara one after the other
apare some, others, 1/pl/m
aparigraha mfn destitute, without possessions, non-acceptance, renouncing, deprivation, destitution
a-pariharaṇīya mfn. not to be avoided, inevitable, not to be abandoned or lost, not to be degraded,
aparimeya 51/2 immeasurable, illimitable,
aparokṣa 51/3 not invisible, perceptible, in the sight of, directly knowable
aparyāptam *(a pari √āp)* 1/s/n ppp. incomplete, insufficient, unlimited
apasmāra the desire to ignore the Truth HH epilepsy, want of memory, confusion of mind,
apaśyat 1/s/imperf./act he saw, mfn not being in view of, not noticing, not considering,
apatat fell
apātra 54/1 n. unworthy, undeserving
apatya n. offspring, child, descendant, *-tā* f. state of childhood,
apāvṛnoti 54/3 opens, uncovers, reveals
apāvṛnu open! reveal! 1/s/pres/impv
apāvṛta 54/3 mfn. open, unconcealed, unrestrained, self-willed,
apāyin mfn going away, departing, vanishing, perishable, 56/2

api 55/1 as a separable adv. and, also, besides, surely, very, even, even now, though, moreover, and, too, although, expresses placing near or over, uniting to, when used at the beginning of a sentence it indicates a question,
apibat drank
api ca moreover
apihita mfn. placed into, concealed, covered

*āpnoti*142/1 reaches, 1/s/pres/indic/act
√ *āp* he/she/ it reaches, attains
āpnuvan pres.act.part. overtaking, meeting with, reaching
āpnuyām I should attain, I should reach, 3/s/opt/act √*āp*
apohana 56/3 reasoning, arguing, denying,
apradāya not offered, not offering
apraiṣyat he sent
aprakāśas 57/2 not shining, unenlightened, dark, not visible,
aprākṛta 59/1 mfn. not principal, not original, G. 50 non-material, 'is eternal' HH
apramāda m. care, vigilance, mfn careful, cautious, mindfully guarding, n. (*am*) carefully, with attention
aprameya 58/3 mfn. immeasurable, unlimited, unfathomable
aprāpya ind. not attaining or reaching. gerund *a pra*√*āp*
apratīkāra 57/3 mfn unopposing, unresisting, without remedy
apratiṣṭha 58/1 mfn. having no solid ground, fluctuating, unsafe
apṛcchat asked
apriya uncherished, unloved, disliked,
apsaras f.a beautiful heavenly nymph
āpti f. 142/2 reaching, meeting with, obtaining, attaining, abundance, fortune, fitness, aptitude
āptum 142/1 to reach, obtain, gain infin. √*āp*
apūrva 56/2 mfn unprecedented, unrecorded, not having existed before,
āpūrya ind. filling, (gerund)
āpūryamāṇa becoming filled or full pres/mid/part *ā*√*pṝ*
āra m. brass, iron, a corner, a spoke,
ā-rabhate begins, commences, engages
ārādhana 150/2 mfn. propitiating, rendering favourable to one self, (*am*) n. homage, worship, adoration, *(ā)* f. worship, homage,
arāla mfn curved, crooked,
ārāma 150/1 m. delight, pleasure
aramat rejoiced
ā-rambha 150/1 m. undertaking, beginning, a thing begun, origin
*āraṇyaka*149/3 mfn. forest, wild, forest-born, name of a class of religious and philosophical writings closely connected with the Brāhmanas, the name indicating written or studied in forests, the *upaniṣad*s are considered to be attached to them, forest discussion of *vedā* ,
araṇya 86/3 n. a foreign or distant land, a wilderness, desert, forest
ārāt ind. from a distant place, distant, to a distant place, far from, near, directly, immediately,
arati 86/3 f. dissatisfaction, discontent, anxiety, regret, distress,
aravinda n. a lotus, Indian Crane, copper,
arāya m. an evil spirit
arcana 90/1 mfn. honouring, praising, n. f. homage paid to deities and to superiors,
√*arc* 89/3 shine, be brilliant, praise, sing, honour, *arcitum* infin. to shine
arc 2. shining, brilliant
ardha half, the half, side, part, place, region,
ārdra mfn wet, fresh
argha m. price, offering, worth,
arghya mfn of price (or) that may be priced, n. an offering of water or a garland,
arha 93/3 mfn meriting, deserving, obliged, proper, fit, worthy of
arhati is worthy, is able, is capable
√*arh* 93/3 to be worthy of
be allowed to do anything
be obliged or required to do ..
he ought, should (with infinitive)
ari 87/3 1. faithful, attached to
mfn. envious, hostile, m. an enemy
arisūdana slayer of the enemy, name for *Kṛṣṇa*
ārjava 151/3 straightness, honesty, sincerity, rectitude, virtue
arjayitvā 90/1 *arjayati* he acquires, past part. having acquired,
arjuṇa a prince and a principal in the *bhagavad gītā*

arka 89/1 m. the sun, a ray, flash of lightning, copper, praise, hymn
arṇava mfn agitated, foaming, m. a wave, flood, ocean, sea,
arodat cried, wailed
ārogya 151/2 n. freedom from disease, health, mfn healthy, giving health,
ārohaṇa mfn. 151/2 mfn arising, ascending, n. the act of rising, a carriage, ladder, staircase
ārohati climbs
āropa 151/1 m. imposing (as a burden), burdening with, placing in or on, super-imposition, arousing consciousness
arpana 92/3 mfn. procuring, consigning, n. inserting, fixing, offering, entrusting, giving back,
arpita 92/3 fixed upon (eyes or mind) placed, entrusted, thrown, delivered,
arṣati √ *ṛṣ* to flow, flow quickly, moves with a quick motion,
arṣat he ran (*īṣā up*)
ārta mfn. pained, distressed,
artha 90/2 m.n. wealth, prosperity, substance, worth, aim, purpose, cause, motive, reason, thing, object, object of the senses
artham or *arthe* for the purpose of, for the sake of, on account of, for (frequently ifc.),
arthārjana 91/2 acquisition of property,
arthāya for the purpose of, 4/s/m
arthin mfn having an object, desiring, seeking, needy, wishing for, begging, 91/3 active, industrious, one who wants or desires anything, longing for,
arti 90/2 f. pain, trouble, misfortune,
ārti 149/2 pain, injury distress
ārūdha 151/1 mfn. mounted, ascended, undertaken, reached,
aruṇa mfn the colour red, ruddy, reddish,
arundhatī wife of *Vasiṣṭha,* f. name of the morning star,
ārurukṣu 151/1 mfn. desirous to rise, ascend or advance

arvāk 93/2 ind. before (time), from a certain point (with 3rd),
āryaḥ noble one, Aryan,
Aryaman 93/1 chief of the departed spirits
āryaputraḥ son of a noble one
√*ās* 159/3 to be present, exist, to sit, sit down, rest, dwell in, abide, remain, continue, continue doing anything,
āsa there was, m. posterior of the body, ashes, dust, n. a bow,
āśā 157/1 f. wish, desire, hope, region
asādhu mfn not good, evil, disgrace, m. a wicked man, n. anything bad or evil, ind. interjectn. bad! shame!
āsādya attaining, approaching, having attained/approached
asaha 120/1 mfn not able to , intolerant of, impatient,
asakta 118/1 unattached, detached from worldly feelings, not hanging on to, not clinging
āsakta 160/1 mfn. fixed or fastened to, attached to, intent on,
aśakta 112/3 mfn. unable, incompetent
āsaktamanas 160/1 mfn. having the mind deeply engaged in or fixed upon (any object), intent on, devoted to, absorbed in
asakti 118/1 f. being detached from worldly feelings or passions
āsam I was
aśama 113/1 disquietude, uneasiness, 'not resting'
asamartha 119/1 mfn. unable to, not having the intended meaning, n. incapability of
asambhūti f. non-existence (unborn), destruction, *prakṛti* as primal material cause
asaṁdigdha mfn not indistinct, undoubted, unsuspected, certain, (*am)* ind. without any doubt, certainly,
āśaṁkā f. fear, apprehension, doubt,
asaṁkhya mfn countless,
asaṁmūḍha mfn free from delusion, deliberate,
asaṁsakta 117/3 unconnected, not joining, separate, indifferent,

asaṁsakti the fifth stage of realisation, "attachments very close to the individual begin to drop
asaṁśaya 117/3 m. absence of doubt, certainty, surely, without doubt
asaṁśaya 117/3 m. absence of doubt, certainty, surely, without doubt
asaṁśayam adv. without doubt, surely
asaṁyama m. non-restraint (as of one's senses
asaṁyata 117/2 mfn not kept together, not shut (as a door), unbridled,
āsan they were
aśana 112/2 1. reaching, reaching across 2 n. eating, food
āsana 159/3 2.√ *ās* to sit, be present, exist,
āsana n. seat, sitting, sitting down, sitting in particular posture, the manner of sitting forming part of the eightfold observances of ascetics
asaṅga 118/1 m. free from ties, independent, m. non-attachment, non-inclination, non-impediment, generally without obstacle,
aśani m. a bolt of lightning, the tip of a missile, a hailstone,
āsanna 160/2 mfn. seated down, set down, near, proximate, (*am*) nearness, end, death
aśanāyāti (or -nayā) desires food, is hungry
aśānta 113/1 restless, violent, wild
āśāpāśa trap of hope, shackles in the form of hope
asapatnam n. unrivalled, undisturbed,
āśāpratīkṣe hope and expectation,
asàra 120/2 mfn spoiled, unfit, sapless, without strength or value
aśas 113/1 mfn cursing, hating, aversion
aśastra n. unarmed, without weapon,
aśāśvata mfn impermanent, inconstant
asat 118/2 not being, not existing, unreal, non-being, untruth
asat sat false existence
asatas of the non-existent, of the unreal, pres.part. *a*√*as* 6/s/n
asatkṛta 118/2 mfn badly treated, not treated respectfully or properly, n. offence
asau 18/1 (see *adas*) pron. that, he, a certain 1/s/m or f. he, she, that
āśaya 157/3 m. resting place, the mind, heart, soul, abode, receptacle,
āścarya 158/1 n. a wonder, appearing rarely, curious, miracle, mfn marvellous
āścaryavat adv. like a marvel, wondrously
aśeṣa 113/3 without remainder, entire, perfect, all, wholly
asi 120/2 m. a sword or knife
asi 2/pres/indic/act of *as* to be thou art, you are
asi m. a sword, knife (for killing animals),
āsi you are
asiddha 120/3 mfn. imperfect, incomplete, unaccomplished,
asiddhi f. non-attainment, failure, want of proof, conclusion not warranted by the premises,
āsīḥ you (s) were
āśi f. eating, P. to sharpen, make zealous,
āśina 157/1 aged, eating 2. √*aś*
āśīs 157/2 asking for, prayer, wish, blessing, benediction,
āsīt *as* 1/s/impf/act was
āsīta he might sit, he should sit, 1/s/opt/mid √*ās*
Asitaḥ Devala a legendary sage
aśīti eighty,
aślīla mfn ugly, vulgar, coarse,
aśma 114/1 a stone
asmāt 5/s from this therefore
āsma pron. we (pl) were
asmābhiḥ pron. by us pl.
asmabhyam pron. for us pl.
asmad pron. personal pronoun base, I we, us, at beginning of a compound
asmadīya by our,
asmadīyaiḥ our
asmākam pron. of us, ours, our 6/pl.
aśman m. 1. stone, f. *aśmā* 2. thunderbolt, 3. vault of heaven,
asmān pron. us 2nd pl.
asmāsu pron. in us pl.
asmat pron. from us (pl.
asmi verb to be 1/s/pres/act I am

asmin pron. 7/s in this
aśnan eating pres/act/part √*aś*
aśnat 114/1 part. eating
asnāvira 123/1 mfn. without sinews
asnihyat fell in love
aśnute attains, reaches, 1/s/pres/indic/mid √*aś*
a-śocya 114/1 mfn. the state of being not to be lamented
aśoka name of a tree
aśokavṛkṣa a kind of tree with magnificent red flowers
aśoṣya not to be dried, withered *a*√*śuṣ*
aspṛha 123/2 mn desireless
aśraddadhānana 114/2 mfn not trusting in
aśrama mfn indefatigable,
āśrama 158/2 a halting place, one of 4 stages in the life of a *brāhman, (brahmacārin*- student of the *veda, grīhastha*- household life, *vānaprastha*- forest life, - *saṁnyāsin*- abandoner of worldly concerns) *āśramin* belonging to..one of the 4 stages,
a hut, college, school, a wood or thicket, a hermitage
aśrauṣam I have heard 3/s/aorist/act √*śru*
āśraya 158/2 that to which anything is closely connected or on which anything depends or rests, resting place, place of refuge, shelter,
āśrayet should cling to or lean on, 1/s/opt/act *ā*√*śri*
āśrita 158/3 atttaching ones-self to, joining, having recourse to, seeking refuge or shelter from, subject to, depending on, concerning, practising, observing, using
āśritya 158/3 part. employing, practising, having recourse to,
taking refuge in, depending on
asṛj or *asṛk* n. blood,
aśṛṇot listened
asṛṣṭānna 121/3 mfn one who does not distribute food, not offered, (as in sacrificial food not offered to Brāhmaṇas)

aśru 14/3 n. a tear (as in crying)
asta mfn thrown, cast, n. home, esp. of the sun, m. setting (the sun or other luminaries, end, death,
āsta pron. you (pl) were
aṣṭa eight
aṣṭādaśan eighteen,
aṣṭadhā eightfold
āstam pron. you two were
āstām pron. they two were
astam 122/1 n. home, m. setting (as of the sun), end, death, ind. at home, home,
aṣṭan eight,
aṣṭāṅga yoga of *patañjali* the eightfold *yoga* of p... consisting of *yama, niyama, āsana, prāṇāyāma, pratyāhāra, dhyāna, dhāraṇā, samādhi*
aṣṭāvakra a wise counsellor of king *Janaka*
āste √*ās* to sit, be present, 159/3 sits, to be present, to exist,
1/s/pres/indic/mid sits
asteya n. not stealing, '.. to be fair, equitable, is the human law, to steal is against the law'
asthāpayat placed, put
āsthāya having recourse to, following, practicing, (gerund),
āsthita 161/2 mfn abiding being, existing, attained, obtained, established, seated in, staying or sitting on,
asti verb √*as* 117/1 to be present, to rest, to exist, live, be present, 1/s/pres/act/indic he, she or it is, f. being,
asthi or *asthī* n. a bone, a fruit kernel,
asthira 123/1 mfn. unsteady, trembling transient, doubtful, changeable
āsthita 161/2 mfn. staying or sitting on, abiding, one who has undertaken or performed, being, existing
āstikya faith, respect for the teaching of the scriptures
astra n. arrow, weapon,
astu let there be, let it be 1/s/impv/act √*as*
asu 121/1 m. breath, life
āśu 157/3 mfn. fast, quick, going quickly, ind. quickly, immediately,

aśubha 113/3 bad, vicious (as thought or speech), sin

aśuci unclean, impure,

asukhi unhappy, miserable

asura 121/1 mfn. spiritual, incorporeal, divine, (*as*) m. a spirit, good spirit, supreme spririt, the chief of the evil spirits, an evil spirit, demon, ghost, opponent of the gods, demons of the first order in perpetual hostility with the gods, (*ī*) f. a female demon

asūra n. absence of sunlight, (*e*) ind. in the night

āsura 160/3 mf(i)n. spiritual or divine, belonging or devoted to evil spirits, demonic, m. an *Asura* or demon,

asurī f. a female demon

āsurī 160/3 female demon, surgery

asurya 121/2 mfn. incorporeal, spiritual, divine, demoniacal
n. spirituality, divine nature, the collective body of spiritual beings

asūrya mfn. sunless, demoniacal, inaccessible, unknown,
(am) ind. at night

aśuśrūṣā 113/3 non-desire of hearing, disobedience from desid. √*śru*

aśuśrūṣāve 4/s/m of above- to one who does not wish to listen ,

asūyā f. impatience, envy,jealousy,

āsva pron. we two were

aśva a horse

ā√svad to eat, consume, *svadati*, caus. *svādayati*, eat with relish,

āsvādana 162/1 n. the act of eating, tasting, enjoying

aśvamedha m.horse sacrifice

asvargya 124/1 mfn. not leading to heaven

ā√śvās 159/2 to breathe again or freely, take heart or courage, revive

āśvāsayām āsa he caused to take heart caus/peri/perf *ā√śvas* + √*ās* 1/s/perf (used in the sense of continuing)

aśvatara m. mule, f. (*ī*)

aśvattha 115/3 'under which horses stand', the holy fig tree,

aśvin 116/1 mfn. possessed of horses, consisting of horses, mounted on horseback, a cavalier, name of two divinities – they bring treasures to men and avert misfortune and sickness

Aśvatthāmān a *Kaurava* warrior 'having the strength of a horse'

asya pronoun - of this

asya fut/pass/part of √ *as* is likely to be

asyām in it, in this, 7/s/f

āsyam mouth, face,

āt ind. afterwards, then, further, also, therupon, *ād id* then indeed,

atad not that

ataḥ hence, from here, from this, then, from that time, therefore,

atandra 12/1 mfn. free from lassitude, alert, unwearied

atandrita as above

ātaṅka 134/2 disease, sickness, apprehension, fear

ātapa 134/2 mfn causing pain or affliction, m. heat (esp. from the sun), sunshine,

atapaska 12/1mfn one who neglects austerities

ātapavāraṇa n. umbrella, parasol,

atarat crossed

atas 12/1 ind. hence, so, from this, hence, from here,

ātatāyin 134/2 having one's bow drawn, endeavouring to kill someone, a murderer, warrior,

atattvārthavat 12/1 mfn not conformable with the nature of truth, without true purpose, not concerned with truth

ata-ūrdhvam 12/1 ind. henceforth, afterwards

atha 17/3 ind. an auspicious and inceptive particle, then, now, and,

atha kim what else? how else? quite so, assuredly, sure enough,

athāpi thus

atharva 4th division of the Veda

athavā 17/3 ind. or, rather, however
ind. is it not so, what? or, rather, however, or else, but, otherwise, when repeated, either or,

or rather, or perhaps, is it not so?
however
atho 17/3 ind. now, likewise, next, or, and,
ati- 12/2 a verbal prefix expressing
overmuch, passing, going,
excessive, intense, beyond,
surpassing, over,
excessiveness, excessively,
intensity,
atibhāravāhana mfn excessive-burden-
carrying,
atibhūmi f. excess, extensive land,
culmination, eminence, superiority,
atibhūmiṁ gam to go to excess,
reach the climax ,
atibodha m. increase in knowledge
atiricyate it exceeds, it surpasses, *ati √ric*
1/s/pres/mid
atiśayaḥ mfn pre-eminent, superior,
m. pre-eminence, eminence,
ātiṣṭha undertake, perform, carry out
2/s/impv/act *ā√sthā*
atiṣṭhat stood
atithi m. 14/1 a guest, a person entitled to
hospitality, name of *Agni*
atisvapna too much sleeping, oversleeping,
atīva ind. very, very much, too, quite,
supassing (with 2nd), exceedingly,
ativartate he goes beyond, he transcends,
1/s/pres/indic/mid *ati √vṛt*
atimānitā f. excessive pride, arrogance
ati √muc to avoid, escape, giving up
atīndriya mfn transcending the senses,
beyond the realm of the senses,
n. soul, spirit, the mind,
atirikta 15/2 mfn left with or as a
surplus, left apart, redundant, unequalled,
atiśānta m. completely at rest,
completely peaceful,
atisarga m. the act of parting with,
giving away, granting permission
atisarjana n. the act of giving away,
granting, liberality, a gift, sending,
atiśaya mfn pre-eminent, superior,
m. pre-eminence, eminence,
superiority, excess,
ati √sṛj to glide over or along,
to send away, dismiss, abandon,
to remit, forgive, give away, present,
atisṛjya 16/1 to be dismissed, or given up
atīta 16/2 gone by, passed away, dead,
transcended, gone beyond,
atitārin 14/1 crossing,
atitārya to be crossed or passed over
or overcome
atītya going beyond, transcending,
gerund *ati√ī*
atīva very
ativartate moves beyond, transcends,
1/s/pres/mid *ati√vṛt*
ātmā 135/1 the Self (in all)
ātmabhāvasthaḥ situated in one's own
being, dwelling in one's own being
ātmaja son
ātmajā daughter,
ātmajña 135/2 knowing one's Self,
6/s knower of the Supreme Spirit
ātmajñāna " .the experience of the Self,
not as this and that, but as Itself".
HH
ātmaka Apte 78/2 made up or composed of,
(*am*) n. of the nature of, consisting
of,
ātmakṛpā the grace of the Self,
ātman the Self 135/1 the highest
personal principle of life, the
individual soul, the Self,
ātmanaḥ his
ātmanivedana 135/2 n.offering oneself to a
deity
ātmārāma 136/1 m one who rejoices
in his own Self
ātmasāt √kṛ to appropriate,
ātmavaśa 135/3 mfn. dependent on one's
own will, self-controlled,
self-restrained
ātmavat 135/3 mfn. having a soul, self-
possessed
ātmavān possessed of the Self, full of the
Self m.
ātmavat 135/3 mfn. having a soul, prudent,
composed, self-possessed,
ātmavanta as above
ātmavibhūtayas self powers or
manifestations 1/pl/f
ātmavinigrahas control of the aggregate

of body and organs
ātmikā having the nature of Self
āṭopa m. swelling, pride, flatulence, a multitude, redundancy, haste,
atra here, with regard to (this)
atrāntare meanwhile, meantime, on this occasion, at this juncture,
atra tatra sarvatra here, there, everywhere
aṭṭālaka m. a watch-tower,
aṭṭālikrā f. a high mansion,
atudat was hit or struck,
ātura 135/1 suffering, sick, afflicted with sorrow, affected by,
atyadbhūta mfn n. extremely marvellous
atyāgī who do not resort to renunciation,
atyanta 16/3 beyond the proper end or limit, excessively, endless, thoroughly,
ātyantika 136/1 continual, uninterrupted, infinite, endless, entire, universal
atyartha 17/1 excessively, exceedingly, beyond, beyond the proper worth
atyaśnata mfn eaten too much,
atyaya m. end. passing, lapse, passage, passing away, perishing, death,
atyeti outruns
atyucchrita raised too high, *aty-ud -√śri*
atyuṣṇa very hot
aucitya n. fitness, suitableness, decorum,
audāsīnya 237/3 indifference, apathy, disregard,
aupamya 238/3 n. the state or condition of resemblance or equality, comparison, analogy
aupaniṣada 238/2 mfn. contained or taught in an *upaniṣad*, a follower of the *U°*, a *vedāntin*
auṣadha 240/2 consisting of herbs, a herb, medicine, medicine in general
autsukya n. anxiety,
āvābhyām pron. by/for/from us two
avācya 106/3 not to be spoken
avadat said
avadāta mfn cleansed, clean, clear, pure, blameless, excellent, of white splendour, dazzling white, clear, intelligible, m. white colour,
avadhāna n. attention, attentiveness, intentness,
avadhārya 100/1 mfn to be ascertained or known, aware that,
avadhi m. attention, a term, limit, conclusion, termination, environs, (G) supernatural cognition, transcendental knowledge, clairvoyance, limit,
avadhya inviolable, not to be harmed,
avadya mfn censurable, blamable, low, inferior, disagreeable, n. anything blamable, want, imperfection, vice, blame, shame, disgrace,
avagacchati goes down, understands,
avagaccha understand! 2/s/impv. *ava√gam*
āvaha 155/1mfn. bringing, conveying, bringing to pass, producing, what bears or conveys, m. inviting, invitation,
avahāsa 106/2 jest, joke, laughing
avahela f.n. disrespect, disregard, (*ayā* 3rd) ind. without any trouble, quite easily,
avajānanti they despise or treat with contempt 1/s/pres/indic/act *ava √jñā*
avajñāta 98/2 mfn. despised, disrespected
avakāśa m. 1. an open place, 2. opportunity, occasion,
avalambate 103/2 rest on, 1/s/pres/indic/mid depends upon,
avalepa m. pride, insult, arrogance,
āvali m. (*ī*) f. a continuous line, series, dynasty, a row, range,
avalokana 103/3 seeing, viewing, observing
avalokya ind. having seen, mfn to be looked at
āvām *pron.* we/us two
avamāna 101/3 disrespect, contempt, dishonour
avamāna 101/3 disrespect, contempt, dishonour
avanata mfn bent down
avani f. course, bed of a river, stream, earth,
avanipāla ruler of the earth
avantiḥ name of a city (now Ujjain)
avāpnoti 107/1 to reach, obtain, get, gain, 1/s/pres/act. to cause to obtain anything, he attains

avāpnu 107/1 *avāpnuhi* to reach, obtain, attain. *-nuyāt* opt.act. 1/s should attain
avāpya ind. having attained/obtained
avāpsyasi you will attain, you will incur
avāpsyatha you shall attain, you shall achieve, 2/pl/fut/mid *ava √āp*
avāptavya to be attained or reached gerundive
avāptum infin. to attain, reach *ava √āp*
avāpyate it is attained or reached, 1/s/pres/indic/pass *ava √āp*
avara 102/2 mfn below, inferior, low, mean, posterior, West, n. the lowest, the meanest
āvaraṇa 'the limiting of the limitless or superimposing one limit on another' such as 'the presumption of snake over rope. This superimposition causes agitation (*vikṣepa*). 156/1 mfn. covering, hiding, concealing, (am) n. the act of covering, concealing, (in phil. mental blindness),
āvaraṇaśakti f. the power of illusion
avardhata grew
avarodha 1. mfn hindrance, obstruction, injury, harm, seclusion, imprisonment, an enclosure, confinement, a covering, a lid, fence, pen, the inner apartments, the queen's or women's apartments, 2. m. moving down, a shoot or root sent down by a branch,
āvarta 156/1 m. turning, winding, an eddy, turning round, deliberating
avaśa 104/1 mfn. unsubmissive to another's will, independent, unrestrained, free, 104/2 f. wrong desire,
avasādayet one should degrade, cause to sink, render downhearted, dispirit, 1/s/caus/act/opt *ava √ sad* 104/3
avasāna mfn not dressed, 2. n. limit, end conclusion, where the horses are unharnessed, stopping or resting place, residence, a chosen building site, conclusion, termination, cessation, death, boundary, of a word, last part of a compound, end of a phrase, end of a line of verse or the line itself,
avasara 105/1 m. rain, occasion, moment, favourable opportunity, seasonableness, appropriate place for anything, leisure, a year, 7th *(e)* ind. at the right moment,
avasat dwelt
avaśeṣa n. leavings, remainder, (*am*) ind. so as to leave as a remnant,
avaśiṣyate 104/2 to be left as a remnant, remain, 1/s/pres/pass remains,
avaṣṭabhya 104/2 resting on, supported by
avasthā state, state of experience, state of consciousness, condition,
avasthātum 105/3 to stand, to remain standing, infinitive of *ava √sthā*
avasthita 106/*1* mfn. standing near, having it's place or abode, abiding, resident, continuing to do anything, stationed, placed
avastutvāt 105/3 n. because of unreality
avaśya mfn necessary
āvaśyaka mfn necessary, inevitable, (*am*) n. necessity, inevitable act or conclusion,
avaśya mfn necessary (*am)* ind. necessarily, surely, of course, indeed,
avaśyā f. hoar frost, dew,
avaśyāya m. hoar frost, dew,
avasyu mfn desiring favour or assistance, desirous of helping or assisting,
avaṭa m. a hole, vacuity in the ground,
avata m. a well, cistern,
avataṁsa m. ear-ring,
avatāra an incarnation of *Viṣṇu,* descent, manifestation (of a deity),
avatarati comes down, descends,
avatiṣṭhati 105/3 remains standing, stays, abides, takes his stand, remains firm
avātsīḥ you have lived 2/s/aorist 5. *√vas*
avayava 102/2 a limb, member, part, portion,
āvayoḥ pron. of/in us two
avekṣe I see, I behold, 111/1 *ava √īkṣ*

1/s/pres/indic/mid

avekṣya looking at, perceiving, beholding,

āveśa 155/3 m. joining one's self, taking possession of, absorption of the faculties in one wish or idea, intentness, devotedness to an object, possession, anger, wrath, pride, arrogance, indistinctness of idea, 'agitative charge or aggressiveness'

aveśita entering, abiding in,

āveśya having caused to enter, fixing, concentrating
caus.gerund *ā√viś*

avibhakta 109/2 mfn. undivided, not shared, joint, (*am*) n.

avidvāṁa the unwise perf.act.part *a √vid*

avidhipūrvakam 108/3 ind. not according to Vedic rule, in the absence of fixed rules,

avidita 108/3 mfn. unknown
(am) ind. so that nobody knows

avidyā 108/3 mfn. unlearned, unwise, 1/s/f ignorance, spiritual ignorance, illusion, (personified as *māyā*)

avihvala 110/3 not disquieted, unperturbed

avijñeya mfn not to be known or understood gerundive, unknowable, not distinguishable, not discernible,

avikampa unwavering,

avikārya mfn. invariable

avikriya 107/3 unchangeable

avikṛta 107/3 mfn unchanged, not prepared being in its natural condition

āvila mfn turbid, foul, not clear, confused,

avināśa 109/1 m. non-destruction

avināśin imperishable

avināśyanta not perishing, not lost or dying

avipaścit 109/1 mfn. unwise, ignorant

avirata mfn uninterrupted, continuous, not desisting from, (*am*) ind. continuously,

aviruddha 109/3 mfn. unobstructed, unimpeded, not incompatible with, consistent with, not opposed to, not encountering resistance from

ā√viś to go or drive in or towards, approach, enter, settle, reach, obtain

aviśeṣa 110/1 m. non-distinction, non-difference,

aviśiṣṭa " a synonym for *nirguṇa*" HH uniformity

aviṣṭa *m.* taken possession of, fallen into, overcome by, ppp. *a √viś*

āviṣṭa 155/1 *ā√viś*, mfn. entered, being on or in, intent on, subject to, possessed, engrossed, filled (by sentiment)

āviśya entering, approaching, having entered or approached, gerund *ā√viś*

āviveśa entered

ā √vṛ 156/1 to cover, hide, conceal

avraṇa not wounded

avratī (A) p60 desireless (E) p132 passionless

āvriyate he is covered, he is enveloped 1/s/pres/indic/pass *ā √vṛ* 156/1

ā √ vṛt 1.turn or draw round or back or near 2. f. a turning towards or home, entering, turn of path or way, course, process, direction,

āvṛta 156/1 mfn. enveloped, covered, concealed,

āvṛtta turned round, stirred,

āvṛtti return, turning towards, entering, reversion, retreat, flight, rebirth

āvriyate he is covered, he is enveloped 1/s/pres/indic/pass *ā√vṛ* 156/1

āvṛtya ind. enveloping, covering, obscuring, having enveloped, spread or pervaded

avyabhicāra 111/3 m. non-deviation, not going astray or wandering, non-transgression, unwavering
-cārin mfn. as above, permanent

avyākṛta 112/1mfn. undeveloped, un-expounded, n. elementary substance from which all things were created, considered as one with the substance of Brahman

avyakta 111/2 mfn undeveloped, not manifest, invisible, imperceptible, "..the unmanifest nature of the Absolute, .. it is here that the divine regulations are held and may be

known" LM, unmanifest (in seed or causal form),
m. the Universal Spirit,
avyavasāya m. irresolute, wavering,
avyavasāyin mfn not dtermined or resolute,
avyaya 111/3 2. an indeclinable word, a particle, imperishable, undecaying, words or particles which do not change their grammatical form whatever the position in a sentence. not liable to change
aya 84/2 m. ifc. going √*i*
ayam m. pron. 1/s this
āyāma 148/2 m. stretching, extending, restraining, stopping
ayanṣu 7/pl/n in positions, progress, movements
ayaśas 85/1 n. infamy, disrepute, bad reputation, disgraced,
ayas n. metal, iron, an iron weapon,
āyāsa 148/2 effort, exertion, (bodily or mental), trouble,
āyāsadam suffix *dam* indicates an adverb of time, (W 1103b) persistent effort,
a-yat 84/3 mfn. not making efforts
a-yata mfn unrestrained, uncontrolled
āyata mfn long, wordy
āyatana 148/1 n. resting place, home, house, abode, an altar, a plot of ground,
ayathā 84/3 ind. not as it should be,
ayathāvat incorrectly, wrongly,
a-yati no ascetic,
āyāti 148/3 coming near, arrival, coming from, coming back, comes to, reaches, attains,

āyāti 148/3 to reach, attain
āyatta dependent on,
āyātu 1/s/pres/impv/act may cease
aye ind. an interjection showing surprise
ayi ind. a voc. particle , introducing encouragement or a kind enquiry
ayīva very, exceedingly,
ayodhyā a capital city, home of *Rāmaḥ*
ayogata without yoga
ayomaya mfn made of iron,
āyudha 149/1 n. a weapon, implement, gold used for ornaments,
ayukta 85/3 mfn. not yoked, not harnessed, not connected, not united, not joined, (*am*) ind. not yoked,
āyus n. activity, liveliness, life, period or duration of life, long life, age
babhūva he/she/it was or became 1/s/perf/act √*bhū*
baddha baddha 720/2 mfn bound, tied, fixed, fastened, tied, bound by the fetters of existence..., 1/s/m that which binds or fetters the embodied spirit, bound
baddhavā having bound
bādha mfn distressing, m. distress, a molestation, affliction, *(ā)* f. injury, detriment, hurt, damage, suspension, annulment (of a rule), obstruction, a contradiction,objection, absurdity,
bāḍham certainly, yes,
bādhate he troubles, he attacks
badhira mfn deaf,
badhnāti binds
badhura mfn handsome,
bādhyamānā pres.pass.part. (she) being troubled
bahala mfn thick, abundant, bushy (tail), deep or intense (colour),
bahavaḥ 1/p/m many
bahis ind. outside, as prep. outside of,
bāhi 726/3 ind. out, forth, outwards,
bahu 724/2 much, many
bahudhā 726/2 many times, in many ways, variously, repeatedly
bāhu m. arm, fore-arm,
bahukālam ind. for a long time
bahula much, many, dense, copious,
bāhulya n. abundance, commonness, state of being usual, usual order of things, *-āt* in accordance with the usual order of things, *-ena* mostly,
bahumāna m. esteem, respect,
bahūni many 1/pl/n
bahuvacana case-endings and personal terminations in number, plural,
bahuvāram ind. many times, often
bahuvidha mfn of many kinds or sorts
bāhya 730/3 mfn being outside,

outer, external, expelled from caste or communitym. a corpse, the outer part, exterior, ibc. outside, without,

bāhyatas ind. outside, externally,

baka m. heron, crane, fig. a hypocrite, cheat, rogue,

bakula m. name of a tree,

bala 722/3 n. power, strength, might, force, vigour,

bāla 728/3 young, a child, childish, foolish, a boy under 5
- *vat* suffix "like" like a child,

balāt ind. forcibly

bali 723/3 tribute, offering, gift

bālaka m. little boy (*-ka* diminutive)

balāka m. crane,

bali 723/3 tribute, offering, gift, portion of meal or sacrifice offered as tribute, tax,

bālikā girl, young woman,

bāliśa 729/3 mfn childish, ignorant, 1/s/m a fool

baliṣṭha mfn most mighty, very strong.

balivarda or *balīvarda* m. bull, ox,

ballava m. cowherd, cook, f.(*ī*)

bālya 729/3 n. boyhood, childhood, immaturity of understanding,

bāṇa m. an arrow, cow udder, , (*ā*) f. the feathered end of an arrow, n. the body, 'aggregate of body and senses' (Gam.),

baṇḍa mfn maimed, defective, crippled,

bandha mfn 720/3 binding , tying, bondage, imprisonment, custody, m. a binding, (in phil.) mundane bondage, attachment to this world, 2. band, string,

bandhu m. connection, relation, association, friend, companion
bandhūn 2/pl/m relatives, kinsmen

bandhana 721/1mfn binding, tying, a bond, tie, m. a relative, friend,

bāndhava m. kinsman, relation, friend,

bandhu 721/1 m. connection, relation, association, kinship, a relative, kindred, a friend, a husband, a brother,

bandin m. prisoner, a praiser, bard,

barbara mfn stammering, m. foreigners (applied to non-Aryans by Aryans), a man of lowest origin, a wretch,

barha m.n. tail feather,

bāṣpa m. a tear (as in crying)

bāṣpākala mfn agitated by tears, inarticulate through tears,

bata alas!

baṭu m. boy, lad, youth,

bhā 750/3 1. to shine, be bright or luminous, shine forth, appear

bhā 2 f. light, brightness, splendour

bhadra 745/3 √*bhand* mfn blessed, auspicious, fortunate, happy, good, gracious, prosperous, friendly, kind, excellent, fair, beautiful, lovely, pleasant, dear, good i.e. skilfull in (7th), great, (*am* and *ayā*) ind. happily, fortunately, joyfully,

bhādra m. name of a rainy month from mid–August to mid-September,

bhāga 751/2 a part or portion

bhagavan 743/3 holy, glorious, illustrious, used as a form of address to gods, demigods, and saints, O Blessed One,

bhagavān the Lord, the greatly fortunate, your lordship,

bhagavat mfn ' possessing good fortune', fortunate, prosperous, glorious, blessed, heavenly, venerable, holy, lordly, m. the divine or adorable one,

bhagin mfn fortunate, happy, splendid, prosperous, perfect, glorious,

bhāgin mfn 751/3 entitled to or receiving or possessing a share, partaking of.

bhāgineyaka m. sister's son,

bhaginī f. sister,

bhagīratha m. an ancient king who brought the Ganges down from heaven,

bhāgīratha mfn of *bhagīratha* , f. (*é*) the stream of B°, the Ganges,

bhāgya n. lot, fate, esp. happy lot, luck, *bhāgyena* luckily,

bhaikṣa 766/3 living on alms

√*bhaj* 743/1 cl1 P *bhajati* A *bhajate* to serve, honour, revere, love, adore,

P to divide, distribute, allot or apportion to, share with, adore, A. to grant, bestow, obtain as one's share, partake of, enjoy, DP in *sevā* (cl 1) serving, *viśrāṇana* (cl 10) giving

bhaja 2/s/pres/impv/act (you) cultivate

bhajāmi I share with, I love, I reward 3/s/pres/indic/act √*bhaj*

bhajana n. the act of sharing, possession, ifc. reverence, worship, adoration, devotional singing,

bhājana n. a vessel. pot, receptacle, a fit object,

bhajante they get or obtain 1/pl/pres/mid

bhajati 743/1 he honors, loves or worships

bhāk from root *bhāj* 752/1 enjoying, devoted to, to serve, honour, love, adore, enjoy,

bhakṣita eaten

bhakta 743/1 mfn attached or devoted to, loyal, faithful, honouring, worshipping, serving, m. a worshipper, devotee, n. food or a meal, cooked rice, any edible grain boiled with water, a vessel, a share, portion,

bhakti 743/1 f. distribution, partition, share, belonging to, attachment, devotion, fondness for, devotion to, homage, worship, piety, faith or love

bhaktimān full of devotion

bhalla mfn auspicious, favourable,

bhallaka m. a bear

bhāma m 1. light, brightness, splendour, 2. rage, fury, (*ā)* f. a passionate woman,

bhāṇḍāra m. a storehouse,

bhaṅga 744/3 mfn breaking, bursting, m.the act of breaking, splitting, a wave, a water-course, a bend,

bhaṅgara mfn fragile,

bhaṅgi f. breaking, a bend, curve, circumlocution, mode, manner,

bhānu m. the sun, appearance, brightness, light or a ray of light, lustre,

bhāra m. burden

bharataḥ *Bharataḥ*

bhārataḥ descendant of *Bharataḥ* a name for *Yudhiṣthira,*

Bharatarṣabha Bull of the *Bharatas (Arjuna)*

bhāratī goddess of speech, (Sarasvatī),

bhartā supporter, bearer, sustainer

bhartṛ 748/1 m. one who bears or carries or maintains, a bearer, protector, maintainer, a husband, (*trī*) wife

bhāryā wife

bhāsa 756/1 m. light, lustre, brightness, impression made on the mind, fancy, a bird of prey, vulture,

bhāṣā speech, conversation, language, definition,

bhāsate 755/3 he/she/it shines, appears, or is appearing, ,

bhāṣate (or *–ti*) speaks, says, tells

bhāṣase you speak, say 2/s/pres/act √*bhāṣ*

bhāsayate causes to shine or illuminate

bhasita mfn reduced to ashes, n. ashes,

bhāṣitum (infinitive), to speak

bhāskara m. the sun,

bhasman 750/3 devouring, consuming, pulverizing, (what is pulverized by fire) ashes,

bhasmāntam reduced to ashes, (the body)

bhasmasāt ind. with √*kṛ* to reduce to ashes,

bhastrā f. a leather bag, bellows,

bhāṣya commentary to a major work

bhaṭa m. soldier, combatant,

bhāti 750/3 √*bhā* to shine, be bright or luminous, shine forth, to appear as, be, exist, exists or shines, 'that which exists proclaims itself through its brilliance and is known to be there; this is called *bhāti'* HH 'The word bhāti is the act of knowing, known, so it is directly related to knowledge. The knowledge is again only one and it arises from that which is in existence. ... includes knowledge of existence and knowledge of ignorance, ... knowledge of the Brahman and knowledge of the world'.

bhatsanā f. threat
bhaumavāra Tuesday *bhauma* 768/3 name of the planet Mars whose day is Tuesday, also to do with the earth and production from the earth, earthy, corn, grain
bhava 748/3 m. coming into existence, birth, life,
2/pres/impv. √*bhū* you be, be! exist! become! let be,
bhāva 754/1 becoming, being, existing, turning or transition into, occurring, appearance, state of being anything, true state, manner of being, that which is or exists, way of thinking or feeling, being or living creature, states of existence,
'the emotional realm' HH
bhavad in comp. for *bhavat,* Your Honour,
bhavadīya your honour's your,
bhāvaka 755/1 mfn causing to be, effecting (comp.), imagining, fancying, having a taste for the beautiful or poetical, singing with expression, m. sentiment, affection,
expression of amatory sentiments,
bhavān a form of *bhavat,* a respectful form of address – your honour, your worship, (lit. the gentleman or lady present) 2/s/m you
bhavana n. dwelling, residence, house,
bhāvana 755/1 mfn causing to be, forming in the mind, conception, fancy, thought, imagination,
m. a creator, producer, efficient,
bhāvanā 755/1 f. causing to be, manifesting, imagining, thought, the act of producing or effecting, feeling of devotion, faith in, reflection, contemplation, right conception or notion, emotional intent, "sometimes used as emotion and being" HH "the individual is free in *bhāvanā.* This should be taken as dedication. An individual can dedicate any *bhāvanā* to anyone. He can deliberately create a *bhāvanā* within himself and work accordingly. even in miserable conditions, people become happy or in happy conditions become miserable because they choose it like that." HH "the emotion with which the work is being done, the real motive with which the first move into the activity was made". HH "The *bhāvanā* is the most basic factor of all activity. That must be pure. It should be a dedication, an offering to the Absolute, or a service to *samaṣṭi*. That will bestow on it the pleasure of the Lord and give it the most glorious meaning." HH
bhavantas 1/pl/ honorific, your lordships
bhavaroga 'the disease of existence' HH
bhāvasaṁśuddhis purity of being, purity of heart, absence of manipulation
bhavat mfn being, present, *bhavat* m.f. respectful address, you sir, your honour,
bhavata be! become! pl.
bhavati verb to be 1/s/pres/indic/act he/she becomes
bhavatu let it be! 1/s/act/ impv.
bhāvayantas cherishing, fostering, pres. part. 1/pl/m *bhū*
bhāvayanti root *bhū* to think about, consider, 760/2 1/pl/causative *bhū* they consider
bhāvayata may you cherish, or foster, may you cause to be, may you increase the well-being of, 2/pl/caus/opt/act *bhū*
bhāvayantu may they cherish or foster, may they cause to be, may they increase the well-being of 1/pl/caus/impv/act *bhū*
bhāve in meaning or in intention 7/s
bhavet verb to be, 1/pres/opt he should be/become , it would be
bhāvin mfn becoming, being, existing, wont to be (ifc.), about to be, future, imminent, predestined, inevitable,
bhāvinbuddhi mfn one who has cultivated or purified his mind,
bhaviṣyāmaḥ we shall be, we shall exist,

1/pl/fut/act √*bhū*
bhaviṣyasi 2/s/fut you will be
bhaviṣyat 750/1 mfn about to become or be, future, n. the future
bhāviṣyati 760/1 1/s/fut/act. of *bhū,* will come into being, he will be, it will arise
bhaviṣyatkāla future tense
bhavitā he, she, it will become, will be, 1/s/periphrastic future
bhāvitaḥ transformed into, caused to become, caus. part.
bhavitum infinitive of verb to be *bhū* 760/1 to become
bhāvya 755/2 about to be or be effected or performed, future or what ought to be,
bhaya 747/1 n. fear, alarm, dread, danger, apprehension
bhayaṁkara mfn causing or inspiring fear, fearsome,
bhayānaka 747/2 fearful, terrible, dreadful, m. the sentiment of terror, a tiger
bheda 766/1 m. breaking, splitting, cleaving, opening, expanding, a cleft, separation,
bheka m. a frog, a cloud, a timid man, f. (*ī*)
bheryas 1/pl/f large drums
bheṣaja 766/3 curing, healing, medicine, *bheṣajam* 2/s/n a remedy
Bhīma a powerful warrior, brother of *Arjuna*, tremendous, awful
√*bhī* 1.cl3 to fear, be afraid of
bhī 2. 758/1 f. fear, apprehension, fright
√*bhid* cl7split, cleave, break, cut or rend asunder, pierce, destroy, *bhinatti, bhintte,*
bhidura mfn fragile, brittle,
bhīta mfn afraid, fearful, (*am*) ind. timidly, n. fear, danger,
bhikṣā 756/2 f. the act of begging or asking,
bhikṣu 756/3 one who subsists entirely on alms, 1/s/m a mendicant
bhīmaḥ *Bhīma 758/1* terrible, awful
bhīmakarman formidable in action
bhinna 757/1 changed, altered, different from, broken, distinct from, other than,
bhīru mfn timid,
bhiṣaj mfn healing, m. healer, physician,
bhīṣaṇa mfn terrible,
Bhīṣma famous warrior, 'awesome', 'terrible' great uncle of *Arjuna* but fighting for the opposing *Kuru* army,
bhīta mfn afraid, fearful, (*am*) ind. timidly, n. fear, danger,
bhīti f. fear,
bhitti f. a wall,
bhiyas 758/1 m. fear, apprehension
bho 768/2 used in addressing another, Oh Your Honour, Sir, voc. of *bhavat,*
bhoktāra enjoyer, eater
bhoga 767/2 2 m. experiencing, feeling, sense enjoyment,
bhojana n. a meal,
bhojya 768/2 to be enjoyed or eaten, a festive dinner + *māna* 809/1 respect, honour. pres/mid/part. feasted or honoured
bhokṣyase you shall enjoy, you shall eat, 2/s/fut/mid √*bhuj*
bhoktā 759/2 [under *bhuj* to enjoy, use, possess], f. the enjoyer,
bhoktāra m. enjoyer, eater
bhoktṛ 760/1 m. one who enjoys or eats, enjoyer, eater, experiencer
bhos Oh!
bhrama 769/3 confusion, mistake, error, mistaking anything for, illusion, wandering or roaming about, turning round, revolving
bhramara m. a bee, bumble-bee, a young man, lad, a potter's wheel,
bhramati he/she/it wanders or roams about 1/s/pres/indic/act √*bhrams* 769/2
bhramabhūta 769/3 being an error, erroneous, unreal
bhramati 769/2 wanders or roams about, 1/s/pres/act he she or it roams
bhrāmayan causing to move, causing to wander, revolving, caus/pres/part
bhrānta 770/1 moving about unsteadily, being in doubt or error, confused, perplexed, deluded

bhrānti 770/1 f. confusion, error, mistaking something for, false impression of, supposing anything to be or exist, illusion,

bhraṣṭa mfn fallen, dropped, broken down, decayed, lost, gone, fled or escaped from, strayed or separated from, depraved, vicious, a backslider, f. a fallen or unchaste woman,

bhrātṛ a brother or an intimate friend,

bhrātṝn brothers, 2/pl/m

bhṛgu 765/1 name of a mythical race of men associated with bringing fire to men, name of a *ṛṣi* (supposed author of the *ṛk veda*)

bhṛṅga m. a bee,

bhṛśa 765/3 mfn mighty, strong, often, powerful, abundant, vehement, (often ibc.), *(am)* ind. frequently , greatly, strongly, violently, excessively,

bhṛt 764/3 mfn. bearing, carrying, bringing, maintaining, supporting

-bhṛt a bearer

bhṛta 764/3 mfn borne, carried, gained, acquired, ifc. filled, full of, hired, paid, m. a dependant, a servant, mercenary,

bhṛtya m. (one who is to be maintained), a servant,

bhrūḥ 770/3 f. an eyebrow, the brow

bhruvos 6/du/f of the 2 eyebrows

√*bhū* 1. 760/1/2 cl 1 P A *bhavati*, (*te*) to become, be, arise, come into being, exist, be found, live, stay, abide, happen, occur, to fall to the share of, belong to, be on the side of, assist, serve for, tend to, be occupied with, devote oneself to, thrive or prosper in, be of consequence or useful, A. fall or get into, attain to, obtain, to obtain it, be successful or fortunate,

bhuja m. an arm (of the body), trunk, branch, bough, a bending, curve,

bhūja f. a winding, coil (of a snake), the arm or hand, the side of any geometrical figure,

bhujaga m. snake,

bhuṅkṣva enjoy! 2/s/impv √*bhuj*

bhuṅkte root *bhuj*, 759/2 1/s/pres/indic/mid eats

bhūmi m. ground, earth, element earth, soil, ground, foundation, floor,

bhūmipa *m.* king

bhūmipaḥ king,

bhūmṛt m. mountain, king,

bhūmyām on the ground

bhuñjīthāḥ you should enjoy or experience yourself, or make use of , (*īṣā up* protect yourself), 2/s/opt/mid

bhuñjiya I should enjoy, I should eat, 3/s/opt/mid √*bhuj*

bhuṅkte he enjoys, he eats, he possesses 1/s/pres/indic/mid √ *bhuj*

bhūpati m 761/2 "lord of the earth' a king, monarch, prince

bhūriśas 764/1 manifoldly, variously , in diverse ways,

bhūrloka m. this earth

bhūs it should be, it should arise 1/s/aor/subj √*bhū*

bhūṣaṇa n. ornament, jewel,

bhūta mfn become, been gone, past, (n. the past), actually happened, true, real, (n. matter of fact, a reality), existing, present, ifc. being or being like anything, consisting of, mixed or joined with,
m. a son, child, n. that which is or exists, any living being (divine, human, animal or vegetable), the world, a spirit (good or evil), a ghost, demon, goblin, an element, one of the 5 elements, or a *tanmātra (subtle-element),* well-being, welfare, prosperity, 761/3 n. that which is or exists, an element, a being or creature, vampire, goblin, ghost,

bhūtādi 762/2 original or originator of beings, the origin of beings, the beginning of beings,

bhūtastha abiding in beings, existing in beings, 761/3 living on the earth, residing in the elemants,

bhūtabhṛt sustaining beings, supporting beings

bhūtabhāva m. state of being

bhūtabhāvana m causing beings to be, causing beings to come into existence, causing welfare in beings,

bhūtagaṇa 761/3 the host of living beings, a multitude of spirits or ghosts

bhūtagrāma 761/3 any aggregate or elementary matter, the body, see also *bhūta,* 761/3 any living being and *grāma* 373/1 people 7/s in all beings

bhūtakāla past time or past tense

bhūtāni n.pl. beings, creatures

bhūti 762/3 f. existence, being, well-being, thriving, prosperity, might, power, wealth, fortune, riches,

bhūtvā having become, having been

bhuvana –760/3 being, man, the world, world, earth, *bhuvi* on earth

bhūya 763/3 m. more, very much being, becoming more, more numerous, greater, larger, most, moreover, still more, once more, again, generally, usually,

bhūyāya 4/s/n to oneness with, for becoming Brahman

bhūyiṣṭha 763/3 mfn. most numerous or abundant or great or important, chief, principal (*am*) ind. mostly, chiefly

bibharti 764/3 bears, carries, upholds

bībhatsa mfn loathsome, disgusting,

bibheti he fears, is anxious about, 1/s/pres √*bhī* 758/1 cl3

biḍāla m. a cat, the eye-ball,

bīja 732/2 n. seed (of plants), semen, seed-corn, grain, primary cause or principle, source, analysis, truth (as the seed or cause of being),

bījaprada 732/3 m. yielding or sowing seed, a generator, who deposits the seed

bila n. cleft, hollow, cave, hole,

bimba m.n. the sun disk or moon disc, a disk made of gold or silver, a mirror, an image, shadow, m. a lizard, chameleon,

bindu m. a drop, spot, pearl, coloured mark,

boddhyavyam to be known or enlightened, to be learned, gerundive √*budh*

bodha 734/2 knowing understanding, becoming or being awake or conscious, awakening, consciousness,

bodhamātra m. the full and simple measure of anything, pure consciousness,

bodhayanta enlightening, causing to enlighten, awakening, pres/act/caus/part. √*budh*

bodhi m. enlightenment,

bodhisattva m. an aspirant for enlightenment whose essence is perfect knowledge, one who is on the way to perfect knowledge and has only one birth to go, a Buddhist saint,

bodhātman 734/2 m. the intelligent and sentient Self, (Jainas),

brahmā the name for cosmic *buddhi* is *brahmā* HH 'The primal manifestation of the *nirguṇa brahman* into *saguṇa brahman* in the imagery of the creative deity is known as *brahmā*. It is a figurative term used for the point of departure from the *nirguṇa*. This is the state of the universal *buddhi*' HH. "... when one thinks and reasons with one's *buddhi*, one is acting as *brahmā* on the individual level" 738/1 the one impersonal universal spirit manifested as personal Creator and as the first of the triad of personal gods

brahma 738/1 in a compound for

Brahman 737/3 n. the one self-existent Spirit, the Absolute, truth, One without a second,

brahmabhūta 739/2 mfn. become absorbed in *Brahman,* n. identification with *Brahmā*

brahmabhūyā 739/2 n. identification with or absorption into Brahman *brahmacārin* 738/2 practising sacred study as an unmarried student, observing chastity and obedience,

brahmaloka 739/3 the world or heaven of *brahmā* (a division of the universe and one of the supposed residences of pious spirits) "where there are beings who have acquired great merits .."

brahmabhūtas 739/2 absorbed in Brahman, at one with Brahman

brāhma 741/1 relating to *brahma* or *brahmā,* holy, sacred, divine, relating to sacred knowledge, prescribed by the veda, scriptural

brahmacārin 738/2 mfn. practising sacred study as an unmarried student, observing chastity

brahmacarya 738/2 n. study of the veda, the state of an unmarried religious student, a state of continence and chastity,

brahmajajñam one that is born from *Brahmā* and illumined,

brahman 737/3 lit.n. growth, expansion, a sacred word, the sacred syllable Om, religious or spiritual knowledge, the one self-existent impersonal Spirit, the one universal Soul(or one divine essence and source from which all created things emanate or with which they are identified and to which they return, the Self-existent, the Absolute, the Eternal, (not generally an object of worship but rather of meditation and knowledge,) m. the Creator,

brāhmaṇa mfn. relating to or given by a *brāhman*, befitting or becoming a *brāhman*, m. one who has divine knowledge, a *brāhman*, a man belonging to the first of the classes or castes, generally a priest but often in present day a layman engaged in non-priestly occupations although the name is strictly only applicable to one who knows and repeats the *Veda*

brāhmaṇas the explanatory part of the *veda*- rules for recitation, legends

brahmāṇḍa 740/2 brahmā's egg, the universe

brahmanirvāṇa 'blown out", ceasing to exist, in Brahman

brahmāstram name of a terrible weapon

brahmāsūtrāṇi a harmony of *sūtra*s. teaching the single truth. "I am Brahman"

brahmavidyā 740/1 f. knowledge of the 'the one self-existent Being', sacred *knowledge*

brāhmī 742/1 the *śakti* or personified energy of Brahmā

brāhmī sthitiḥ the state of Brahman, Brahmanic position,

bravīmi 1/s/pres/indic/act I tell, I speak

bravīsi 2/s you tell, say

√2. *bṛḥ* pious effusion or utterance, outpouring of the heart in worshipping, 735/3 to increase, expand, DP in growing, increasing, expanding, sounding

G.96 the Absolute Reality, or all-pervasive principle of the universe, it has nothing similar to it and nothing different from it, the nature of *Brahman –sat* existence absolute, *cid* consciousness absolute, *ānanda* bliss absolute

bṛhaspati 737/1 head priest of the gods with whom he intercedes for men, god of wisdom, planet Jupiter,

bṛhat 735/3 lofty, high, tall, extended or bright, name of a man, name of a *marut,* name of various *sāman*s (a metrical hymn or song of praise) composed in *bṛhatī* form, name of *Brahman,* big, strong,

bṛhatsāma 736/1 having the *bṛhat-sāman* for a *sāman* (see above)

brūhi 742/1 √*brū* 2/s/mid/*lot* (impv) speak, say, tell

brūte 742/1 he says, tells, speaks, 1/s/pres/indic/mid

brūvan *brū* 742/1 to speak say, part. speaking

brūyāt should speak,

bubhukṣā 735/1 f. desire to enjoy anything

bubhukṣu 735/1 mfn wishing to be or become anything, wishing to become powerful or prevail, desiring power or personal change, 735/1 mfn wishing to eat, hungry, desirous of worldly enjoyment,

bubhutsā 734/2 desire to know, curiosity about

budbuda 733/1 a bubble m/1/plu often used as a symbol of something transitory

buddha 733/2 awake, awakened, expanded, conscious, intelligent, wise

buddhayā . through judging it to be, 3/s

buddhayas insights, enlightenments, 1/pl/f

buddhi 733/3 f. reason, the organ of discrimination, reflects the light of the *ātman*, intellect, the power of forming and retaining concepts and general notions, intelligence, reason, discernment, judgment, mind, perception, the name for cosmic *buddhi* is *brahmā,*
'*buddhi* is used in two main ways: reason or common-sense, intelligence to help deal with worldly affairs; and discrimination between conscious and inanimate, which is known as *viveka*, to exorcise the ghost of *ahaṅkāra* or *prakṛti*.'
reflects the light of the *ātman*

buddhimān m. full of wisdom, wise, enlightened, intelligent,

buddhitva understanding, having the nature of Buddhi,

buddhiyoga 734/1 devotion of the intellect, intellectual union with the Supreme Spirit, yoga of discrimination

buddhiyuktas he who is disciplined in determination through buddhi, 734/1 mfn endowed with understanding, intelligent,

buddhvā 733/2 understanding, having learned, having awakened, gerund, √ *budh*

budha 734/1 mfn clever, awaking, wise, intelligent, m. a wise or learned man, the planet Mercury,

ca and, also, (when more than two words are connected it is used with the last only),

caila 402/3 made of cloth, piece of cloth, bred in clothes (insects),

caitanya 402/2 consciousness, intelligence, spirit, Universal Soul or Spirit

caitra m. name of the 2nd spring month,

cakita mfn trembling, timid, frightened, n. timidity,

cakra 380/3 n. a wheel, a discus, a circle, G100. Centres (6) of energy in the subtle body where the (*nādi)* channels converge. These junctions, *cakras* or centres of consciousness regulate the body mechanism.

cakravartin mfn rolling every where without obstruction, supreme, m. an emperor, supreme, holding the highest rank,

cakravāta m. the whirlwind demon

cakrin 381/3 mfn bearing a discus

cakṣu 382/1 m. the eye,

cakṣus *m.* seeing, n. light, clearness, the act of seeing, faculty of seeing, sight, a look, the eye

cala 391/1 mfn. moving, trembling

calati 391/1 moves, is agitated, moved from one's usual course, is disturbed

cāmara mfn coming from the yak (*cam*), m. a chowrie (a fly-whisk made from the bushy tail of a yak,)

camatkāra m. admiration, astonishment,

caṁcala mfn moving to and fro, unsteady, inconstant, flickering, inconsiderate, m. the wind, a lover, libertine,

caṁcu f. beak,

caṇḍa mfn impetuous, wrathful, n. heat, passion, wrath, (*am*) ind. violently, in anger,

caṇḍāla m. a Chandāla man or man of the most despised class of society,

candana m. sandalwood,

caṇḍila m. a barber,

candra m. moon, glittering, shining, having the hue of light,

candramas m. moon, moon god,

candrikā f. moonlight,

cāṇūra *Cāṇūra*
cāpaḥ a bow, (as in bow and arrow), arc, rainbow,
capala mfn fickle, shaking,
capalā f. lightning,
cañcala 382/2 mfn. moving to and fro, shaking, flickering, movable, unsteady, inconstant, inconsiderate, intensive, from √cal 391/1
cāndra mfn. lunar, m. a lunar month *ī* f. moonlight
cāndramasa n. lunar
candramasi 7/s in the moon
cāṇūraḥ Cāṇūraḥ (a demon),
cāpa 393/1 m.n.a bow, an arc, a rainbow,
capeṭa m. a slap with the open hand,
cara 389/2 mfn moving, movable, walking, wandering, living, practising, m. spy
carama mfn last, ultimate, final,
caraṇa 1. m.n. foot, ifc. pl. 'the feet of the venerable', a pillar, support, root, a school or branch of the Veda, n. going round or about, motion
carata part. living, wandering
carati 389/1 *car* – to move, walk, go 1/s/pres/indic/act walks, moves, grazes,
cārin 393/3 mfn moving, ifc. living, being, moving, walking or wandering about, acting, doing, proceeding,
carita 389/3 gone to, attained, done, 2. conduct, behaviour, proceedings, deeds,
caritra n. an adventure, conduct,
caritrā f. tamarind tree,
carman skin, leather, pelt, bark, parchment
cāru mfn lovely, pretty, pleasant, fair
cāṭa 391/3 a cheat, rogue. Apte – one who wins the confidence of the person he wishes to deceive, *-vahas,* like , in a cheating way, in an ingratiating way
cāṭu flattery,
catur 384/1 four , *-vidhā* 967/3 division,
catura mfn clever, swift, dextrous,
caturdaśa fourteen
caturtha fourth
caturvidhā the 4 divisions - those born from the womb, those born from eggs, those born from vapour or sweat, those born from seeds or sprouting in the 4 divisions
catvāra four
ced 401/3 ind. (*ca + id*) if (never begins a sentence or half-line)
cela cloth
ceṣṭa 402/1 mfn action, bodily activity,
ceṣṭamāna pres.part. acting,
ceṣṭā 402/1 f. behaviour or manner of life, action, effort, activity, doing, endeavour, exertion, performance
cet if
ceṭa m. a servant,
cetam n. mind
cetana 397/3 mfn.distiguished, visible, intelligence, conscious, sentient, m. an intelligent being, man, soul, mind, f. (*ā*) intelligence, consciousness, understanding, sense
cetas 398/1 n. splendour, consciousness, intelligence, thinking soul, heart, mind,
cetasāḥ thoughts, 1/pl/n
chadman n external covering, deceptive dress, disguise, pretext, pretence, deceit, fraud
chala 405/2 n. fraud, deceit, pretense, delusion
chanda mfn pleasing, inviting, alluring, m. appearance, look, shape, pleasure, delight, appetite, desire, n. pleasure,
chandas 1. roof, deceit
chandas 2. 405/1 desire, longing for, incantation, hymn, metre, the science of metre, singing of verses
chandatas 404/3 ind. at will, at pleasure, according to choice,
channa mfn covered, covered, over,
chāgaḥ a goat, coming from a goat,
chātra m. pupil, disciple,
chatra n. umbrella,
chaviḥ f. beauty, colour, aura,
chāyā 406/1 shade, shadow, a shady place, shelter, protection, a reflected

image, reflection, shading or blending of colours, lustre, light, colour, gracefulness, beauty,

√*chid* 406/2 to cut off, amputate, cut through, infin. *chettum*

chidra n. hole, defect, weak spot,

chindanti they cut, they pierce √*chid*

chinna 406/3 mfn cut, cut off, taken away

chittvā ind. cutting away, having cut away

cibuka n. chin, tongs,

cid 397/3 in compounds for cit 395/2 /3 thought, intellect, spirit, consciousness

cid pure uninfluenced consciousness, "is experienced as consciousness" HH (see *cit*) "unlimited consciousness" HH "Cid is *akhaṇda* and it is also known as *ātmajñāna*, the experience of the Self, not as this and that, but as Itself". HH

cidābhāsa "consciousness of knowledge or appearance of knowledge on the consciousness" "That consciousness which shines or seems to reflect in the *antaḥkaraṇa*". HH 'all experiences are called *cidābhāsa,* that is the illusion of being conscious' HH

cidātman 397/3 pure thought or intelligence, *cid/cit* 395/3 pure thought or intelligence + *ātman* 135/1 essence, nature, character, 6/s whose nature is consciousness,

cidrūpa 397/3 n. wise, the Universal Spirit as identified with pure thought, consciousness

cihnam n. a sign, mark,

cikīrṣu desiring or intending to do or make 1/s/desiderative √ *kṛ*

cikitsā 395/2 medical attendance, practice or science of medicine, medical treatment,

cikitsaka m. physician

cīna m. chinese, a kind of deer, a thread,

cinmātra adj. 397/3 consisting of pure thought, pure consciousness

cinmātra 397/3 consisting of pure thought, *cin* in comp. for *cit, cit* 5. 395/3 pure thought, *mātra* –(suffix) in full measure, entirely, only , pure consciousness

cinmaya 397/3 consisting of pure thought, pure consciousness,

chinna mfn cut, cut off, taken away, nibbled,

√*cint* 398/1 cl 10 *cintayati*, cl 1 *cintati,* to think, have a thought or idea, reflect, consider, to think about, reflect upon, direct the thoughts towards, care for, to find out, to take in to consideration, treat of, to consider as or that,

cintayet 1/s/pres/opt/act he should reflect

cintā f. thought, care, anxiety, consideration, anxious thought about, (in comp.) worry anxiety,

-cinta mfn worry,

cintāmaṇi m. a wish-fulfilling jewel, philosopher's stone,

cintānurodhī *cinta* 398/1 thought, care, anxiety, *anurodhin* 37/3 complying with, compliant, thought compliant,

cintayanta directing thought to, meditating on,

cintayati 398/1 *cint* 1/s/pres/act he or she thinks

cintayet he should think of, he should reflect on, 1/s/caus/opt/act √*cint*

cintya to be thought or imagined, 1/s/m gerundive

cira 398/2 n. long, lasting a long time, at all times, ever, for a long time, mfn long,

cirajīvikā f. a long life

cirakāra mfn slow, working slowly,

cirakārin mfn slow, making slow progress

cirantana f. (*ī*) old, ancient, m.pl. the ancients,

cirāt after a long time,

cireṇa after a while, after a long time,

√*cit* 395/2 to perceive, observe, be conscious of, know, 5. *cit* 395/3 thought, intellect, spirit, soul, consciousness, *cin* =*cit* 395/3 5.*cit* pure thought, spirit, soul, intellect, consciousness, influenced consciousness in *antaḥkaraṇa,* " in *cit* are involved all concepts from *adhyātma* and *vyavahāra* (spiritual knowledge and practical knowledge with which the individual relates himself to the universal", HH "limited consciousness" HH (see *cid*) "*cit* is closely associated with the *antaḥkaraṇaḥ* and it is changeable, destructible. *cid* on the other hand is unchangeable, indestructible. *Cit* is powered by *cid* and the light of *cid* shines in the *cit* and goes through its modifications." HH

citā f. funeral pyre,

citi 1. f. pile, stack, funeral pile, collecting, gathering, a heap, multitude, an oblong, understanding, 2. f . 395/3 understanding, thought, intellect, spirit, m. the thinking mind,

cīt-kāra m. the sound *cīt* the braying of an ass, noise,

citra 396/1 mfn conspicuous, excellent, distinguished, bright, clear, bright-coloured, clear (a sound), various, different, wonderful, n. a picture, sketch, a wonder, anything bright or coloured which strikes the eye, a bright or extraordinary appearance, a brilliant ornament, the ether, sky,

citraratha 397/1mfn having a bright chariot, m. the sun, the polar star, the king of the Gandharvas

citraśālā f. a room of pictures

citrita decorated,

citta 395/3 n. the heart, mind, memory, thought, storehouse of *saṁskāra,* mfn noticed, aimed at, longed for, appeared, visible,

cittahārin mfn mind or heart captivating,

cittavṛttaya m. movements of the mind,

cittavṛtti 396/1 continuous course of thoughts, (as opposed to concentration), thinking, imagination,

cora m. thief,

corayati steals

corya n. theft,

cūḍa m. a tonsure,

cūḍā f. tuft of hair left on the crown of a child's head after the tonsure ceremony,

cūḍāmaṇi m. crest-jewel,

cumbakamaṇi m. magnet,

cūrṇita 401/2 mfn crushed

cyavati moves from one's place, deviates

-da giver

dā *dhatu* give

dadat giving pres/act/part

dadāmi I give, 3/s/pres/indic/act

dadāti 473/2 1/s/pres/indic/act he, she, or it gives

dadau he gave 1/s/perf/act √*dā*

dadhāti he puts, places, allots

dadhi n. curds,

dadhmau 1/s/perf. √*dhmā* he blows, sounded, blew,

dadṛśivān having seen

dagdha mfn. burnt, scorched, consumed by fire, tormented, pained

dagdhvā having set alight

dahati burns *Dh° dah*

dāhayati sets light to

dailya m. demon,

dainya 497/2 n. wretchedness, affliction, depression, meanness

Daitya 497/1 a son of *Diti*, a demon

daiva 497/2 mfn. belonging to or from the gods, divine, from chance, or fate, destiny,

daivapara m. fatalist,

daivī peculiar or relating to the gods, coming from gods, divine

daivī saṁpatti divine properties

dakṣa 465/1 able, fit, suitable, capable, m. ability, faculty, strength, power, esp. spiritual power, will,

dakṣiṇa mfn. South, right (as relative position), able, clever, straightforward, candid, sincere, m. the right (hand or arm),

(am) ind. to the right,
dakṣiṇā f. donation to a priest for services, a gift, donation, a prolific cow, 465/2
dakṣiṇataḥ ind. from the right or south on the right side or southward
dakṣināyana n. southern sun phase
dakñiëī + *kṛ* to place on the right,
dākṣiṇya mfn worthy of a sacrificial fee, n. politeness, kindness, skill, consideration, dexterity,
dākṣya 475/1 n. cleverness, skill, fitness
dala n. a leaf, petal,
damaḥ control of mind, speech, senses, body, self-restraint, 'is self-control, the control of the organs of action' '... not to have self-control is against the law'
damanya 469/3 to subdue √*dam*
ḍamara m. a tumult, riot, an evil omen,
ḍāmara mfn causing tumult, extraordinary, surprising, m. surprise, a lord,
damayantī name of *bhīma*'s daughter,
damayatām of rulers pres/part. 6/pl/m
dambha 469/3 deceit, fraud, hypocrisy
dāmbhika mfn deceitful, deceiver,
dambhin mfn deceiver, m. hypocrite,
dampati m. master of the house, as dual – master and mistress,
daṁśati he bites
daṁṣṭra 464/3 m. tusk, fang
dāna 474/1 n. the act of giving, giving up, gift, generosity, charity, benevolence,
dānakriya act of giving, charity
dānava 474/3 m. a class of demons
daṇḍa m. a staff (stick), 466/2 a stick, staff, staff given at investiture, power over
daṇḍaya punish! impv.
daṇḍayati punishes
dantaḥ m. tooth, ivory, a tusk
dantin 469/1 mfn tusked, m. an elephant
dantura mfn uneven, jagged, having projecting teeth
dāra 2. 475/3 a wife, hole, rent, cleft,
dāraka m. boy, son
darbha m. grass-tuft, grass used at ceremonies esp. *kuśa* grass,
daridra n. °*draḥ* ; °*drā* poor, without riches, *Dh*° *drā* in making haste, being in need
darpa m. pride, impudence, arrogance,
darpaṇa m. a mirror,
darśa mirror. 470/3 *darśa* looking at, viewing. root *dṛś* 491/1 to see, -*madhya* in the middle, standing between, belonging to neither or both parties *ādarśamadhyaste* 7/s existing in a mirror (ref. A and C)
darśana 470/3 mfn showing, knowing, seeing, experiencing, contemplating, ifc. seeing, looking at, 'knowing', exhibiting, teaching, n. seeing observing, looking, noticing, observation, perception, inspection, examination,
visiting, audience, meeting, experiencing, contemplating, observation, discernment, understanding, intellect, opinion, intention, view, doctrine, philosophical system,
the eye, the becoming visible or known, presence,
darśanagocara m. range of vision,
darśanīya mfn visible, worthy of being seen, good-looking, beautiful,
darśaya cause to be seen, allow me to see, show! 2/s/caus/impv/act √*dṛṣ*
darśayām he revealed, peri. perf. √*dṛś* with *āsa* from root *ās* 1/s/perf
darśibhıḥ by the seers, by the perceivers, by the discerners, by the knowers, 3/pl/m *dṛś*
darśita mfn manifested, shown, past/pass/caus/part
dāru mfn liberal, breaking, splitting, n. wood, log or billet of wood,
dāruṇa mfn harsh m. cruel, severe
daśa ten
daśadhā in ten ways
daśā 473/1 f. state or condition of life, condition, circumstances, a weft, fringe, lamp-wick,
dāsa m. 1. foe esp. supernatural foe, evil

demon, 2. foe of the gods, infidel, 3. servant, slave, *dāsé* female slave, servant of God,
daśama tenth
daśan ten
daśana 472/3 m. a tooth, a bite, peak,
daśarathaḥ father of *rāmaḥ*, a king
dāsya 477/2 n. servitude, slavery, service
dāsyante they will give, 1/pl/fut/mid √*dā*
dāsyati he will give
dasyu 473/1 m. robber, thief, demon,
dātavya to be given (gerundive √*dā*)
dātṛ m. giver, donor mfn generous,
datta 467/2 1. protected, 2. given, granted, m. a son given for adoption,
datvā ind. having given
dauhitra 499/3 m.daughter's son,rhinoceros,
daur 499/1 bad-heartedness, wickedness, depravity, *daur-bala,* weakness, impotence
dava m. forest-fire, burning, fever,
daviṣṭha mfn (superlative) remotest, ind. very far away,
dāya 474/2 a gift, a present
dayā 469/3 sympathy, compassion
dāyāda m. heir, son or distant kinsman,
dāyaka m. heir, mfn giving,
dayālu mfn compassionate,
dayayāḥ please, by showing mercy,
deha m. n. 496/3 the body, manifestation
dehabhṛt 497/1 mfn. embodied, corporeal, m. a living creature, life, vitality, the embodied one, the *ātman*
dehatyāga m. death, giving up the body,
dehi give! (s.)
dehin 497/1 mfn. having a body, corporeal, a living creature, man, m. (*dehī*) the spirit, soul (enveloped in the body), the Self
dehi dayayā please give, please pass deliberation, examination, (discursive thought), + *nir* – without
deśa 496/2 m. place, part, country, kingdom, locality
deśīya belonging to the country,
dese in or at the proper place 7/s
deva 492/2 mf(ī)n. heavenly, divine, m. a deity, god, shining one, universal power or deity
Devadatta god-given (Arjuna's conch-horn)
devadeva God of Gods
devakula n. temple,
devara m. husband's brother,
devarṣis m.divine seer 1/s/m
devasva 495/1 n. *deva* property
deva svabhāva divine nature,
devatā 495/3 f. goddess, godhead, divinity, nymph, name of the organs of sense, ind. with divinity, i.e. with a god (gods) or among the gods,
devayajña sacrifice or worship for the divine
devayajya n. worship of the gods, a sacrifice,
devī a feminine deity, goddess, queen, lady,
devīvat like a queen, goddess
devṛ m. husband's brother,
deya 492/2 to be given or presented,
dhairya 520/2 n. intelligence, forethought, calmness, patience, gravity, fortitude, firmness, 2. n. constancy, 'patience as an aspect of constancy, as Absolute is constant'
dhakṣya mfn burn, consume by fire
dhakṣyati will burn, will set alight,
ḍhāla n. a shield
ḍhālin mfn armed with a shield,
√*dham* to blow, or to blow a conch shell, *dhamati* blows
dhāman 514/3 n. dwelling place, house, abode
dhana 508/2 n. wealth, riches, the prize,
dhāna mfn holding, containing, n. receptacle, case, seat, the site of a habitation, coriander,
Dhanaṁjaya conqueror of wealth (*Arjuna*)
dhanika mfn rich,
dhanu 509/1 1/s/m a bow (as in bow & arrow)
dhanudharas m. an archer or bowman
dhānuṣka bowman,
dhanuvedaḥ m. the science of archery
dhanya 509/1 mfn fortunate, happy, auspicious, good, virtuous,

the blessed_.
dhānya mfn cereal, n. cereal, grain, corn
dhara 510/1 mfn.holder, holding, bearing
dharā the earth
dhārā f. stream, jet, shower, edge, blade, a leak or hole in a pitcher, the pace of a horse (5 specified), uniformity, sameness, custom, usage,
dhāraṇa 515/1 mfn holding, bearing, keeping (in remembrance), retention, preserving, protecting, maintaining, possessing,
dhāraṇā 515/2 f. the act of holding, supporting, maintaining, concentration of the mind(joined with the retention of breath), understanding, intellect, memory, steadfastness
dharaṇī f. the earth, tubular vessel of the body,
dhāraya 515/2 holding, bearing
dhārayan resolving, maintaining, believing, being convinced pres/caus/act/part.
dhārayati carries, maintains, preserves, employs, practises, restrains, suppresses, remains,
dharma 510/3 m law, virtue, morality, righteousness, correct conduct, duty, right, justice
[√*dhṛ* 519/1 in holding, supporting] the law, that which upholds, system of duties, rewards, punishments, etc., Will of the absolute (fine laws of the universe), Universal justice ensuring happiness, freedom and virtue. (an aspect of *puruṣārtha*)
dharmacārin mfn virtuous, observing the law, fulfilling one's duties, dutiful,
dharmārthakāmamokṣa a traditional expression for "the 4 objectives of life" *dharma* 510/3 justice, virtue, doing one's duty, right action *artha* 90/2 wealth, prosperity. *kāma* 271/3 pleasure, sensual pleasures, *mokṣa* 835/1 freedom, liberation 7/pl /m in the matter of meritorious behaviour, prosperity, pleasure, and freedom
dharmakṣetra in the field of virtue
dharmaśāstra the Laws of *Manu* according to *dharma,* any lawbook,
dharmastha m. judge, 'abiding in the law'
dharmasthānam n. tribunal,
dharmika mfn righteous, just, virtuous,
dhārmika mfn righteous, just, virtuous,
dharmya 513/1 mfn. legal, legitimate, usual, customary, just, virtuous, endowed with properties, suitable to righteous
dhāryate it is sustained or supported 1/s/pres/indic/caus/pass √*dhṛ*
dhātā the establisher or arranger
dhātāra the supporter, one who places or puts
dhātṛ m. creator
dhātrī nurse,
dhatte 513/2 to be given, put,place, intend, middle voice to accept, obtain, 1/s/pres/ accepts,
dhātu 513/3 element of words, grammatical or verbal root or stem, mineral,
dhāvaka m. washerman, orerunner, mfn running,
dhavala mfn dazzlingly white,
dhāvasi you (s) run ,
dhāvata m. a runner
dhāvati 516/1 runs, runs after, seeks for, 1/s/pres/indic/act seeks
dhenu 520/1 mfn. yielding or giving milk, f. a cow
√*dhī* 516/3 cl 3 A *dīdhīte* to perceive, think, reflect, wish, desire,
dhī m. thought, mind, mental attitude, intelligence, reflection, meditation, devotion, prayer, understanding, intelligence, wisdom, knowledge, science, art, mind, disposition, intention, design, notion, opinion, 'the intellect in the employment of obedient service, listening to discourses, reception of good ideas, accepting these ideas, analysis, science of meaning or semantics and

philosophical or spiritual principles is the human law, To misuse the intellect is against the law.'

dhik expletive expressing annoyance (with 2nd case)

dhikkṛta mfn reproached, derided, n. reproach, contempt,

dhīmān *dhī* 516/3 intelligent, wise, learned *dhīmān* 1/s/m the wise man

dhīmat mfn wise, intelligent, sensible,

dhīra 517/1 mfn steady, constant,composed, intelligent, wise, one of steady mind, the wise one,

dhīradhī 517/1 *dhīra* steady, steady-minded, *dhī* 516/3 2. understanding, wisdom, one of steady wisdom

dhīrya n. prudence,

dhīvara m. 'a very clever or skilful man', a fisherman,

dhobī the washerman

dhṛṣṇu mfn daring, courageous, doughty,

dhṛta 519/2 2/s– borne, maintained, measured, continuing, existing, being, kept back, supported , held firmly,

Dhṛtarāṣṭra 519/2 a powerful king

dhṛti 519/2 f. holding, seizing, keeping, firmness, constancy, satisfaction, content, joy, resolution, patience '*dhṛtiḥ* means *dhairya* or patience as an aspect of constancy, as Absolute is constant', HH.

dhṛtvā having put on

dhruva 521/2 mfn. fixed, firm, immovable, constant, permanentsure, eternal, n. the fixed point (from which a departure takes place), the pole star, air, atmosphere, *(am)* ind. firmly, constantly, certainly, surely,

dhūliḥ f. dust,

dhūma 518/1 m. smoke, vapour, mist

dhūmra mfn purple, gray, m. a camel, incense,

dhūpa m. incense, perfume,

dhur f. a yoke, burden, load, top, summit, place of honour (at the head, in front, in presence of,),

dhūrdhara m. chief, leader,

dhurīna 517/2 leader, chief

dhūsara mfn dusty, grey

dhvaja m. a banner or standard, flag,

dhvaṁsa m. the perishing, destruction, (*ī*) f. a mote in a sunbeam,

dhvaṇi m. sound, echo, noise,

dhvasira mfn covered, dusty, sprinkled,

dhyāna 521/1 n. meditation, reflection,

dhyāyanta meditating on, thinking of, pres/act/part √*dhyā*

dhyāyat 521/2 mfn. thinking, meditating, contemplating,

diganta m.the horizon, remote distance, mfn being in the remote distance,

dīkṣā f. preparation or consecration for a religious ceremony, dedication, initiation, any serious preparation, complete resignation or restriction to, consecration,

dilīpa m. ancestor of Rāma

ḍimba m. an egg, a chrysalis, new-born child, a child, a young animal,

dinam 478/1n. a day

dīna 480/3 sad, miserable, wretched, disturbed

dīnatā 480/3 scarcity, weakness, timid (A. humility), timid

dinakara m. the sun

dinanātha m. the sun

dinapati the sun,

dīnāra m. denarius, name of a gold coin,

ḍiṇḍama m. drum, clamour, great noise, loud assertion,

dīpa 481/1 m. a light, lamp, lantern

dīpita 481/2 mfn. set on fire, inflamed, excited, illuminated, manifested m. an illuminator, enlightener,

dīpti f. brightness, light, splendour, beauty

dīptimat 481/3 mfn. bright, splendid, brilliant,

dīrgha mfn long in space, time and sound, lofty, high, tall, deep,

dīrghadarśin far-seeing,

dīrghasūtratā "such characters would take ten hours to do a job which could easily be done in two hours.." HH

dīrghasūtrī 482/3 dilatory, procrastinating

dīrghāyus long-lived,

diś f. direction, point, cardinal point, quarter of the heavens,
diśā 480/2 f. direction, region point of the compass
diśas 480/2 direction, region, quarter
div m. sky, heaven, heaven personified as father (of the dawn),
divā ind. by day, during the day,
divānaktam day and night,
divārātram day and night,
divasa m. a day, heaven,
divātana mfn daily, diurnal, m. a crow,
divaukas m. god, an inhabitant of heaven, a deity, 'having heaven as a dwelling',
divya 2. mfn divine, heavenly, celestial, wonderful, magical,
n. the divine world or anything divine, pl. the celestial regions, the sky, heaven, an ordeal, oath, solemn promise, cloves, m. barley,
f. a kind of perfume,
dīyate it is given, bestowed, 1/s/pres/indic/pass √*dā*
doha mfn. milking, yielding, granting, m. milking, milk
dohana mfn giving milk, a milker, yielding profit, f. milk-pail, n. milking, milk, milk-pail,
dolā litter, hammock, swing,
dolāya (*dolāyate)* to swing like a dooly, waver,
ḍoma m. a man of low caste living by singing and music,
dos n. arm, fore-arm, side of a trangle or square,
doṣa 498/2 m. evening, darkness,
2. m. fault, vice, deficiency, badness, wickedness, offence, wrong, weakness, sin, crime, guilt, harm, bad consequence,
doṣā f. darkness, night,
doṣmat mfn strong-armed, having arms,
drāghiman m. length, degree of longitude,
drāk instantly, quickly,
drākṣā f. vine, grape, made of grapes,
drakṣyati he will see
draṣṭa m. a seer, sees mentally, 'the witness' the pure consciousness comprehending all objects (G),
draṣṭṛ m. spectator, observer, witness,
draṣṭum to see, to behold (infin. √*dṛṣ*)
draupadeyās sons of *Draupadī*
draupadī wife of the Pandava brothers,
dravati 502/1 runs, hastens, dissolves, melts
draviḍa m. Dravidian,
draviṇas 501/1 n. movable property, substance, wealth,
dravya 501/1 n. a substance, thing, object, the ingredients of anything, property
dṛḍha 490/2 fixed, firm, hard, solid steady, resolute, persevering, shut fast, strong massive
droha 502/3 m. injury, mischief, harm, wrong, perfidy, treachery
Droṇa a *Kaurava* warrior and martial arts master
dṛś 491/2 to see, to see with the mind, to understand, to see by divine intuition, having the quality of - seer
dṛś 2. m. seeing, viewing, looking at, knowing, discerning, f. sight, view, look, appearance, the eye, theory, doctrine, (in compounds) look, appearance,
dṛṣad f. stone, esp. the lower mill-stone,
dṛṣṭa mfn seen, perceived, discerned, n. perception, observation,
dṛṣṭānta 491/3 m. example, paragon, standard, allegory, type, illustration, instance, exemplification, a *śāstra*, death,
dṛṣṭapūrva mfn seen previously, seen before
dṛṣṭavān having seen, perf/part
dṛṣṭāye so as to be seen,
dṛṣṭi f. vision, attitude, opinion, system, notion, doctrine, intelligence, wisdom, glance, eye, theory, mind's eye, beholding, consideration, regard, m. eyesight, glimpse, glance,
dṛṣṭī 492/1 f. seeing, viewing, beholding, (also with the mental eye), view, opinion, sight, the mind's eye, wisdom, intelligence, the faculty of seeing, wisdom,
dṛṣṭin 492/1 mfn.having an insight into, or familiar with anything, having the

looks or thoughts directed onto anything,

dṛṣṭipāta m. . glance,

dṛṣṭiṣu seeing, sight, hence any sense experience, 7/pl (in the matter of) sensory experiences

dṛṣṭvā gerund, having seen, seen

dṛśya 491/3 mfn. visible, conspicuous, to be looked at, any visible object

dṛśyamānā pres.part. being perceived, perceiving,

dṛśya 491/3 visible, to be looked at, part. will be appearing

dṛśyate √*dṛś* to see 491/2 1/s/pres/indic/pass is seen

druma a tree,

druta mfn quick, speedy, swift, quickly or indistinctly spoken, flown, run away, dissolved, melted, fluid, (*am*) ind. hastily, rapidly, without delay, m. a scorpion, a tree,

dugdha 483/3 mfn. milked, milked out sucked out, impoverished, n. milk, 2.√*duh*

duhitṛ f. daughter,

duḥkha 483/2 mfn uneasy, uncomfortable, unpleasant, difficult, n. pain, sorrow, trouble, difficulty, (*am*) ind. with difficulty, scarcely, hardly,

duḥkhahā . sorrow destroying, pain destroying, *duḥkha* √*han* 1/s/m

duḥkhatara n. greater hardship, greater pain, greater misery comparative

duḥkhena ind. unhappily

dukhin mfn unhappy (person),

duḥkhita mfn sad, pained, distressed,

dundubhi m.f. drum, a poison,

dur the form taken by *dus* before voiced letters, in comp. denoting 'bad' or 'difficult' etc. n. great crime or wickedness,

dūra mfn. distant, far, remote, n. distance, remoteness, a long way, ind. (*am*) far, far from

durācāra m. bad conduct, wicked,

dūram 489/2 ind. distant, far, remote

durāsada 485/1 mfn. dangerous to approach, unheard of unparalleled,

durāśaya m. evil-minded, malicious, m. the subtle body which is not destroyed by death,

dūrastha 489/3 mfn. being in the distance, remote,

dūrāt ind. far away, from a distance, from afar,

durātman mfn, evil-minded, villain

duratyaya 484/2 mfn. inaccessible, unfathomable, (*ā*) f. difficult to penetrate, difficult to master,

durbala 486/1 of little strength, weak, feeble,

durbhāgya mfn unfortunate, unlucky, n. ill-luck,

dur-buddhi 486/1 f. weak-mindedness, foolish, ignorant, malignant, evil-minded

durdivasa m. bad or rainy day,

dūre 489/2 ind. far away, away from

durga 487/2 mfn difficult of access or approach, impassable, unattainable, n. a difficult or narrow passage, a citadel, rough ground, roughness, difficulty, danger,

durgati 485/2 f. misfortune, distress, poverty

durgraha 485/2 m. seizing badly, cramp, illness, obstinacy, mfn difficult to seize, catch or attain,

durjana m. bad person, scoundrel, mfn malicious, wicked,

durlabha 486/3 scarce, rare, hard to find

durlabhatara more difficult to attain, harder to attain, comparative

durmati 486/2 f. bad disposition of mind, envy, hatred, m. fool, blockhead

durmitra 486/2 mfn unfriendly

durnigraha 486/1 mfn. difficult to be restrained or conquered

durnirīkṣya difficult to see or look upon, gerundive *dus nis* √*īkṣ*

durvāra mfn hard to be restrained, irrepressible, irresistible,

Duryodhana dirty fighter, chief of the *Kuru* army, son of *Dhṛtarāṣṭra*,

dus prefix evil, ill, bad, difficult, hard,

slight, inferior, opp. to *su*
dūṣaṇa mfn corrupting, spoiling, violating, n. the act of corrupting, dishonouring, detracting, disparaging, objection, adverse argument, refutation,
duścaritra having false or bad character
dūṣi 489/1mfn corrupting, defiling, (the mind), f. a poisonous substance,
duṣkṛta 487/3 mfn wrongly or wickedly done, evil action, bad action
duśpūra 488/1 mfn difficult to be filled or satisfied, insatiable
duṅprāpa mfn difficult to attain, hard to reach, *duṣ pra √āp*
duṣṭa evil, spoilt, corrupted, defective, bad
dūta m. messenger, ambassador, envoy,
dvaidha 507/2 mfn twofold, double n. a state of duality, duplicity
dvaita 507/2 duality
dvandva 503/2 pair, couple, male and female, a pair of opposites, a copulative compound or any compound in which the members if uncompounded would be in the same case and connected y the conjunction "and"
dvāpara yuga 503/3 the bronze age, (864,000 years) 3rd of the 4 traditional ages, the age of heroes, qualities no longer pure
dvāra n. door, gate, entrance,
dvaya 503/2 mfn (from and in comp. *dvi*) twofold, double, of 2 kinds or sorts,
dve, dvau two
dvedhā ind. in two, in two kinds or ways,
dveṣa 507/1 aversion, dislike, hostility
dveṣṭa 506/3 *root 2. dviù* hates, *dveṣṭi* dislikes.
dvi two
dvidhā ind. in two parts, 'in two ways',
dvija twice-born, a member of one of the 3 highest castes
dvijottama highest of the twice-born
dvipa m. elephant,
dvīpa m. island
dvīpin 507/1m. tiger, panther, leopard
dvirepha m. bee
dviṣ (in compounds) hating, f. hate, m. (*as*) hater, foe, enemy,
dviṣ 1. in comp. for *dvis,* twice
dvis twice,
dvitaya mfn consisting of two, twofold, double, n. a pair, couple,
dvitīya mfn second, forming the second part or half of anything, m. companion, fellow, the 2nd in a family, n. the half (ibc. or ifc.),
dvitīyā 506/2f. female companion or friend, wife, the second case, a second
dvivacana (in gram.)the dual and its endings,
dvividha 505/3 mfn. twofold, of 2 kinds
dyotana 500/2 mfn. shining, illuminating enlightening, a lamp, n. shining, being bright, illumination
dyuti 500/1 f. splendour, lustre, brightness
dyūtakāra m. gambler,
dyūta 500/2 n. play, gaming, gambling
e 227/2 a particle of recollection, addressing, censure, contempt, compassion,
e *ā-√i eti* to come near or towards, go near, approach, reach, attain
ebhyaḥ pron. this (indefinite) 4/pl or 5/pl from these
√edh cl1 *edhate, -ti,* to prosper, increase, become happy, grow strong, grow big with self-importance, become insolent, become intense, extend, spread,
edha 231/3 m. fuel, mfn. ifc. kindling
ehi come! impv
√ej *ejati* to stir, move, shake, tremble he/she/it moves
eka 227/3 one. alone, solitary 1/s/m a certain,
eke some
ekadā once (upon a time), at the same time
ekadhā ind. in one way, together, at once, simply, singly,
ekāgra 230/1 one-pointed, closely attentive, intent, undisturbed, close and undisturbed attention, intentness in the pursuit of an object,
ekāgratā 230/1 f. intentness in the pursuit of one object, close and undisturbed attention, 'one-pointed attention'

ekāgrya 230/1 mfn closely attentive, n. close attention, concentrating
ekaika mfn one by one, one by itself, one singly, each one singly, every single one,
ekākin 231/1 mfn alone, single, solitary,
ekākṣara having one syllable, the sole imperishable thing,
ekam n. unity, a unit
ekāntika 230/2 mfn. devoted to one aim or object or person or theory
ekāntam 230/2 ind. solely, only, exclusively absolutely, necessarily, invariably, a lonely place,
ekarasa 229/1 m. the only pleasure, mfn. having only one pleasure or object of affection, unchangeable, 'on an even keel'
ekarṣi or ekariṣi the only or chief *ṛṣi*
ekastha mfn standing together, standing as one, remaining in the same place, resting or abiding in one 1/s/m/n
ekatara one of two, either, other,
ekatra ind. at one place together, in one place,
ekatva 228/1 n. oneness, unity, union singularity
ekavacana singular (in grammar)
eke some
ema *(m), eman* n. a course or way
ena a pronoun base
ena 3rd case of idam
enā ind. here, there, thus, then
enas n. mischief, crime, sin, evil, unhappiness, misfortune,
enam 232/1 pron he, she, it (previously referred to)
enat pron. this Supreme Lord (*īṣā up*)
eṣā pron. 1/s/f this
eṣā f. wish
eṣaḥ pron. 1/s/m of *etad* this, "*eṣaḥ* denotes *aham* and not *idam* which is used for all that is not *aham*" HH "This, the *prājña*, the mere consciousness undifferentiated, is the lord of all, the omniscient and resides in each *antaḥkaraṇa*, the cause of everything and the beginning and end of all existence." HH
eṣām pron.6/pl of these
eṣyasi you shall come or attain 2/s/fut/act √*i*
etad 231/2 this, this here, referring to what precedes, ind. in this manner, thus, so, here, at this time
etādṛś mfn such, such like, so formed, of this kind, similar to this
etādṛśa such .... *yat*..... that
etān 2/pl/m these
etasya pron. 6/s of this
etat-kahaṇe ind. in this moment, now
etat-para mfn intent on or absorbed in this
etat-tulya 231/3 mfn similar to this, equal to this
etāvan 231/3 of this measure/quantity, so great,
etāvat 231/3 of such extent, so great, so far, such is, so much (and no more)
ete 1/pl/m these
eteṣām pron. 6/pl/m of these, to them
eti he goes, he attains 1/s/pres/indic/act *ā*√*i*
eva 232/2 ind. only, even, so, indeed, truly, indeed, only, alone, just,(emphasizes previous word)
evam 232/2 ind. thus, in this way, in such a manner, likewise, so
-ga goer, (in compounds) going, ifc. mfn singing,
gaccha go! (singular)
gacchan going from root *gam* to go 346/3 pres/act/part.
gacchata go! (pl)
gacchati he/she/it goes
gaccheh you would go
gacchet should go
gaccheyam I shall go,
gadā f. mace, club, a series of sentences,
gādha mfn shallow, fordable, m. desire, cupidity,
gadin 344/3 mfn armed with a club, sick
gadgada mfn stuttering,
gagaṇa n. the sky, heaven, atmosphere,
gahana 352/1 mfn deep, dense, impenetrable, hard to understand,
gahvara 352/1 m. a cave, cavern, arbour, mfn thick, impenetrable

gaja m. elephant
gajendra 342/2 a princely elephant,
gala m. throat, neck, a reed, rope,
gāli f. verbal abuse,
galita 350/3 lost, perished, melted, dissolved
gām ind.? the earth, the planets, a cow,
gama 348/1 m going, a road,
ifc. mfn going, riding on,
gamana n. a going, (on a journey) , undergoing, attaining,
gamas you should undergo, partake of
gambhīra mfn deep, (voice, character, navel) m. the lemon tree, a lotus, a hiccup,
gāmin 353/3 mfn. going anywhere, going or moving on or in or towards or in any particular manner
gamiṣyati will go 1/s
gamyate it is attained, reached, gone to 1/s/pres/pass √*gam*
gaṇa m. a group, troop, crowd, host,
gāna n. song, singing, a sound,
gānadhārī wife of *Dhṛtarāṣṭra*
gaṇḍa m. the cheek,
gaṇḍaka m. rhinoceros,
gandha 345/1 m. smell, odour, fragrance, scent
gandharva m. celestial musician
Gāṇḍīva the name of *Arjunas* bow
gaṅgā f. the Ganges, a goddess, 'one who goes swiftly'
gantā going to, goes, will go,
gantāsi thou shalt go 2/s/peri/fut/act
gantavya to be attained, to be gone, to be approached, be accomplished gerundive √*gam*
garala m. n. poison, venom of a snake,
garbha 349/2 m. the womb, the inside, middle, sleeping chamber, foetus, seed, ifc. containing, filled with,
gardabha m. donkey, ass, *(ī)* f. she-ass,
garīyas 348/3 mfn. (comparative), heavier, extremely heavy, greater than, more precious or valuable, very honourable, dearer than
garīyān m. glorious, worshipable, more venerable, heavier
garta m. 'earth-cut' ditch, hole, a high seat, throne, the seat of a war-chariot, a chariot, a table for dice,
garuḍa a mythical bird, 'devourer', the vehicle of Viṣṇu,
garva 350/2 pride, arrogance
garvita° proud
gata 347/1 gone, gone to any state or condition, arrived at, being in, attained, restored 1/s/m
gatāgatam going and coming, what comes and goes, going to and fro,
gatakleśa *gata* 347/1 gone, gone away. *kleśa* 324/1 pain, affliction, free from pain
gatarasa 347/2 mfn having lost its flavour or sap, withered, tasteless,
gatasandeha 347/2 2/s free from doubt
gatavyatha free from concern, 'whose anxiety is gone' 1/s/m
gati 347/3 going, arriving at, obtaining, passage, progress, way path, road , destination, condition, f. motion, gait,
gātra 352/1 n. īnstrument of moving, a limb or member of the body
gatvā ind. having gone
gauṇa mfn indirect, indirect meaning, secondary, relating to a quality, having qualities, attributive, subordinate, secondary, unessential,
gaura mfn white, pale, shining, brilliant, clean, beautiful,
gaurakṣya n. cattle-tending
gaurī a name of *Pārvati,*
gautama patronymic from Gotama, name of Buddha,
gāyati sings
geha 363/2 n. a house, dwelling, habitation
ghana 376/1 mfn a striker, killer, destroyer, compact, solid, material firm, hard
ghana m. cloud,
ghaṇṭā f. a bell or gong,
gharma m. warmth, heat, sunshine
ghaṭa m. 375/1 a jar, pitcher, jug,
ghāta m. blow, bruise, mfn killing, injuring,
ghātayati he causes to slay 1/s/caus/act √*han*

ghaṭākāśa *ghaṭa + ākāśa*
space in a jar or jug
ghna 379/3 killing, striking
ghnata those who are killing, those who are about to kill, pr.part √*han*
ghora mfn dreadful, horrible, terrible
ghoṣa 378/1 m. indistinct noise, the soft sound heard in the articulation of the sonant consonants,
g,gh,j,jh,ḍ,ḍh,d,dh,b,bh,ṅ,ñ ,n,m,y,r,l,v,h, the vowels and *anusvara*
ghrāṇa 379/3 mfn smelled, smelling, m. smelling, smell, odour
ghṛṇā f. a warm feeling towards others, compassion, tenderness, aversion, contempt,
ghṛta n. butter – clarified and then hardened, (anglo-indian *ghee*)
gir mfn addressing, invoking, praising, f. speech, praise, song, verse,
gira 355/1 speech, speaking, voice
giri 355/2 m. a mountain, hill, rock giving up, 1/s/pres/impv/mid let him give up
gīta 356/1 mfn. sung, chanted, praised in songs, n. singing, song, (*ā*) f. a song, sacred song or poem
glāna feeling aversion or dislike, wearied, exhausted, sick, exhausted
glāni 374/3 f. exhaustion, languor, lassitude,
go f. *gau* m. a bull or cow, 2. flesh, 3. the earth,
gocara 364/1 m. pasture for cattle,range, field for action, offering range or field or scope for action,
gola m. a globe or ball,
gomukha m. a trumpet, a crocodile,
gopa m. cow-herd, keeper in general,
gopālaḥ m. a king, a cowherd,
goptā m. a defender, protector,
gotraja 364/3 mfn born in the family, m. a relative,
govindaḥ Govinda, the Lord, grace, love, attachment, cow-finder, cow-master,
√*gṝ* 363/1 to call, invoke, praise, extol
graha 372/1m. seizing, taking, accepting, a planet (as affecting men's destinies)
grāha 372/3 mfn seizing, receiving, large marine animal, conception, notion of,
grāhya 373/1 373/1 mfn to be received or accepted or gained, to be overpowered, to be picked or gathered, to be seized or taken or held, to be captured or imprisoned, to be taken in marriage, to be received in a friendly or hospitable way, to be perceived or recognized or understood, to be understood in a particular sense, meant, to be accepted as a rule or law,
grāma m. village
grāmaṇīḥ m. head-man of a village,
grantha 371/1 m. a book, tying, binding, stringing together, a knot, a literary work, a verse or couplet, honeycomb,
granthi 371/1 m. a knot, tie, knot of a cord, unreal and illusory complexity and ignorance,
grāsa m. mouthful, food, mfn swallowing,
grasamāna swallowing, devouring, pres/part/mid √*gras*
grasiṣṇu 371/2 mfn accustomed to swallow or absorb
grāvan m. stone, esp. stone for pressing the Soma,
√*gṛdh* cl4 361/2 endeavour to gain, covet, desire,
gṛdha m.. or *gṛddha* ppp.. coveting, desirous of,
gṛdhraḥ m. vulture, mfn desiring greedily,
gṛha 361/3 m.n. *a* house, a home, a servant, a family,
gṛhāṇa just accept, please take now, √*grah*
gṛhastha mfn householder (2nd stage of traditional life),
gṛhiṇī house-wife, mistress of the house,
gṛhīta mfn grabbed, grasped, taken,
gṛhītvā having grabbed, taking, grasping
gṛhṇāti 371/2 root *grah*, takes, seizes grabs, receives, accepts
gṛhnan grasping pres/act/part √*grah* 371/3
grīṣma m. summer,
grīva m. neck, nape of the neck,

gr̥ṇanti they extol 1/pl/pres/act
grīva 374/1 m. the neck, nape of the neck, f. (*ā*)
guccha m. bundle, bunch,
guḍa 356/3 globe or ball, lumpy sugar, treacle, molasses, an elephant's trappings or armour, a ball for play
guḍaka m. ball, molasses,
guḍākeśa O Thick-Haired One *(Arjuna)*
guhā cave, hidden place, ind. in secret, the heart,
guhya 360/3 to be covered or concealed, secret
guhyatama most secret (superlative)
gulpha m. ankle,
guṇa quality, characteristic, attribute,
In Vedānta philosophy, there are three major guṇas that serve as the fundamental operating principles or 'tendencies' of *prakr̥ti* (universal nature) which are called: *sattva*, *rajas*, and *tamas*. The three primary gunas are generally accepted to be associated with creation (*rajas*), preservation (*sattva*), and destruction (*tamas*). They are the three basic qualities of nature which determine the inherent characteristics of all created things,357/1 . *–āḥ* pl. the attributes of nature (*sattva, rajas* and *tamas*), " the whole creation is in the grip of the *guṇā* and they never stay the same, so they keep on changing all beings and all situations. Everyone, wherever he is placed, whether at level one or even at level nine, is tossed by them. Some are totally affected while others are only outwardly affected. This means that one of the *guṇāḥ* may be predominant now and after a few moments, another, and yet after a few more moments, you may be caught by another *guṇa*. Thus the fluctuation of *guṇāḥ* will keep on forcing changes in all beings and in all situations." HH, a single thread or strand of a cord, string or thread, rope, a garland, a bowstring, chord, a multiplier, coefficient, subdivision, species, kind, a quality, peculiarity, attribute or property or virtue,
guṇabhedata 357/2 ind. according to the difference of quality, i.e. according to the guṇā relationships at the time
guṇāḥ the 3 constituents of the universe
guṇamayī 1/s/f made or produced by the *guṇa*
guṇānvita 358/1 endowed with virtues, excellent, associated with the *guṇā*
guṇātītas g + ppp. *ati* √*ī* going beyond the *guṇa*, transcending the *guṇa*
guru 359/2 m. a spiritual parent, teacher, or guide, G133 6. "The root *gu* stands for darkness; *ru* for its removal. The removal of the darkness in the heart is indicated by the word *guru*." , 'one who is firmly convinced that he is the supreme consciousness, one whose mind is rooted in the highest reality, one who has a pure and tranquil mind, one who has realized identity with Brahman" mfn heavy, important,
gurukr̥pā the grace of the teacher
gurūkti . words from a *guru*
ha a particle emphasizing a previous word or simply used as an expletive in poetry, m. m. water, a cipher (representing zero), meditation, auspiciousness, sky, heaven, paradise, blood, dying, fear, knowledge, the moon, battle, a horse, pride, a physician, cause, motive, m.f. laughter, n. the supreme spirit, pleasure, delight, a weapon, the sparkling of a gem, calling, mfn mad, drunk,
ha vai once upon a time
hā expresses astonishment or satisfaction, water, the arithmetical figure which expresses zero, meditation, auspiciousness, sky, heaven, paradise, blood, sex, dying, fear,
hā hā alas! alas!
haituka 1304/1 having a cause or reason,

founded on some motive,
caused, motivated

hala m. a plow, the earth, water,

hāna 1296/2 gone or departed, the act of abandoning, relinquishing, giving up

hanu f. jaw, a weapon, death, disease, a prostitute,

hanumān or *hanumat* wisest and most capable of monkeys

haṁsa the one caste in the golden age,
haṁsa 1286/1 a swan, 'the Universal Soul or supreme Spirit', the soul or spirit,

hanana mf a killing, a killer, n. the act of striking or hitting, killing,

hāni 1296/2 f. abandonment, relinquishment, decrease, diminution, damage

hanta 1288/2 ind. an exclamation here, look, see, oh, alas,

hantāra slayer, killer

hanti he slays, he kills, 1/s/pres/indic/act.

hantum to kill, slay, infin. of √*han* slay

hanumān wisest and most capable of monkeys

hanyamāne in being slain or killed pres/mid/part. 7/s/m

hanyate he is slain, killed 1/s/pres/indic/pass

hanyus they should kill, they may kill, 1/pl/opt/act √*han*

hara mfn (only ifc.) bearing, carrying, bringing, conveying, taking √*hṛ*

hāra m. necklace, mfn bearing, carrying

haraḥ 1289/1 a name of *śiva,* destroyer,

harati seizes, carries away 1/s/pres/act

hari 1.mfn bearing, carrying,
2.mfn brown, tawny, yellow, (esp. horses), m. yellow, reddish-brown,
1289/3 a lion, a horse, steed,

hari 1289/3 m. the Lord, a name of – *Vāyu, Indra, Viṣnu- Kṛṣṇa*

hariṇa mfn yellowish, greenish, a deer, antelope, the sun, 'full of rays' (Gam.),

harita mfn green,

harmya n. a strong building, dwelling, region of darkness, mfn living in houses,

harṣa 1292/2 joy, pleasure, bristling, erection, excitement, lust, desire,

hāsa m. laughter, laughing, a joke, fun,

hasati laughs

hasta m. hand, an elephant's trunk,

hastin m. elephant
hastāt 5/s/m from the hand

hāsya to be laughed at, (*as*) m. laughter, ridicule,

hata° mfn slain, killed √*han*

hāṭaka n. gold,

haṭhayoga 1287/1 a kind of forced yoga, 'in which physical activity of control of body and breath predominates'

hātum 1296/2 infin. to relinquish, give up, to renounce,

hatvā part. having killed,

havis n. an oblation or burnt offering, sacrificial gift or food,

haya 1288/2 m. a horse, yak,

he ind. O used as in O King

helā 1305/2 sport, play, disrepect, contempt, L. carelessness, levity,

hemanta m. winter, the cold season,

hetavaḥ causes, 1/pl/m

hetu 1303/3 m. impulse, reason for, motive, the cause, by reason of

hetunā by/with reason, from reason 3/s/m

hetvābhāsa m. fallacious semblance of an argument,

heya 1297/1 to be left or abandoned, rejected, 1296/1 to be gone

hi 1297/3 ind. for, because, on account of, of course, truly, indeed

hima m. snow, frost, the cold, winter,
n. ice, snow,
f. cold season, winter,

himādri m. Himalaya mountain

himālaya 1299/2 abode of snow, snowy,

himapāta m. snowfall,

hiṁsā see 1297/3 f. hurt, injury, wrong, desire to hurt, harm

hiṁsātmaka mfn cruel by nature, violent natured,

hiṁsra mfn harmful, harming,
m. a savage or cruel man

-hīna 1296/2 mfn abandoned, left devoid

of, free from, without, (am) n. deficiency, want, absence,

hinasti 1297/3 he/she injures, wounds, kills, destroys 1/s/pres/indic/act.

hīnayāna the 'small or lesser vehicle' referring to *theravāda* (classical) buddhist schools

hiraṇmaya mfn. golden, gold-coloured

hiraṇya mfn golden, made of gold, n. gold, imperishable matter,

hiraṇyagarbha '...the seed-form of the creation as the golden egg or womb' HH. 1299/3 a golden egg, in which the Self-existent *Brahma* was born as *Brahmā* the Creator, who is therefore regarded as a manifestation of the Self-existent, possessed of the twofold power of knowledge and action, called *Sūtra* when conceived of as the principle of action

hita 1298/2 mfn beneficial, wholesome, favourable, good (as in diet), set, m. a friend, benefactor, pl. veins or arteries,
n. anything useful or suitable or proper, benefit, advantage, profit, service, good, welfare,
the means to the end,

hitā f. a causeway, a pl. noun. of particular veins or arteries. 'a *hitā* nerve constitutes part of the subtle body'. HH

hitakāmyā 1298/2 desire for another's welfare,

hitvā 1296/2 ind. having left or abandoned, with the exception of, excepting, letting alone, slighting, disregarding,

ho ho alas ! alas! (stronger than *aho*)

homa m. pouring into the fire, oblation, sacrifice, (older word is *āhuti*),

homi m. fire, clarified butter, water,

hotṛ m. an offerer of an oblation or burnt offering (with fire), sacrificer, priest,

hrada m. pool, lake, a ray of light, ram,

hrāsa m. diminution, loss,

hraswa mfn short, weak,

hṛd 1302/2n. the heart (as seat of feelings and emotions)
hṛdi 7/s/n in the heart

hṛdaya 1302/3 n. the heart as seat of feelings and sensations, mind as centre of mental operations,

hṛdaye + √*kṛ* to take to heart, take seriously,

hṛddeśe in the region of the heart

hṛdya mfn being in the heart, internal, inward, inmost, innermost, pleasing or dear to the heart, beloved, agreeable, pleasant, pleasant to the stomach, savoury or dainty (food),

hrī 1307/2 2. f. shame, modesty, shyness, timidity

hṛśīkeśaḥ bristling haired, erect haired, a reference to *Kṛṣṇa*

hṛṣṭa mfn delighted

hṛṣṭaroman 1303/2 hair standing on end

hṛṣyati 1303/2 rejoices, exults, is glad or pleased

hṛta 1302/1 taken, taken away

hṛtstha 1302/3 mfn. standing or abiding in the heart

hriyate he is carried on, he is conveyed 1/s/pres/indic/pass. √hṛ

huta 1301/1 mfn. offered in fire, poured out, burnt, sacrified, the oblation, the pouring out

hutabhuj m. fire, south-east, plumbago,

hutāśa 1301/1 oblation-eater, fire

hyaḥ yesterday,

i ind. an interjection

√*i* cl. 2 go, flow, walk, advance, go away, arise from, come from, run, ayati, ayate

ibha 167/3 m. an elephant, fearless, servants, dependents,

icchā f. desire, inclination, wish , in math.- a question or problem, in gram.-the desiderative form, ind. according to wish or desire,

icchāmi I would like, I desire √*iṣ* 3/s/pres/indic/act

icchānicchāvivarjane *icchā* (above) + *an for a* not *anicchā* 29/2 undesirous, averse, *vivarjana* 988/3 the act of avoiding, shunning, leaving, 7/s in the matter of abandoning desire and aversion

icchasi 169/1 √*iṣ* 2/s/pres/act. seek for, desire, you wish

icchati he/she desires, wants

iḍā 164/2 f. refreshing draught, vital spirit, stream or flow of praise and worship, a partic. artery on the left side of the body, a tubular vessel (one of the principal channels of the vital spirit, that which is on the right side of the body)

idam pron. 1/s/n this, (see pronoun section), 'this world diversified through names and forms, and the object of direct perception'

idānīm now, at this moment, in this case, just, even, now-a-days,

iḍenya 170/2 praiseworthy, to be invoked or implored, adorable

īdṛś or *īdṛk,* mfn endowed with such qualities, such

īdṛśa 170/2 mfn. such, endowed with such qualities. of such a kind, of this kind

īḍya 170/2 praiseworthy, to be invoked or implored, adorable

iha 169/3 ind. in this place, in this world, now, at this time, here,

iha, 169/3 ind. here, in this place, now, at this time,

īhā f. wish, effort, exertion, activity,

ihāmutra in the other world, in the life to come, in this world and the next, now and hereafter

ihaloka m. this world, this life,

īhate 171/2 endeavours to attain, seeks for, wishes for

īhita 171/3mfn sought, wished, desire, effort

ijya 164/2 mfn. to be revered/honoured

ijyate it is performed, offered or sacrificed 1/s/pres/pass √*yaj*

√*īkṣ* 170/1 to see, look, view, behold, *īkṣate* 1/s/pres/indic/mid sees

īkṣaka m. a spectator, beholder,

īkṣaṇa n. 170/1 look, view, sight, from √*īkṣ* to see, look, see in one's mind, regard, consider, foretell

īkṣate he/she sees, observes

ikṣurasa 164/1 m sugarcane juice,

ikṣvākave to or for *Ikṣvāku*

iḷenya 170/2 praiseworthy, to be invoked or implored, adorable

imam 2/s/m this

imāni pron. (indefinite) these 1/pl/n

ime 1/pl/m these

indhana m. fuel, n. kindling, lighting, fuel, wood, grass etc. for this purpose,

indra m. *Indra*, Lord of the minor gods, universal *manas*, thunder,

indrajāla 166/2 magic, illusion,

Indrajit eldest son of *Rāvaṇa*

indriya 167/2 n. power, force, power of the senses, fit for or belonging to Indra, *indriyāṇi* the senses, -five of knowledge (*jñānendriya*) and five of action (*karmendriya*)

indryagocara mfn field of action of the senses, field perceptible to the senses, object of the senses

indriyanigraha control of the senses, 'mastery over sensory organs of knowledge and perceptions. Mastery over senses requires choice of perceptions conducive to righteous life.' 'Not to master the senses of knowledge or to pervert the senses of knowledge is against the law.'

indriyagrāma all the senses collectively,

indriyārtha sense-objects, objects of the senses, anything exciting the senses,

indu m. moon, a bright drop, a spark,

iṅgate 164/1 it moves or agitates, goes to or towards, flickers or stirs, 1/s/pres/indic/mid √*iṅg*

īpsā 170/2 f. asking, desire, wish to obtain

īpsu 170/2 striving to contain/obtain,

irasya 168/1Nom. P. *-ti,* to be envious, to be angry

īrṣā f. impatience, envy of another's success

√*iṣ* 1. cl 1. to seek, search, *eṣati, eṣate,* cl 4 *iṣyati,* cl 9 *iṣṇāti,* cause to move quickly, throw,

cast, deliver a speech, proclaim, impel, animate
iṣ 168/3 mfn. moving quickly, speedy
√*iṣ* 3. cl 6. to desire, wish, seek for, obtain, strive for *icchati, icchate*
iṣ 169/2 mfn ifc. seeking for
iṣ f. wish
iṣ f. anything drunk, refreshment, enjoyment, libation, the refreshing waters of the sky,
√*īṣ* 171/1 1. cl2. *īṣte* (*Ved*) *īṣe* belong to, dispose of, be powerful, behave like a master, allow
īṣ 2. m. master, lord, the Supreme Spirit
īṣa mfn. owning, possessing, one who is completely master of anything, powerful, supreme, a ruler, master, lord, m. master, lord, the supreme spirit
f. (*ā*) power, dominion
īṣ, *ṭ*, m. master, lord, the Supreme Spirit, mfn. power, dominion one who lords it over is *īṭ*
īṣ cl 1 A (with prep. also P), *īṣate* (*ti*), to go, to fly away, escape, to attack, hurt, to glean,
īṣā by the Lord 3/s/m
īṣat 1. attacking, hurting,
2. a little, slightly
īṣāvāsya n. to be clothed or pervaded by the Supreme
iṣita mfn. moved, driven, willed, directed, caused, quick, speedy
iṣta 169/2 1. mfn sought, wished, desired, loved, 2. sacrificed, worshipped with sacrifices, reverenced, respected, approved,
m. a lover, a husband, sacrifice
n. wish, desire,
iṣṭāpūrta the merit of sacred rites, the fruit of sacrifice
iṣṭakā f. brick used in the sacred fireplace,
iṣṭakāmaduh 169/2 f. granting desires, the name of the cow of plenty
iṣṭikā f. brick used in the sacred fireplace,
iṣṭvā worshipping, offering, having worshipped, (gerund)
iṣu m. arrow,
Iśvara 171/1 able to do, master, Lord,
īśvarabhāva 171/1 royal or imperial state, lordliness, exercising rulership
itaḥ adv. from here, from hence, from this world, in this world
itara 164/3 another, different from, other, may indicate a contrary idea to the preceding word, e.g. *sukhetareṣu* in happiness and distress, in a tatpuruṣa compound may express an idea implied in the contrary of that idea e.g. *dakṣiṇetara* - the left hand,
itas adv. from here, from hence, from this world, in this world, from this time, now,
itas itas here, there
itastataḥ 165/1 adv. hither and thither
iti 165/1 ind. signifying the end of thought or speech, thus, in this manner,
itihāsa 165/2 'so indeed it was' tradition, history, traditional accounts,
ittham ind. thus, in this way,
iva 168/3 ind. like, as it were, as if, seems,
iyam pron. 1/s/f this
iyant mfn so great, so much
iyat mfn so much, only so much, so large, only so large,
ja mfn(in cpds. ifc.) born, born from, growing in, living at, 'belonging to, connected with', m. a son of, a father, birth,

jā f. a race, tribe, ifc. a daughter,
jaḍa 409/3mfn cold, frigid, motionless, inert, void of life, inanimate, unintelligent, stupid,
jaḍadhī dull-witted
jāḍya 417/2 n. coldness, chilliness, insensibility, dullness, absence of soul or intellect, inactivity
jagadiśvara 408/2 Indra, world-lord
jāgara 417/1 mfn. awake or watchful, m. waking, wakefulness
jāgarita 417/1 mfn. n. waking, waking state,
jagarti 417/1 to be awake or watchful 1/s/pres/indic/act. awakes
jāgarti 417/1 awaken, be attentive

to 1/s/pres/indic/act awakens,
f. waking, vigilance,

jagat 408/1 mfn moving, movable, living, m. pl. people, mankind, n. that which moves or is alive, the world , the universe

jagatpati 408/1 Lord of the Universe,

jagatyām 7/s/f on the earth

jagdha 407/3 mfn. eaten, exhausted by, n. a place where anyone has eaten

jaghana m.n. the hinder parts, the buttocks, hip,

jaghanya 408/3 mfn. hindmost last, latest lowest, worst, vilest, least, least important, of low origin or rank

jāgrat 417/1 m. waking, the waking state,

jahāti 1296/2 root *hā*, to give up, renounce, resign, 1/s/pres/ind/act. gives up, leaves, casts off,

jahi kill! destroy!
2/s/impv/act √ *han*

jāhnava 420/2 m. the Ganges, (the daughter of Jahnu)

jala 414/2 n. water, any fluid, the element water with the property of taste,

jāla mfn watery, n. a net (for fish or birds), a hairnet, a snare, a cob-web, mail-coat, lattice window, the webbing of web-feet, lion's mane, a cluster (buds etc.), collection, multitude, kind, species, m. a small cucumber,

jalada m. cloud,

jaladhi m. ocean, a lake,

jālakāra m. spider,

jālma mfn despicable, cruel, inconsiderate,

janādhipa m. ruler of men

jāmātṛ m. son-in-law, brother in law, husband,

jambūka m. a jackal, a low man,

jana 410/1 m. a man, living being, person, people, person, √ *jan* in coming into existence

janaka m. father, *Janaka,* father of *Sītā,* king of *Videha*

jānan knowing pres/act/part

jānāna 426/1 in comp for *jñāna* pres.mid. part. knowing

jananī f. mother

janapada m. district, community,

janarava m. gossip, rumour,

janārdana m. agitator of men, mover of men (*Kṛṣṇa)*

janasaṁsad 410/3 an assembly of men, an assembly of common people

janasamūha jana 410/1 living being , people, *samūha* 1170/3 assemblage, multitude, a multitude of people,

jānāti root *jñā* 425/2 to know
1/s/pres/indic/act knows

janavāda m. gossip, rumour,

janayet should cause to give birth to or arise, or produce, 1/s/opt/act/caus

jāne I know 3/s/pres/indic/mid √*jñā*

jaṅgama 408/2 moving, living, 'moving on feet'- (Gam.), f. a living being,

janma in comp. for *janman*

janmamṛtyū birth and death

janman 411/3 birth, re-birth

jantu 411/2 a child, offspring, a creature, living being. pl. *jantavas*

jānu n. knee,

japa *412/1* muttering, whispering, muttering prayers

japamālā f. rosary,

japayajña muttering prayers as a sacrifice

jara mfn becoming old, m. the act of wearing out, wasting,

jāra mfn becoming old,
m. lover, sweetheart,

jarā the act of becoming old, old age

jaraṭha mfn old, bent, drooping,

jarayanti they are wasting, wearing out, becoming old √*jī*

jarāyu mfn withering, dying away,
n. the cast off skin of a snake,

jarjara mfn decayed, broken, divided,

jāspati m. head of a family,

jaṭā f. having matted hair, tangled locks,

jāta 417/2 mfn. born, grown, produced, a son, happened, become, present, apparent, manifest,
n. birth, race,

jātāni born, brought into existence,
1/pl/n

jaṭāyu king of the vultures

jaṭhara mfn hard, old, n. belly, womb,
jāti 418/1 f. birth, production, re-birth, the form of existence (man, animal etc.), fixed by birth, position assigned by birth – rank, caste, race etc. class, classification,
jātsaya of the born 6/s/m
jātu 418/2 ind. at all, ever, some day, once, once upon a time,
java 416/2 mfn. swift, m. speed, velocity, swiftness
javīyas mfn. quicker, faster
jaya m. victory
jāyā wife, 'bringing forth'
jayājayau victory and defeat (1/dual/ m *dvandva* comp.)
jayanta mfn victorious, m. the moon,
jāyante they are born, originated 1/pl/pres/pass
jayati conquers,
jāyate √ *jan* 410/1 produced, caused, is caused, born, brought forth, is born 1/s/pres/pass
jayati root *ji* 420/2 excel, surpass, conquers, wins, to conquer (the passions),
jayema we should conquer, we should prevail, 3/pl/opt/act
jayeyus they should conquer, 1/pl/opt/act
jayya part. to be conquered, gained,
jetāsi you will conquer 2/s/peri/fut √*ji*
jhaṁjhā mfn roaring,
jharā f. waterfall,
jharjharita mfn bruised, wasted, withered,
jhaṣa 429/1 a large fish, the sign Pisces, sun-heat, a desert,
jhaṣiti 428/3 ind. at once, instantly immediately,
jhillī f. a cricket, a lamp wick,
jhillika m. a cricket,
jighran 421/1 mfn smelling
jigīṣatām of those who desire victory desid/pres/part/act 6/pl/m √*ji*
jihāsā 421/3 desire to abandon or give up
jihvā 422/1m. the tongue, forms of flame,
jijīviṣāmas we desire to live 3/pl/desid/act √*jīv*
jijñāsu mfn 421/1 desirous of knowing
jīmūta m. thundercloud, a cloud, mountain,
jina mfn victorious, m. victor, a *Buddha*, an *Arhat (Jaina)*,
jīrṇa 422/2 mfn. old, worn out, m. an old man n. old age
jita mfn won, acquired, defeated, conquered, subdued, given up,
jītitavyam should be lived,
jitvā having conquered
jīva 422/2 mfn living, existing, alive, ifc. living by, causing to live, vivifying, m.n. alive, any living being, existence, life, m. the principle of life, vital breath, the living or personal soul (as distinguished from the universal soul), G.148 -consciousness inseperably qualified by the internal organs. G 147, the phenomenal self subject to experience and empirical changes- a blend of *puruṣa* and mind, G. a blend of the Self and not-Self with a wrong identification each of the other, consciousness qualified by the internal organs. In truth the Self is ever free, this is about what we think ourselves to be –erroneously,
'the transmigrating individual soul',
jīvabhūta consisting of the *jīva*s, or souls, or spiritual beings, 422/3 become alive, endowed with life
jīvana 423/2 enlivening, a living being, *jīvane* 7/s in life, in living
jīvana mfn giving life, enlivening, (said of the wind, sun, etc.), m. a living being, wind, a son, manner of living, living by, making alive, n. (*am*) life, manner of living, livelihood, means of living, enlivening, making alive,
jīvanmukta 423/2 emancipated while still alive, liberated while living
jīvavīcayaḥ waves of individual existence
jīvati 422/2 lives, is or remains alive,

1/s/pres/indic/act. lives

jīvikā f. livelihood,

jīvita 423/2 life, living, lived through (a period of time), returned to life, enlivened, animated, n. a living being, life, duration of life, livelihood,

jīvitās 1/pl/m lives, as in their lives

jīvite from root *jīv* 422/2 to live, 1/s/pres/mid/indic being alive, to live

-jña knower of (at end of a compound)

jña 425/3 2.mfn knowing, wise, m. a wise and learned man,

√*jñā* 425/2 root, to know, perceive, apprehend, understand

jñāna 426/1 n. knowing, knowledge, , the higher knowledge, 'wisdom', true knowledge. 'The primary knowledge is Pure Consciousness or *svarūpajñāna* (knowledge in itself) i.e. not other than the Self'
'The secondary sense, and the one most commonly used, is the expressionor reflection of the Pure Consciousness in *antaḥkaraṇa*. As such it could be lofty or otherwise, and it may be valid (*pramā*) or invalid (*apramā*), unlike the word "knowledge" in the West, which usually refers to valid knowledge only. In the scriptures of course the secondary sense refers to spiritual knowledge such as in the Upanishads or conversation with a fully realized man.' see *vijñāna* and *prajñāna*
higher knowledge, knowing, becoming acquainted with higher knowledge (derived from meditation on the Self),

jñānābhāsa "The limited manifests in the *antaḥkaraṇaḥ*. That consciousness which shines or seems to reflect in the *antaḥkaraṇaḥ*. is called *cidabhāsa*. in this reflected light of knowledge is the knowledge one acquires from the creation, communication, operative skills, etcetera. All this is known as *jñānābhāsa"*.

jñānadīpa 426/1 the lamp of knowledge,

jñānagamya 426/2 mfn. attainable by understanding (*am*) n. goal of knowledge,

jñānasvarūpa 'The primary knowledge is Pure Consciousness or *svarūpajñāna* (knowledge in itself) i.e. not other than the Self'

jñānavān wise man, man of wisdom 1/s/m

jñānavat 426/2 endowed with knowledge, having spiritual knowledge, intelligent, wise

jñānin 426/2 mfn. knowing, wise, a wise one, m. a fortune-teller, astrologer, a sage,

jñānendriyāṇi five senses of knowledge, seeing, hearing, touch, taste, smell

jñāsyasi you will know, thou shalt know 2/s/fut/act √*jñā*

jñāta 425/3 *jñāta* mfn understood, comprehended, known,

jñātatattva knowing the truth,

jñātvā ind. having known or understood,

jñātavya to be known

jñāti m. kinsman, relative,

jñeya 426/2 mfn. to be known, to be learnt or understood or inquired about, (the object of knowledge) – gerundive 1/s/m

joṣayet should cause to enjoy or delight 1/s/opt/caus/act

jugupsā 423/3 dislike, abhorrence, censure

juhosi you offer (in sacrifice) 2/s √*hu*

juhurāṇa mfn. crooked, deceitful, √*hvṛ* to deviate or diverge from the right line, go crookedly or wrongly or deviously
m. the moon

juhvati they offer, they sacrifice, 1/pl/pres/indic/act √*hu*

juṣṭa 424/1 mfn. pleased, propitious, liked, agreeable, usual

jvāla m. flame, torch,

jvalana mfn combustible, flaming, shining, m. a fire, n. blazing,
jvalati 428/2 burns brightly, blazes, glows
jvara 428/1 m. fever, fever of the soul, mental pain, affliction, grief
jyā f. bowstring, superior power, force,
jyaiṣṭha name of a month, May-June,
jyāyas 426/3 mfn. superior, greater, larger, stronger, most excellent, older,
jyāyasī better, superior, 1/s/f comparative
jyeṣṭha 426/3 mfn most excellent, pre-eminent, first, chief, best, greatest, m. the chief, greatesteldest, eldest brother, n. what is most excellent, f. the eldest wife, the middle finger, misfortune, a small house lizard, (*am*) ind. most, extremely,
jyotis n. light (of sun, dawn etc.), as pl. the heavenly bodies, stars,
jotiṣa m. the sun, the illuminator, n. science of astronomy and planetary influence, 427/2 mfn. luminous, brilliant, shining, belonging to the world of light, celestial, spiritual, pure 'the brilliance of light' LM

jyotiṣām of the lights, of stars 6/pl/n
jyotsnā f. a monlit night, moonlight, pl. light, splendour,
ka who? what ? 1/s/m
kā who? what? 1/s/f
ka 4. 240/3 a *Taddhita* affix used in forming adjectives or added to nouns to express diminution, deterioration or similarity e.g. *putraka* a little son, *aśvaka* a bad horse or like a horse
kabandha m.a heavenly being cursed to live in a *rākṣasa* body
kāca m. glass,
kaccit is it that? has it? has this? used in questions expecting the answer 'yes' ibc. marks the uselessness, badness or defectiveness of anything e.g. -*akṣara* n. a bad letter, bad writing, with *na* in no way or manner,
kadā 248/1 when?
kadācana at any time, at any time whatsoever
kadācid (t) 248/1 at some time or other, at any time, at any time whatever, one day
kadācit at one time, one day,
kadācana at any time
kadācit 248/1 at some time or other, at any time, at any time whatever, one day
kadalaḥ or *kadalī* (f.) banana tree
kadāpi ever (after *na*) never
kaiḥ by whom? with whom? 3/pl/m interrog.
kaikeyī mother of *Bharata*
kailāsa m. a Himalayan peak, 'crystalline', 'abode of bliss',
kaivalya 311/3 isolation, absolute unity, detachment from all other connections, beatitude, established in unity, detachment of the soul from matter or further transmigration
kais by what, 3/pl/n
kajjala n. collyrium (an eye-salve),
kāka m. crow
kakud f. a peak, summit or hump, a chief or head
kakum or *kakubh* f. a peak, summit, space region, pony tail hair, a wreath of *campaka* flowers, splendour, beauty,
kāla 278/1 mfn black, m. a period of time, time (in general), the right or appropriate time,
kalaha m. strife, contention, quarrel,
kālam 278/1 2/s for a certain time, death, time of death
kalaṅka m. spot, stain, mark
kalaśa m. pot, jar, pitcher,
kalatra 260/3 n. a wife, consort,
kalayatām of the calculators or regulators, pres/part/act √*kal* 6/pl/m
kāle in time, at the proper time 7/s
kālena in course of time
kalevara 262/2 m.n. the body
kāliyaḥ *Kāliyaḥ* a serpent demon
kaliyuga iron age, 432,000 years, selfishness, ignorance and conceit prevail,

kalila 262/1 mfn. full of, covered with, impenetrable, n. a thicket, confusion
kalmaṣa 263/1 n. stain, dirt, darkness, moral stain, mfn. impure, sinful
kallola – 263/3 m. a wave, billow
kalpa fourteen *manvantaras,* one day in the life of *brahmā,* one *manvantara* = 71 cycles of the 4 *yugas,* mfn practicable, feasible, possible, proper, fit, able, m. a sacred precept, ordinance, manner, way, manner of acting, proceeding, practice, one side of an argument, an alternative, investigation, research, resolve, ifc. having the form or manner of anything, similar to, resembling, like but with a degree of inferiority, almost,
kalpādau at the beginning of a kalpa
kalpakṣaya 262/3 the end of a kalpa, destruction of the world
kalpana 263/1n. creating in the mind, assuming anything to be real. (*ā*) f. making, manufacturing, preparing, fixing, settling, arranging, imagining, creating in the mind, assuming anything to be real, fiction, hypothesis, form, shape, image,
kalpāṇa mfn noble, good, blessed, n. good fortune,
kalpānta 262/3 the end of a *kalpa,* (cycle, a day of *brahmā,* 4320 million years) the end of a cycle
kalpate 308/2 is ordered or regulated, is or becomes fit, is adapted well managed, succeeds, prepares, arranges, happens, becomes, occurs, creates, makes, executes, brings about, contrives, invents 1/s/pres/indic/mid
kalpita 263/1 mfn made, fabricated, imagined
kalyāṇa 263/2 mfn. beautiful, agreeable, illustrious, noble, virtuous, good, beneficial, auspicious
kalyāṇakṛt 263/2 mfn doing good, virtuous
kam 1. particle emphasizing the previous word in an affirmative sense, 2. interrog.whom? which?
kāma 271/3 m. longing, desire, 'sex energy' pleasure, enjoyment, love, esp. sexual love or sensuality ,
kāmabhāj mfn partaking of sensual enjoyment, enjoying all desires,
kāmabhāja partaker in enjoyment, fit for enjoyment,
kāmabhoga m. gratification of desires, sensual gratification,
kāmacāra 272/1 mfn moving freely, following one's own pleasure, unrestrained, independent, following one's own desires m spontaneous action
kāmadhena = *kāmadhuk* f. the cow of plenty, the wish-giving cow,
kāmakāmī m. desirer of the objects of desire
kāmakāra 272/1 mfn. fulfilling the desires of anyone, m. the act of following one's inclinations, spontaneous deed, free will,
kamala 252/1m.n. a name of *Brahmā,* a lotus, lotus-flower, mfn pale-red, rose-coloured, *ja* 407/3 born or descended from, *Brahmāja*, born of the lotus,
kamalapattrākṣa lotus petal-eyed, *Kṛṣṇa*
kāmam ind. at will, gladly, indeed, certainly, willingly, according wish or desire
kāmarūpam desire-form, having the form of desire,
kāmātman 272/3 mfn whose very essence is desire, whose selves are desirous, given to lust, sensual
kāmavaśa 272/3 m. subjection to love (lust), *vaśa* 929/2 will wish desire, *vaśaga* 929/2 being in the power of, subject, enamoured, subject to the power of lust
kambala m. blanket, woollen cloth,
kampate he trembles, shakes
kaṁsa *Kaṁsa*
kāmyā 273/3 mfn desirable, beautiful,

amiable, lovely, agreeable, to one's liking, agreeable to one's wish, f. wish, desire, longing for or striving after

kaṇa m. a small grain, (as of dust or rice),

kāṇa mfn one-eyed, blind, pierced, perforated, m. a crow,

kanaka 248/2 n. gold, a thorn-apple, mfn of gold, golden,

kānana n. forest, grove, a house,

kāñcana 268/2 n. gold, money, wealth, property, the filament of the lotus, mfn golden, made of gold, m. a covenant binding for life, a form of temple,

kañcuka mfn armour, mail, m. snake-skin, husk, shell, cover, envelope,

kañcukin m. chamberlain,

kāṇṭa m. an arrow, a bow (for arrows),

Kandarpa 249/3 love, lust, god of love

kanduka m. a ball, saucepan, pillow, betel-nut,

kaniṣṭhaka mfn smallest, f. *–ikā* little finger

kaṅkana ring shaped ornament, a bracelet

kāṅkṣā 268/1 f. wished, desired, expected

kāṅkṣe I will wish for, desire, 3/s/fut/mid/ √*kāṅkṣ* 268/1

kaṇṭaka m. a thorn, prickle, fish-bone, sting

kāntāra 271/1m.n. a large forest, a difficult road through a forest, living in the world compared to a difficult road through a forest

kaṇṭha m. throat, using the *kaṇṭhaḥ* mouth, throat, and tongue position,

kānti f. desire, wish, loveliness, beauty, splendour, female beauty, personal embellishment, brightness

kanyā daughter, maiden,

kapāla n. 1. cup or dish, 2. cover or lid, 3. cranium, skull, egg-shell,

kapaṭa m. n. trickery, fraud,

kapi-dhvajas m. banner of the monkey , mfn monkey-bannered, (*Arjuna*)

kapi m. monkey, ape

Kapila a sage and founder of the *Sāṁkhya* philosophical system

kapila n. brown (monkey colour)

kapola m. cheek,

kapota m. dove, pigeon,

kara 253/1 1. m. a doer, maker, causer, doing, making, causing, producing, the act of doing, making etc. a hand, trunk, 2. a ray of light, sunbeam, moonbeam,

kāra 274/2 n. making, doing, working, a maker, doer, m. ifc. an act, action, a term used in denoting a letter or sound or indeclinable word, effort

kārā f. prison, gaol,

kārāgṛham n. prison, gaol,

kāraka 1. mfn. making, doing, acting, who or what does or produces or creates, n. instrumental in bringing about the action denoted by a verb, (*karman, karaṇa, kartṛi, sampradāna, apādāna, adhikaraṇa*)

karāla 255/2 mfn. cleaving asunder, formidable, dreadful, terrible, a kind of deer

kāraṇa 274/2 1. n. cause, reason, the cause of anything, instrument, means, motive, origin, agency, instrumentality,

karaṇa 254/1 doing, making, effecting, causing, clever, skilful, a writer, (in Gram.) a sound or word as an independent part of speech (or as separated from context; in this sense usually n.), the act of making doing, producing, instrument, means of action, method, cause, means

kārayan causing to act, causing action, 1/s/pres/caus/act part.

kardama m. mud,

karhi ind. when? at what time? (with *svid, cid or api*) at any time, (with *cid* and a particle of negation) never or at no time,

karhicit 260/1 at any time

kārikā f. 274/3 concise statement of doctrines,

karin mfn 'possessing a hand', an elephant,

kariṣyati will do or make

karişyasi you will do or make
karma 258/3 act, action,
karma 258/2,3 for *karman* in cpds.
act, action, work, any religious act or rite (as sacrifice, oblation etc., esp. as originating in the hope of future recompense and as opposed to speculative religion or knowledge of spirit),
the accumulated effect of deeds in past, present or future, 'as one sows so shall one reap',
karma-bandha bondage of karma TP compound
karmacodanā 258/3 the motive impelling to ritual acts, inducement to action, inducer of all actions 1/s/f
karmaja 258/3 bor n of action *karma* √*ja*
karmakāṇḍa 258/3 that part of the śruti which relates to ceremonial acts and sacrificial rites
karmakṛt 258/3 mfn. performing any work, skilful in work
karmamarga 'the way of action'
259/1m. the course of acts, activity
karman 258/2 n. act, action, performance, business, office, special duty, occupation, obligation (ifc. the first member of the compound being the person who performs the action or the person or thing for whom the action is performed or a specification of the action, any religious act or rite, work, labour, activity, action consisting in motion (Nyāya phil.), product, result, effect, organ of sense or of action, (in gram.) the object (of a sentence or an action), action with implied reference to the effect of deeds in past, present or future,
karmāṇi actions, works 1/pl/n
karmānuṣṭhānam 259/2 act of practising one's duties, acting appropriately
karmaphala n. fruit of action
karmendriyāṇi five senses of action, speaking, grasping, moving, evacuating, generating
Karṇa a *Kaurava* warrior, half-brother of *Arjuna*
karṇa m. ear
kārpaṇya 275/3 n. pitiful circumstances, poorness of spirit, weakness,
karomi I do, I make,
3/s/pres/indic/mid √*kṛ*
karoṣi you do 2/s/
karoti 301/2 1/s/pres/act he or she makes or does, puts on, performs,
karotu verb *kṛ* 1/s/impv/act
let him/her do, he or she may do
karṣa 259/3 m. the act of drawing, dragging, ploughing, agriculture
kartā abstract noun from *kṛ* 300/3
the doer, the creator 1/s/m
kartṣra m. creator, maker,
kartavya 'the will of the Absolute as the laws of nature reflecting through the framework of the individual'
The little Absolute has to respond to the big Absolute. The interaction is the *kartavya*.' fut/pass/part √*kṛ*
257/3 to be done or made or accomplished, that which ought to be done, duty, obligation
kartavyatā 257/3 f. that which ought to be done, or made or accomplished, part. obligation, duty
kārtika m. name of a month,
kārtikeya god of war,
kartṛ 257/3 mfn. one who makes or does or acts, a doer, maker, agent, author (in grammar) the agent of an action (who acts of his own accord [*sva-tantra*]), the active noun, the subject of a sentence
kartṛtva 258/1 n. agency, means of action, state of performing action,
the state of being the performer or author of anything
kartṛtā 258/1 the state of being the agent of the action,
kartum 257/3 *kartu* , *kartum* infinitive of *kṛ* to do, to do, (needing) to be done,

karuṇa 255/2 mfn mournful, miserable, compassionate, (*ā*) f. pity, compassion, m. pity
kāruṇya 275/1 n. compassion, kindness,
kāsāra m. pond, pool,
kārya 276/1 mfn to be made or done, fut.pass. part. (gerundive)
kāryate is caused or forced to perform, 1/s/pres/indic/pass/caus √ *kṛ*
kaśā f. a whip,
kaṣāya mfn red, astringent, dull, 265/3 attachment to worldly objects, " a screen which fogs the subtle body" (Jaiswal),
kaścana 240/3 any, anyone, at all, in any way
kaścid 240/3 anyone, someone,
kāśī the city of Benares, Varanasi,
kaśmala 265/2 foul, dirty, impure, timid, m.n. consternation, stupefaction, dejection, despair,
kasmin pron. 7/s in whom
kaṣṭa n. hardship, mfn evil, wrong, bad,
kāṣṭha n. stick of wood, log, firewood,
kasya pron. whose
kasyacid of anyone, of anyone whatever
kaṭa m. a mat, hip
kaṣaka 243/3 m. a bracelet of gold
katama who or which of many
katara who/which of two
kathā story, tale,
katham 247/2 ind. how?
kathayanta speaking of, explaining pres/act/part 1/pl/m
kathayata please speak, please tell,
kathayati tells
kathayiṣyanti they will relate, they will tell, 1/pl/fut/act
kaṭhin mfn hard, cruel, firm, stiff, harsh,
kathita° told
kaṭhora mfn cruel, hard, stiff, offering resistance, sharp, piercing,
kathyate 247/1 from *kath* to converse, to be called, be regarded or considered as, 1/s/pres/indic/pass it can be described
kati 246/3 how many? some, several,
katipaya mfn indef. several, some, a few,
kaṭu 244/1 pungent, acrid, sharp
kaumāra n. childhood , youth, mfn juvenile, youthful,
kaumudī f. moonlight,
kaupīna 316/2 a loin cloth, a small piece of cloth worn over the genitals by poor persons. *-tva-* part. *–tve* 7/s in having a loin cloth, having nothing but a loin cloth,
kauśala 317/3 n. well-being, welfare, good-fortune, health, prosperity
kausalyā f. *Kausalyā*
kautuka 316/1 n. curiosity, interest in anything, eagerness, impatience,
kautūhala m. curiosity,
kavaca m. armour,
kavi 264/2 mfn. gifted with insight, intelligent, knowing, enlightened, wise, m. (*ḥ*) a wise man, sage, seer, prophet, poet, seer of the *krānta* (past), seer of all, 'there is no other seer but this'
kavya mfn a sacrificer , sacrificial priest, n. (*am*) an oblation of food to ancestors,
kāvya mfn endowed with the qualities of a sage or poet,descended or coming from a sage, prophetic, inspired, n. poetry, poem, m. happiness, welfare, pl. poems, f. intelligence,
kāya 274/1 2. m.the body, trunk of a tree, body of a lute,
kayā 253/1 ind. 3/s/ *ka* in what manner? by what?
kāya 274/1 2. m. the body, trunk of a tree, ind. bodily,
ke which two, which many,
kecid some, whoever
keli 309/3 sport, amorous sport,
keliśikṣayā 3/m/s by amorous practises
kena pron. by or with whom? what or which?
kenacid with anything
kendra n. centre, m. the centre of a circle, the equation of the centre, the argument of a circle, the argument of an equation,
kesara m. hair, mane,

keśa m. hair, a mane, kind of perfume,
keśava o handsome haired one
voc/s/m a name for *kṛṣṇa*
Keśi a demon in the form of a
horse slain by *Kṛṣṇa*
ketu m. brightness, flag, banner,
pl. beams, a chief, leader, intellect,
discernment, unusual phenomena
e.g. comet, meteor, rays, beams,
kevala 309/3 mfn exclusively one's own (not
common to others), alone, only,
mere, sole, one, excluding others,
not connected with anything else, n.
alone, absolute, entire, whole, all
one, mere, (*am*) ind. only,
keyūra m. an armlet worn on the upper arm,
kha n. 1. hole, hollow, 2. opening,
aperture of the human body,
3. hole in the hub of a wheel,
4. void space, the sky, air, ether,
m. the sun,
khādata eat! (pl)
khādati eats
khaḍga m. sword, scimitar, rhinoceros,
khādita mfn eaten
khādiṣyati will eat
khaga m. bird
khala m. a rogue, threshing floor, granary
khalu 338/2 ind. indeed, verily, certainly,
may emphasize the previous word,
please, pray (in entreaty)
khaṇḍa mfn broken, m. a break, section,
piece, a continent, part,
khaṅga 335/1 see *khaḍga* 335/3 a sword,
scimitar, sacrificial knife
khañja mfn lame,
kheda 340/1 m. lassitude, depression,
exhaustion, sadness,
khela 340/3 moving, trembling, sport, play,
pastime,
khidyate 339/3 is wearied , suffers pain,
khinna 340/1 mfn depressed, distressed,
afflicted,
khura m. hoof, razor,
khyāti f. assertion, view, idea, perception,
knowledge, being well-known,
fame,
kīdṛś(a) *(ī)* what kind of..?

kila ind. indeed, certainly, (follows the
word it emphasizes),
m. play, trifling,
kilbiṣa 284/2 n. fault, offence, sin, guilt
kim 282/2 ind. interrogative, what,
why, expecting the answer 'no',
sometimes used as a question
marker without meaning,
kimapi somewhat, much more, still further
kimartham why?
kim bahunā 724/2 "what occasion is there
for much talk?" i.e. "in short"
kiṁ ca moreover
kimiti wherefore? why?
kimiva wherefore?
kiṁśuka m. name of a tree,
kiṁ tu (*kiṁtu)* but, however
kiṁ vā perchance?
kim + *vadantī* 282/3 1/s/f "what
do they say" ,
(it is) a common saying
kimicchasi what would you like?
(at meals), what do you desire?
kiñcana 283/1 something, anything,
(with negation), in no way, nothing,
anything
kiñcid 283/1 whatever , anything,
something
kiraṇa m. dust, very minute dust, a ray or
beam of light, a sun or moon-beam,
kirīṭa 284/1 any ornament used as a crown
kirīṭina crowned
kīrtana 285/1 n. mentioning, repeating,
saying, √*kīrt* recite, repeat,
celebrate, praise, glorify (with gen.),
'praise-singing' HH
kīrtayat 285/1 mfn mentioning, celebrating,
praising glorifying pres/caus/part
kiśalaya n. sprout, shoot,
kiṣkindhā the capital city from which
sugrīva was exiled
kiśora m. a colt, the young of any animal,
(*ī)* f. young, a female colt,
kīrti 285/1f. good report, fame, renown,
glory, lustre
kīṭa m. worm, caterpillar, faeces,
ifc. an expression of contempt,
kitava m. gambler, rogue, f. *vī* addicted to

gaming

kiyat mfn how great, how large, how far, how much, of what extent, of what qualities, little, small, unimportant,

klaibya n. 324/1 impotence, unmanliness, weakness, timidity, cowardice

kleda 323/3 m. wetness, dampness

kledayanti they cause to become wet, 1/pl/pres/indic/caus/act √*klid*

kleśa 324/1 m. pain, affliction, distress

klṛpta mfn arranged, made, ready, in order, created

kokila m. an Indian Cuckoo

kolāhala m.n. uproar, confused cry, din,

komala mfn tender, soft, sweet, charming

koṇa m. a corner, angle, the number 4, the sharp edge of a sword, club,

kopa m. anger, fury, passion,

kopāt angrily

kośa 314/1 m.a cask, cover, sheath, treasure,

koṭara n. hollow of a tree, hollow,

koṭi f. a crore, =10,000,000 or 100 *lakh*

√*kṛ* 301/1 Cl 8 P *karoti* A *kurute* to do, make, perform, accomplish, cause, effect, prepare, undertake, to do anything for the advantage or injury of another, to execute, carry out (as an order or command), to manufacture, prepare, work at, elaborate, build, to form or construct one thing out of another, to employ, use, make use of,

krakaca m.n. a saw,

√*kram* 319/3 Cl 1 P A *krāmati*, or *kramati* or *kramate,* also Cl 4 P *krāmyati* or *kramyati,* to step, walk, go, go towards, approach,

krama m. a step, course, process, sequence, succession, series, method, manner, going, proceeding,

krameṇa ind. step by step, gradually,

kratu 319/1 m. plan, intention, desire, will, intelligence personified, conviction, determination, a firm belief

kratumaya mfn. endowed with intelligence, identified with a conviction

kṛcchra mfn distressful, troublesome, n. trouble, difficulty, hardship,

krīḍati plays

kriyā means activity. 'There is only one activity in truth. The entire creation is this activity, manifesting the glory and substance of the Absolute. At different times this activity may be called –speaking, writing, resting, going or living, but at all times it is manifesting the substance of the absolute. Name and form change but the Absolute does not. The ocean and its waves are of the same substance; the waves are in motion and ever changing, but the substance, water, remains the same.' L..M., verbs in general, action (as the general idea expressed by any verb). The activity in a sentence, the verb. the form of the *kriyā* can express a range of aspects of the activity such as its time or mood.

kriyā rites, offerings

kriyā'dvaita 321/1 n. efficient cause (as resigning all to God)

kriyamāṇa ..that "which would gather in the future through the activities performed by the person."
pass.part. √*kṛ* being performed, performed
the *saṁskara* of the future produced by present action
being done or performed, pres/pass/part √kṛ

kriyate it is performed, done, made 1/s/pres/pass √*kṛ*

kriyāviśeṣaṇa a word which "expands the remainder" from a verb, bringing out a previously unmanifested character, (an adverb)

krodha 322/1 m. anger, wrath, passion, (used with 7th),

kroḍa 323/1 m. the interior of anything, cavity a cave, the breast, chest,

krośa m. call, calling distance,

krośati cries out

kṛp to mourn, long for

kṛpā 305/1 f. pity, tenderness, grace, compassion (with gen. or loc.)
kṛpālu mfn merciful,
kṛpaṇa 305/1 inclined to grieve, miserable, wretched, feeble
kṛpāya to mourn, grieve, lament,
Kṛpa a *Kaurava* warrior and instructor in arms
kṛpaṇa 305/1 mfn miserable, poor, wretched,
kṛśā lean,
kṛṣaka m. a ploughman,
kṛṣi 306/1 f. ploughing, cultivation, the harvest, the earth
kṛṣṇa Great lord, reincarnation of *Viṣṇu*
kṛṣṇa° black, the dark lunar fortnight
kṛsnavat as if it were all, as if it were the whole,
-kṛt maker
kṛta mfn done, made, performed,
kṛtajña grateful, knowing what is right, correct in conduct,
kṛtakṛtya 302/1 one who has attained any object or purpose, contented, satisfied with, his duties fulfilled
kṛti 303/2 f. the act of doing, making, performing, manufacturing, composing, action, activity, literary work, a production, a literary work,
kṛtī see *kṛti* 303/2 and *kṛtin* 303/2 one who has gained his end. satisfied, contented ,
kṛtvā 304/1 gerund, having done, gained,
kṛttama the best (person) to act,
kṛta yuga or satya yuga golden age, 1,728,000 years , people realised the Self and remembered without difficulty
kṛta-niścaya resolved - *kṛta* made *niścaya* conviction, certainty
kṛtānta 303/1 mfn. causing an end, bringing to an end, whose end is action, destiny, fate, doctrine, dogma
kṛtartha 303/1 one who has attained, successful, satisfied, contented
-kṛte for the sake of (with 6th)
kṛtin mfn one who acts, active, expert, clever, skilful, knowing, learned, good, virtuous, pure, pious, obeying, doing what is enjoined, successful,
kṛtrima mfn artificial, not natural, adopted, fostered,
kṛtsna 304/3 mfn. all, whole, entire n. water, f. (*ā*) totality, completeness
kṛtvā having done, having put on, made
kṛtya 303/3 to be done or performed, duty
kruddha mfn irritated, provoked, angry with
krudh f. anger, wrath,
krudhā f. anger,
krūra 322/3 mfn wounded, hurt, sore, cruel, fierce, pitiless, harsh
kṣālayati washes, wipes
kṣam 326/2 bear patiently, be patient
kṣamā 326/2,3 patience, forbearance, forgiveness, 'to forgive is the *dharma* , the human law , and not to forgive is against the law.'
kṣamī forgiving, remaining unperturbed even when abused or assaulted
kṣāmaye I beg pardon, request indulgence 1/s/caus/mid √*kṣām*
kṣāmya part. to be borne patiently,
kṣaṇa 1. 324/3 m. any instantaneous point of time, instant, twinkling of an eye, moment, measure of time (4 min.), leisure, opportunity,
kṣaṇam for a moment
kṣaṇika mfn transient, momentary,
kṣānta 326/3 mfn. borne, endured, enduring, patient,
kṣānti 326/3 f. patiently waiting for anything, patience, forbearance, endurance, the state of saintly abstraction
kṣapā f. night, ind. (3rd) at night,
kṣapaṇaka m. a mendicant, a Jaina mendicant who wears no clothes,
kṣapita 326/1 mfn. destroyed, ruined
kṣāra mfn pungent, saline, caustic, biting, m. any caustic, corrosive substance,
kṣati 326/1 injury, hurt, loss, want, Apte 170/2 *kṣati* decline, decay, diminution 1/s/f reduces
kṣatriya m. the second class or caste, warriors, kings, statesmen,

n. the power or rank of the sovereign,

kṣātra 325/3mfn relating to the warrior class, n. the dignity of a ruler or governor,

kṣaya 327/3 1.m. dominion,
3. loss, decay,
4. mfn. dwelling, residing

kṣema 332/3 m. giving rest or ease or security, at ease, habitable, peace

kṣematara n. greater ease, greater tranquillity, (comparative)

kśetra 332/1 the field, land, any geometrical figure, place of origin, place where anything is found, the body (considered as the field of the indwelling soul)

kṣetrajñā 332/3 the conscious principle in the corporeal frame, the knower of the field,

kṣetrapati m. farmer, landowner,

kṣetre in/on the field 7/s/n

√*kṣi* 1. to rule or govern, *kṣit* ruling
2.to abide, stay, dwell
3. f. abode, going, moving
4. to destroy, corrupt, ruin

kṣīṇa 328/2 diminished, wasted, lost, worn away

kṣipati throws or shoots, (√*kṣip*)

kṣipram 329/1 quick, speedy, swift

kṣīṇa mfn reduced (to nothing), thin, wasted,

kṣipra 329/1 mfn. quick, speedy, swift, n. (*am*) a measure of time (*am*) ind. quickly, immediately, directly,

kṣīra n. milk, milky sap,

kṣiti f. dwelling, abode, piece of ground or land, the earth, the ground, destruction, the period of destruction of the universe,

kṣobha 331/1 m. agitation or disturbance

kṣubhyati (yate) 331/2 shakes, trembles, is agitated, or disturbed,

kṣudhā f. hunger

kṣudhita mfn hungry,

kṣudra 330/2 very small, little, base, low

kṣura m. a razor, arrow barb, cow's hoof,

ku- a prefix indicating badness, smallness, deficiency,

kubera *Kubera*, the god of wealth

kubuddhaya mfn unintelligent,

kubuddhi 286/2 having vile sentiments, stupid, wrong opinion, part.

kuca m. the female breast, teat,

kūjana n. warbling, cooing, rumbling,

kukkura m. a dog

kukkuṭa m. a cock,

kula 294/2 n. herd, troop, family, community, flock, number

kūla n. shore, bank, slope,

kulin mfn well-born, also *kulīna*

kumāra m. 'easily dying' a child, boy, youth, son, a prince
(-ī) a young girl 10-12, daughter

kumbha 293/1 m. a water jar, pitcher, jug,

kumbhīra m. a shark, gangetic crocodile,

kumuda m. a white lotus, red lotus, camphor

kuñja m. bower,

kuñjara m. elephant, anything pre-eminent of its kind,

Kuntī mother of Arjuna and his brothers,

Kuntīputra son of *Kunti*

kūpa m. a well, cave, hollow

kupita mfn angry

kūrma m. tortoise,

kupyati 291/2 *kup* to be excited, agitated, angry, *kupyati* is angry

kuru 301/1 2/s/impv/act of *kṛ* to do do/ make, perform!

Kuru 294/1 name of a people of India and of their country, a person of that tribe

Kurukñetra an extensive plain north of *Delhi*

kurunandana O descendant of Kuru, voc.

kuruṣva do! make! 2/s/mid/impv √*kṛ*

kurute √ *kṛ* 300/3 he does, makes, acts

kurvan pres. act. part. of *kṛ* 300/3 performing, doing, acting, making,

kurvāṇa doing performing, making, pres/mid/part.

kurvanti they do, perform, make 1/pl/pres/indic/act √*kṛ*

kurvat 294/2 doing, acting as an agent, or servant, present, actual,

kurvīta he should do, 1/s/mid/opt √*kṛ*
kuryām I should perform or do or make, 3/s/opt/act √*kṛ*
kuryāt he should act, perform, make, do 1/s/opt/act
kuśa 296/3 a grass with long pointed stalks
kuśala 297/2 mfn right, proper, good , auspicious, fit for, able, virtue, n. welfare, well-being, happiness, (*am*) ind. well, properly, (in comp.) happily, cheerfully,

kuśala 297/2mfn right, proper, good , auspicious, well, healthy, in good condition, prosperous, fit for, competent, conversant with, (*am*) n. welfare, well-being, happiness,
kuṣṭha m. leprosy,
kusuma n. flower
kusumākara m. Spring , (abounding with flowers)
kūṭa 1.n. the bone of the forehead, horn, m.n. a summit or peak, the highest, most excellent, first, a heap, multitude, part of a plough, an iron mallet, a deer trap, a concealed weapon, illusion, fraud, trick, untruth, falsehood, enigma, elemental uniform ethereal substance,
kutas m. whence, from where, from whom, wherefore, how?
kutaścid 290/2 from or through any or some,
kūṭastha 299/3 2/s immovable, uniform, unchangeable (as the soul, spirit, space, ether, sound), standing at the top, keeping at the highest position,
kuṭhāra m. axe,
kuṭila mfn crooked or bent,
kuṭīra m. a hut,
kutra where?
kutracidapi anywhere (or with preceding *na* not anywhere, nowhere
kutracit 290/2 somewhere, wheresoever, anywhere,
kuṭumba n. household, family,
kuṭumbin m. householder,
kva interrogative, 7/s in whom, in what place, where? if repeated with another question expresses great incongruity or incompatibility
kvacit 324/2 kva where, + indefinite article, anywhere, anywhere whatever, at some time,
labdha 896/2 gained, taken, seized, arrived at, got at, found,
labh *Dhātu* to find
lābha 897/1 m. acquisition, gain, profit, meeting with, finding
lābhālabhau gain and loss, (dual *dvandva* compound)
labhate finds,
labhante they (pl) find or attain 1/pl/pres/indic/mid √*labh*
labhasva attain! find! 2/s/impv
labhet he should obtain, find or get 1/s/opt/act
lāghava 899/3 n. swiftness, rapidity, speed, alacrity, versatility, skill, lightness, an auspicious time for action,
laghu 893/3 light, easily digested, short,
laguḍa m. cudgel,
laharī f. a large wave, billow,
lajjā 895/2 f. shame, modesty, embarrassment n. causing shame,
lakṣa n. 1. mark, token, 2. a hundred-thousand, 3. a mark for aiming at,
lākṣā f. a kind of red dye from the cochineal beetle, lac,
lakṣaṇa 892/1 mfn. indicating, expressing indirectly, (*ā*) f. a line or symbol
lakṣman n. a good or lucky mark or sign,
lakṣmaṇa brother of Rāma
lakṣmī consort of *Viṣṇu,* the power of increase and prosperity
lakṣya 893/1 mfn to be marked, characterized, defined, to be indicated or expressed, to be kept in view or observed, observable, perceptible, visible, n. an object aimed at, a target, prize, an aim, mark, goal,

lālā f. saliva,
lālasa 900/3 eagerly longing for, desirous of, totally given up to
lalāṭa n. forehead, brow,
lampaṭa mfn greedy, covetous,
laṅga mfn lame, limping, m. lameness, union, association, a lover,
lāṅgala n. a plough, a palm tree, kind of flower, penis
lāṅgūla n. tail,
laṅkā the island where *rāvaṇa* lived
lapsyate will find
latā f. a creeper, a slender woman, a whip, a string of pearls, a streak, line,
laukika 909/2 mfn worldly, common, usual, m. common or ordinary men, men of the world, men in general, people, mankind, (*am*) n. worldliness,
lavaṇa 898/3 mfn salty, briny, m. salt,
lāvaṇya n. the taste or property of salt, beauty, loveliness,
lavaśas ind. in small pieces, bit by bit,
laya 903/2 m. melting, dissolution, disappearance, or absorption in, Apte 477/3 mind absorbed, 903/2 spiritual indifference, making the mind inactive or indifferent (G p.175) dissolution, absorption, to merge, said to be a precursor to *samādhi*, dissolution
lekha m. a writing, letter, line, stroke, manuscript, written document,
lekhā f. a scratch, streak, line, furrow, the act of drawing, painting, writing, a drawing, likeness, figure, impression,
lekhinī pencil
leliha 903/1 m.constantly licking, a serpent
lelihyase you lick 2/s/intens/*lih*
lepa 902/3 spot, stain, impurity, (A) attachment,
leśa m. a little, particle, little bit,
leśataḥ ind. very slightly,
√*lih* to lick,
likhanaphalaka n. writing table
likhati writes
līlā 903/2 play, sport, game,
līlayā 4/s for diversion,
limpati 902/2 smears, anoints with, stains
liṅga 901/3 a mark, spot, sign, token, a sign of gender or sex, male organ (in gram.) gender
liṅgin 902/2 mfn having a mark or sign, characterized by, bearing false signs, a hypocrite, one whose external appearance coincides with inner character, having a subtle body
√*lip* 902/2 Cl 6.1. P A *limpati (te)* to smear, anoint with, stain, soil, pollute, defile, to inflame, kindle, burn, pass. *lipyate (ti)* to be smeared, to be attached to, stick, adhere, etc.
lipi f. rubbing over, writing, painting, drawing, anything written, letter, manuscript,
lipyate is smeared, defiled, contaminated, 1/s/pres/indic/pass
lobha 905/1 m. perplexity, impatience, covetousness, eager desire for, avarice, 'greed' HH
locana 1. mfn enlightening, 2. (*as*) n. eye,
loha 908/3 mfn red, reddish, copper-coloured, iron, steel, gold or any metal, a weapon, a fish-hook,
lohakāra m. blacksmith,
lohita mfn red, red-coloured, reddish, made of copper, metal, m. red, redness, n. any red substance, f. (*ā*) blood,
loka 906/1 m. space, room, place, a region, the world, heaven, ordinary life, common practice or usage
lokādi m. the beginning of the world, the creator of the world
lokāḥ inhabitants, people, humanity
lokasaṅgraha 907/1 the propitiation or conciliation of men, the whole of the universe, aggregate of worlds, the welfare of the world
lokavat 907/1 mfn. containing the worlds, ind. as in the ordinary life
lola mfn 1. moving hither and thither, uneasy, 2. anxious for, desirous of, greedy, fickle, longing for,

lolupa 908/2 very destructive,very desirous, eager longing for, longing,
lomaharṣa m. thrill or shudder,
loman n. the body-hair of men and animals, a tail,
lopa m. omission, want deficiency, absence, (in gram.) dropping, elision,
loptum inf. to cut off,
loṣṭa 908/2 a lump of earth or clay
lubdha 904/3mfn bewildered, confused, greedy, covetous, avaricious, n. a hunter, a lustful man,
lubdhaka m. a hunter, a greedy man,
lupta mfn deprived, robbed, plundered,
ma 771/1 m. time, poison a magic formula,
mā 804/1 ind. a particle of prohibition or negation- not, that not, do not
mac-citta 777/2 mfn. having the mind fixed on me, thinking of me
mad 1. base of the first person pronoun
√*mad* 777/3 to rejoice, be glad
mada 777/3 m. hilarity, rapture, lust, excitement, inspiration, intoxication, 'pride of possession' HH
madana m. passion, love or the god of love, a kind of embrace, a bee, beeswax, *(ā)* f. any kind of intoxicating drink, musk, n. the act of intoxicating,
madarthe 7/s/m for my sake, 'of me in purpose'
madāśraya m. dependent on me , taking refuge in me,
madbhakta worshipping me, devoted to me
madbhāva my state of being, originating from me
mādhava m. mfn relating to spring, vernal, descendant of *Madhu* (*Kṛṣṇa*),
madgataprāṇāḥ 1/pl/m those who have concentrated the vital breath on me,
madgatena by going to me,
madhyama mfn. middle, middlemost, central, m. In Sanskrit grammar the *madhyama puruṣaḥ* (middle or second person of the verb) is expressed as 'you' e.g. *gacchasi* - you (2/s) go. An aspect of speech or sound manifestation, "when the move is made to one of the possibilities and the sound related to the knowledge to be expressed has risen only in the mental realm of the being, then it is called *madhyamā"* HH
madhu m. honey, mfn sweet,

madhukāra (or *-kara*) 'honey-maker' a bee,
madhulih m. 'honey-licker', a bee,
madhura mfn sweet, (of speeches) honeyed, charming, delightful, melodious,
mādhurya 809/1 loveliness, beauty, charm, sweetness or tenderness, sweetly speaking
Madhusūdana a name of *Kṛṣṇa*, slayer of *Madhu* (not the ancestor above)
madhya mfn central, moderate, n. middle, middle-most, intermediate, central, impartial, neutral, of a middling size, quality or quantity
madhyastha m. standing in the middle, neutral
madhye (+ 6th case) in the middle of
madirā f. liquor,
madīya mfn mine, my own,
madvyapāśrayas trusting in me, taking refuge in me, one to whom I am the refuge, 1/s/m *mat vi apa ā* √*śri*
madya n. wine
madyājinas those who are devoted to me (those sacrificing to me)
Magadha an ancient country (now a part of Bihar and of western Bengal)
māgha m. a month corresponding to January/February,
maghavan mfn abounding in liberal gifts, generous, esp. as m. a rich patron or lord who institutes a sacrifice and pays the priests, Indra – 'rewarder of priests and singers', the generous one',
√*mah* 794/1 cl1,10, *mahati, mohayati*, elate, exalt, arouse, magnify, esteem highly, honour, revere, worship,

mahā 794/3 used in compounds for *mahat* or *mahant,* used for *mahat* as an independent word in 2nd s. *mahām* = *mahāntam*

mahā 794/3/2 great, mighty,

mahābaho O mighty armed one

mahābhārata an epic story

mahābhūmi f. a great country, a vast region

mahābhūtāṇi five subtle elements (properties*), śabda, sparśa, rūpa, rasa, gandha*

mahāhrada 802/1 m a great tank or pool

mahākāśa m. 'the limitless space held in consciousness' HH

mahānubhāva mfn of great might, mighty

mahāpuruṣa 797/2 m. a great or eminent man, a great sage or saint, the great soul, the Supreme Spirit, a realised being

mahārāja 799/3 m. a great king, supreme sovereign,

mahārathās 'those whose chariots are great' –great warriors 1/pl/m

maharṣayāḥ the great seers, m.pl.

maharṣi 794/2 m. any great sage or saint

mahāśaya 801/1 "great receptacle", the ocean, having a noble disposition, gentleman, high-minded, magnanimous, open, sometimes a term of respectful address, sir or master, the master,

mahat 794/2 mfn great, mighty, strong, n. G.181 the Great Intellect, The first evolute of primordial nature (*prakṛti*). It is the cosmic aspect of the intellect and, along with the intellect, ego, and mind, it is the cause of the entire creation. It is also called *buddhi* which is the psychological aspect of the intellect in individuals. It is both eternal and non-eternal. Its special function is determination. From it evolves egoity.

mahatā mfn long, great, extended, f. greatness, mightiness,

mahatattva 794/2 n. 'the great principle (name of universal *buddhi*)', the intellectual principle as source, 'the great That Thou', "here are universal feeling of existence and individual feeling of existence," the subtle world,

mahati 7/s/m in the great, in the mighty

mahātman 796/1 mfn. high-souled, magnanimous, having a great or noble nature, exceedingly wise eminent, distinguished, the Supreme Spirit,

*mahāvākya*800/2 n. a principal sentence, the name of 12 great utterances of the *upaniṣads*

mahāyuga one cycle of the four yugas 4,320,000 years,

maheśa 802/2 great lord or god, a name of *śiva*

maheśvara 802/2 Great Lord

maheśvāsā mighty archers (*mahā iṣu āsās* mighty arrow hurlers) 1/pl/m

mahi mfn great,

mahī 803/2 the great world, the earth, earth as substance, the base of a triangle

mahī-kṛte for the sake of the earth,7/s/m

mahiman 803/1m. greatness, power, majesty,

mahī-pate voc. O Lord of the Eart

mahīyate √ *mah* is worshipped, honoured highly esteemed, 1/s/pass/pres

mahilā f. woman,

mahiṣa m. buffalo, f. (*ī*),

mahodadhi 802/2 1/s/m the great ocean

mahyam pron. for me

maitra 834/1 mfn. friendly, amicable, benevolent, kind, belonging or relating to Mitra, m. 'friend of all creatures', friendship,

maitrī f. friendship, friendliness, benevolence, goodwill,

makara 771/2 m. a kind of sea-monster, crocodile, f.(*ī*)

makāra 771/1 the letter or sound *ma*

makṣika m. (*ā*) f. a fly, bee,

mākṣīkaḥ m. spider,

mala 792/1 m.n. dirt, filth, dust, impurity

(physical and moral) "*mala* is due to the *saṁskārāḥ* which form a thick layer of dirt in the subtle body" (Jaiswal)
mālā f. crown, wreath, garland,
mālākāra m. gardener,
malaya m. name of a mountain,
mālawa m. Malva –name of a country in west-central India,
malīmasa mfn dirty, foul,
malina mfn dirty, filthy, impure, soiled,
mālinya 814/2 n. foulness, dirtiness, impurity
mālya 814/1 n. wreath, garland
mām pron. me (2nd)
mama pron. 6/s my, of me
māmaka m mine, my
mamatā 789/1 sense of "mine", egotism" 1/s/f ownership
māmikā my, mine, my own 1/s/f
mamatva 789/1 the state of mineness,
māṁs or *māṁsa* n. meat, flesh,
māṁsala mfn fleshy
√*man* 783/1 cl8 *manute, manyute* to think, believe, imagine, suppose, to regard or consider anyone or anything, consider, to remember, meditate on,
māna 809/1 m.n. regard, respect, honour, arrogance, pride
mana(s) 783/3 the mind (in its widest sense) in phil. the internal organ of perception and cognition, the faculty or instrument through which thoughts enter, considered perishable, the information gatherer, an instrument of knowing, the lower level of mind which thinks, deliberates
manāḥ m. form of *manas* when used in a *bahuvrīhi* compound,
manāk 784/1 ind. a little, in a small degree, even slightly, at once, immediately, slightly, merely,
manas 783/3 mind, mind detached
manana 783/3 mfn. thoughtful, careful, thinking, reflection, meditation, intelligence, understanding, (esp. intrinsic knowledge or science, as one of the faculties connected with the senses, homage, reverence, 2nd stage of reflection, (*śravanam, manana, nididhyāsanam) q.v.* G.185 … removes the doubt of an aspirant regarding the nature of the object (*prameya*) to be contemplated. reflection is to be employed so as to get an intellectual conviction of the truth. It is the constant thinking of the Absolute (Brahman).
manasaḥ than the mind, more than the mind, of the mind, from the mind
mānasa 810/1 belonging to the mind or spirit, mental, spiritual (opp to corporeal), expressed only in the mind, conceived or present in the mind, the mental powers, mind, spirit, heart, performed in thought , mentally, deriving from mind
mānava 809/3, a human being, man, boy, youngster, Manus, ancestors of man
manavāṇīkriyā mind, word and deed
manave to Manu 4/s/m
manda 787/3 mfn slow, dull-witted, tardy, apathetic, dull, m. the planet Saturn, a stupid or slow elephant, f. (*ā*) a pot, vessel, ink-stand,
mandākinī Ganges, (going slowly),
maṇḍala 775/3 circular, round, globe, circumference, orbit of a heavenly body, a disk, territory, province
maṇḍana 775/3 mfn adorning, being an ornament to, n. ornament, decoration
mandana mfn 787/3 gay, cheerful
mandaṁ mandam very slowly
maṇḍapa m.n. open hall or pavilion (erected on festive occasions), tent, temple, arbour, bower,
mandara mfn slow, tardy, sluggish m. Mandara , a sacred mountain, heaven, a mirror,
mandāra m.n. coral tree, name of a man,
mandira n. house, palace, temple,
maṇḍuka m. frog

maṅgala n. welfare, luck, 2. anything lucky, auspicious or of good omen,
māṅgalya 806/1 mfn conferring or indicating happiness, auspicious, m. welfare, propitiousness, luck,
maṇi m. pearl, gem,
maṇigaṇa 774/3 pearls
manīṣā f. thought, reflection, wisdom, intelligence, concept, idea,
manīṣī ruler of the mind, a saintly person, intelligent man, philosopher
manīṣikā 784/2 f. wisdom, intelligence
manīṣin mfn thoughtful, intelligent, wise
mañjara n. a cluster of blossom, panicle,
mañjarī f. a cluster of blossoms, bud, flower, foliage, a parallel line,
mañju mfn beautiful, lovely, charming,
mañjula mfn beautiful, pleasing, lovely,
mañjuṣā f. basket,
manmanā mind fixed on me
manmatha m. god of love, love,
manmaya 777/2 mfn. consisting of or proceeding from me, full of me, like me,
manobuddhi mind and intelligence f.
manogata 785/1mfn. mind-gone, existing or concealed in the heart or mind, n. thought, opinion, notion
manomaya 785/2 consisting of spirit or mind, mental, associated with the mind,
manoratha 785/2 m. "heart's joy", fancy, illusion, desire,
maṅsyante they will think, they will believe 1/pl/fut/mid √*man*
manthara mfn slow, dull,
mantra 785/3 m. 'instrument of thought,' speech, sacred text or speech, a prayer or song of praise, a sacred formula addressed to any individual deity, G187 a sacred word or phrase of spiritual significance and power.
mantradīkṣā initiation of an aspirant through giving/accepting of *mantra*, *dī* – what is given or the person capable of bestowing divine grace, *kṣa* – one who is capable of assimilating,
When the *Guru* initiates His disciple with the *mantra*, He also bestows His sensitive power of intuition and empowers the disciple with His '*sankalpa*' (benign resolve) as well. *Mantra* = *mananam* (reflection) + *antar* (interior, inner,); that which is to be reflected upon in the heart.
mantrin 786/3 mfn wise or eloquent, a king's counsellor, minister, a conjurer, in chess – the queen,
manu 1.m. man, mankind, Manu a lawgiver, father of mankind, mfn thinking, intelligent, wise,
manuja m. man, sprung from Manu,
mānuṣa m. pertaining to man, human, man, (*ī*) woman,
manusmṛti the laws of *Manu* according to *dharma*
manuṣya m. human, man, men mfn manly, useful or friendly to man,
manuṣyāṇām of men, of mankind
manuṣyajajña m. sacrifice for mankind
manvantara 7 cycles of the 4 *yugas*, supervised by one *Manu* (Lawgiver)
manyatā f. one thinks to know, belief
manyate thinks, imagines 1/s/pres/indic/mid √*man*
manye I think or believe, 1/s/pres/indic/mid √*man*
manyu m. 1. mood (temper of mind), 2. anger, rage, heat of temper,
marakata n. emerald,
*maraṇa*789/3 n. death, the act of dying
maraṇe in death 7/s
mārdava 813/2 n. softness, gentleness, kindness, leniency towards all beings
mārdavena ind. gently
mārīcaḥ uncle of *rāvaṇaḥ*
marīci chief of the storm gods, 790/1 a particle or ray of light
mārga *m.* a way, road or path
mārgaśīrṣa m. a month (approx November/December)
mārjāra m. a cat, (the cleaner), f. *(ī)*

markaṭa m. ape,
marmāra m. murmur,
marta 791/1 m. mortal, a man
martya 791/1 mfn who or what must die, mortal, m. man, person, the world of mortals, the earth
martyaloka mortal world, world of mortals
maru m. a waste, desert,
marubhūmi f. wilderness, desert,
marut pl/m the storm gods, 790/2 the flashing or shining ones
maruta 790/3 m. wind, a god
māruta mfn relating or belonging to the Maruts,
maryādā f. limit, a frontier, boundary,
māsa 814/3 m. the moon, a month,
maśaka m. mosquito, biting insect,
māsala 815/1 m.a year
masṛṇa mfn smooth, mild, bland,
mastaka n. m. head, top, skull, summit
māstu *(mā astu)* let there not,
mat may indicate any singular form of *aham* i.e. my, me etc.
mat pron. from me
mata 783/1 ppp. *mata* thought, believed, thought to be, regarded as, imagined, opinion,
māta 804/2 mfn. formed, made, composed
mātaṅga m. elephant,
mātari 7/s of
mātariśvā air, lord of the atmosphere,
mate thought, thought to be 1/du/f
maṭha m.n. a hut, cottage, monastery, esp. the hut/cell of an ascetic or student, a cloister, college (esp. for young Brāhmans), temple, m. a cart or carriage drawn by oxen,
mathurā f. a city in the north Indian state of Uttar Pradesh, an ancient city,
mati 783/2 f. thought, design, intention, devotion, prayer, determination, inclination, 'as the thought ...'
matkarmakṛt performing my action
mat-paras 777/2 mfn. me intent on, with me as highest
matparāyaṇaḥ with me as supreme aim or object
matprasādāt from or through my grace
mātṛ 2. 807/1 mother, air, space
-mātra merely
mātra 804/3 the full measure of anything, or (in cpd.) merely, the one thing and no more, nothing but, only,
mātra 804/2 elementary matter, measure,
mātrā f. material, measure, quantity
mātrata(s) 804/3 ind. from the first moment of , f. being as much as, no more nor less than,
mātṛkā f. "the basic forces which initiate all formal and informal creation of causal, subtle, and physical bodies. They have in them all those qualities which are seen to be manifest in this creation." HH
matsama-(tva) 777/2 resemblance of me, *mat* 777/2 for *mad* me, *-sama* 1152/1 same, like, like me,
matsamsthā 777/2 f. union with me
matsara 776/2 mfn exhilarating, intoxicating, selfish, greedy, envious,m. selfishness, jealousy, hostility, passion for, 'envy' HH
matsthāni in me abiding, living, resting, 1/pl/n
matsya n. fish
mattaḥ 5/s pron. *mat* from me *+taḥ* adv. abl. term. from me
mātula m. maternal uncle
matvā past part. having considered or meditated on, having thought,
mauli m. head, diadem,
mauna 836/3 n. silence, taciturnity
-maya made of
mayā by me, with me, 3/s/m
māyā 811/1 f. illusion, unreality, deception, trick, magic G. 189 the principle of appearance. The force which shows the unreal as real and presents that which is temporary and short-lived as eternal and ever-lasting. The force that conceals our divinity.
mayā pron. by me
mayi pron. 7/s in me
mayūkha m. ray of light, flame, brightness,

mayūra m. peacock,
me pron. 6/s of me, my
medas n. fat, marrow, corpulence,
medha m. broth, sap, pith, essence
medhā f. mental vigour or power, intelligence, wisdom, worldly intelligence,
medhas n. sacrifice,
medhāvin 833/1 mfn possessing wisdom, wise, m. a learned man, teacher
medura mfn fat, dense, unctuous, bland,
megha m. cloud,
mekhalā f. girdle, (of Munja –grass),
melana n. meeting,
meṇaṭha m. elephant-keeper,
meru a famous sacred legendary mountain (not possible to identify geographically)
meṣa m. ram, (*ī*) ewe,
meṭha m. elephant –keeper,
mīlati 819/1√*mīl* to close the eyes 1/s/pres/indic/act closes the eyes
milati meets (with 3rd)
mīmāṁsā 818/3 f. profound thought or reflection, consideration, investigation, examination, discussion, examination of the Vedic text, the *Pūrva-mīmāṁsā* usually called the *mīmāṁsā,* concerning itself chiefly with the correct interpretation of Vedic ritual and text, 'calls for understanding of the will of the Absolute and expects one to put it into practice exactly as prescribed, Only then the result follows. In *Uttaramīmāṁsā* (also known as *Vedānta*) it has been presented differently, The real understanding of the unity of the Absolute and the individual brings all these two parts together and one becomes the Absolute oneself.'
mīna m. fish,
miśra 817/3 mfn. mixed, mingled, blended
mithas ind. together, mutually, among each other, in turns,
mithilā a city, capital of *Videha* the, kingdom of *Janaka*
mithuna mfn paired, forming a pair, m. a pair (male and female, but also any couple or pair, in later language mostly n. ifc. f. *(ā)*, n. pairing, copulation, a pair, couple, the other part, complement or companion of anything, a kind of small statue at a temple entrance, honey and ghee, (in gram.) a root compounded with a preposition, *-tva* n. the state of forming a pair
mithyā 817/1 ind. contrarily, wrongly, vainly in vain, improperly, incorrectly, illusion, not in reality, only apparently,
mithyācāra 817/1 improper conduct, acting hypocritically, a hypocrite
mitra n. 816/1 friend,
mlāni f. decay, dejection,
mleccha m. barbarian, foreigner,
mocitaḥ turned loose, released,
moda m. joy,
modate rejoices √2. mud
modiṣya I shall rejoice √*mud*
mogha 835/2 mfn. vain, fruitless, useless, (*am*) in vain, uselessly, without cause
moha 836/1 m. loss of consciousness, perplexity, ignorance, delusion, error "attachment or infatuation" HH
mohayati 825/1 causes to err or fail, stupefies, bewilders, caus. √ *muh*
mohita 836/2 mfn. stupefied, bewildered, deluded
mokṣa 835/1 freedom, liberation from the bondage of *saṁsāra*
mokṣa 835/1 m. emancipation, liberation, release from worldly existence or transmigration,
mokṣakāma 835/1 emancipation, liberation, freedom, *kāma* 271/3 wish, desire, - one who longs for liberation
mokṣārthe intent on liberation
mokṣyase you shall be released or liberated 2/s/fut/pass √*muc*
mṛd 830/2 f. earth, clay,

mṛdā f. clay,
mṛdaṅga m. drum,
mṛdu mfn soft, weak,
mṛga m. deer, 828/2 a forest animal or wild beast,
mṛgayā f. hunting,
mṛgendra 829/1 m. king of beasts, a lion
mriyate dies
mṛṇāla n. f.(ī) 'liable to be crushed', edible fibrous lotus root or lotus stalk fibre,
√*mṛś* 831/1 1. to touch (physically or mentally), consider, reflect, deliberate, DP in *āmarśan* rubbing, stroking, touching, handling,
mṛśā 831/1 ind. in vain, wrongly,
mṛta 827/2 mfn dead, deceased, departed
mṛttikā f. clay
mṛtyu 827/3 m. death, dying
mṛyate he dies, he is dead, 1/s/pres/pass.
√1. *mud* cl10 822/2 P *modayati* to mix, mingle, blend
√2. *mud* cl1 A *modate* to be glad, happy, rejoice
3. *mud* f. joy, delight, gladness, intoxication, frenzy
mudā f. joy,
mūḍavat ind. like a fool
mūḍha 825/2 mfn bewildered, confused, deluded, foolish, simple
mūḍhadhī 825/2 silly-minded, simple,
udrā f. name of partic. finger/hand signs or signals, a seal, signet-ring, any ring, any stamp, print, mark or impression, a stamped coin, rupee,
muhur occurring repeatedly, recurring, at every moment
muhur muhur again and again
muhurmuhuḥ 825/1 suddenly, at once, in a moment, at every moment, constantly,
muhūrta m.n. 1. moment, 2. an hour (30th of a day, 48 minutes,
muhyati he is deluded, confused, 1/s/pres/indic/act
mūka 825/2 mfn silent, speechless, mute, f.crucible,
mukha n. mouth, face,
mukhara mfn loquacious,
mukhya first, chief,
mukta 820/3 liberated (one who is....), free from bondage, let go, free, loose, liberated, with 5th – freed,
muktā f. pearl,
mukti 821/2 f. liberation, setting or becoming free, giving up, final beatitude, [√ *muc* in liberating, or gladdening, delighting]
muktvā ind. having been liberated,
mukula n. bud, the body, the soul,
mukuṭa m. diadem, tiara, crown,
mūla 826/2 n. firmly fixed, rooted, a root
mūlaccheda 826/2 cut up by the roots
mūlādhāra G 195 the *cakra* or spiritual centre at the base of the spine where the Kuṇḍalinī (latent spiritual power) lies dormant
mūlya n. price, capital,
mumukṣu 821/2 mfn desirous of freeing,eager to be free, striving after emancipation, m one who strives after liberation,
mumukṣubhiḥ by the seekers of liberation desiderative noun 3/pl
mumurṣā f. death wish, impatience with life,
mumūrṣu mfn wishing to die, about to die, moribund,
muñcati root *muc* 820/3 to loose, liberate, relinquish, quit, to free oneself, get rid of 1/s/pres/act/ he, she, it rejects
muṇḍa mfn bald, hornless,
muni 823/1 m. a sage, saint, seer, sage, ascetic, silent one,
munijana m. monk
mūrdha(n) 826/1 the forehead, head in general, skull, the foremost or topmost part of anything, roof (of the mouth), a mouth position for pronunciation,
mūrkha mfn foolish, stupid, m. fool,
mūrta 824/1 mfn formed, substantial, material, embodied, incarnate
mūrti 824/1 f. consisting or formed of, manifestation, embodiment, form, material elements, any solid body or material form,

mūṣaka m. thief, mouse, rat, Mousey as name of a man,

mūṣika m. mouse, rat,
mūṣakākhyā f. the name 'Mousey',
muṣṭi m.f. fist, clenched hand, stealing,
-na used to form adjectives or participles
na ind. not, no, nor, neither, with indef. pron. no if repeated (*na na)* or with an (*a*)generally forms a strong affirmation, with 3rd or 5th case indicates deficiency, often joined with other particles, it may also like *(a)* form compounds meaning – that not, lest, for fear lest, like, as, as it were,
na... vā neither... nor
nabhas n. 527/3 sky or atmosphere, ether (as an element), period of life, age, mist, clouds, vapour, m. period of life, age, clouds, rainy season, the nose or smell, a rope,
Naciketā a name in the *Kaṭha Upaniṣad* meaning – that which is unperceived i.e. spirit
nacira 523/1 mfn. not long (in time), (*am*) ind. shortly, soon,
nacirena ind. shortly, soon
nāda m.a loud sound, roaring, bellowing,
nadī f. river, also *nadaḥ* (m),
nāḍi f. 2. f. any tube or pipe, esp. a tubular organ of the body e.g. a vein, artery, nervous system,
nāga m. snake, elephant, also a class of demons, ordinary men (Buddhist), name of a tribal group,
nagaram/ nagarī n./f. city, town,
nagna mfn naked, bare, m. a naked beggar,
naikṛtika mfn dishonest, vile, wicked, given to destroying the livelihood of others,
naimittika 570/3 mfn occasional, special, accidental, work not usually known in advance – arising out of a situation or need
naipuṇa mfn or *naipuṇya* n. dexterity, experience in, skill, requiring skill, completeness, totality,
nairaśya 570/2 n. hopelessness, non-expectancy, despair at,

naiṣadha mfn pertaining to Niṣadha, m. prince of the Niṣadhans, i.e Nala
naiṣkarmya 570/2 n. freedom from action, inactivity, state beyond *karma,* abstinence or exemption from acts and their consequences
naiṣṭhika Apte 304/2 mfn 1. final, last, concluding, 2. decided, definitive, 3. fixed, firm,
nāka 532/3 m. 'where there is no pain', vault of heaven, firmament, sky, the sun, mfn painless,
na kadāpi never (not ever)
na kutracidapi nowhere at all
na kutracit nowhere
nakha n.m. nail, (on fingers or toes),
nakra m. a crocodile, the nose, f. a swarm of bees or wasps,
nakṣatra 524/2 n. a star or any heavenly body, collectively the stars
nakta n. night, (*am*) by night
nakula m. a mongoose, a *Pāṇḍava* prince,
nala (or *naḷa*) m. reed, stalk, name of a prince of Niṣadha, chosen by Damayantī to become her husband in preference to the gods,
nala m. a monkey architect
nalinī f. 'the reedy one' name of a mythical river, day lotus,
nama 536/1 ind. by name, named, called
nāmadhātu verbs derived from nouns or nouns derived from verbs.
nāman name in general including proper names and nouns
-nāman named
namas a bow, salutation to (with 4th),
namaskāra m. making of *namas,* adoration, greeting (in a form of worship),
namaskuru be reverent, make obeisance, 2/s/impv. *namas* √*kṛ*
namas-√*kṛ* do homage,
namasya 528/2 *-ti* to pay homage to or worship, be humble or deferential, mfn. deserving or paying homage

namati bows
nameran they should bow, 1/pl/opt/mid
nāmnā ind. by name, called
namra mfn bent, humble,
nānā 535/1 ind. variously, various, differently, f. coin,
nanāndṛ f. sister- in -law,
nānāvidha 535/2 of various sorts, multiform, manifold
nanda or *nandana* m. son,
nandanam causer of joy
nandita mfn overjoyed
nanu ind. not, not at all, never, certainly, surely, indeed, a particle implying kindness or reproach, or perplexity,
nāpita m. barber,
naptṛ m. grandson,
napuṁsaka m. a eunuch, neuter,
napuṁsakaliṅga neutral gender, " not pertaining to generation"
nārada m. an immortal sage,
narādhama m. vile man, wretch, hostile,
narādhipa m. lord of men, king, prince,
nara 528/3m. a man, a male, a person ,
nāra 536/3 mfn relating to or proceeding from men, human, mortal, spiritual, m. man, water, calf, n. multitude of men,
naraka 529/3 m.n. place of torment, hell
nāraṅga m. orange colour, an orange, orange tree,
narapuṅgavas man bull, bull of a man
narayāna n. palanquin,
nārāyaṇa m. son of the primal man, synonym of *Viṣṇu*
nārī 537/1 a woman, a female, wife, any object regarded as feminine,
nārikela m. coconut, fermented coconut drink,
narman n. fun, jest,
nas pron. us, of us, to us, for us
nāsā 538/1 f. the nose, the two nostrils,
nāśa 538/1 m. being lost, destruction, disappearance, annihilation,
nāśana mfn 538/1 destroying m. destruction, removal, causing to be lost or to perish
nāśayati destroys
nāsikā f. nose, nostril
nāśita mfn lost, destroyed,
naṣṭa 532/1mfn. lost, disappeared, perished, spoiled, in vain
nastātmanas who have lost their selves
nāstika m. an atheist or non-believer, mfn atheistic,
naśvara mfn perishable,
naṭa m. dancer, mime, actor, (these form a despised caste), f. (*ī*)
nāṭaka n. play,
nātha n. a refuge, m. a protector, lord,
natvā ind. having bowed
nāṭya n. dance, dancing, the costume of an actor,
nau f. boat, ship,
naukā f. boat, ship
nava or *navan* nine
nava mfn new, 530/3 fresh, recent, young, modern,
nāva 538/1 1. m. a shout of joy or triumph 2. a boat, a ship, f. *(ā)*
navakṛtva nine times,
navam ninth
navanīta n. fresh butter
nāvika m. boatman,
navīn mfn new
naya 528/2 m leading (of an army), conduct, behaviour, prudent conduct or behaviour, good management, polity, wisdom, prudence, reason, principle, system, method, an opinion or viewpoint (Jaina), mfn fit, proper
nāyaka m. leader, chief
nayana n. eye
nayati leads fut. *neñyati,* past *anayat*
nayet he should lead or direct 1/s/caus/opt/act √*nī*
nāyikā f. heroine in a drama, noble lady, coutesan, mistress,
nediṣṭha mfn the nearest, next, very near, (*am)* ind. next, in the first place, (*āt*) ind. from the neighbourhood,
nedīyas mfn nearer, very near, ind. near, hither, *-yastā* f. nearness, neighbourhood,
nejaka m. washerman,

nema mfn half, several, one, one...other m. portion, dancing,
nepathya n. (in drama) the part of a theatre behind the scene (where costumes were changed etc.),
neṣyati will lead
netṛ m. leader,
netra n. eye (as guiding organ), a leader, guide, n. leading, guiding, conducting, m. a leader, guide,
ni- 538/3 prefix to verbs or nouns, down, back, into, within, (with nouns has a sense of negation or privation e.g. down-hearted). often may be translated as 'without' *ni, niḥ, nir, nis, niś,* have the same meaning and are used in appropriate sandhi situations
nī *for nis* (before *r*)
√*nī* Cl 1 P A *niyati (te)* to lead, guide, conduct, direct, govern,
nibaddha mfn securely bound, tied to,
nibadhnāti 550/1 see *ni*√*bandh* he binds, fetters,
ni √*bandh* to bind on, tie, fasten to, join
nibadhyate he is bound 1/s/pres/indic/pass *ni* √*badh*
nibha mfn ifc. resembling, like, similar,
nibiḍa or *niviḍa* mfn without spaces, close, compact, thick, dense, firm, full of, abounding in,
nibodha know! understand! 2/s/impv/act
ni√*budh* to learn or hear anything, to attend or listen to, to know, understand P *nibodhati*
nīca mfn a low or vile person, mfn low, not high, dwarfish, depressed (navel), short (hair, nails), deep, lowered (voice),
nīcaiḥ ind. low, below, underneath, humbly, modestly,
ni √*cāy* to regard with reverence, honour, worship, observe, perceive
nicāyya looking on (meditating on) something as one's own Self
nīḍa m.n. resting place, esp. bird's nest,
nidarśana mfn pointing to, showing, indicating, announcing, teaching, pleasing, n. seeing, viewing, sight, appearance, vision, showing, proof, evidence, example, refutation of an argument, a sign, mark, omen, a system, scheme, injunction, precept, ordinance, authority, text,
nidhana 548/3 mfn having no property, poor, n. domicile, settling down, conclusion, end, death, destruction
nidhāna 548/3 mfn containing anything, n. putting or laying down, depositing, a hoard or treasure
nidhi m. a place for deposits, a receptacle, treasure, *apāṁ nidhi* the ocean, sea,
nididhyāsana 549/1 n. profound and repeated meditation, contemplation, the third stage of reflection. (see *śravanam mananam,)* G 205 .. removes the contrariwise tendencies of the mind, ..a continuous stream of ideas of the same kind as those of Brahman, one of the principal aids to liberation, assimilating the teaching by inquiry within until the teaching becomes one with the seeker,
nidrā f. sleep, slumber, sleepiness, sloth, non-perception,
nidrālu mfn sleepy,
nidrāṇa 548/2 mfn. asleep, sleeping
nidrāti falls asleep 548/2 1/s/pres/indic/act sleeps
nidrita 548/2 mfn asleep, sleeping
nigacchati 545/3 settles down upon or near, enters, resorts to, undergoes, attains
nigaḍa m. the heel chains for an elephant, mfn bound, fettered,
nigraha m. keeping down or back, binding, restraining, coercion, suppression,
nigṛhīta 546/1 mfn. held down or back, seized, caught, harassed, attacked
niḥ- 538/3 for *nis* before a sibilant and rarely before *k, kh, p, ph.* (with nouns has a sense of negation or privation e.g. destitute of and may often be translated as 'without'
nīhāra m. mist, heavy dew,

nihatya ind. striking down, killing, having killed, gerund *ni√han*
nihita 564/3 mfn. laid, placed, deposited, located (in) with loc. given, bestowed, laid (as dust by rain), encamped, uttered in a deep tone,
niḥsaṁdigdha mfn not doubtful, certain
niḥsaṁśaya mfn undoubted, certain,
niḥśeṣa mfn without remainder, whole, finished, passed away,
niḥspṛha free from desire or longing,
niḥśreyasa 538/3 mfn. having no better, best, most excellent,
n. the best, ultimate bliss, final beatitude or knowledge that brings it
niḥsaṁkalpa *nih* without, *saṁkalpa* 1126/3 will, desire, purpose, intent, without intent desire or purpose,
nija 547/1 innate, native, own,
nikāma m. desire, wish, pleasure, ibc =(*am*) according to wish or desire, to one's heart's content, abundantly, at will, excessively, mfn desirous, covetous,
nikara m. a heap, pile, a multitude, a bundle, mass, collection, pith, sap, essence, suitable gift, a treasure, the best of anything, an honorarium.
nikaṣa m. rubbing in, smearing, f. a roller, harrow, m.f. the touchstone,
nikaṣā 544/2 ind. near to (with acc.), proximate, in the middle, between
nikaṭa mfn. being at the side, near
m. or n. nearness, proximity,
(*am*) ind. near to, towards
niketa m.n. a mark, sign, a house, habitation, a stage in the life of a Brāhman, state of being,
niketana 545/1 n. a house, mansion, habitation, temple, m. an onion,
nikhila 545/2 mfn complete, all, whole, entire, *(ena)* ind. completely,
nikṛtya 545/1 f. wickedness, dishonesty,
nikṣepa 545/2 m. putting down, throwing or casting on, a deposit, pledge, trust, sending away,
nikṣipya ind. having thrown
nikuñja m. an arbour, a thicket,
nīla mfn blue, m. a monkey architect
nīlamaṇi m. a sapphire,
nimagna sunk (with 7th), fallen into (water)
nimba 551/3 the *nimb* or neemb tree, (it has bitter fruit and it's leaves are chewed at funerals)
nimeṣa m. closing or winking of the eyes,
nimeṣonmeṣayoḥ 6/du. of opening and shutting the eyes
nimiṣa 551/2 m winking, shutting the eye, n. the interval of a moment, in a moment,
nimiṣan closing the eyes pres/act/part *ni √miṣ* 551/2
nimiṣ 551/2 to shut the eyelids, wink, fall asleep , *nimiṣati* closes the eyes
nimitta 551/1 n. a mark, target, sign, omen, cause, reason *nimittāni* 1/2/pl/n
nimna *-tā* f., *-tva,*n. depth, lowness, profundity,
nindā 549/2 f. blame, censure, reproach
nindāyām 7/s/f in blame
nindati 549/2 1/s/pres/ind/act he blames, censures, despises
nindita 549/2 mn blamed, censured, despicable, condemned
nipāta m. falling down, descending, alighting, falling from, into or upon,rushing upon, decay, (in gram.) irregular forms, exceptions, particles. words without gender or number are without endings so they appear in a sentence already complete
nipuṇa mfn clever, adroit, skilful, sharp,
nir- 539/2 for *nis*, see *nis* 543/2
543/2 ind. out, forth, away. also used as a prefix to verbs and nouns in which case it takes the meanings- out of, away from, without, destitute of, free from, also may be used as a strengthening particle – entirely, very liable to be changed to *niḥ, nir, niś, niṣ,* or *nī*
nīra n. water, juice, liquor,
nirahaṃkāra *nir* without, *ahaṃkāra* 124/2 conception of one's individuality, ego, 1/s/m egoless

nirāhāra nir without *āhāra*162/3 food, taking food, without taking food, fasting
nirākāra 540/1 mfn formless, shapeless, incorporeal, m. heaven, the Universal Spirit, god,
nirākula mfn clear, steady, serene, unconfused, calm, n. clearness, calmness ,
nirālamba mfn independent, friendless, alone, self-supported,
nirāmaya 540/1 freedom from illness, health, welfare, complete, entire, pure,
*nirañjana*539/2 spotless, pure, simple, unpainted, stainless, void of passion or emotion,
nirantara 539/2 having no interval, uninterrupted, continuous perpetual, constant,
nirapekṣa 539/3 regardless of, indifferent to, independent of, disinterested, unaffected by prior, consideration, without expectation,
nīrasa mfn without juice, sapless, dried up, withered, tasteless, without sentiment
nirāśa 540/2 mfn. without any hope or wish or desire, free from expectation,
nirāśis 540/2 mfn. hopeless, despairing without desire or wish, indifferent,
nirāśraya mn not dependent or resorting to
nirasta 553/1mn rejected, removed, destroyed, shot (arrow), spat out,
nirātaṅka 134/2 mfn free from fear or pain, comfortable, not feeling/causing it,
nīrava mfn noiseless, *(am)* ind. silently,
nirāvaraṇa mfn unveiled, manifest, evident,
nirāyāsa mfn not causing trouble or fatigue,
nirbandha 555/3 m. perseverance, insisting upon
nirbhara 541/2 mfn without weight or measure, measureless, ardent, vehement, deep, abounding in,
nirbodha 541/2 see *nirbuddhi* 541/2 dull, stupid,
nirbuddhi mfn unintelligent, stupid, m. idiot, fool,
nirdeśa 555/2 pointing out, indicating, directing, command, instruction, designation,
nirdhūta mfn shaken, agitated, harassed,
nirdhyāi 555/3 to think of, reflect upon, meditate, to meditate
nirdhyāta mfn thought of, meditated,
nirdoṣa without evil, guiltless, see 2. *doṣa* 498/2
nirdvaṃdva 541/2 indifferent to the pairs of opposites, e.g. pain and pleasure,
nirgacchati comes out, goes out, leaves,
nirgata mfn departed
nirguṇa 541/1 devoid of all qualities or properties, having no epithet, (said of the Supreme Being), "synonym for *para Brahman* and *aviśiṣṭa*" HH
nirguṇatva having the nature of being without *guṇā*
nirīkṣe I see, I behold, *3/s/mid, nir √īkṣ*
nirindriya mfn impotent, without manly vigour or strength, a barren cow, having no organs of sense ,
nirjana mfn unpeopled, lonely, desolate,
nirjhara m. a waterfall, cataract, cascade, a mountain torrent, burning chaff, an elephant, (ī) f. a river,
nirmala without stain or impurity n.
nirmama mfn unselfish, disinterested, esp. free from all worldly connections, regardless of, indifferent to,
nirmāna free from pride or arrogance
nirmukta 556/2mfn loosed, separated, liberated,
nirṇaya m. taking off, removing, complete ascertainment, decision, settlement, determination, (in logic) deduction,
nirnimitta mfn without reason or motive, causeless, having no ego motive, free from cause,
nirodha 554/1 m. confinement, imprisonment, restraint, check, suppression, suppression of pain, covering up, hurting, injuring, aversion, disfavour, dislike, a state of intense concentration in which

the distinction between subject and object is destroyed, control (of the mind),

ni √rudh 553/3 to hold back, stop,

niruddha mfn. held back, withheld, stopped

nirudhya gerund confining, suppressing, having confined or restrained,

niruṇaddhi, confines, restrains, holds back,

nirupādhi (and *–dhika*) mfn without attributes or qualities, absolute, unconditioned,

nirūpayati he sees, describes

nirvaira mfn without enmity, amicable,

nirvāṇa 557/3 mfn. blown or put out, extinguished (as a lamp or fire), set (as the sun), calmed, quieted, dead, deceased (having the fire of life extinguished), lost, disappeared, immersed, plunged, immovable, n. blowing out, extinction, cessation, vanishing, disappearance

nirvāsa m. leaving one's home, banishment,

nirvāsita mfn exiled, banished, dismissed,

nirveda 557/3 complete indifference, disregard of worldly objects, loathing, disgust for,
542/2 mfn not having the Vedas, infidel,

nirvikalpa mfn not admitting an alternative, free from change or differences,
2. *nirvikalpa* G209 nonconceptual, the highest state of *samādhi*, 'free of judgement',
'devoid of all imaginations' (Gam.),

nirvikalpa samādhi unqualified unity HH

nirvikāra 542/1 m. unchangeable, uniform, normal, unchanged,

nirvimarśa Apte 293/1 void of reflection, unthinking, 542/2 unreflecting, inconsiderate,

nirviṣaya mfn having no dwelling place or expelled from it, supportless, hanging in the air, having no object or sphere of action, not attached to sensual objects,

nirviśeṣa mfn showing or making no difference, undiscriminating, without distinction, not different from, same, like, n. absence of difference, likeness,

nirvṛta mfn satisfied, happy, tranquil, at ease, contented, n. a house,

nirvṛti 558/1 f. complete satisfaction, bliss, emancipation, final beatitude, attainment of rest, extinction (of a lamp), destruction, death,

nirvṛtta mfn sprung forth, originated, developed, accomplished, finished, ready, grown out (fruit)

nirvṛtti mfn having no occupation, destitute, 2.f. originating, development, growth, completion, termination,

nis- 543/2 ind. out, forth, away. also used as a prefix to verbs and nouns (with nouns has a sense of negation or privation - often may be translated as without), in which case it takes the meanings- out of, away from, without, destitute of, free from, also may be used as a strengthening particle – entirely, - liable to be changed to *niḥ, nir, niś, niṣ,* or *nī*

niś- 542/3 for *nis* in comp.

niṣ- for *nis* before *k, kh, p, ph,* *see nis- / niś-* above, 2. Cl 1 P. *neṣati,* to moisten, sprinkle,

niśā f. night, a vision, dream, turmeric,

niśācaraḥ m. night-wanderer, a kind of demon, a jackal, an owl, a snake, mfn night-walking,

niṣaṅga m. clinging to, attachment, quiver,

niṣanna mfn dejected,

nisarga m. voiding excrement, giving away, granting, bestowing, relinquishing, abandoning, natural state or condition,

niścala 542/3 mfn motionless, immovable, fixed, steady, invariable, unchangeable

niścarati moves away, wanders away

niścaya 561/2 conviction, certainty, "to differentiate the two (see *cid* and *cit*) is called *niścaya* (resolution) ." HH

niścayabodha. (E. p.434) sure-knowledge,
niścayin 561/2 of firm opinion or resolution,
niścayī one who has come to know
niścita 561/2 mfn one who has come to a conclusion, or formed a certain opinion, ascertained, determined, n. certainty, decision, knowing with certainty
niścitya 561/2 ind. having ascertained or decided, surely, without doubt,
niṣedha 562/1 hindering, prohibition, keeping off , prevention,
niṣiddhi f. prohibition, defence, warding off,
niśītha m. midnight, night,
niṣkarman mfn inactive, exempt from or neglecting religious or worldly acts,
niṣkarmya ind. being inactive,
niṣkṛti f. complete development, restoration, cure, requital, atonement, expiation, removal, doing away, escaping, avoiding, neglecting,
niṣkriya 543/1 n. the actionless One the Supreme Spirit, *-tā* f. inactivity, neglect of (comp.)
niṣprapañca 543/2 mfn subject to no expansion or manifoldness, pure, honest,
*nispṛha*564/2 mfn free from desire, not longing for (7th, or comp.), abstaining from (5th),
niṣṭha mfn resting upon,
niṣṭhā 563/1 to give forth, emit, yield mfn. *niṣṭha* being in or on, situated on, grounded on or resting on, depending on, relating or referring to, f.(*ā*)state, condition, position, steadiness, devotion, attachment, application, skill in
niṣṭhura mfn hard, rough, harsh, severe,
niṣūdana 562/1 m.removing, destroying, n. killing, slaughter,

nīta mfn led, guided, brought, gained, obtained, well-behaved, correct, modest, entered, gone or come to, n. wealth, corn, grain,

nitamba m. the buttocks, the ridge or side or swell of a mountain, the sloping bank or shore of a river,
nitānta mfn extraordinary, excessive, considerable, important, (*am*) ind. very much, in a high degree,
nitarām ind. downwards, in a low tone, completely, entirely, wholly, by all means, at all events, especially, in a high degree,
nīti moral (of a story), statesmanship 565/1 f. leading or bringing, guidance, management, conduct, prudence, righteousness, moral conduct, morality,
nītiśāstra n. doctrine or science of political and social ethics,
nitya 547/2 mfn innate, native, one's own, continual, perpetual, eternal, ifc. constantly dwelling or engaged in, intent upon, devoted or used to, ordinary, usual, fixed, necessary, obligatory, always, m. the sea, ocean, f. a ploughshare, (*am*) ind. always, constantly, regularly, by all means, ever, eternal
nityānitya 547/3mfn eternal and perishable, permanent and temporary, who discriminates the eternal from the transient,
nityatva having the nature of the eternal, steadfastness, constancy
nīvārakaṇa m. wild rice grain,
nivartanti they return, they turn back 1/pl/pres/indic/act *ni√vṛt* 560/1
nivartate it turns away 1/s/pres/indic/mid he returns, turns back, is born again
nivartitum 560/1 to turn back, return from, return into life, be born again, infin. *ni-√vṛt*
nivāsa 559/1 m. living, dwelling
nivasati he lives
nivāta 559/2 1. sheltered from the wind, calm,
niveśaya cause to enter or approach, 2/s/caus/impv/act *ni√viś*
2 unhurt, uninjured, safe, secure

nivṛta 558/1 satisfied, happy
nivṛti f. covering, enclosing,
nivṛti f. complete satisfaction or happiness, emancipation, final beatitude,
nivṛtta 560/1 turned back returned, retreated,
nivṛtti 560/2 returning, ceasing action, rest, ceasing, cessation, abstaining from, desisting,
nivṛtti f. 694/1 in-active life (see *pravṛtti*), inactivity, 560/2 ceasing, cessation, ceasing from worldly acts, abstaining from action, inactivity, rest, repose, attainment of rest, emancipation, liberation "renunciation" HH non-participation (*pravṛtti* = participation),
niyama 552/1 any fixed rule or law, necessity, obligation, a rule or precept, limitation, restriction, obligation, agreement, vow, certainty, the ten traditional Niyamas

1. are:*hṛ*: remorse, being modest and showing shame for misdeeds
2. *santoṣa* contentment; being satisfied with the resources at hand - therefore not desiring more
3. *dāna* giving, without thought of reward,
4. *astikya* faith, believing firmly in the teacher, the teachings and the path to enlightenment,
5. *īṣvarapūjana* worship of the Lord, the cultivation of devotion through daily worship and meditation, the return to the source;
6. *siddhānta śravaṇa* scriptural listening, studying the teachings and listening to the wise of one's lineage;
7. *mati* cognition, developing a spiritual will and intellect with the guru's guidance,
8. *vrata* sacred vows, fulfilling religious vows, rules and observances faithfully
9. *japa* recitation, chanting mantras daily
10. *tapas* the endurance of the opposites; hunger and thirst, heat and cold, standing and sitting etc.*ahiṁsa* 'harmlessness' is sometimes included , another version is- modesty, contentment, giving without thought of reward, faith, worship –devotion and meditation, scriptural study, developing spiritual will and intellect, fulfilling rules, vows and duties, chanting of mantras, endurance of adversity, self-surrender,

nīyamāna pres.part. mfn being brought,
niyamānāsu 7/pl at the time of distribution,
niyamita 552/2 mfn regulated, prescribed, bound by, destined to be, governed, guided
niyamya 552/2 ind. having restrained or checked, or bound, mfn. to be restrained, limited, restricted or defined, controlling, subduing
niyata 552/1 mfn. held back or in, fastened, put together, restrained, obligatory, mandatory, customary
niyata-mānasa 552/1 of subdued mind or spirit, whose mind is subdued,
niyati f. the fixed order of things, necessity, destiny, fate, restraint, restriction, self-restraint,
niyojana. mfn enjoining, urging, n. the act of tying, fastening,
niyojayasi you cause to yoke, you urge, 2/s/pres/indic/caus/act *ni √yuj*
niyojita 552/3 mfn. connected with, attached to, appointed, directed
niyokṣyati will impel, enjoin, command 1/s/fut/act *ni √yuj*
no 571/1 ind. and not, not
nṛ 567/3 m. a man, hero, person, mankind, people, in gram. a masculine word nom. *nā*
nṛloka m.the world of men
nṛṇām *nṛ* 567/3 a man, hero, person, mankind, people *nām* 6/pl/m of men
nṛpa m. king
nṛpati m. king, prince,
nṛtya n. dance,
nṛtyati dances

nu 567/1 1. at the beginning of a verse, ind. now, still, just, at once, so now, now then, indeed, surely
nahi nu by no means,
nakir nu no-one, nothing at all, etc.
nūnam ind. in all probability, assuredly
nūpura 567/3 m. an anklet, toe ornament,
nūtana mfn of now, recent, young, new,
nyac low, directed downwards,
nyācam ind. bending down,
nyāsa giving up, renunciation *ni* √ *2. as*
*nyāya*572/2 m. that into which a thing goes back, an original type, standard, rule, a general or universal rule, in the right manner, a logical or syllogistic argument or inference, likeness, analogy
nyāyya mfn regular, normal, right, (*am*) ind. rightly, properly,
nyuna mfn less, inferior, defective,
odana m.n. grain boiled with milk, porridge, rice,
ogha m. a flood, a heap,
ojas mfn. odd (as opposed to even) n. bodily strength, vigour, energy, vitality, light, splendour, lustre
oka n.m. a house, home, refuge, a bird,
om 235/3 ind. a word of solemn affirmation and respectful assent, the *praëava* sound, the object of profound religious meditation, the highest spiritual efficacy being attributed not only to the whole word but also to the three sounds *a, u, m* of which it consists.
ośadhi(ī) f. a herb, plant, medicinal herb, an annual plant,
oṣṭha 236/1 the lip
√pā 1. class 1 *pibati* drinks
pac 1. to spread out, make clear or evident
pac 2. to cook, bake, ripen, mature, bring to perfection or completion, mfn cooking, baking,
pacati 575/1 cooks, bakes, roasts, boils, ripen, mature
pada 583/1 a word, an inflected word, the stem of a word in some cases, a foot, a foot as a measure, a step, a footing, position, standpoint, rank
pāda 617/1m. the foot, column, pillar, a wheel, a foot as a measure, the foot of a tree, foothill, a ray, a fourth part
padāni words
pādapa m. plant esp. tree, 'drinking with its feet', footstool, foot-cushion,
padārtha 583/3 the meaning of a word, substance, topic, that which corresponds to the meaning of a word, a thing, object, man, person, a category, objects of experience, substance,
padārthābhāvanī the sixth stage of realisation, "the constituent elements of the creation begin to lose their lustre for the aspirant" " the glory of the form, the pleasures of the senses, the beauty, the rhetoric and everything to lure the mind, does not lure anymore." HH "Every *padārtha* is said to have existence and therefore to have some essence. So the word indicates its negation, not its existential negation but only the negation of its essential attraction." HH
pādasevana 617/3 n. 'foot-salutation', service, duty
padāti m. foot-soldier, pedestrian, peon,
padavī f. track, path, way,
paddhati f. path, row, footpath, track, a class of expositional writing,
pade pade 583/1 at every step, at every whatever happens,
padma m.n. lotus
pādukā f. shoe, slipper, sandals, the sandals of the guru
padya n. a verse,
pakṣa m. a wing, side, faction e.g. *aripakṣaḥ* enemy faction
pakṣapāta m. partiality, a partisan, adherent,
pakṣin m. bird, 'winged',
pakṣman n. eyelash, the hair of a deer, filament of a flower, a thin thread,

palāyati 610/1 flees, runs away, escapes,
1/pl/pres/indic/act they run away,
palāyate he flees
palāyiṣyate will flee,
palita mfn gray, hoary, old, aged,
pallava m. shoot, twig,
pallī f. small village, hut,
palvala n. a pond, puddle, pool,
pāṁsu m.pl. dust, sand, crumbling soil,
dung, manure, pollen,
pāṇa = *pāṇi* 615/2 m. the hand
paëava m.a cymbal or drum
pañca 1. spread out, a measure in music, 5
pañca in comp for *pañcan* 578/2 five
pañcadhā ind. five-fold, in five parts,
in five forms,
pañcakṛtva five times,
pañcama fifth,
pañcan five,
pañcatva n. fiveness, dissolution of the
body into the five elements i.e.
death, with *gam* – die,
pañcīkaraṇa the interpenetration of the
five causal elements
pañcamahāyajña five great sacrifices to the
deva – the divine
ṛṣi s – the sages
pitṛ s – the fathers or ancestors
manuṣya s – men
bhūta s – lower beings
pañcan five,
pāṇḍava adj. pertaining to the Sons of
Pāṇḍu
pāṇḍava -anīkam army of the Sons of
Pāṇḍu TP cpd. , 2/s/m or n
pāṇḍavāḥ 1/pl/m the sons of *Pāṇḍu*
pāṇḍavaḥ 1/s/m son of *Pāṇḍu* (*Arjuna*)
paṇḍita 580/3 mfn. learned, wise,
a learned man
pāṇḍitya 616/1 scholarship, erudition
pāṇḍu mfn whitish, pale, m. name of a
prince of the Lunar Race,
pāṇḍura mfn white, pale,
paṅga mfn lame,
pāṇi 615/2 m. the hand
paṇitṛ m. a trader,
pañjara m. cage, body, skeleton, ribs,
paṅka n. mud, mire,
paṅkila mfn muddy, miry,
paṅkti f. set or series or row of five,
row in general,
pāntha m. wayfarer, visitor, wanderer,
panthā f. see *panthan*,
panthan m. road, path, way,
pāpa 618/2 mfn wicked, evil, bad , sin,
essence of bad action
pāpā wicked woman
pāpman 619/1 evil, unhappiness
pāpmāna pres.part.being a devil, being evil
pāpmanā f. sinful, sinfulness,
para 1. 586/1 mfn far, distant, remote (in
space), opposite, ulterior, beyond,
after, highest, supreme, far, remote,
more than, other than, another,
superior, supreme, later, subsequent
parā *1.* 586/1 f. of *para,* name of
a sound in the first of its 4 stages,
'pure consciousness and knowledge
in substance' HH
ifc. highest point or degree, final
beatitude, chief matter or paramount
object, engrossed in, intent upon,
parā 2. prefix - away, off, alongside, on
parabrahman 587/1 n. the supreme spirit
or *Brahman,* " a synonym for
nirguṇa Brahman" HH
parāc mfn averted, turned away from,
paradharma 586/3 the duties of another or
of another caste
parādhīna mfn ifc. entirely engaged in,
intent upon or devoted to,
parāga m. pollen, dust, fragrant powder
used after bathing, sandal, fame,
celebrity, independence
parāhṇa m. the afternoon,
parājitya ind. having overcome
parakīya mfn belonging to another, strange,
hostile,
parākrama m. bold advance, attack, valour,
courage, strength, energy, power,
paraloka m. the other or future world,
param 586/2 ind. beyond,afterwards, later,
parama 588/1 mfn (superl. of *para)* most
distant, remotest, last, chief, highest,
primary, best, worst, n. highest
point, extreme limit, chief part or

matter or object, (ifc. f. (*ā*) consisting chiefly of, completely occupied with , devoted to, intent upon, (*am*) ind. yes, very well,

paramā 588/1 f. devoted to or intent upon

paramādvaita 588/3 the highest being without a second, pure, non-duality, supreme non-duality

paramahaṁsa 588/2 an ascetic of the highest order, a religious man who has subdued all his senses by abstract meditation,

parāmarśa m. seizing, pulling, bending (a bow), violation, remembrance, recollection, reflection, consideration, judgment, (in logic) inference, conclusion,

paramarṣi m. a great or divine sage

parāmarśin 590/3 calling or bringing to mind, referring to (memories, opinions)

paramārtha 588/3 m. the highest or whole truth, spiritual knowledge

paramārthatā 588/3 the highest or whole truth, spiritual knowledge, reality, transcendence, consciousness, abstract noun transcendence,

paramātma 588/2 being entirely the soul of the universe, the Supreme Self

paramātman 588/2 the Supreme Spirit

paraṁbrahman 588/2 the Supreme Spirit

parameśvara 88/3 supreme lord, Supreme Being,

parampara mfn one following the other, proceeding from one to another, successive, repeated, (*am)* ind. successively, uninterruptedly, *-tas* ind. successively, continually, mutually,

paramparā succession, one to another

paramtapa m. scorcher of the foe

pārasa m. Persian,

paraspara 589/1 mfn mutual, each other's, ind. one another, each other

parastāt beyond, further (with 6th), towards, beyond, above, from afar off, from before or behind, afterwards, later, at the end,

paraśu m. a hatchet, axe

parāsu mfn one whose vital spirit is departed or departing, dying or n. dead, death, exhaustion,

paraśvas ind. the day after tomorrow,

parasya of another

parataram ind. higher, superior, (compar.)

paratas ind. farther, far off, afterwards, behind, *itas-paratas* here-there, high above in rank, after (in time), beyond, above (in rank),

paratra ind. elsewhere, in another place, in a future state or world, hereafter

parāyaṇa 587/3 n. final end or aim, last resort or refuge, principal object 1. f. (*ā*) intent upon, wholly devoted to, 2. going away, final end, departure

pārāyaṇa 619/3 n. going over, reading through, perusing, studying, (esp.) reading a Purāṇa or causing it to be read, the part of the Vedā that deals with the understanding of the world and its process of manifestation.

pareṇa (with 2nd) beyond, after, farther, past, thereupon, afterwards, later, than,

pari 591/2 beyond, outside of, adv. outside

pari 591/2 prefix round, around, about, round about, fully, abundantly, richly, against, opposite, in the direction of

paribhāva m. contempt, disregard,

paribhavana n. humiliation, degradation,

paribhāvana 598/2 n. cohesion, union, f. (*ā*) thought, contemplation

paribhāvaya 2nd present imperative. *Cinmayānanda* – says that *paribhāvaya* indicates a state of utter balance within and total oblivion of outer happenings.

paribhūḥ one who exists above all 'transcendent', enclosing, containing, pervading, guiding,

pari √*cakṣ* 593/3 to overlook, pass over, despise, condemn, mention, relate,
paricāra 593/3 mfn moving, flowing, m. a servant, follower,
paricāraya(ti) to attend on, wait on
paricārayasva perform your own service, get your own service performed, e.g. washing of feet etc.
paricchanna mfn covered, veiled, clad
paricakṣate they regard as, see as, they declare 1/pl/mid
paricaryā attendance, service, worship, doing service 593/3
paricintayan meditating on, reflecting on pres/act/caus/part *pari* √*cint*
paridahyate it is burned, it burns 1/s/pres/indic/pass. *pari* √*dah*
parideva m. 595/3 lamentation
paridevana n. lamentation, complaint,
paridhāna n. putting or laying round, putting on, dressing, clothing, f. closing or concluding a recitation,
parigraha 593/1 m. laying hold on all sides, surrounding, enclosing, assuming a form, comprehending, summing up, taking, accepting, receiving, getting, attaining, property, gift, present, acquisition, possession, a house, abode, root, origin, foundation, hospitable reception, getting, attaining, property, possessing,
parihāsa mfn jesting, joking, ridiculing, deriding, m. a jest, joke,
parijana m. a surrounding company of people, servants, followers, a single servant, *-tā* the condition of a servant, service,
parijñāna 594/2 n. perception, thorough knowledge, discrimination
parijñātā the knower, the experiencer,
parikliṣṭam 592/2 ind. reluctantly, grudgingly,
parimala m. fragrance, or a fragrant substance, perfume, copulation, connubial pleasure, a meeting of learned men, soil, stain, dirt,
parimāṇa n. measure, circumference, size, weight, number, amount,
parimārgitavya to be sought for or realized, gerundive *pari* √*mārg*
pariṇāma 594/3 m. change, alteration, transformation into (instr.), development, evolution, ripeness, maturity, result, consequence, issue, end, a figure of speech by which the properties of any object are transferred to the object with which it is compared.
pariṇāmin mfn changeable, subject to transformation, developing, bearing fruits or consequences,
pariṇatiḥ f. result, change, alteration,
pariṇayati he marries
paripraśna 597/3 m. question, interrogation
pariṣad mfn surrounding, besetting, f. assembly,
parisamāpyate it is fully comprehended, attain consummation, culminate, get merged, it is finished, 1/s/pres/indic/pass *pari sam* √*āp*
pariśrama m. fatigue, exertion, trouble, pain,
pariśuṣyati dries up, *pari* √*śuṣ* 1/s/pres/indic/act
parisvajate he embraces
paritāpa 595/1 m. glow, scorching heat, pain, agony, grief, sorrow, repentance
paritas 595/2 ind. all around, everywhere, as prep. with 2nd round-about,
paritoṣa m. delight in, satisfaction,
paritrāṇa 595/3 n. rescue, preservation, protection or means of protection, refuge, retreat, deliverance(abl.) from, the hair of the body, moustaches,
parityāga 595/2 m. the act of leaving, giving, renouncing, forsaking,
parityāgin mfn leaving, forsaking,
parityajati he completely abandons,
parityajya ind. at a distance from, excepting, having left or abandoned, with the exception of, leaving a space, having renounced

parivāda m. blame, reproach, accusation, detraction,
parivāra m. a retinue, a cover, covering, surroundings, followers, a sheath, scabbard, a hedge round a village, L. that which surrounds,
parivartana mfn causing to turn round, n. turning or whirling round, moving to and fro, revolution, end of a period of time,
parivrāja m. a wandering mendicant, ascetic of the 4th and last order (who has renounced the world,
parivṛta mfn surrounded by, covered with, veiled in, filled by, full of (comp.) n. a place for sacrificing,
parjanya 606/1 m. a raincloud, cloud, rain, rain personified or the god of rain
parṇa 606/2 n. a leaf, feather, pinion, feather of an arrow,
parṇagṛha n. leaf-house
parokśa 589/1mfn unknown, unintelligible, past, completed, (ibc.) in an invisible or imperceptible manner, beyond the range of sight, invisible, absent, unknown,
pārśva mfn near, proximate, n. side, immediate neighbourhood,
pārtha son of *Pṛṭhā* - *Arjuna* referring to his mother *Kuntī* or *Pṛṭhā*
pārthiva mfn of or belonging to the earth, m. king, prince,
paruṣa mfn knotty (as reed), spotted, dirty-coloured, , harsh, sharp, unkind, m. a reed, an arrow, (*ā*) a kind of riddle, n. harsh speech, abuse,
pāruṣya 621/2 n. roughness, harshness (esp. of speech), violence, squalor
parvan n. knot, joint, limb, break, pause,
parvata mfn consisting of knots or ragged masses, of a mountain, m. hill, mountain, rock, cloud-mountain,
parvatī f. consort of *Śiva*, the power of law
paryagāt (V) cannot estimate, must know, (Gam.) is all pervasive –like space
paryanta 607/1 ind.end, to the end of , as far as, end, extremity, bounded by
paryāpta mfn obtained, gained, finished, completed, large, abundant, many, sufficient for, adequate, equal to, a match for, (*am*) ind. fully, completely, enough, one's fill, willingly, readily, abundant, sufficient, equal
paryavatiśṭhate he/she/it becomes steady, steadies, stands, 1/s/pres/indic/mid
paryupāsate 608/3 sits round, is present at, partakes of, practises, worships 1/pl/pres/indic/mid
paryuṣita mfn having passed the night, having stood for a time or in some place, not fresh, stale, insipid,
pāśa 623/3 a snare, trap
pāśāna m. a stone,
paścāt ind. 612/2 afterwards, beyond, from behind, in the rear, westwards, hereafter, later, at last
pāścātya western, last,
paścima mfn last, westerly, final,
paśu 1. ind. see, behold!
2. m. cattle, domestic animal,
paśya 611/2 mfn. beholding, rightly understanding, seeing,
paśya see!, behold! 2/s/impv √*paś* 2/s/impv/act see!
paśyan pres/act/part. seeing
paśyanti they see 1/pl/pres/indic/act
paśyantī "the poised state of action" HH (2nd state of speech or sound)
paśyasi 2/s/pres/indic/act. you see
paśyata 611/2 part. visible, conspicuous, seen, see!
paśyati 611/2 *paś* to see, *paśyati* sees or beholds
paśyet he should see or perceive 1/s/opt/act *paś*
paṭa 579/1 a woven cloth, cloth
pata flying, falling 1/s/pres. imperative it may descend
paṭaha m. a drum,
patākā f. 'flying'a banner or flag, a flag, banner, flagstaff, good fortune, auspiciousness,
pātaka 616/3 mfn. causing to fall, n. that which causes to fall, sin, crime
patākinī f. an army,

pāṭala mfn pale red, pink,
pātāla n. hell, underworld,
pāṭaliputram n. capital of Magadha, now Patna,
pataṅga 581/1 a flying insect, moth, bee etc
patati falls
patatu *pat* 580/3, 1/s/pres. imperative, fly! fall down!
patha m. road, path way, see *panthan*,
pāṭha m. study, reading, recital
paṭhaka mfn knowing the way, a guide,
pāṭhaka m. a reciter, reader,
paṭhati reads, studies, recites, teaches,
pātheya n. provisions, food for a journey,
pathi on the path or road loc/s/m
pathika m. traveller,
pati m. husband, lord
patita 581/2 mfn fallen, descended, happened, occurred
patitvā ind. having fallen
patnī f. wife, lady, mistress,
patra n. page, leaf, leaf of paper, wing,
pātra 612/3 n. a drinking vessel, a cup, dish, bowl
pātre to a/the (proper/worthy) person 7/s
pattrin m. arrow, bird,
pattana n. a town
patti m. foot-soldier,
paṭu mfn 1. sharp, 2. fig. clever,
paura m. a townsman, citizen,
pauruṣa 651/2, mfn manly, human, n. manhood, virility, manliness,
pauruṣeya mfn made by man, man-made,
paurvadehika 651/3 mfn. belonging to or derived from a former body or existence, done in a former life
pautra grandson
pautrī granddaughter,
pāvaka 623/2 mfn. pure, clear, bright, (said of Agni, Surya and other gods) m. fire, flame
pavana 610/3 m. purifier, wind or the god of wind, breeze, air,
pavitra 611/1 m. a means of purification, filter, a means of purifying or clearing the mind, mfn pure, holy,
payas n. milk, water
payodhara m. a cloud or breast,
pelava mfn soft, tender, delicate, fine,
peṣala mfn lovely, clever, artificially formed, adorned, decorated,
peṭa mfn a box, basket, bag, a multitude, retinue, m. the open hand with the fingers extended,
phala n. fruit (esp. of trees), the kernel or seed of a fruit, a nutmeg, menstrual discharge, fruit –metaphysically – consequence, effect, result, retribution (good or bad), gain or loss, reward or punishment, advantage or disadvantage, benefit, enjoyment, compensation, the issue or end of an action, a gift, donation, the point of an arrow, a shield, a ploughshare, a spot on a die,
phalahetavas those who are motivated by the fruit of action,
phālguṇa name of a month in Spring,
phalaka n. a plank, board, bench
phalākāṅkṣin mfn desiring fruit (results)
phaṇā f. a snake's hood,
phaṇin 716/1 m. 'hooded' a serpent
phaṇī m. a snake
phaṭā f. a snake's hood,
phena 718/3 m. foam, froth, scum,
phenila mfn foaming,
phulla mfn burst open, expanded, blooming
phuṭa n. a snake's hood,
piba mfn drinking, who or what drinks, drink! s.
pibata drink! pl.
pibati he/she drinks
piccha n. tail-feather (bird or arrow),
pīḍā 629/2 f. pain, suffering, violation, damage, torture, a chaplet or garland for the head,
pīḍita mfn distressed, troubled, tormented
pīḍyate 629/2 root *pīḍ*, pass. to hurt or harm, to be pained or afflicted,
pīna mfn thick, brawny, swollen, fat
pinākin m. Śiva
piṇḍa m. a ball of rice offered to ancestors, a ball, globe, lump, piece, body, has the sense of individuality as opposed to universality,

piṅga mfn reddish-brown, tawny
piṅgalā 624/3 f. reddish-brown, tawny, a partic. vessel of the body, the right of 3 tubular vessels which according to yoga are the chief passages of breath and air
pipāsā 627/3 f. desire to drink, thirst,
pipasat 627/3 mfn wishing to drink, thirsty
pipīla m. ant,
pipīlikā f. ant,
piśāca m. vampire, goblin, ghost
piśita n. flesh,
piśuna mfn back-biting, slanderous, wicked, base,
pīta mfn yellow, drunk
pitāmahaḥ great father, grand-father, the Creator,
pīṭha n. chair, stool, bench
pitṛ 626/2 a father, fathers, virtuous ancestors
pitṝn fathers, 2/pl/m
pīyūṣa 630/1 nectar, cream, the drink of immortality produced at the churning of the ocean of milk
- *vat* like nectar
plava 715/2 mfn. swimming, floating, a float, boat, small ship, bird, frog etc.
plavaga m. frog, monkey,
plavana n.swimming, plunging into or bathing in, leaping, jumping over (comp) mfn inclined, stooping down towards, m. monkey,
plavate he jumps
plutvā having jumped
poṣakā f. a nourisher, feeder, maintainer
poṭa m. the foundation of a house, putting together, uniting, mixing, (*ā*) f. a hermaphrodite or a woman with a beard, a female servant or slave, *(ī)* f. the rectum, a large alligator,
pota 650/1 m.n. a vessel, ship, foundation of a house,
m. a young animal,
pra 652/1 ind. prefix – before, forward, in front, on, forth, (as a separate word) forth, away, (as prefix to an adjective) excessively, very much, (in nouns of relationship) great,
2. mfn filling, fulfilling, like, resembling, n. ifc. fulfilment,
prā 701/3 √ to fill *prāti* fills
3. lengthened form of *pra* (prefix meaning before, forward, in front, on, forth) in compounds
prabala mfn powerful, strong, mighty, important (as a word), dangerous, ifc. abounding in, (*am*) ind. greatly,
pra √bhā 683/3 shine forth, begin to become light, shine, gleam, seem, look like, reveal, to illuminate, enlighten,
pra √bhāṣ to speak, tell, declare, manifest, call, name, explain, talk to,
prabhā 683/3 f. light, splendour, radiance
prabhava 684/2 mfn. prominent, distinguished. m. production, source, origin, cause of existence (as father or mother or the Creator), coming to be, f. *ā* springing or rising or derived from
prabhāva mfn power,
prābhava n. superiority,
prabhaviṣṇu Lord of Creation, creator
prabheda m. difference, splitting, piercing,
prabhṛta 685/1 mfn. brought forward, introduced, ind. beginning with, from – forward or upward,
prabhṛti f. bringing forward, offering (sacrifice or praise), beginning, from then onward (with 5th)
prabhu 684/2 mfn excelling, mighty, powerful, rich, abundant,
m. a master, lord, king,
prabhūta mfn come forth, risen, appeared, ifc. become, transformed into, much, abundant,
pl. many, numerous,
prabodha m. awaking (from sleep or ignorance), becoming conscious, consciousness, opening (of flowers), manifestation, appearance (of intelligence), waking, wakefulness, knowledge, understanding,
prabravīmi I shall say 1/s/fut/act
pra√brū 683/3 *-bravīti, -brūte*, to exclaim

proclaim, announce, declare, teach, praise, celebrate, speak kindly to, say, tell, relate

prabrūhi speak!

prāc eastern,

pracchādya ind. having covered

prācīna mfn turned towards the front or eastward, eastern, easterly, old, former, prior, preceding, ancient,

prācīra m.n. an enclosure, fence, hedge, wall

prada mfn. giving, yielding, bestowing, causing, *pradā* f. a gift

pradāya 679/3 m. a present

pradeśa m. (ifc. *ā* f.) pointing out, showing, indication, direction, decision, determination, appeal to a precedent, an example (in gram. law etc.), a spot, place, region, country, a short while, a wall, the distance from tip to tip of thumb and forefinger, one of the obstacles to liberation (Jainas) 'atomic individuality',

prādeśa m. ifc *ā* the span of the thumb and forefinger, place, country, mfn a span long,

pradhāna n. a chief thing or person, the most important or essential part of anything, ibc. the principal or first, chief, head of, primary or unevolved matter or nature, supreme or universal soul, intellect, understanding, (in gram.) the principal member of a compound, (in Sāṁkhya) the original germ of the material universe,

prādhānya n. predominance, prevalence, ascendancy, supremacy, *-tas* ind. in regard to the highest object or chief matter, chiefly, mainly, m. a chief or most distinguished person,

pradigdha 680/1 mfn. smeared over, stained, n.a dish prepared with meat, m. a kind ofgravy

pradīpa m. lamp, light

pradīpta mfn burst into flames, alight, lit

pra√diṣ 679/3 to point out, show, ordain,

pradiṣṭa mfn pointed out, indicated, fixed, ordained,

pradoṣa 1. mfn corrupt, bad, wicked, m. defect, fault, mutiny, rebellion, 2. m. the first part of the night, evening, (*am*) ind. in the evening, in the dark,

prādur ind. out of doors, forth, be visible or audible, appear, arise, exist,

praduṣyati 680/1 becomes worse, deteriorates, is polluted, falls (morally)

pradviñ 680/3 mfn disliking, hating,

pragacchati goes forward

prāha he told, he communicated 1/s/perf/act *pra √ ah*

prahāra m. a blow or thump, striking, hitting, a necklace,

praharaṇās 1/pl/n striking, throwing

pra-√has *-hasati* to burst into laughter, ridicule,

prahasant smiling, laughing, pres.part. 1/s/m

prahāsyasi you shall leave or abandon, 2/s/fut/act *pra√hā*

Prahlada a prince of the Daityas

prāhna m. before midday,

pra √hṛṣ 701/2 to rejoice, be glad or cheerful,

prahṛṣyet one should rejoice, 1/s/opt/act

prāhus they call, they say 1/pl/perf/act *pra √ah* with present meaning)

praiti (pra √i cl 2) comes forth, appears, begins, goes on, advances, goes forwards, comes to, arrives at, departs (dies)

praja mfn bringing forth, bearing

prajā 658/2 f. propagation, birth, offspring, children, family, descendants, a creature, animal, man, mankind, people

prajahāti 700/3 deserts, gives up, abandons, 1/s/pres/indic/act

prajahi kill!, destroy! 2/s/impv/act *pra √han* 700/2

prajānan being well aware of pres.part. *pra √jñā*

prajānāti distinguishes, discriminates 1/s/pres/indic/act *pra√ jñā*

prajāpati sacrifice (a divine power), Lord of the Creatures, 'the first embodied being – Gam.'
m. 658/2 'protector of life', creator, a father, son-in-law, prince, king, the planet Mars, a partic. star,
prājāpatya son of *prajāpati*
prajña 659/1 mfn. wise, prudent, knowing, conversant with
prājña 702/1mfn intelligent, wise, clever, m. a wise or learned man, intelligence dependent on individuality,
(ā) f. intelligence, understanding,
prajñā f. 659/2 wisdom, intelligence, knowledge, discrimination, judgment,
prajñāna mfn prudent, wise, easily known, n. wisdom, knowledge, intelligence, discrimination, sometimes translated as 'consciousness' (e.g. Māṇḍūkya Up.) , wisdom as the outcome of *vijñānam* and practical application,
pra √kāś to become visible, appear, shine
prāk 703/3 in comp. for *prāñc,* directed forwards, facing, in front previous, prior (see *prāñc* 703/3)
prakara mfn doing much or well, m. aid, friendship, usage, custom, respect, seduction, 2. m. a scattered heap, mulitude, quantity, plenty,
prakāra m. sort, kind, nature, class, species, way, mode, manner,
etena prakāreṇa in this way,
kena prakāreṇa in what way? how?
prakāraiḥ in one way or another,
prakāratā f. speciality,
triprakāra of three kinds,
prakāravat mfn belonging to a species
prakaraṇa n. production, creation, treatment, discussion, explanation, book, chapter, a subject, topic, a kind of drama, treating with respect, doing much or well,
prakāśa 653/1 m. visible, shining, bright, manifest, light
prakāśate 653/1 to become visible, appear, manifest, illumine
prakāśayate causes to appear or shine, caus.
prakāśayati 653/1 causes to appear or shine, illumine, display 1/s/pres/indic/caus/act *pra √kāś*
prakāśe ind. publicly,
prakṛta mfn made, done, produced, accomplished, prepared, appointed, charged, commenced, begun or one who has begun, put forward, mentioned, genuine, real, *-tā* f. being begun or in process, *-tva* n. being the subject of discussion,
prākṛta 703/1 original, normal, ordinary, unrefined, provincial, vernacular m. a low or vulgar man, With *laya* or *pralaya* –resolution or re-absorption into *prakṛti*, the dissolution of the universe, dialects akin to sanskrit,
prakṛti 654/1 f. nature, whole of Creation, manifest *vyakta* and unmanifest *avyakta*, includes the 3 guṇā
prakṛtija 654/1 mfn springing from nature, innate, inborn
prakṛtistha mfn existing in material nature, being in the original or natural state, genuine, unaltered, unimpaired,
prakṛtyā ind. by nature, naturally,
prāktana mfn former, prior, previous, preceding, old, ancient,
pralambhana 689/2 n. over-reaching, that by which anyone is deceived, deceiving
pralāpa 689/2 m. prattling, chattering, raving, internal chattering,
pralapan speaking pres/act/part *pra √lap*
pralaya m. dissolution, presided over by Śiva the dissolver or destroyer,
pralayānta mfn ending in death
pralīna mfn dissolved, reabsorbed into (7th), disappeared, lost, died, dissolving, dying, when one dies, tired, wearied,
pralobha m. allurement, seduction,
pramā 685/3 f. basis, foundation,measure, scale, right measure, true knowledge, correct notion, *-tva* n. accuracy of perception,
pramāda 685/2 m. intoxication, madness,

insanity, an error, mistake, carelessness about through acting without prior consideration, through spontaneous action, inadvertence, negligence,

pramādī idle people

prāmādika mfn arising from carelessness, erroneous, faulty,
-*tva* n. erroneousness, incorrectness,

pramāṇa 685/3 n. measure, scale, proof, standard, a measure of any kind, right measure, standard, authority, a means of acquiring *pramā* or certain knowledge,
(*pratyakṣa* sense perception,
anumāna inference,
upamāna analogy,
śabda or *āptavacana* verbal authority or revelation,
anupalabdhi or *abhāvapratyakṣa* negative proof,
arthāpatti inference from circumstances), any proof or testimony or evidence, a correct notion, right perception, oneness,

pramātha 685/2 m.stirring about, tormenting, destruction of enemies

pramathabhāṣā A type of uttering. 'This is a state of abundance of energy either through ecstasy or some other intoxicating situation through emotional charge. In this state, when rajas would be predominant, then the uttering would be rather erratic and profuse. They may not respond to rules.'

pramāthin mfn stirring about, tearing, rending,

prameya 686/1 n. the thing to be proved, the object of knowledge, mfn to be measured, measurable, to be proved, provable,

pramoda m. excessive joy, delight,

prāṁśu mfn high, tall, long, strong, intense,

pramucyate is liberated or released, becomes freed
1/s/pres/indic/pass *pra* √*muc*

pramudita mfn delighted, pleased, glad,

pra-mukha mfn. turning the face towards, first, foremost, honourable
-*tas*, before the face of, in front of

pramukta mfn. loosened, untied, released, forsaken, abandoned, given up, renounced,

prāṇa 705/1 2. m. the breath of life, breath, respiration, spirit, vitality, pl. life, a vital organ, vital air; the 5 vital airs are known as *prāṇa* – upwards, *apāna*, downwards, *vyāna* – that by which these two are held, *samāna* – that which carries the grosser material of food to *apāna* and brings the subtler material to each limb, and *udāna* which brings up or carries down what has been drunk or eaten, *prāṇāḥ* pl. life,

prāṇamaya 705/3 consisting of vital air or breath,

pranamya making obeisance,
ind. having bowed (gerund),

pra-ṇaś 659/3 √*1.ṇaś* *ṇaśati* reach, attain
√2. *naś* *ṇaśati/ ṇaśyati* to be lost, disappear, vanish

pra-ṇaṣṭa mfn . destroyed, lost

pranaśyāmi I am lost or destroyed

praṇava 'the first word is called the *praṇava* sound and is uttered as *om*, which is composed of *a,u* and *m.'*

praṇava 660/3 the mystical or sacred symbol *om*

praṇaya m. a leader, guidance, conduct, manifestation, display, setting forth an argument, affection, confidence in (7th), love, attachment, friendship, favour, (ibc. *āt, ena,* °*yopetam* ind. confidentially, affectionately, openly, frankly), desire, longing for, an entreaty, request, reverence, obeisance, final beatitude,

prāṇāyāma 706/1 m. the name of specific breathing exercises,

prāṅgaṇa n. a court, yard, courtyard, a kind of drum,

prāṇin 706/1 m. breathing, living, alive
m. a living being or creature

praṇipāta 660/2 mfn prostating oneself,

bowing respectfully before
prañjalayaḥ with palms joined (a reverent gesture)
prāñjali mfn joining and holding out the hollowed open hands,
prānta m.n. (ifc f. *ā*) edge, border, margin, verge, extremity, end, a point, tip (of a blade of grass), ibc. finally, eventually,
prapadyante they take refuge in, they resort to, 1/pl/pres/indic/mid *pra√pad* 682/1
prapadye I take refuge or resort to 3/s/mid
prapañca 681/3 m. manifestation, development, manifoldness, expansion, diversity, phenomenon,
pra-panna 682/1 mfn. arrived at, fallen at a person's feet, suppliant
prapaśya see! behold! 2/s/impv
prapaśyat 682/2 mfn. well-discerning, judicious, sensible, intelligent
prapaśyāmi I see, I perceive 3/s/pres/indic/act *pra √paś*
prapaśyati 682/2 to see before one's eyes, observe, behold, 1/s/pres/indic/act sees
praphulla mfn blooming forth, blooming, covered with blossoms or flowers, expanded, opened wide, smiling, shining, cheerful, pleased,
prapīta mfn swollen out, swollen up, distended,
prāpita mfn restored (to), led, conveyed or conducted to, possessed of, caused to attain to or arrive at,
prapitāmaha a paternal great grand-father
prāpnoti 707/2 attains to, obtains, receives, 1/s/pres/indic/act he attains
prāpnuyīt he should attain or reach 1/s/opt/act *pra √āp*
prāpta 707/3 mfn come to, arrived, present, attained to, reached, meet with, find, to meet with (events), met with *pra√āp*
prāpti 707/1 f advent, occurrence, reach, range, extent, reaching, arrival at
prāptis attainment, obtaining, reaching' arrival at, f.
prāpya ind. obtaining, attaining, having encountered, having attained
prāpyate it is attained, obtained or reached, 1/s/pres/pass *pra√āp*
prārabdha 708/2 begun, undertaken, (G) accumulated past actions, the fruits of which are experienced now, events related to the past,
prārabdha "This is what man gets in his present life and is the effects of his deeds which are ripe for use." HH "If one has performed good activities in the past, then good situations are presented in life, and if bad, then only bad situations confront him." HH "..presents itself as favourable or unfavourable situations for man's development"... HH 1967 S2 p3/4 "When some event begins at the call of *prārabdha* the chain of events will follow its full course mechanically. Unless it is fully redeemed in the course of time, nothing will stop it" HH the circumstances one encounters due to good and bad *saṁskāra* '...has all that which the individual could use as his own capital in the present life'
prārabhate he undertakes, commences, begins, performs, 1/s/pres/indic/mid *pra ā √rabh*
prārambha m. beginning,
pra√arth 708/3 *prārthayate (*occ.*-ti)* to wish or long for, desire, to ask a person, to look for, search, have recourse to,
prārthanā f. prayer, devotionals,
prārthayati asks for
prārthayante they seek, they ask for 1/pl/pres/indic/mid *pra √arth*
prasabha 697/1 n. forcibly, violently
prasāda 696/3 m. clearness, brightness, calmness, tranquillity, kindness, absence of excitement, serenity of disposition, good humoured, grace, a propitiatory offering or gift

(of food), gift, gratuity, well-being, welfare, graciousness, kindness, grace, a favour, aid, mediation, free gift, gratuity, the food presented to an idol, well-being, welfare, √*sad*

prāsāda m. lofty seat, building on high foundations, palace,

prasakta 696/2 mfn. attached, adhering, devoted to, fixed or intent upon,

pra √*śam* 695/1 to become peaceful,

praśaṁsā f. praise, fame, glory, a poem of praise, laudatory comparison,

praśāmyati 695/1 to become calm or tranquil, cease, fading away,

prasaṅga m. adherence, attachment, inclination or devotion to, indulgence in, fondness for, (*ena*) ind. zealously, eagerly, evil inclination or illicit pursuit, union, connection,

praśānta mfn. tranquillized, calm, quiet, composed, indifferent

prasaṅga 696/2 adherence, attachment, indulgence in, fondness for

prasanna 696/3 clear, bright, pure, plain placid, tranquil, correct, just, gracious, kind

praśānta 695/1 mfn. calmed, quieted, composed. ppp.
indifferent, extinguished

praśasta 695/1mfn praised, commended, happy, auspicious,

praśāstu let him rule, impv.

prasaviṣyadhvam may you bring forth, bring forth, 2/pl/impv/fut/act
pra √*su*

prasīda be merciful, 2/s/impv/act *pra* √*sad*

prasīdati is pacified, calmed down, settles down, becomes placid, grows clear and bright, becomes clear or distinct, falls into the power of,

prasiddhyet it should be accomplished, it might be accomplished, it should succeed or should be attained, 1/s/opt/act *pra* √ *sidh* 697/3

prasita mfn bound, fastened, diligent, attentive, attached or devoted to, engaged in, engrossed by, occupied with, lasting, continuous,
2. n. pus, matter,

praśna 2. m. a question, demand, interrogation, query, a short section or paragraph (in books),

praśnaya m. support, modesty,

prasṛta 698/2 mfn. come forth, issued from, resounding, widespreading, extending over or to

prasṛṣṭa mfn let loose, dismissed, set free, undirected, uncontrolled, permitted

prastara m. ifc. (*ā*) f. anything strewed forth or about, a couch of leaves and flowers, a couch, a flat surface, flat top, level, a plain, a rock, stone, a gem, jewel, a leather bag, a paragraph, section,

praṣyati sends

prātaḥ in comp. for *prātar* ,at the dawn, early

pratāpavān mfn. 1/s/m full of dignity, full of power, full of strength

prātar 706/2 in the early morning, at dawn, at daybreak, next morning, tomorrow

pratāraṇa n, ferrying over, carrying across, passing over, crossing, deceiving,

pratāya m. majesty

prathama 678/3 mfn (for *pra-tama* superlative of 1. *pra*), foremost, first, earliest, primary, original, prior, former, preceding, initial, chief, principal, most excellent, (*am*) ind. firstly, at first, for the first time, first of all, just, newly, at once, formerly, previously, In Sanskrit grammar (*ā*) f. the first or nominative case and its terminations, the first person (verbs) and its terminations,
the *prathamā puruṣaḥ* (first person of the verb) is he, she or it e.g.
gacchati - he, she or it goes

prathamam firstly

prātharāśa m. breakfast

prathita 678/3 mfn divulged, published,

known, known as, celebrated,

prati 1. ind. a prefix to roots, their derivative nouns and other nouns, sometimes *pratī*
towards, near to, against, in opposition to, down, upon, back again, in return, down upon, upon, on,
-before nouns it also expresses likeness or comparison, or
-forms indeclinable compounds of various kinds, e.g. *praty-agni*
- as a preposition with usually preceding 2nd case, in the sense of towards, against, to, upon, in the direction of e.g. *śabdam prati* in the direction of the sound, *agnim prati* or *praty-agni* (ind.) against the fire, also opposite, before, in the presence of, in comparison, on a par with, also with 5th or *–tas*
in the vicinity of, near, beside, at, on, at the time of, about, through, may be used distributively to express – at every, in or on every, severally, also – in favour of, for, on account of, in regard to, concerning,

prāti 1. √*prā* fills f. filling

pratibhā f. an image, light, splendour, appearance, fitness, suitableness, intelligence, understanding, presence of mind, genius, wit, an image or appearance,

pratibhāsa(te) 668/3 to manifest oneself, appear, to appear to the mind,

prātibhāsika 706/3 mfn. having only the appearance of anything, existing only in appearance,

pratibhū m. a surety, security, bail,

pratibimba n.reflection (as in a mirror), likeness,

pratibodha 668/2 m. awaking, waking, perception, knowledge,

pratībodha m. vigilance,

pratibodhaka mfn awakening (with 2nd), m. a teacher, instructor,

pratidhvani m. echo

pratigacchati returns

pratihāra m. striking against, touch, contact, (esp. tongue with teeth for pronunciation of dentals), a door, gate, door-keeper, (*ī*) f. a female door-keeper, a juggler, juggling, trick, disguise,

pratijāne I admit, acknowledge, approve, 3/s/pres/indic/mid *prati* √*jñā*

pratijānīhi 2/s/impv/act of above, be aware!, become aware!

pratijña mfn acknowledging,

pratijñā 665/3 to admit, acknowledge, acquiesce in, consent to approve vow, promise

pratijñā f. admission, acknowledgement, assent, agreement, promise, vow, an assertion, declaration, affirmation, a proposition, the proposition to be proved, a complaint, indictment

pratijñāta mfn promised, admitted, acknowledged, agreed, declared, asserted, alleged, agreeable

pratīkam n. symbol, face,

pratikāra mfn acting against, counter-acting, m. requital, compensation, retaliation, reward, retribution, revenge, opposition, prevention, remedy,

pratīkāra = *pratikāra* m. counteraction, remedy, revenge, etc.

pratīkṣa mfn looking forward to, expectant of, f. (*ā*) expectation, consideration, attention, respect, veneration waiting for

pratīkṣate he watches for, anticipates, look at, beholds, perceives,

pratikūla mfn 'against the bank' contrary, adverse, opposite, inverted, wrong, refractory, inimical, unpleasant,

pratimā m. a creator, maker, framer, *(ā)* f. an image, likeness, symbol, a picture, statue, figure, idol, measure, extent,

pratinidhi m. substitution, a substitute, representative, proxy, surety, a resemblance of a real form, an image, likeness, statue, picture, similar, like, *pratīpa* mfn 'against the stream', going in an opposite direction, meeting, encountering, adverse, contrary, opposite, reverse, disagreeable, m. adversary, opponent, (*am*) ind. against the stream, backwards,

prātipadika the "stem" of a word, the crude form or base of a noun in its uninflected state

pratipadyate he attains, he enters, reaches,

pratipatti f. gaining, obtaining, acquiring, perception, observation, ascertainment, knowledge, intellect, supposition, assertion, admission,

prati√paś look at perceive, see, to live, experience, to consider

pratiśruti f. an answer, promise, assent,

pratiṣṭha mfn standing firmly, steadfast, resisting, leading to, ending with (ifc), famous, n. point of support, centre or base of anything,

pratiṣṭhā 671/2 f. standing still, resting, remaining, steadfastness, stability, perseverance in, a standpoint, resting place, foundation, stay, support, a receptacle, homestead, dwelling house, limit, boundary, state of rest, quiet, tranquillity, comfort, ease, pre-eminence, superiority, fame, celebrity

pratiṣṭhāpya establishing, causing to fix causative gerund *prati √sthā* to be placed or fixed or located,

pratiṣṭhita mfn standing, stationed, placed, situated in or on, abiding or contained in, fixed, firm, rooted, founded, resting or dependent on, established, proved, ordained for, applicable to (7th), secure, thriving, well off, transferred to (7th), undertaken,

pratīta mfn acknowledged, recognized, known, convinced of, trusting in, resolved upon, satisfied, cheerful, having recognized, respectful, clever, *prati√i*

prativadati answers or replies

pratiyotsyāmi I shall fight against 3/s/fut/*prati √yudh*

pratta mfn. given away, offered, presented granted, from *pra √dā*

pratyac mfn backward, south-western, f. southwest,

pratyaham ind.everyday, daily, day by day,

pratyāhāra 677/2 m. drawing back, abstraction, withdrawing of created things, re-absorption or dissolution of the world; in gram. the comprehension of a series of letters or roots etc., into one syllable by combining for brevity the first member with the *anubandha* of the last member, a group of letters so combined, e.g. *ac*, or *hal*

pratyakṣa 674/2 mfn present before the eyes, perceptible, visible

pratyakṣatas ind. before the eyes, visibly

pratyanīkeṣu in opposing armies 7/pl

pratyavadat (he) repeated verbatim

pratyavāya m. backsliding, reversal, sin,decrease, reverse, contrary course, opposite action,

pratyaya m. belief, conviction, trust, faith, assurance or certainty of, proof, conception, assumption, notion, idea, ascertainment, definition, analysis, solution, explanation, grond, basis, motive, cause, an ordeal, want, need, fame, notoriety, a subsequent sound or letter, the term for a verb or noun ending,

pratyeka mfn each one, every one, (ibc. or *am* ind.) one by one, one at a time,

pratyupakāra 678/1 returning a service or favour, gratitude

pratyuṣa m. the daybreak, dawn,

pratyūṣa m. the daybreak, dawn,

prauḍha 714/3 mfn raised or lifted up, full-grown, mighty, violent, impetuous (as love), thick, dense (as darkness), full (as the moon), proud, arrogant, audacious, ifc. filled with, full of, f. (*ā*) a married woman aged 30-55 n. a violent or impetuous woman,

pravadati 690/3 speaks out, proclaims, declares,
pravakṣyāmi I shall speak or talk
pravakṣye I shall speak of, I shall explain, 3/s/fut *pra√vac*
pravāla 691/3 a young shoot, sprout, new leaf,
pravaṇa mfn prone,
pravartate 693/2 -*√vṛt* to be set in motion or going, sets about, engages in, commences, happens, is intent upon, comes about,
pravartita 693/3 mfn. caused to roll on or forwards, set in motion, set up, established, built, made,
pravāsa m. dwelling abroad,
praveśa 692/3 entering, entrance, penetration,
pravibhakta mfn (having been) divided or distributed, one who has received his share,
pravilīyate is melted away, dissolves, vanishes, 1/s/pres/indic/pass *pra vi √lī*
pravīṇa mfn skilful, clever, versed in (7th),
pra√viś P.A. *–viśati (te),* to enter, go into, resort to, to reach, attain,
prāviśat (he,she) entered
praviśati enters 1/s/pres/act
praviśya having entered
pravṛddha 694/1 fully developed, increased, intense, prosperous, mighty, strong,
prāvṛṣ f. the rainy season, the rains, the monsoon,
pravṛṣṭa mfn begun to rain or pour down,
pravṛṣṭe ind. when it rains,
pravṛtti participation HH (cf. *nivṛtti* – non- participation)
pravṛtta 693/3 mfn round, globular, driven up (as a carriage), circulated (as a book), set out from (*-tas*), come forth, resulted, arisen, happened, going to, bound for, engaged in, commenced, begun, proceeding, existing, occupied with, busy, n. with *karman* (action) –causing a continuation of mundane existence,
pravṛttau 7/s/m in beginning activity,
pravṛtti 694/1 f. active life as opposed to in-active life, moving onwards, progress, manifestation, active life consisting of the wish to act, knowledge of the means, & accomplishment of the object, giving or devoting oneself to, course or tendency towards, inclination/predilection for (7th or comp.), application, use, employment, conduct, behaviour, practice, the applicability or validity of a rule, continuance, prevalence, fate, destiny, news, tidings,
pravyathita 699/2 mfn affrighted, distressed
prayacchati 687/3 he holds out towards, presents, extends, offers
prāya m. 708/1 m. going forth, starting, departure from life, probably, ifc. consisting in, mostly, like,
prayāga m. place of sacrifice, a sacrifice, a horse, confluence of Yamunā and Gaṅgā rivers,
prayāṇakāle at the time of departure, at the time of death 7/s/m
prayanti they progress, go 1/pl/pres
prāya(s) 708/2 ind. for the most part, probably, commonly, likely, perhaps, ifc. consisting in, mostly,
prayāsa m. exertion, effort, pains, trouble, high degree,
prāyaśas ind. for the most part,
prayaścitta n.penance, atonement,
prayata 687/3 dutiful, careful, prudent, pure, controlled, intent on devotion, well prepared (for a sacred rite), ritually pure, self-subdued, m. a holy or pious person, *-tā* f. *–tva* n. purity, holiness,
prayatate he tries
prayāti he/she/it goes forth, sets out, departs or dies *pra √yā* 688/1 1/s/pres/indic/act
prayatna, 687/3 active efforts, continued exertion, activity, action
prāyena ind. mostly, generally, as a rule,

prayoga 688/2 m. joining together, connection, position, addition (of a word), hurling, casting (of missiles), offering, presenting, undertaking, beginning, commencement, application, employment, use, a design, plan, device, practice, experiment,

prayojana n. occasion, object, cause, motive, purpose, design, aim, end, (in phil.) a motive for discussing the point in question, *-vat* mfn having or connected with or serving any interest or purpose, interested, serviceable, useful, °*t-tva* having a cause, caused, produced,

prayujyate 688/2 it is used or employed, it is fit or suitable

prayukta 688/2 mfn. yoked, harnessed, ordered, directed, used, employed

pṛcchati asks

pṛcchāmi I ask

prekṣā f. seeing, viewing, beholding, looking on (at a performance), a public show or entertainment, ifc. the being understood or meant as,

prekṣāgṛham n. theatre, venue,

prema 711/2 1. love, affection, 2. in comp. for *preman*

preman 711/2 m.n. love affection, kindness, tender regard, love

prepsā 712/3 f. wish to obtain, desiring

prepsu mfn. wishing to attain, seeking, longing for, supposing, assuming (*-nā*) 3/s/m

preṣ (*pra√iṣ*) 1. cl1. to go, move, *preṣate* 2. *preṣyati* to drive on, urge, impel, direct

preṣita mfn set in motion, urged on, directing, dispatched on an errand, sent forth,

preṣyati he sends

preta 711/3 mfn. departed, dead, a dead person, deceased, vampire, goblin, ghost, the spirit of a dead person, an evil being, *pra√i*

pretya 712/1 ind. having died, after death, in the next world, hereafter, having desisted, desisting,

prīta 711/1 mfn beloved, dear to, delighted

prītamanās mfn whose mind is cheerful, gladdened in mind

prīti 711/1 pleasurable sensation, pleasure, joy, gratification personified, kindness, favour, grace, love, attachment

prītipūrvakam ind. kindly, affectionately

priya 710/1 mfn beloved, dear to, devoted to, beloved

priyacikīrṣā 710/1 f. the desire of doing a kindness to, or serving,

priyakṛttama mfn the best accomplisher of what is dear (comparative) doing that which pleases most,

prīyamāṇa mfn being delighted, joyous pres/pass/part

prīyamāṇāya to the delighting one, to the one who is beloved pres/mid/part 4/s/m

priyatara mfn dearer, more pleasing, (comparative)

pṛṣṭa 647/3 mfn (having been) asked, inquired, questioned, demanded, wished for, n. a question, inquiry,

pṛṣṭha a ridge, the back or rear of an animal, the upper side, surface,

pṛthag see *pṛthak*

pṛthak 645/3 ind. widely apart, separately, separately, severally, without,(+5th)

procyamāna proclaimed, explained, pres/pass/part. *pra √vac*

procyate it is said, declared or stated 1/s/pres/indic/pass *pra √vac*

prokta 690/2 mfn. announced, told, said, ppp. *pra √vac*

proktavān declaring, having declared, perf/act/part 1/s/m *pra √vac*

prota 713/2 mfn sewed, strung on, fixed on or in, contained in , set, inlaid, woven

pṛṣṭa 647/3 mfn (having been) asked, inquired, questioned, demanded, wished for, n. a question, inquiry,

pṛṣṭha a ridge, the back or rear of an

animal, the upper side, surface, 'standing forth prominently', the heights, top (of a hill or palace),
pṛṣṭhata m. at the back,
pṛthagvidha 646/1 of diverse kinds, existing in many forms, manifold, various
pṛthak 645/3 ind. widely apart, separately, separately, severally, without (+5th),
pṛthak pṛthak one by one, in turn,
pṛthaktvena 645/3 singly, one by one
pṛthivī 646/1 f. the earth or wide world, earth regarded as one of the elements,
pṛthu mfn broad, wide, expansive,
pṛthvī 647/1 f. the earth, an element,
puccha n. tail
pūjā 641/1 f. honour, worship, respect, reverence, veneration,
pūjana n. reverencing, honouring, worship, respect, attention
pūjita 641/2 mfn. honoured, received or treated respectfully, worshipped, adored, ppp. 1/s/m treated respectfully
pūjya mfn worthy of worship, to be worshipped, gerundive
pulakā m. bristling hair (pl.) (through pleasure rather than fear),
puṁliṅga n. masculine gender, consciousness, the essence of man, man; power to beget, set in motion; the powerful; generation, the penis,
puṁs 630/3 Cl 10 *puṁsayati* to crush, grind, DP in *abhi-vardhana* crushing, grinding, troubling,
2. m. a man, a male being, (in gram.) a masculine word, a human being, a servant, attendant, the soul, spirit, spirit of man,
punaḥ again *(punar)*
punaḥ punaḥ again and again
punar (or *punaḥ)* ind. 1. back, home,
with *ā-gam* -go back,
with *vac* -reply,
2. again, anew, further, moreover,
3. but, on the other hand,
punaḥ punaḥ (punaḥ punar) again and again,
punarbhava, 633/3 adj. born, new birth, transmigration,
punarjanma rebirth
puṅgavas bull, hero
puṇya 632/1 mfn auspicious, propitious, good, right, merit, essence of good action, meritorious act, moral or religious merit,
puṉs 630/3 a man, a male being, a masculine word, a human being, see *puṁs*
pur f. 1. fullness, 2. a rampart, wall, stronghold, fortress, city, castle, town, the body (considered as the stronghold of the city), the intellect,
pura n. city, fortified town, citadel,
purā 634/3 ind. long ago, before, formerly, of old, in a previous existence, at first, in the beginning
pūra mfn filling, making full, satisfying, m. a large quantity of water, flood,
puraḥsara mfn going before, m. forerunner, ifc. having ... as forerunner, accompanied by ...
purāṇa 635 mfn belonging to ancient times, ancient, a class of sacred works, legends, history, science, study, discussions, not growing, *(ī)*f.
puras kṛ to place in front or at the head,
purastāt ind. before, forward, in or from the front, in the first place, in or from the East, Eastward, above,
puratas ind. before (in place or time), in front or in presence of (with 6th or in comp.)
purātana 635/1 mfn. belonging to the past, former, old, ancient
purī f. citadel,
purīṣa n. crumbling earth, loose earth, dirt, excrement,
pūrṇa 642/1 mfn full, filled with, fulfilling, satisfying, complete, perfect, filled, abundant, fulfilled, ended, complete, all, entire, satisfied, contented,
m. particular measure, kind of tree, water, n. fulness, plenty, abundance,
pūrṇimā f. the night or day of full moon, an auspicious time,

purodhas 635/2 'placed at the head' chief priest of a king

purohita mfn set before or in charge esp. of priestly service, m. priest, house-priest of a prince,

puruṣa 637/1 m. the soul and original source of the universe, the Supreme Being, person, "the light of the *ātman* illuminating the *antaḥkarana* (mind)." L.M. one who lives in the city i.e. in the *antaḥkaraṇa,* '...There is nothing higher than the *puruṣa.* He is the culmination. He is the highest goal'. HH 'The truth of existence is that the *puruṣa* or *ātman* is the Absolute: within this the universe has its existence.' HH

puruṣārtha spiritual endeavour – HH .. the efforts he will make to realise himself '
637/3 any object of human pursuit, any one of the 4 aims or pursuits of existence,
kāma -gratification of desire,
artha - acquirement of wealth,
dharma - discharge of duty or virtue,
mokṣa final emancipation)
puruṣārthe 7/s in the goal of life

puruṣottama 637/3 highest among men or spirits

pūrva 643/1 mfn. former, prior, before, East, being before or in front, preceding, previous to, to the east of, eastern, m. an ancestor, forefather, pl. ancients or ancestors, an elder brother,
(*am*) ind. before, formerly (+7th), the day before,

Pūrva-mīmāṁsā see *mīmāṁsā*

pūrveṣita 644/3 mfn known from former times, former

pūṣā the sun, nourisher

pūṣan a Vedic deity, surveyor of the universe, protector of the universe, the sun

puṣkala 639/1 much, many,

puṣkara n. blue lotus

puṣṇāmi √*puṣ* 638/2 I thrive or flourish

puṣpa 639/2 n. a flower, blossom *-ika* suffix = pertaining or relating to offerings as of flowers

puṣṭa mfn well fed, fat

pustaka n. book

puṣṭi 639/1 f. well nourished condition, fatness, growth, increase, prosperity, wealth, comfort, completeness

puṭa m.n. fold, cavity, pocket, slit, concavity, a cloth worn to cover the genitals (also *ī*), a horses hoof, an eyelid, m. a cup or basket made of leaves, a casket, enveloping or wrapping for cooking, a cake or pastry filled with stuffing, n. a nutmeg,

pūta 640/3 mfn. cleaned, purified, pure, clear, bright, m. a conch shell,

pūtanā a demoness

pūti 641/1 1. purity, purification
2 641/3 putrid, foul-smelling

putra 632/2 a son, child. - *ka* diminutive- little son Oh son,

putrikā f. daughter, doll,

√*ṛ* 223/2 Cl 1.3.5. P *ṛcchati, iryati, ṛnoti, ṛṇvati,* to go, move, rise, tend upwards, go towards, meet with, fall upon or into, reach, obtain, to fall to one's share, occur, befall, to advance towards a foe, attack, invade, hurt, offend, move, excite, erect, raise, cast through, pierce, DP in (cl1) *gati, prāpaṇa,* (Cl 3) in *gati,* (Cl 5) in *hiṁsā*

√*ṝ* not listed, DP in *gati* going

√*rā* 871/2 (or *rās*) Cl 2 P A *rāti,* t*(te)*, to grant, give, bestow, impart, yield, surrender, DP in *dāna* giving, granting,

√*rabh* 867/1 (or *rambh)*Cl 1 A *rabhate,* (*ti), rambhate (ti),* to take hold of, grasp, clasp, embrace, to desire vehemently, to act rashly, DP in *rābhasya* longing for, being eager, embracing,

rabhasa m. violence, impetuosity, energy,

rapid, fierce, wild, hurry, haste, speed, passion, mfn impetuous, violent, ifc. eager for, desirous of,

rābhasya 877/1 n. velocity, impetuosity, delight, joy, pleasure

√*rac* 860/3 Cl 10 P *racayati* to produce, fashion, form, make, construct, complete, cause, effect, to compose, write, to place in or on, to adorn, decorate, cause to make or do, cause to move (a horse), DP in *pratipatna* arranging, preparing, making ready,

√*rad* 866/2 Cl 1 P A *radati (te)* to scratch, scrape, gnaw, bite, rend, dig, break, split, divide, to cut, open (a road or path), lead (a river into a channel), to convey to, bestow on, give, dispense, DP in *vilekhana* splitting, rending, gnawing, digging,

√*radh* 866/3 or *randh* Cl 4 P *radhyati* to become subject to, be subdued or overthrown, succumb, to be completed or matured, to bring into subjection, subdue, to hurt, torment, caus. *randhayati* to make subject, deliver over to, torment, afflict, annihilate, to cook, prepare food, DP in *hiṁsā* injuring or *saṁrāddhi* success, accomplishment,

√*rādh* 876/2 Cl 5.4. P *rādhnoti, rādhyati, rādhati, rādhyate* to succeed (said of things to be accomplished or finished), to succeed (said of persons), be successful, thrive, prosper, be ready for, submit to, be fit for, partake of, attain to, to accomplish, achieve, perform, make ready, prepare, to propitiate, conciliate, gratify, hurt, injure, exterminate, DP in *vṛddhi* (Cl 4) prospering, *saṁsiddhi* completing, finishing,

rādhas n. gracious gift, blessing,

√*rag* 860/2 Cl 1 P *ragati* to doubt, suspect, *āsvādana* tasting, Cl 10 P *rāgayati* DP (Cl 1) in *śaṅkā* doubting, (Cl 10)

rāga 872/1 m. feeling or passion, vehement interest in, desire, the act of colouring or dyeing, colour, hue, tint, red colour, redness, inflammation, any feeling or passion,

rāgātmaka 872/2 mfn impassioned, composed of or characterised by passion,

raghu m. ancestor of Rāma,

rahas 871/1 loneliness, secrecy, solitude,

rahasi n. privacy, solitude, secrecy, loneliness, solitude, a secret,

rahasya 871/2mfn. secret, private, concealed,

rahita 871/2 mfn left, forsaken, deserted, lonely, solitary, separated or free from

rāj mfn shining, radiant, m. a king, sovereign, chief, anything the best of its kind,

rāja ifc for *rājan*

rājadhānī f. a king's residence, capital,

rājagṛha n. palace

rajakaḥ a washerman, dyer of clothes,

rājan m. king

rajanī or *rajani* f. night,

rājaputra m. prince

rājarṣi m. a royal seer

rajas 863/2 n. one of the three guṇā "the force of motion within *prakṛti*" HH. including the qualities of activity, urgency, and variability, passion, movement, energy,

rajasa born of *rajas*, *raja,sic* , mfn unclean, dusty, dark, living in the dark,

rājasika 875/2 mfn belonging or relating to the quality *rajas*, endowed with or influenced by the quality of passion, passionate,

rajata 863/1 mfn silvery, made of silver,

rājate √*rāj* 872/3 reigns, shines, appears or looks like, illuminates, he she or it shines, 872/3 he reigns, directs, rules, 1/s/pres/indic/mid

rājavat ind. like a king, as towards a king,

rājayoga 873/3 a constellation under which princes are born, an easy

way of meditation, 'the royal way to total unity' HH
rājī f. line
rajjuḥ 861/1 f.m. rope, cord, string, line, a braid of hair,
rajjusarpa 861/1 *rajju* a rope, *sarpa* 1184/1 a snake, a rope -snake, a snake in a rope, a rope seen as a snake,
rājñī f. queen,
rajoguṇamaya n. a quality of the universe, having the quality of rajas
rājyam 875/1 kingdom, kingly, princely, country, realm,
rājyam +*kṛ* he reigns
rakṣa protect! 859/3 guarding, watching, protecting, a watcher, 860/1 an evil being or demon
rakṣā f. protection, a guard, sentinel
rakṣaka m. protector, guardian
rakṣaṇa 859/3 m. protector, f. guarding, protection, n. the act of guarding, watching, protecting, preservation
rākṣasa m. cruel man-eating ogre
rākṣasī f. female of above
rakṣati protects, saves
rakṣika m. protector,
rakṣita mfn saved,
rakṣitṛ m. protector, watcher,
rakta mfn reddened, reddened, n. blood,
√*ram* 867/2 cl1 *ramate (-ti,)* to stop, stay, make fast, calm, set at rest, to delight, make happy, *ramayanti* they delight, please or cause to delight 1/pl/caus.
rāma 'causing rest', dark, dark-coloured, black, pleasant, beautiful, *Rāmaḥ*
rāmā a beautiful woman, a woman, a dark woman, vermillion
ramaṇīya mfn charming, to be enjoyed, pleasant, agreeable, delightful,
ramate 867/2 delights, 1/s/pres/indic/mid rejoices at, stand still, rests,
rāmavat like *Rāmaḥ*
rāmāyaṇa the story of *rāmaḥ*
rambha *867/2* a prop, staff, support
rambhā f. banana palm,
raṇa 863/3 m.n. delight, combat, battle as an object of delight,
raṇakṣetra n. the field of battle,
randhra n. a hole,
raṅga m. 1. colour, paint, dye, hue, 2. theatre, amphitheatre,
rañj 861/2 to be dyed or coloured, to redden, grow red, glow, to be affected or excited, attracted,
rañjana 863/3 pleasing, delighting, n. colour, giving pleasure,
√*ras* 1. cl1 to roar, yell, cry, sound, reverberate, to praise, *rasati* DP in *śabda* sounding
√*ras* 2. cl 10 to taste, relish, feel, perceive, *rasayati,* DP in *āsvādana* 162/1 tasting or *snehana* 1267/3 delighting
rasa 869/2 1/s/m the best or finest or prime part of anything, G.254 the essence of things, delight of existence, essence, taste or inclination or fondness for, desire, pleasure, flavour, 1/s/m taste for,
rasā f. moisture, a mythical stream round the earth and atmosphere, earth,
rāsabha m. ass, jackass, donkey,
raśanā f. cord, strap, rein, girdle,
rasanā f. sense of taste, tongue,
rasātmakas mfn having the nature or essence of juice or flavour,
rāśi m. troop, host, heap, zodiac sign,
rasika mfn tasty, m. connoisseur,
raśmi 869/2 m. a string, rope, ray of light, beam, splendour,
rāṣṭra n. m. kingdom, sovereignty, a people, nation, subjects,
rasya 871/1 mfn. juicy, tasty, savoury,
rata 867/2 pleased, amused, gratified, delighting in, devoted or attached to, fond or enamoured of, intent upon
ratha m. chariot,
rathika m. charioteer, valiant one,
rathin m. charioteer, warrior who fights from a chariot, a *kṣatriya,* driver,
rathya m. a horse,
rathyā f. a highway, street,

rati 867/3 f. pleasure, enjoyment, passion, rest, repose, attachment
ratna n. gift, blessing, riches, treasure, (as something bestowed or given), a jewel, precious gem,
rātri 876/1 f. *(ī)* night, the darkness or stillness of night
rava m. cry, yell, howl,
rāvaṇaḥ *Rāvaṇaḥ* -king of the demons
ravi 869/1 m. the sun or sun-god, a particular form of the sun, a mountain
raya m. current, speed, the stream of a river, impetuosity, ardour,
rāya a prince or king, also see *arāya,* 888/1 *rās, rāyam* etc.from √*rai,* goods, wealth, riches
4/s *rāye* for the sake of wealth
ṛc f. a hymn of praise,
ṛcchati 223/2 reaches, obtains, goes towards 1/s/pres/indic/act √ *ṛ*
ṛddha 226/1 mfn. increased, thriving, prosperous, abundant, wealthy
rekhā f.a scratch, streak, stripe, line, a continuous line, row, series, outline, drawing, sketch,
reṇu m. dust, pollen,
ripu 880/3 mfn. deceitful, treacherous, m. an enemy, adversary, foe,
rīti f. manner, style,
ṛju 225/2 mfn straight, honest, upright, ind. unswervingly, precisely, in the right manner, correctly,
ṛk a division of the Veda, a hymn,
ṛkṣa m. a bear,
ṛṇa mfn (having gone against or transgressed), guilty, n. guilt, debt, duty,
rocate 881/3 shines, is bright or radiant, is pleasing (with 4th),
rodati cries, wails
rodha mfn growing, sprouting,
rodhana mfn obstructing, impeding, m. planet Mercury, f. a dam, bank, n. shutting up, confinement, stopping, checking, preventing,
roditvā ind. having cried
roga 888/3 m. 'breaking up of strength' disease, infirmity, sickness,
rohati climbs
roma 889/3 3. m. a hole, cavity, the city Rome, n. water, n. body hair
romaharṣaṇa mfn causing the hair to bristle,
romapulaka m. bristling of the hair,
romāśca m. bristling of the hair,
roṣa 885/1 m. anger, rage, wrath, passion,
roṣaṇa mfn angry, wrathful, passionate, enraged
ṛṣabha 226/3 m. a bull, a male animal in general, mfn best,
ṛṣayas the seers, wise men 1/pl/m
ṛṣi m. a seer or sage
ṛṣiyajña m. sacrifice for the sages
ṛta 223/2 mfn. proper, right, fit, brave, honest, true, worshipped, respected, n. (*am*), fixed or settled law, order, divine truth, truth in general, righteousness, right,
*ṛtambhara*223/3 mfn. bearing the truth within one self, f. with and without
ṛtambharā f. intellect or knowledge which contains the truth within itself,
ṛte 226/1 ind. excepting, besides, without, unless, (with 5th),
ṛtu m. 1. a fixed and settled time esp. time for sacrificing, 2. time of year i.e. season, 3. the menses,
ṛtvij mfn offering at the appointed time, m. a, priest in the ritual, pl. priests,
ruc, 881/3 to shine, be bright, long for *rocate* longs for,
ruci f. light, lustre, splendour, beauty, pleasure, liking, taste, relish, appetite, zest, pleasure in, desirous of, longing for,
rucira mfn bright, beautiful, splendid,
ruddhvā ind. restraining, having restrained,
rūḍha 885/2 mfn. mounted, risen, ascended
rudhira 884/2 mfn red, blood-red, bloody
rudra Rudra, destroyer
√*ruj* 882/3 Cl 6 P *rujati (te)* to break, break open, dash to pieces, shatter, destroy, to cause pain, afflict, injure, caus. *rojayati,* DP in *bhaṅga* breaking to pieces, destroying, in *hiṁsā* hurting,

ruj f. pain, disease, sickness,

rujā 882/3 f. breaking, fracture, pain, sickness, disease, m. sickness, disease induced by passion or love

rūkṣa 885/3mfn rough, dry, arid, dreary

ruṇḍa mfn maimed, mutilated, m. a headless body,

rūpa 885/3n. form, beauty, any outward appearance, or colour, shape, or figure, consisting of, like to

rūpaka mfn having form, figurative, metaphorical, illustrating by figurative language, m. rupee,

rūpakabhāṣā A type of utterance. When one has to indicate function and properties of non-physical things, then the poets resort to these styles where similes illustrate with the help of physical forms.

rūpita 886/3 mfn formed, represented, exhibited, characterisation

rūpya 886/3 mfn beautiful, well-shaped, n. beautiful, silver,

sa m. he, that, 1111/2 6. the base for the nom. case of the 3rd person pron. *tad,*
1111/2 7. ind an inseparable prefix expressing junction, conjunction, possession, similarity, equality, (compounded) with, together with, having, containing, having the same,

sā 1111/2 pron. f. she or that

śabala mfn dappled, spotted, filled with,

śabda m. sound, voice, word, space, ether, property of sound

śabda-brahman 1053/1 n. word-brahman, the Veda considered as a revealed sound or word, and identified with the Supreme

śabdādi m 1053/2 the objects of sense beginning with sound,

sabhā f. an assembly, congregation, meeting, council, social party, society, good society,

sabhāgya mfn having good fortune, fortunate,

sabhāpati m. president,

sabhya mfn being in an assembly –hall or meeting-room, fit for an assembly or court, suitable to good society, courteous, polite, refined, civilised, m. an assessor, judge, assistant,

sabuddhi 1229/2 mfn wise, clever, intelligent

sacarācara both the animate and inanimate, both the moving and unmoving, (*cara acara*)

saccaritra mfn virtuous, n. good conduct, true or good character

saccidānanda *sat, cid, ānanda* truth, consciousness, bliss,

sacetā f. calm in mind,

sacetas 1131/1 mfn. having the same mind, unanimous, M. conscious,

śacī f. 1048/1 the rendering of powerful or mighty help, assistance, aid, kindness, favour, grace, skill, dexterity, name of Indra's wife,

sacinta 1131/1 mfn absorbed in thought thoughtful

saciva m. an associate, companion, friend,

sadā 1139/2 ind. always, ever, perpetually,

sadācāra 1137/2 m.behaviour of the good or wise, 'just action' HH

sadana causing to settle down or remain, n. a seat, palace, abode, residence,

sadātana mfn continual, perpetual,

ṣāḍava m. a sweetmeat,

sadbhāvanā sadbhāva 1137/2 real being, existence, real state of things, 'pure feelings' HH

sadguṇa 1137/2 m. a good quality, virtue, mfn. having good qualities, virtuous

sādhaka 1201/1 effective, efficient (G p.261) one who practises spiritual disciplines, *sādh* –to go straight to the goal, a spiritual aspirant

sādhana 1201/1 mf(*ī* or *ā*)n. leading straight to a goal, guiding well, furthering, effective, efficient, productive of, (*ā*) the act of mastering, overpowering, any means of effecting or accomplishing, propitiation, worship, adoration G.p261 self-effort, spiritual discipline, (from the verb root *sādh* to go straight to the goal, make straight (a path)), (D.P. completing, finishing), the way, generally- the means to release or liberation

sādha 1201/1 m. accomplishment, fulfilment, achievement of the goal

sādhāraṇa mfn belonging or applicable to many or all, universal, generic, like, equal, similar to, behaving alike m. a twig of bamboo, n. something in common, a league or alliance with, a common rule or one generally applicable, a generic property, (*am*) ind. commonly, generally,

sādhāraṇabhāṣā a type of utterance. 'This is the ordinary, according to fact, language, fully grammatical and simple without any exaggerations.'

sadharma m. the same nature or qualities, mfn having the same nature or qualities, subject to the same law,

sādharmya 1202/2 identity of nature with, likeness or homogeneity with

śādhi (you) correct! 2/s/impv/act

sādhu 1201/2 mfn good, virtuous, m. a saint, sage, f. (*vī)* a chaste or virtuous woman, faithful wife,

sādhuḥ sādhuḥ well done!

sādhuḥ, sādhvī (f) good, virtuous

sādhya 1202/1 what is to be accomplished, attained, a class of celestial beings

sādhyābhāva 1202/1 absence of the thing to be proved

sādhyābhāvāt 5/s because nothing is to be accomplished

sādhya 1202/1 mfn to be accomplished, perfection, G.p263 the subject, that which is to be proved

sādhyate 1200/3 1. √*sādh* go straight to any goal or aim, attain an object, be successful, prosper, 1/s/pres/mid he is successful

sadoṣa mf n having deficiency, faulty, together with the night,

sadṛś mfn fit, proper, just, right,

sadṛśa 1140/1 like, resembling, similar to, fit, proper, right, worthy,

sadyas 1140/1 ind. in the very moment, in the present, immediately, on the same day, at once,

sagadgada 1125/1 mfn with stammering

sāgara 1198/2 m. the ocean

saguṇa 1125/1 having qualities, qualified, worldly

saguṇa brahman the *Brahman* with all *guṇa* and manifestations,

saḥ 111/2 pron. he (or that with masculine nouns),

saha + 3rd together with, with,

Sahadeva a *Pāṇḍava* prince (means – accompanied by the gods)

sahaja mfn born with, innate, natural, m. natural state or disposition, n. emencipation during life, ibc. by birth, by nature, naturally,

sāhasa mfn precipitate, rash, foolhardy, m.n. punishment, fine, ifc. f. (*ā*) n. boldness, daring, rashness, any reckless act,

sahasā suddenly, forcibly, quickly, at once, unexpectedly, fortuitously,

sāhasika mfn bold, daring, rash, cruel, brutal, m. a robber,

sahasra 1195/2 a thousand

sahāya m. a companion, follower, adherent, assistant, helper,

sāhāyya n.used with *Dh° kṛ* to mean giving help – the person being given help is put in the 6th case

sāhāyyam kariṣyati will give help

sahiṣṇutā 1193/2f. patience, forbearing, tolerance,

sahita 1. 1193/2 mfn. borne, endured, supported, 2. 1195/1 joined, conjoined, united

saikata mfn sandy, gravelly, a sandbank, any bank or shore,

śaila mfn stony, rocky, made of stone, stone-like, rigid, m. a mountain, rock, crag,

saindhava m. salt, a horse

sainika m. soldier

śaila mfn stony, rocky, made of stone, stone-like, rigid,
m. a mountain, rock, crag,

sainya mfn belonging to or coming from an army, m. a soldier, an army, a guard, a body of troops, army,

√*sajj* 1131/2 to attach to, root *sañj* 1132/3 to be attached, *sajjate* 1132/3 1/s/pres/pass. attached, is attached

sajja mfn fixed, prepared, ready for, equipped, fit for everything, dressed in armour, armed, fortified, having a bowstring, strung, placed on a bow-string,

sajjā f. equipment, armour, mail, dress, decoration,

sajjana m. good or virtuous man (*sat* + *jan*)

sajjī ready (for), (in comp. for *sajja),*

sajji +*kṛ* he prepares, makes ready,

śāka n. vegetable, greens,

śākabhakṣa mfn vegetarian,

śakala m.n. a chip, piece, ½ an eggshell,

sakala 1. mfn having a soft or low sound,
2. mfn consisting of parts, divisible, complete, possessing all parts, entire, whole, all, wholesome, sound,

sākam 1197/2 ind. together, jointly, at the same time, along with

sākāra 1197/3 mfn having form, beautiful

śākhā 1062/3 f. a branch, limb of the body, a division, sub-division, a branch or school of the Veda

sakha m. a friend, companion, attended or ifc. accompanied by ,

sakhi n. friend, companion,

sakhī f. a female friend or companion, a woman's confidante, a mistress,

sakhya 1130/3 n. friendship, intimacy with, fellowship, community

śaknomi I am able, I have the power to 3/s/pres/indic/act √*śak*

śaknoti is able,

śakra 1045/1 mfn strong, powerful, mighty (referring esp. to Indra)

sakṛt 1.mfn acting at once or simultaneously, ind. at once, suddenly, forthwith, once, formerly, ever, at once, together,

sākṣād(t) ind. with the eyes, with one's own eyes, before one's eyes, evidently, clearly, openly, manifestly, in person, in bodily form, personally, visibly, really, actually, immediately, directly, witnessing, a witness *sākṣicaitanya* 'the *ātman* or *brahman*' HH

sākṣāt ind. with the eyes, with one's own eyes, before one's eyes, evidently, clearly, openly, manifestly, in person, in bodily form, personally, visibly, really, actually, immediately, directly,

sākṣin 1198/1 adj. seeing with the eyes, witnessing, observing, witness of the ego or subject as opposed to that which is external to the mind, the witness,

sakta 1132/3 mfn clinging or attached to, fixed or intent upon, directed towards, addicted or devoted to,

śakta 1044/2 mfn able, competent for, equal to, capable of

sakthi n. thigh, thigh-bone,

śakti 1044/2 f. power, ability, strength, might, effort, energy, capability, the power or force of a *deva* as his wife

sakti f. attachment, entwinement,

śaktimāna the powerful or that containing all qualities, having the qualities, pres/mid or pass/part.
'The *śakti* belongs to that thing *śaktimāna,* which exists embodying different measures in different things and these measures are ordained by the *śaktimāna* himself.'
'The *śaktimāna* is the Absolute and is seen as sun and sunlight, moon and moonlight, fire and heat. The way the forces work creates the visible world.'
'*śaktimāna* is the conscious being, the Self, and *śakti* emanates from this *śaktimāna.* The *śakti* cannot be separated from the *śaktimāna* under any circumstances'

śakuna m. a bird, a partic. kind of bird (a vulture, kite, Pondicherry eagle),
śakuni m. a bird-catcher,
śakya possible, able , capable of being, to be conquered or subdued, liable to be compelled, direct, explicit, literal,
śakye I am able 1/s/pres/mid
śakyase you are able, you can 2/s/pres/indic/pass. √*śak*
śālā f. a house, mansion, building, hall, large room, shed, workshop, stable,
śalabha m. grasshopper, locust, moth type,
salila n. water,
salīla mfn playing, sporting (not in earnest), (*am*) ind. playfully, with ease,
śālin mfn possessing a house or room ifc. possessing ...., versed in,
sallakī 1059/2 a plant boswellia thurifera, The sallakī is a medium sized tree with herbal uses for humans and animals. It has similar leaves to those of the bitter neem tree.)
śalya n. spear, dart, thorn,
śalyaka m. hedgehog, porcupine,
śalyoddhara 1059/2 the extraction of thorns or arrows
śam n. welfare, happiness, blessing, 2. 1054/2 ind. blissful, auspiciously, fortunately, happily, well,
sam prefix with, together with, along with, altogether, (opp. to *vi*)
śama m. tranquillity, calmness, rest, equanimity, quietude or quietism, absence of passion, abstraction from eternal objects through intense meditation, (*śāmaṁ* √*kṛ* to calm oneself, be tranquil), pacification, alleviation, cessation, extinction,
sama 1152/1 same, equal, like, identical with, similar, equal, like,
-sama same, equal,
sāma a division of the Veda
samā 1152/1 f. a year, a plain, equanimity, imperturbability, similarity, right measure or proportion
ind. in like manner, alike, equally, together with, exactly, precisely, honestly
samabuddhaya even-minded, dispassionate, indifferent
samācara perform! accomplish! 2/s/impv *sam ā* √ *car*
samācaran performing, practising, observing, pres.part.act *ā*√*car*
samacittatva n. steadiness of thought, evenness of mind,
samadarśana 1152/2 mfn of similar (or *sama*) appearance, looking on all things or men with equal or indifferent eyes, *samadarśina* regarding all things impartially, seeing the same
samādhātum to keep, to place (infin.)
samādhi 1159/3m. joining with, intense contemplation, a unifying concentration, completion, profound meditation, bringing into harmony, meditation, absorption, union, intense application or fixing the mind on, a state beyond experience and expression,
samādhibhāṣā 'a sort of uttering recorded when someone reached a state of *samādhi*. This state, being a state of union and complete peace would produce very nominal use of sound. Thus it is symbolic, and although just few sounds, it would explain much about the subject for which it was intended.'
sam-adhi- √*gam* 1154/1 to go towards together, come quite near, approach,
samadhigacchati he approaches, comes near, surpasses
samāgata 1159/1 mf. come together, assembled, *sam-ā-*√*gam*
samagra 1153/3 mfn. all, entire, whole, complete, (*am*) adv. wholly, together, in the aggregate
sāmagrī f. totality, entirety, completeness, esp. a complete collection of implements or materials,
samāhartum to destroy, annihilate, *hartum* = infinitive of *hṛ*

samāhita 1160/1 mfn put or held together, joined, combined, devoted, one who has collected his thoughts or is absorbed in abstract meditation, quite devoted to or intent upon,

samāja m. meeting with, falling in with, a meeting, assembly, party, a quantity, plenty, abundance, an elephant,

samakṣa 1153/2 being within sight or before the eyes, present, visible (*am, āt, e, atas*) ind. visibly, manifestly, in the presence of

samālocya ind. having considered,

samam ind. in like manner, alike, equally, similarly, together with or at the same time with, just, exactly, precisely, honestly, fairly,

sam√am A. –amate to ask eagerly, solicit, win over, to fix or settle firmly,

sāman 1205/1 1. n. acquisition, property, wealth, abundance, 2. calming, tranquillizing, kind or gentle words for conciliation or negotiation, 3. a metrical hymn, or song of praise, a partic. kind of sacred text or verse as arranged for chanting, the collection of *sāmans* the *sāmaveda,* any song or tune sacred or profane (also the hum of bees),

samāna mfn (connected with 1., 2. *sama*), same, identical, uniform, one, alike, similar, equal, homogenous (sound or letter), moderate, common, general, universal, all, whole (number), being (=*sat* after adj.), virtuous, good, (*am*) ind. like, equally with (3rd), m. an equal, friend, digestive function of prāṇa

samānatā f. or *samānatva* n. equality with, community of quality,

samanta 1155/1 mfn. having the ends together, contiguous, neighbouring, ind. on all sides, around,

sāmanta mfn being on all sides, bordering, limiting, m. a neighbour, a vassal,

samantāt ind. from all sides, on all sides

samantatas ind. on all sides, around, wholly, completely, 'having the ends together' , contiguous, in all respects, neighbouring, adjacent,

samanvita 1155/2 mfn fully endowed with, connected or associated with, accompanied by, going along with,

sāmānya mfn equal, alike, similar, joint, common to, whole, entire, universal, common, common-place, vulgar, ordinary, insignificant, (*am*) n. equality, similarity, identity, normal state or condition, universality,

samāpti f. complete acquisition (as of knowledge or learning), completion, perfection, reconciling differences,

samara m. coming together, meeting, concourse, confluence, hostile encounter, conflict, struggle, war,

samārambha m. enterprise, undertaking, spirit of enterprise, beginning,

samartha mfn having a similar or suitable aim, object or meaning, suitable or fit for (6th or comp.), very strong or powerful, competent, capable of, having the same grammatical construction, m. a word with force or meaning, significant word, the construction or coherence of words in a significant sentence, n. ability, competence, conception, intelligibility,

sāmarthya 1205/3 n. sameness of aim or object, or meaning or signification, belonging or agreeing together, adequacy, accordance, fitness, suitableness, the being entitled to, justification for, ability or capacity for, efficacy, power, strength, force , the force or function or sense of a word,

samāsa 1. 1158/2 throwing or putting aggregation, connection, union, totality, (in grammar) a compound word
2. 1163/2 m. abiding together, connection

samāsama mfn du. equal and unequal

samāsena adv. with brevity, briefly, in brief,
samasta 1158/1 combined, united, all
samasta 1158/1 united, whole, inherent in or pervading the whole of anything, the aggregate of all the parts, everything
samaṣṭi 1158/1 reaching, attaining, conclusion, totality, collective existence, the state of being an aggregate, the universe as a single person or whole
sāmāsika 1206/2 mfn comprehensive, concise, relating or belonging to a *samāsa,* m. or n. a compound word
samatā 1152/2 f. sameness, impartiality, equanimity,
samatīta mfn the departed, the crossed over, the dead, gone or passed by,
samatva n. equality with equanimity, indifference, equableness
samavasthita 1157/3 mfn standing or remaining firm, present equally
samaveta mfn come together, assembled,
samāviṣṭa 1162/3 mfn entered together or at once, filled with, imbued with,
samāvṛta mfn enveloped, covered
samaya m. a time, coming together, meeting or a place of meeting, intercourse with (3rd), coming to a mutual understanding, agreement, treaty,
samayā ind. through, into the middle of or midst of anything, entirely, thoroughly, in the neighbourhood of, near (with 2nd.) 2. in comp. for *samaya*),
śambala n. m. provisions for a journey, envy, jealousy,
sambandha 1177/3 m. binding or joining together, close connection or union or association, conjunction,
sam-bandhi(n) 1177/3 mfn. a relation, kinsman, joined or connected with
sambhava 1179/1 coming together, being, existence, possibility, origin, source, birth, production, cause, reason, arisen or produced from
saṁbhavāmi I come into being, I originate myself, 3/s/pres/ind/act *sam √bhū*
saṁbhāvitasya of the honoured, of the famous, past passive causative part. 6/s/m
sambhrama 1179/3 m. whirling round, haste, hurry, flurry, confusion, agitation, activity, eagerness, zeal, awe,
śambhu or *śambhū* mfn being or existing for happiness or welfare, granting or causing happiness, beneficent, benevolent, helpful, kind, Śiva,
sambhūta 1179/2 mfn being or come together, made or composed of, proceeding from, produced by, originating in
sambhūti f. the fact of being born, birth, origin, production
sambodha 1178/1 m. perfect knowledge or understanding, *-na* mfn. awaking, arousing, recognizing, perceiving, reminding, the act of causing to know, calling to, the vocative case or its termination
saṁcaya 1132/1 collection, gathering, accumulation, dense, thick
saṁchinna 1132/3 mfn. cut to pieces, sever
saṁdaṁśa 1143/1 m. a pair of tongs/nippers,
saṁdeha 1143/3 m. a conglomeration of material elements (said contemptuously about the body), mfn doubt, uncertainty about,
saṁdeśa 1143/2 m. communication of intelligence, message, information, errand, direction, command, order to, a present, gift, the message words, *sandeśavacana* see *saṁdeśa* and *vacana*
saṁdhā f. intimate union, compact, agreement, a promise, vow, design, intention, mixture, a boundary, limit, fixed state, condition,
saṁdhyā f. time of junction (of day and night) , du. morning and evening twilight, morning twilight (of a *yuga),* prayers recited at dawn,
saṁdigdha mfn smeared over, covered with,

confused, confounded with, questioned, questionable, doubtful, dubious, uncertain, unsettled, (*am*) n. an ambiguous suggestion or expression,

saṁ√dṛś 1144/1 P.A. to see together or at the same time, see well or completely, behold, view, perceive, observe, consider, A. and pass. to be seen at the same time, appear together with, to look like, resemble, be similar or equal, to be observed, become visible, caus. *–darśayati* to cause to be seen, display, show,

saṁdṛś f. sight, appearance, a beholding,

saṁdṛśyante are seen 1/pl/pres/pass

saṁgata mfn come together, met, friendly to, the results of good company, n. coming together, alliance, association, friendship,

saṁgati f. coming together, meeting with, going or resorting to (7th), association etc.,

saṁgha m. (*sam* +√*han*) 'close contact or combination', any collection or assemblage, heap, multitude,

saṁghāta 1130/1 mfn close union, complexity, striking or dashing together, killing, combination, (E) p. 102 the body-complex – sense-organs, mind, intellect and ego, organism, organic whole

saṁgraha m. holding together, maintenance, 1129/2 bringing together, assembling (of men), (in phil.) agglomeration (*=saṁyoga),* sum, amount, totality, keeping, guarding, protecting, a ruler,

saṁgrāma 1129/3m. an assembly of people, host, troop, army, battle, war

saṁhāra 1123/2 m. end, conclusion, destruction, bringing together, collection, accumulation, (esp. the periodical destruction of the universe at the end of a *kalpa* – 262/3 4,320,000,000 years, a day of *Brahmā*)

samidh 1164/3 mfn. igniting, flaming, burning, f. firewood, fuel,

samidha fuel, wood, m. fire,

samiddha mfn. set alight or on fire, lit, kindled, ignited

samīkṣya ind. contemplating, regarding, *sam-*√*īkṣ* gerund

samīpa 1165/1 mfn proximate, adjacent, close by, n. nearness,

samīpe ind. near

samīra also *samira* m. wind, breeze, air,

samitiṁjaya 1/s/m victorious in battle,

Saṁjaya the narrator of the B.G.a minister in the court of King *Dhṛtarāṣṭra,*

saṁjāyate is born, is produced, *sam*√*jan* 1/s/pres/indic/pass

saṁjanayan 1/s/m pres. part. *sam* √*jan* producing, bringing forth

saṁjña 1. 1133/2 to agree together, be of the same opinion, be in harmony with, to obey, acknowledge, know well, understand
2. 1133/3 one who has recovered consciousness,

saṁjñā 1133/3 f. agreement, mutual understanding, harmony, consciousness, clear knowledge or understanding, any noun having a special meaning, used for technical terms & definitions which have a specific technical meaning, lit. containing all knowledge (of the named thing)

saṁjñārtham ind. for the purpose of knowing, for information, for the sake of a sign,

saṁjñita mfn. made known, communicated, known as, called

saṁkalpa 1126/3 m. conception, idea, or notion formed in the heart or mind, will, purpose, resolution

saṁ-kara 1126/2 mfn soothing, m. intermixture, commingling, confusion, offspring of a mixed marriage,

śaṁkara another name for *śiva*

saṁkāśa m. having the appearance of

saṁkaṭa mfn a narrow strait, Slender –

name of a gander, narrow passage – a strait, a difficulty 'narrow strait',
saṁketa m. sign, signal, gesture, agreement, compact, stipulation, assignation with (6th), engagement, appointment, allusion, hint, a short explanation of a grammatical rule, condition, provision,
saṁkhya 1128/1 mfn. counting up, reckoning, n. conflict, battle, war,
saṁkhyā f. number, numeration, calculation, summing up, reasoning, reflection, reason, intellect, name,
Sāṁkhya 1199/1 an adherent of this doctrine, a dualistic philosophy of 2 realities – spiritual and *prakṛti*
saṁkoca 1126/1 m. limitation, 1125/3 draw in, withdraw, internalises, goes within, contraction, shrinking together, restriction,
saṁkruddha mfn greatly enraged, incensed
saṁkṣobha m.1128/1 agitation, excitement
saṁkula 1126/1 mfn filled, disordered.
sammāna m.n. honour, respect, homage, n. the act of measuring out, equalizing, comparing,
sammoha 181/1 m. stupefaction, unconsciousness, ignorance, delusion,
sammūḍha mfn uncertain, confused, ppp. *sam √muh*
sammukha mfn facing, confronting, fronting, being face to face or in front of, present, before the eyes,
sāmna 1205/2 relating to *sāmans* (which see) f. a sort of metre
saṁnibha 1147/1 mfn resembling, like,
saṁnidhāna n. juxtaposition, nearness,
saṁnidhāne 7/s in the vicinity of,
saṁnihita 1146/3 mfn deposited together or near, contiguous, proximate, present, close, near, at hand, upon, proximate, well-seated,
saṁniviṣṭa 1147/2 mfn. seated down together with,
saṁniyamya ind. controlling, subduing, having subdued, gerund *saṁ-ni-√yam* 1147/1

saṁnyāsa 1148/1 thrown down, laid aside, relinquished, renunciation of the world, profession of asceticism
saṁnyasta 1148/1 ppp. renounced, abandoned, given up
saṁnyasya relinquishing, renouncing gerund *sam ni √as*
saṁnyāsa 1148/1 m. putting or throwing down, laying aside, resignation, renunciation of the world, giving up the body, sudden death
saṁnyāsin mfn 1148/1 laying aside, giving up, m. one who abandons..
sampad 1172/1 f. benefit, blessing, good fortune, prosperity,
sampada 1172/1 mfn furnished with,
sampādana mfn procuring, bestowing, accomplishing, carrying out, n. the act of procuring/bestowing, bringing about, carrying out, making, effecting, preparing, putting in order,
saṁpadyate 1171/3 turns out well, becomes full or complete, succeeds, prospers
saṁpanna 1172/1 mfn furnished with, endowed with, perfect, accomplished, excellent,
sampanna mfn fallen or turned out well,accomplished or endowed with
samparka 1173/2 m. mixing together, mixture, conjunction, union, association, touch,
saṁpaśyan seeing, observing pres.part.
sampat 1172/1 (in comp. for *sampad),* benefit, blessing, success, prosperity,
saṁpatti f. prosperity, welfare, good fortune, success, turning out well, concord, properties
– two types available
sāmānya saṁpatti
worldly properties
daivī saṁpatti divine properties
sampluta 1177/2 mfn. flowed or streamed together, flooded with water
sampra√dā 1175/1 to give completely up or deliver wholly over, surrender,

hand down by tradition, teach, impart,
-*na* the act of giving or handing over completely, presenting, bestowing, (in gram.) the idea expressed by the dative case, the recipient to which the agent causes anything to be given
saṁprakīrtita 1173/3 mfn mentioned, designated, called, declared
saṁprāpta mfn 1177/1 well reached or attained, become, one who has become
sāmprata mfn seasonable, proper, correct, L. mfn of now, present, (*am*) ind. at present, now,
samprati ind. directly opposite, close in front of (2nd), rightly, in the right way, at the right time, exactly, just, now, at this moment, at present, immediately or at once (with impf.),
sampratti 1174/2 ind. directly over-against or opposite, rightly, in the right way, at the right time, exactly, just, at this time, now, immediately, at once
saṁpravṛtta 1176/2 mfn. gone forward, proceeded, arisen, existent, present, near at hand, commenced, passed, gone by
saṁpravṛtti f. coming forth, appearance, occurrence
saṁprekṣya ind. having perceived, seen, looking at, focusing the eyes on, gerund *sam pra* √*īkṣ*
sampujya 1173/1 to salute deferentially, honour greatly, revere, part. greatly honouring or respecting,
sampūrṇa mfn complete,
samrāj m. a universal or supreme ruler, a sovereign lord, paramount sovereign,
samṛddha mfn prosperous, prospering, accomplished, succeeded, flourishing, fortunate, full-grown (trees), complete, whole, entire, abundantly endowed with, rich,
saṁṛddhavega mfnincreased haste, great speed,
śaṁsati 1043/3 √*śaṁs* recites, repeats, praises, extols,
saṁsakta 1118/3 mfn sticking fast, occupied with, intent upon, devoted to, given to mundane pleasures, enamoured,
saṁsaṅga m. connection, conjunction,
samsāra 1119/3 transmigration, worldly illusion(s), circuit of mundane existence,
saṁsāra repeating births in various bodies
samsāravān perf.act. part. worldly
saṁsarga 1119/3 mfn commingling, combining, m. mixture or union together, blending, conjunction, connection, contact, association, society, sexual union
saṁsārin 1119/3 m. a living or sentient being, animal, creature, man,
saṁśaya 1117/3 m. lying down to sleep, uncertainty, doubt in or of, irresolution, hesitation, danger, a doubtful matter, difficulty, danger, risk,
saṁ-siddha 1119/2 mfn. fully or thoroughly performed or accomplished, satisfied, contented, one who has attained beatitude
saṁ-siddhi f. complete accomplishment or fulfilment, perfect state, beatitude, the last consequence or result
saṁśita sharpened, ready, rigid (as a vow), -*vrata* firmly adhering to a vow or obligation, honest, virtuous
saṁskāra 1120/2 impression on the mind of acts done in a former state of existence, a mental creation or conformation of the mind, (such as that of the external world, regarded by it as real), latent impressions,
saṁskṛta 1120/3 mfn put together, constructed, perfected, purified, refined, m. a word formed according to accurate rules, a learned man, sanskrit
saṁsmaraṇa 1122/2 n. the act of remembering, recollecting
saṁsmṛtya ind. remembering, having remembered,
saṁspardhā f. emulation, rivalry, jealousy,

saṁsparśa 1122/1 m. close or mutual contact, touch, conjunction, perception, sense
saṁsparśaja mfn born of contact or touch
saṁsṛti 1119/3 passage through successive states of existence/transmigration
saṁstabhya ind. ind. having supported or strengthened or encouraged, having supported or composed the mind firmly (in affliction), having taken heart or courage, together sustaining, upholding,
saṁstava 1121/1 m. praise, commendation
saṁstha mfn standing together, existing,
saṁsthā f. staying or abiding with, shape, form, manifestation, appearance, established order, state, standard, rule, direction, quality, property, nature, conclusion, completion, a complete liturgical course,
-gāra m.n. a meeting house,
-japa m. a closing prayer,
saṁsthāna mfn standing together, like, resembling, n.f. staying or abiding in, (comp.), standing still or firm (in battle), being, existence, life, strict adherence or obedience to, abode, dwelling place, shape, form, appearance, beauty, splendour, nature, state, condition, an aggregate, whole, totality, conclusion, end, death,
-vat mfn being, existing, having various forms,
saṁsthāpana 1121/3 n. fixing, setting up. establishment
saṁtāpa 1142/2 m. distress, torment, agony
saṁtarati 1142/3 cross or traverse together, bring safely over, rescue, save
saṁtata mfn stretched or extended along, spread over, covered, continual, perpetual, uninterrupted,
saṁtuṣṭa mfn quite satisfied or contented, well pleased or delighted with
samuddhartā f. deliverer, uplifter
samuddhartṛ mfn deliverer, uplifter, m. an uptearer, extirpator,
samudra 1166/3 m. the sea, ocean, mfn stamped, sealed, marked,
samudyata 1168/2 part. raised up, lifted up, offered, presented,
samupāśrita 1170/1 mfn leaning against, one who has recourse to(2nd), supported by, resting on, resorted to
samrāḍ 1181/3 in comp. for *samrāj* 1181/3 a universal or supreme ruler
samudbodha becoming consciousness
samudbhava 1168/2 existence, production, origin, coming to life again, revival, cause of being
samudraḥ ocean
sam-udyama 1168/2 m. lifting up, raising, setting about, readiness to or for
samudyata 1168/2 part. raised up, lifted up, offered, presented, in raising, arising, arose
samūha 1170/3 m. assemblage, multitude, aggregate, sum, totality,
samūha sweep together, gather up 2/s/impv *sam* √*ūh*
samupasthita mfn approaching, coming near, standing near, approximated,
samutpanna mfn arisen, sprung up together, produced, occurred, happened, taking place,
samuttha 1166/1 mfn. rising up, risen, appearing, derived from
saṁvāda 1114/2 m. speaking together, conversation, dialogue,
saṁvardhita mfn brought to complete growth, brought up, reared, raised, cherished,
sāṁvatsara mfn yearly, annual, perennial, m. an astrologer, almanac-maker, a lunar month, black rice,
saṁveṣṭita mfn surrounded by
saṁ√*vṛt* 1116/2 to come together, grow, become, turn or go towards,
saṁvṛtta 1116/3 mfn arrived, fulfilled, become,
saṁvigna mfn starting back, recoiling

sāmya 1207/2 n. equality, evenness, equilibrium, likeness, sameness
samyag in comp for *samyañc* 1181/2 mfn. going along with or together,

turned together or in one direction, combined, united, entire, whole, complete,

samyagājñā m. right understanding,

samyag-jñāna 1181/3 n. real knowledge G279 One of the 3 jewels of Jainism, a specialized knowledge of the essence of the Self and not-Self. It is without any defects and beyond all doubt.

samyak ind. correctly, in one or the same direction, in the same way, at the same time, together, (with √*sthā*)in one line, straight, completely, wholly

saṁ-yama 1112/1 m. holding together, restraint, control, esp. control of the senses, self-control

saṁyama 1112/1 m. holding together, restraint, control of the senses, self-control, concentration of mind (comprising performance of *dhāraṇā, dhyāna,* and *samādhi*), effort, exertion,

saṁ-yamin 1112/1 mfn. one who subdues his passions, self-controlled

samyañc 1181/2 going along with or together, proper, true, right

saṁ√*yat* 1111/3 unite, meet together

saṁyata 1111/3 mfn. held together, held in, self-contained, self-controlled, subdued, restrained

śāmyate is extinguished

śāmyati 1053/3 1/s/pres/indic/act. to be quiet, calm, rested, content, satisfied, to cease or be extinguished, is still,

saṁyāti meets with encounters 1/s/pres/indic/act *sam* √*yā*

saṁyoga 1112/2 m. conjunction, combination, connection, union or absorption with or in, contact (in phil.) direct material contact, (in gram.) , a conjunct consonant, (combination of 2 or more consonants), dependence of one case on another, total amount, sum, agreement of opinion, being engaged in,

saṁyuga n. union, conjunction, conflict, war

san in comp. for *sat,*

sana mfn old, ancient,

√*san* to gain, acquire, possess, enjoy, *sanati, sanate sanoti* or *sanute*

śanais 1051/3 mfn moving slowly ind. quietly, softly, gently

śanaiḥ śanaiḥ little by little, gently

śanakais ind. quietly, gently, slowly,

sanātana 1141/1 mfn eternal, perpetual, permanent, ancient

saṁcita .." that which has been collected (in the *citta)* over a long time." HH G.281 unripe actions
the store of inactivated *saṁskāra* in the causal body

sandhi or *saṁdhi 1144/3* mfn. containing a conjunction or transition from one to the other, junction, connection, combination, union with, totality, the whole essence, euphonic junction of final and initial letters in grammar, place or point of connection or contact

sandhim etya getting connection

sāndra mfn thick, dense, oily, intense,

saṅga 1132/3 m. sticking, clinging to, association with or attachment to, contact, 'the company or environment in which he would find himself and with which he would work' HH76

saṅgati 1128/2 f. coming together, connection with, contacting together, connection with, contacting,

saṅgavarjita mfn free from attachment,

śani m. planet Saturn,

sanīḍa m. proximity,

sañjā f. special names, classifications

sañjayati √*sañj* 1132/3 causes attachment 1/s/pres/caus.

śaṅka 1047/1 m. doubt, fear, hesitation,

śaṅkā 1047/1 f. fear, doubt, care, alarm, apprehension, fear, distrust, suspicion of, doubt, uncertainty, hesitation

saṅkalpa 1126/3 m. conception, idea, or notion, formed in the heart or mind, will, purpose, resolution, belief (by *Manas)*

śaṅkara or *śaṁkara* 'causing prosperity, auspicious, beneficent', great philosopher, re-established the vedic tradition, first *śaṅkarācārya,* a name for *Śiva,*

śaṅkarācārya a fully realized man appointed to the highest position as spiritual leader in the tradition of *advaita vedanta* established by *śaṅkara.* There are 4 such positions in Indiain the north, south east and west,

śaṅkha 1047/2 m.n.a conch shell or horn,

saṅkoca m. contraction, shrinking together, diminution, humbling one's self, shyness, crouching down,

śaṅku m. a peg, nail, spike, pillar, post, arrow,

sannyāsa m. giving up the body, complete renunciation, monkhood, profession of ascetism, sudden death,complete renunciation

sannyāsin 1148/1 m. laying aside, giving up, one who abandons. the fourth stage of life – complete renunciation as a wandering mendicant

śānta 1064/2 mfn tranquil, calm, peaceful, free from passions,

śāntadhīḥ 1/s/m serene-minded

santāna m. offspring, family, n. child,

śāntānanda the bliss of tranquillity, the bliss of peace

śāntamanas mfn composed in mind

śāntasaṁkalpaḥ he whose mind is freed (from anxiety, distraction etc.)

santi they (many) are, form of verb *as*

śānti 1064/3 f. peace, tranquillity, quietness of mind, absence of passion, alleviation of evil or pain, indifference to objects of pleasure or pain, propitiatory rites for averting evil or calamity i.e offering water for washing feet, cessation, abatement, extinction, peace, welfare, prosperity, good fortune, happiness, bliss,

santoṣa m. contentment

santyaj saṁ √tyaj to relinquish altogether, totally surrender,

sānu n.m. top, surface, ridge, back,

sānurāgā 1203/1 f. feeling or betraying passion, affectionate, enamoured of, passionate

sapadi ind. at the same instant, on the spot, at once, immediately, quickly,

śāpa m. a curse

śāpatha m. an oath, curse,

śapati he curses,

saphala mfn together with fruits, fruitful, not emasculated, having good results, productive, successful,

sāphalya n. successful, fruitfulness, success

śapta mfn cursed

saptama seventh

saptan seven

śara m. arrow

sāra m. substance, pith, course, motion, the substance, essence, heart or essential part of anything,

śarad f. autumn,

śārada mfn autumn, new, shy, diffident, modest, recent, mature, m. cloud, year, autumnal sunshine, n. fruit,

sarala mfn straight (not crooked), right, correct, upright, sincere, candid, honest, artless, simple, outstretched,

sārameya m. descendant of the bitch, dog, *Saramā,* name of certain dogs,

śaraṇa 1057/1 mfn. protecting, guarding, defending, n. place of shelter, refuge,

saraṇi f. a road, path, way,

saras n. a lake, pond, pool, tank, a trough, pail, water,

sarasa 1183/3 containing sap, moist, wet, tasty, elegant, bodies of water,

śarāsata n. a bow (for arrows),

sārathi m. a charioteer, coachman, leader, a helper, assistant, the ocean,

sarasvatī consort of Brahmā, the power of

wisdom, 1182/2 the mother of goddesses, bestower of vitality, renown and wealth, connected with speech, eloquence, learning and wisdom, name of a sacred river

śaravya mfn capable of wounding, f. an arrowshot, shower of arrows, an arrow, missile, arrow personified, n. a target, aim,

sārdham ind. jointly, together, along with,

śārdūla m. tiger, ifc. the best of ...

sarga 1183/3 m. letting go, voiding, primary creation, chapter, book, begetting, a created being, a creature,

śarīra 1057/3 n. the body, that which perishes, the bodily frame,

sarit f. a river, stream, a thread, string,

śarita f. praise,

śarkarā 1058/2 1/s ground or candied sugar, brown sugar,

śarman 1058/2 shelter, refuge

sarpa 1184/1 m. a snake,

sarpis n. clarified butter, (warm & fluid or cold and hard) , so not different from *ghṛta* 'ghee'

sārtha mfn having an object, or business, attained its object, successful (as a request), having property, wealthy, significant, important, useful, m. a caravan of traders or pilgrims, a troop, collection of men,

śaru f.a missile, an arrow or spear,

sarva inflected as a pronoun,
1184/3 adj. mfn whole, entire, all, every, (m.s. everyone, pl. all, n.s. everything), sometimes strengthened by *viśva*, of all sorts,, manifold, various, different, with negation- not any, no, none, not everyone, not everything, with another adjective or in comp. altogether, wholly, completely, in all parts, everywhere,
(am) ind. completely,

sarvabhāva 1186/2 m. whole being or nature, whole heart or soul, complete satisfaction, all objects, with one's whole soul,

sarvabhūta 1186/2 mfn being everywhere, n. all beings, m.n. the maker or cause of all things or beings,

sarvabhūtahite in the welfare of all beings

sarvabhūtastha 1186/3 mfn. present in all elements or beings

sarvabhūteṣu in all beings 7/pl/n

sarvadā ind. always, at all times, ever

sarvadṛś 1185/3 all seeing, all organs of senses

sarvadevata mfn relating to all the deities, *sarvadevatā* 1/pl/m all the gods,

sarvagata 1185/1 of universal diffusion, omnipresent, all going, n. universal diffusion, omnipresence,

sarvahara mfn appropriating everything, inheriting all of a person's property,

sarvaiśvarya 1189/1 n. the sovereignty of every one, sovereignty over all

sarvam ind. completely,

sarvanāman words which can be applied to all i.e. pronouns. e.g. me, mine, you, they, which, who

sarvārambha 1188/3 m. entire energy in the beginning of a work, *-eṣu* 7/pl fully dedicated at the beginning of all actions,

śarvarī f. the star-spangled night, twilight,

sarvārtha m. all objects, all aims, all matters

sarvaśaḥ altogether, wholly, entirely, on all sides, in all respects, adv.

sarvata 1189/1 mfn all-sided, on all sides, everywhere,

sarvatas ind. from all sides, in every direction, everywhere, around, entirely, completely, thoroughly,

sarvathā 1189/2 ind. however, in whatever way, in every way, in every respect, by all means, altogether, entirely

sarvatra ind. 189/2 at all times, always, everywhere

sarvatraga mfn everywhere going, omnipresent

sarvaveda mfn having all knowledge

sarvavedas mfn having complete property

m. one who gives away all his property to the priests after a sacrifice,

sarvavedasa accompanied by a gift of all one's goods (as a sacrifice)

sarve all 1/pl/m

sarveṣu 7/pl/n in all

sarveśvara 1188/3 m. the Lord of all, a universal monarch,

ṣaṣ six,

sasa mfn sleeping, m. herbs, grass, corn,

śaśaḥ / śaśakaḥ rabbit, hare,

śaśaka m. hare, rabbit,

śāsana 1068/3 mfn punishment, correction, chastisement, dominion, rule, order, command, edict, teaching, instruction, discipline

saśara 1191/3 mfn. furnished with an arrow, together with an arrow

saśarīra 1191/3 m. with the body, embodied

śaśi 'that which contains the rabbit' i.e. the moon

ṣaṣṭha mfn the sixth, a sixth, the sixth part,

śastra n. weapon, axe, knife, n. invocation, praise(applying to any recited verses – as opposed to sung verses), reciting, recitation,

śāstra 1069/1 n. an order, command, precept, rule, teaching, instruction, direction, advice, good counsel, scripture, any instrument of teaching, any sacred book or composition of divine authority, a body of teaching, scripture, science, what is taught,

śastrabhṛt m. weapon-bearing

śāstrakṛpā the grace of scripture

śastra-saṁpāta mfn clash of weapons

śāstravidhi 1069/2 m. scriptural injunction

sasmitam ind. with a smile, smilingly

śaśvat 1060/3 perpetual, endless

śāśvata 1068/3 mfn. eternal, constant perpetual, all, (*am*) for evermore, eternally

śāśvatam ind. for evermore, eternally

śāśvatva n. constancy, eternity

sasya n. m. corn grain, fruit, a crop of corn

śasya as above

sat 1134/2 present part. of 1. √*as* being, existing, occurring, happening, being present, real, actual, true, good, right, beautiful, wise, venerable, honest, "that which exists in truth" HH

śata a hundred, any large number,

śāta mfn sharpened, whetted, sharp,

sat sat true existence

śata 1048/3 n. a hundred

satas of the real, of the true, of the existent, pres.part √*as* 6/s/n ind. equally, like,

satata 1138/1 mfn. constant, perpetual, (*am*) ind. constantly, ever, always

śatāyuṣaḥ an age or a life of a hundred years 1050/3

satī 1. f. (fem of *sat*) her ladyship, your ladyship, a good and virtuous or faithful wife, n. 1134/2 being, existing, being present,

satkāra 1134/2 m. kind treatment, honour, favour, reverence

śaṭha 1048/2 mfn. false, deceitful, m. a cheat, rogue

ṣaṭpāda m. a bee,

satpuruṣa 1134/3 m. a good or wise man, 'man of truth: usually presumed as subtle form' HH

śatru 1051/1 m. an enemy, foe, rival, a victorious opponent,

śatrughna Śatrughna

satsaṅga 1134/3 m. intercourse or association with the good, holy company, a meeting of the wise or pious, 'good company' HH, see *saṅga*

sattā f. existence, being, goodness,

sattva 1135/2 being, existence, entity, reality, true essence, nature, disposition of mind, spiritual essence, life, essence, the quality of purity or goodness, regarded as the highest of the three *guṇā* because it renders a person true, honest, wise and a thing pure and clean, material or elementary substance.

the qualities of purity, intelligence and brightness

sattvabuddhimāna sattva 1135/2 the highest of the 3 *guṇā*, disposition of mind, the quality of purity or goodness, renders a person true, *buddhi* 733/3 intelligence, reason, the discriminative faculty, a person of pure reason

sattvaguṇa one of the three *guṇā*

sattvāpatti the fourth step of realisation, natural growth of *sattva* in being, mind and body

satvaram ind. quickly

sattvasaṁśuddhi 1135/2 f. purity of nature or disposition, purity of mind or heart

sāttvika 1200/1 mfn. spirited, vigorous, energetic, relating to or endowed with the quality *sattva* i.e. 'purity' or 'goodness', pure, true, honest, virtuous, good, internal, caused by internal feeling or sentiment, natural, not artificial, unaffected (style),

satyā 1135/3 f. speaking the truth, sincerity, truthful

satya 1135/3 mf(*ā*) n. true, real, actual, honest, good, (*am*) n. truth, reality *sat* = existence + termination *ya* = pertaining to, pertaining to true existence = truth

satyadharma 1136/1 the law of truth, eternal truth,

satyam 1135/3 truth, reality, truthfulness in speech, see above, unfailing truthfulness of speech, sincerity, 'the Truth, that which really exists. To perceive that which really exists, to conceive the truth as it ought to exist and speak the truth as it does and has existed in the mind is the aspect of human law, *dharma*. To deviate from the truth is against the law.

satyatā f. reality, truth, love of truth,veracity

satyatas ind. in truth, really, truly

satya yuga the golden age, 1,728,000 years

savikalpa 1190/3 mfn possessing variety or admitting of distinctions, differentiated, admitting of an alternative or option or doubt

Saubhadra son of *Subhadrā*

saubhāgya n. welfare, good luck, success, prosperity, happiness, beauty, charm, grace, affection,

śauca n. cleanliness, ' the act of purification, bodily, intellectually and emotionally. '... not to purify body, mind and heart is against the law,'

śaucika m. cleanser, cleaner,

saucika ' one who lives by his needle' m. a tailor

Saumadattis a *Kaurava* warrior 1/s/m son of *Somadatta*

saumya 1254/1 mfn relating to soma placid, gentle, mild, auspicious, happy, cheerful

śaunaka a famous householder,

saunika m. a butcher, a hunter,

śaurya 1093/2 n. heroism, valour, prowess, might

śava m.n. a corpse, dead body, n. water

śāva m. the young of an animal, mfn relating to a dead body, dead, tawny coloured, n. defilement by corpse contact or death of a relation,

sāvadhāna mfn attentive, heedful, careful, intent upon doing anything, (*am*) ind. attentively, carefully,

śāvaka m the young of an animal,

savayas mfn of like strength or age, m. comrade,

savijñāna 1190/3 mfn. endowed with right understanding, with discrimination

savikāra 1190/3 with its developments or derivatives, undergoing or with modification or transformation,

savitṛ m. a stimulator, rouser, vivifier, 'the divine influence and vivifying power of the sun', name of a sun-deity, or 'lord of all creatures'

savya mfn left, left hand, m. left arm or hand,

savyasācin 1191/3 voc. o ambidextrous archer (Arjuna), ambidextrous,

savyatha mfn distressed, sorrowful,

śaya 1055/3 mfn abiding, resting, sleeping, of cool temperament, m. sleep, sleeping, a bed, couch, a snake, lizard, abuse, the hand,

sāya n. the close of day, evening, (*am*) ind. in the evening, at eventide, m. a missile, arrow, n. unloosing, unyoking, turning in, going to rest,

sāyaka m. a missile, arrow, sword,

śayālu mfn sleepy, sluggish, slothful, m. a dog, jackal, the boa snake,

śayana mfn lying down, resting, sleeping, n. a bed, the act of lying down, resting, sleeping,

śayāna mfn lying down, resting, sleeping,

śayita sleeping, asleep

śayitā will sleep 1/s/peri.fut.

śayyā f. bed, couch, mfn sleep, refuge,

śekhara m. crest, crown, diadem, chaplet,

sena 1246/2 n. the body, mfn dependent on another, in comp. for *senā,*

senā f. army, missile, dart, armament,

senānī m. a general, chief,

sendriya 1246/3 possessed of manly vigour or potency together with the organs of sense, having sense organs

śeṣa m. remainder, leavings, residue,

śete 1077/1 √ *śī* lies down, falls asleep 1/s/pres/indic/mid sleeps

setu m. a bridge, causeway,

√*śev* 1088/3 Cl 1 A *śevate* to worship, serve,

√*sev* 1247/1 Cl 1 A *sevate (ti),* to attend upon, honour, obey, to dwell or stay near or in, to remain or stay at, live in, frequent,

sevā 1247/1 f. going or resorting to, service, attendance on, worship, homage, reverence, devotion to

sevakaḥ m. attendant, servant, mfn dwelling in, inhabiting, practising, using, employing, revering, worshipping,

sevate he/she serves, honours, obeys

sevin mfn frequenting, inhabiting, going or resorting to, attending on, serving

sevita 1247/2 mfn. dwelt in, visited, frequented, followed

śibikā f. a palanquin, litter,

śibira n. a royal camp or tent, any tent,

sīdanti they sit √*2. sad* 1138/2 to sit 1/pl/pres/indic/act

siddha 1215/1 2. mfn. accomplished, fulfilled, one who has attained his object, endowed with supernatural faculties, sacred, holy, divine, illustrious

siddhānta m. established end, final end or aim or purpose, demonstrated conclusion, settled doctrine, received or admitted truth, any established scientific text,

siddhi 1216/2 f. complete attainment, fulfilment, perfection, 'mastery or independence , realization of the Self', HH, supernatural faculties

śīghra 1077/3 mfn quick, speedy, rapid

śīghram ind. quickly, rapidly, fast,

śīkara m. spray, drizzle, mist, a fine drop

sikatāḥ f.pl. sand,

śikhā f. tuft or braid of hair, top, peak,

śikhara mfn peaked, m.n. peak, summit,

śikhari(n) 1070/3 m. a peaked mountain, any mountain, mfn. pointed, peaked

śikhin m. peacock, a cock, bull, horse,

śikṣā pronunciation (one of the *vedāṅgas*), art, teaching,

śilā rock or large stone,

śīla 1079/1 n. habit, custom, usage, natural or acquired way of living or acting, practice, conduct, nature, disposition, tendency, character,

śilpa 1073/3 n. decoration, ornament, artistic work, variegated or diversified appearance, the art of variegating, skill in any art or craft or work of art, ingenuity, mfn variegated,

śilpin m.artist, craftsman, artisan,

sima mfn whole, all, every, entire,

sīman m. a hair parting, n. a boundary, border, limit, f. a ridge marking the boundary of a field or village, a bank, shore, the horizon,

siṁha m. lion, the powerful one, a lion, a hero or eminent person,

sindhu m.f. a river, stream, esp. the Indus, m. flood, waters, ocean, sea,
sirā a stream, water, a nerve, vein, artery, tendon, a bucket
sīra m.n. a plough, m. an ox for ploughing, draught-ox, the sun,
śiras 1072/2 n. the head, skull, peak, chief, leader, head, foremost,
śīrṣa n. the head, skull, upper part, tip,
śiśira mfn cold, chilly, frigid, m.n. dew, hoarfrost, the cold season,
śiṣṭa 1076/3 1. left, remaining, residual, remains, 2. taught, directed, ordered, disciplined, cultured, educated, m. a learned or well-educated or wise man, a chief, counsellor,
śiśu m. young, child,
śiṣya m. to be taught, scholar, student
śīta mfn cold, cool, chilly, frigid, dull, apathetic, sluggish, indolent,
sita mfn bound, tied, fettered, white, pale, bright, light, pure, m. white, Venus (planet), sugar, moonlight, a handsome woman, n. silver, sandal, a radish,
sitā f. sugar,
sītā *Sītā*, a princess, wife of *Rāma*, fabled to have sprung from a furrow, 1218/2 f. a furrow, the track or line of a ploughshare
śītala mfn cold, cool, cooling, shivering, frosty, cold i.e. free from passion, f.*(ā)* free from passion, cool,
śithila mfn loose, flaccid, unsteady,
Śivaḥ 1074/1 mfn. auspicious, propitious, benign, fortunate, kind, benevolent, friendly, harmonious, conscious, true, m. happiness, welfare, liberation, final emancipation, the Auspicious one, the dissolver of creation, destroyer
Skanda god of war,
skandha m. shoulder, tree-trunk, a king, prince, sage, heron, a branch, creeper,
ślāghya mfn honourable, to be praised,
ślakṣṇa mfn slippery, smooth,
ślatha mfn loose, relaxed, flaccid, weak,
śleṣman m. phlegm,
śloka m. (thing heard) i.e. sound, fame, a verse esp. the '*anustubh*' a classic *śloka* form (stanza) in which many stories or scriptures are written,
sma or *smā, ṣma, ṣmā* 1271/2 ind. indicates the past in a present tense sentence , gives a past sense,
sma 1271/2 ind. indeed, certainly
smaḥ we (pl) are
smaran mfn remembering, thinking of
smaraṇa 1272/1 n. the act of remembering or calling to mind, remembrance, reminiscence, recollection of (gen. or comp.), memory, handing down by memory, tradition, traditional teaching or record or precept, mental recitation (of the name of a deity)
smarati 1271/3 he remembers, thinks of 1/s/pres/act/indic.
√*smṛ* to remember, think of, be mindful of,
śmaśāna n. the place for burning the corpses and for burying the bones, cemetery,
śmaśru n. beard, moustache, beard-hairs,
smera mfn smiling, friendly, expanded, evident, proud, abounding in, full of, m. a smile, laugh,
smita mfn smiled, smiling, expanded, blossomed, n. a smile, gentle laugh,
smṛta 1272/2 mfn. remembered, recollected, referred to, called to mind, thought of, handed down, taught, prescribed, enjoined by *smṛti* or traditional law
smṛti f. memory, "all that was heard and retained in memory is *smṛti* when recorded" HH , what has been remembered, the teaching of great sages, secondary to *śrūti*, includes Laws of *Manu* etc.
snāna n. bath
snāyu f.n. any sinew or ligament in a

human or animal body, tendon, muscle, nerve, vein, the string of a bow,

sneha 1267/2 m. n. oiliness, viscidity, tenderness, attachment to, affection, oil, grease, fat,

snehana 1267/3 mfn anointing, lubricating, feeling, affection, n. unction, lubrication, rubbing or smearing with, being or becoming oily, feeling, affection

snigdha 1267/2 mfn oily, sticky, viscous, glossy, resplendent

snihyati (+7th) falls in love, he loves

so'ham *saḥ* pron. 1/s he + *aham* pron. 1/s I (am) he

śobha 1092/1 mfn bright, brilliant, handsome, m. lustre, name of a class of gods, √*śubh*
f. (*ā*) splendour, brilliance, lustre,

śobhana mfn beautiful, brilliant, splendid, excellent, glorious, magnificent, propitious, auspicious, virtuous, moral, correct, right,
ifc, superior to or better than,
f. (*ā*) a beautiful woman,
n. the act of adorning, causing to look beautiful, anything propitious or auspicious, welfare, prosperity,

śobhate √*śubh* 1083/1 to beautify, embellish, 1/s/pres/indic/mid he adorns, 1083/1 to shine, be bright, or splendid, 1/s/pres/indic/mid shines gloriously,

śocati 1081/1 root *śuc* to grieve, suffer, 1/s/p/a he or she regrets or grieves,

śocitum infinitive to mourn, to grieve

sodara m. brother, (*ī*) f. sister

ṣoḍaśan sixteen,

soḍhum to endure, bear, tolerate, infin. √*sah* 1192/3

śoka 1091/1 mfn. burning, hot, m. sorrow, grief, anguish, pain

śokātiga mfn having crossed over sorrow, free from mental unhappiness, overcoming sorrow,

soma m. a drink of the gods, the moon,

somapā 1250/1mfn. soma-drinker,

somavāra Monday, *soma* 1249/3 juice, extract from the *soma* plant, one of the most important *Vedic* gods to whom many hymns were dedicated, identified with the moon or the god of the moon, the moon or moon-god.

śoṇita n. blood,

sopāna n. staircase, ladder,

śoṣa 1092/2 mfn. drying up

śoṣayati causes to dry up, wither 1/s/pres/indic/caus/act √*śuṣ*

spanda m. activity, vibration, motion,

spardhā 1268/2 mfn emulous, envious f. emulation, rivalry, envy,

sparśa mfn touching, m. sense of touch, contact, touching

spaṣṭa mfn clearly perceived or discerned, distinct, clear, evident, plain, real,

sphāra mfn extensive, wide, large, great, abundant, violent, strong, m. a shock, slap, bang,

sphāṭika m. a drop of water, n. crystal,

sphīta mfn swollen, enlarged, thriving, prosperous, successful, much abundant, heavy (with rain, a cloud), dense (as smoke),

sphoṭa ..a point which expands and in its expansion is its activity. This expansion is very fast, an explosion in consciousness. A *sphoṭa* is a sound, a creative desire, a single particle of consciousness, and it holds the cause, the action and its effects. It also holds the law governing the movement of cause, through action into effect. This is the first step in speech when the forces of *parā* are gathered to a point for action. L.M.

sphuliṅga m. a spark,

sphuraṇa 1271/1 springing or breaking forth, expansion, manifestation

sphurati 1270/3 starts into view, becomes evident, appears,

spṛhā 1269/3 f. eager desire, longing

spṛśan mfn touching

spṛśati he touches,

sphūrti 1271/1 breaking forth visibly,

manifestation.

sphuṭa mfn open, opened, expanded, blossomed, evident, manifest, clear,

śrad-dadhāna 1095/3mfn. having faith, trustful, full of faith

śraddhā 1095/3 f. to have faith, faithfulness,

śrāddham n. funeral rites, last rites,

śraddhāmaya mfn made of faith, full of faith

śraddhāvat mfn assenting, consenting,

śraddhāvirahita mfn devoid of faith, disbelieving,

śraddhayānvita imbued with faith

śraddhayā with faith

anvitāḥ 47/2 endowed with

sraj mfn turning, twisting, winding, f. a wreath of flowers, garland,

śrama m. toil, effort,

śramaṇa mfn making effort or exertion, toiling, labouring, one who performs acts of mortification or austerity, an ascetic, monk, devotee, religious mendicant, a Buddhist monk or mendicant, also applied to a Jain mendicant now more commonly called Yati,

sraṁsate it falls, it drops 1/s/pres/indic/mid √*sraṁs*

śrānta mfn exhausted, wearied,

sraṣṭṛ m. a creator, the Supreme Creator, the creator of the universe, mfn loosened, relaxed, hanging down, one who emits, discharges,

śrauta 1103/2 mfn relating to the ear or hearing, to be heard, audible, relating to sacred tradition,

śravaṇa 1096/3 n. the act of hearing, that which is heard, acquiring knowledge by hearing the truth. The first stage of reflection. (see *mananam, nididhyāsanam*), m. ear,

srāvaṇa m. a month (=July-August),

śreṣṭa mfn classic,

śreṣṭhas best, most splendid, most excellent 1/s/m superlative

śreyas mfn (comparative) better, preferable, n. the higher good, the supreme good, comparative, prosperity

śṛgāla m. a jackal or fox, a rogue, cheat,

śrī 1098/2 to burn, flame, diffuse light, f. diffusing light or radiance, light, lustre, radiance, splendour, glory, high rank, majesty, royal dignity, honorific prefix – sacred, holy, respectful title,
mfn mixing, mingling, cooking,

śrībhagavān the Blessed Lord, the Blessed One

śrī kṛṣṇa Great Lord, (re-incarnation of Viṣṇu)

śrīmad bhāgavatam a famous *pūrāṇa* – the life and exploits of *Kṛṣṇa*

śrīmān m. mister, sir,

śrīmat 1100/2 mfn splendid, glorious

śrita 1098/2 clinging or attached to , gone to, approached, served, part. approaching

sṛjāmi √*sṛj* 1245/1 to let go or fly, emit, pour forth, emit from oneself, create, produce, I create, 3/s/pres/indic/act

sṛjati he sheds,

sṛṅga n. the horn of an animal, a tusk, a peak, crag, summit,

sṛṅgāra m. love, sexual passion or desire,

sṛṅkā f. necklace

sṛṅkala m. a chain,

sṛṅkhala m. a chain, a young camel,

śṛṇu listen! 2/s/impv

śṛnvan hearing pres/act/part 1/s/m

śṛṇoti 1100/3 1/s/pres/indic/act hears,

śṛṇu listen, hear 2/s/impv.

śṛṇuta listen! pl. impv.

śṛṇute hear! 1100/3

śṛṇuyāt he should hear/listen 1/s/opt/act √*śru*

śṛṇvan pres/act/part. hearing

śromata n. celebrity, renown, glory,

śroṣyati he will hear, listen,

śrotas n. the ear

srotas n. the current or bed of a river, a river, stream, torrent, water,

śrotavya to be heard or listened to, audible, worth hearing, n. the moment for hearing, 'it must be heard'fut.part.

śrotṛ one who hears, hearing, a hearer

śrotra n. the organ of hearing, ear, the act of hearing or listening to, comprehending the Veda or sacred knowledge

śrotriya 1103/1 mfn learned in the Veda, conversant with sacred knowledge, docile, modest, well-behaved, m. a Brāhman versed in the Veda, theologian, divine,

śroṣyasi you will hear or listen 2/s/fut/act

śrotavyasya of the to-be-heard, with that which is to be heard, 6/s/m gerundive

srotas 1274/3 a river-bed, a river, stream

śrotriya 1103/1 learned in the Veda, conversant with sacred knowledge,

sṛṣṭa 1245/2 mfn let go, discharged, thrown etc. given up, abandoned, brought forth, produced, created, provided, filled or covered with, engrossed by, intent upon (3rd),

sṛṣṭi 1245/2 f. letting go, letting loose, emission, production, procreation, creation, the creation of the world, nature, natural property or disposition, liberality, Creation, presided over by Brahmā

sṛṣṭvā having created, having sent forth, having let go,

sṛta 1244/3 mfn. running, going, gone, passed away

sṛti 1245/1 f. a road, path, wandering, transmigration, aiming at,

√*śru* 1100/3 cl5 to hear, listen or attend to, study, learn, be attentive, obey

śruta mfn heard, listened to, been heard, n. oral tradition, sacred knowledge, anything heard from the teacher, that which is learned, learning,

śrutasya of the heard, of that which has been heard, 6/s/m ppp.

śrutavān heard, one who has heard

śruti f.'verbal testimony' HH, what has been heard, the *veda*, - word of the Lord, hearing, listening, the ear, organ or power of hearing, that which is heard or perceived with the ear, sacred knowledge orally transmitted from generation to generation, the Veda, as eternally heard by certain holy sages thus differing from smṛti (remembered and handed down in writing) learning, scholarship,

śrutimat having ears, having hearing, possessed of knowledge, learned, having the veda as source or authority,

śrutvā ind. having heard

śrūyatām let it be heard! listen! (impv.)

stabdha mfn firmly fixed, supported, immovable, paralysed, stubborn, obstinate, dull, proud, arrogant

staḥ pron. two are, they two are

stamba 1257/3 a clump or tuft of grass,

stambha m. a post, pillar, column, stem, support, propping, pretentiousness, arrogance, fixedness, stiffness, paralysis,

stana m. breast, chest, nipple,

stanita mfn thundering, sounding, n. thunder, loud groaning,

stavaka m. praise, eulogy, a praiser,

stena 1260/2 m. a thief, robber

-stha suffix, dweller,fixed, staying, standing, abiding, being situated in, standing in,

stha you (pl.) are

stha 1262/3 mfn. standing, staying, abiding, existing, being in on or among

√*sthā* to stand, stand firmly, stay, remain, continue condition

sthaḥ you (two) are

sthairya n. stability, constancy, perseverance

sthala n. a place, chapter of a book,

sthāna n. a place, 1263/1 n. the act of standing, standing firm, being fixed, staying, abiding, maintenance, basis,

sthāṇu mfn standing firmly, stationary, firm, fixed, immovable, m. a stump, trunk, post, pillar (also as a symbol of motionlessness),

sthāpana mfn causing to stand, maintaining, preserving, fixing, determining, storing, keeping, fixed order or regulation, establishing, establishment, dialectical proof, n. causing to stand, placing, fixing, foundation, m. erecting an image etc.

sthāpaya(ti) to cause to stand, cause to be situated, 2/s/caus/impv/act √*sthā* (he, she, or it) places,

sthāpayitvā ind. causing to stand, having caused to stand, caus. gerund

sthāvara 1264/1standing still, immovable, L. not endowed with the power of locomotion, stationary beings, (herbs, plants)

sthāvira mfn firm, thick, massy, sturdy, full-grown, old, m. old man,

sthira 1264/3 mfn. firm, hard, solid, compact fixed, immovable, notion less, still, constant, steadfast, faithful, trustworthy, firmly resolved to,

sthita 1264/1 mfn standing (firm), staying, resting or abiding in

sthitadhī 1264/2 mfn. steady-minded, firm, unmoved, calm, whose meditation is steady

sthitaprajña 'the man with unshakeable wisdom', Chapter 2 *bhagavad gītā*, v.55 'Essentially, he does everything with utmost attention, great ease and without any claims' HH

sthiti 1264/2 f. standing firmly, abiding, continued existence, staying, remaining,

sthūla mfn thick, dull, gross, tangible

stimita mfn wet, moist, fixed, motionless, still, calm, tranquil, soft, gentle, (*am*) ind. pleased, n. moisture, stillness, motionless,

stoka m. a drop (water etc), a spark, mfn little, small, short, (*am*) ind. a little, slightly, gradually,

stotra 1259/2 n. praise, a hymn of praise, name of the verses or texts which are sung (as opposed to being recited)

strī f. a woman, female, wife, the female of any animal, (in gram.) the female gender,

strīliṅga feminine gender, creative power which brings to birth, the power of the powerful

striyāḥ women 1/pl/f

strīya 1261/2 °*yati* to desire a woman or wife

stuti 1259/1 f. praise, adulation

stuvati 1259/1 praises, lauds, extols

√*su* 1219/2 Cl 1 P A *savati (te)* to go, move,

su 5. 1219/3 ind. prefix good, much, greatly, very, right, virtuous, beautiful, easy,

√*sū* 1. 1239/3 Cl 6 P *suvati (te), savati, -sauti,* to set in motion, urge, impel,

śubha 1083/2 mfn splendid, suitable, fit, good, blessed, auspicious, beautiful, n. anything bright or beautiful, beauty, charm, good fortune, auspiciousness, happiness, bliss, welfare, prosperity, benefit, service, good or virtuous action,

śubhamastu farewell

śubhecchā f. pure desire, good impulse, the starting point, "Every desire contains a purpose to be fulfilled and a good impulse in this context is Self-realization or Liberation" "willingness to follow *viveka* and willingness to follow *aham*" HH

śubhra radiant, shining, beautiful, splendid, clear, bright-coloured, white, 'free from attributes' (Gam.), m. white (the colour), sandal, heaven,

śuc f. sorrow, pain, brightness, lustre, mfn shining illumining,

sūcaka mfn pointing out, indicating, pointing to, informing, betraying, m. a denouncer, informer,

śuci 1081/1mfn clear, clean, pure, pure (in a ritual sense), honourable (in business), light, bright, beaming,

sūci or *sūcī* f. a needle or any sharp-pointed instrument, the sharp point or tip of anything, a rail or balustrade,

an elephants trunk,
sucira mfn for a long time,
sūdana 1242/2 killing, destroying
śuddha 1082/1 mfn cleansed, clean, pure, taintless
śuddhacaitanya 1082/1 n. pure intelligence, pure consciousness
śuddhacinmātra pure awareness,
śuddharūpin 1082/1 having the nature of purity,
śuddhi 1082/2 f. cleansing, purification, purity, holiness, freedom from defilement, purificatory rite, setting free, rendering secure, exculpation, acquittal, innocence, (established by trial or ordeal), quittance, discharge (of a debt), verification, correction, truth, clearness, certainty,
suddhyupāsya a form of address indicating respected by the wise,
sudhā f. welfare, 'good drink' the beverage of the gods, nectar, the nectar of honey or flowers, juice, water, milk,
sudhī 1225/3 f. intelligence, good sense or understanding, mfn wise,
śūdra fourth caste or class, servants, labourers
sudurācara 1225/1 mfn. very ill-conducted, very badly behaved or wicked, a profligate
sudurdarśa m. difficult to see,
sudurlabha mfn hard to find, difficult to obtain
suduṣkara mfn difficult to do or achieve
sugrīva king of the monkeys
suhṛd 1239/3 m. good-hearted, a friend,
suhṛt (in comp. for *suhṛd*), friend
sujña mfn. knowing well, conversant with anything
sujñāna n. easy perception or intelligence, good knowledge, f (*ā*) possessing good knowledge, easy to be understood
sujñeya well-comprehended,
śuka m. parrot, 'the bright one', the planet Venus,
sūkara m. swine, boar,
sukha 1220/3 mfn pleasant, comfortable, happy, prosperous, virtuous, n. ease, easiness, comfort, pleasure, prosperity, happiness, joy, delight in,
sukhī mfn one who loves pleasure (?), happy,
sukhin mfn possessing or causing happiness or pleasure, happy, joyful, pleasant, m. a religious ascetic,
sukhita mfn happy
sukhena ind. happily
śukla 1080/2 bright, light, white, pure, spotless, the bright ½ of a lunar month,
śukra 1080/1 mfn. bright, resplendent, clear, pure, spotless, the essence of anything,
sukṛta 1220/2 n. a good or righteous deed, meritorious act, virtue, doing good, benevolent 1220/2
śukti 1080/1f. a pearl oyster or oyster shell
sūkṣma 1240/3 mfn subtle, intangible, intangible matter, the subtle all-pervading Spirit
sūkṣmatvāt 1240/3 5/s from subtlety or fineness, because of or through subtlety or fineness
sukumāra mfn tender, young, delicate,
śūla m. a dart or spear, stake, spike,
śūlā f. a stake, a prostitute,
sulabha 1232/3 mfn easy to be obtained or effected, feasible, easy, trivial
sumana 1230/3 mfn very charming, beautiful, handsome, m. wheat,
sumanas mfn. good-minded, benevolent, kind, gracious, agreeable, wise, intelligent, calm of mind
sumitrā *Sumitrā*
sundara 1227/1 mfn beautiful, charming, handsome, noble,
suniścitam ind. definitely, with certainty
sūnṛta mfn joyful, glad, friendly, kind, n. pleasant and true speech, sweet discourse, f. (*ā*) gladness, joy, kind and true speech,
sūnu m. an inciter, 2. m. a son, child,

a younger brother, daughter's son,
śūnya 1085/1 empty, void, a riderless horse, vacant, without aim or object, void of thinking, (*am*) solitude,
śūnyacitta 1085/2 mfn vacant-minded, not thinking
sūpa m. sauce, soup, broth, a cook, pot,
supatha 1227/2 m.n. a good road, virtuous course, good conduct, mfn. having a good road
supta 1230/1 fallen asleep, asleep, *vat* – like , like those fallen asleep
śūra mfn mighty, bold, m. man of might,
sura 1234/2 m. a god, divinity, deity
sūra the sun, a wise or learned man
surā f. spirituous liquor, wine, water,
surabhi mfn sweet-smelling, fragrant, charming, pleasing, lovely, famous, good, virtuous, friendly, a friend, m. fragrance, perfume,
suragaṇāḥ the multitudes of gods m.pl.
śurās heroes, 1/pl/m
surendra lord of the gods
sūri m. a learned man, sage, L. he who engages priests to perform a sacrifice for his benefit and pays them for it, a sacrifice-master,
śurpanakhā *Śurpanakhā*
sūrya 1243/1 m. the sun or its deity,
sūryakara 1243/2 m.a sunbeam,
śuṣka mfn dried,
suśobhita 1237/2 mfn shining brightly,
suśrānta 1237/2 mfn very tired, greatly exhausted,
śuśruma we have heard, we heard
śuśrūṣā f. obedience, reverence, service,
suṣṭhu mfn highly praised or celebrated, aptly, well,
susukha 1239/1 mfn very easy or pleasant
suṣumnā G305, the subtle central nerve, the principal nerve
suṣupta 1237/3 fast asleep, *suṣupta* 1237/3 deep sleep, in phil. complete unconsciousness
suta 1219 1. mfn impelled, urged, allowed, authorized,
2. mfn pressed out, extracted, m.a Soma libation,
3. mfn begotten, brought forth, a son, child, offspring, (*sutau* du. = 'son and daughter'), a king,
sūta 1241/2 m.a charioteer, driver, groom
sūtaputra son of a charioteer (*Karna*)
sūtra 1241/3 n. a thread, yarn, string, , that which like a thread runs through or holds together everything, rule, direction, a short sentence or aphoristic rule, any work or manual consisting of strings of such rules... a terse statement,
sūtradhāra 1242/1 thread-holder, architect, carpenter, puppet-master
sūtrātman 1242/1 m. the *ātman* or Self like a thread through the universe
suvarṇa mfn golden, n. gold,
suvicāraṇā f. good thoughts and reasoning
suvijñeya 1233/2 mfn. easy to be, easily comprehensible, distinguished,
suvirūḍha 1233/3 mfn. fully grown up or developed
sūyate it produces, creates, impels, 1/s/pres/indic/mid √*sū*
sv for 5. *su* 1219/3 good, excellent, right, virtuous, (due to sandhi),
śva(ḥ) m. or ind. tomorrow,
sva one's own, his, her or its own
sva 1275/1 own, one's own, my own, *svam* his own

svabhāva 1276/1 m. (ifc. *ā*)native place, own condition or state of being, nature, impulse, disposition,
-*vāt* rom natural disposition,
-*vena* by nature, naturally,
-*taḥ* ind. intrinsically,
-*tas* ind. inherently,
-*ta* adv. with 5/s sense, natural disposition
svābhāva m. own non-existence,
svabhāvaja mfn born of own nature, innate, natural,
svābhāvika 1283/3 belonging to or arising from one's own nature, "(knowledge).. that which is

provided by the Will of the Absolute to the individual. Natural knowledge is in the design of the individual."
HH 'a *svābhāvika* is created by human beings for their welfare. A *svābhāvika* is also natural but is hidden from the individual and is discovered by intellectual insight. This is learnt and is subject to change.'

svaccha mfn very transparent or clear, pellucid, crystalline, bright-coloured, clear, distinct (as speech), pure (as the mind or heart), healthy,

svacchanda 1275/2 own or free will, independently, uncontrolled,

svācchandya 1283/2 independence, freedom

svadhā 1280/1 an axe, knife,
1278/1 inherent or self power, spontaneously, willingly, freely

svadharma own duty or duty of one's own caste, one's own rights,

svādhīna mfn independent,

svādhyāya m. reciting or repeating the scriptures to one's self,
study of scriptures and discourses between the aspirant and the wise,
'...it removes all doubts, resolves questions and enlightens the way'. HH

svādu mfn sweet, savoury, dainty,

svāgata n. welcome, greeting, well come,

śvaḥ tomorrow

svaḥ we two are

svaira mfn going where one likes, doing what one likes, wilful, independent, unrestrained, walking cautiously, voluntary, optional, *(am)* n. wilfulness, (*am*) ind. according to one's own will or pleasure, easily, spontaneously, at random, slowly, softly,

svairin mfn free, independent,

svajana 1275 m. own people, own kindred

svakarman n. one's own deeds or duties

svalpa mfn little, very small

svāmi 1284/1 in comp. for *svāmin*, master, lord, a spiritual preceptor, learned *brāhmin* or *paṇdit*

svāmin m. master, husband, owner,

śvan m. a dog, f. (*ī*)

svanuṣṭhita mn well performed,

√*svap* to sleep, 1280/2 root

śvāpada m. a beast of prey,

svapada 1276/1 one's own place or abode, own position or rank, *svapade* 7/s in one's own Self

svapan sleeping pres/act/part.

svapiti he sleeps

svapna 1280/3 m. sleep, sloth, sleepiness, dreaming, n. a dream,

svara m. a vowel (long, short or extended), air breathed through the nostrils,
a voice, sound, noise,
tone in recitation, accent,

svāra m. sound, noise (snorting horse), tone, accent, the *svarita* accent,
mfn relating to sound or accent, having the *svarita* accent,

svārāj 1282/1 king of heaven

svārāma 1277/3 mfn delighting in oneself,

svarasa 1276/2 m. one's own pure essence

svarga 1281/2 mfn. (or *suvarga*) heavenly, celestial, going or leading to or being in light or heaven, m. heaven, heavenly bliss. *ārohaṇa* mfn. 151/2 arising, ascending, n. the act of rising *svargārohaṇa* rising to heaven

svargakāma 1281/3 mfn desirous of heaven

svarganarakau 1281/3 1/du heaven and hell

svargya mfn. occupying or dwelling in heaven

svarṇa 1282/1 n. gold, a kind of red chalk,

svarūpa 1276/2 n. own form or shape, condition, character, nature, in reality, natural form,

svarūpastha 1262/3 abiding, abiding in your true nature, situated in himself,

śvasan breathing pres/act/part √*śvas* 1105/3

svaśarīra 1277/1 n. one's own body or person, his/her own body or person,

svasṛ sister,

śvaśrū f. mother-in-law and the other wives,mother in law,
svastha 1277/1mfn abiding in one's self, in one's natural state, (the natural state is that the senses are subordinate to the Self), being oneself, healthy
svāsthya 1284/3 n. self-dependence, comfort, contentment,
svasti 1283/1 n.f.well-being, luck, success, good fortune, hail!, farewell!
svasti iti may it be well
śvaśura m. father-in-law,
svatantra n. self-dependence, independence, self-will, freedom, mfn self-dependent, self-willed, independent, free, uncontrolled, of age, full grown,
svātantrya 1283/3 following one's own will, freedom of the will, independence, *svātantryāt* 5/s of one's own free choice, freely, through freedom,
svātman 1277/2 m. own self, one-self *svātmani* 7/s/m in your own Self
svatva 1275/2 n. proprietary right to, self-existence, independence, relationship to one-self,
svayam pron. ind. self, thyself, him-self, yourself etc.e.g. *svayam vṛtavān* I chose it myself
svayambhū 1278/3 mfn. self-existing, independent, name of *Brahman*, ' m.(-*ḥ*)... 'is the first-born of his own accord' HH, he who exists by himself
svayaṁvara m. self-choice, esp. free choice of a husband, which was allowed to girls of the warrior caste,
sve in own 7/s/ *sva* , *sve sve* repeated for emphasis
sveccha ibc. according to one's wish, at will, freely, voluntarily,
svecchā f. one's own wish or will, ibc. at pleasure, according to one's own wish,
svecchayā ind. according to desire
śveta mfn white, bright,
svid 1284/3 ind. particle of interrogation, inquiry or doubt, 'do you think?, indeed, perhaps, any'
svīkṛta 1279/1 mfn appropriated, making one's own, claimed,
svīya mfn relating/belonging to one's self, own, proper, characteristic, m.pl. one's own people or kin, f.(*ā)* one's own wife, a wife solely attached to her husband,
śvobhāvaḥ 1106/1 tomorrow's state of affairs, the affairs or occurrences of tomorrow, ephemeral, whose existence is subject to doubt as to whether they will exist tomorrow or not,
syāla 1273/2 brother-in-law 1/s/m
syām I should be 3/s/opt √*as*
śyāma dark, black, dark blue, a name for *kṛṣṇa,*
syāma we should be, we might be 3/pl/opt/act √*as*
śyāmala mfn dark coloured, m. black,
√*syand* move swiftly

syandana 1273/1 mfn. moving on swiftly, running (as a chariot), m. chariot,
syāt 1273/2 1/s/opt/act verb to be – *as,* expresses possibility, perhaps it is, it may be, perchance, it should be, might it be
syāt he should be , one becomes, 1/s/opt/act √*as*
śyena m. eagle, falcon, hawk,
syus they should be, should they be 1/pl/opt/act √*as*
ta m. a tail, the breast, womb, hip, a warrior, thief, wicked man, a jewel, nectar, n. crossing, virtue,
tāḥ they f.pl. pron.
tad 434/1 that, this, pron 1/s/n n. this world, ind. there, thither, in that place, then, in that case, therefore, accordingly, thus, in this manner, with regard to that, on that account, so, also, equally, *tad tad* this and that, various, different, respective, *yad tad* whosoever, whichsoever,

any, every,
ind. *tadapi* even then, nevertheless, notwithstanding,
tadyathā 'in such a manner as follows', namely,

tadā 434/3 ind. then, at that time, in that case then (corel. of *yadā* – when…then) ,

taḍāga n. a lake or pond,

tadānīm ind. then, at that time,

tadantara 434/1 mfn. nearest to anyone, (*am*) ind. immediately upon that, thereupon, then

tadarthīya 434/1mfn intended for that, undertaken for that end, relating to that, meant for this

tadātmānas they whose selves are fixed on that BV compound

tadbuddhayas whose minds are absorbed in that, BV comp.

taḍit ind. lightning,

tāḍita mfn beaten, struck, punished,

tadīya mfn pertaining to him, her, it, them, such,

tādṛś mfn such,

tādṛśaḥ 442/1 in such a manner, such a one

tādṛśāḥ 442/1 *tādṛśa* mfn anybody whosoever, such like, such a one pl. those like (e.g. him)

tadvat ind. in this way, so, likewise,

tadvidas the knowers of this (or that) pl.

ṭagara mfn squint-eyed, m. borax,

tāḥ tāḥ such and such

tāḥ pron. 1/pl/f those

taijasa 455/1 mfn. originating from or consisting of light (*tejas*) bright, brilliant

taila n. oil,

tais tais by these and those

tajjalān *tajja* – sprung from that, *-lān*, produced, absorbed and breathing in that, 'is born from that Brahman, therefore it is called *tajja*, and it is *talla* because... it gets merged in that very Brahman, becomes wholly identified with that; and it is *tadana* because it continues to live, to function on that very Brahman during its existence.'

tajjña 433/2 (*taj* for *tat* -that*)* knowing That, a knowing man, familiar with, *jña 425/3* intelligent, wise, a wise and learned man,

takra n. buttermilk mixed with water,

takṣa m. a wood-cutter, carpenter, mfn cutting through,

tala m.n. surface, level, flat roof, the part underneath, base, bottom,

tāla m. slapping the hands together, the flapping of an elephants ears, the palmyra tree, a dance, a cymbal,

tale at the foot of, ifc. = on

talpa m. couch, bed,

tālu 445/2 the palate, name for palatal sounds,

tam pron. 2/s that, him

tām pron. her (2nd)

tam tam 434/1 this and that

-tama 438/2 2. an affix forming the superlative degree of adjectives and rarely of substantives, added (in older language) to adverbs and (in later language to verbs, intensifying their meaning, ind. in a high degree, much

tamas 438/1*,* darkness, night, one of the 3 *guṇa(*s) having the qualities of ignorance, illusion, stability, decay, dullness, inertia, 'it is of the nature of indifference and serves to restrain. It is heavy and enveloping.' G. 314

tāmasika 443/1 mfn. relating to the quality *tamas*

tāmbulam n. betel,

ṭaṁkāra m. howl, cry, clang, twang etc.

tamoguṇa a quality (darkness or ignorance) of nature,

tamomaṇiḥ m. firefly, a kind of jewel,

tāmra mfn of a coppery-red colour, made of copper, n. copper,

tān those (many) 2nd m. them,

tanayaḥ/yā mfn propagating a family, belonging to one's family, a son, du. son and daughter,

tandrā twilight, "neither sleep nor the waking state; always lost somewhere in between" HH L. f. fatigue,

tandrālu mfn weary, tired, sleepy,

taṇḍula m. rice, grain, (after threshing and winnowing),

tāni pron. 1st or 2nd pl/n , those,

ṭaṅka m.n. a spade, hoe, hatchet, stone-cutter's chisel, leg, m. a sword, scabbard,

tanmātra 434/3 n. merely that , a rudimentary or subtle element (5 in number), from which the grosser elements are produced

tanniṣṭhās they whose basis is that, they whose foundation is That BV compound *tan-ni-sthā*

tantra n. a loom, thread, warp of a web, division of a work, fundamental doctrine,

tantrī f. lute,

tantu 436/1 a thread, cord, string, line

tanu 435/2 mfn. thin, slender, f. the body, person, form, self

tanumānasā f. the third step in realization, experience that impurities and impediments are lessening

tanutra n. armour,

tanu-trāṇa n. body protection,

√*tap* 436/3 2. *tapati* to give out heat, be hot, shine, shine upon, make hot, heat , *tapyate* to rule,

tapa 436/3mfn. causing pain or trouble, m. discipline, heat, warmth, austerity

tāpa 442/2 m. pain (mental or physical), sorrow, affliction,

tapanta pres/part burning, consuming, illuminating

tapas disciplined action, (austerities) which purifies and enhances energy, unswerving performance of one's duties, disciplined action that purifies and enhances energy

tāpasa m. an ascetic, the moon,

tapasvin 437/2 m. practising austerities, an ascetic,

tapasya 437/2 1. *(-ti)* to undergo (perform) austerities, 2 produced by heat, devout austerity

tapasyasi 2/s you perform (austerities)

tāpatritayadūṣita impure through 3-fold misery, (the 3-fold misery – from one's body/mind/intellect, from the beings and objects around one, from accidents like floods and earthquakes)

tapodhana m. ascetic, mfn rich in austerities

tapovana n. hermitage,

tapta mfn heated, inflamed, hot, refined (gold etc.), fused, melted, molten, practiced (austerities), undertaken,

-tara 438/3 surpassing (comparative affix intensifying meaning)

tāra 443/3 carrying across, a saviour, protector, high, loud, shrill, good, excellent, well-favoured, crossing, saving

tārā f. a star, universal Divine Mother, pupil of the eye,

tāraka m. a helmsman, a raft, n. a star, the pupil of the eye, the eye, the eye, mfn causing or enabling to pass or go over, rescuing, liberating, saving, ifc. f. (*ā*)

tarala mfn tremulous,

taraṁga 438/3m. across-goer, a wave,billow

tarati 454/2 he passes across or over, gets through, attains an end or aim *Dh° tṛ*

tarhi then

tarī m. f. boat,

tariṣyasi you will pass over or transcend, 2/s/fut/act/ √tṛ sorrow, affliction,

tarjanī f. 'threatening finger', the fore-finger,

tarka m. conjecture, supposition, reasoning, inquiry, speculation, doubt, the number 6,

tarpaṇa mfn satiating, refreshing, (esp. of gods and deceased persons) by presenting to them libations of water), n. (*am*) refreshment, food, satisfaction, f.(*ā*) ifc. fuel

tarpaṇīyaḥ to be satisfied

taru m. tree

taruṇa mfn young, tender, fresh, juvenile,
-*ka* n. sprout,
-*tas* adverbial suffix, through, by

taskara m. robber, thief,
ifc. a term of contempt,

tasmai pron. to that, to him,

tasmāt 441/2 pron.5/s from that , on that account, therefore

tasmin pron. in that, in him

taṣṭṛ m. carpenter, builder of chariots,

tasya pron. 6/s his, of him

tasya tasya on him, on whoever he is

tasyāḥ pron. 6/s her, of her

tasyai pron. to her

tat pron. that, (in a compound represents any form of pronoun *tad*)

taṭa m. a slope, declivity, shore,

tāta 441/3 voc/s/m a term of affection addressed to a junior, dear one, O son

tata 435/1 mfn extended, stretched, diffused,

tatas tataḥ what next

tat tat that (see *yat yat)*

tāṭakā Tāṭakā

tatas 432/2 ind. used for the 5th case thence, after that, from that , from there, from this point, therefore

taṭastha mfn standing on a slope or bank, m. an indifferent person (neither friend nor foe), n. a property distinct from the nature of the bodyand yet that by which it is known, spiritual essence,

tatas tatas from thence from there

tathā so, just so, 433/3 ind. in that manner, so, thus, likewise, as well
(correlative of *yathā* as... so)
(correlative of *yathā* as... *tathā* so)
in order that...... thus,
yathā yathā..... tathā tathā
to what degree..... to that degree...
the more................ the more....

tathāpi 433/3 even thus, then even, even then, nevertheless,

tathā-astu let it be so,

tati so many 1/2/pl.

tatkṣaṇa 432/3 *tatkṣaṇāt* 5/s from the same moment, immediately

tatpara 433/1 mfn. having that as one's highest object or aim, totally devoted or addicted to, attending closely to, mfn. following that or thereupon,

tātparya intention (as in the original intention of an author) (K),

tatsamakṣam in public, in the presence of others, before the eyes, adv.

tatra 433/2 ind. in that, there, over this, about this,

tatrabhavān refers to a respected person,

tatrāntare meanwhile,

tatra tatra there is, here and there, everywhere, to every place,

tat tad (*tad tad*) this or that, this and that

tat u that very thing, that Brahman,

tattva 432/3 n. true or real state, truth, reality, "thatness", truth

tattvabodha 433/1 m knowledge or understanding of truth

tattvajña 433/1 1/s/m knowing the truth, knowing the true nature of, knowing thoroughly,

tattvamasi *tat tvam asi* 'thou art that'

tattvata 432/3 *tattva* – true or real state, truth, true principle, from *tad* + *tvam* – that art thou-
by the truth about, in truth, truly

tattvavid mfn truth-knowing

tau pron. 2/du/m they 2, those 2

tava pron. your, of you

tāvaka mfn thy, thine,

tāvat 445/3 so great, so many, for so long, meanwhile, now, at that time, just, (correl. with *yāvant)* as long as ..... so long ....,

tayā pron. 3/s. f. by or with her,

tayoḥ pron. of/in those two

te pron. they (two) or 6/s your, those many m. or
4/s to thee, to you

454/2 n. a sharp edge, point of a flame, ray, glow, glare, splendour, brilliance, light, fire, vital power, spirit, essence, majesty, dignity, authority the element fire with the properties of form and beauty, vigour,

tejasvin 454/3 mfn brilliant, splendid, bright, powerful, energetic, violent, inspiring respect, dignified, noble,

tejorāśi 454/3 m. mass of splendour, all splendour,

tena 454/3 pron. 3/s by him, by that

thoḍana n. covering,

tigma mfn sharp, hot,

ṭīkā f. a commentary esp. on another commentary,

tīkṣṇa 448/3 sharp, hot, pungent, fiery, acid, harsh, rough, rude, vehement

tikta mfn bitter, pungent, m. a bitter taste,

tila m. the sesame plant or its seed,

timira mfn dark, gloomy, n. darkness, darkness of the eyes, partial blindness, iron-rust

tīra n. a shore, bank

tiras 1. prep. through, across, beyond,
3. ind. crossways, sideways, aside, so as to pass by, apart from,

tirohita mfn hidden ,

tīrtha 449/1 n. a ford, passage , way, place of pilgrimage, a sacred or holy place

tīrtvā ind. having crossed over, crossing over

tiryag see *tiryañc*

tiryak see *tiryañc*

tiryaktva n. the nature of beasts

tiryaṅ see *tiryañc*

tiryañc 1. mfn directed across, horizontal,
2. m.n. beast (going horizontally as opposed to man being upright),

tisraḥ three (fem)

tiṣṭha stay!, stand!

tiṣṭhanta existing, standing, situated pres/act/part √*sthā*

tiṣṭhasi 448 *tiṣthad* (see *sthā*) 1262/2 to stand, stand firmly, to stay, remain, continue in any action or condition, 2nd pres. act. you remain

tiṣṭhataḥ 1262/2 stands firmly, remains, to be, abiding, living,

tiṣṭhati 1262/2 remains, stands

tiṣṭhatu 1/s/pres/impv/act. let remain

tithi m.f. a lunar day,

titikṣā 446/2 endurance, forbearance, patience

titikṣasva you must endeavour to endure 2/s/impv/mid/desid √*tij*

tīvra mfn severe, violent, intense, fierce, of rigorous austerities, *(am)* ind. severely,

toka n. creation, progeny,

toṣa 456/1 satisfaction, contentment

toya 456/1 n. water

traiguṇya 462/1 the 3 *guṇā*

trailokya n. the three worlds, of the earth, the gods and in between

tras 457/3 to be afraid of , *trasyati* 1/s/pres/act/indic he fears

trāsa m. fear, terror, anxiety, fright,

traya mfn triple, threefold, consisting of 3

trāyate 462/1 protects, preserves, 1/s/mid

tredhā in three ways,

treta yuga the Silver Age 1,296,000 years, man started to want something for himself

tri 3

tṛī 454/2 cl1 *tarati* to pass across or over, cross over, float, swim, get through, attain an end or aim, fulfil, accomplish

tridhā in three ways, 3 parts, 3 places, triply,

trikarmakṛt one who undertakes 3 types of sacrifice- sacrifice, study of the Vedas and charity, or ceremonies, repeating the Veda, gifts

trīṇi 457/3 3

trividhā threefold, triple

tripuṭa 459/2 mfn. threefold, a kind of pulse, a kind of measure,

tris ind. thrice, three times,

tritaya 461/3 a triad, group of three,

tṛṇa n.grass

tṛpta 454/1 satisfied with, satiated,

tṛṣ mfn longing for
f. thirst, strong desire,

tṛṣā f. thirst, strong desire,
tṛṣṇā 454/1 f. thirst, avidity, desire,
tṛtīya° third
tu 449/3 but, however, though, expletive, indeed, rhythmic filler
tubhyam pron. for you 4/s
tuccha mfn empty, vain, small, little, trifling, n. anything trifling,
tudati strikes, hits *Dh°* *tud*
tulā f. balance, scale, weight, equality,
tulanā 451/2 rating, equality with, comparison, part. compared
tulya 451/3 equal to, of the same kind, similar, like
tumula 1/s/m tumultuous, noisy
tuṅga mfn tall, high, m. a height, mountain, top, peak,
turīya 451/1 the 4th state of spirit, pure impersonal spirit or Brahman *turãya* the seventh or last step of realisation, "the being itself, the Self alone without a second" HH, the underlying sub-stratum of the waking, dreaming and deep-sleep states, the self beyond the changing modes of existence, "Truth is that which has the capacity to witness all these states." HH
turya fourth,
tūrya n. a musical instrument
tuṣāra mfn cold, frigid, m. dew, frost,
tūṣṇīka mfn silent,
tūṣṇīm 453/1 ind. silently, quietly
tuṣṭa pleased, satisfied,
tuṣṭi 452/1 m.f. satisfaction, contentment
tuṣyati 452/1 is satisfied or pleased
tūṣṇīm bhava be silent, (silent become)
tūṣṇīm 453/1 silently, quietly
tuṣyati 1/s/pres/indic/act is content, is satisfied
tva or *tvat* or *tvad* mfn one, several, thy, your, base of the 2nd personal pron.
tvac 463/3 2. f. skin, hide, bark,
-tvād (t) by reason of, because,
tvadānīm 463/2 ind. sometimes
tvadanya 463/2 mfn. other than thee
tvadīya thine, your,
tvadrik ind. towards you
tvādṛk mfn like you, of your kind
tvādṛśa mfn like you
tvak 463/3 in comp for 2. *tvac*
tvam you pron. 1 or 2/s you, thou, that one, applied to *puruṣa* – the Self.
tvām pron. 2/s to you
tvara 464/1 hastily,
tvarā f. haste, speed, hastily, quickly
tvaramānā rapidly, in great haste
tvaṣṭṛ m. workman, 2. Twashtar, the artificer of the gods, former of fruit of the womb, giver of growth and long life, father of Saranyū,
tvat from you (s)
tvatsama like you, same as you
tvayā pron. 3/s by you
tvayi 7/s pron. in you
tviṣ f. violent agitation, fury, light, brilliance, splendour, glitter, beauty, authority,
tyad or *tad* pron. he, she, it, that
tyāga 456/3 m. abandoning, renouncing
tyāgī m. abandoner, renouncer
tyaja 456/3 *tyaj* leave, avoid, quit, let go, dismiss, impv. set aside
tyaja leave alone!
tyajas n. abandonment, difficulty, danger, alienation, aversion, envy, m. 'offshoot', descendant,
tyajati leaves, abandons, gives up
tyajet one should abandon or renounce 1/s/opt/act √*tyaj*
tyājya 457/1 ind. to be left or abandoned
tyakta 456/3 mfn left, abandoned
tyaktena 3/s by or with an abandoned ... by that detachment, through detachment, (*īṣā up.*)
tyakta jīvitās they whose lives are at risk
tyaktum √ *tyaj* 456/3 infinitive form to let go, dismiss, surrender, renounce,
tyaktvā ind. having left, having abandoned, abandoning, sacrificing, relinquishing
u ind. an interjection of compassion or anger, a particle implying assent or

command, and, also, further, on the other hand, particle of emphasis, may be used to indicate a conclusion
ubha/ubhaya both
ubhaya 216/2 both, of both kinds, in both ways,
ubhayatas ind. from or on both sides, to both sides (with 2nd or 6th), in both cases, on both sides of ,
ucca 172/3 mfn. high, lofty, elevated
uccais ind. aloft, high, above, upwards, from above, loud, accentuated, intensely, much, powerfully, loudly, high
ucchaiḥśravasa m. 'high sounding' the name of Indra's horse,
ucchiṣṭa 173/3 left, rejected, stale
ucchoṣaṇa 174/1 mfn. making dry, parching
ucchṛṅkhalā 174/1 mfn unbridled, uncurbed, unrestrained, self-willed, perverse,
ucita mfn proper, usual, delightful, agreeable, acceptable, convenient,
ucyate 1/s/pres/pass. is called, it is said, it is spoken, he is said to be, he is called, 1/s/pres/indic/pass. 912/1 root *vac* to speak, to be spoken or said, to resound, to be called or accounted,
ud prefix, expresses superiority in place, rank, station, power; up, upwards, upon, on, over, above, (or implying separation and disjunction), out, out of, from, off, away from, apart, (may also imply) publicity, pride, indisposition, weakness, helplessness, binding, loosing, existence, acquisition, *sometimes repeated in the Veda to fill out the verse,
udadhi mfn holding water, m. 'water-receptacle', a cloud, the ocean, sea, river,
udagra mfn tall, fierce,
udāhāra m. an example or illustration, the beginning of a speech,
udaharat lifted, lifted up
udāhṛta 185/3 mfn described, explained, called, entitled, declared,
udaka 183/2 n. water, the ceremony of offering water to a dead person, ablution (ceremonial),
udāna 184/2 breathing upwards, one of the five vital airs of the -body, (that which is in the throat and rises upwards), the navel, an eyelash, a kind of snake, the breath at death,
udapāna 183/2 m.n. a well
udara 184/2 n. the interior or inside of anything, belly,
udāra 185/2 exalted, high, lofty, noble
udāsīna 185/3 mfn. sitting apart, indifferent, free from affection, inert, inactive
udāsīnavat as if sitting apart etc.
udaya 186/1 rising, rising of the sun, dawning, appearance, development,
udbhava 190/2 existence, generation, origin, birth, springing from
udbhāva m. production, generation, birth, rising (of sounds), production,
udbhavati arises, is born,
udbhūta 190/2 mfn come forth, produced, arise, arising, visible, distinct,
uddharati lifts,
uddharet one should rise up, lift up, raise up 1/s/opt/act *ud* √ *dhṛ*
uddhati 188/3 f. haughtiness, pride, arrogance,
uddeśatas ind. pointedly, distinctly, by way of explanation, for example,
uddiśya 188/1 ind. with regard to, for the sake of, with reference to, having shown or explained, aiming at
udeti *ud*-√*e* 186/3 *udeti* to go up, rise, 1/s/pres/act/indic it rises
udharati lifts, lifts up
ūdhas n. udder,
udhavati he arises, or is born
udita mfn. risen, ascended, high, tall, lofty, conceited, in creased, visible 2. 186/2 said, spoken, proclaimed, declared, authoritative, right, ppp of √*vad*
uditvā ind. having said
udvega 192/1 mfn. going swiftly, a runner, courier, trembling, waving
udvigna 192/1 mfn terrified, sorrowful,

anxious, worried mind,
ud √vij *udvijati* 192/1 agitated, to fear, to be agitated, shudder, tremble, be afraid of, 1/s/pres/indic/act he fears
udvijet one should shudder or tremble, 1/s/opt/act
udyamya gerund ind. flourishing, brandishing, having flourished,
udyāna n. small wood, garden,
udyat 190/3 mfn rising, a star,
udyanti 3/pres/indic/act/plu they are rising
udyata mfn upraised, uplifted, elevated, high, eager for, intent on, undertaken, commencing, active preparation, trained, exercised, disciplined,
ugra mfn terrible, fierce, powerful,
ūhana n. transposition, change, reasoning,
ūhanī f. a broom,
ujjvala mfn blazing up, luminous, splendid, light, burning, clean, clear, lovely, beautiful, glorious, full-blown, expanded, (*as*) m. love, passion, (*am*) n. gold *(ā)* f. splendour, clearness, brightness,
ukāra 171/3 the letter or sound *u*
ukta 171/3 mfn. uttered, said, spoken, ppp. of √*vac*
uktavān pres.part. speaking, saying,
ukti f. speech, saying, sentence, a worthy speech or word, statement,
uktvā ind. speaking, having spoken, gerund √*vac*
ulba 219/1 n.a cover, envelope, membrane
ulkā f. a meteor, torch,
ullāsa 219 m. light, splendour, coming forth, becoming visible, appearing, happiness, merriness, increase, growth, chapter,section, division of a book,
ullekha m. mentioning, speaking of, description, intuitive description, causing to come forth or appear clearly,
ulūka m. owl,
umā *umā* f. flax, turmeric, splendour, light, wife of *Śiva*
ūna mfn lacking, wanting, deficient, short of the right quantity,
unmāda 194/1 m. mad, insane, extravagant, insanity, madness, hysteria,
unmārga m. wrong path or way, evil way,
unmatta mfn disordered in intellect, distracted, frantic, mad
un√mīl P. *unmīlati* 194/2 to open the eyes 1/s/pres/indic/act opens the eyes
unmiṣan opening the eyes, pres/act/part *ud √miṣan*
unmiṣati opens the eyes, winks, blinks
unnata mfn high, tall, prominent, lofty, eminent, sublime, great, noble,
unnati f. elevation, rising, ascending, swelling, height, advancement, prosperity,
upa prefix, towards, near to, by side of, with, together with, under, down, (opp. to *apa*)
upabhoga m. enjoyment, gratification,
upacāra m. approach, service, attendance, courtesy, proceeding, procedure, established use (of a word), act of civility, obliging or polite behaviour, reverence, a figurative or metaphorical expression, offerings to a deity,
upādāna 213/2 n. the act of taking for oneself, perceiving, learning, acquiring, accepting, including, cause, motive, material cause,
upadekśyati he will point out, instruct or teach, 1/pl/fut/act *upa √ diś*
upadeśa 199/1 m. specification, teaching, instruction, advice, prescription, initiation, reference, communication of the initiatory mantra or formula
upadeṣṭāram or *upadeṣṭā* 199/1 one who teaches, a guru or spiritual guide, *tara* – surpassing, comparative 2/s surpassing guru
upādeya 213/2 to be taken or received, not to be refused, acceptable
upadhāna mfn placing upon, (*am*) n. the act of placing or resting upon, a pillow, cushion,

upadhāraya understand, comprehend, consider, reflect 2/s/pres/indic/caus/act *upa √dhṛ*
upadhārya mfn to be comprehended, ind. having taken or held up etc.
upādhi 213/2 m. a qualification, disguise, limitation, deception, deceit, that which is put in the place of another thing, a substitute, substitution, an attribute, point of view, aim, reflection on duty, G.328 adventitious condition, limiting condition,
upādhyāya m. teacher, preceptor,
upadraṣṭā the Witness, he who while staying nearby does not Himself become involved 1/s/m 199/2
upadrava m. any grievous accident, misfortune, harm, outrage, calamity, mischief, national distress
upagacchati 196/2 he/she/it approaches, goes near, comes toward, attains,
upagraha m. seizure, confinement, a prisoner, handful of *kuśa* grass, alteration, change, addition, propitiation, conciliation, – the *pada* or grammatical voice of a verb, , there are 3 voices- active (*kartari prayoga)*, middle (*ātmanepada)*, and passive (*karmaṇi prayoga)*
upa √han 211/3 beat, hit at, strike, touch
upahanyām I should destroy or smite 3/s/opt/act above
upahāra m. offering, oblation (to a deity), a gift or present to a superior,
upahāsa m. ridicule
upahāsapātra n. a laughing stock,
upahata 211/3 mfn hurt, damaged, injured, overpowered, covered, *upa-√han*
upahṛta 212/2 mfn brought near, offered, taken, collected
upaiti approaches, attains, 1/s/pres/indic/act *upa √i*
upajāyate it is born, it is produced, 1/s/pres indic/pass *upa√jan*
upajīvaka mfn living upon, subsisting by, depending on, subject to, a dependent, servant, f.n. subsistence, livelihood,
upajuhvati they offer, they sacrifice, 1/pl/pres/indic/act *upa √hu*
upakalpita mfn assigned, prepared
upakāra 195/2 m. help, assistance, benefit, service, favour,
upakrama m. beginning, the act of coming or going near, approach, setting about, undertaking, commencement, the rim of a wheel,
upakṣepa m. threat, allusion, throwing at, threatening, mention, hint, poetical or figurative style
upala m. a rock, stone, jewel, a cloud, upper mill-stone,
upalabdhi f. obtainment, gain, observation, perceiving, perception, becoming aware, understanding, mind,
upalabhyate is perceived, is perceptible or attainable *upa √labh* 205/3
upalambha m. obtainment, perceiving, ascertaining, recognition,
upālambha m. abuse, taunt, reproach,
upalipyate is defiled or smeared
upama 203/2 mfn highest, uppermost, similar to
upamā 203/3 1.ind. in the closest proximity or neighbourhood, 2. f. comparison, resemblance, equality, similarity
upamāna n. comparison, analogy
upameya mfn comparable with, n. that which is compared, the subject of comparison,
upāṁśu mfn in a low voice, in a whisper,
upānah f. sandal, shoe,
upaniṣad 201/1 a class of philosophical writings (100+) regarded as the source of the Vedantic and some other philosophies,
upānta mfn near to the end, last but one, n. proximity to the end or edge or margin, border, edge,
upapadyate goes towards or against, arrives at, enters, comes, is fit for, occurs, happens, is according to the rules, suitable to1/s/pres/indic/mid/pass *upa √pad*

upapanna 201/3 mfn one who has approached a teacher (as a pupil), one who has approached for protection, one who has obtained or reached, gained, happened, fallen to one's lot

upapatti f. happening, occurring, taking place, proving right, resulting,

uparāga m. the act of dying or colouring, colour, darkening, influence, an eclipse, affecting, misbehaviour, ill-conduct, reproach, abuse,

uparam stop!

uparama m. cessation, stopping, expiration, leaving off, desisting, giving up, death,

uparamati stops, ceases,

uparamet he should cease, he should be quiet, 1/s/opt/act *upa √ram*

uparata 204/3 mfn. ceased, stopped, quiet, indifferent, ceasing to exist, from *upa√ram*

upari ind. on top, above, upon, on, (as a separable prep. with 2nd, 6th, 7th), over, above, upon, at the head of, on the upper side of, beyond, in connection with, with reference to, with regard to, towards, after,

uparotsīḥ 2/s/aorist *upa√2. rudh* you lock in, shut up, besiege, obstruct, hinder, press, trouble, importune,

√upās 3. *upa* + *√ās* to sit near, serve, honour, revere, be devoted to, worship, see *upāsana*

upaśama 207/3 m. the becoming quiet, stopping, cessation, calmness, patience,

upasaṁgamya having approached, gerund

upāsana 2. 215/1 *am, ā*, n. f. the act of sitting or being near at hand, serving, service, homage, adoration, worship (consisting of 5 parts , viz. *abhigamana* or approach, *upādāna* or preparation of offering, *ijyā* or oblation, *svādhyāya* or recitation, and *yoga* or devotion). Grimes p.330 It is of 3 kinds (1) *aṅgāvabodhopāsana* – something is worshipped or meditated on as a limb of a rite e.g. a piece of grass is thought of as a deity, (2) *pratīkopāsana* – an idol or picture is worshipped as God, (3) *ahaṁgrahopāsana* – the worshipper equates himself with a deity, 'in the realm of devotion and service' HH '*upāsanā* means being close or united through physical, mental and emotional means.'

upaśānta 207/3 mfn calmed, appeased, ceased, (conditioning) extinct,

upasarga 210/2 m. a *nipāta* or particle joined to a verb or noun denoting action... These are used like prefixes and are said to 'change the direction' or sense of the word to which they are prefixed.

upāsate they worship or honour 1/pl/pres/indic/mid *upa √ās*

upasevate 210/3 frequents, abides or stays at, visits, serves, does homage, honours, worships

upāsita mfn. served, honoured, worshipped, one who serves or offers worship,

upāśrita 214/3 mfn. having recourse to, taking refuge with, relying upon clinging to, adhering to, beset with

upāśritya resorting to, following, depending on, taking refuge in

upastha 211/1 mfn 'the part which is under', a seat or stool, lap, the generative organs,

upāsya 215/1 1. 1. mfn to be revered or honoured or worshipped
2 ind. having served or worshipped,

upavana n. garden, grove, plantation,

upavāsa m. a fast, fasting, abstinence in general, kindling a sacred fire, a fire altar,

upaviśa sit down!

upāviśat sat down 1/s/imperf/act *upa ā √viś*

upaviśati sits down

upaviśya having sat down

upavīta mfn invested with the sacred thread, n. being invested with the sacred thread, the sacred thread or cord,

upāya 215/2 plan, trick, method, that by which one achieves one's aim, a means or expedient, way, stratagem, artifice, method, coming near, approach, arrival,

upa √*yā* 204/2 to come near, go near, or towards, approach

upayoga m. employment, use, enjoyment, consuming, an agreement, fitness, acquisition (of knowledge), good conduct, observing established practices,

upekṣā 215/3 f. overlooking, negligence, disregarding, indifferent,

upeta 215/3 mfn. one who has come near or approached, arrived at, abiding in, endowed with, initiated

upetya mfn to be set about or commenced, ind.having approached, approaching

uraga 217/2 m. a serpent, snake

uras n. breast, chest (of the body),

ūrdhva 222/1 mfn rising or tending upwards, high, elevated, above, in the latter part, subsequent, after, raised, *(am)* ind. upwards, above, afterwards (with 5th),

ūrjas n. vigour,

ūrjita 221/3 n. strong, mighty, powerful,

ūrṇā f. wool,

ūru 221/2 m. thigh, shank, mfn wide,

urvī f. the earth,

uśanas 219/3 name of the planet Venus

uśanā ind. with desire or haste, zealously

uṣas f. morning red, dawn, (personified) Dawn,

uśitvā having dwelt, dwelling, gerund √ 3. *vas*

ūṣmapa 223/1 steam-eater

uṣṇa n. heat, mfn hot,

uṣṇīṣa m. turban,

uṣṭra m. camel, f. *(ī)*, bufalo, cart,

ut ind. a particle of doubt or deliberation

uta 175/2 2. sewn, woven
2.ind. and, also, even, often used for emphasis, indeed,

utkala m. a porter, a bird-catcher, present day Orissa,

utkaṇṭha mfn ready, eager,

utkhāthin mfn rugged,

utkrāmanta pres/part departing, stepping away, leaving the body

utkrāmati 176/3 steps out, goes out or away, passes away, dies

utpala n. the blossom of the blue lotus, any water-lily, any flower, 2. fleshless, emaciated,

utpatita mfn springing up, risen, ascended,

utpattavya mfn to be produced or born,

utpatti f. arising, birth, production, origin, resurrection, profit, productiveness, producing as an effect or result, giving rise to, occurrence,

utsādana 182/1 n. putting away or aside, suspending, interrupting, destroying, overturning

utsādyante they are withdrawn, disappear, a 1/pl/pres/indic/pass/caus *ud* √*sād*

utsāha 182/1m. power, strength, energy, perseverance, strenuous and continuous exertion, fortitude, joy, happiness

utsaṅga m. the lap, hip, a horizontal area,

utsanna mfn obliterated, disappeared,

utsava m. enterprise, beginning, a festival, jubilee, joy, gladness, blossoming,

utsīdeyus they would sink down or perish 1/pl/opt/act/ *ud* √*sad*

ut √*sṛj* 182/2 let loose, set free, open, lay aside, abandon, send forth

utsṛjāmi I set free, let loose, send forth,

utsuka mfn eager, anxious, attached to,

uttama mfn best. In Sanskrit grammar the *uttama puruṣaḥ* or best person is the 3rd person i.e. I or we e.g.

uttamāṅga 178/1 the head (highest limb)

Uttamaujas a warrior 'of highest power'

uttamavidām of those who know the highest

uttara 1. 178/1 mfn. upper, higher, superior, northern, left, later, following, subsequent, future, *(am)* n. , answer, reply, upper surface or cover,

the following member, the last part of a compound
superiority, competency, result
uttarāyanam n. the northern phase of the sun
uttha 179/3 standing up, rising
utthita mfn . √*sthā* risen, rising
utthitā f. state of activity or readiness to serve,

uttiṣṭha stand up 2/s/impv/act *ud*√*sthā*
uttiṣṭhate 179/3 comes forth, arises, results, 1/s/pres/indic/mid arises
uttiñṭhati he/she stands, stands up, *ud*√*sthā*
uvāca he said, he spoke, 1/s/perf/ act √*vac* speak,
va 910/1 2. m. air, wind, the arm, the ocean, water, addressing, reverence, conciliation, auspiciousness, a dwelling, a tiger, cloth, n. a weaver, mfn strong, powerful,
vā or, as well as, also,
vā... vā either... or
√*vā* 557/2 cl.2 to blow (as the wind), to procure or bestow anything (acc.) by blowing, to blow towards or upon, DP in *gati* going, or *gandhana* 344/3 blowing
vā yadi vā whether... or if...
yadi vā... vā whether.... or...
√*vac* 912/1 to speak, say, tell, utter, announce, declare, mention, proclaim, recite, describe,
vāc 936/1 f. speech, voice, talk, language, sound, a word, saying, phrase, sentence,
vaca mfn. speaking, talking
vacana 912/3 mfn. speaking, a speaker, indicating, n. command, statement, the act of speaking, utterance, word, speech,
vacas 912/3 n. speech, voice, word, singing, song (of birds), advice
vācāṭa mfn talkative, boastful,
vācyartha 937/3 m. directly expressed meaning,
vada speak! say! impv.
vāda 939/3 mfn. speaking of or about, causing to sound, playing, m. speech, discourse, proposition, argument, doctrine, demonstrated conclusion, result
-vāda m. the 'doctrine of ...'
vadan mfn saying, pres.part.
vadana n. 916/2 speaking, the mouth, face
vadati says, speaks
vādayati plays (an instrument)
vadha m. killing, slaughter, murderer,
vādhrīṇasa m. rhinoceros,
vadhū f. bride, woman,
vādi in comp. for *vādin* 940/1 mfn saying, speaking, a speaker, learned, wise,
vādin 940/1mfn. saying, talking about, proclaiming, m. teacher of any doctrine, speaker
vādin 940/1mfn. saying, talking about, proclaiming, m. teacher of any doctrine, speaker, disputant, accuser, plaintiff, prosecutor,
vāgmin 937/1 eloquent, speaking well,
vāgvistara m. prolixity, diffuseness (in speech)
vāha 949/1 mfn bearing, drawing, m. the act of a draught animal, any vehicle, conveyance, car, a bearer, porter,
vahāmi 933/2 √*vah* I lead, carry, bear
vāhana mfn carrying off, n. 1. beast of burden, beast for riding, team, vehicle, 2. the carrying,
vāhanā f. army,
vahati carries
vāhinī f. army,
vahni 933/3 m. any animal that bears or draws along, horse, team, charioteer, rider, bearer of oblations,
fire in general or the god of fire, the digestive fire,
vai 2.*vai* 1019/3 a particle of emphasis – certainly, truly indeed, common in poetry as an expletive
vaidehī a name for *Sītā*
vaidya 1. mfn having to do with science, m. physician,
vaikharī 4th stage in the manifestation of

sound or speech, "when the sounds are manifest in the physical form, through the use of tongue and mouth, and are expelled to vibrate in the open space, then it is called *vaikharī*"

Vainateya 1023/2 a name of Garuda the bird transport of *Viṣṇu*

vaira n.m. enmity, hostility, mfn hostile

vairāgya 1025/2 n. freedom from all worldly desires, indifferent to worldly objects, and to life, renunciation, aversion, distaste for, life (A) detachment, 'power of detachment' HH

vairasya 1025/2 n. tastelessness, disgust

vairi 1025/1 m. an enemy

vaiśākha m. a month, (April-May),

vaiṣayika 1027/2 m. belonging or relating to an object of sense, sensual

vaiśvānara 1027/1 mfn. relating or belonging to all men, omnipresent, known or worshipped everywhere, universal, general, common, consisting of all men, the sun, sunlight, name of the supreme Spirit or intellect when located in a supposed collective aggregate of gross bodies, the digestive fire of all men, name of Agni or fire,

vaiśya m. the third class or caste, merchants, producers, farmers

vaivasvata mfn coming from or belonging to the sun, relating or belonging to Yama, m. Vaivasvata (son of the sun – Death), O Death,

vaitṛṣṇya 1022/1 n. freedom from desire, indifference to,

Vaivasvata 1026/1 a *Manu* the son of *Vivasvat* the Sun

vajra 913/1 m. n. thunderbolt, a mythical weapon, diamond,

vāk statement, in comp for *vāc*

vakra mfn crooked, 2. fig. disingenuous, ambiguous,

vakṣas n. the breast, bosom, chest,

vaktā he/she will speak 1/s/peri fut, mfn speaking, fluent speaker, an instructor,

vakti 912/1 root *vac* 1/s/pres/indic/act speaks

vaktṛ m. speaker,

vaktra n. mouth, face

vaktum infin. of *vac* 912/1 to say , speak, utter

vākya n. a sentence lit. that which is spoken, 936/2 n. word, speech, saying, assertion, statement, command, a statement, a sentence, a rule, an argument, mode of expression

vākyasiddha 'whatever one would say would duly come to pass'

vāla m. bristle, hair, animal tail-hair,

valaya m.n. bracelet,

valgu mfn handsome, beautiful, attractive,

valī f. a fold, wrinkle, a wave,

vālī brother of *sugrīva*

valkala m. tree-bark,

valkya m. bark of a tree,

vallabha m. beloved, a favourite, friend,

vallarī or *vallī* f. a creeper, creeping plant

valmīka m. ant-hill,

vālmīki a sage who wrote the *Rāmāyaṇa*

vālukā f. sand, gravel, powder,

vāma mfn lovely, pleasant, n. a lovely thing, a joy, left, on the left side, any dear or desirable good, wealth,

vāmana mfn dwarfish, short in stature, a dwarf, small, minute, short (also of days), bent, inclined,

vami f.nausea, vomiting, m.fire, a cheat,

-vāmin dweller,

vamra m. ant, f. (*ī*),

vaṁśa 910/1 m. lineage, race, family, a dynasty, offspring, L. cane ,stock or stem of bamboo,

vaṁśa m. flute

vana n. 917/2 forest, wood, grove

vānaprastha a forest dweller, the third stage of life for a *brāhman*

vānara m. monkey

vanaukas m. forest-dweller, anchorite, a forest animal, a wild-boar, ape,

vāñchā 939/1 f. longing for, desire,

vañcaka mfn cunning, deceitful, m. a

jackal, a tame or house mongoose, a low or vile man,

vāñcati 938/3 1/s/pres/act/indic. of √*vāñch* to desire 938/3, he/she desires

√*vand* 919/1 to praise, celebrate, laud, show honour, do homage, venerate, worship, adore

vanda mfn. praising, extolling

vandana (m) n 919/2 the act of praising, praise, reverence, worship, adoration, offering gratitude, thanking,

vandanam thank-you,

vandhya n. barren,

vandya 919/2 mfn to be praised, saluted, praiseworthy,

vaṅga m. Bengal, m.n. cotton, n. tin or lead

vāṇī 939/2 f. sound, voice, music, speech, language, words, eloquent speech or fine diction, 'following true perception with exact expression'

vaṇij 915/2m. a merchant, trader, commerce

vaṇijya trade, traffic, commerce

vāṇija 939/2 a merchant, trader,

vanitā f. a loved wife, mistress, any woman

vāṅ-manasa 937/2 speech and mind,

vāpi whether,

vāpī f. oblong pond, lake, well,

vapra m.n. a rampart, earthwork, mound, slope of a hill, table-land, the gate of a fortified city, a sown field, any field, dust,

vapus 920/1 mfn. having form or a beautiful form, handsome, n. form, figure, esp. a beautiful one, nature, essence, ifc. the body,

vapusāt ind. into the form of a body,

vara 1. *vara* 921/1 m. enclosing, circumference, space, environing
2. *vara* 922/1 select, choicest, best, most excellent, valuable, precious
3.choosing,
L. 1.m. choice, wish, a thing to be chosen as gift or reward, gift, reward, *varam vṛ* wish a wish, make a condition, *varam dā* give a choice, grant a wish, *prati varam* or *varam ā* according to one's wish,
2. mfn most excellent or fair, best, *varam...na ca* the best thing is.. and not ....
(ifc. TP.) best of such and such, the best such and such,

vara/ varam n. a boon,

vāra 943/3 1. the hair of any animal's tail (esp. that of a horse), 2. keeping back, restraining, anything enclosed or circumscribed in space or time – appointed times, times e.g. 3 times, a moment, occasion, opportunity, a day of the week

varaḥ wish

vāraḥ a turn

varāha m. boar,

vāraṁ vāram time and again, sometimes,

vāraṇa 944/1 mfn warding off, restraining, all-resisting, invincible, relating to prevention, dangerous, forbidden m. an elephant, armour, mail. the act of restraining or keeping back or warding off

vārāṇasi Benares,

varas n. width, room, expanse, space,

varcas n. vitality, vigour, the illuminating power in fire and the sun, splendour, fig. glory,

vardhate he/she/it grows

vardhiṣyate will grow

varga m. group, division, class,

vāri 943/1 1/s water, rain, fluidity,
, a water-pot, pitcher, jar,

vāridhi 943/2 m. the sea, the ocean
5/s/m from the ocean

variṣṭha 921/2 1. mfn. (superlative) widest, broadest, largest,
most extensive, 923/1 mfn. the most excellent or eminent among,
best, most preferable among, better than, chief (in a bad sense) – worst, most wicked,

varja mfn. (ifc) free from, devoid of

varjaka mfn. (ifc.) shunning, avoiding

varjana 924/1 n. leaving, avoiding, excluding, neglect, omission,

exception, hurting,
varjita 924/1 mfn. excluded, abandoned, avoided, deprived of, wanting, without,
varman n. envelope, coat of armour,
varṇa 924/2 1/s/m a covering, exterior or outer appearance, colour, a class of men, order, caste, the four classes or castes -
brāhmaṇa – priests, teachers,
kṣatriya- warriors, kings, statesmen,
vaiśya – merchants, producers, farmers, *śūdra* – servants, labourers
varṇanā f. description, the act of painting, colouring etc.
varṇavyavasthā 924/3 f. the caste-system, institution of caste
varṣa 926/3 mfn raining, m. rain, raining, the rains, a cloud, a year, shower,
varṣā rain f.pl. the rains (monsoon),
vārṣika mfn annual,
vārṣṇeya, voc. 'O clansman of *vṛṣṇi*' *(Kṛṣṇa)*
varta m. subsistence, livelihood,
vartamāna 925/2 mfn. turning, moving, existing, living, abiding, present, *(ā)*f. the terminations of the present tense, n. presence, the present time, (in gram.) the present tense,
vartamānakṣepa 925/2 m. denying or not agreeing with any present event or circumstances
vartamānatā 925/2 f. or *tva* n. the being present, the condition of present time, the dwelling or abiding in (with loc.)
vartate 1009/1 turns, revolves, proceeds, is, lives, exists 1/s/pres/indic/mid he lives
varte (or *vartate*) I turn, move on, live, continue 3/s/pres/indic/mid √*vṛt*
varteyam I should continue 3/s/opt/act √*vṛt* 1009/1
varti or *ī* f. a bandage round something, a lamp wick, a lamp,
vartikā f. a lamp wick, a stalk, a paint brush, colour, paint,
vārtīka m. a businessman, a kind of quail,
vartin resting, abiding, behaving properly towards
vartma in comp. for *vartman*
vartman 925/3 n. the track or rut of a wheel, path, road, way, course,
vārttā f. news,
vārttikā f. business,
vartula mfn round, circular, globular, a ball,
Varuṇa the supporter, supreme vedic god,
vaśa 929/2 m. will, wish, desire, power, control, dominion, influence,
vāsa 947/2 1. n. cloth, clothes, garment 2. m. abiding, dwelling, abode, habitation, perfume,
vāsanā: 947/3 f. thinking of, longing for, desire, the impression of anything remaining unconsciously in the mind, the present consciousness of past perceptions, latent tendencies, idea, imagination,
vasanta m. spring,
vāsara 1. (Vedic)of the dawn, (Classic) time of dawn, day in general
vāsas n. garment, clothing,
vasati lives, dwells,
vasati f. a dwelling, home, residence,
vaśī 929/3 having mastery, a ruler a sage with subdued passions
vāsin dweller
vasiṣtha a sage, wrote the Supreme Yoga,
vāsita 947/2/3 mfn.infused, steeped, perfumed, scented,affected with, influenced by, spiced, seasoned (as sauces), caused to dwell or live in, peopled, populous (as a country), n. the art of rendering populous, knowledge (esp. derived from memory = *vāsanā*),
vāstava 948/3 substantial, real, true, genuine, fixed, demonstrated, n. an appointment,
vastra f. becoming light, dawning, n. clothing, garment, cloth,
vastu 932/3 n, the seat or place of anything, thing, object, article, (in phil.) the "real" , the real as opposed to the unreal adv.
vāstu m.n. dwelling, the site or foundation

of a house, site, ground,
vastutā f. ifc. the state of being the object of,
vastutas in fact, in reality,
vasu 930/3 mfn excellent, good, beneficent, n. goods, wealth m. 1. good (of gods), 2. m.pl. the good ones the Vasus, a class of gods closely associated with Indra,
Vāsudevānanda
Vasudeva was the father of *Kṛṣṇa* so another name for *Kṛṣṇa* is *Vāsudeva* which indicates the relationship by the addition of a measure of the letter *a*. Therefore *vāsudevānanda* can mean the bliss of *Kṛṣṇa* which could be another way of saying the bliss of the Absolute. Other meanings may also be derived.
vasu-dhā mfn yielding good, f. the earth, the land,
Vāsuki king of serpents,
vaśya 929/3 mfn. to be subjected, subdued, obedient to another's will, dutiful, humble, at the disposal of, a slave
vaśyatā f. obedience, humility, being under the control of,
-vat a suffix – like, as
vaṭa m. a kind of fig tree, the Banyan tree, a kind of bird, cowry shell, a chess pawn, sulphur,
vāta 934/2 blown, the wind
vataṁsa m. an ornament, garland, crest,
vātāyana mfn moving in the air or wind,
m.'fleet as the wind' a horse,
n. 'wind passage' a window, air-hole, loop-hole,
a balcony, roof-terrace,
vaṭhara mfn stupid,
vatsa m. dear child, a child,
vatsa m. calf, young, yearling,
vatsala mfn tender, kind, loving,
vatsara a year, the year personified,
vayam we pron. 1/pl
vayas n. a bird, any winged animal, bird (collective),
2. food, meal, (enjoyment),
3. strength –of body and of mind, health, the time of strength – youth, marriageable age, any age or period of life, years (of life),
vāyasa m. a bird, crow, turpentine,
vāyos of the wind 6/s/m
vāyuputraḥ -Hanumān son of the wind,
vayasya m. a friend, a contemporary,
vāyu 942/2 m. air, wind, the element air, has the property – touch
the god of the wind, breathing, breath, a vital force,
vayuna 920/3 mfn. moving, active, alive, agitated, restless, distinctness, clearness, knowledge, wisdom
vāyuputra son of the wind - *hanuman*
veda 1015/1 1. knowledge, true or sacred knowledge or lore, name of 4 celebrated works - *rgveda, yajurveda, sāmaveda* and *atharvaveda*. The concluding portions of each (*vedanta* – end of the *vedas*) are the *upaniṣad*s
veda he knows, 1/s/perf/act √*vid*
vedana mfn announcing, proclaiming,
n. perception, knowledge, making known, proclaiming,
feeling, sensation,
f. (*ā*) pain, torture, agony,
vedāṅga support (limb) of the Veda in six sciences – pronunciation, metre and singing of verses (poetry), grammar, meaning of words, astronomy and planetary influence, sacrifices and ritual
vedānta 1017 m. end of the *veda* – see above. One of the great branches of Indian Philosophy, (called *Vedanta* either as teaching the ultimate scope of the *veda* or simply as explained in the *upaniṣads* – its chief doctrine is that of *advaita* i.e. that nothing exists in reality but the One Self or Soul of the Universe called *Brahman* or *Paramātman* and that the *jīvātman* or individual human soul and indeed all the phenomena

of nature are really identical with the *paramātman*.....

vedāntin 1017/2 follower of the *vedānta* philosophy,

vedas 2. n. knowledge, property, wealth, science,

vedavid 1016/1 mfn. knowing the Veda, conversant with it

vedayajña sacrifice for the divine,

vedhas mfn 1. worshipper of the gods, worshipping, pious, devoted,
2. (generalised) faithful, true, (used of Indra), creator (Brahmā and others),

vedi m. a wise man, teacher, Pandit, f. knowledge, science, a seal ring,

veditum to know (infin. √*vid)*

vedya n. the to-be-known, the object of knowledge, 1/s/n gerundive √*vid*

vega 1013/3 m. rush, dash, speed, haste, rapidity, quickness, impetus, momentum, agitation, shock, jerk, outbreak, outburst (of passion),

vegena ind. quickly,

velā f. 1. end-point, limit, 2. esp. limit of time, point of time, hour, last hour, 3. sea-shore

veṇi f. weaving, braiding, a braid of hair, braided stream (*veṇī*),

veṇu m. reed esp. bamboo reed, a flute,

vepas 1018, n. trembling, quivering

vepathu 1018/2 m. quivering, trembling

veśa m. settler, neighbour, dwelling small farmer, tenant, neighbour, house, dwelling, brothel, trade, business,

veṣa m. work, management, activity, dress, apparel, artificial exterior, assumed appearance, often for *veśa,* mfn working, active, busy,

veśman n. dwelling, house, chamber,

vetāla m. vampire, goblin, ghost,

vetana n. wages,

vettha you know 2/s/perf/act √*vid*

vetti √*vid* 1. 963/2 (he, she, it) knows,

vi 1. m. a bird,
2. ind. an artificial word = *anna*
3. ind. in two parts, apart, asunder, in different directions, to and fro, about, away, away from, off, without,

may denote 'through' or 'between' as a preposition with 2nd case.

as a prefix to verbs, nouns and other parts of speech derived from verbs to express – division, distinction, distribution, arrangement, order, opposition or deliberation,

may express- outwards, in different directions, in all directions.

sometimes gives a meaning opposite to the idea contained in the simple root, or intensifies that idea,

in some cases does not seem to modify the meaning of the simple word at all,

may be used in forming compounds not immediately referable to verbs, in which cases it may express difference in terms of change or variety,

vibhā 2. mfn shining, bright, f. light, lustre, splendour, beauty,

vibhāga 977/2 separation, differences, distribution, apportionment, a share, portion, separation, distinction, difference, roles division,

vibhakta 977/2 mfn. divided, distributed among, parted, one who has received his share, one who has caused partition, isolated, secluded, n. seclusion, solitude,

vibhakti f. inflection of nouns, declension, an affix of declension, case, lit. division, separation, modification, partition

vibhāvin vibhāvin 978/3 mfn inherent cause,

mighty, powerful, arousing a particular emotion,
ifc. causing to appear,

vibhīṣaṇaḥ brother of *rāvaṇa*

vibhīṣikā 978/1 f. frightening, terrifying, the act of terrifying, fear, an object of fear, frightened,

vibhrama 979/2 doubt, error, mistake, restlessness, unsteadiness, excess, intensity, agitation, disturbance,

vibhraṣta 979/2 mfn. sunk, fallen, disappeared, useless, vain, gone, lost, strayed from, deprived of

vibhu or *vibhū* 978/3, being everywhere, far-extending, all-pervading, omnipresent, eternal, abundant, plentiful, a Lord, ruler, sovereign, king - *vibho* voc sing - Oh, all pervading One

vibhūti 978/3 mfn. penetrating, pervading, plentiful, powerful, f. expansion, development, multiplication, manifestation of might, superhuman powers

vibhūtimat mfn powerful, splendid,

vibudha 1. destitute of learned men,
2. mfn very wise or learned, m. a wise or learned man, teacher, a god

vicacakṣire 1/pl/perf *vi-√cakṣ*
they explained

vicakṣaṇa 958/2 mfn. conspicuous, visible, bright, radiant, clear-sighted, wise

vi√cal 958/3 to move about, shake, waver

vicālayet he should cause to waver
1/s/caus/act/opt *vi√cal*

vicālyate he is shaken or moved
1/s/pres/indic/caus/pass

vicāra 958/2 m. consideration, reflection, discrimination, mode of acting or proceeding, investigation, inquiry, examination, self-inquiry, hesitation, deliberation,

vicārita 958/3 mfn when deliberated, considered, when examined, settled, decided,
n. deliberation, hesitation, doubt,

viccheda m. separation,

vicetas 1. unintelligible, 2. mfn. visible, clearly seen, discerning, wise

vīci m. a wave, ripple, f. f. going or leading aside or astray, aberration, deceit,

vicikitsā 959/1 f. doubt, uncertainty, question, inquiry *vi √4. cit*

vi √4. cit to perceive, discern, understand, Desid. *vicikitsati* to wish to distinguish,

vicitra mfn very variegated, 2. differently coloured, varied, 3. (full of variety and surprises) entertaining, beautiful,

vid cl 1 P. *veòati* to call, cry out,
2. f. a bit, fragment,
cl.2 to know, understand, learn, perceive, be conscious of

vid 2. 963/3 mfn. knowing, understanding, planet Mercury, f. knowledge, understanding,

vida mfn. ifc. knowing, knowledge, discovery, m. knowledge, discovery,

vidagdha 1. mfn undigested, 2. mfn burnt up, consumed, digested, decomposed, spoiled, turned sour, clever, shrewd, knowing, m. a clever man, a scholar,

vidagdha śākalya a clever man, scholar, *pandita*

vidāhin 965/3 mfn burning, scorching, hot, pungent, acrid,

viḍamba mfn imitating, representing, m. mockery, derision, distressing, annoyance,

vidambate 962/1 to imitate, copy, deceive

vidambita mfn deceived, imitated, transformed, distorted, low, abject, n. an object of ridicule or contempt, despicable object,

viddhi 968/1f. a rule, law, rules of behaviour 1/s/m code of behaviour, understanding, intelligence,

viddhi 963/2 from root *vid* to know, understand, perceive, learn, be conscious of – 2/s/impv/act. know!
viddhi yathā know that,

viddhi sutrāṇi state the rules of grammar in Pāṇini's grammar,

videśa m. another country, foreign country, abroad, °*ga* going abroad,

√*vidh* cl6 to worship, honour, dedicate *vidhati, vidhema* we offer

vi √*dhā* 967/2 *vidadhāti* to distribute, grant, apportion, bestow,

vidhā f. division, part, portion, kind, sort,

vidhāna 967/3 mfn disposing, arranging, regulating, acting, performing, possessing, prescription, precept, disposing, n. order, measure, regulation, rule

vidhātṛ mfn distributing, arranging, m. creator, maker,

vidhavā f. widow, country without a king,

vi-dheya 968/2 to be bestowed or procured, to be enjoined, governed or controlled, docile, compliant, subject or obedient to

vidhi 967/2 1. m. a worshipper, one who does homage 968/1 2. m. a rule, formula, law, direction,

vidhihīna 968/1 mfn destitute of rule, unauthorised, opposed to what is enjoined, contrary to injunction

vidhidṛṣṭa 968/1 mfn. prescribed by rule

vidhivākya 'divine rules', G343 injunctive sentences containing the essence and purport of the Veda

vidhīyate it is granted, it is given 1/s/pres/indic/pass *vi*√*dhā*

vidhu mfn lonely, solitary, m. the moon, miserable, helpless,

vidhura mfn alone, bereft, 2. suffering, lack, miserable, 3. disagreeable, n. trouble, adversity, m. a widower,

vidhvaṁsa m. ruin, destruction, hurt, injury, cessation (of a disease), violation (of a woman), insult, offence,

vidita 963/3 mfn. known, understood, perceived, learnt, knowing, m. knower, a learned man, sage,

viditvā knowing, having known

vidmas we know, 1/pl/pres/indic/act √*vid*

vidrava m. running away, flight, panic, melting, liquefaction, censure, reproach, intellect, understanding,

vidrāva m. flight, retreat, liquefaction,

vidruma 1 treeless, 2. m. a young sprout or shoot, coral,

vidu mfn intelligent, wise, m. the hollow between the frontal globes of an elephant,

vidus 3/pl/perf 1. √vid 963/2 they knew or with present meaning, they know,

viduṣā f. very learned man, understanding, possibly – an apparently learned man,

vidūṣaka m. a jester, mfn witty, facetious,

viduṣkṛta mfn free from sins or faults or transgressions,

vidvān the wise, the wise one part. √*vid*1/s/m

vidvas mfn one who knows, knowing, understanding, learned, intelligent, wise, mindful of, familiar with, skilled in (2nd, 7th, comp.), m. a wise man, sage, seer,

vidyā 963/3 f. scholarship, science, learning, philosophy, knowledge, 'The knowledge or *vidyā* belongs to the *ātman* and out of *vidyā* comes the world. having taken a form, it must perish and go back to *vidyā* again' HH

vidyā 'is implied as *adhyātmavidyā*, the knowledge of the Self,'

vidyāt may it be known, let it be known 1/s/opt/act √vid

vidyate 1/s/pres/indic/pass 2. √*vid* 963/2 it is known, understood, perceived, learned, is conscious of, has an understanding of,

vidyut f. lightning

vigata 956/3 mfn free, disappeared, ceased, gone, free from, devoid of

vigataspṛha mfn gone away desire, whose desire has gone away,

vighna m. a breaker, destroyer, an obstacle, impediment, hindrance,

vigraha 957/2 keeping apart or asunder, the body, embodied, (in gram.) separation of a word, quarrel, war with, individual form or figure,
viguṇa 950/2 mfn deficient, imperfect, wicked, bad
vihaṅga mfn sky-going, flying, m. a bird
vihara 1003/2 m. taking away, removing, separation
vihāra 1003/3 m. distribution, transposition, arrangement or disposition, too great lengthening or drawling in pronunciation, sport, play, pastime, enjoyment, pleasure, walking for pleasure or amusement
vihasya 1003/1 *vi* √*ha* to laugh loudly at, laughing at
vihāya 1003/2 ind. notwithstanding, leaving behind, setting aside, at a distance from, forsaking
vihīna 1003/2 mfn entirely abandoned or left, absent, free from
vihita 953/2 mfn improper, unfit, not good, 1003/2 distributed, apportioned, bestowed, ordered, determined, ordained,
vihvala mfn agitated, perturbed, distressed
vijana mfn free from people, solitary, deserted, lonely,
vijānat 961/1 mfn knowing, understanding m. a wise man, sage
vijānāti 961/1 he distinguishes, discerns, knows, 1/s/pres/indic/act.
vijanita 959/3 mfn born, begotten
vijānītas they two know, understand, 1/du/pres/indic/mid
vijānīyām I should understand or comprehend, 3/s/opt/act *vi* √*jñā*
vijānīmaḥ we are aware, we understand, we know, 3/pl/pres/act *vi*√*jñā*
vijara mfn not growing old, m. a stalk
vijaya 960/1 m. contest for victory, victory, conquest
vijita conquered, subdued
vijña 961/1 mfn. knowing, intelligent, wise, discerning, m. a wise man, a sage,
vi√*jñā* 961/1 to distinguish, discern, observe, ascertain, know, understand, have right knowledge, become wise or learned,
vijñāna 961/2 the act of distinguishing or discerning, understanding, comprehending, has been used in the sense of 'right apprehension' in *Advaita* text, has been used with the sense of 'proper analysis of the *jñānam* q.v. also see *prajñānam*
vijñāpta mfn informed, made known, reported,
vijñāta mfn discerned, known, understood
vijñāya mfn recognizable,
vijñāna 961/2 n. the act of distinguishing or discerning, understanding, comprehending, intelligence, knowledge, faculty of right judgement, consciousness, pure knowledge, nothing but intelligence,
vijñānata mfn knowing, wise,
vijñānamaya mfn consisting of knowledge
vijñānamayakośa the sheath of intellect,
vijṛmbhita 960/3 mfn become expanded, appearance, manifestation,
vijugupsate 957/2 shrinks away from, wishes to conceal from, dislikes, hates,
vijvara mfn 950/3 free from distress or anxiety, cheerful, free from fever or pain, exempt from decay,
vikaca 1. mfn hairless, bald, 2.mfn opened, blown, shining, resplendent, brilliant, expanded,
vikala 953/3 mfn crippled, impaired, exhausted, weakened
vikalpa 955/2 m. alternative, option, different, doubt, conflicting ideas,
vikalpanā 955/2 f . false notion or assumption, fancy, agination
vikalpita 955/2 mfn from *vikalpa* diversity, imagination, arranged, false notion, imagined,
vi√*kamp* 953/3 to tremble greatly, quiver,
vikāra 954/2 change of form or

nature, transformation, coming into being, changing, and passing away

Vikarṇa a Kaurava warrior, 'without ears'

viklava mfn overcome with fear or agitation, confused, bewildered, distressed, timid, shy, unsteady,

vikrama m. a step, stride, pace, going, proceeding, walking, valour, courage, heroism, power, strength, force, intensity, high degree, stability, duration, a foot,

vikrānta mfn striding forth, courageous

vikraya m. sale, selling,

vikṛti 954/3 f.change, modification, agitation,

vīkṣ 1004/2 to look upon, regard, see, see in the heart,

vikṣepa 956/2 m. inattention, distraction, confusion, "due to non-stop use of the subtle body" (Jaiswal)

vikṣipta 956/2 mfn agitated, scattered,

vīkṣya pres.part. seeing,

vilagna 984/3 mn fastened or attached to,

vilambhāt with delay

vilāpa m. lamentation,

vilapati laments

vilāsa 985/1 m. shining forth, appearance, manifestation, joy,

vilasati 985/1 gleams, flashes, shines forth, sports, plays,

vilaya 985/3 m.disappearance, dissolution, decomposition, n. corrosion, melting, corroding,

vilokya 986/1 to be or being looked at, visible,

vimala 979/3 mfn stainless, spotless, pure

vimāna mfn devoid of honour, disgraced, measuring out, traversing, traversing the sky, m. disrespect, dishonour, m.n. a car or chariot of the gods, a horse, ship, boat, n. measure, extension, the science of (right) measure or proportion (partic. the state of the body with regard to remedies etc),

vimārga m.a wrong road, evil course, mfn being on a wrong road,

vi-marśa 981/*1* m. consideration, deliberation, critical test, examination, reasoning, discussion, knowledge, intelligence,

vimatsara mfn free from greed, malice or envy

vimohayati causes to confuse, confuses, deludes, 1/s/pres/indic/act *vi√muh*

vimokṣana 981/2 mfn liberating from, untying, loosening, liberating

vimokṣyase you shall be liberated 2/s/fut/pass *vi√muc*

vi- √mṛś 981/1- *mṛśati* to touch (with the hands) stroke, feel, (mentally), be sensible or aware of, perceive, consider, reflect on, deliberate about, investigate, examine, *√mṛś* 831/1 1. to touch (physically or mentally), consider, reflect, deliberate,

vimṛśa 981/1 reflection, consideration,

vimṛśata mfn reflecting,

vimṛśya 981/1 ind. having deliberated or considered, reflecting on

viṁśati twenty

vimucya ind. relinquishing, abandoning, having relinquished or discarded,

vimuñcati 980/2 980/2 he shuns, avoids, keeps off, relinquishes, frees oneself, rejects, abandons, gives up

vimūḍha 980/3 mfn not foolish, ifc. perplexed as to, m.simple, dull, deluded,

vinā ind. without (after 3rd), except

vīṇā f. lute, lightning,

vinadya mfnsounding forth, vibrating,

vinaṅkṣyasi you will be lost, you will perish 2/s/fut/act *vi √naṣ*

vināśa 969/3 m. destruction, loss

vināśvara 969/2 m .liable to be lost or destroyed

vinaśyatsu 7/pl among the perishable

vinaśyati 969/2 is lost or destroyed

vinaya 971/3 mfn separating, m. taking away, 2. leading, guidance, training, discipline, decency, modesty,

vindati knows, understands, perceives,

learns, experiences, feels, considers as, takes for, √ 3. *vid*

vindhya m. an east-west range of hills north of the Deccan, a hunter,

viniścita 971/2 mfn. firmly resolved upon, determined, settled, certain, (*am*) ind. most certainly, decidedly

vinirgata 970/3 liberated or freed from, gone out, come forth 2/s

vinirmukta 971/1 liberated, escaped, free

vinirvṛtta 971/1 proceeded, come forth, completed, finished

viniścaya 971/2 m. deciding, settling ascertainment,

vinivartate 971/2 turns back, returns, turns away, ceases from, renounces

viniyamya restraining, subduing, gerund mfn to be restricted or limited,

viniyata 970/2 mfn. restrained, checked, regulated, limited,

vinoda m. driving away, removal, diversion, sport, pleasure, amusement, eagerness, vehemence,

vipakṣa mfn 'deprived of wings', an opponent, adversary, enemy, in logic – a counter statement,

vipaṇa m. selling, sale, wager, shop, market-place, the organ of speech,

vipaṇin m. shopkeeper,

viparīta 974/1 mfn. turned round, reversed, inverted, being the reverse of anything, opposite, contrary to, perverse, wrong, inauspicious

viparivartate it revolves, exists 1/s/pres/indic/mid *vi pari* √*vṛt*

viparyasta 974/2 mfn overthrow, opposite of, contrary, turned over, reversed, opposite,

vipaścit 972/3 mfn. inspired, wise, learned, the intelligent Self, -intelligent because its nature of consciousness is never lost, versed in,

vipat 973/3 P. *–patati,* to fly or dash or rush through, to fly apart, fall off, burst asunder, *-pātayati* to cause misfortune or calamity

viphala mfn bearing no fruit, useless, ineffectual, futile, idle,

vipina n. forest, grove, thicket,

viplava mfn having no ship or boat, confused (as words), m. confusion, trouble, disaster, evil, calamity, misery, affray, revolt, loss, damage, shipwreck,

vipra mfn stirred or excited inwardly, inspired, wise (said of men and gods), a sage, seer, singer, poet, a priest, the moon, a brāhmana,

viprakarṣa m. dragging away, carrying off, remoteness, distance, difference, contrast, the separation of 2 consonants by inserting a vowel,

vipralambha m. deception, deceit, disappointment, disjunction, quarrel, disagreement, separation of lovers, disunion, disjunction,

viprati √*pad* 975/2 to go in different or opposite directions, be perplexed, be mistaken have a false opinion about,

vipratipanna mfn. averse, gone in different directions, having a false opinion,

vipriya mfn disaffected, disagreeable, unpleasant to, n. anything unpleasant or hateful, offence, transgression,

vipula mfn wide, thick, large, extensive, long, abundant, numerous, important, m. a respectable man, f. (*ā)* the earth, *-tva* largeness, greatness, extent, width,

vīra mfn brave courageous, heroic, m. warrior, a brave or eminent man

virāga 952/1 passionless, without feeling, aversion, dislike,

virāgatā f. indifference

viraha 982/3 absence from, lack, want

virahita mfn deserted, abandoned, lonely,

virāj 982/3 2. mfn. ruling far and wide, the first progeny of Brahmā, sovereign, excellent, splendid, a ruler, chief, f. excellence, pre-eminence, high rank, dignity, majesty, 1. m. the king of birds,

virājati 982/3 reigns, rules, is illustrious, shines forth, shines out, appears as

virakta 981/3mfn discoloured, changed in disposition, estranged, disaffected, averse, indifferent to, having no interest in, unattached,

virakti 982/1 f. change of disposition or feeling, alienation of mind, freedom of passion, aversion,

virala 982/2 rare, scarcely found

virama 982/2 cessation, end

virāma m. stop! cessation, termination, end, grammatical stop at end of line or verse,

viramati stops

virāṭ in comp. for 2.*virāj* , '..the macrocosm universe in full manifestation' HH.
-'the cosmic person embodied in the gross universe', 'who exists as fire, air and the sun'

viraṭa m. the shoulder

virata 982/2 stopped, ceased, ended

virati *virati* 982/2 f. cessation, stop, pause, end, one who has given up, resigned, abstention, desistence from, detachment,

virodha m. opposition, hostility, quarrel, contradiction, inconsistency, calamity, misfortune,

virodhin mfn hindering, disturbing, opposing, obstructing, besieging, blockading, dispelling, removing, adverse, hostile, opposed, contradictory, rivalling with, contradictory, contentious, quarrelsome,

virūpa mfn many-coloured, variegated, multi-form, manifold, various, altered, changed, deformed, less by one, m. jaundice, n. deformity, difference of form, the act of disfiguring,

vīrya 1006/3 n. (ifc.) manliness, valour, strength, power, energy, splendour, lustre, dignity, consequence, f. (*ā*) vigour, energy, virility, heroic deed, mfn. strong, powerful, 'power of potentiality' HH

vīryavān valorous, full of heroism, the most powerful, the omnipotent,

viś 989/1 *Dhatu* to enter in, to pervade,

viṣa 995/2 m. a servant, attendant, n. poison, venom, anything active

viśada 989/3 mfn bright, brilliant, shining, splendid, beautiful, white, spotless, pure, calm, easy, cheerful, clear, intelligible, tender, ifc. skilled in, fit for,

viṣāda 996/3 m. depression, despondency, despair

viṣādī m. despondent, depressed,

viśāla mfn great, broad, huge, vast, illustrious, eminent, ifc. abundant in, full of,

viṣama 996/3 mfn uneven, rough, irregular, difficult, dangerous, bad, wicked

viṣāṇa n. a horn, a tusk, crab-claws, a peak, top, point, summit, the chief or best of a class or kind,

viśārada mfn experienced, proficient, learned, wise, holy,

visarga 1001/1 m. sending forth, letting go, liberation, emission, discharge, a release of breath, shown as :

viśati 989/1 retires, resorts to, enters,

viśaya 991/1 m. the middle, centre, doubt, uncertainty,

viṣaya m. object of the senses – sounds, textures, colours, tastes, smells 997/1 m. an object of the senses, sphere of influence or activity, anything perceptible by the senses, sphere (of influence or activity),

vi-ṣīdati 996/2 is exhausted or dejected,

viṣīdan despairing, despondent, pres.part.

viśeṣa 990/2 distinction, difference, characteristic difference, peculiarity, a kind, species, individual, distinction, excellence, (in gram.) a word which defines or limits the meaning of another word, (in phil.) particularity, individuality,

essential diference or individual essence,
viśeṣatas ind. especially, particularly, above all, individually, singly, according to the difference of.., in proportion to (comp.),
viśeṣaṇa 991/1 mfn distinguishing, discriminative, specifying, qualifying, distinctive (as a property), n. the act of distinguishing, distinction, discrimination, particularization, (in gram.) a word which - particularizes or defines, attribute, adjective, species, kind, 'brings out a quality of a *nāman* (an adjective)' "the act of expanding the remainder"
viśiṣṭa mfn 'left apart', separated, distinct, distinguished, particular, peculiar, excellent, that which is qualified, characterized by (3rd or comp.), chief or best among (6th), better or worse than (5th or comp.),
*viśiṣṭa brahman " * a synonym for *saguṇa brahman"* HH
viśiṣṭādvaita 990/2 n. qualified non-duality
viśiṣyate is distinguished, better or superior 1/s/pres/pass *vi √śiṣ*
viślatha mfn relaxed, loose,
vismaraṇa 1002/2 the act of forgetting, oblivion
vismarati he forgets,
vismaya 1. 953/1 free from pride or arrogance, 2. 1002/2 m. wonder, surprise, amazement, bewilderment, pride, arrogance,
vismita mfn amazed, astonished,
vismṛta 1002/2 forgetful of all,
vismṛti f. forgetfulness, loss of memory, oblivion,
viṣṇu sustainer of the universe, preserver, universal *citta*
viṣṇu purāṇa famous book
viśrabdha mfn confiding, confident, fearless, tranquil, calm, trusting in, relying on, (*am*) ind. quietly, confidingly, without fear or reserve, confidently, without hesitation,
viśrabdhatva n. trustworthiness,
viśrāma 992/1 rest, repose, calm,
viśrambha m. relaxation of the organs of utterance, cessation, trust, confidence in, absence of restraint, familiarity, intimacy,
viśrānta 991/3mfn rested or ceased from, stopped reposed,
visṛjāmi I send forth, I create 3/s/pres/indic/act *vi √sṛj*
visṛjan excreting, discharging, pres/act/part *vi√sṛj* 1001/1
visṛjya 1001/2 mfn. to be sent out or let go, to be produced or effected, effect
throwing down, having cast aside gerund *vi √sṛj*
viśruta 1.mfn flowed forth, flowed away, 2. mfn heard of far and wide, heard, noted, notorious, famous, known as, passing for, named, pleased, happy,
viṣṭabhya supporting, having stopped, gerund *vi√stabh*
vistara 1001/3 mfn extensive, long, m. spreading, expansion, a multitude, pl. great wealth or riches, detail, particulars,
vistaraśa in detail (adv.)
vistara 1001/3 mfn extensive, long (as a story), spreading, extension, a multitude, assembly, high degree, intensity
viṣṭhita 999/1 mfn. standing apart, scattered, standing, fixed, standing or being on or in, specially exist, being present or near, situated
viśuddha 991/2 mn. completely cleansed or purified, clean, clear, pure, free from vice, virtuous, honest,
viśuddhabodha m. a fully realized man
viśva 992/2 mfn all, everyone, whole, entire, universal, all pervading, omnipresent, n. the whole world, the universe, (in phil.) m.the intellectual faculty, Grimes 351, the

individual form of the Self having egoism in a gross body while awake, the form of the Self in its waking state according to *Advaita Vedanta*

viśvāmitra *Viśvāmitra*

viśvāsa 995/1 m. confidence, trust, faith or belief, reliance,

viśvasākṣin 994/1 mfn all-seeing,

viśvatas mfn from or on all sides, universally

-vit knower ,

viṭa m. a bon-vivant, boon-companion, rogue, knave,

vīta 1004/1 1. mfn gone, approached, 2. gone away, departed, disappeared, 4. worn out, useless

vitamanyu mfn free from anger or sorrow,

vitamas mfn free from darkness, light

viṭapa 961/3 a branch of a tree, twig, shoot,

vītarāga 1004/2 mfn dispassionate, calm, (*vita-* gone away *raga-* passion), desireless, tranquil, unattached

vitarka m. conjecture, supposition, doubt, uncertainty, a dubious or controversial matter, reasoning, deliberation, purpose, intention, a teacher, instructor in divine knowledge, a partic. class of *yogī*

vītaśoka 1004/2 mfn free from the disturbance of sorrow, m. the *aśoka* tree,

vitata 962/2 mfn spread out, extended, diffused, drawn (as a bow-string), bent (as a bow)

vītatṛṣṇaḥ 1004/2 mfn free from all passions or desires

vitṛṣṇatva 950/3 n. freedom from desire

vitta 963/2 mfn known, understood, celebrated, notorious, famous for, m. wealth, fame, money,

vittārtha m. one who knows the matter, an expert

Vitteśas another name for *Kubera*

vivāda m. a dispute, quarrel

vivāha m. fetching home of the bride, wedding, marriage, a partic. wind

vivāha + kṛ he gets married

vivardhana 989/1 mfn 2. augmenting, increasing, furthering, promoting,

vivarjita mfn avoided, left, abandoned by, destitute or deprived of, free or exempt from (3rd or comp.), that from which anything is excluded (ifc.), excepting, excluding,

vivarṇa mfn pale, colourless, low, vile, m. a man of low caste or outcaste,

vivarta 988/3 m. 'the revolving one' name of the sky, turning round, revolving, rolling onwards, changing from one state to another, alteration, transformation, illusion,

vivartate 988/3 changes from one state to another, turns, revolves, 1/s/pres/indic/mid rolling onwards

vivartavāda a method of asserting the Vedanta doctrine (maintaining the development of the universe from brahma as the sole real entity).

vivaśa mfn deprived or destitute of will, powerless, helpless, unwilling, involuntary, spontaneous, unrestrained, independent,

vivasvat 987/1 mfn. shining forth, diffusing light, name of the sun,

viveka 987/3 m. true knowledge, right judgement, the power of separating the invisible Spirit from the visible world, truth from untruth, reality from illusion, "The result of *viveka* is such that in appreciation of the separation of the two, there is no binding force for the limited knowledge. In *viveka* the limit is broken and the vision goes beyond the limit. It transcends." HH 'discrimination between the conscious and inanimate' HH 'Only through true understanding, (*viveka)* can one experience *aham* and segregate *ahaṅkāra*' HH "*Viveka* is the reasoning system to acquire the truth about the Self." HH

vivekin 988/1 mfn discriminating, examining distinguishing, investigating,

vivikta 987/3 mfn separated, discriminated, isolated, alone, solitary, pure

vivṛddha 989/1 mfn grown, increased,

enhanced, n. (*am*) grown powerful, increased,

viyat mfn going apart or asunder, being dissolved, passing away, vanishing, n. the sky, heaven, air, atmosphere, ether,

viyoga 981/3 m. disjunction, separation

viyukta 981/3 mfn detached, separated, disunited

√vṛ 2. cl 5,9 1007/3 to choose, select, ask, for or on behalf of, ask or request that,

√vraj 1049/3 to obtain, attain to, 2/s/pres/impv/act become

vraja m. a way, road, n. wandering, roaming, ifc. m.f (*ā*) a fold, stall, cow-pen, cattle-shed, station of herdsmen, a herd, flock, swarm, troop, host, multitude,

vrajeta he might go, he should travel, he should proceed 1/s/opt/mid *vraj*

vraṇa m. a wound, sore, flaw, blemish,

vrata 1042/2 n. will, command, law, vow ordinance, rule, obedience, service

vrāta 1043/1 m. a multitude, flock, assembly, group

vṛddha mfn old, grown larger, aged

vṛddhi mfn old

vṛddhi 1011/1 growth, increase, rise, success, gain,

vrīḍā f.shame, modesty, bashfulness

vrīhī m. rice,

vṛjina 1009/1 mfn bent, crooked, false, wicked

vṛka m. wolf

vṛkṣa m. tree

vṛṇe I ask for, I seek for 3/s/mid/pres/ mid cl 9

vṛṇīṣva you ask for 2/s/impv *√vṛ* cl9

vṛṅkte excludes 1/s/pres/mid *vṛj*

vṛṇoti chooses,

vṛṣṇi 1013/2 manly strong, powerful, nickname of tribe (of *Kṛṣṇa*)

vṛṣṭi f. rain

vṛṣabha same as *vṛṣan,* bull as type of greatness and might etc., of Indra – most mighty one,

vṛṣan mfn all that was distinguished for its strength and virility, 1. man as opposed to a castrated person, 2. stallion, bull, bear, etc. 3. of gods – manly, mighty, great, of Indra and others,

vṛt 1009/1 lives or exists

vṛta chosen, selected, preferred,

vṛthā 1007/3 f. at will, at pleasure , i.e. not for the sake of he gods, in vain, ind. aimless

vṛtta mfn turned, set in motion (as a wheel), round, rounded, circular, occurred, happened, ifc. continued, lasted for a certain time, completed, finished, absolved, past, elapsed, gone, quite exhausted, deceased, dead, studied, mastered, existing, effective, unimpaired, become..., acted or behaved towards, fixed, firm, chosen, m. a tortoise, a kind of grass, a round temple, n. a circle, the epicycle, occurrence, transformation or change into (ifc.), appearance, formed or derived from (ifc.), procedure, practice, action, mode of life, conduct, behaviour

vṛttānta mfn alone, solitary, m. news, report,

vṛtti 1010/1 f. rolling, mode of life or conduct, course of action, behaviour, moral conduct, common practice, mode of being, nature, disposition, state, being, existing, devotion to, occupation with, working, activity, function, the use of a word in a particular way, (in gram. – a complex formation which requires explanation or separation into its parts e.g. some compounds), a commentary

vy-ā-√cakṣ 1036/3 cl2. to explain, comment upon, rehearse,

vyācacakṣire they explained, they spoke clearly, 1/pl/perf.

vyadadhāt has allotted or distributed in the proper way

vyadārayat it caused to burst, it tore, it rent, 1/s/caus/imperf/act *vi √dṛ*

vyādhi m. disease,
vyāghra 1036/2 m. a tiger
vyagra mfn inattentive, distracted, agitated, (*am*) ind. in an agitated manner,
vyagrā 1029/1 distracted, engrossed by, eagerness, intentness 1/pl/m eager to attain
vyāharan uttering, pronouncing, speaking, pres/act/part see *vy ā* √*hṛ* 1039/3
vyāhṛti 1039/3 f. utterance, speech, declaration, mystical utterance partic. of *bhūr, bhuvaḥ, svar*
vyāja 1036/3 deceit, deception, fraud,
vyajana n. a palm-leaf used as a fan, a fan,
vyākaraṇa 1035/3 n. separation, distinction, explanation, detailed description, grammatical analysis, grammar, grammatical correctness, polished or accurate language, the science of grammar
vyakta mfn. adorned, embellished, beautiful, caused to appear, manifested, apparent, visible, manifest creation
(*am*) ind. apparently, evidently, certainly,
vyaktam 1029/2 ind. apparently, evidently, certainly
vyakti f. visible appearance or manifestation, becoming evident or known or public,
vyakti f. visible appearance or manifestation, becoming evident or known or public, (in gram.) gender, the proper form of any word, case, inflection,
vyākula mfn intently engaged in or occupied with (comp.), mfn confused, puzzled, full of,
vyāmiśra mfn. mixed together, blended, manifold, of various kinds
vyāmoha 1038/2 m. loss of consciousness, delusion
vyàna whole body breath, one of the *prāṇas*
vyanunādayan causing to resonate, thunder, howl, *vi-anu-*√*nad*
vyāpādaya kill!
vyāpādayati he kills
vyāpādayiṣyati will kill
vyāpādya having killed
vyāpaka 1037/2 mfn pervading, diffusive, comprehensive, widely spreading or extending, spreading everywhere, (as an attribute always found (like smoke)), all pervading,
vyāpāra 1038/1 m. occupation, employment, exertion, activity,
vyapāśraya 1028/3 1. mfn. devoid of reliance or support, self-centred, self-dependent
place of refuge, shelter, support, secession from worldly attachments,
vyapaśritya taking refuge in, having recourse to, gerund
vyāpatti f. falling in to misfortune, suffering injury, loss, ruin, death
vyāpta 1037/2 mfn pervaded , (as the universe by spirit), spread through, pervaded, filled with, permeated
vyāpya 1037/3 permeable, the site or locality of universal pervasion, proof, reason, cause, pervading, having pervaded,
vyartha mfn useless, unavailing, unprofitable,
vyāsa the sage who composed the *Mahābhārata* and compiled the *Veda*
vyasana n. separation, individuality, attachment, throwing one's self away (upon a thing), passionate devotion to a thing, an overpowering passion, vice,
vyaṣṭi 1034/3 f. attainment, success, singleness, individuality, a separated aggregate, (such as a man) viewed as a part of a whole, individual acting as a separate unit
vyathā f. feeling of painful unrest, agitation, perturbation,
vyathate is agitated, churned up,
vyathayanti they cause to tremble 1/pl/caus/act √*vyath*
vyatikara m. a mixing, confusing, confusion, disaster,
mfn acting reciprocally,

m. reciprocity, reciprocal action, contact, contiguity, ifc. performing

vyatitariṣyati 1030/1 will pass completely across, overcome, 1/s/fut/act

vyatireka 1030/2 m. distinction, difference, separation, exclusion, negation, logical discontinuance, (opp. to *anvaya* q.v.), contrasting of things compared in some respect to each other.

vyatītāni passed away, gone away, *vi ati* √*i* 1/pl/n

vyavahāra m. doing, performing, action, practice, conduct, procedure, way of acting, way of acting with others, intercourse, usage, custom, ordinary life, common practice, common life or practice or action, (in phil.) practical existence, + *ika* – relating to the above,

vyavasāya m.determination, resolve, purpose

vyavasitā mfn determined, resolved, ended,

vyavasthā 1033/3 f. respective difference, abiding in one place, statute, law, rule, steadiness, fixity, constancy, establishment, state, condition,

vyavasthita 1034/1 mfn stationed, established, persevering in, placed in order, contained in, settled,

vyavasthiti f. being placed apart or separate, separation, distinction, difference, staying, abiding, perseverance, constancy, steadfastness

vyavasthitān ppp. 2/pl/m *vi-ava-*√*sthā* arrayed, drawn up in battle order,

vyaya mfn going asunder or to pieces, passing away, changeable,
m. loss, expense,

vyoman 1041/2 mfn one who cannot be saved, n. heaven, sky, atmosphere, ether (as an element), space thoroughly occupied or penetrated by, pervaded

vyudasya having rejected or abandoned *vy ud 2.* √*as* 1040/2

vyūḍha 1. mfn led home, married, divided, distributed, arranged, transposed, altered, expanded, developed, wide, broad, large, compact, firm, solid, arrayed, drawn up in battle formation,

vy √ *1. ūh* push apart, place asunder, remove

vyūha *(you)* remove, place apart, 2/s/impv

vyūha m. placing apart, distribution, battle array,

vyutpatti f. learning, production, origin, derivation, etymology, perfection, growth, proficiency (esp. in knowledge), comprehensive learning or scholarship, difference of tone or sound,

ya pron. who, which, what,
ya ya whoever, whichever, whatever, whosoever,
ya ka ca, ya ka cid, ya ka cana, anyone soever no matter who,
ya if anybody
ya and .... he..
m. a goer or mover, wind, joining, restraining, fame, barley, light abandoning,
f. going, a car, restraining, religious meditation, attaining, the vulva,

yācaka m. beggar,

yaccittam yat pronoun – who or which, *citta* 395/3 the heart or mind, whose mind,

yācñā 850/2 f. begging, asking for, asking alms, mendicancy, any petition or request, prayer, entreaty

yad who, which, what, whichever, whatever, that, also used to introduce direct assertions,
yad....tad....., since...... therefore.....
yad...tasmāt... inasmuch as... therefore
tad...yad... then... when..
yad... tatas... when...then...
m. = *puruṣa,*

yadā 844/1 ind. When, at what time, whenever,

yadā.... tadā... when..... then....

yādas 851/2 n. a large aquatic animal, a sea monster, semen, water, river

yadi ind. if, or else, or rather, or

yadi api even if

yadi...tarhi ... if...then....
yadṛccha 844/3 ind. spontaneity, unexpectedly, accident, chance, *yadṛcchayā* 3/s by accident, accidentally, that which is presented or happens by chance
yaddṛṣṭam yat 844/2 who, which, what, whoever, whatever, *dṛṣṭa* 491/3 seen, beheld, considered, seen in the mind, visible, apparent 2/s what is seen
yadi ind. if, or else, or rather, or in case that
yadi ... tarhi if..... then...
yadṛccha 844/3 mfn spontaneous, accidental f. (*ā*) self-will, accident, chance, spontaneously, that which happens by chance,
yadṛcchayā (ibc. or ind.) by luck, by chance, by good fortune, by accident,
yādṛś 851/2 which like, as like, of whatever kind or nature
yādṛśa anyone whatever, anybody whatsoever
yad vā whether, if, if either
yadvat 844/3 in which way, as, correlative of *tadvat* as/so
yadyad whatever
yadyāpi although
yāga m. sacrifice, offering, oblation,

yaḥ 838/1 pron. he who, who or which,
yaḥ.... saḥ... (he who..... he...)
yajanta m. a sacrificer, worshipper,
yajante they sacrifice, they worship, 1/pl/pres/indic/mid √*yaj*
yajña 839/2 m. worship, devotion, act of worship, devotion, sacrifice
yajñabhāvita 'sacrifice produced', brought into being by sacrifice,
yajñāśiṣṭa 840/1 n. the remnants of a sacrifice after the gods and priests have consumed their share
yajus a division of the *Veda*, n. a sacrificial prayer or formula
yakṣa 838/2 a ghost or spirit,(usually benevolent), attendant to Kubera
yama 846/1 m. the act of checking or curbing, suppression, restraint, the Lord of death, controller and ender of all, death,
yāma mfn of or coming from Yama, m. course or going, course (of a feast), watch of the night,
yama & niyama = behaviour codes of conduct, *yama* =a traditional code of restraints-non-violence, truthfulness, non-stealing, continence faithfulness when married), patience, steadfastness, compassion, honesty, neither eating too much or too little, purity in body, mind and speech, 'control of body and senses and observance of moral injunctions' (Gam.)
yāmika m. watchman,
yāminā f. night,
yam yam whatever,
yamunā f. a river,
yān whom, 2/pl/m
yāna mfn leading, conducting (to or in), m. way, path, teaching n. wagon, vehicle (fig. Buddhist)),
yānti they go, 1/pl/pres/act √*yā*
yantra n. a prop, support, barrier, a means or implement for holding, a fetter, band, tie, a surgical instrument esp. a blunt one e,g, tweezers, any instrument or apparatus, engine, machine, restraint, force, -*eṇa* ind. forcibly, violently,
yantraṇa n. or f. (*ā*) restriction, limitation, pain, constraint, force, compulsion, n. guarding, protection,
yaśas 848/2 n. beautiful appearance, beauty, splendour, worth, honour, glory, fame
yaśodā name of *Kṛṣṇa*'s mother,
yaṣṭi f. staff, stick, pole, pillar, support,
yasya who, whose
yas yas whoever
yāsyasi you shall go, you shall come, 2/s/fut/act √*yā*

yat pron. who, which
yata 845/2 mfn restrained, controlled,
yatacetas 845/2 mfn. restrained or subdued in mind
yatamānas controlled, restrained,
yātanā f. requital, esp. punishment, pains of hell, torment,
yatas 841/2 ind. wherefore, for which, reason, for, since, because
yatatas of the striving, of the one who strives, pres.act.part. √*yat* 6/s/m
yatati he strives, stretches
yattmavān m. controlled in mind, self-controlled
yat yat whatever
yatas yatas whensoever, wheresoever
yat yat...... sat sat whatever.... that
yathā 841/2 ind. as, like , according as, correlative *tathā* 433/3 ind. so
yathābhāgam according to each share, each in his respective place,
yathā tathā 841/3 in whatever manner, as..... so....
yathāprāpta 842/2 as met with, the first met with, the first that is met with or occurs.
yathāprāptavartī
yathāprāpta 842/2 as met with, the first met with, the first that is met with or occurs. *vartī* 925/3 see *vartin* resting, abiding, behaving properly towards one who rests in life's situations as they arise
yathārtha 843/1 accordant with reality, conformable to truth, true, right (*am*) ind. suitably, according to one's dignity, - *ta* truly
yathāsthiti 843/3 accordant with usage, certainly, assuredly,
yathāsukham ind. according to ease or pleasure, at ease, at will or pleasure, comfortably, agreeably,
yāthātathya 851/1 a real state or condition, truth, *-ta* as it should be, consistent with endeavour and result,
yatheṣṭam according to wish
yathokta mfn as said or told previously just as .... said,

yati, yatin 841/1 mfn. an ascetic, a devotee, one who has restrained his passions and abandoned the world,
yati as many as, as often,
yāti 849/1 √*yā* to go to, proceed, 1/s/pres/indic/act goes,
yatna 841/1 m. activity of will, volition, effort, 5/s *yatnāt* through effort
yatna yatna ind. in or to which place or where, wherein, in which
yatnavat 841/1 possessing energy, making effort, aspiring after, striving
yatra where, if, when, since
yātrā 849/3 f. going, setting off, journey, support of life, maintenance, way, means, expedient
yatra tatra in whatever, in whatever place, anywhere, to any place whatever, at any rate, indiscriminately,
yatra tatra .... tatra tatra wherever there is .... there is
yatra yatra 841/2 ind. wherever
yatra.... tatra where..... there..
yauvana n. youth
yauvarājyam immediate heir to the throne,
yava m. orig. any grain or corn yielding flour, later, barley-corn, barley,
yāvad as many, as much, until, as often, as frequent, as far, as long, as old
yāvajjīvam 852/2 life-long, lasting for life, as long as life
yāvān *(yāvat, yāvad)* as much, so much , having which measure, how great, how much 1/s/m
yavana m. a greek, a swift horse, wheat,
yāvat as many, as much, until, as often, as frequent, as far, as long, as old (with 2nd) during, up to, till
yāvatī fem. of above
yāvat ..... tāvat....
as long as .... for so long....
yaviṣṭha mfn youngest, esp. of a fire just born or just set on the altar,
yavīyas mfn younger, lesser, worse,
yayā pron. 3/s/f by which, with which
ye pron. 1/pl/m who

yena ... saha together with whom, by which

yena 3/s pron. by or with whom ind. in which manner, on what account, why

yeṣām pron. of whom, among whom 6/pl/m

ye ye all things

yoddhukāma m.anxious to fight, hungry for battle,

yodha m. a fighter, warrior, battle, war,

yodhamukhya m. prominent warrior

yodhavyam to be fought, √*yudh* gerundive, 1/s/n

yodhin mfn ifc. fighting, m. a warrior, conqueror,

yoga 856/2 m. a yoke, team, vehicle, the act of yoking, joining, attaching, use, application, a means, method, work, connection, use, application or concentration of thoughts, abstract contemplation, meditation (esp. self-concentration), abstract meditation and mental abstraction practised as a system ... to teach the means by which the human spirit may attain complete union with the Supreme Spirit

yogabala 857/1 n. the force of devotion, the power of magic

yogabhraṣṭa mfn fallen from yoga, lost from yoga

yogācāra m. 'one whose practice is yoga', a Buddhist Mahāyāna School,

yogadhāranā 857/1 f. continuance or perseverance in meditation or concentration

yogakṣema 856/3 m. acquisition and preservation of property, protecting or holding on to what has been acquired

yogavittama having best knowledge of yoga

yogayukta 857/1 mfn. immersed in deep meditation, absorbed in yoga, steadfast, disciplined, yoked steadfast in yoga

yogī 857/3 m. usually called *yogin,* a contemplative saint, devotee, or ascetic a *yogin,* pl. *yoginas*

yogya mfn of use, suited for use, fit, fitting,

yojana n. joining, yoking, harnessing, that which is yoked or harnessed, a team, vehicle, course, path, (also applied to words addressed to the gods), (sometimes m. f. *ā* ifc.*),* a distance (traversed in one harnessing),

yoktavya to be joined or yoked or united (as the mind) to be prepared or practised, gerundive √*yuj*

yoni 858/2 m.f. womb, source, origin,

yoṣit f. young woman, maiden,

yotsyamānān those who are about to give battle, √*yudh* 854/3 fut/mid/act/part. 2/pl/m

yotsye I will fight, I shall fight 3/s/fut/mid √*yudh*

yuddha 854/3 mfn fought, encountered, conquered, n. battle, fight, war, opposition , (*am*) with *kṛ* makes battle)

yuddha-viśārada m. skilled in battle, battle-skilled,

Yudhāmanyus 1/s/m name of a warrior 'fighting with spirit'

Yudhiṣṭhira son of *Kuntī* and *Dharma*, eldest of the *Pāṇḍava* princes

yudhya fight! join battle! 2/s/impv/act

yudhyasva fight! join in the battle! 2/s/impv/mid

yuga 854/1 an age of the world of which there are four – *satya* or *kṛta, tretā, dvāpar*a and the present *kaliyuga* (432,000years). also a yoke or team

yugapad 854/1 ind. together, at the same time, simultaneously, (being in the same yoke)

yuge yuge from age to age, in age after age

yujyasva join, engage, yoke!, yoke thyself!, join thyself, 2/s/impv/mid *yuj*

yujyate it is used, 1/s/pres/indic/pass

yukta mfn yoked or joined or fastened, or attached or harnessed to, set to work, made use of, engaged in, intent upon, ready to, prepared for (4th), absorbed in abstract

meditation, concentrated, attentive, skilful, clever, experienced in, joined, united, connected with, disciplined, applied, auspicious, favourable, prosperous, thriving, (in gram.) primitive (as opposed to derivative),
added to, increased by (ifc.), connected with, concerning (ifc.), subject to, dependent on (ifc.), (*am*) ind. fitly, suitably, justly, properly, rightly,
m. fit, proper, n. a team, yoke, junction, connection, fitness, suitableness, propriety,

yuktacetasa those whose thought is steadfast, whose mind is steady

yuktatamas most devoted, most steadfast, superlative of *yuktas*

yuktātmān of steadfast self 853/3 mfn. concentrated in mind, ifc. wholly intent upon,

yukte 7/s/m joined, in yoke

yukti 853/3 f. union, junction, combination, practice, usage, suitableness, fitness, propriety, meditation on the Supreme Being, contemplation, union with the universal spirit, reasoning, argument, proof, deduction from circumstances, reason

yuktyā 853/3 (see *yukti*) 3/s by means of reasoning, by logical argument,

yunakti √*yuj* to yoke, join, make ready, use, concentrates the mind on, engages,

yuñjan practising, performing yoga, disciplining, concentrating

yuñjat he should practice/concentrate 1/s/opt/act √*yuj*

yuñjīta he should concentrate the mind on, come into union with, discipline himself, 1/s/opt/mid √*yuj*

yūpa m. post, pillar, sacrificial post,

yuṣmābhiḥ by you pron. 3/pl.

yuṣmabhyam pron. for you 4/ pl.

yuṣmad you

yuṣmadīya pl. your,

yuṣmākam of you pl.

yuṣmān you pl. 2nd

yuṣmāsu in you pl.

yuṣmat pron. from you pl.

yūtha n. herd, flock,

yuvābhyām pron. by/for/from you two

yuvām pron. you two 1st or 2nd

yuvan 855/2 mfn young, youthful, adult, (applied to men and animals), strong, good, healthy, m. a youth, young man, young animal,

yuvayoḥ pron. of/in you two

yuvatiḥ f. young woman

yuvayoḥ pron. of/in you two

yūyam you pl. 1st

yuyodhi destroy! remove!

yuyutsu 855/2 mfn. wishing to fight, desire for war, combativeness,

yuyutsavaḥ desiring to fight or do battle, √*yudh* 1/pl/m desiderative adj.

Verb/Upasarga List

Frequently used roots are given with basic meanings and prefixed meanings.

root class, Parasmai, Ātmane, meaning

ah to say, call, speak,
pra+ declare to be
akṣ 5 P to reach,
aṁs 10 PA to divide
an 2P to breathe,
pra+ to be alive, breathe,
aṅgīkṛ 8 PA to accept,promise, admit,
añj 1 PA to bend, to worship,
pari+ to twist,
7 P to anoint,
vi+ to reveal, show,
āp 5 P to obtain, reach, gain,
abhi+ reach to a thing, attain,
desid. strive to win,
caus. carry out fully,
ava+ to secure, come upon,
fall in with, incur,
pari+ to be competent,
pra+ to get, reach, arrive
sam + to complete,
vi+ to pervade,
arc 1 PA to worship
arh 1 P to deserve,
arj 1 P to gain, to earn,
upa+ to earn
arth 10 PA to request,
abhi+ to beg,
pra+ to ask, so wish,
prati+ to challenge,
arthayati(te) to seek for an object,
abhi+ ask, entreat,
pra+ desire, sue for,
aś 5 A to pervade, reach, enjoy,
aś 9 P to eat,
pra+ to taste, eat, partake of,
as 2 P to be,
as 4 P to throw,
apa+ to cast away,
abhi+ to practice, direct one's
attention to, study,
ni+ to put down, throw down,
deposit, commit,
parini+ throw down over,
stretch over,
nis+ throw out, root out,
sanni+ to give up,
vi+ cast or throw away,
vipari+ to upset,
vyati+ throw over, cross,
ās 2 A to sit, to be,
adhi+ to occupy, take one's place in,
put on (e.g.shoes),
ud+ to be indifferent,
upa + to serve, worship, sit by,
sit waiting for,
asūyati Nom. envies,
aṭ 1 P to wander,
ātmasāt + *kṛ* to appropriate,
av 1 P to deserve,
pra+ show favour,
be attentive or heedful,
bādh 1 A to thwart,
adhi+ to harass,
anu+ to vex,
apa+ to drive away,
ava+ to restrain,
pari+ to ward off,
pra+ to repel,
vi+ to distress,
bandh 2 PA to bind,
ā+ to hold fast,
anu+ to combine,
ni+ to check, bind, fasten,
write down,
nis+ to importune,
pari+ to surround,
pra+ bind on, form a series,
sam+ bind together, connect,
ud+ to suspend,
bhā 2 P to shine,
ā+ to look like, illumine, shine upon
ava+ to appear,
nis+ shine forth from (5th),
pra+ shine forth, begin to be light,
prati+ to illumine,
ud+ to shine forth,
bhaj 1 PA to share, adore,
ā+ give a person, deal out to,
pravi+ divide,

	saṁvi+ divide a thing with a person, present a person (3rd) with a thing (2nd),		*vi+* to fail,
	vi+ to divide,	*bhrasj*	6 P to fry
bhaṇ	1 P to speak,	*bhū*	1 P to become,
bhañj	7 P to break,		*abhi+* to overcome, oppress,
	ava+ to destroy,		*abhisam+* enter into, become by a process of change,
	nis+ to defeat,		*anu+* to experience, attain,
	sam+ to shatter,		*parā+* to vanquish
	vi+ to dispel,		*pari+* to surpass, surround,
bharts	1 P to threaten,		*pra+* to be produced, to rule,
	abhi+ to mock		*sam+* to be possible,
	ava+ to abuse,		*sam+*caus. to honour,
	nis+ to deride,		*ud+* to arise,
bhāṣ	1A to say,	*bhuj*	6 P to curve,
	ā+ to converse,	*bhuj*	7PA to enjoy, eat,
	abhi+ to address,		*anu+* reap the fruit (of good or evil deeds),
	ava+ to revile,		*sam+* to enjoy,
	pari + to explain		*upa+* to enjoy,
	*pra+*to declare	*budh*	4 A to awake,
	prati+ to reply, speak back,		*anu+* to think of,
bhās	1 A to shine,		*ava+* to perceive,
	ā+ to appear,		*pra+* to awake,
	ava+ to shine,		*prati+* to observe, awake,
	prati+ make a show, appear well,		*ud+* to awake,
bhī	3 P to fear,		*sam+* to recognise,
bhid	7 P to split,		*ud+* to awake,
	antar+ to plot,		*vi+* to learn,
	pra+ split forth or open,	*brū*	2 PA to say,
	prati+ to betray,		*anu+* to repeat,
	ud+ to pierce,		*apa+* try to console a person,
	vi+ to destroy, split asunder,		*ava+* to console,
bhṛ	1 PA, 3 P, to hold,		*nis+* to explain,
	ā+ bear to, bring to,		*pra+* to proclaim,
	apa+ carry off, take away,		*prati+* to answer, speak back to,
	ava+ bear down, ward off,		*upa+* to invoke,
	ni+ to fix,	*cakṣ*	2 A to appear, look upon, speak,
	pra+ bring forward, offer,		*ā+* to look on
	sam+ to prepare,		*sam+* look upon, consider,
	upa+ to procure, bring to,		*vi+* appear far and wide, shine,
bhrāj	1 A to shine,	*cal*	1 P to go,
bhram	1 P, 4 P to roam, wander around,		*vi+* to shake,
	pari+ to turn round,	*cam*	1 P to sip,
	sam+ to fall into error, be confused,		*ā+* to rinse the mouth,
	vi+ to be perplexed, shine,	*car*	1 P to move,
bhraṁś	4 PA to fall,		*ā+* to practise, approach, set about,
	pari+ to escape,		*abhi+* to offend, trepass against,
	pra+ to disappear,		

anu+ to follow,
apa+ go off, be absent,
parā+ move away from,
pra+ to set forth,
samā+ proceed, do, perpetrate,
ud+ go up, rise (of the sun), caus. cause to go out, evacuate,
udā+ rise up out of,
upa+ to serve, come to (esp. in order to serve), attend, wait upon politely, proceed with, undertake,
vi+ move in different directions, wander about, caus. cause to go hither and thither in thought, ponder,

chad 10 P to cover,
ā+ to cover, conceal,
pari+ envelope, cover over,
pra+ cover, dress oneself with,

chid 7 PA to cut,
ā+ to rob,
apa+ to sever,
pari+ to divide,
ud+ to destroy, cut out,
vi+ to separate, cut asunder,

ci 5 PA to collect,
ā+ to heap up,
ava+ to gather,
nis+ to ascertain,
pari+ to recognise, find out,
sam+ gather together, collect,
ud+ to arrange, heap up, collect,
vi+ to select,
vinis+ ponder, consider,

cint 10 P to think,
anu+ to remember,
pari+ to reflect,
sam+ to ponder, think to oneself,
vi+ to discern, reflect,

cirāyati Nom. he delays

citrayati Nom. decorates,

cṛt 6 P to tie, hurt, shine,
pra+ caus. drive on, inspire,

cud 10 P to urge,
abhi+ to impel,
pra+ to command, drive on, further, inspire,
sam+ to stimulate,

cumb 1 P to kiss,

cur 10 PA to steal,

curṇ 1 A to waver, fail,

cyut 1 P to drip, fall,

dā 2 P to cut,
ava+ to cut off,
samava+ cut in pieces and collect

dā 3 PA to give,
ā+ to receive, take, grasp,
anu+ to yield, grant, admit,
pari+ to entrust, deliver over,
pra+ give, grant, impart,
prati+ to give back,
upā+ A. to acquire, appropriate,
vi+ to distribute,

dah 1 P to burn,

dal 1 P to burst,

dam 4 P to be tamed,

ḍamb 10 P to push, throw,
vi+ to deceive,

daṁś 1 P to bite,

daṇḍ 10 P to punish,

daridrā 2 P to become poor,

day 1 A to have pity,

dhā 3 PA to lay, hold, maintain,
ā+ to deposit, set in or on, put on (wood on the fire), take on, take or take away,
abhi+ to address, put on, designate, name, address, speak to,
adhi+ A. to wear,
antar+ to conceal, put in the interior,
(a)pi+ to close, cover,
ava+ to heed, put down in, esp. down into water,
ni+ to entrust, lay down, set down (sacred fire),
pari+ to put on, put around,
pra+ set forward,
prati+ to adjust,
pratini+ to substitute,
sam+ to dispose,
samā+ to concentrate, put upon,
samni+ lay down together,
upa+ put on (brick/stone on altar),
upasamā+ set together (wood onto a burning fire), put (fuel) on,
vi+ to prescribe, distribute, spread abroad, arrange, determine,

vyā + pass. be separated, be sick,
ḍhauk 1 A to approach,
dhāv 1 P to run,
abhi+ to rush at,
anu+ to pursue, run after,
ava+ to drip down,
pra+ to run away, flow, run,
samupa+ run on to,
upa+ run to,
dhe 1 P to suck,
dhīrayati encourages,
dhmā 1 P to blow,
ā+ to inflate, blow up,
nis+ to blow out,
dhṛ 1 P to hold,
dhṛ 10 P to hold, owe,
ava+ to determine,
nis+ to pick out,
upa+ to support,
dhṛṣ 1 P to be bold,
ā+ venture against,
prati+ hold out against, withstand,
dhū 9 PA to shake,
ava+ to shake off, shake down,
dhvaṁs 1 PA to perish,
dhvan 1 P to sound,
dhyai 1 P to meditate,
abhi+ to desire,
anu+ to reflect,
ḍī 1 A, 4 A to fly,
ud+ to fly up,
dih 2 P to smear,
dīp 4 A to blaze,
ud+ to flame up,
diś 6 PA to show,
ā+ to prescribe, point out to,
anu+ to refer to,
apa+ to feign, to show,
nis+ to specify,
pra+ point out to, designate,
sam+ to assign,
samā+ point out to, direct,
ud+ to point out,
upa+ to instruct,
vyapa+ make a false show of,
div 10 to suffer, lament,4 PA to play,
du 1 to go, 5 P to burn, suffer,
dṛ 6 A to heed,
ā+ to respect,
dṝ 9 P to tear,
ā+ to split,
ava+ to burst,
vi+ to tear,
dṛp 4 P to become crazy,
dṛṣ 1 PA to see,
anu+ to behold,
pra+ to foresee,
prati+ appear before one's eyes,
sam+ to perceive, behold,
upa+ to observe,
vi+ pass. be seen far and wide,
dru 1 P to melt, run, 5 P to hurt,
ā+ run to, make an attack, charge,
abhi+ to assail,
anu+ to pursue,
apa+ to flee,
ati+ run past or by, escape,
pra+ to rush upon,
samupa+ run to rush at,
upa+ to hasten, run to,
vi+ to flee, burst,
druh 4 P to hurt,
abhi+ to do harm,
duh 2 PA to milk,
duḥkhayati P afflicts,
duḥkhāyate A feels pain,
dyut 1 A to gleam,
abhi+ to shine,
ud+ to shine forth,
vi+ to flash,
gad 1 P to speak,
ni+ to declare,
gāh 1 A to plunge,
ava+ to dive,
upa+ to penetrate,
gai 1 P to sing,
ava+ to censure,
gal 1 P to drip, fall, perish,
galbh 1 A to be bold,
gam 1 P to go,
ā+ to come to, go to, return,
abhi+ to approach,
abhyā+ come unto, visit,
adhi to acquire, go to attain,
antar+ go within, enter,
anu+ to follow, go after,

api+ go unto, join,
ava+ to know, come down,
nis+ to go out, proceed from,
prati+ to return, come back,
sam+ A. to meet,
samā+ to meet, assemble,
samupā+ to go to together,
ud+ to rise, go out, proceed from,
upa+ to approach, go unto,
upā+ approach,
vi+ to pass away, go asunder,

gaṇ 10 PA to count,
ava+ to disregard
pari+ to consider,

garh 1 A to censure,

garj 1 P 10 PA to roar,

ghaṭ 1 A to strive, to happen,
sam+ to be united,
vi+ to break down,

ghrā 1 P to smell,

ghṛṣ 1 P to rub,
sam+ to vie with,
ud+ to scratch,

ghuṣ 1 P to proclaim,

ghūrṇ 1 A,6 P to whirl,

gṝ 6 P to swallow,
ud+ to vomit,

grah 9 PA to seize,
ā+ to persist in
anu+ to favour,
ava+ to resist,
ni+ to check,
pari+ to clasp,
prati+ to accept, take hold of
sam+ to collect, hold together,
vi+ separate, make a division, quarrel, fight,

granth 9 P to fasten,

gras 1 A to swallow,
sam+ to destroy,

guh 1 PA to hide,

guṇ 10 PA to multiply,

gup to shun, abhor,

hā 3 A to go

hā 3 P to leave,
pari+ to forsake,
vi+ to cast off,

han 2 P to kill,
ā+ to beat, strike upon,
abhi+ to smite,
apa+ to drive away,
ava+ strike down, bring to nought,
ni+ to fall upon, strike down, slay,
pra+ to strike,
pari+ strike around, encompass,
prati+ to check, strike back at, strike against so as to transfix,
sam+ to join, strike together,
ud+ force up,

has 1 P to laugh
ava+ to deride,
pari+ to ridicule,
pra+ laugh out, laugh,
vi+ laugh out,

hi 5 PA to send,
pra+ to despatch,

hiṁs 7 P to injure,

hlād 10 PA to refresh,
ā+ to gladden,
pra+ to gladden, refresh

hṛ 1 P to take,
ā+ to obtain, eat, fetch, receive,
abhi+ to offer,
anupra+ throw in the fire or on a fuel pile,
apa+ to take away,
ava+ move down,
pari+ to avoid, carry around,
pra+ to strike, attack,
pratyā+ get back again,
pravyā+ utter, speak,
sam+ to check, bring or draw together, contract, withdraw,
samā+ to collect,
ud+ to lift, rescue, take out,
udā+ say, tell,
upa+to offer,
upasam+ bring or draw together to one's self,
vi+ to enjoy oneself, take apart, divide, pass one's time, esp. pleasantly, enjoy one's self, wander about,
vyā+ to utter, bring out,
vyava+ to behave, move hither and thither, go to work, proceed,

hreṣ 1 PA to neigh
hrī 3 P to be ashamed,
hṛṣ 1 P, 4 P, to rejoice,
hrus 1 PA to decrease,
hu 3 PA to sacrifice,
hve 1 P to call,
ā+ to summon,
ā+ A. to summon,
i 1 A to go,
ā+ to come near, hither,
with *punar* go back,
abhi+ go unto, become embodied in
abhipra+ to intend,
abhyā+ to approach, go near,
adhi+ to study, learn,
antar+ go within, retire,
withdraw,
anu+ accompany, go after,
anuparā go forth (along a path),
apa+ to depart, go off, slink away,
ati+ *to* go beyond, transcend,
leave behind, escape,
ava+ approach,
ni+ go into or in, (e.g. *nyāya*)
parā+ go away, depart,
pari+ to circumambulate,
walk round (the fire),
pra+ go forward or onward,
come out, be prominent,
prati+ go against, go back,
withstand,
sam+ come together, assemble,
samanu accompany, go after,
samava+ to assemble,
samupa+ to obtain, come hither,
ud+ to arise,
upa+ to approach,
upā+ go unto,
vi+ go asunder, separate, disperse,
viparā go away separately,
īh 1 A to strive,
īkṣ 1 A to see,
anu+ to seek,
apa+ to expect, to need,
ava+ to look after, look
after one's self, i.e. look behind or
around,
nis+ look after, contemplate,
pari+ to examine, investigate,
prati+ to wait for,
sam+ look upon, behold, perceive,
upa+ to neglect, overlook,
vi+ to look, look on,
indh 7 A to kindle,
īr 2 A to move, arise,
pra+ caus. drive or steer a vessel
onward ,
sam+ caus. bring together i.e. into
shape or form , create,
samud+ to utter,
ud+ rise up, caus. rouse, send out,
announce,
īrṣ 1 P to envy (with 4th)
iṣ 6 P to wish,
abhi+ seek for
anu+ 4 P to search, seek after
prati+ to accept
īś 2 A to rule, to be able,
jāgṛ 2 P to awaken,
jakṣ 2 P to eat,
jalp 1 P to murmur,
pari+ to prattle,
sam+ to converse,
jan 4 A to be born,
ā+ breeding (as with horses),
lineage,
abhi+ pass. be born unto,
be destined for from birth,
pra+ be born, caus. procreate,
sam+ to arise, happen, be produced,
upa+ to be born, arise,
jap 1 P to mutter,
upa+ to whisper,
jhaṇajhaṇāyati Nom. he,she,it rattles
ji 1 P to conquer,
ava+ to deprive of,
nis+ to overcome,
parā+ A. to defeat,
ud+ to conquer, pass. be conquered,
vi+ A. to vanquish, subdue,
jīv 1 P to live,
anu+ to live upon,
ati+ to survive,
ud+ to live again,
upa+ to maintain oneself,
jñā 9 PA to know,

ā+ to attend to, notice,
abhi+ to recognise, know,
anu+ to permit,
ava+ to despise,
pari+ carefully observe, find out,
pra+ to know, know what to do,
prati+ to promise, allow,
pratyabhi+ recognize,
sam+ A. to agree,
samanu+ to wholly acquiesce in,
vi+ *to* ascertain, understand, know,

jṝ 4 P to grow old,

jṛmbh 1 A to yawn,
ud+ to expand,

juṣ 6 PA to relish,
abhi+ to frequent,
anu+ to visit,

jval 1 P to blaze,

kal 10 P to drive (cattle),
anusam+ to lead along after

kamp 1 A to tremble,
anu+ to feel pity,

kaṇ 1 P to sound

kāṅkṣ 1 P to wish,
ā+ to long for,
abhi+ to desire,

karṇ 10 PA to pierce, bore,
ā+ to hear,

kāś 1 A to shine,
ā+ to look on,
ava+ be visible, lie open,
pra+ shine out, become clear,
pra+ to shine,
vi+ to bloom,

kās 1 A to cough,

kath 10 P to tell,

khād 1 P to eat,

khan 1 PA to dig
ā+ dig, burrow,
ni+ to bury
ud+ to uproot,

khid 4 A to suffer,

khyā 2 P to tell,
ā+ to declare, show, narrate, name
parisam+ reckon up completely,
pratyā+ to deny, turn away, repulse,
sam+ to count, tell together, sum up,
vyā+ show to discriminately,

klam 1,4 P to be tired,

kḷp 1 A to be fit for,
pari+ to decide,
vi+ to doubt,

kliś 4 A to suffer
9 P to torment,

kṛ 8 PA to make, do, perform,
ā+ bring hither, prepare, fashion,
adhi+ to refer to, put in office,
alam+ to adorn,
anu+ to imitate,
apa+ to harm, injure,
āvis+ to reveal,
namas+ to salute,
pari+ to surround, make ready, adorn,
pariṣkṛ+ to polish,
pra+ carry forward, accomplish, set before, make the subject of discussion or treatment, (buddhism) put a plan before oneself,
prati+ to remedy, to counteract,
sam+ put together, prepare, consecrate, abide by rites,
saṁskṛ+ to refine
tiras+ to abuse,
upa+ to help, do someone a service, bring something to someone,
upas+ to decorate,
vi+ to change,
vipra+ to tease,
vyā+ to explain, separate, analyse,

kṛ 3 P mention with praise

kṛ 3 P pour out, scatter abundantly (e.g. hailstones)
ā + scatter abundantly, cover over, fill,
ava+ strew (loose earth) throw in,
samā+ bestre, cover,
vyati+ be scattered in various directions,

kṝ 6 P to scatter,
ā+ to spread,
sam+ to mix,
ud+ to carve,
upa+ to buy,
vi+ to strew, to sell, sell for (w 3rd)

kram 1 PA 4 P to go,
ā+ to attack, step near to, come upon, overpower
abhi+ to approach,
abhyud+ caus. cause to step out,
ati+ to cross, o step beyond, excel, overcome
nis+ to leave, go out,
parā+ step forth, advance boldly (show one's strength or courage),
pari+ go around, circumambulate,
pra+ step forward, set out, start from
sam+ come together, approach, enter
samati+ excel,
ud+ go out, depart (vital spirit), caus. cause to disembark,
upa+ A. to begin, approach,
vi+ move away or on, proceed,

krand 1 P to cry
ā+ to cry out,

krī 9 PA to buy,
pari+ A. to hire,
vi+ A. to sell,

krīò 1 P to play,

kṛṣ 1 P to pull,
ā+ to attract, draw on, draw from (a source),
ni+ to lessen,
pra+ draw forward, place in front,
ud+ to enhance, elevate,

kṛt 6 P to cut,
ud+ cut out/off/up, butcher,

kruś 1 P to cry,
ā+ to carry out,
anu+ to pity,
vi+ to call aloud,

kṣal 10 PA to wash,
pra+ to cleanse,

kṣam 1 A 4 P to suffer, forgive,

kṣaṇ 8 P A to hurt,

kṣi 1 P to decay,
5, 9 P to destroy,
apa+ be afflicted, suffer loss (pass.)

kṣip 6 PA to throw,
ā+ to allude, throw at,
adhi+ to offend,
ni+ to entrust, throw down,
sam+ to abridge, dash together in a heap, destroy,
vini+ lay down separately/orderly

kṣu 2 P to sneeze,

kṣubh 4, 9P to shake,

kṣud 7 PA to crush

kṣudh 4 P to be hungry,

kūj 1 P to hum, warble,

kup 4 P to be angry, (with 4th)
pra+ be angry, boil with rage,

kus = *kuś* 4 P to embrace,

kuts 10 A to abuse,

lā 2 P to take,

labh 1 A to obtain, find,
pra+ to deceive,
upa+ to perceive,
upā+ to blame,
vi+ to hand over
vipra+ to mock at,

lag 1 P to adhere,
ava+ to linger
vi+ to cling to,

lakṣ 10 P to mark,
ā+ to observe,
upa+ to consider,
vi+ to perceive,

lal 1 P to frolic, play

lamb 1 A to hang down,
ā+ to grasp,
ava+ to cling to,
pari+ to linger,
vi+ to delay,

laṅgh 1 PA to cross, leap,
ati+ to transgress,
ud+ to cross,
vi+ to leap,

lap 1 P to chatter,
ā+ to address,
apa+ to deny,
pra+ to prattle,
sam+ talk with,
vi+ to lament,

laṣ 1 P to desire,
abhi+ to long for,
ud+ glance, play, be overjoyed,
vi+ glance play, be overjoyed or wanton,

las 1 P to shine,

lī 4 A, 9 P, to adhere,

abhi+ to clasp,
ava+ to lurk,
ni+ to cling,
pra+ to disappear,
vi+ to perish,

lih 2 PA to lick,

likh 6 P to scratch,
ā+ to sketch,
abhi+ to write,
ava+ to erase,
pari+ to copy,
pra+ to draw,
ud+ to polish,

lip 6 PA to anoint,
anu+ smear over, cover with,
vi+ besmear,

loc 1 A to see, behold,
ā +to appear or be seen,
bring to sight or mind,
paryā+ reflect, deliberate,
samā+ reflect,

lok 10 P to behold,
ā+ to consider,
ava+ to look at or upon,
vi+ look at, inspect, behold,

lū 5 P 9 PA to cut,

lubh 4 P to covet,
pra+ to allure,
upa+ caus. to entice,
vi+ caus. to seduce,

luṇṭh 10 P to plunder,

lup 6 P to break,
ava+ to snatch,
pra+ to rob,
vi+ to lacerate
vyā+ to dispel,

luṭ 4 P, 5 P, to wallow,

mā 2 P, 3A, to measure,
anu+ to infer, re-create in imagination, conceive,
nis+ to fashion, make out of,
pari+ to estimate, measure around, limit,
pra + measure,
prati+ to imitate,
upa+ to compare, measure with,
vi+ measure out,
vinis+ lay-out (garden),

mad 4 PA to rejoice,
pra+ to neglect,
ud+ to be mad,

man 1 A, 4A, to think,
abhi+ to desire, put one's mind upon
anu+ to agree, approve,
apa+ to despise,
ava+ to despise, look down upon,
sam+ to esteem,

manth strong form of *math* 9 PA to churn,
nis+ to thrash,
ud+ to stir up,
vi+ A. to tear,

mantr 10 PA to consult,
ā+ to take leave,
abhi+ to address,
ni+ to invite,
sam+ to consult,
samni+ invite together

marg 10 PA to seek,

mi or *mī* 9PA to lessen, bring low, bring to nought,
pra+ bring to nought, pass. come to nought, perish,

miṣ 6 P to wink,
ni+ to close the eyes, fall asleep, wink,
ud+ to bloom,

miśrayati Nom P mixes

mlai 1 P to fade,

mṛ 6 A to die,

mṛd 9 P to crush,
abhi+ to trample
ava+ to rub,
pari+ to pound,
pra+ to devastate,
vi+ to lay waste,

mṛj 2 PA to cleanse,
apa+ to wipe away (also fig. guilt),
pra+ to stroke, wipe off, polish,
sam+ to rub
vi+ to smear,

mṛś 6 P to touch,
abhi+ touch
vi+ to consider,

muc 6 PA to release,
ā+ to put on,
abhi+ to discharge,

ati+ to avoid,
ava+ A. to take off,
nis+ to loosen,
pari+ to abandon,
ud+ to free,
vi+ to loosen, e.g. a bond (with 2nd), loosen from (with 5th), untie, free, pass. be freed or separated from or be deprived of (with 3rd or 5th),

mud 1 A to rejoice,
ā+ to be fragrant,
anu+ to approve,
pra+ to rejoice,

muh 4 P to lose sense,
ati+ to be at a loss,
pari+ to be confused,
vi+ to faint,

murch 1 P to faint,
sam+ to coagulate,

nam 1 P to bow,
ā+ bow down to,
ava+ to stoop, bow down,
pari+ to change into,
samud+ rise,
ud+ to rise, raise, arise,
upa+ to occur,

namaskṛ to pay homage,

nard 1 P to roar,

naś 4 P to perish,
vi+ to be lost,

nī 1 PA to lead,
ā+ to fetch, bring to, mix,
abhi+ to act (as actor), bring to,
anu+ to request, try to win or conciliate by friendly words,
apa+ to carry away,
nis+ to decide,
pari+ lead around a cow, or a bride in the wedding ceremony,
parinī+ to marry,
pra+ bring forward (one's feelings or sacrificial components),
sam+ to unite,
vi+ to dispel, lead, guide, train,
ud+ to raise, bring up, rescue,
upa+ to offer, take unto oneself, (teacher who receives a youth and confers spiritual re-birth),

nij 3 PA to cleanse
ava+ to purify,

nind 1 P to blame,

nu 2 P to shout,

nud 6 PA to impel,
apa+ to drive away,
nirṇud to remove
praṇud to dispel,

pā 1P to drink,
ā+ to absorb,

pā to protect,

pad 4 A to fall,
ā+ to gain, happen, get into trouble,
anu+ to agree,
ati+ to postpone,
pra+ to seek refuge,
prati+ to receive, step to, enter upon get into a condition,
sam+ to succeed, turn out well,
ud+ to arise, go out of, come into existence, be produced,
upa+ to occur, happen,
vi+ to fail, fall apart,
vyā+ fall away, perish,
caus. destroy, kill,

pāl 10 P to protect,
pari+ to expect,
prati+ to observe,

pat 1 P to fall,
abhi+ to rush at
ati+ to neglect,
ni+ to fall down, fly down,
anu+ to fly after, pursue,
parā+ to fly off,
praṇi+ to prostrate oneself
samni+ fall together, come together
samud+ to fly up together,
ud+ to fly up

pīḍ 10 P to afflict, press,
ā+ press out,

piṣ 7 P to grind,

plu 1 A to float or leap,
ā+ bathe,
ava+ to submerge,
samā+ bathe,
ud+ spring up
upa+ hover unto,

vi+ to drift,
pṝ 3 P,9 P to fill,
ati+ bring across,
pari+ to fulfill,
pra+ to complete,
sam+ to fulfill, becomes full,
prā to fill,
ā+ to fill
prach 6 P to ask,
ā+ to take leave,
pari+ to enquire, ask,
sam+ to converse, consult with,
vi+ find out by asking,
prakaṭayati Nom P to manifest,
prath 1A to spread out
vi+ to spread out wide,
psā 2 P to chew, eat
pū 9 PA to purify
niṣpū to winnow,
pūj 10 P to worship,
adhi+ to honour,
pari+ to venerate,
puṣ 4 P,9 P to nourish,
pyai 1 A to swell,
ṛ 1 P to go, 5 P to injure,
ā+ get into trouble,
nis+ dissolve connection with,
sam+ meet, go along with,
caus. deliver to, consign,
ud+ to rise, raise,
upa+ go against, transgress,
rā 2 P to give,
rabh 1 A to grasp,
ā+ to begin, take hold upon, touch
anvā+ take hold of from behind,
prā+ to undertake,
pari+ to embrace,
sam+ to become excited, take hold of each other (for dance, battle,..),
samā+ undertake,
samanvā+ hold onto each other (said of several),
rac 10 P to fashion,
ā+ to prepare, caus. make happy, satisfy,
upa+ to construct,
vi+ to compose,
rādh 5 to prosper,
ā+ caus. to propitiate,
apa+ to offend,
rah 1 P to separate, abandon
vi+ separate from, abandon, leave,
rakṣ 1 P to protect,
abhi+ to observe,
pari+ to guard,
pra+ to save,
sam+ to preserve,
ram 1 A stop, stay, make fast rest, abide, find pleasure in,
ā + P stop,
abhi+ A. stop, find pleasure,
upa+ stop, *uparata* ceased,
vi+ P. stop, pause,
rañj or *raj* 4 PA to be glad,
abhi+ to be devoted,
anu+ to love, take the tinge of,
apa A. to lose colour,
sam+ A. to redden,
vi+ to lose interest, lose colour, be indifferent towards,
raṭ 1 P to cry,
ṛdh 6,2,4,5,7, P to grow, increase, prosper, succeed,
sam+ to be fulfilled,
ric 7 PA to empty,
ati+ pass. to surpass,
ud + pass. to excell,
ruc 1 A to please, to shine,
abhi+ to please,
ati+ to shine,
pra+ to shine forth,
prati+ appear good to, please,
rud 2 P to cry,
pra+ to wail,
vi+ to weep,
rudh 7 PA to obstruct,
ā+ to besiege,
anu+ 4 A to obey,
ava+ to confine,
ni+ to check,
prati+ to resist,
upa+ to molest,
vi+ 4 A to contend,
ruh 1 P to ascend,
ā+ to ascend, seat oneself upon, climb (tree), ascend (hilltop, life,

place), embark upon (boat, ship), fig. get into danger,
ā+caus. to ascribe,
adhi+ to mount,
ava+ to descend,
pra+ to grow
sam+ to grow,
vi+ to shoot up,

ruj 6 P to break,
ā+ to tear,
pra+ to shatter,

rūp 10 P to represent, form,
ni+ to observe,
pra+ to explain,
vi+ to disfigure,

sā = *so*

sad 1 P to sit,
ā+ to find, sit upon, lie in wait for, get to, reach,
ava+ to collapse,
ni+ sit down, take one's seat, set, install as,
niṣad + to sink,
pra+ to be pleased, be favourable or gracious,
sam+ to lose heart, to sit together,
ud+ to perish
vi+ sink, be dejected, come to grief,
viṣad + to be dejected,

śam 4 P to be calm,
pra+ to be quiet, come to rest, stop,
upa+ to cease, be quiet, stop,

śaṁs 1 P to praise
ā+ A. to hope, wish, bless,
abhi+ to accuse,
pra+ to extol, praise,

sañj 1 P to adhere,
ā+ to fasten,
ava+ to entrust to,
pra+ to result, follow,

śaṅk 1 A to fear,
ā+ to be apprehensive
abhi+ to distrust,

śap 1 PA to curse,

śās 2 P to rule
ā+ A. to hope,
anu+ to instruct,
pra+ to rule,

ścut 1 P to trickle,

sev 1 A to serve,
ni+ to frequent,
samā+ to practice
upa+ to reverence,

śī 2 A to lie (down),
ā+ lie in,
adhi+ to dwell, dwell in,
anu+ to repent, lie down after another,
ati+ to surpass,
prati+ to importune
sam+ to hesitate, be in doubt,
upa+ lie by,

sic 6 PA to sprinkle,
ā+ pour into,
abhi+ pour upon, sprinkle, anoint, consecrate,
ava+ pour upon,
ni+ pour down or in (semen)
ud+ to be arrogant,

sidh 1 P to drive away,
apa+ to ward off,
niṣidh to forbid
pratiṣidh to forbid

sidh 4 P to succeed,
sam+ to be accomplished

śiṣ 7 P to remain,
ud+ leave remaining,
vi+ to distinguish, hence distinguished, eminent,

skhal 1 P to stumble,
pari+ to stagger,
vi+ to falter,

śliṣ 4 PA to cling to,
ā+ to embrace,
sam+ to clasp,
vi+ to be loosened,

smi 1 A to smile,
pra+ to laugh,
anu+ caus. to remind,
vi+ to forget
vi+ to be astonished,

smṛ 1 P to remember,

snā 2 P to bathe,

snih 4 P to love,

spand 1 A to throb,

spardh 1 A to compete

sphāy 1 A to swell
sphur 6 P to quiver,
sphuṭ 1 P to burst,
spṛdh 1 A to emulate, compete,
spṛh 10 P to long for,
spṛś 6 P to touch,
upa+ to caress, touch,
so = *sā* 4 P to finish,
adhyava+ to resolve, decide upon, undertake,
ava+ to conclude, unbind, unharness, turn in, go to rest, go home,
udava+ set out,
vyava+ to decide, determine,
sṛ 1 P to move,
ā+ run to, run
abhi+ to assail,
anu+ to follow, go after,
apa+ to depart, remove, take out,
ava+ go down,
nis+ to emerge, go out, caus. drive out,
pra+ to gush, go forth,
pra+caus. to stretch,
sam+ flow together, wander
upa+ go to, approach,
śṝ 9 P to crush,
sṛj 6 PA to emit, hurl, utter,
ati+ to grant,
pra+ to renounce,
ud+ to discharge,
vi+ to dismiss,
sṛp 1 PA to creep,
ud+ creep out or up,
upa+ approach gently,
vi+ move apart, disperse, move about,
śram 4 P to grow weary,
pari+ to be exhausted,
vi+ to rest, stop,
sraṁs 1 A to fall,
vi+ to collapse,
śrambh 1 or *srambh* A to be negligent, usually with *vi,*
vi+ to trust in, confide,
śri 1 PA to lean, rest on,
ā+ to seek refuge, lean upon, seek support,
adhi+ to resort to,
pari+ A. lay about, enclose,
pra+ lean forward,
upa+ A. lean against,
śru 5 P to hear,
ā+ to listen,
prati+ answer, say yes to, make a promise to, not turn a deaf ear to – answer,
sam+ hear, accede to the request of,
vi+ be heard of far and wide, be famous,
sru to shed, emit,
prati+ to promise,
stambh or *stabh* 9 P to prop, support,
ava+ to fix,
sam+ to benumb,
ud+ prop up,
vi+ to check, prop apart,
sthā 1 PA to stand,
ā+ take one's place at, resort to
abhi+ set the foot upon, vanquish, withstand,
adhi+ to dwell, stand upon,
anu+ to perform, take one's place by, support, devote oneself to a thing, carry out a plan, accomplish
anūpa+ A. approach one after another,
anuvi+ spread oneself over, pervade,
ava+ to stand still, stand off, abide, remain,
ni+ to be versed in, stand in, rest on,
pari+ stand round about, encompass, restrain,
pra+ A. to set out, go off, caus. send away, dismiss,
prati+ stand, be established, get a foothold,
pratyud+ rise up to meet (in respect)
sam+ A. remain with, come to a standstill, get through, finish,
samud+ rise up, spring up,
samupa+ approach one after another
ud+ stand up, rise up, spring up,
upa+ to wait upon,

utthā to rise,
vi+ A. spread itself,
vyava+ to remain,

ṣṭhīv 1 P to spit,
stṛ 5 PA to strew,
ā+ to cover, spread out,
anu+ cover over,
ava+ to scatter,
upa+ spread upon,
vi+ to spread,

stu 2 P to praise,
su 5 PA to press,
sū 2 A to beget, set in motion,
śubh 1 A to look beautiful,
śuc 1 PA to grieve, shine, burn,
ā+ bring hither by flame,
abhi+ burn, *anu+* to regret,
apa+ drive away by flame,

sūd 1 A to put in order, guide aright
10 P to kill,
niṣud to destroy

śudh 4 P to purify, become pure,
sukhayati Nom P delights,
sukhāyate Nom A feels happy,
svād 1 A to taste,
ā+ to relish,

svan 1 P to resound,
svañj 1 A to clasp,
pari+ to embrace,

svap 2 P to sleep,
śvas 2 P to breathe, get one's breath, become quiet, caus. quiet, comfort
ā+ to revive,
abhipra+ blow forth upon,
ni+, nis+ to sigh, breathe out,
pra+ blow forth,
ud+ to expand,
vi+ to confide in, have confidence, be unsuspecting,

svid 1 P to sweat,
svīkṛ 8 A to agree,
syand 1 A to flow,
taḍ 10 P to beat,
pari+ to strike,
vi+ to wound,

tan 8 PA to stretch, extend, spread over,
ā+ to pervade,
adhi+ to string (a bow)
ava+ to descend,
pari+ to clasp, surround, envelope,
vi+ to spread, stretch out, cover,

tap 1 P to heat, suffer, practice austerities
tap 4A to be heated, to suffer, do penance, be purified,
tarj 1 P, 10 P, to threaten,
abhi+ to revile,
vi+ to threaten,

tark 10 PA to surmise,
tṝ 6 PA to cross,
abhyud+ come out of the water to, cross the water to,
at+ to overcome,
ava+ to descend esp. divine beings as men,
nis+ to overcome,
pra+ take to the water, start on,
ud+ to escape, come up out of the water,
vi+ to bestow, cross through, traverse,

trā 4 A to rescue, (form of *tṛ* ?)
trap 1 A to be ashamed,
tras 1 P to tremble,
apa+ to flee,
pari+ to be afraid,
sam+ to dread,

tṛh 7 P to crush,
tṛṣ 4 P to be thirsty,
tud 6 P to strike,
tul 10 P to weigh,
tuṣ 4 P to be pleased,
pari+ to be satisfied,
sam+ to rejoice in,

tvar 1 A to hasten,
tyaj 1 P to abandon,
pari+ to forsake, leave to one's fate
sam+ to give up,

ud or *und* 7 P to flow or issue out, wet,
sam+ flow together, wet,

ūh 1 PA to push, attend to, expect, guess, suppose,
apa+ to remove,
api+ to grasp, understand,
prati+ to impede,
vi+ to arrange troops,

ujjh 6 P to leave,
ukṣ 1 PA to sprinkle, wet, emit,
pra+ sprinkle before one for consecration,
uñch 1,6 P to gather, glean,
pra+ to wash away, wipe out,
uṣ 1 P to burn,
vā 2 P to blow,
ā+ blow here,
nis+ to go out (flame etc.), be extinguished,
parā+ blow away,
pra+ blow or move forward,
vi+ blow asunder, scatter to the winds,
vac 2 P to say, speak,
abhyanu+ say with regard to, say after the teacher, learn, study,
anu+ to recite, repeat (prayers), say,
nis+ to explain, speak out clearly,
pra+ to announce, tell forth,
prati+ to reply, answer,
sam+ say together,
vi+ to explain,
vad 1 P to speak, say,
ā+ speak to,
abhi+ to address, speak to, salute,
apa+ to abuse,
pari+ to blame,
pra+ speak forth, say, declare to be,
pratyabhi+ caus. A.salute in return,
sam+ A. to converse, consider,
vi+ A. to quarrel,
vah 1 PA to bear, to carry, to flow,
ā+ to cause, bring hither or to,
apa+ to carry away,
ati+ to pass (time),
nis+ to carry out,
pari+ lead about,
pra+ to blow, carry onward,
sam+ carry, carry together,
ud+ to marry, bear or bring up, lead a bride from her father's house,
vi+ to marry, lead away (the bride from her parent's house),
vam 1 P to vomit,
van 8 PA to desire,
vañc 10 PA to cheat, go crookedly,
vāñch 1 PA to desire,
vand 1 A to salute, honour, praise,
vap 1 P to sow, strew,
ā+ throw upon, strew,
abhi+ bestrew,
apa+ cast away, fig. destroy,
ni+ throw down,
nis+ throw out, deal out (oblation),
vas 2 A to put on,
vas 1 P to dwell, live,
ā+ to abide, take up one's abode in, occupy, enter upon,
adhi+ to occupy,
ni+ to dwell (men and beasts),
pra+ to live abroad,
prati+ have one's dwelling,
ud+ caus. remove from its place,
upa+ to stay, to fast, stay with, wait,
vi+ to depart,
vāsayati Nom P perfumes,
ve 1 P to weave, interweave,
vep 1 A to tremble,
veṣṭ 1 A to wind round
pari+ caus. to surround,
ud+ caus. to loosen,
vic 7 P to sift,
vi+ to discern,
vid 2 P to know,
anu+ know thoroughly, from end to end
*ni+*caus. to inform, cause to know, announce, communicate,
vid 6 P to find,
anu+ to find,
vij 3 PA to separate,
vij 6 A, to shake,
ud+ to shudder,
vīj 1 P to fan
viś 6 PA to enter,
ā+ to overpower, enter, go into,
abhini+ A. to resort to, settle down to, be inclined towards,
ni+ A. to retire, go in, go home,
pra+ to enter, get into,
sam+ enter together, i.e. make their appearance together,
sampra+ go in,
upa+ to sit down, settle down upon

vṛ 5 PA to cover,
ā+ to cover,
abhi+ cover,
anu+ to conform, cover over,
apa+ to depart, uncover, open,
ati+ to surpass,
ni+ to return, keep down, suppress, ward off,
nis+ to arise, uncovered
nirvṛta – pleased, contented, free from care (not covered over),
pari+ to turn round, surround,
pra+ to set out, cover,
sam+ to be, to occur,
samā+ cover,
sampra+ A. cover completely,
upa+ to approach,
vi+ uncover, open, make open or clear, illumine

vṛ 5,9, PA to choose, prefer,
ā+ to choose, desire,

vraj 1 P to go,
ā+ come hither, go to,
pari+ to wander, wander around,
pratyā march or go back

vṛdh 1 A to increase,
pra+ grow on, grow up,
sam+ grow, caus. cause to grow, bring up, nourish, feed,
*vi+*grow, increase,

vṛṣ 1 P to rain,

vṛt 1 A to turn, turn round, revolve,
ā+ P. turn hither, A. turn, roll back
abhyparyā+ turn around to,
anu+ roll after, follow, continue,
ni+ turn back, flee, turn away, turn from, abstain,
nis+ roll out, develop, come into being, evolve itself, create from (with 5th),
pari+ turn around, move in a circle,
pra+ turn or move forward, set out, begin, set about, engage in,
caus. set in motion,
pratini+ turn back from (5th),
sam+ unite, take shape, form itself, come into being,
samā+ turn back to meet, go home (esp. a pupil who has finished his studies),
ud+ turn out, fly asunder,burst open,
upā+ turn to here,
vi+ turn away, part with,
caus. whirl about,

vyadh 4 P to pierce,
apa+ to cast aside,
nis+ to slay,

vyath 1 A to suffer,

yā 2 P to go,
ā+ to come,
ati+ to overcome,
anu+ to follow,
nis+ to go out,
pra+ to set out, go forth,
samā+ assemble, come together,
ud+ go forth, go out,
upa+ to approach, go or attain to,

yāc 1 A to beg,
abhi+ to implore,
anu+ to beseech,
sam+ to solicit,

yaj 1 PA to worship,
ā+ get a thing as a result of sacrifice,

yam 1 P to curb, sustain, support,
ni+ to check, restrain,
pra+ to bestow,
pratipra+ offer in turn, pass (food) (with 6th),
sam+ to curb, hold or reach out, hold together,
samud+ raise, set about,
ud+ to strive, undertake, raise (the arms or weapons),
upa+ hold onto, take hold of,
A. take to wife, marry,
vi+ hold asunder, stretch out,

yat 1 A to strive
pra+ to endeavour,

yuj 7 PA to join, prepare, employ
abhi+ to accuse,
anu+ to instruct,
ni+ to appoint, fasten to,
pra+ apply, use,
sam+ to unite, join together,
ud+ to get ready,
upa+ to use, enjoy,

English Index

transitive – a label applied to a verb which takes a direct object e.g. the Mongols destroyed Kiev. many verbs may be transitive or intransitive. An example of intransitive use is- Susie arrived early. An intransitive verb is one which cannot take a direct object. English examples are – arrive, snore, elapse, hibernate and stroll. Sanskrit does have some intransitives. (X)

Sanskrit Index/ Glossary

ādeśa a substitute, substitute form or letter

gamaḥ a grammatical augment,

aghoṣa unvoiced, an unvoiced sound is one in which the vocal chords do not vibrate e.g. zzzzzz can be felt vibrating when a finger is placed against the throat but the sound ssssssss can not.

alpaprāṇaḥ 'small breath' unaspirated – referring to the pronunciation of sounds,

anadyatanaḥ 'not of today' a tense not referring to the current day, e.g. periphrastic future, past imperfect or perfect tense

āṅgaḥ base or stem, mfn (in gram.) relating to the base (*aṅga*) of a word

antaḥstha 'in-between' semi-vowel

anunāsikaù a sound pronounced through the nose and mouth

anusvāra m. after-sound, the nasal sound marked by a dot above the line and which belongs to a preceding vowel, *-vat* mfn having the *anusvāra*

anusyūta mfn sewed consecutively, strung together, or connected regularly and uninterruptedly,

ardhaspṛṣṭa 'half–contacted' sibilant sounds

avagrahaḥ 'held apart, separated' represents a *lopa a* sound. m. separation of the component parts of a compound, or of the stem and certain suffixes and terminations, the mark or the interval of such a separation, mark of the elision of an initial '*a*',

avyaya 111/3 2. an indeclinable word, a particle, imperishable, undecaying, words or particles which do not change their grammatical form whatever the position in a sentence.

bahuvrīhi 'much rice' a compound the principal of which is outside the word e.g. he who has much rice i.e. is wealthy

daṇḍa stick, the vertical stroke used in forming letters, the vertical line at the end of a sentence.

devanāgarī the Indian script most commonly used by Sanskrit scholars

dhātu verbal roots

dīrgha long, the long (double) measure of a vowel

dvandva 503/2 pair, couple, male and female, a pair of opposites, a copulative compound or any compound in which the members if uncompounded would be in the same case and connected by the conjunction "and" ,

dvigu 'worth 2 cows' the name of a class of *karmadhāraya* compound that begins with a number,

gaṇaḥ list, the verb root classifications

gati (in gram.) a term for prepositions and some other adverbial prefixes e.g. *alam* when immediately connected with the tenses of a verb or with verbal derivatives 347/3

ghoṣa voiced

guṇaḥ strengthened vowel

jihvāmūlīyaḥ formed at the base of the tongue, *kh* or *ù* before *k*

kaṇṭha throat, sounds made from the throat

kāraka 1. mfn. making, doing, acting, who or what does or produces or creates, n. instrumental in bringing about the action denoted by a verb, 6 kinds- *kartṛ, karman, karaṇa, sampradāna, apādāna, adhikaraṇa* these concepts should be studied with the vibhakti endings which express them

The 6th case is not included because it expresses a relationship between 2 nouns (not between noun and verb.

karaṇa 254/1 doing, making, effecting, causing, clever, skilful, a writer, (in Gram.) a sound or word as an independent part of speech (or as separated from context; in this sense usually n.), the act of making doing, producing, instrument, means of action, method, cause, means

karman the object of the action

kartṛ the agent or subject of the action

karmadhāryaḥ tatpuruṣa a compound the members of which refer to the same object and would be in the same case if the compound were dissolved.

kartari prayogaḥ active (agent) sentence construction, the subject is the agent of the action

kṛdanta –(*pāṇini s* name for) participles

kriyā *Kriyā* is the sanskrit word for verbs and they are formed from roots called *dhātu.* For instance the *dhātu* for *kriyā* is *kṛ* 300/3 - to do, make, perform, accomplish, cause, effect, prepare, undertake. Strictly speaking to be correct the meaning should be listed as do, make etc., because "to" do is the infinitive form of the verb but the meanings are easily understood as they are listed.

verbs in general

kriyāviśeṣaṇa a word which "expands the remainder" from a verb, bringing out a previously unmanifested character, (an adverb)

ktvānta a gerund with a *tvā* ending, meaning carried out the action e.g. *bhūtvā* having become

lakāra the ten tenses/moods

laṭ	present indicative,
liṭ	perfect – remote past action not witnessed by speaker,
luṭ	periphrastic future – not of today,
lṛṭ	simple future,
leṭ	subjunctive (only in Vedic Sanskrit)
loṭ	imperative –command, demand,
laṅ	imperfect – past, not of today,
liṅ	optative, potential, what should, ought, could, might, be done,
luṅ	past, of today,
lṛṅ,	aorist conditional, would have

liṅga gender

mahāprāṇa 'great breath' aspirated,

mātrāḥ measure

mūrdhaḥ roof (of the mouth), a mouth position

napuṁsakaliṅga 523/1 neutral gender, " not pertaining to generation"

nāmadhātu verbs derived from nouns or nouns derived from verbs.

nāman name in general including proper names and nouns, adjectives, pronouns and adverbs

nāsikaḥ nose, nasal

nipāta irregular forms, exceptions, particles. words without case, gender or number i.e. without endings so they appear in a sentence already complete. *nipāta* – an indeclinable particle . ..all adverbs including particles and interjections (MW) e.g. *ca* meaning 'and'.

padapātha words without sandhi

parasmaipada 'word for another' the active form of verbal words

pluta the protracted measure of a vowel, (beyond *dirgha)*

pradhānaḥ the principal member of a compound

prātipadika the "stem" of a nominal

pratyaya *pratyaya* an affix or suffix to roots forming verbs, substantives, adjectives and all derivatives, the term for a word ending

puṁliṅga 523/1 masculine gender, consciousness, the essence of man, man; power to beget, set in motion; the powerful; generation

puruṣa person *prathamaù* first, *madhyamaù* second (middle), *uttamaù* third

samāsa compound word

saṁhitā put together, joined, attached, composed of, uninterrupted as a series of words

saṁjñā used for technical terms & definitions which have a specific technical meaning lit. containing all knowledge (of the named thing)

saṁyoga 1112/2 m. conjunction, combination, connection, union or absorption with or in, contact (in phil.) direct material contact, (in gram.) , a conjunct consonant, (combination of 2 or more consonants), dependence of one case on another, total amount, sum, agreement of opinion, being engaged in

saṁyukta 'connected' a complex vowel

saṁdhi euphonic combination

sarvanāman words which can be applied to all i.e. pronouns. e.g. me, mine, you, they, which, who

sparśa 1269/1 touching, sense of touch, contact, touching

spṛṣṭaḥ 1269/2 formed by complete contact of the organs of utterance (all consonants except sibilants, semi-vowels and h).

sthānaḥ point of articulation

strīliṅga feminine gender, creative power which brings to birth, the power of the powerful

subanta a word taking a nominal ending i.e. a nominal

śuddha a pure simple vowel

sup a nominal ending

taddhita 434/2 m. an affix forming (derivative) nouns from other nouns. *taddhita* is an example of this and means 'good for that or him'

tālu the palate, name for palatal sounds

tatpuruṣa 'his man' the name and an example of a class of compounds in which the second term is the main one.

tiṅ a verb ending

tiṅanta 'having a *tiṅ* ending' a verb

upadeśa an original utterance –includes the *maheśvarāṇi sutrāṇi* , *dhātu* (verbal roots), *āgama* (a grammatical augment), *ādeśa* 137/3(a substitute, substitute form or letter), *pratyaya* (an affix or suffix to roots forming verbs, substantives, adjectives and all derivatives, and *upasarga* (below)

upagraha – voice, there are 3 voices- active *kartari prayoga*, middle *ātmanepada*, and passive *karmaṇi prayoga*

upasarga prefixes to verbs or *nāmadhātu* (see below) which change the direction or sense of the word to which they are prefixed. a particle joined to a verb or noun denoting action . Practically it may be thought of as a pre-fix .

vacana speaking, used to express number in grammar e.g. *ekavacana* speaking of one, lit. the act of speaking

vākya a sentence lit. that which is spoken

vibhakti inflection of nouns, declension, an affix of declension, case. lit. division, separation, modification, partition

virāma stop, pause, end of a word or sentence, a vertical stroke to indicate this

viśeṣaṇa brings out a quality of a *nāman* (an adjective) 20

vṛddhi 1011/1 the second modification or increase of vowels under certain conditions, a strengthened vowel,

vyākaraṇa 'taken apart', grammar ,

special application of words in *Pāṇini's* work

ādhikāra sutrāṇi these are statements that govern particular following groups of *sutrāṇi* in *Pāṇini's* work

paribhāṣā sutrāṇi explain how to understand the *sutrāṇi* which define the laws of grammar in Pāṇini's exposition.

pragṛhya 656/2 mfn to be taken or seized or accepted, (in gram.) to be taken or pronounced separately, not subject to the rules of *saṁdhi* , ind. having taken or grasped, carrying away with

pratyāhāra the system that identiies relevant groups of sounds

viddhi sutrāṇi state the rules of grammar in Pāṇini's work.

Pāṇini has allocated special meanings for use of the 1st, 5th, 6th, and 7th vibhakti when describing *saṁdhi* rules.

1st	the replacement (*ādeśa*) , (the name of the replacement sound),	
5th	that after which there is replacement (*purva*)	'after'
6th	that which is replaced (*sthānin*)	'in place of'
7th	that before which there is replacement (*uttara*)	'before', 'in the presence of'

anuvṛtti are unseen words from previous *sutrāṇi*

nityam sutrāṇi limit the scope of previous *sutrāṇi*

it letters are indicatory only

lopa indicates non-appearance or invisibility

sandhi terms

purva the one before or the one underneath

uttara the one following or the one above

sandhi the one in-between and encompassing

sandhāna the one that actually unites

saṁhitā 1123/1 put together, joined, conjunction, union, connection, 'part of the way the whole universe works'

Abbreviations

(A) to (W)	references to bibliography sources
acc	accusative case
act	active voice
adj	adjective
adv.	adverb
aor	aorist
caus	causative
comp.	compound
denom	denominative
desid	desiderative
du	dual number
f	feminine
ifc	at the end of a compound
impf	imperfect tense
impv	imperative tense
ind	indeclinable
inf	infinitive
HH	His Holiness Śrī Śāntānanda Saraswatī
LM	Leon McLaren
loc	locative case
m	masculine
mfn	masculine, feminine or neuter = adjective
mid	middle voice
n	neuter gender
opt	optative tense
part	participle
ppp	past passive participle
pass	passive voice
perf	perfect tense
pl	plural
pres	present tense
pron	pronoun
s	singular
Ved	Vedic
voc	vocative case – used to address somebody (oh Ràma)
1	1st case – nominative (the subject)
2	2nd case – accusative (the object)
3	3rd case – instrumental (by or with)
4	4th case – dative (to or for something)
5	5th case- ablative (from or through)
6	6th case – genitive (of something)
7	7th case – locative (in or on something)

Bibliography and Reference List

A Sanskrit-English Dictionary – Sir Monier Monier-Williams, Motilal Banarsidass, Delhi, 1993 (all page references unless otherwise noted)
(A) Aṣṭāvakra Saṃhitā – Swami Nityaswarupananda, Advaita Ashrama, Mayavati 1981
(Apte) The Student's Sanskrit English Dictionary – VS Apte, Motilal Banarsidass, Delhi 1997
(B) Sanskrit Manual – Roderick S. Bucknell –Motilal Banarsidass, Delhi 1996
(C) Ashtavakra Gita translated by Hari Prasad Shastri –Shanti Sadan London 1961
(E)Aṣṭāvakra Gītā – Commentary by Swami Chinmayananda – Central Chinmaya Mission Trust – Revised Edition May 1997 – Mumbai
(F) Teach yourself Sanskrit –Michael Coulson, Teach Yourself Books, Hodder, England 2001
The Sanskrit Language – an Introductory Grammar and Reader, WH Maurer, Curzon, 1995
(G) A Concise Dictionary of Indian Philosophy – John Grimes, SUNY, NY, 1996
(H) A practical aid for the study of Sanskrit Dhātus – The School of Economic Science, London 2003
(HH)Quotations from his Holiness Śrī Śāntānanda Saraswatī, Śankarācārya
(I) Dhātu Pātha – Hill and Harrison – Duckworth 1991
(J) The roots, verb-forms and primary derivatives of the Sanskrit language –WD Whitney reprint 1994 Motilal Banarsidass Delhi
(K) Wikipedia
(LM) Quotations from Mr. Leon McLaren in various publications
Laghu Kaumudi of Varadaraja James R Ballantyne reprint 1995 Motilal Banarsidass, Delhi
The Siddhanta Kaumudi of Bhattoji Dikshita (Vasu) reprint 1982 Motilal Banarsidass, Delhi
(O) A Sanskrit Manual (for High Schools) Parts 1 and 2, R.Antoine S.J. Xavier Pubn. Calcutta,
(P) Pāṇini
A Concise Elementary Grammar of the Sanskrit Language, Jan Gonda, The University of Alabama Press 1966
A Sanskrit Grammar for Students A.A. Macdonell reprint 1997 Motilal Banarsidass, Delhi
Devavāṇīpraveśikā – An introduction to the Sanskrit Language – RP Goldman & SJS Goldman 1980 et al, University of California, Berkeley
Introduction to Sanskrit, parts 1 and 2 - Thomas Egenes 1989, 1985 Motilal Banarsidass, Delhi
Pāṇini –His Description of Sanskrit Jag Deva Singh
Sanskrit Grammar for Beginners – Second Edition – Max Müller –Hippocrene Books, New York 2004 (M)
Sanskrit Grammar – William Dwight Whitney – Bodhi Leaves Corp. Delhi reprint 1990 (W)
School of Economic Science London Sanskrit Faculty numerous texts
The Penguin Dictionary of English Grammar – R.L. Trask , Penguin 2000 (X)
The Bhagavad Gita Winthrop Sergeant SUNY 1994
Bhagavad Gita translated by Swami Gambhirananda, Advaita Ashrama fifth impression May 2000
Secondary Suffixes in Sanskrit Grammar Dr. D K Das Sanskrit Book Depot 2002
A Sanskrit Grammar for Students Arthur A Macdonell Motilal Banarsidass, Delhi
A Sanskrit Reader Charles Rockwell Lanman 1885 Motilal Banarsidass, Delhi
A Sanskrit Primer Edward Delavan Perry 1936 Motilal Banarsidass, Delhi

Printed in Great Britain
by Amazon

42920598R00183